HOLTMATH 11

Bye Dale Doran Mackenzie Midyette Teshima

Holt, Rinehart and Winston of Canada, Limited

Authors
Marshall P. Bye/Calgary, Alberta
William A. Dale/School District #71, Courtenay,
British Columbia
Kevin Doran/Peel Board of Education, Ontario
Leona MacKenzie/York Board of Education, Ontario
Robert Midyette/Calgary Board of Education,
Alberta
Roger Teshima/Calgary Board of Education, Alberta

Director, Art and Design Mary Opper
Art Direction and Design by Julia Naimska
Assembly and technical art by David Hunter
Cover by Tiit Telmet

Executive Editor Ken Leland
Developmental Editors Colin Garnham and
Anna-Maria Malizia
Senior Production Editor Sharon Dzubinsky
Assistant Production Editor Sharon Tomas

Canadian Cataloguing in Publication Data
Main entry under title:

Holtmath 11

For use in grade 11.
Includes index.
ISBN 0-03-921957-7

1. Mathematics - 1961-   -Juvenile literature.
I. Bye, Marshall P., 1928-

QA107.H645 1988   510   C88-093263-5

The metric usage in this text conforms to the
standards established by the Canadian General
Standards Board.

Printed in Canada
1 2 3 4 5   92 91 90 89 88

Acknowledgements
P. 27 © 1968 United Feature Syndicate, Inc. P. 447 courtesy
of Scotiabank. P. 121 adapted by permission of Princeton University Press.

Photograph Credits
Miller Services Ltd.: P. 9 Roberts B25971, P. 44 W. Wittman
141-13, P. 67 Camerique 0708, P. 121 Roberts R26168,
P. 173 Roberts B23945S, P. 200 Camerique W1127, P. 229
Lambert LP6110, P. 240 Andre Boucher 324B, P. 280 Lambert
LA4344R, P. 296 J. Marshall TO-AIR-77-1, P. 331 Roberts
F13851, P. 369 Camerique G1161, P. 416 Roberts S23293,
P. 430 Roberts B7687A. P. 112 courtesy The Royal Bank
of Canada.

Every reasonable effort has been made to trace the owners of
copyrighted material and to make due acknowledgement. Any
errors or omissions drawn to our attention will be gladly rectified
in future editions.

The authors of HOLTMATH 11 wish to thank the following
reviewers for their invaluable comments and suggestions during
the developmental stage of the text.

Don Buntain and Ken Robinson
Wentworth County Public School Board
Dundas, Ontario

J.G. Crompton
West Park Secondary School
St. Catharines, Ontario

Russel Donnelly
Calgary RCSS District #1
Calgary, Alberta

Georgina V. Kelly
Parkview Education Centre
Bridgewater, Nova Scotia

David N. Spencer
Steveston Senior Secondary School
Richmond, British Columbia

Brian Thorkelson
Vincent Massey High School
Brandon, Manitoba

John Turnbull
Matthew McNair Secondary School
Richmond, British Columbia

CONTENTS

VARIATIONS IN COMPUTERS

The programs in the pupil text are written for use with Apple computers. The same programs can be run on Commodore and Radio Shack TRS-80 models if the following changes are made.

1. All programs should begin with the statement NEW to clear the memory.

2. All programs should be proceeded by:
HOME—for Apple
SHIFT/CLR—for Commodore
CLEAR—for TRS-80.

3. RETURN is used on both Apple and Commodore models; ENTER is used for TRS-80.

4. When the TRS-80 is turned on, the letters CASS appear on the screen. Press the key L before starting to type in the program.

5. The exponent symbols are keyed and displayed as follows:

Computer	Key	Display
Apple	∧	∧
Commodore	↑	↑
TRS-80	↑	[

FOREWORD TO THE STUDENT AND TEACHER

There are several unique features that we, the authors, have included in this book. We feel that a word of explanation about each is desirable.

The Calculator

The calculator, when used appropriately, helps to foster exploration and experimentation, assists in the development and reinforcement of concepts, and facilitates and encourages problem solving. We believe that each student should have a calculator readily available. In the text, we suggest specific instances where a calculator might be used to solve problems and to assist in the development of concepts, but it is not intended that the use of the calculator be restricted to these cases only. At the discretion of the teacher, it is recommended that students be encouraged to use calculators more generally, especially in those cases where the emphasis is not on manual calculation skills but rather on thinking, planning, or understanding in a problem-solving situation. Though we believe the student should learn when it is useful and desirable to use a calculator, the calculator is not a replacement for the learning of basic facts and mental computation.

Problem Solving

The problem-solving process developed in this book is useful in learning mathematics as well as in solving problems. It is a way of thinking through new concepts and ideas logically. To assist students in developing the ability to solve problems in the broadest sense, we emphasize problem solving in four different modes.

a. In the display for most of the lessons there is a description of a practical situation in which mathematics can be used to solve a problem. This lends credibility to the "need" for the mathematics about to be developed by indicating where and how such a concept or skill is used.

b. In the exercises, more practical problems are presented for solution based on the skills developed in the display. We endeavor to pose the problems in a "real-life" context.

c. A four-step problem-solving model is developed in Chapter 1. It is suggested that this procedure be used with all types of problems. The handling of routine-type problems using algorithms is just another strategy to be employed. Scattered throughout the text are specific "process" problems which can be solved using one or more of the strategies outlined in Chapter 1.

d. Some problems require an "insight" or a change in your normal thought pattern in order to solve them. They are not designed to be "tricky" but rather to require the student to have some special inspiration, insight, or hunch. While some may be solved using the problem-solving model presented in Chapter 1, all can be solved using a creative mental leap. Typically, problems of this type are presented in the Brainticklers.

Historical Notes

Mathematics is the product of the efforts of men and women throughout history. We believe mathematics is more interesting when students know something about the lives and times of these people. At times we encourage the readers to extend their knowledge of mathematicians through a section titled "Using the Library".

We hope you enjoy developing your skills and learning about mathematics in the year ahead.

The Authors.

M. P. Bye	L. MacKenzie
W. A. Dale	R. Midyette
K. Doran	R. Teshima

SYMBOLS

h	hours	$\sqrt{x}$	square root of a number
$\propto$	proportional to	$\triangle$	triangle
{ }	the set of	$\pm$	plus or minus
$\because$	since	L.S.	left side of an equation
$\therefore$	therefore	R.S.	right side of an equation
|	such that	U	universal set
ϵ	belongs to	$\subset$	is contained in
N	set of Natural numbers	$\cup$	union
W	set of Whole numbers	$\cap$	intersection
I	set of Integers	$\varnothing$	null set
^+Q	positive Rational numbers	$a:b$	ratio of a to b
^-Q	negative Rational numbers	$\cong$	congruent to
Q	set of all Rational numbers	$\ncong$	not congruent to
$\overline{Q}$	set of all Irrational numbers	$\sim$	similar
R	set of all Real numbers	$\doteq$	approximately
C	set of Complex numbers	$\llcorner$	right angle
$>$	greater than	$\angle$	angle
$<$	less than	$\overline{AB}$	line segment AB or measure of line AB
$\geq$	greater than or equal to	$\overleftrightarrow{AB}$	line AB
$\leq$	less than or equal to	$\overrightarrow{AB}$	ray AB
$\neq$	does not equal	$\parallel$	parallel to
$f(x)$	the value of an expression at x	$\perp$	perpendicular to
$f^{-1}(x)$	the inverse of f at x	sin	sine ratio
Δy	difference in y-values	cos	cosine ratio
$^\circ$C	degrees Celsius	tan	tangent ratio
$\rightarrow$	maps onto	csc	cosecant ratio
π	approximately 3.141 592	sec	secant ratio
$|x|$	absolute value (magnitude) of x	cot	cotangent ratio
...	and so on	Σ	sum of
(x, y)	ordered pair	$\overline{y}$	mean
$P(x)$	probability of x	$\vec{a}$	vector a

CHAPTER ONE

POLYNOMIALS AND PROBLEM SOLVING

Tune Up

1. Find the Greatest Common Factor (GCF) of these sets of numbers.

a. 2, 4, 6   **b.** 13, 52, 130

c. 21, 189, 7   **d.** 16, 32, 26

2. Find the GCF of each.

a. x^3, x^2, x^5 **b.** $3xy$, $6x$, 12

c. $5x^2y^3$, $3x^5y^2$, y^2 **d.** $7a^3$, a^5b, $14a^4b^9$

3. In your own words, state the Pythagorean Theorem. Draw and label an appropriate diagram to help with your explanation.

4. Find the Least Common Multiple (LCM) of each.

a. 14, 12, 9   **b.** 7, 17, 27

c. x, y, z **d.** $12x^2$, $3xy$, $5x^3y^3$

5. Two airplanes leave an airport. One plane flies on a course defined by the equation $3x - 2y = 12$. The other plane flies on a course defined by the equation $x - 4y = 8$. The planes are flying at different altitudes.

a. On a regular coordinate grid, sketch the paths that the planes will take.

b. Will the paths ever intersect? If so, estimate the point of intersection.

6. In your own words, define these terms.

a. perimeter   **b.** area

c. volume   **d.** surface area

e. degree of a polynomial

7. Find the length of the hypotenuse in this right triangle.

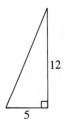

8. State the order of operations. How would the order of operations be used to evaluate this expression? $(3)(54) \div (9)(6) - 8 + 1$

9. Solve.

a. $3x = 12$ **b.** $7x = -42$

c. $5x - 1 = 14$ **d.** $4x + 4 = 4$

e. $5x - 12 = 23$ **f.** $6x - 18 = -42$

10. Two posts are 85 m high. They are joined at the top by a cable that is 150 m long. The cable hangs from the two posts so that it is 10 m above the ground at its lowest point. How far apart are the two posts?

11. Multiply.

a. $3(x + 6)$ **b.** $2x(x - 1)$

c. $2a(a + b)$ **d.** $3y(x + 2y)$

e. Explain the distributive property over multiplication.

1·1 Polynomials

A **term** is a number or letter or a combination of numbers and letters joined by multiplication or division. **Algebraic expressions** are comprised of one or more terms separated by addition or subtraction. The letters or **variables** represent unknown quantities. These are examples of algebraic expressions.

$22,\qquad -5y^3,\qquad 4x - 2\sqrt{7},\qquad 8xyz,\qquad \frac{3x-2y}{x+y},\qquad 3a^2 - 2b + \frac{4a}{7b}$

The first expression consists only of a number called a **constant**. In the expression $8xyz$, each term is the **coefficient** of the product of the other three terms. The number 8 is the **numerical coefficient**, while the x, y, and z are the **literal coefficients**.

> A **polynomial** is an algebraic expression which contains one or more terms. The exponents of the variables in a polynomial are **whole** numbers.

A polynomial is classified according to the number of terms it contains.

Name	Number of Terms	Examples
*mono*mial	1	$3,\ -18m,\ 8xy^2$
*bi*nomial	2	$k-4,\ x^2+2,\ a+6b^2$
*tri*nomial	3	$3r-2s+10t,\ 3x^2+x+12$

Although there are specific names for polynomials with more than three terms, they are generally referred to as polynomials of four terms, five terms, and so on. A polynomial can be evaluated by substituting specific values for the variables.

Example

Evaluate $4x^2 - 3xy$ for $x = 2$ and $y = -5$.

$$\begin{aligned} 4x^2 - 3xy &= 4(2)^2 - 3(2)(-5) \\ &= 46 \end{aligned}$$

Exercises

1. Copy and complete.

a. The term $3m^2n$ contains a literal [redacted] and a [redacted] coefficient.

b. The numerical coefficient of ab^3 is [redacted].

c. A polynomial containing three terms is called a [redacted].

d. In the polynomial $3s^2 - 15s + 8$, the number 8 is called a [redacted].

2. Classify each polynomial according to the number of terms.

a. $5a$ **b.** $12m^2 - mn + 5n^2$

c. $3xy + 8yz$ **d.** $6p^3q^2$

e. $m^2 + 10m - 2$ **f.** $2x^2 - y^2$

3. Which are polynomials? For those which are not polynomials, explain why they are not.

a. -25 **b.** $4x^{-2}$

c. $\frac{1}{2}x^3 + 8$ **d.** $\sqrt{3}k + 5$

4. Evaluate the expression for $p = 3$, $q = -2$, and $r = 5$.

a. $2p + 4q - r$ **b.** $6q - 3r$

c. $p^2 + q^2 + r^2$ **d.** $6p^2 - 2r^2$

5. If the area of a triangle is given by $A = \frac{1}{2}bh$, find the area of the triangles.

a. $b = 15$ cm, $h = 8$ cm

b. $b = 8$ cm, $h = 34$ cm

c. What is the coefficient of h in the area equation?

1·2 Add and Subtract Polynomials

To add or subtract polynomials, the coefficients of the **like terms** are combined. In a polynomial, like terms contain exactly the same variables raised to the same degree. A polynomial is simplified if all the like terms have been combined.

Example 1

If x represents 6 m and y represents 5 m, then find the perimeter of this field.

One way of finding the perimeter is to substitute the values into all the individual expressions and then find the sum. However, for some shapes, this would require many substitutions. To simplify the number of calculations, gather all the like terms and then make the substitution into one expression.

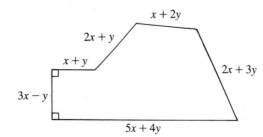

$$P = (3x - y) + (x + y) + (2x + y) +$$
$$(x + 2y) + (2x + 3y) + (5x + 4y)$$
$$= (3x + x + 2x + x + 2x + 5x) +$$
$$(-y + y + y + 2y + 3y + 4y)$$
$$= 14x + 10y$$

Therefore, the perimeter is $14(6) + 10(5)$ or 134 m.

Example 2

Subtract. $7pq - 2p$ from $4p^2 + 5pq$

$$(4p^2 + 5pq) - (7pq - 2p) = 4p^2 + 5pq - 7pq + 2p$$
$$= 4p^2 - 2pq + 2p$$

Multiply by -1.

Exercises

1. Find an expression for the perimeter.

a.

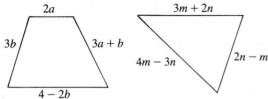

b.

2. Add or subtract the polynomials.
a. $(5a + 3b) + (2a - 7b)$
b. $(-4p + q) + (3p - 10q)$
c. $(6u + 5v) - (12u - 3v)$
d. $(x^2 + 7x - 12) - (2x^2 - 3x + 1)$

3. Simplify by adding.
a. $12ab + 3a^2b + 4ab^2$ and $6ab - 2a^2b - 15ab^2$
b. $7pq + 21pq^2 - 5pq^3$ and $pq - 14pq^2 + 9pq^3$
c. $-3x^2yz + 5xy^2z + 8xyz^2$ and $6x^2yz + 11xy^2z - xyz^2$

4. Calculate the length of the fourth side of the quadrilateral if the perimeter is $10x + 6y$.

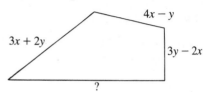

5. Write a simplified expression to represent the perimeter of an equilateral triangle with one side equal to $-3x + 5y$ cm.

3

1·3 Multiplication of Polynomials

The product of two polynomials is found by using the distributive property of multiplication over addition. Find the area of the rectangle with side lengths of $2x + 7$ cm and $3x + 2$ cm.

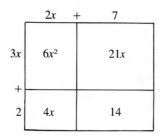

The area of the rectangle is the sum of the areas of the individual smaller rectangles.
$6x^2 + 21x + 4x + 14 = 6x^2 + 25x + 14$

The area of the rectangle is $6x^2 + 25x + 14$ cm².

Example 1

Multiply. $(3x + 1)(x + 5)$
$(3x + 1)(x + 5) = 3x^2 + 15x + x + 5$
$\qquad\qquad\qquad = 3x^2 + 16x + 5$

When multiplying two binomials, think of the word **FOIL**. Each letter represents terms that are multiplied.

F—first terms
O—outside terms
I—inside terms
L—last terms

The simplified expression can be verified by substituting values for the variables in the original expression and then in the simplified expression. If the results are the same, then the expression has been simplified. For example, if $x = 2$, then in Example 1, $(3(2) + 1)(2 + 5) = 49$ and $3(2)^2 + 16(2) + 5 = 49$. Therefore, the simplification has been done correctly.

Example 2

The area of a trapezoid is found using the formula $A = \frac{1}{2}h(a + b)$. Find the area of this trapezoid.

$A = \frac{1}{2}[4m + n][(2m - 5n) + (8m + 3n)]$

$\quad = \frac{1}{2}[4m + n][10m - 2n]$

$\quad = \frac{1}{2}[40m^2 + 2mn - 2n^2]$

$\quad = 20m^2 + mn - n^2$

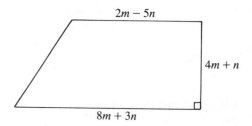

The area of the trapezoid is $20m^2 + mn - n^2$ square units.

Exercises

1. Write a polynomial expression that will represent the area of each rectangle.

a.

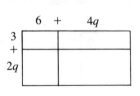

b.

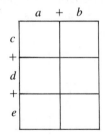

2. Copy and complete. Explain what you have done in the steps that you complete.

a. $(2x - y)(x + 3y) = 2x^2 + \blacksquare - \blacksquare - \blacksquare y^2$
$= \blacksquare$

b. $[2 - (2x - y)]^2 = \blacksquare - 4(2x - y) + \blacksquare$
$= 4 - 8x + \blacksquare + 4x^2 \blacksquare$

3. Find the product.

a. $2a(5ab - 3b)$ **b.** $-4x^2(7 + 2y)$

c. $(6p^2 - 5q)(4p)$ **d.** $4(3x^2 + 5x - 2)$

e. $3mn(2m^2 - mn - 9n^2)$

f. $(12a + b - 8c)(-3b)$

4. Find the product and simplify.

a. $(x + 1)(x - 3)$ **b.** $(x - 2)(5x + 3)$

c. $(6p + 1)(6p - 1)$ **d.** $(4 - 3a)(5 - a)$

e. $(3k + 4)(12k + 5)$ **f.** $(2s - 3t)(5s + 4t)$

g. $(5y + 2z)^2$ **h.** $(5 - 3ab)^2$

5. If the radius of a circle is given by the expression $(a + 4b - c)$ units, then find an expression for the area of the circle.

6. Simplify.

a. $2(x - 4)(2x - 5)$ **b.** $-3(6 - p)(1 + 3p)$

7. Expand and simplify.

a. $(a + 5)(2a - 1) + (3a + 2)(6a + 1)$

b. $3x(x - 2) - (2x + 1)(2x - 1)$

c. $(5m + 3n)^2 + (4m - n)(2m + 3n)$

d. $(8x - 3)(x + 5) + 2(x + 4)(3x - 4)$

e. $(5 - 2x)^2 - (x + 3)^2$

f. $5(a + 3b)(2a + b) - 2(4a - b)(a - b)$

g. $3(p - 2q)^2 + 2(p - 2q)(p + 2q)$

8. Find the area of the figure.

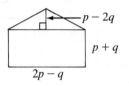

9. Simplify. Verify your answer by substituting a value for x.

a. $(x + 8)(2x + 1) - (3 - x)(3 + 2x)$

b. $2(3x + 2)(x - 5) + (x - 4)^2$

10. Find the sum of $(4a - b)(9a + 5b)$ and $(a + 3b)(2a + b)$.

11. Simplify.

a. $[3 + (a + 2b)]^2$ **b.** $[(x - y) - 4]^2$

c. $[p^2 + (q - 3r)]^2$ **d.** $[(x + 2) - 5y]^2$

e. $(3m + 4n - p)^2$ **f.** $(2u - v - w)^2$

g. $[(a^2 + b^2) + 1][(a^2 + b^2) - 1]$

h. $[x^3 + (2x - y)][x^3 - (2x - y)]$

i. $(y^2 + 6y - 4)(y^2 + 6y + 4)$

j. $(m - 3n + p)(m + 3n - p)$

k. $(4a - b - 5c)(4a + b + 5c)$

12. To the product of $(2x - y + 5z)$ and $(x + 2y - 3z)$ add $(3x - 3y + z)^2$.

13. Simplify by gathering like terms.

a. $(3p + 2q)(p + q) + (p - 5q)^2$

b. $(a - 6c)(3a + b) + (a - b)(a + 2c)$

c. $(4m + n)^2 + (m - 4n)^2$

d. $(a^2 + 2)(a^2 - 2) + (3a^2 - 5)^2$

e. $(3x + y)(x - 2y) - (x - 8y)(x + 2y)$

f. $(u - 4v)^2 - (2u + v)(2u - v)$

g. $(2p^2 + 3)^2 - (p^2 - 8)^2$

h. $(a^2 + bc)(a^2 - bc) + (3bc + a^2)^2$

Using the Library

Girolamo Cardano is one of the most extraordinary characters in the history of mathematics. Research the life of this man, and write a report stating his actual profession, his most noted work, and summarize one of the many stories told about him.

1·4 Common Factor

To factor an expression, write it as a product of simpler terms or expressions. One way to factor an expression is to find the GCF of all terms in the expression and use it as one of the factors. This is called **common factoring**.

For example, factor $16x^2y + 8xy^2$.

The GCF of the numerical coefficients is 8.
The GCF of the literal coefficients is xy.
The GCF of the two expressions is $8xy$.

Therefore, $16x^2y + 8xy^2 = 8xy(2x + y)$.
This is shown on the diagram to the right.

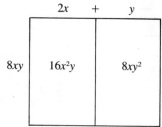

Example 1

Factor.
$16r^2s - 4rs^2t + 20rst^2$
$= 4rs(4r - st + 5t^2)$

Example 2

Express as a product.
$x(x + 2) - 5(x + 2)$
$= (x - 5)(x + 2)$

> The common factor may be a binomial or a trinomial.

Example 3

Factor.
$3p(r - 2) + 5q(r - 2) + 4(r - 2)$
$= (r - 2)(3p + 5q + 4)$

Exercises

1. Find the GCF.

a. $4a - 18b$
b. $5x^2 + 25x$
c. $75m + 30n$
d. $3a^2 - 5ab^2 - 7a^2b$
e. $8p^2 + 24$
f. $c^2 + 6cd - c + 5c^3d^5$
g. $36km^2 - 27km$
h. $10h + 25h^2 - h^3$
i. $35r^2 + 5r + 3r^6$
j. $7xy - 42xy^2 - x^2y^2$

2. Factor. Verify your factors by substituting values for the variables in the original expression and the factored expression.

a. $2k^2 + 8k - 4$
b. $10s^2 - 40st - 60st^2$
c. $8a^2 + 10ab - 6abc^2$
d. $15x^2y - 20xyz + 40xyz^2$
e. $18p^2s^2 + 27ps^2 + 6ps$
f. $12 - 48mn - 36n^2$
g. $54c + 9cd - 30c^2d^2 - 3cd^3$

3. The area of a rectangle is given by $15a - 45b + 5c^2$ cm². Find two possible expressions for the lengths of the sides.

4. Express each as a product.
a. $12mn + 20m$
b. $5s + 5st^2$
c. $2\pi r^2 + 8\pi R^2$
d. $-18p^2 - 6pq^2$
e. $9xuv + 15yuv - 6zuv$
f. $4r^3s^2 - 5r^2s - r^2s^2 + 8rs$

5. Factor.
a. $4m(p + q) + 5n(p + q)$
b. $r(x - 2) - 6(x - 2)$
c. $b(3x + 1) - c(3x + 1)$
d. $r(2p - 5) + (2p - 5)$
e. $2x(m - 4) - 3y(m - 4) + z(m - 4)$
f. $4a(2a + b) + 3b(2a + b) - c(2a + b)$

6. Find an expression for the shaded area.

$2(2x - 5)$

1·5 Solving Linear Equations

An equation is a mathematical statement asserting the equality of two expressions. Every equation has the property that by adding or subtracting the same constant from both sides of the equation, or by multiplying or dividing both sides of the equation by the same number, the equality does not change.

Example

Solve.

a. $3(m - 3) + 2 = 2(4 - m)$
$$3m - 9 + 2 = 8 - 2m$$
$$3m - 7 = 8 - 2m$$
$$3m + 2m = 8 + 7$$
$$5m = 15$$
$$m = 3$$

b. $3(x - 2)(x + 1) = (3x + 5)(x - 3)$
$$3(x^2 - x - 2) = 3x^2 - 4x - 15$$
$$3x^2 - 3x - 6 = 3x^2 - 4x - 15$$
$$-3x - 6 = -4x - 15$$
$$-3x + 4x = -15 + 6$$
$$x = -9$$

All equations can be verified by substituting the value into the original equation.

$$3(3 - 3) + 2 = 2(4 - 3)$$
$$2 = 2$$

$$3(-9 - 2)(-9 + 1) = (3(-9) + 5)(-9 - 3)$$
$$264 = 264$$

Therefore, $m = 3$ is the correct solution.

Therefore, $x = -9$ is the correct solution.

Exercises

1. In your own words, describe the mathematical operations which have been applied to obtain each equivalent equation.
$$4(3x + 2) - 5x = 2(x - 1)$$
$$12x + 8 - 5x = 2x - 2$$
$$7x + 8 = 2x - 2$$
$$5x = -10$$
$$x = -2$$

2. Solve. Verify your solution.

a. $3 - 2y = 5y + 6$

b. $3t + 8 = t + 8$

c. $5m + 2 - (m + 1) = 9$

d. $6p + 4(3 - p) = 15$

e. $s - 2 = 10 - (3s - 5)$

f. $2(4x - 5) - 3 = 3(x + 2)$

3. Solve.

a. $(3x^2 - 2x + 12) - (3x^2 - x + 6) = 0$

b. $4x^2 - 5x - 1 = (2x + 1)(2x - 3)$

c. $14 - (x + 3)(x - 3) = (2 - x)(4 + x)$

d. $3x(2x - 3) + 8 = (x - 1)(6x - 5)$

e. $(8x + 3)(x + 2) = (2x - 1)(4x - 9)$

f. $(x - 2)^2 - (x + 5)(x - 5) = 2x$

4. Find the masses of two objects if the sum of their masses is 33 kg and the mass of one object is 6 kg more than twice the other.

5. The perimeter of Port Severn Park is 8.6 km. If the width is increased by 0.5 km and then tripled, it would be equal to the length. Find the dimensions of the park.

6. The measure of the largest angle of a triangle is 2° less than 4 times the smallest angle. The third angle is 8° more than half the largest angle. Find the measure of the three angles.

7. Solve for x.

a. $\dfrac{x}{4} - 5 = 6$

b. $\dfrac{3}{5}x + \dfrac{2}{5} = 1$

c. $3x - 4 = 7$

d. $2x - 7 = 12$

e. $0.9x - 0.4 = 0.3$

f. $2x - 0.5 = 18.8$

g. $\dfrac{x}{6} - \dfrac{2x}{3} = -3$

h. $\dfrac{5x - 3}{2} - \dfrac{3x - 2}{3} = 20$

i. $\dfrac{x}{5} - \dfrac{x}{7} = 4$

j. $\dfrac{x + 4}{3} - \dfrac{x + 4}{4} = x + 4$

1·6 Word Problems

Equations can be used to solve problems. Although the problem may be stated in a sentence, it is possible to translate the facts of the problem into an equation and then solve that equation.

Example

Cosmetsales sold $4 000 000 more in cosmetics than twice the sales of Cosmetworld. Cosmetiks sold $10 000 000 less than three times the sales of Cosmetworld. If all three cosmetic outlets have a combined sale of $126 000 000, then how much in sales did each store have?

Let x represent the amount of cosmetics Cosmetworld sold in millions of dollars.
The amount of sales Cosmetsales had is $(2x + 4)$ million dollars.
The amount of sales Cosmetiks had is $(3x - 10)$ million dollars.

$$x + (2x + 4) + (3x - 10) = 126$$
$$6x - 6 = 126$$
$$6x = 132$$
$$x = 22$$

Cosmetworld sold $22 000 000 worth of cosmetics, Cosmetsales sold $48 000 000 worth of cosmetics, and Cosmetiks sold $56 000 000 worth of cosmetics.

Exercises

1. Claims are often made by countries on the number of armaments in that country. Write an expression for each claim.
a. x has 18 more submarines than y.
b. m has 1500 fewer tanks than twice that of n.
c. x has twice the satellites of m and r.

2. Five years ago, Twyla was twice Craig's age. If Craig's present age is k years, then write an expression to represent Twyla's present age.

3. A box contains 15 coins in dimes and quarters. If there are n dimes, then write an expression to represent the total value of the coins.

4. Two computer manufacturers claim to have sold a total of 38 000 computers in one year. If Compworld has sold 2000 more than three times Compstore, then how many computers did each store sell?

5. Find two numbers such that their sum is 86 and one number is 8 more than the other.

6. The price of two compact disk players is such that their difference is $110. If the price of the less expensive one is tripled and the price of the more expensive one is increased by $150, the sum of the numbers is $880. Find the price of the two compact disk players.

7. A car travelling at a certain rate takes 3 h to travel from London to Niagara Falls. If the rate of travel is increased by 20 km/h, the time to travel the same distance is decreased by 1 h. Find the distance from London to Niagara Falls.

8. Three video retailers are competitors. Outlet Y claims that it rented 3 times as many videos as Outlet M. Outlet A claims it rented 70 000 more than Outlet M. Also, Outlet Y claims that it rented twice as many videos as Outlet A. If all claims are true, then how many videos did each outlet rent?

9. The length of a rectangle is 3 cm less than four times its width. If the perimeter of the rectangle is 54 cm, find the dimensions of the rectangle.

1·7 The Four-Step Model

There are many strategies and methods that can help you solve problems. Mathematics can help to interpret a problem, organize the data so that the problem becomes easier, and obtain a solution. The process of problem solving can be organized into a series of four steps.

1. Understand the Problem   **2.** Develop a Plan
3. Carry Out the Plan   **4.** Look Back

Since steps 2 and 3 often involve the same strategies, they are combined below.

Understand the Problem
- Note key words and phrases.
- Identify important facts.

a. State what is given and what is wanted.
b. Omit irrelevant information.
c. Place all necessary information on a diagram.
- Determine if there are hidden assumptions.
- Consider other interpretations.

Develop and Carry Out a Plan
- Look for patterns.
- Guess and check.
- Use direct computation.
- Draw a diagram.
- Find a table of values.
- Solve a simpler problem.
- Use reasoning.
- Work backwards towards a solution.
- Use formulas or equations.

Look Back
- Write a conclusion.
- Ensure the answer is reasonable.
- If necessary, justify your solution.
- Make and solve a similar problem.
- Solve the problem a different way to ensure a correct solution.
- Generalize the solution.

Example 1

Tanya and Max leave home on bicycles and ride to Burlington 100 km away. Max can average 25 km/h, while Tanya takes one hour longer than Max to ride to Burlington. Max and Tanya must attend the same function in town at 14:00. When should each leave home? How fast will Tanya be riding?

Understand the Problem
We must determine how long Max and Tanya will be riding, and then find how fast Tanya is moving. When solving any problem, ask yourself if all the necessary information is given. What further piece of information will allow us to solve the problem.

Develop a Plan
Knowing how long Max takes to ride to Burlington allows us to find how long it takes Tanya to travel to town. The formula of distance = rate × time can be used to find the necessary information.

Carry Out the Plan
From the formula $d = rt$, the time it takes Max to ride to Burlington is

$$t = \frac{d}{r}$$
$$= \frac{100}{25}$$
$$= 4$$

Max takes 4 h to ride to Burlington and should leave home at 10:00. Tanya takes 5 h for the same ride and should leave home at 09:00. We can now find how fast Tanya will be riding.

9

$$r = \frac{d}{t}$$
$$= \frac{100}{5}$$
$$= 20$$

Tanya will average 20 km/h.

Look Back

In the Look Back section of any problem, you should write the solution to the problem, and also consider different ways of solving the same problem. In this case, formulas were used to solve the problem. However, if you did not know the formulas, the problem could still be solved by finding patterns. For example, we could set up a table of values to determine how far Max travels each hour until he reaches Burlington 100 km away. This would then tell us how long it would take Tanya to reach Burlington. Then divide the total distance by the length of time to find her average speed.

Example 2

The dimensions of a square are changed to form a rectangle. The width of the rectangle is 20 cm longer than the side of the square and the length is 30 cm less than 3 times the side of the square. The area of the rectangle is 300 cm² greater than 3 times the area of the square. Find the dimensions of the square and the rectangle.

Understand the Problem

Find the dimensions of the square and the rectangle.
Sketch the square and the rectangle and label all relevant information.
Let x represent the length of the square.

Develop a Plan

Write and solve equations relating the areas of the square and the rectangle.

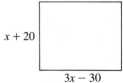

Carry Out the Plan

The area of the square is x^2 cm².
The area of the rectangle is $(x + 20)(3x - 30)$ cm².
Since, the area of the rectangle is 300 cm² more than 3 times the area of the square, then
$$(x + 20)(3x - 30) = 3x^2 + 300$$
$$3x^2 + 30x - 600 = 3x^2 + 300$$
$$30x = 900$$
$$x = 30$$

Look Back

The square has dimensions of 30 cm by 30 cm and the rectangle has dimensions of 50 cm by 60 cm. The area of the square is 900 cm² and the area of the rectangle is 3000 cm².
Since the area of the rectangle is 3 times the area of the square plus 300, the solution is verified.

Problems can be solved in a number of different ways. Try a variety of strategies and approaches to every problem. Remember, do not give up after one try. Your method of solution may not solve the particular problem, but it may be applicable to a different problem.

Exercises

1. Why was a diagram used in Example 2 but not in Example 1? Explain.

2. In Example 1 of the display, are the speeds obtained for the two cyclists reasonable? Explain.

3. The sum of three numbers is 55. The second number is 6 more than the first and the third is one more than twice the first. Find the numbers.

4. The sum of one third a number and two fifths of the same number is 176. Find the number.

5. The sum of the interior angles of a polygon of n sides is $90(2n - 4)°$. Find the number of sides of a polygon if the sum of its interior angles is $1080°$.

6. The length of a rectangular garden is 4 m longer than its width. If each dimension is increased by 2 m, then the area is increased by 24 m². Find the dimensions of the original garden.

7. Kari invested $5000, part of it at 10%/a and the rest at 12%/a. If the total interest earned in one year was $556, then how much was invested at each rate?

8. In a stairway, there are 24 steps of uniform height. If each step was made 3 cm higher, then only 20 steps would have been required. How high is each step?

9. Craig jogs a specified distance at 15 km/h and then returns by bicycle at 24 km/h. If he takes a total of 39 min, then how far did he run?

10. At 09:00, Jill leaves home for Jasper driving at an average speed of 60 km/h. Her brother Terry leaves from the same house at 09:20 and follows Jill into Jasper. If Terry drives at an average speed of 70 km/h, then how far will Jill have driven before he passes her?

11. Find three consecutive even integers whose sum is 114.

12. A boat sails from a dock downstream and back to the dock in 18 min. The boat averages 40 km/h in still water and the current is flowing at 8 km/h. How far downstream did the boat travel measured to the nearest kilometre?

13. An aunt is 3 times as old as her nephew. In eight years, she will be four years older than twice his age. Find their present ages.

14. The sum of the ages of Mark's two sons is equal to his own age of 51 a. Twenty-one years ago, Mark's older son was twice as old as the younger son.
a. Find the present ages of the sons.
b. How old was Mark when the sum of his sons' ages was half his age?

15. Ken received a bonus of $94 500 paid over 6 a. In each successive year, he is paid twice as much as the previous year. How much was the payment in the fifth year?

16. Adult tickets for the drama production were $4.00 each, while the student prices were $3.50 each. If a total of 640 tickets were sold for $2330, then find the number of each type of ticket sold.

For Exercises 17 and 18, read and discuss the problem with two of your classmates. Decide what strategy is best to solve the problem, explain the selection, and then solve the problem independently.

17. The middle digit of a three-digit number is 9. The sum of the three digits is 16. If the hundred's digit and the one's digit are reversed, the new number is 2 more than twice the original number. Find the original number.

18. Rules for a mathematics contest state that 5 points will be awarded for each correct answer but one point will be deducted for each incorrect response. Grant scored a total of 78 points on the 24-question contest. How many questions did Grant answer correctly?

1·8 Understand the Problem

In the previous section, you were introduced to the four-step model as a whole. In this section, we will look at the Understand the Problem and the Look Back steps in more detail. To Understand the Problem, you consider three basic components: the given information, what is required to solve in the problem, and the skills that may be used to solve the problem. The Look Back step is related closely to the Understand the Problem step as you should be looking for other ways to solve the same problem or attempting to increase the understanding of a process by making a similar problem and having one of your classmates attempt a solution.

Example

Starting with the number 99, reach the number 100 only by adding 11 or subtracting 7.

Understand the Problem
Starting with the number 99, we are asked to obtain the number 100 by a series of additions of 11 and subtractions of 7. These are the only operations that we are allowed to use.

Develop a Plan
Use systematic trial and a series of operations to get 100 from 99.

Carry Out the Plan
One possibility is $99 + 11 - 7 - 7 + 11 - 7$. Notice that we either add or subtract depending on whether the sum is over or under 100. For example, $99 + 11 = 110$. Since this is greater than 100, the next procedure was to subtract 7.

Look Back
Are there other solutions?
What did we do?
Will a graphic representation help?

Can we generalize the solution?
Can we solve the problem another way?
Can we make and solve a similar problem?

A graphic representation is started for you. The completion of this chart will be left as an exercise.

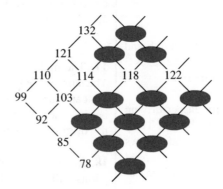

The strategy of making a similar problem can help you to understand the problem so that when you meet another similar problem, the strategy will be apparent. You will meet this strategy several times in this set of exercises.

Exercises

1. Show another way of reaching 100 for the example in the display.

2. Copy and complete the chart in the Look Back section of the display.
a. How many different routes are there to 100?
b. What is the minimum number of steps to 100?
c. Is there a maximum number of steps? Explain.

For Exercises 3, 4, and 5, state the given information, the required information, construct a diagram to solve the problem, and generalize the solution process in your own words.

3. Starting with the number 375, obtain the number 376 by the calculations of adding 13 and subtracting 17.

4. Given the number 484, reach the number 496 by adding 8 and subtracting 12.

5. Starting with the number 56, reach the number 7.5 by adding 4 and dividing by 2.
a. Solve the problem in a different way.
b. Can you use the graphic method used in the example to generalize this problem? Explain.
c. Make a similar problem by solving the same problem without dividing.

6. Is it possible to reach 17 by starting at 107 and using only additions of 11 and divisions by 3?
a. Explain some of the strategies that you might try.
b. Is there a way to solve the problem without dividing? If so, create a similar problem and challenge two of your classmates to solve your problem.

7. Construct a problem similar to the one in the display by using only the calculations of addition and finding the square root. Exchange your problem with two of your classmates.

8. Make a problem similar to the one in the display by using only the calculations of squaring and subtraction. Exchange your problem with two of your classmates.

9. Is it possible to make up a question using addition and subtraction for which there is no solution? Explain.

Solve these problems using any method.

10. Simplify $\frac{5+7}{10} + \frac{7}{15}$. Show all the ways that this question can be solved.

11. A.T., the "Mathematics Wizard", stated that "the expression $(a + 24n)^{\frac{1}{2}}$ produces all primes except 2 and 3 when n is a whole number". Is A.T. correct? Explain.

12. Which multiple of 7 added to 9 gives a 0 in the unit's digit?

Historical Note

George Polya (1887-1985)
George Polya, a noted professor at Stanford University, was an ambitious and curious student. Whenever he performed an experiment, or read a book on a subject, there were questions that disturbed him: "The solution seems to work, but how is it possible to invent such a solution? How could people discover such facts? How can I discover or invent such facts?"

Here is one of George Polya's more famous problems. See if you can solve it.
"A traveller, stopping at an inn, discovered that the innkeeper was an old friend. The innkeeper told the traveller that he had three children. The product of their ages was 72 and the sum of their ages was the same as the number of rooms at the inn. The traveller knew the number of rooms in the inn but he told the innkeeper that he needed more information to find the ages of the children. The innkeeper told the traveller that the oldest loves to ride horses. What are the ages of the children?

1·9 Using Algebra

In many "word problems", you are asked to solve an equation for a single variable. However, not all problems need to be solved completely for a single variable. Sometimes, it is more convenient to consider an equation as a single entity, solve an equation for an expression as opposed to a variable, and then to use the value of the expression to solve the remainder of the problem. It will be necessary to use your knowledge of algebra, as well as a wide range of mathematical skills, to solve many of these problems.

Example

Using the equation $6(3x - 5) = 12$, evaluate the expression for $\dfrac{3x - 5}{2}$.

Understand the Problem
In this question, we are **not** asked to solve for x. However, we are required to evaluate an expression. In this case, to find the value of one half of $3x - 5$.

Develop a Plan
Both expressions have a common factor of $3x - 5$. Therefore, treat $3x - 5$ as a single entity, find the value of $3x - 5$ from the equation, and substitute this value into the expression. In this way, we do not have to find the value of x to find the value of the expression.

Carry Out the Plan
$6(3x - 5) = 12$

$\dfrac{6(3x - 5)}{6} = \dfrac{12}{6}$

$(3x - 5) = 2$

Substitute 2 for $3x - 5$ in the expression.

$\dfrac{3x - 5}{2} = \dfrac{2}{2}$

$= 1$

Look Back
The value of the expression $\dfrac{3x - 5}{2}$ is 1. Notice how it was convenient to consider $3x - 5$ as a single entity rather than to solve for x. You also could evaluate the expression by finding the value of the variable from the equation and then substituting it into the expression. In this case, when solving for x, fractions will be introduced into the expression and there is a stronger possibility of error. However, if you wish to verify your answer, solve for x and substitute it into the expression. If you are careful, the same result will appear.

Exercises

1. Solve for x.
a. $3x - 9 = 27$
b. $5x + 8 = 52$
c. $4x + 8 = 2x - 6$
d. $9 - 8x = 12 + 3x$
e. $13x - 9 - 23x + 27 = 0$
f. $42x - 86 = 26 - 34x$

2. Using the equation $7(2x + 3) = 49$, evaluate these expressions.

a. $3(2x + 3)$
b. $\dfrac{2x + 3}{3}$
c. $10x + 15$
d. $4x + 6$
e. $\dfrac{8x + 12}{4}$
f. $\dfrac{5(4x + 6)}{7}$

14

3. From the equation $8(5x - 1) = (5x - 1) + 21$, evaluate the expression $5x - 1$.
a. Evaluate the expression $5x - 1$ in a different way.
b. Which way do you prefer? Explain.

4. From the equation $7(x - 8) = 2(x - 8) - 28$, evaluate the expression $x - 8$.

5. From the equation $8(x - 5) = 81$, evaluate the expression $2x - 10$.

6. From the equation $3(x - 11) = 8$, evaluate the expression $5x - 55$.

7. From the equation $5(x + 2) = x + 5$, evaluate the expression $2x + 4$. (*Hint*: Express $x + 5$ in terms of $x + 2$.)

8. From the equation $8(x - 3) = x - 9$, evaluate the expression $5x - 15$.

9. If $\dfrac{3x - 6}{5x} = 0$, then evaluate the expression $x - 2$.

For the remainder of the exercises, use any strategy you wish to solve the problem. Explain why you chose the particular strategy in each case.

10. If $\dfrac{1}{3 - \dfrac{x}{3 - x}} = \dfrac{1}{3}$, then find the value of x.

11. If $4a - 4b = 12$, then find the value of the expression $b - a$.

12. For any two positive numbers r and s, where r and s are both greater than one, and such that $r = 3s$,
a. find the least common multiple of r and s.
b. find the greatest common divisor of r and s.

13. Write three monomials whose sum is a monomial.

14. The difference between two fractions is $\frac{6}{13}$. Find the two fractions if they are both in lowest terms and they both have different denominators.

15. Write three monomials whose sum is a binomial.

16. Write three monomials whose sum is a trinomial.

17. Write a binomial and a monomial whose sum is a binomial.

18. Write a trinomial and a binomial whose difference is a monomial.

19. The average of two numbers is $z + w$. If one of the numbers is z, then find the other number.

20. From the equation, $x^5 y^4 z^2 - x^3 y^4 z^4 = 0$, find a possible value of $x^3 y^3 z^2$.

21. From the equation $(x^2 + 3x + 2)^{x^2 - x} = 1$, find a possible value of $x - 1$.

22. From the equation $[(x + y)^2]^{2x - x^2} = 1$, find a possible value of $x - 2$.

23. Write a trinomial and a binomial whose difference is a binomial.

24. Write two trinomials whose difference is a binomial.

25. The product of two numbers is 24 and the sum of their squares is 52. Find the negative difference of the two numbers.

26. A toy manufacturer has given a $200 credit in merchandise to one of its customers. The customer may have either the $8 trucks or the $12 wooden trains. Make a list of the possible choices the customer has to obtain the $200 credit exactly.

1·10 Develop and Carry Out a Plan

Some problems can be solved by the first strategy that comes to mind. However, for the majority of problems, it will be necessary to attempt a solution using more than one strategy before arriving at a solution. Because of the nature of most problems, it is advisable to think of a strategy that could be used successfully before attempting to solve the problem. By developing a plan before attempting the problem, you may be able to save many unnecessary calculations. Some of the strategies that can be used to solve problems are listed.

- Look for patterns.
- Direct computation.
- Construct a table of values.
- Use reasoning.
- List all possibilities.

- Systematic trial.
- Draw and label a diagram.
- Solve a simpler problem.
- Work backwards towards a solution.

Example

A.T., the "Mathematics Wizard", stated that in a jar full of coins there is $111.17 with exactly 25 pennies. Is A.T. correct?

Understand the Problem
We must determine whether A.T. is correct in saying that there can be 25 pennies in a jar containing $111.17.

Develop a Plan
1. Since there is a definite amount of money involved, attempt to write an equation from the given information, and then solve the equation.

2. Use reasoning (or critical analysis) to determine whether there is a flaw in A.T.'s reasoning.

Carry Out the Plan
1. Let n, d, q, h, and D represent the number of nickels, dimes, quarters, half dollars, and one dollar coins respectively. Therefore, the equation is $5n + 10d + 25q + 50h + 100D + 25 = 11\ 117$. Since there are no other relations from which to write equations, this strategy will not yield a solution. Therefore, return to the Develop a Plan step and try the next strategy.

2. One way to check A.T.'s reasoning is to remove 25 pennies from the jar. Once the 25 pennies are removed, $110.92 remains in the jar. Since it is impossible to have a value of $0.92 without more pennies, A.T.'s reasoning is incorrect.

Look Back
Many of the problems that you will encounter can be solved in a number of different ways. These other strategies should be explored in the Look Back section of your solution. This case is no exception. You could have solved a simpler problem by asking if there is any way to have a total of $1.17 using 25 pennies. This is done by knowing that $110.00 can be formed by one hundred ten $1.00 coins. You will then be able to find quickly that there is no combination of silver coins that will produce a total that is not a multiple of 5. Since 17 is not a multiple of 5, it is impossible to have $1.17. Are there other strategies that could have been used to solve the problem?

Exercises

1. What other strategies could have been used to solve the problems in the display? Discuss with classmates the various strategies used. Which strategy do you prefer?

For Exercises 2 to 4, read and discuss each problem in a small group. Decide which strategy you would choose to solve the problem and explain why you chose that strategy. Record those strategies you think will yield a solution.

2. From a ten-dollar bill, Ming receives $2.85 change consisting of quarters and dimes. He says that he was given a total of 15 coins: 9 quarters and 6 dimes. Does his answer satisfy the given conditions?

3. Jock would like to divide his 300 ha farm into 15 equal parts. He would then plant 9 parts with cauliflower, 1 part with cabbage, and 5 parts with carrots. How many hectares of cauliflower, cabbage, and carrots will this ratio give?

4. For a class camping trip in Banff, Shelley has been selected to buy the hotdogs and buns for the weekend trip. She is required to purchase 264 hotdogs and buns. When Shelley gets to the store, she finds that there are 12 wieners per package and 8 buns per package. If the wieners cost $2.69 per package and the buns cost $1.09 per package, then what is her total bill?

5. Ken is one year older than twice Colin's age. In six years Ken will be five years younger than twice Colin's age. How old will Ken and Colin be in six years if the sum of their present ages is 40?

6. Twenty chairs are to be placed around a room so that each wall has 6 chairs. How can this be done?

7. Find the value of a and b in the expression if each letter represents a single unique digit.

$$\begin{array}{r} 325a \\ -\ a763 \\ \hline a4bb \end{array}$$

8. Is it possible to receive $2.85 in quarters and dimes if 16 coins are used?

9. The sum and product of 3 consecutive natural numbers are the same. What are the numbers?

10. Find the sum of these numbers.
$$400 - 398 + 396 - 394 + \ldots + 4 - 2$$

11. Lynne mistakenly multiplies a number on her calculator by 25 instead of dividing by 25. If the number on the calculator is 23 750, then what is the correct answer to the problem?

12. In the equilateral triangle, the value of y is 7. What is the area of the triangle?

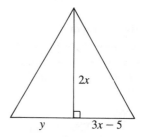

13. Oscar is climbing a 21 m rope. Every 30 s he climbs 3 m and then slips back 2 m in the next 30 s. At this rate, how long will it take him to climb the rope?

14. These numbers were presented to a contestant on a game show: 3, 12, 21, 96, 51, 30, 60, 123, 72, and 6. The contestant was asked to make a sum of 200 using any combination of the given numbers. Is it possible? Explain.

15. It takes Fatima 24 min to row a boat 60 m against the current of a river and 16 min to row the same distance with the current. If she rows at a constant pace, then what is the speed of the river?

1·11 Perimeter and Area I

The perimeter of a geometric figure with straight sides can be calculated by adding the lengths of the individual sides. Area is the amount of surface taken by an object. The table gives the perimeter and area formulas for some of the more common geometric shapes.

Figure	Symbols	Perimeter Formula	Area Formula
Square	s	$P = 4s$	$A = s^2$
Rectangle	ℓ, w	$P = 2(\ell + w)$	$A = \ell w$
Parallelogram	a, b, h	$P = 2(a + b)$	$A = bh$
Triangle	a, b, c, h	$P = a + b + c$	$A = \dfrac{bh}{2}$
Trapezoid	a, b, c, d, h	$P = a + b + c + d$	$A = \dfrac{h(a + b)}{2}$

Example

The Metro Zoo Committee is planning to build a new enclosure for the Plains Buffalo. The zoo has an area available as shown in the diagram. The enclosure requires a moat 1 m wide and 6 m deep; and a 4 m high fence on the outside of the moat. A landscaper estimated that the fence and moat together would cost $230/m and the landscaping on the interior of the enclosure would cost $7.50/m². Calculate the total cost for constructing the enclosure.

Understand the Problem

To calculate the cost of the fence and moat we need to calculate the perimeter. To calculate the landscaping cost we need the area of the enclosure.

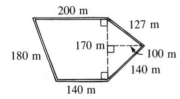

Develop a Plan

To calculate the perimeter of the enclosure, find the sum of the outside dimensions. Multiply the result by the charge per metre for the fence and moat to find the cost of enclosing the exhibit. To calculate the area of the enclosure, find the sum of the area of the trapezoid and the area of the triangle, and multiply the result by the landscaping cost.

Carry Out the Plan

The perimeter of the enclosure is 787 m. Therefore, the cost of the moat and the fence is 787×230 or $181 010. The area of the trapezoid and triangle can be found using the formula

$$A = \frac{h(a + b)}{2} + \frac{bh}{2}$$
$$= \frac{170(140 + 200)}{2} + \frac{170 \times 100}{2}$$
$$= 37\ 400$$

Therefore, the cost of landscaping is $37\ 400 \times \$7.50$ or $280 500.

Look Back

The total cost to the zoo is the sum of the two separate costs. In this case, the cost to the zoo is $181 010 + $280 500 or $461 510.

Exercises

1. In your own words, define the terms "perimeter" and "area".

2. Calculate the perimeter of each figure.

a.

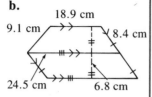

8 m   11 m   15 m

b.

18.9 cm
9.1 cm
8.4 cm
24.5 cm   6.8 cm

3. The Peterson's wish to install a ceramic-tile deck around their rectangular swimming pool. The pool measures 10 m by 12 m and the deck is to be 2 m in width.
a. Find the perimeter of the pool.
b. Calculate the perimeter of the outer edge of the tiled deck.
c. Calculate the area of the tiled deck.

4. The Citadel in San Cristoble, Mexico, is surrounded by a moat and a safety fence. A fence costing $23.76/m was installed along the inner edge of the moat as a safety measure. Find the cost of installing the fence.

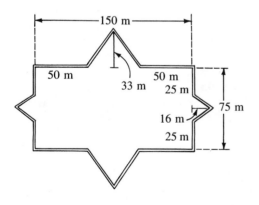

150 m
50 m   50 m
33 m   25 m
75 m
16 m
25 m

5. Calculate the cost of painting Joe's sculpting studio with two coats of paint. The studio is square (7.62 m on each side), the walls are 4 m high, the roof of the studio has three skylights 1 m in diameter, and 1 L of paint costs $6.90 and covers an area of approximately 10 m².

6. Deidre purchased a hotel in Salmon Arm. She decides to refurbish the hotel in the original style. She can re-do the old roller blinds with new fabric or replace them altogether. Material with the required width of 1.7 m could be purchased for $15.35/m. There are 10 windows measuring 3 m by 1.7 m and 12 windows measuring 1 m by 1.7 m. Fringe for the border running along the bottom edge costs $1.80/m. Pull tabs cost $1.50 each. To replace the blinds altogether, it would cost $43 for the smaller size and $67 for the larger size. To save as much money as possible, should she refinish or replace the blinds?

7. One bolt of wallpaper has a width of 53 cm and a length of 10 m. Calculate the minimum number of bolts needed to cover the walls of a room measuring 3.7 m by 4.6 m with a wall height of 2.4 m if you must allow 10% extra wallpaper for matching the pattern. The doors and windows in the room cover a total area of 10 m², and the wallpaper chosen costs $17.80 per bolt.

8. From the area of a parallelogram, show how to obtain the formula for the area of
a. a triangle.   **b.** a trapezoid.

9. Show that the diagonals divide a rectangle into four equal areas.

10. Diana built a cottage on Vancouver Island overlooking the ocean. The cottage is situated on an 80 m by 130 m property. She wants to surround the property with pine trees for privacy. Find the total cost of the trees if she plants trees every 1.5 m, the nursery charges $6.25 per tree, and the nursery plants them for $1.25 per tree.

11. Find the area of a regular pentagon with sides of 10 cm if the **apothem** (distance from the geometric centre to the midpoint of one side) is 6.8 cm. Use a calculator if one is available.

1·12 Perimeter and Area II

The circumference (perimeter) and area of circles also can be found using formulas. In this case, the area of a circle is πr^2, where r is the radius of the circle and π is about 3.14, and the perimeter of a circle is $2\pi r$. A **sector** of a circle is part of a circle bounded by two radii and the contained arc. The area of the sector can be calculated as a fraction of the area of a complete circle using the formula $\frac{\text{angle}}{360}\pi r^2$.

Example

A campsite has a circular hot tub with a circumference of 24 m. The owners wish to put a circular patio around the hot tub. If its width is to be the same as the radius of the hot tub, then find the cost to build the patio if cement costs $2.15/m² and a student will charge $0.75/m² to pour the cement.

Understand the Problem
The circumference of the hot tub is 24 m.
The cost of the cement is $2.15/m² and the cost of pouring it is $0.75/m².
Draw and label an appropriate diagram to summarize the information. If the radius of the hot tub is known, then the area of the patio can be found.

Develop a Plan
Use the circumference formula to find the radius of the hot tub. Then the radius of the total area covered is twice the radius of the hot tub. The area covered by the cement is the difference of the total area and the area covered by the hot tub. Multiplying the area covered by the patio and the combined cost will give the cost of the patio around the hot tub.

Carry Out the Plan
$C = 2\pi r$
$24 = 2 \times 3.14 \times r$
$r \doteq 3.8$
The radius is found using this calculator keying sequence and the answer rounded to one decimal place.
24 ÷ (2 × 3.14) = **3.8216561**

Total radius is 2×3.8 or 7.6 m. Therefore,
Area of cement = Total area − Area of hot tub
$$= \pi R^2 - \pi r^2$$
$$= \pi(R^2 - r^2)$$
$$\doteq 3.14(7.6^2 - 3.8^2)$$
$$\doteq 136.0$$

Look Back
The total cost of the patio will be $136.0 \times (2.15 + 0.75)$ or about $394.40.

Exercises

For all exercises in this section, use a calculator if one is available.

1. If the perimeter of an object and the circumference of a circle are the same, which will occupy more area?

2. Calculate the perimeter and area of each. Draw and label an appropriate diagram.
a. a circle with a radius of 5.23 m
b. a circle with a radius of 101.5 m

3. Calculate the cost to fence a circular enclosure whose radius is 50 m when fencing costs $24.70/m.

4. A sheep tethered on a rope can eat a circular patch of grass with a 10 m radius in one day. Calculate the area of this patch.

5. Joey observes the sheep in Exercise 4 and sees money to be made by renting out his 3 sheep as lawnmowers. Ali hires Joey to mow his lawn with the sheep. If the lawn is rectangular and measures 45 m by 15 m, how long will it take Joey to have the lawn cut completely? (*Hint*: How long is one day?)

6. The diameter of the trunk of a pine tree is approximately 30 cm at its base. Slices of the base of the trunk are made into coffee tables. Find the area of the top of a coffee table made from a slice of this tree trunk.

7. A tree specialist has to measure the area of the stump of a tree but it is not a perfect circle. Initially, the specialist covers the stump with 11 disks, each having a radius of 5 cm, so that almost all of the stump is covered. Then, in the same way, she covers the stump with 24 disks, each having a radius of 2.5 cm. In each case, the area of the stump is approximated by adding the areas of the individual disks. Calculate the approximated area in each case. Which is the more accurate measurement?

8. Calculate the area of the track shown if it is 7 m wide and the ends are semicircular in shape.

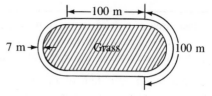

9. Compare the areas of two circles if one has a radius of twice the other.

10. Find the radii of the inner circle and the outer circle if a washer has an area of 10 cm². (*Hint*: Draw and label an appropriate diagram.)

11. A sector of a circle with a radius of 12 cm has an inner angle of 70°. Calculate the perimeter and the area of the sector.

12. A sector of a circle with radius 50 cm has an area of 760 cm². Calculate the sector angle.

13. A goat is tied to the corner of a 12 m by 16 m barn on a rope that is 8 m in length. Find the area of the grass surrounding the barn that the goat can eat.

14. A square lawn has a side length of 16 m and encloses a circular flower bed with a radius of 7 m. How many 1 kg bags of fertilizer for the garden are needed if it is applied at the rate of 60 g/m²?

15. State a relationship between arc length and sector area for a given radius.

Braintickler

Draw one square on a page and count how many squares there are in total. Draw a second square on a page and divide it into 4 equal squares. How many squares are there in this diagram? Draw a third square on a page, divide it into 9 equal squares, and decide how many squares there are in this diagram. Continue this pattern and determine how many squares there are on a checkerboard?

1·13 Surface Area

The surface area of a solid is the sum of the areas of the faces. In most shapes there are several faces or surfaces. For example, a right prism has six faces, and a triangular-based pyramid has four faces. To find the surface area of a shape, calculate the area of each face or surface and find the sum.

In the example, the problem of finding the surface area of a cylinder is solved through a series of questions. Each question suggests a strategy or approach that could be used to solve the problem. While reading this example, answer each question and complete the indicated steps.

Example

Calculate the surface area of a cylinder with a radius of 14 cm and a height of 23 cm.

Understand the Problem
Surface area is the area covered by the faces. Can the situation be simulated to help understand the problem? Will a drawing help to understand the problem?

Develop a Plan
The situation can be simulated by using a tin can. The top and bottom can be removed and the side cut and flattened into a rectangle. A drawing may be beneficial. A net is a two-dimensional drawing of the surfaces of the object. The area of the individual surfaces can be calculated and then added to find the total surface area.

Carry Out the Plan
If a tin can is not available, then try drawing and labelling an appropriate diagram.

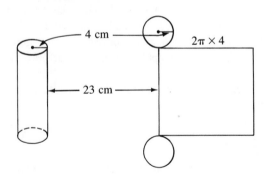

The area of the two circles and the rectangle is $2\pi(4)^2 + 2\pi(4)(23)$ or about 678.24 cm².

Look Back
The surface area of this cylinder is about 678.24 cm². By using the net, the problem of finding the surface area was broken into simpler parts by finding the area of the circles and then adding the area of the rectangle. This procedure can be generalized into a formula. Let h represent the height of the cylinder and r represent the radius. Therefore, we can calculate the surface area of a cylinder using the formula $2(\pi r^2) + 2\pi rh$ or $2\pi r(r + h)$. Make and solve a similar problem to find a general formula for the surface area of a square-based pyramid, a right prism, and a triangular prism.

Exercises

1. In your own words, define the term "surface area".

2. What does each product represent in the expression $2\pi r^2 + 2\pi rh$?

3. Calculate the surface area of each shape. Generalize the procedure to find the formulas for the surface area of a right prism, a triangular prism, and a square-based pyramid. Use a calculator if one is available.

a.

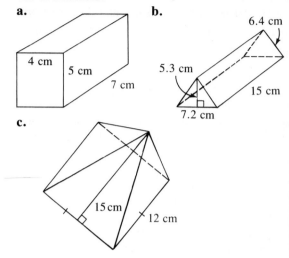

b.

c.

4. Calculate the surface area of each shape.

a.

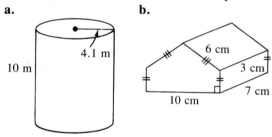

b.

c.

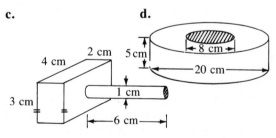

d.

5. Akim makes aluminum boxes in the shape of a rectangular solid for gifts. One size he makes has a length of 10 cm, a width of 6 cm, and a height of 4 cm. The cost of aluminum is $48.50 for each 60 cm by 60 cm sheet. Calculate the cost of the aluminum for 100 boxes.

6. Calculate the area that can be decorated for a rectangular cookie tin measuring 12 cm by 6 cm by 5 cm.

7. Increase each of the dimensions of the box in Exercise 6 by 25%. What is the percentage increase in surface area?

8. The physics lab has an oblique glass prism with the measurements shown. Calculate the surface area of the prism.

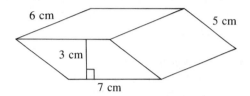

9. Tincans Limited makes decorated cylindrical containers with a fitted top that overlaps by 0.5 cm. The cost to the company is related to the size of the can and the amount of surface-area decoration. The can with a radius of 5 cm and a height of 10 cm costs $0.50 for the tin and $1.75 for the decoration. Determine the cost of producing a can having a radius of 5 cm and a height of 5 cm if the cost of the decoration is proportional to the surface area.

10. Mei-Lee bakes cakes for special occasions. One of her specialties is a three-layer fruit cake with almond icing. The icing and decorating costs $0.12/cm². The top layer of the cake has a diameter of 8 cm, the middle layer has a diameter of 12 cm, and the bottom layer has a diameter of 16 cm. Each layer is 6 cm high.
a. Draw and label an appropriate diagram of the cake.
b. Calculate the surface area of the cake.
c. Calculate the total cost of the cake to a customer. (*Hint*: The bottom of the cake will have no icing.)

11. Find the surface area of a solid hemisphere whose diameter is 13 m. (*Hint*: The volume of a sphere is $\frac{4}{3}\pi r^3$.)

1·14 Volume

A cone and a pyramid both have a volume equal to one third the volume of a corresponding cylinder or prism respectively. The volume of a cylinder or a prism is the product of the area of the base and the height. For example, the volume of a cylinder is $\pi r^2 h$, where h is the perpendicular distance from the midpoint of the base to the top. Therefore, the volume of a cone is $\frac{1}{3}\pi r^2 h$. However, the solution to many problems will require more than just the application of the formula.

Example

A wheelbarrow is made in the shape of an inverted "truncated pyramid" with the top edges 60 cm each and the bottom edges 30 cm each. Its slant height (the perpendicular distance from the midpoint of a base to the vertex) is half the slant height of the total pyramid and is 35 cm. Calculate the volume of the wheelbarrow.

Understand the Problem

To draw and label an appropriate diagram, we must know the meaning of "truncated pyramid". Truncated means that a portion has been cut off, and in this case, the vertex of the pyramid has been removed.

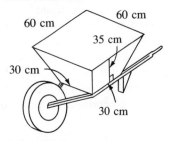

Carry Out the Plan

Let h represent the height of the completed pyramid.
$$h = \sqrt{70^2 - 30^2}$$
$$\doteq 63$$
The height of the total pyramid is about 63 cm. Therefore, the volume of the total pyramid would be about $\frac{1}{3}(60 \times 60 \times 63)$ or about 75 600 cm³. Since half of the pyramid is removed, the base will have a length of 30 cm and the height will be approximately 31 cm. Therefore, the volume of the removed portion of the pyramid is approximately $\frac{1}{3}(30 \times 30 \times 31)$ or 9300 cm³. Therefore, the volume of the wheelbarrow is 66 300 cm³.

Develop a Plan

Because the wheelbarrow uses only part of the pyramid, we must find the volume of the whole pyramid and then subtract the volume of that part that has been removed. The volume of any solid is the product of the area of the base and the height. These diagrams are drawn to complete the pyramid.

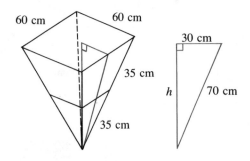

Look Back

The volume of the wheelbarrow is about 66 300 cm³. Note that the height of a pyramid is the perpendicular distance from the base to the vertex. It is most common for the slant height to be given when describing a pyramid. Be careful to draw and label the diagram correctly.

Exercises

For all exercises, use a calculator if one is available.

1. Develop a formula for the volume of a square-based pyramid using the slant height, s, and the length of the base, b.

2. Using the diagram, develop a general formula for the volume of a frustum. In this case, s is the slant height of the entire pyramid and s_1 is the slant height of the removed portion.

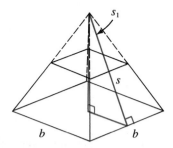

3. A hopper for holding grain is in the shape of an inverted square-based pyramid. The base length is 152 cm and the slant height of the pyramid is 170 cm.
a. Draw and label an appropriate diagram.
b. Find the volume of the hopper.
c. Cut off the end of the hopper to allow sand to run out a perpendicular distance of 18 cm from the vertex of the pyramid. If a door is to be added to keep the grain in the hopper, then find the area of the door.

4. Determine the volume of the frustum. Show that the ratio of the radii is the same as the ratio of the slant heights.

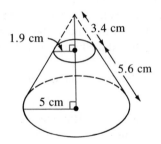

5. A cylindrical can has a radius of 36.5 mm and a height of 20.4 cm. It holds three tennis balls so that the bottom of the first ball and the top of the third ball touch the bottom and top of the can respectively. Find the amount of air left in the can when the three tennis balls are placed in the can and the can is sealed shut.

6. Generalize a formula for the volume of a frustum using the diagram and the variables given.

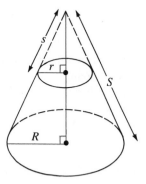

7. A spherical balloon has a diameter of 23 cm. Find the percent increase in volume if the balloon is inflated to a diameter of 30 cm.

8. The radius of a sphere equals half the length of one side of a cube and it fits tightly inside the cube.
a. Draw and label an appropriate diagram.
b. Find the ratio of the volume of the cube to the volume of the sphere.

9. For a square-based pyramid with a height of h cm, if the base length is doubled, then how will the volume of the pyramid change?

10. A store sells cantaloupes in two sizes. One has a diameter of 12 cm and the other has a diameter of 20 cm. The smaller cantaloupe costs $1.99 and the larger cantaloupe costs $3.29. Assuming that both cantaloupes are spherical, which is the better buy? Explain.

11. The slant side of a cone is s metres. What will happen to the volume of the cone if the radius is doubled?

1·15 Look Back

The purpose of the Look Back step when solving any problem is to cause you to focus on the process used to solve the problem in order to have a better understanding of the solution. Here are some of the strategies that can be carried out in the Look Back step.

- Restate the problem in your own words.
- Ensure the answer is reasonable.
- Make and solve a similar problem.
- Check for other solutions.
- Write a conclusion.
- Explain or justify the solution.
- Solve the problem in a different way.
- Generalize the solution.

Example

Two lines from Lord Tennyson's poem, ''The Vision of Sin'', read:
Every minute dies a man,
Every minute one is born.
Charles Babbage wrote Lord Tennyson suggesting the lines be changed to:
''Every moment dies a man,
Every moment $1\frac{1}{16}$ is born.''

If the approximate number of births each minute is 260, and the number of deaths in the same time is 96, then find the mixed number that should be used in place of the $1\frac{1}{16}$.

Understand the Problem

If $1\frac{1}{16}$ people are born every moment, then in 16 moments 17 people are born. (Verify this.) In the same time, how many will die?

Carry Out the Plan

If 3 births and 2 deaths occur every moment, then the line would be: Every moment $1\frac{1}{2}$ is born.''
What would the line read if there were 2 births and 3 deaths? We can use the same method for a rate of 260 births to 96 deaths. This is left as an exercise.

Develop a Plan

Solve a simpler problem using more convenient numbers. Use this simpler method to solve the problem.

Look Back

a. Write a conclusion to the problem.
b. Make and solve a similar problem.
The births-to-deaths rate has been dropping over the last few years. In some countries, the births to deaths in the year 2000 is projected to be 1.001 to 1. Rewrite the last line to Babbage's suggestion for the year 2000.
c. Generalize the solution.
If the births-to-deaths rate is a to b, then what fraction is used in the line? What can you say about the fraction if the births-to-deaths rate decreases? increases?
d. Can you solve the problem a different way?

Wherever possible, verify the solution to a problem in the Look Back step. This will be especially important in future chapters when the solution to a problem is **extraneous**.

Exercises

For Exercises 1 and 2 refer to the example in the display.

1. In your own words, restate the problem.

2. Complete each part in the Look Back step.

3. Two pattern nets for a cube are shown. Copy each net into your notebooks. Place the digits 1 to 6 on the faces so that when the cube is assembled the sums of the opposite faces are the same.

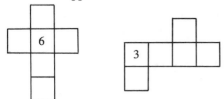

a. Will a model help?
b. What is the sum of the opposite faces that will be constant?
c. Use systematic trial to find the opposite numbers. Then find the numbers on the proper faces by visualizing the cube when it is folded. Predict the numbers on the remaining faces and then fold to check.
d. We can name the six faces of a cube as top, bottom, left, right, front, and back. Label the four remaining faces on the net so that when the cube is assembled, the names will be on the proper faces.
e. Draw a net for a cube and place the letters MACK on the faces so that they will appear on the top, bottom, and opposite sides of the cube when it is folded.

4. Suppose an item is on sale for a 25% discount but there is a 6% sales tax. The clerk offers to calculate the sales tax then the discount or the discount then the sales tax. Answer each part and decide which method is better for the consumer?
a. Is it sufficient to try just one price?
b. Generalize the answer to this question.
c. Does the way the tax is calculated make any difference to the amount of tax paid to the Government?
d. Which way is the best for the business? Explain.

5. A new device on a car motor will save 20% in fuel, while another device will save 30% in fuel, and a third device will save 50% in fuel. What is the total saving if all three devices are used on a motor?
a. Explain why you would know immediately that an obvious answer of 100% is incorrect.
b. A store puts an item on sale for 30% discount. Since it doesn't sell, another discount of 40% is placed on the item. Since it still doesn't sell, a further discount of 30% is placed on it. Find the total savings on the item.

6. Can you help Peppermint Patty find how far it is from Town A to Town B?

a. Explain how you arrived at your solution.
b. Solve the problem in a different way.
c. Make a similar problem and challenge one of your classmates to solve it.

Braintickler

Which is correct?
"The whites of the egg *are* yellow."
"The whites of the egg *is* yellow."

1·16 Computer Application— Word Problems

James opened his change jar to find $15.95 in nickels, dimes, and quarters. There are 9 fewer quarters than nickels. If he had 10 more dimes, then James would have twice as many dimes as quarters. How many of each coin did he have? The computer can be used to check a solution to a problem by systematic trial. In this case, we will find the number of quarters.

Let x represent the number of quarters.
Then $2x - 10$ represents the number of dimes and $x + 9$ represents the number of nickels.

```
10  REM A PROGRAM TO DETERMINE THE TOTAL
20  REM NUMBER OF NICKELS, DIMES, AND QUARTERS
30  REM IN $15.95
40  INPUT "THE TOTAL VALUE OF THE COINS $"; T
50  INPUT "GUESS THE NUMBER OF QUARTERS "; X
60  LET TX = 0.25 * X + 0.1 * (2 * X - 10) + 0.05 * (X + 9)
70  PRINT "THE VALUE WHEN X = "; X; " IS $"; TX
80  INPUT "IS THIS THE AMOUNT IN THE CHANGE JAR? TYPE YES OR
NO."; A$
90  IF A$ = "NO" THEN 50
100 PRINT "THERE ARE "; X; " QUARTERS, "; 2 * X - 10; " DIMES,
AND "; X + 9;" NICKELS."
110 END
```

Exercises

1. In this program, why is it necessary only to guess the number of quarters and not the number of dimes or the number of nickels?

2. Which line in the program calculates the total value of the coins?

3. Which line in the program prints the number of quarters, nickels, and dimes?

4. In line 80 of the program, the variable A$ appears. In the BASIC language, this allows the user to type a word into the computer and have that word stored in the memory. Explain the purpose of line 80 in this program.

5. How does this program end?

6. Verify the program in the display by algebraically solving the linear equations.

7. Modify the program so the user must guess the number of nickels instead of the number of quarters and then have the program print the number of nickels, dimes, and quarters.

8. Omar had $8 in nickels, dimes, and quarters. He had 4 dimes less than three times the number of quarters, and 12 nickels less than 7 times the number of quarters. Modify the program from the display to find how many nickels, dimes, and quarters Omar had.

9. "Computers are an integral part of everyday life and their use should never be restricted, especially during mathematics and science examinations." Write a short report either agreeing or disagreeing with this statement.

1·17 Chapter Review

1. Evaluate each expression for $a = -2$, $b = 3$, and $c = 4$.

a. $5a - 3b + 2c$ **b.** $2(a + 2b) + c$

c. $4b - a^2$ **d.** $3(5a^2 + b^2) - 2c$

2. Add the polynomials.

a. $(8x - 4y) + (5x - 4y)$

b. $(-2a + 18b + c) + (4a - 6b - 9c)$

c. $(7x^2 + 3x - 10) + (4x^2 + 15x - 3)$

d. $(-5m^2 + 6mn + n^2) + (2m^2 - 2mn + 15n^2)$

3. Subtract the polynomials.

a. $(3x + 14y) - (5x - 6y)$

b. $(8x - 3y) - (2x + 9y)$

c. $(4x + 10y) - (7x - 4y)$

4. Find the sum of the polynomials. $(8a - 12b + 7c)$, $(-3a + 6b + 18c)$, and $(10a + b - 5c)$

5. Perform the indicated operations.

a. $(6x + 14y - 8z) - (5x - 3y + 10z) + (-4x + 7z)$

b. $(2m + 15n - p) - (3n - 8p) + (4m + 7n)$

6. Find the product.

a. $(5ab^2)(-3a^2b)$ **b.** $(2xy^2z)(8x^2yz)$

c. $(x + 9)(x - 3)$ **d.** $(x - 5)(x - 6)$

e. $(4x + 3)(2x + 9)$ **f.** $(6x - 1)(6x + 1)$

g. $(2x + 5)(2x + 5)$ **h.** $(3 - 2x)(4 + x)$

7. Perform the operations and simplify.

a. $3(a - 7b) + 2(5a + b)$

b. $8 - 4x(x - 3y) + 2(5x^2 - 6xy)$

c. $(3a + 2b)^2 - (3a - 2b)^2$

8. The sides of a trapezoid are 2 cm, 4 cm, $(x + 3)$ cm, and $3(3x - 5)$ cm. Find the perimeter of the trapezoid.

9. Solve for the variable.

a. $2x + 5 - 8x = 12 - 4x$

b. $5t - 3(4t - 1) = 2(3t - 8)$

c. $4(2x + 3) = 5(x - 2)$

d. $6m - 2(m - 4) + 3(m + 4) = 0$

10. If the surface area of a closed right cylinder is given by $A = 2\pi r^2 + 2\pi rh$, then find the expression for the surface area in factored form.

11. Find three consecutive even numbers such that three times the first number is 20 more than twice the third.

12. A box contains 44 dimes and quarters. If the value of the quarters is 50 cents more than the value of the dimes, find the number of each type of coin.

13. Two sisters purchased a magazine for $2.60 with a five-dollar bill. They received the change in nickels and dimes and they shared it equally. If both girls received three more nickels than dimes, then how many coins did each girl receive?

14. In your own words, define the terms "area" and "volume". State the formula for the volume of each shape.

a. sphere   **b.** square-based pyramid

c. cone   **d.** cylinder

15. Leslie arranged for a one-year mortgage at the current bank rate of 14%/a. If the interest on the mortgage had been 12%/a, then Leslie could have borrowed another $700 without paying any additional interest. How much money was borrowed?

16. A straight line, with endpoints at $(3,0)$ and $(3,5)$, is "spun" (rotated) about the x-axis.

a. What type of shape will this rotation produce?

b. Find the volume of this shape.

17. If Bradley had $3 more in his pocket, then he would have twice as much money as Jenette. If Bradley gave Jenette $15, then he would have $1 more than Jenette. How much money does each person have?

1·18 Chapter Test

1. Evaluate for $p = 3$ and $q = -2$.
a. $6q + 8p$
b. $2p - 7q - 10$
c. $5p^2 - q^2$
d. $4(p + 3q) + (p + 5q)$
e. $(4p - 5)(q + 3)$
f. $3(p + 2)(3q + 8)$

2. Add the polynomials.
a.
$$\begin{array}{r} 5x - 3y + 8z \\ x + 11y - 2z \\ -2x + 4y + 5z \\ \hline \end{array}$$
b.
$$\begin{array}{r} 12a + b - 6c \\ 8b + 5c \\ 3a - 15b - 3c \\ \hline \end{array}$$

3. Subtract the polynomials.
a.
$$\begin{array}{r} 2p - 9q - 7r \\ 8p + 4q - 10r \\ \hline \end{array}$$
b.
$$\begin{array}{r} 4x^2 + 15xy - 3y^2 \\ -x^2 + 6xy + 3y^2 \\ \hline \end{array}$$

4. Perform the indicated operations and simplify.
a. $(8a + 3b - 2c) + (-4a + b + 6c) - (a - 9b + 5c)$
b. $(-5x + 10y + z) - (2x - 3y + z) - (11x + y - 3z)$
c. $(6x^2 - 5x - 12) - (-x^2 + 14x + 3) + (2x^2 + 9x - 5)$
d. $(4m^2 - mn - n^2) + (8mn - 3n^2) - (m^2 - 2n^2)$

5. In your own words, define the terms "perimeter" and "surface area".

6. The length and the width of a rectangle are $(5p - 3q)$ cm and $(2p - q)$ cm respectively. Find the expression which represents the area of the rectangle.

7. Expand and simplify.
a. $6(2x + y) + 3(x - 5y)$
b. $12a - 4(3a + 2b) + 5(a - 3b)$
c. $2(6p + 5q) - 3(4p - q) + (2p + q)$
d. $(x - 3)(2x - 3) + (3x + 5)(2x + 1)$
e. $(4x - 3)(x + 2) - (2x + 5)^2$
f. $2(5x - 6)(x + 1) + 4(x - 3)(x - 2)$

8. Sarah jogs to the store at a rate of 16 km/h and then walks back home at a rate of 8 km/h. If she takes 2 h to complete the trip, then how far does Sarah live from the store?

9. Jim invests an amount of money at 6%/a for one year. If he had increased the amount by $400, the investment would have paid 8%/a and the amount of interest he currently receives would have doubled. How much money did he invest?

10. Solve for the variable.
a. $8x + 12 - 3x = 9 - 2x - 7$
b. $5(2n - 3) + 3(n + 2) = 4$
c. $2(2a + 5) - (9a - 4) = 3a$
d. $3(4x + 1) = 2(x - 6) + 5$
e. $(2x - 9) + 4(5x + 3) - 3(3x + 1) = 0$

11. Find two numbers whose sum is 88 such that twice the smaller number is 8 more than the larger number.

12. Find the volume of a pyramid with a regular pentagon as the base, a base length of 4 m, a slant height of 7 m, and an apothem of 4.7 m. (*Hint*: Draw and label an appropriate diagram.)

13. Calculate the surface area and the volume of each.
a. a cube of side length 4 cm
b. a test tube with a diameter of 4.5 cm

14. Omar designed a metal lamp shade in the form of a truncated pyramid. The width of one side of the base is 30 cm and the width at the top is 10 cm. The distance along the slant edge between the bottom and top bases is 18 cm. The metal used is 3 mm thick.
a. Calculate the volume of metal used in 100 of these lamp shades.
b. The sheet metal for these lamps costs $9.78/m². At what price would Omar sell these shades to have a 70% profit?

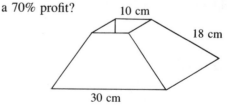

RATIONAL EXPRESSIONS

Tune Up

1. Simplify by collecting like terms.
a. $x + 3y - 2x - y$
b. $3a - 6b - 5a + b$
c. $(m - 2p) + (4p + 7m)$
d. $ax^2 + 2y + by - 4x^2$
e. $4a(x^2 + 1) - a(x^2 + 1)$

2. Multiply.
a. $(3a)(a)$ **b.** $(2x)(-3y)$
c. $(5r)(-2s)$ **d.** $(-ax)(2b)$
e. $(3ax)(4ax)$ **f.** $(-ab)(-ab)$

3. Expand using the distributive property.
a. $4(x + y)$ **b.** $-5(2x - y)$
c. $-a(3x - 2y)$ **d.** $(5x + 3y)(3a)$
e. $-4x(3x - y + 5z)$ **f.** $a(3x + 2y - 7z)$

4. Evaluate the expression for $x = 2$, $y = -3$, and $z = 1$.
a. $4x - y + z$ **b.** $x + 3y - z$
c. $-3(2x + y - 5z)$ **d.** $x(4y - 5z)$
e. $5y(x - 2z)$ **f.** $(z - x + 2y)(-2y)$

5. Fatima wishes to cover her swimming pool which is $(3x + 2y)$ m long and $(5y)$ m wide for the winter. If $x = 2$ m and $y = 4$ m, how much plastic covering, in square metres, would Fatima need to cover her pool?

6. Determine the amount of fencing needed to surround the field given that $x = 4$ cm and $y = 5$ cm.

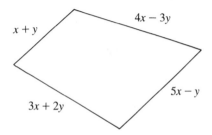

7. Factor.
a. $2x + 4y$ **b.** $3x - 9y + 24$
c. $2ax + 5ay$ **d.** $-ab + 3ab$
e. $5ax - 20axy$ **f.** $abx + aby - 3abz$

8. The area of a rectangle is expressed as $(3x^2 + 7x + 2)$ and its width is $(x + 2)$.

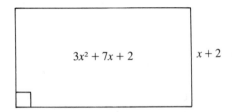

a. What is the expression which describes the length?
b. Determine the perimeter of the rectangle if $x = 6$.

2·1 Products of Polynomials

Expanded forms of polynomials sometimes yield special products. Some of these special products will be discussed in this section. For example, find an expression for the nonshaded area in the diagram.

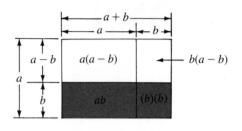

The area of the nonshaded rectangle, whose sides have dimensions of $(a + b)$ units and $(a - b)$ units, is given by $(a + b)(a - b)$ or $a(a - b) + b(a - b)$. This product can be simplified.

$a(a - b) + b(a - b)$
$= a^2 - ab + ab - b^2$
$= a^2 - b^2$

$$\boxed{(a + b)(a - b) = a^2 - b^2}$$

The product of all polynomials can be found using the area model. However, the distributive property, or the FOIL method, also will yield the product of polynomials.

Example

Find the products using the FOIL method and the distributive property.

a. $(2x + 4y)^2$
$= (2x + 4y)(2x + 4y)$
$= 4x^2 + 8xy + 8xy + 16y^2$
$= 4x^2 + 16xy + 16y^2$

$$\boxed{(ax + by)^2 = a^2x^2 + 2abxy + b^2y^2}$$

b. $(x - y)(x^2 + xy + y^2)$
$= x(x^2 + xy + y^2) - y(x^2 + xy + y^2)$
$= x^3 + x^2y + xy^2 - x^2y - xy^2 - y^3$
$= x^3 - y^3$

$$\boxed{(x - y)(x^2 + xy + y^2) = x^3 - y^3}$$

Exercises

1. Find the product.
a. $(x + 3)(x - 7)$ **b.** $(x + 2)(x - 4)$
c. $(x + 4)(x - 7)$ **d.** $(x - 9)(x + 1)$

2. Find the product.
a. $(2x - 4)(3x - 6)$ **b.** $(5x - 1)(3x + 2)$
c. $(x - 9)(2x - 6)$ **d.** $(ax + 4)(bx - 7)$

3. Expand by multiplying.
a. $(3x + 4)(3x - 4)$ **b.** $(2x - 7)(2x + 7)$
c. $(4x + 2)(4x - 2)$ **d.** $(ax - b)(ax + b)$

4. Multiply.
a. $(3x + 2)^2$ **b.** $(4x + 1)^2$
c. $(2x - 5)^2$ **d.** $(7x - 5)^2$
e. $(ax + b)^2$ **f.** $(ax - b)^2$

5. Find the product of $x + y$ and $x^2 - xy + y^2$.

6. Copy and complete these general statements. Use the products of Exercises 1 to 4 as a guide.
a. $(ax - b)(ax + b) = \rule{2cm}{0.4pt} - b^2$
b. $(ax + b)^2 = \rule{2cm}{0.4pt}$
c. $\rule{2cm}{0.4pt} = a^2x^2 - 2abx + b^2$

7. Multiply.
a. $(a + 3)(a^2 - 3a + 9)$
b. $(m - 4)(m^2 + 4m + 16)$
c. $(5 + y)(25 - 5y + y^2)$
d. $(2x - 3)(4x^2 + 6x + 9)$
e. $(3b + 5)(9b^2 - 15b + 25)$
f. $(5a - 2b)(25a^2 + 10ab + 4b^2)$
g. $(x + y)(x^2 - xy + y^2)$
h. $(x - y)(x^2 + xy + y^2)$

2·2 Factoring $x^2 + bx + c$

Recall that the product of two binomials of the form $(x + a)(x + b)$ has a solution of $x^2 + (a + b)x + ab$. In the next several sections, you will learn how to find the binomial factors that produced the product. This is called **factoring** a polynomial. To factor a trinomial of the form $x^2 + bx + c$, two integers are found so that their product is c and their sum is b.

Example 1

Factor. $x^2 + 12x - 45$

Use systematic trial to find two integers whose sum is 12 and whose product is -45.

$(-1)(45) = -45$; sum is 44
$(1)(-45) = -45$; sum is 44
$(3)(-15) = -45$; sum is -12
$(-5)(9) = -45$; sum is 4
$(5)(-9) = -45$; sum is -4

$\boxed{(-3)(15) = -45\text{; sum is }12}$

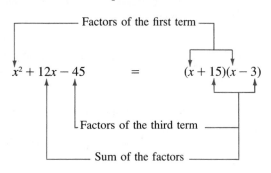

Factors of the first term

$x^2 + 12x - 45 \qquad = \qquad (x + 15)(x - 3)$

Factors of the third term

Sum of the factors

Example 2

Factor.

a. $3p^2 - 12pq - 36q^2$
$= 3(p^2 - 4pq - 12q^2)$
$= 3(p - 6q)(p + 2q)$

$-4 = (-6) + (2)$
$-12 = (-6)(2)$

b. $k^5 + 9k^3 + 8k$
$= k(k^4 + 9k^2 + 8)$
$= k(k^2 + 1)(k^2 + 8)$

Exercises

1. Find two factors whose product is given in Column A and whose sum is given in Column B.

	Column A	Column B
a.	-30	1
b.	16	10
c.	15	-8

2. Factor.

a. $x^2 - 5x - 14$ **b.** $x^2 - 4x + 4$
c. $x^2 + 7x + 12$ **d.** $x^2 - 7x + 6$
e. $x^2 - 2x - 15$ **f.** $x^2 + 4x - 32$

3. Find all integral values of k such that the trinomial is factorable.

a. $x^2 + kx - 12$ **b.** $x^2 + kx + 15$
c. $x^2 + kx - 24$ **d.** $x^2 + kx - 9$

4. Express as a product of factors.

a. $x^2 - 2xy - 3y^2$ **b.** $p^2 + 12pq + 27q^2$
c. $m^2 - 11mn - 12n^2$ **d.** $r^2 - 9rs + 20s^2$

5. Factor. Check by multiplying your factors.

a. $x^2 + 7x - 8$ **b.** $t^2 + 3t - 18$
c. $x^2 - 14x + 24$ **d.** $x^2 + 14x + 48$

6. Factor completely.

a. $x^4 + 5x^2 + 6$ **b.** $x^4 - x^2 - 20$
c. $s^4 + 6s^2 - 27$ **d.** $p^4 - 13p^2 + 30$

7. Factor completely.

a. $2x^2 + 10x - 12$ **b.** $3x^2 - 18x + 24$
c. $2x^2 + 6x - 80$ **d.** $5x^2 + 15x - 20$

8. Consider $x + a$ to be a single variable and factor.
$(x + a)^2 + 4(x + a) + 3$

2·3 Factoring $ax^2 + bx + c$

To factor trinomials of the form $ax^2 + bx + c$, where $a \neq 1$, an additional step to the process used in the previous section is presented here.

Consider this product.

$$(3x + 4)(x - 2) = 3x(x - 2) + 4(x - 2)$$
$$= 3x^2 \boxed{- 6x + 4x} - 8$$
$$= 3x^2 - 2x - 8$$

Notice the product of the first and last terms and the product of the two boxed terms in the expansion. They are $(3x^2)(-8)$ and $(-6x)(4x)$ respectively. Both have the same product of $-24x^2$. Using this fact, the final product of many expressions can be factored by working backwards.

$3x^2 - 2x - 8$

$(3x^2)(-8)$

Find two factors of $-24x^2$ such that the sum of the factors is $-2x$. The terms $-6x$ and $4x$ satisfy this condition.

$3x^2 - 2x - 8$
$= 3x^2 - 6x + 4x - 8$ Substitute $-6x + 4x$ for $-2x$ and group to find a common factor.
$= (3x^2 - 6x) + (4x - 8)$
$= 3x(x - 2) + 4(x - 2)$ Notice the common factors.
$= (x - 2)(3x + 4)$

This is called the method of **decomposition**.

Example 1

Factor.

a. $20x^2 - 7x - 3$
$= 20x^2 - 12x + 5x - 3$
$= (20x^2 - 12x) + (5x - 3)$
$= 4x(5x - 3) + (5x - 3)$
$= (5x - 3)(4x + 1)$

Product $= -60x^2$
Sum $= -7x$
$ = -12x + 5x$

b. $6x^2 - 19xy - 7y^2$
$= 6x^2 - 21xy + 2xy - 7y^2$
$= (6x^2 - 21xy) + (2xy - 7y^2)$
$= 3x(2x - 7y) + y(2x - 7y)$
$= (2x - 7y)(3x + y)$

This method also works with more complicated expressions. Remember, when factoring any expression, check for a common factor first.

Example 2

Factor.

a. $6x^2 + 2x - 20$
$= 2(3x^2 + x - 10)$
$= 2(3x - 5)(x + 2)$

b. $2(x + a)^2 - 3(x + a) - 5$
Let $(x + a)$ be represented by a single variable m.
$2m^2 - 3m - 5 = (2m - 5)(m + 1)$
Replace m by $(x + a)$.
$= [2(x + a) - 5][x + a + 1]$

Exercises

1. Find two integers whose product is the first number and whose sum is the second number.

a. -40; 3 **b.** 36; -13
c. 18; 9 **d.** -28; -3

2. In your own words, explain the method of decomposition.

3. Find the integral values of p such that the polynomial is factorable.

a. $2x^2 + px - 5$ **b.** $4x^2 + px + 3$
c. $3x^2 + px - 8$ **d.** $2x^2 + px + 9$

4. Factor by decomposition. Explain the reason for each step in the solution.

$5x^2 - 6x - 8$
$= 5x^2 - 10x + \blacksquare - 8$
$= \blacksquare(x - 2) + 4(\blacksquare)$
$= (x - 2)(\blacksquare)$

5. Factoring can be checked by finding the product of the factors. Verify that the expression $8x^2 + 14x - 15$ factors to become $(4x - 3)(2x + 5)$.

6. Factor and check by multiplying.

a. $3x^2 - 8x + 5$ **b.** $6x^2 - 11x - 2$
c. $16x^2 + 24x + 9$ **d.** $8x^2 + 34x + 15$

7. Factor using the method of decomposition.

a. $2x^2 + 7x - 4$ **b.** $3x^2 - 7x - 6$
c. $2x^2 - 7x - 15$ **d.** $3x^2 + 11x - 4$
e. $3k^2 - 8k + 4$ **f.** $2s^2 - 3s - 5$
g. $2t^2 - 11t + 12$ **h.** $3m^2 - 2m - 5$

8. Factor completely. The first one is started for you. Remember to look for a common factor first.

$24x^2 + 40x + 6$
$= 2(12x^2 + 20x + 3)$
$= 2(12x^2 + \blacksquare + \blacksquare + 3)$
$= 2(6x(\blacksquare + 3) + \blacksquare + 3)$
$= 2(\blacksquare + 3)(\blacksquare + 1)$

a. $4x^2 - 2x - 30$ **b.** $8x^2 - 18x + 4$
c. $12x^2 - 4x - 8$ **d.** $15x^2 + 27x + 12$

9. The area of a rectangle is given by the expression $3x^2 - x - 2$ square units. If one side is given by the expression $(x - 1)$ units, is it possible for the other side to have a length of $(3x + 2)$ units?

10. Factor completely. (*Hint*: An expression is factored completely when all the factors have been found.)

a. $4x^2 + 4x - 3$ **b.** $6x^2 - x - 2$
c. $12p^2 - 17p - 5$ **d.** $25y^2 + 10y + 1$
e. $3h^2 + 2h - 8$ **f.** $6z^2 - 23z + 15$
g. $8x^2 - 14x + 4$ **h.** $6u^2 + 5u - 4$

11. The area of a triangle is $2x^2 + 3x - 5$ square units. Find possible lengths for the height and base of the triangle.

12. Factor completely.

a. $2x^2 + 5xy - 3y^2$ **b.** $4x^2 - 13xy + 3y^2$
c. $2x^2 + 11xz + 15z^2$ **d.** $2r^2 - 5rq + 3q^2$
e. $5t^2 + 14tu + 8u^2$ **f.** $18x^2 + 9xy - 2y^2$

13. Factor completely.

a. $(x + 3)^2 - (x + 3) - 6$
b. $(x - 1)^2 + 4(x - 1) - 12$
c. $4(x - 2)^2 + 8(x - 2) - 5$
d. $3(x + 5)^2 - 10(x + 5) - 8$
e. $5(x - 3)^2 + 26(x - 3) + 24$

14. Factor completely.

a. $x^2 + 2x - 48$ **b.** $8x^2 - 6x$
c. $5x^2 - 13x - 6$ **d.** $30 + 13x - 3x^2$
e. $8x^2 + 30x + 7$ **f.** $3x^2 + xy$
g. $x^2 - 16x + 48$ **h.** $10x^2 - 23x + 12$
i. $2x^2 + x - 36$ **j.** $3x^2 + 6x - 45$
k. $5ax^2 - 25ax + 30a$
l. $6(a + 2b)^2 - 7(a + 2b) - 20$
m. $4(x - y)^2 + 9(x - y) + 5$

Braintickler

Think of a two-digit number. The ten's digit is multiplied by 5, increased by 7, doubled, and increased by the original value in the unit's digit. The result of these calculations is the original number. What is the number?

2·4 Difference of Squares

In Section 2·1, we saw that the product of $(x + y)$ and $(x - y)$ is the expression $x^2 - y^2$. Any expression that is the **difference of two perfect squares** can be factored as the sum and difference of the square roots of the two perfect squares.

$$x^2 - y^2 = (x + y)(x - y)$$

Example 1

Factor.

a. $9x^2 - 4$

$9x^2 - 4 = (3x + 2)(3x - 2)$

b. $4x^4 - 25y^2$

$4x^4 - 25y^2 = (2x^2 + 5y)(2x^2 - 5y)$

Whenever an expression has been factored, the answer can be verified by expanding (multiplying) the factors.

$(3x + 2)(3x - 2)$
$= 9x^2 - 6x + 6x - 4$
$= 9x^2 - 4$

$(2x^2 + 5y)(2x^2 - 5y)$
$= 4x^4 - 10x^2y + 10x^2y - 25y^2$
$= 4x^4 - 25y^2$

Example 2

Factor.

a. $(p - 2q)^2 - r^2$

Let u represent $p - 2q$.
$= u^2 - r^2$
$= (u + r)(u - r)$
$= (p - 2q + r)(p - 2q - r)$

b. $20k^2 - 45m^2n^2$

Check for a common factor.
$= 5(4k^2 - 9m^2n^2)$
$= 5(2k + 3mn)(2k - 3mn)$

Exercises

1. Why is there no linear or first-degree term in the product of $(x + a)$ and $(x - a)$?

2. Copy and complete.
a. $x^2 - \blacksquare = (x + 12)(x - 12)$
b. $\blacksquare - 81 = (2x + 9)(2x - 9)$
c. $4x^2 - 25 = (\blacksquare + 5)(\blacksquare - 5)$
d. $x^4 - y^4 = (x^2 + \blacksquare)(x^2 - \blacksquare)$
e. $100x^4 - \blacksquare = (10x^2 + 3)(10x^2 - \blacksquare)$
f. Can part **d** or **e** be factored again? If so, then factor and explain why.

3. Factor completely. Check by multiplying.
a. $x^2 - 25$ **b.** $x^2 - 36$
c. $4x^2 - 1$ **d.** $16x^4 - 81$
e. $36x^2 - 25$ **f.** $64x^2 - 9$

4. Factor completely.
a. $(x + 3)^2 - (y - 4)^2$
b. $(5a + 3b)^2 - (a - 2b)^2$
c. $16(2x - 5)^2 - 9(y + 1)^2$

5. Factor.
a. $(2a + b)^2 - c^2$ **b.** $(x - y)^2 - 4z^2$
c. $(4x + 1)^2 - 9$ **d.** $(x - 5)^2 - 16$
e. $36(x + 3)^2 - 25$ **f.** $9(2x + y)^2 - z^2$

6. Factor.
a. $x^2 - (y - z)^2$ **b.** $a^2 - (3b + 4c)^2$
c. $p^2 - (q - 5r)^2$ **d.** $9x^2 - (2u + v)^2$

7. Factor completely.
a. $2x^2 - 18$ **b.** $20x^2 - 5$
c. $\frac{1}{36}m^2 - \frac{1}{4}n^2$ **d.** $\frac{1}{25}p^2 - \frac{1}{81}q^2r^2$
e. $x^4 - 16$ **f.** $x^4 - y^4$

2·5 Perfect Trinomial Squares

In Section 2·4, we saw how to recognize and factor an expression written as the difference of two perfect squares. This section will show how to factor an expression which is a **perfect trinomial square**. A trinomial is classified as a perfect square when these conditions are met.

1. The first and last terms are perfect squares.

2. The middle term is equal to twice the product of the square roots of the first and last terms.

$$x^2 + 2xy + y^2 = (x + y)(x + y)$$

Similarly, $x^2 - 2xy + y^2 = (x - y)(x - y)$
$$= (x - y)^2$$

Example

Factor completely.

a. $a^2 + 4a + 4$
$= (a + 2)^2$

b. $16x^2 - 24xy + 9y^2$
$= (4x - 3y)^2$

c. $2x^2 + 4xy + 2y^2$
$= 2(x^2 + 2xy + y^2)$
$= 2(x + y)^2$

Exercises

1. Identify the perfect trinomial squares and justify your selection.

a. $x^2 + 4xy + 4y^2$ **b.** $4x^2 + 3x + 9$
c. $16a^2 - 8ab + b^2$ **d.** $x^4 - 2x^2 + 1$
e. $3x^2 - 6x + 3$ **f.** $5x^2 - 20xy - 4y^2$

2. Copy and complete so that each is a perfect trinomial square.

a. $x^2 - \blacksquare + 4$ **b.** $\blacksquare + 4xy + y^2$
c. $49 + \blacksquare + 4x^2$ **d.** $3a^2 + 24ab + \blacksquare$

3. Express each as a product.

a. $x^2 + 6x + 9$ **b.** $a^2 - 4a + 4$
c. $a^2 - 2a + 1$ **d.** $9x^2 - 48x + 64$
e. $9y^2 + 12y + 4$ **f.** $12a^2 - 60a + 75$
g. $4 + 20x + 25x^2$ **h.** $4a^2 - 36ac + 81c^2$
i. $9x^2 - 30xyz + 25y^2z^2$
j. $2x^3y + 8x^2y^2 + 8xy^3$

4. In your own words, state the difference between a trinomial that is a perfect square and one that is a difference of squares.

5. If the expression for the area of a square is given by $4a^4 - 16a^2b^2 + 16b^4$, then find an expression for the length of one side of the square.

6. Factoring can be used to assist in calculations. Factor each to evaluate. The first one is done partially for you.

a. $48^2 = (50 - 2)^2$
$= 2500 - 200 + \blacksquare$
$= \blacksquare$

b. 52^2 **c.** 104^2 **d.** 98^2

7. Use the difference of squares to assist in the calculations. The first one is done partially for you.

a. $(88)(92) = (90 - 2)(90 + 2)$
$= 8100 - \blacksquare$
$= \blacksquare$

b. $(76)(84)$ **c.** $(95)(105)$ **d.** $(34)(46)$

8. Factor.

a. $16x^4 - y^8$ **b.** $x^2 - 25y^2$
c. $4p^2 - 9q^2$ **d.** $36m^2 - 49n^2$
e. $16x^4 - 625y^4$ **f.** $p^2 - 4q^2r^2$
g. $x^4 - (2x + 3)^2$ **h.** $x^4 - (5x + 4)^2$

2·6 Completing the Square

Many trinomials are factored by using one of the methods that have been studied so far. However, as is the case with various aspects of mathematics, they also can be factored by using the strategy of **completing the square**.

While we can factor $x^2 - 2x - 15$ by other methods, we will use this polynomial to illustrate the method of factoring by completing the square. Notice that if 1 is added to the grouped terms in the first line of the solution below, then we have the perfect trinomial square $x^2 - 2x + 1$.

$$\begin{aligned} x^2 - 2x - 15 &= (x^2 - 2x) - 15 && \text{Complete the square on the grouped terms.} \\ &= (x^2 - 2x + 1) - 15 - 1 && \text{Since 1 was added in the brackets, 1 is subtracted.} \\ &= (x - 1)^2 - 16 && \text{This is the difference of two squares.} \\ &= (x - 1 - 4)(x - 1 + 4) \\ &= (x - 5)(x + 3) \end{aligned}$$

Since 1 was added in the brackets to **complete the square**, it also was subtracted from the constant to maintain the equivalence of the expression. Since this procedure **always** requires that the square be completed, the choice for the constant to be added is not arbitrary. It is found by taking half the numerical coefficient of the middle term and then squaring.

Example 1

Complete the square and factor completely.

a. $x^2 + 16x$

$$\begin{aligned} &= (x^2 + 16x + 64) - 64 && \left(\frac{16}{2}\right)^2 = 64 \\ &= (x + 8)^2 - 64 \\ &= (x + 8 - 8)(x + 8 + 8) \\ &= x(x + 16) \end{aligned}$$

b. $4x^2 + 16x - 9$

$$\begin{aligned} &= 4(x^2 + 4x) - 9 \\ &= 4(x^2 + 4x + 4) - 9 - 16 \\ &= 4(x + 2)^2 - 25 \\ &= [2(x + 2) - 5][2(x + 2) + 5] \\ &= [2x + 4 - 5][2x + 4 + 5] \\ &= (2x - 1)(2x + 9) \end{aligned}$$

The factors of part **a** are what is expected as x is a common factor. In part **b**, notice that 4 was added inside the brackets and 16 was subtracted outside the brackets. This is due to the factoring of the common factor 4 in the initial grouping. Any constant that is added inside the brackets will be multiplied by the common factor before subtracting.

Example 2

Factor. $x^4 - x^2 + 16$

$$\begin{aligned} &= (x^4 + 16) - x^2 \\ &= (x^4 + 8x^2 + 16) - x^2 - 8x^2 && \text{Add } 8x^2 \text{ to complete the incomplete square.} \\ &= (x^2 + 4)^2 - 9x^2 \\ &= (x^2 + 3x + 4)(x^2 - 3x + 4) \end{aligned}$$

In this case, we grouped the first and the last terms. This was done because $x^4 + 8x^2 + 16$ is recognized as a perfect trinomial square. We then subtracted $8x^2$ from outside the brackets. It is important to understand that the terms can be grouped in any manner, as long as a perfect square trinomial is formed and we are consistent with our additions and subtractions. Example 2 also could have been done by grouping the first two terms and adding and subtracting fractions.

Exercises

1. Factor by completing the square. Are the factors what you would expect?

a. $x^2 + 4x$ **b.** $x^2 - 4x$
c. $4x^2 + 4x$ **d.** $4x^2 - 4x$

2. Factor by completing the square. Are the factors what you would expect?

a. $x^2 + 8x + 15$ **b.** $x^2 - 2x - 15$
c. $x^2 - 4x - 5$ **d.** $x^2 - 5x + 6$
e. $x^2 - 7x - 8$ **f.** $x^2 + 3x + 2$

3. In your own words, explain the concept of completing the square and tell why it works for Exercises 1 and 2 even though they can be factored in other ways.

4. In Example 2, explain why $-8x^2$ is not the correct term to add inside the brackets.

5. Factor by completing the square.

a. $2x^2 + 7x - 4$ **b.** $3x^2 - 9x - 6$
c. $-3x^2 + 8 - 5$ **d.** $x^2 - 3x$
e. $x^2 + 5x$ **f.** $\frac{1}{3}x^2 - x$
g. $\frac{1}{2}x^2 + x$ **h.** $9x^2 + 9x$

6. Factor by completing the square.

a. $x^2 + 4x + 3$ **b.** $x^2 - 7x + 10$
c. $x^2 + 6x + 7$ **d.** $3x^2 - 4x$
e. $5x^2 + 125x$ **f.** $2x^2 + 3x - 2$
g. $6x^2 - x - 2$ **h.** $8x^2 - 2x - 1$

7. The cost of 4 is $0.50. The cost of 40 is $1.00. The cost of 404 is $1.50. What is being purchased?

8. Factor. Use any method that has been developed so far.

a. $6x^2 - 7x + 1$ **b.** $x^2 - 25y^2$
c. $17x^2 - 7x^3 + 12x$ **d.** $3x^2 + 12x + 12$
e. $14x^4 - 56x^2y^2$ **f.** $2a^2 + 3a - \frac{3}{2}$
g. $-75 + 12y^8$ **h.** $2a^2 + 24a + 40$
i. $2x^2 - 3x - 2$ **j.** $y^2 + 6y + 9$
k. $3x^3 - 24y^6$
l. $(x - y)^2 + 4(x - y) + 4$
m. $16(a - b)^2 - 4(a + b)^2$

9. Copy and complete to factor these fourth-degree expressions.

a. $x^4 + 6x^2 + 25$
$= (x^4 \; \blacksquare \; + 25) + 6x^2 - 10x^2$
$= \blacksquare$
$= \blacksquare$

b. $x^4 - 31x^2 + 9$
$= (x^4 \; \blacksquare \; + 9) - 31x^2 + 6x^2$
$= \blacksquare$
$= \blacksquare$

c. $x^4 + 4$
$= (x^4 + 4x^2 + 4) \; \blacksquare$
$= \blacksquare$
$= \blacksquare$

d. $(x^4 + 18x^2 + 81) + 2x^2 - 18x^2$
$= (\blacksquare)^2 - \blacksquare$
$= \blacksquare$

10. Factor by completing the square.

a. $x^4 + x^2 + 1$ **b.** $m^4 + 2m^2 + 9$
c. $k^4 - 3k^2 + 9$ **d.** $p^4 + 4p^2 + 16$
e. $s^4 + 4$ **f.** $4a^4 + 11a^2 + 25$

11. Factor. Use any method.

a. $4x^4 + 6x^2 - 25$ **b.** $x^4 + 6x^2 - 25$
c. $x^4 - x^2$ **d.** $x^8 - x^4$
e. $a^4 - 9$ **f.** $t^6 + t^3$

12. Copy and complete the generalized form.

$$ax^2 + bx + c = a\left(x^2 + \frac{\blacksquare}{a}x\right) + c$$

$$= a\left[x^2 + \frac{\blacksquare}{a}x + \left(\frac{b}{2a}\right)^2\right] + c - \frac{(\blacksquare)^2}{\blacksquare}$$

$$= a\left(x + \frac{\blacksquare}{2a}\right)^2 + \left(c - \frac{\blacksquare^2}{4a}\right)$$

$$= a\left[x - \left(-\frac{\blacksquare}{\blacksquare}\right)\right]^2 + \frac{4ac - b^2}{\blacksquare}$$

Using the Library

Research the term "incomplete square" and write a brief paragraph on why an expression like $x^4 + 4x^2 + 16$ is an incomplete square.

39

2·7 Sum and Difference of Cubes

A cube, with sides of x cm, has a smaller cube with sides of y cm removed from one corner.

The volume of the large cube is x^3 cm³.
The volume of the small cube is y^3 cm³.
What is the volume of the remaining portion?

When the smaller cube is removed, the remaining portion can be divided into three sections.
The volume of section A would be $x^2(x-y)$ cm³.
The volume of section B would be $xy(x-y)$ cm³.
The volume of section C would be $y^2(x-y)$ cm³.

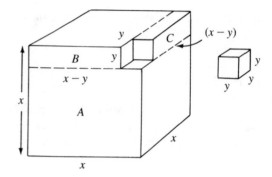

$$x^3 - y^3 = x^2(x-y) + xy(x-y) + y^2(x-y)$$
$$= (x-y)(x^2 + xy + y^2)$$

In a similar way, we can show that $a^3 + b^3 = (a+b)(a^2 - ab + b^2)$.

$$a^3 - b^3 = (a-b)(a^2 + ab + b^2)$$

$$a^3 + b^3 = (a+b)(a^2 - ab + b^2)$$

Example

Factor. Notice how the **cube root** of the terms is used with the general expression.

a. $x^3 - 27y^3$
$a = x, \ b = 3y$
$= (x - 3y)(x^2 + 3xy + 9y^2)$

b. $8p^3 + 1$
$a = 2p, \ b = 1$
$= (2p + 1)(4p^2 - 2p + 1)$

Exercises

1. Show that these statements are true. (*Hint*: Use the distributive property.)
a. $(a - b)(a^2 + ab + b^2) = a^3 - b^3$
b. $(2x - 3y)(4x^2 + 6xy + 9y^2) = 8x^3 - 27y^3$
c. $(x + y)(x^2 - xy + y^2) = x^3 + y^3$
d. $(2r + 3s)(4r^2 - 6rs + 9s^2) = 8r^3 + 27s^3$

2. State the values of a, b, ab, a^2, b^2 and factor.
a. $x^3 - 27y^3$
b. $8 + r^3$
c. $125m^3 + 8n^3$
d. $1 - 27p^3$
e. $x^3 + 1000y^3$
f. $64u^3 - 125v^3$

3. Factor completely. The first one is partially done for you.
a. $x^6 - y^6 = (x^2 - y^2)(x^4 + x^2y^2 + y^4)$
$= \blacksquare$
b. $64a^6 + b^9$
c. $1 - x^{12}$
d. $27a^9 - 125x^{18}$
e. $216x^6 - y^{24}$

4. Expand.
a. $(x + y)^3$
b. $(2a - b)^3$
c. $(a + 3b)^3 - (3a - b)^3$

5. Factor completely.
a. $a^3b^6 + 1$
b. $p^6q^9 - r^3$
c. $16m^3n^3 - 54$
d. $125 + x^3y^9$

6. Factor completely.
a. $27c^3 - 8d^3$
b. $125 - s^3$
c. $\dfrac{m^3}{343} - \dfrac{n^3}{64}$
d. $\dfrac{1}{729} - \dfrac{125p^3}{216}$
e. $\dfrac{r^3}{1000} - \dfrac{s^3}{64}$
f. $\dfrac{1}{64} - \dfrac{27z^3}{8}$

7. A.T., the "Mathematics Wizard", stated that "if we are factoring the sum of cubes, then there is a plus sign in the binomial and a minus sign in the trinomial. This is reversed when factoring the difference of cubes." Is A.T. correct? Explain.

2·8 Factoring Combinations

Factors of a number can be found in various stages. For example, one set of factors of 24 is 2 and 12. However, 12 can be written as a product of another set of factors, 2 and 6, and 6 has factors of 2 and 3. Therefore, 24 can be written as a product of its prime factors as $(2)(2)(2)(3)$.

Just as 24 was factored in stages, polynomials may also be factored in stages by applying a number of factoring methods. Recall the different factoring methods that have been studied so far.

- common factor
- systematic trial
- perfect trinomial square
- completing the square
- factoring a trinomial
- decomposition
- difference of squares
- sum and difference of cubes

Example 1

Factor completely.

a. $6x^2 + 3x - 30$
$= 3(2x^2 + x - 10)$
$= 3(2x + 5)(x - 2)$

b. $6a^2b^2 + 11ab + 5$

Find the factors of $30a^2b^2$ whose sum is $11ab$. In this case, they are $6ab$ and $5ab$.
$$6a^2b^2 + 11ab + 5 = 6a^2b^2 + 6ab + 5ab + 5$$
$$= (6a^2b^2 + 6ab) + (5ab + 5)$$
$$= 6ab(ab + 1) + 5(ab + 1)$$
$$= (6ab + 5)(ab + 1)$$

None of the methods studied in the previous sections, except finding a common factor, will yield the factors of a polynomial with more than three terms. For example, to factor the polynomial $2ax + 8bx + ay + 4by$, you would check for a common factor in all terms. Since one is not readily apparent, a different process is needed to factor this expression. Notice that the first two terms, $2ax$ and $8bx$, have a common factor of $2x$; while the last two terms, ay and $4by$, have a common factor of y. Group the terms together and find the common factor.

$$2ax + 8bx + ay + 4by = (2ax + 8bx) + (ay + 4by)$$
$$= 2x(a + 4b) + y(a + 4b)$$
$$= (2x + y)(a + 4b)$$

In the second line of the solution, there is a common factor of $a + 4b$. Multiplying the factors will give a product that is equivalent to the original expression.

Example 2

Factor completely. $x^2 - y^2 + z^2 - 2xz$

The first three terms are perfect squares, but the fourth term is not. Since the last term of the expression contains the variables x and z, it should be grouped with terms containing the variables x and z to create a perfect trinomial square.
$$x^2 - y^2 + z^2 - 2xz = (x^2 - 2xz + z^2) - y^2$$
$$= (x - z)^2 - y^2 \qquad \text{Difference of two squares.}$$
$$= (x - z - y)(x - z + y)$$

Exercises

For all exercises in this section, use the appropriate method to factor the polynomial completely.

1. Factor.
a. $6ac - 2ad + 21bc - 7bd$
b. $20xz + 12x + 5yz + 3y$
c. $2mp - 12np - mq + 6nq$
d. $12r^2 - 15st + 5rs - 36rt$
e. $6uw - 3uv - 16vw + 8v^2$
f. $24ab + 6ac + 4bc + c^2$
g. $6x^2 - 10x + 9xy - 15y$
h. $9p^2 + 6ps + 12pr + 8rs$
i. $10x^2 - 4xy - 25xz + 10yz$

2. Factor.
a. $5m^2 - 20n^2$ b. $12a^3 - 27ab^4$
c. $12x^2 - 22x - 4$ d. $y^3 - 8y^2 + 16y$
e. $2x^4 - 32$ f. $4p^3q - 4p^2q - 3pq$
g. $2m^4 + 9m^3 - 5m^2$
h. $x^2(x - 3y) - y^2(x - 3y)$

3. Factor. (*Hint*: Group to form a perfect trinomial square.)
a. $m^2 + 10m + 25 - n^2$
b. $9a^2 + 6ab + b^2 - 9$
c. $x^2 - 4xy + 4y^2 - 4z^2$
d. $c^2 + 8cd + 16d^2 - 4a^2$
e. $25p^2 + 4q^2 - 1 + 10pq$
f. $16r^2 - 16t^2 - 8rs + s^2$
g. $9v^2 - w^4 + 4u^2 + 12uv$
h. $9 - a^2 - 2ab - b^2$
i. $25 - 4m^2 + 4mn - n^2$

4. Factor $4p^2 + 16pq + 4q^2 - r^2$ by grouping $4p^2 + 16pq + 4q^2$.
a. Factor the expression by grouping the terms $16pq + 4q^2$.
b. Are the factors the same?
c. Which do you think is the better factored form? Explain.
d. Factor this expression a third way by grouping in a different way.
e. Multiply the expressions in factored form to ensure they produce the original expression.

5. Factor completely.
a. $-24a^3 + 4a^2b + 4ab^2$
b. $q^2(p^2 + 8p + 16) - 9(p^2 + 8p + 16)$
c. $x^8 - 81$
d. $15k^2m^2 - 55km - 100$

6. Factor completely.
a. $3x^4 + 81x$ b. $pq^3 - p^4$
c. $3 + 24(a + b)^3$ d. $x(x - 2y)^3 - x$
e. $a^3b^3 + 125a^3$ f. $2p^2r^4 - 2p^2q^8$
g. $9x^2 + 18x + 9 - y^2$
h. $a^6 - 2a^5b + a^4b^2 - c^2$
i. $a^2(a + b) - b^2(a + b)$
j. $8r^2 + 6r^2s - 5r^2s^2$
k. $x^4 - 2x^2y^2 - 8y^4$
l. $4k^4 + 8k^2t^2 - 12t^4$
m. $2a^5 - 3a^3b^2 + ab^4$

7. Decide which method would be most appropriate and factor completely. Justify your choice.
a. $3ac - 12ad + bc - 4bd$
b. $x^2 + 2x + 1$
c. $x^2 - 7x - 8$
d. $3x^5y - 6x^2 + 12xyz$
e. $2x^2y^2 - 7xy - 4$
f. $8x^3 - 216y^3$
g. $16m^4 - 81n^8$
h. $5(a + b + c)^2 + 11(a + b + c) + 2$

8. A prism has a volume of $x^3 - x^2 - 4x + 4$ m³. Find expressions for the lengths of the sides of the prism.

9. Factor completely.
a. $4x^2y^2 - y^2 - 4x^2 + 4$
b. $x^3y^2 - 1 - x^3 + y^2$
c. $a^3 - 16ab^2 + 2a^2b - 32b^3$
d. $8x^3y^2 + 16x^3 - y^2 - 2$
e. $9y^2 - 4x^2 + 16x - 16$
f. $2m^2n + 6m^2 - 50n - 150$
g. $5p^4 + 5p + 5p^3q + 5q$
h. $25 - 16a^2 - 48ab - 36b^2$
i. $3r^2st^2 - 3r^2s - 3st^2 + 3s$
j. $y^3(x^2 - 16) - x^2 + 16$

10. Factor completely. Verify your factors by multiplying.

a. $3a^2 + 2a - 8$

b. $7y^2 - 3y - 4$

c. $12m^2 - 4n + 6mn^2 - 8m^8 - 18$

d. $x^6 + y^{12}$

e. $(a + b)^4 + 2(a + b)^2 + 1$

11. Factor. Use the method of decomposition.

a. $6x^2 - 19xy + 15y^2$

b. $2a^2 + 7ab - 30b^2$

c. $8p^2 - 10pq^2 - 3q^4$

d. $3m^2 + 14mn + 16n^2$

e. $5r^2 - 21rs + 18s^2$

f. $18u^2 - uv - 4v^2$

g. $3a^2 + 11abc + 6b^2c^2$

h. $x^4 - 7x^2y + 10y^2$

i. $4s^6 + 3s^3t^2 - 27t^4$

j. $2c^2d^4 - cd^2 - 15$

k. $6p^2 + 25pr^4 + 4r^8$

12. Mai was asked to factor the expression and justify the method used. The expression was $25p^2 - 20p + 4 - q^2$ and the answer she gave was $5p(5p - 4) + (2 + q)(2 - q)$.

a. Explain how she arrived at the answer.

b. Has this polynomial been factored completely? Explain.

c. Factor the original expression to check if the factoring is correct.

13. Use the equation $6x - 15 = 9$ to answer the following.

a. Factor the left-hand side of the expression.

b. Divide both sides of the equation by the common factor.

c. Without evaluating x, find the value of the expression $\dfrac{2x - 5}{3}$.

d. Check your solution by solving for x in the original equation and substituting the value into the expression of part **c**.

14. If $x - y = 12$, find the value of the expression $\dfrac{y - x}{4}$.

15. The area of the a triangle is $(4x^2 + 15x + 18)$ cm^3. If x has a value of 4, then find a possible solution for the length of the base and the height of the triangle.

16. If $x + y = 4$, then what is the value of the expression $x^2 + 2xy + y^2$?

17. The volume of the frustum can be found using the formula $V = \dfrac{1}{3}\pi h\left(\dfrac{x^3 - y^3}{x - y}\right)$.

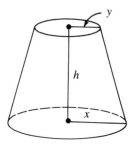

If $x = y$, then this formula can be used to find the area of a cylinder. Using the formula, show that the volume of a cylinder is either πy^2h or πx^2h.

18. Is it possible to factor the expression $(x + 3)^3 + (-x - 3)^3$? Explain your answer. (*Hint:* Try and factor the expression and check the answer.)

Using the Library

Among many of the curiosities connected with π are the mnemonics that have been devised to help remember its value to a large number of decimal places. To evaluate a mnemonic, replace each word in the mnemonic by the number of letters contained in the word. For example, the mnemonic "See, I have a rhyme assisting my feeble brain, its tasks ofttimes resisting" appeared in 1914 in the *Scientific American*. It gives a value of 3.141 592 653 589 for π.

Research A.C. Orr's mnemonic for the value of π. What is the value he uses for π? Devise your own mnemonic for π correct to ten decimal places.

2·9 Evaluating Polynomials

A polynomial may be evaluated by grouping and factoring before substituting values into the polynomial. This method is called **nested factoring** and can be used to find the zeros of a polynomial, the solutions to equations, or the value of an expression at a point. This method is outlined below.

1. Group all the terms of the polynomial except for the constant term.

2. Factor the expression enclosed in the brackets. Check for a common factor first.

3. Repeat this procedure until there are no longer any common factors.

Example 1

Find the value of $x^3 - 4x^2 + 4x + 8$ if $x = 12$.

$$x^3 - 4x^2 + 4x + 8 = [x^3 - 4x^2 + 4x] + 8$$
$$= [x^2 - 4x + 4]x + 8$$
$$= [(x^2 - 4x) + 4]x + 8$$
$$= [(x - 4)x + 4]x + 8$$

Now evaluate the nested form of the expression for $x = 12$. This calculation is easier than in its original form.

$$[(x - 4)x + 4]x + 8 = [(12 - 4)12 + 4]12 + 8$$
$$= [(8)12 + 4]12 + 8$$
$$= 100(12) + 8$$
$$= 1208$$

The nested form of a polynomial can be evaluated using a calculator. For Example 1, the keying sequence is shown.

12 $\boxed{-}$ 4 $\boxed{=}$ $\boxed{\times}$ 12 $\boxed{+}$ 4 $\boxed{=}$ $\boxed{\times}$ 12 $\boxed{+}$ 8 $\boxed{=}$

Not all polynomials are in nested form when the common factors are removed. The other factoring methods also may be helpful in simplifying the expression.

Example 2

Find the area of the washer if R is 3.5 cm and r is 2.5 cm.

The area of the washer is the area of the whole circle less the amount taken for the hole.

$$A = \pi R^2 - \pi r^2$$
$$= \pi(R^2 - r^2) \quad \text{Difference of two squares.}$$
$$= \pi(R - r)(R + r)$$

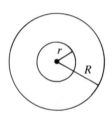

This form is easier to evaluate for the values given.

$$A = \pi(3.5 - 2.5)(3.5 + 2.5)$$
$$= 6\pi$$

Therefore, the area of the washer is 6π cm².

Exercises

When evaluating an expression, use a calculator if one is available.

1. Write the polynomial expressions in nested form.
a. $x^2 + 8x - 3$ **b.** $5x^2 - 4x - 10$
c. $4x^3 + 6x^2 - 12x + 5$ **d.** $8x^5 - 2x^3 + x^2 + 3x - 6$
e. $-6x^3 + 15x^2 + 2x$ **f.** $2x^3 - 9x^2 + 14x - 22$

2. A.T., the "Mathematics Wizard", stated that Example 1 of the display could have been factored as $(x - 2)^2x + 8$. Is A.T. correct? Explain.

3. Write the polynomials in nested form and evaluate using x-values of -2, -1, 0, 1, 2, and 3.
a. $4x^2 - 5x + 3$
b. $x^3 - 2x^2 + 8x - 12$
c. $2x^4 + 3x^3 - 5x + 3$
d. $3x^3 - 4x^2 - x + 10$

4. Evaluate if $x = 5$ and $y = 4$.
a. $2x^2 + xy - y^2$ **b.** $16x^2 - 25y^2$
c. $3x^2 - 2xy + y^2$ **d.** $10x^2 - 29xy + 21y^2$
e. $36x^2 - 84xy + 49y^2$ **f.** $3x^2 - 3y^2$

5. Factor the expression $x^2 + 4x - 5$ using the nested form.
a. Evaluate the expression for x-values of -3, -2, -1, 0, 1, 2, 3, 4, and 5.
b. Which value(s) in part **a** yield a value of zero?

> If an expression is evaluated for a real number q, and the expression becomes zero, then $x - q$ is a factor of the expression.

6. Calculate the values of the polynomial $4x^3 + x^2 - 3x - 5$ for x-values of 1, 1.1, 1.2, 1.3, and 1.4.

7. Use the nested factor form to evaluate the polynomial $x^3 + 2x^2 - 13x + 8$ for x-values of -5.00, -4.99, -4.98, -4.97, -4.96, and -4.95.

8. A Hamilton company makes steel pipes to any diameter required by the buyer. The volume of the steel used in the pipe depends on the diameter required. The larger the diameter, the thicker the steel. The volume of the pipe is given by the formula $V = \pi R^2 L - \pi r^2 L$, where R is the outer radius, r is the inner radius, and L is the length of the pipe.
a. Draw a diagram of a typical length of pipe and label r, R, and L.
b. Factor the equation for the volume.
c. A buyer wishes to purchase a section of pipe that is 120 m in length, and has 50 cm and 45 cm outer radius and inner radius. Find the volume of this pipe.
d. A second buyer required a pipe that had a volume of 1345 m³. If the length of the pipe was to be 320 m and the inner radius was 4 m, then find the ratio of r to R.

9. Use the nested form to evaluate $3x^4 - x^3 - 36x^2 + 60x - 16$ for x-values of 0, 0.1, 0.2, 0.3, 0.4, 0.31, 0.32, 0.33, and 0.34.

10. Find, correct to two decimal places, the value of x that will make the polynomial $3x^3 - 20x^2 + 7x + 30$ have a value of zero.
a. Is the value of x a factor of 30?
b. Check expressions of your choosing to show that an x-value that makes the expression equal zero is a factor of the last constant term.
c. Explain why the x-value must be a factor of the constant term.

11. A dime is placed on top of a 50¢ piece so that the centres of the coins are aligned. If a dime has a radius of about 0.9 cm, and a 50¢ piece has a radius of about 1.3 cm, then find the area of the 50¢ piece that is showing.

12. Factor. Use any method that has been studied so far.
a. $x^2 - 3x - 4$ **b.** $6x^2 - 11x - 35$
c. $2x^2 + 24x + 22$ **d.** $x^2 - 6x + 9$
e. $8x^3 - 8$
f. $16x^{12} - 64y^4$
g. $3x^2 - 4x + 6x - 8$
h. $3abc + bc + 6cd + 9ce$
i. $x^2 + xy - 20y^2$

2·10 Division of Polynomials

Division of a polynomial by a binomial parallels the long-division process with numbers. Just as 13 650 can be divided by 35 using long division, many polynomials can be divided by binomials using the same procedure.

Example 1

Divide. $\dfrac{4x^2 + 19x - 30}{x + 6}$

As is the case with any fraction, the denominator is divided into the numerator.

$$
\begin{array}{r}
4x - 5 \\
x + 6\overline{)4x^2 + 19x - 30} \\
4x^2 + 24x \\
\hline
-5x - 30 \\
-5x - 30 \\
\hline
0
\end{array}
$$

$(4x^2) \div (x) = 4x$
$(4x)(x + 6) = 4x^2 + 24x$
$(4x^2 + 19x) - (4x^2 + 24x) = -5x$
$(-5)(x + 6) = -5x - 30$
$(-5x - 30) - (-5x - 30) = 0$

Therefore, $4x^2 + 19x - 30 = (x + 6)(4x - 5)$. As a check, find the product of the factors to verify that they will produce the original expression.

Polynomials may be without one or more terms, and for convenience, a term with a coefficient of zero is inserted as a placeholder. Also, polynomials may not always give a remainder of zero when divided by a binomial.

Example 2

Divide. $(8x^3 - 52x + 7) \div (2x - 5)$

$$
\begin{array}{r}
4x^2 + 10x - 1 \\
2x - 5\overline{)8x^3 + 0x^2 - 52x + 7} \\
8x^3 - 20x^2 \\
\hline
20x^2 - 52x \\
20x^2 - 50x \\
\hline
-2x + 7 \\
-2x + 5 \\
\hline
2
\end{array}
$$

$0x^2$ is inserted as a placeholder. Why is it 0?

The division can be checked by multiplying the factors. Remember to add the remainder.

$(2x - 5)(4x^2 + 10x - 1) + 2$
$= 8x^3 + 20x^2 - 2x - 20x^2 - 50x + 5 + 2$
$= 8x^3 - 52x + 7$

Since the product plus the remainder gives the original expression, the division has been done correctly.

Exercises

1. Copy and complete this division.

$$
\begin{array}{r}
2x^2 + x - 6 \\
3x - 4\overline{)6x^3 - 5x^2 - 22x + 24} \\
\underline{6x^3 - 8x^2} \\
\blacksquare - 22x \\
\underline{3x^2 - 4x} \\
\blacksquare + 24 \\
\underline{-18x + 24} \\
\blacksquare
\end{array}
$$

2. Refer to Example 2 of the display.
a. Explain why $0x^2$ is used as a placeholder.
b. Explain how the check of the quotient works.

3. When $x^3 + 9x^2 + 18x - 5$ is divided by $x + 5$, the quotient is $x^2 + 4x - 2$ with a remainder of 5. Check this answer by showing that $(x + 5)(x^2 + 4x - 2) + 5$ is equal to the original polynomial.

4. Divide. Check by multiplying.
a. $(x^2 - 18x - 40) \div (x + 2)$
b. $(x^2 - 2x - 24) \div (x - 6)$
c. $(4x^2 + 23x + 15) \div (4x + 3)$
d. $(x^3 - x^2 - 15x - 18) \div (x + 2)$
e. $(4x^3 + 4x^2 - 23x + 12) \div (2x - 3)$
f. $(24x^3 + 61x^2 - 14x - 16) \div (3x + 8)$

5. Arrange the exponents in descending order and divide.
a. $(28x + 16 + 12x^2) \div (3 + 2x)$
b. $(5x^2 - 31x + 10 + 2x^3) \div (2x - 5)$
c. $(10x^2 - 3 - 6x + 3x^3) \div (4 + x)$
d. $(3x^3 - 7x^2 - 6x + 4 + 4x^4) \div (x^2 - 2)$
e. $(34x^2 - 16 - 39x + 33x^3 + 6x^4) \div (3 + x)$

6. Divide. (*Hint*: Insert a placeholder for the term that does not appear.)
a. $(x^4 + 5x^3 - 21x - 9) \div (x + 3)$
b. $(x^3 - 8) \div (x - 2)$
c. $(9x^3 - 16x - 8) \div (3x + 2)$
d. $(15x^4 - 52x^3 + 14x^2 - 1) \div (5x + 1)$
e. $(8x^4 + 2x^3 - 3x - 18) \div (2x^2 - 3)$

7. Divide. $x - y\overline{)x^3 + 0x^2y + 0xy^2 - y^3}$
Does this calculation verify that
$x^3 - y^3 = (x - y)(x^2 + xy + y^2)$?

8. Repeat Exercise 7 to show that
$x^3 + y^3 = (x + y)(x^2 - xy + y^2)$.

9. The area of a rectangle is $(x^3 + 4x^2 + 8x + 5)$ m². If the length of one side of the rectangle is $(x^2 + 3x + 5)$ m, then find an expression for the length of the other side.

Historical Note

Captain Grace Hopper (1907-   )
Captain Hopper has been an active duty officer in the United States Navy for a number of years and was instrumental in the development of computers and computer languages. In order to remind people that things are not always conventional, she has a clock in her office that runs counterclockwise.

Grace Hopper worked on the first large scale computer developed in the United States called the Mark I. She also helped invent the first practical compiler, and the COBOL computer language. Her team was the first to coin the word "bug" to refer to problems in a computer program. The term was used after the Mark I broke down due to a moth getting into the circuitry. The Mark I was considered "state of the art" in 1944 because it could perform three additions each second. Today, computers can perform the same three calculations in 300 nanoseconds, or a billion times as fast. Her advice to all students of computer science is to "get in, start learning, and get as much computer time as possible".

1. How much is a nanosecond?

2. What do the letters in the language COBOL stand for?

3. One test often used with today's computers involves prime numbers. A new Cray X-MP supercomputer was programmed to look for the largest possible prime numbers. The prime found was 65 050 digits in length. The computer took about three hours to complete the 1.5 billion calculations necessary. About how many operations per second did the computer perform?

2·11 Zeros of a Polynomial

We have seen that if two numbers are multiplied together, and their product is zero, then at least one of the numbers must be zero. This is written, if $(a)(b) = 0$, then either $a = 0$, $b = 0$, or a and b are both zero.

> **The zeros of a polynomial** are the values of the variable(s) that make the polynomial equal to zero.

Example

Two frying pans have masses such that one is 2 kg more than the other and the sum of the squares of their masses is 52. Find the mass of each frying pan.

Let x represent the mass of the lighter frying pan. Then the mass of the larger pan is $x + 2$. An equation can be set up as $(x)^2 + (x + 2)^2 = 52$, or $2x^2 + 4x + 4 = 52$. Set the equation equal to zero by subtracting 52 from both sides, factor it, and find the values of x that will make the equation equal to zero.

$$2x^2 + 4x + 4 = 52$$
$$2x^2 + 4x - 48 = 0$$
$$2(x^2 + 2x - 24) = 0$$
$$2(x + 6)(x - 4) = 0$$

These are the zeros of (solutions to) the equation.

$$x + 6 = 0 \qquad \text{or} \qquad x - 4 = 0$$
$$x = -6 \qquad\qquad\qquad x = 4$$

Since mass cannot be negative, the only possible solution for x is $x = 4$. Therefore, the frying pans have masses of 4 kg and 6 kg.

Exercises

1. For what values of x will the polynomials equal zero?

a. $5x$
b. $x(x - 5)$
c. $(x + 3)(x + 2)$
d. $(2x - 5)(x + 1)$
e. $(x - 5)(x + 3)$
f. $-5x(x - 4)$
g. $x(x - 1)(x - 2)$
h. $(5x - 3)(2x + 7)$

2. Find the zeros of the polynomials.

a. $x^2 - 4x - 5$
b. $x^2 + 3x + 2$
c. $x^2 - 36$
d. $2x^3 - 5x^2$
e. $x^2 + 3x - 18$
f. $x^2 - 12x + 27$

3. Group the terms and factor to find the zeros of the polynomial. The first one is done partially for you.

a. $4xy - 5y + 8x - 10$

$= (4xy - 5y) + (8x - 10)$
$= y(4x - 5) + 2(4x - 5)$

b. $8x^2 - 6x + 4xy - 3y$ **c.** $2x + 4xy - 24y - 12$

4. Solve. (*Hint*: Look for a common factor.)

a. $y^3 - 6y^2 - 7y = 0$
b. $4x^2 + 8x + 4 = 0$
c. $2m^2 + 18m - 104 = 0$
d. $5x^2 - 5 = 0$
e. $p^4 + 4p^3 - 12p^2 = 0$
f. $14 - 17x - 6x^2 = 0$

5. Factor to find the value(s) of x that will make each equation true.

a. $2(x + 3) - 4x(x + 3) = 0$
b. $x^2(2x - 1) - (2x - 1) = 0$
c. $x^2(5x - 4) + 2x(5x - 4) + (5x - 4) = 0$

6. Solve.

a. $5x^2 - 11x - 36 = 0$
b. $3x^2 + 4x + 1 = 0$
c. $6x^2 - 5x - 4 = 0$
d. $5x^2 + 25x = 0$
e. $y^2 - 9y + 8 = 0$
f. $4p^2 + 7p + 3 = 0$

7. In a right triangle, the hypotenuse is 8 cm longer than the shortest side, and the third side is 1 cm shorter than the hypotenuse. Find the length of the hypotenuse.

2·12 Factor Theorem

One of the strategies used in problem solving is to look for patterns. For example, the expression $x^2 - 3x - 4$ has a value of 0 when $x = 4$ and when $x = -1$. Note the expression factors to $(x - 4)(x + 1)$. The same pattern occurs when finding the factors of a polynomial with degree greater than two. We look for the zeros of the polynomial first. For example, $x = -3$ makes the polynomial $x^3 + 3x^2 - 10x - 30$ equal to 0. Therefore, $x + 3$ is a factor of the polynomial.

> **Factor Theorem** If $x - q$ is a factor of a polynomial, then q is a zero of the polynomial.
> If q is a zero of a polynomial, then $x - q$ is a factor of the polynomial.

Example 1

For the polynomial $x^3 - 2x^2 - 23x + 60$,
a. determine whether $x = 3$ is a zero of the polynomial.
b. completely factor the polynomial.

a. A calculator could be used to find a zero of the polynomial. In this case, $x = 3$ is a zero of the polynomial.

b. Since $x = 3$ is a solution, one of the factors of the polynomial is $x - 3$. Using long division, the other factor(s) of the polynomial can be found.

$$
\begin{array}{r}
x^2 + x - 20 \\
x - 3 \overline{)\, x^3 - 2x^2 - 23x + 60} \\
\underline{x^3 - 3x^2} \\
x^2 - 23x \\
\underline{x^2 - 3x} \\
-20x + 60 \\
\underline{-20x + 60} \\
0
\end{array}
$$

Therefore, the factors of $x^3 - 2x^2 - 23x + 60$ are $(x - 3)(x^2 + x - 20)$. This expression can be factored further as $(x - 3)(x - 4)(x + 5)$. Notice that there was no remainder and that the zeros of the polynomial (3, 4, and -5) are all factors of the constant term, 60. This is the case whenever you are factoring using the factor theorem.

The factor theorem also can be used to find unknown values in an expression.

Example 2

If $x + 4$ is a factor of the expression $3x^3 + 7x^2 - 22x + k$, then find the value of k.

If $x + 4$ is a factor, then substituting $x = -4$ into the expression will give the polynomial a value of zero.

$$
\begin{aligned}
3(-4)^3 + 7(-4)^2 - 22(-4) + k &= 0 \\
-192 + 112 + 88 + k &= 0 \\
8 + k &= 0 \\
k &= -8
\end{aligned}
$$

Therefore, $k = -8$. Notice that -4 is a factor of -8.

Exercises

1. In your own words, state the meaning of the factor theorem and state the meaning of the zeros of a polynomial.

2. A.T., the "Mathematics Wizard", stated that "to find the zeros of the polynomial $x^3 - 8x^2 - 3x - 6$, only substitute x-values of ± 1, ± 2, ± 3, or ± 6." Is A.T. correct? Explain.

3. In your own words, explain why it is that if a is a zero of a polynomial, then $x - a$ is a factor of the polynomial.

4. If $P(6) = 0$, then state one factor of $P(x)$.

5. Without performing any calculations, determine which of these binomials are possible factors of $2x^3 + x^2 - 18x - 9$. Justify your selection.
a. $x + 1$ **b.** $x - 1$ **c.** $x + 2$
d. $x - 2$ **e.** $x + 3$ **f.** $x - 3$

6. Write all possible factors of these expressions.
a. $x^3 + 3x - 9$
b. $3x^4 + 9x^2 - 4x^3 + 6 - x$

7. Is $x - 2$ a factor of $3x^2 + x^3 - 22 + x$? Explain.

8. For each of the following, perform this sequence of steps to factor each expression.
a. $x^3 + 7x^2 + 2x - 40$
b. $x^4 - 2x^3 + 9x^2 - x - 7$
c. $x^3 + 3x - 36$
d. $m^3 - m^2 - 10m - 8$
e. $y^3 + 3y^2 - 9y - 27$
f. $x^3 - 3x^2 - 2x$
  i) Find all the factors of the constant term.
  ii) Find the factor(s) that make the polynomial equal zero.
  iii) Divide the polynomial by a factor of the polynomial.
  iv) If possible, factor the quotient.

9. Once a factor for an expression has been found using the factor theorem, long division is used to find the other factors. Why will this always lead to a remainder of zero?

10. Find a value of k such that each polynomial is divisible by the given polynomial.
a. $x^2 - 11x + k$; $(x - 3)$
b. $x^3 - 5x^2 - 8x + k$; $(x + 2)$
c. $2x^3 + x^2 - 41x + k$; $\left(x - \dfrac{1}{2}\right)$
d. $3x^3 - 7x^2 + kx - 8$; $(x + 1)$
e. $2x^3 + kx^2 - 13x + 30$; $(x - 2)$
f. $x^4 - 7x^2 + kx - 18$; $(x + 3)$
g. $kx^3 - 11x^2 - 38x - 24$; $(x - 6)$
h. $x^4 - 9x^3 + 30x^2 - 44x + k$; $(x - 2)$

11. Factor completely.
a. $y^3 - 4y^2 + y + 6$
b. $x^3 - x^2 - 14x + 24$
c. $2x^3 + 15x^2 + 4x - 21$
d. $x^4 + 6x^3 - 9x + 4$
e. $2x^4 + 5x^3 - 15x^2 - 10x + 8$

12. Use the factor theorem to prove that $x^3 - y^3 = (x - y)(x^2 + xy + y^2)$.

13. Is $x - 2m$ a factor of $x^2(1 - 2m) + 8m^3 - (0.5x)^2$?

14. A platform is placed at the centre of a square moat. The platform is 2 m × 2 m and the moat is 8 m × 8 m. Peter has to get to the platform to do some repairs but has only two planks that are each 2.9 m in length. How can he get to the platform without getting wet?

15. A third-degree polynomial factors to give $(x - a)(x - b)(x - c)$. What is the first term and the constant term of the original polynomial?

16. A bus driver travels a distance of $x^3 - 2x^2 - 9$ km in $(x - 3)$ h. Find an expression to represent the speed the bus is travelling.

2·13 The Remainder Theorem

What happens when a polynomial is not divisible by a divisor? As in division with whole numbers, there is a nonzero remainder.

Example

Divide the expression $x^3 - 3x^2 + 6x - 4$ by $x - 4$.

Substituting $x = 4$ into the polynomial will give the polynomial a value of 36. Since the value is not zero, $x - 4$ is not a factor of the expression. Verify this using long division.

$$
\begin{array}{r}
x^2 + x + 10 \\
x - 4 \overline{)x^3 - 3x^2 + 6x - 4} \\
\underline{x^3 - 4x^2} \\
x^2 + 6x \\
\underline{x^2 - 4x} \\
10x - 4 \\
\underline{10x - 40} \\
36
\end{array}
$$

Note that the value of the polynomial when $x = 4$ is the same as the **remainder** when the polynomial is divided by $x - 4$.

> **Remainder Theorem**   If a polynomial is divided by a binomial of the form $x - q$, then the remainder is the value of the polynomial evaluated for $x = q$.

Exercises

1. In your own words, explain the remainder theorem.

2. Find the remainder in each. Prove your answer using long division.
a. $(x^4 + 6x^3 - 9x + 4) \div (x - 1)$
b. $(2x^3 - 3x^2 + 6x + 9) \div (x + 2)$
c. $(5x^4 - 3x^3 + 9) \div (x + 1)$
d. $(2x^5 - 3x^4 + 2x^2 - x + 5) \div (x - 4)$

3. When using the factor theorem, the zeros of the expression are factors of the constant term of the expression. Does it follow that if there is a remainder, then the value being substituted for the variable is not a factor of the constant term? Explain.

4. The expression $x^3 - 3x^2 + 2x + k$ was divided by $x - 4$ and a remainder of 2 resulted. Find the value of k.

5. Explain why $x + y$ is not a factor of $x^4 + y^4$.

6. A polynomial was divided by $x + 1$ and the quotient was $x^2 + 2x + 1$ with a remainder of 4. What was the original polynomial?

7. Calculate the value(s) of k such that $kx^4 + k^2x^2 - kx - 6$ leaves a remainder of -2 when divided by $x - 1$.

8. Using the digits 1 through 5 and addition only, arrange the digits to equal a sum of 69.

9. The remainder theorem can be extended so that if a polynomial is divided by $ax - b$, then the remainder is the polynomial evaluated at $\dfrac{b}{a}$.
a. Explain why this statement is true.
b. Find the remainder when $x^3 - x^2 - x - 1$ is divided by $3x - 2$, $2x - 5$, and $4x - 7$.

2·14 Simplify Rational Expressions

Rational numbers are numbers that can be written in the form $\frac{a}{b}$, where a and b are integers and $b \neq 0$.

When a polynomial is divided by a polynomial, the expression is a **rational expression**. These are examples of rational expressions.

$$\frac{22}{3x - 8} \qquad \frac{5x - 7}{5x + 7} \qquad \frac{x^2 - 3x - 8}{x^2 - 7x - 9} \qquad \frac{5x^4 - 7x^3 - 12x - 9}{x^2 - 5x + 12}$$

> A rational expression is the quotient of two polynomials.

The four examples of rational expressions each have polynomials in both the numerator and the denominator. As is the case with any rational number, the denominator cannot equal zero as division by zero is undefined. Therefore, restrictions must be placed on the possible values of the variable(s) before any work is done with the expression.

Example 1

A parallelogram has an area given by the expression $(8x^2 + 4x)$ cm². If the altitude of the parallelogram is $8x$ cm, then find the length of the base.

Understand the Problem

We must find an expression for the length of the base of the parallelogram.

Recall that $\dfrac{\text{Area}}{\text{Altitude}} = \text{Base length}$.

Develop a Plan

By substituting the expressions for the area and the altitude, a rational expression for the base length can be written as $\dfrac{8x^2 + 4x}{8x}$.

Carry Out the Plan

To find the restrictions on the variable, set the denominator equal to zero and solve.

$8x = 0$

$x = 0$

Therefore, $x \neq 0$.

To simplify the expression, factor the numerator and denominator.

$$\frac{8x^2 + 4x}{8x} = \frac{4x(2x + 1)}{8x}$$
$$= \frac{2x + 1}{2}$$

Look Back

The base length is $\dfrac{2x + 1}{2}$ cm.

Notice the restriction on the variable. If $x = 0$, then the parallelogram will have no area and this is impossible. Remember, a rational expression is in simplified form when all factors common to the numerator and denominator have been divided.

Example 2

Simplify.

a. $\dfrac{x^2 + x - 6}{x^2 - 4} = \dfrac{(x + 3)(x - 2)}{(x + 2)(x - 2)} \quad \{x \neq \pm 2\}$
$= \dfrac{x + 3}{x + 2}$

b. $\dfrac{a^3 + 1}{a^2 + 5a + 4} = \dfrac{(a + 1)(a^2 - a + 1)}{(a + 1)(a + 4)} \quad \{a \neq -1 \text{ or } -4\}$
$= \dfrac{a^2 - a + 1}{a + 4}$

Exercises

1. State the restrictions on the variables.

a. $\dfrac{12a^3b}{5ab}$

b. $\dfrac{x^2 - 4x + 4}{4x^2 - 5x - 6}$

c. $\dfrac{x^2 - 3x + 2}{4x^2 - 4x + 1}$

d. $\dfrac{3x^2 + 5}{2x^2 - x - 15}$

e. $\dfrac{x^2 + 6xy + 8y^2}{x^2 - 4}$

f. $\dfrac{3x^2 + 5x + 2}{3x^2 + 3x}$

2. The display suggests finding the restrictions before simplifying the expression. Why is it necessary to find them first?

3. Write a simplified rational expression for the unknown side length for these shapes. The area of the shape is given below the diagram.

a.

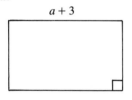

$a + 3$

$a^2 - 9$

b.

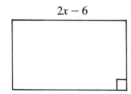

$2x - 6$

$x^2 - 10x + 21$

c.

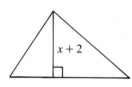

$x + 2$

$3x^2 + 7x + 2$

d.

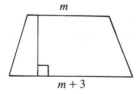

m

$m + 3$

$4m^2 + 14m + 12$

For the remainder of the exercises, state the restrictions on the variables.

4. Simplify.

a. $\dfrac{5xy}{y}$

b. $\dfrac{3x + 7}{7x}$

c. $\dfrac{16a^2b}{-12ab^3}$

d. $\dfrac{5p^3qr^2}{20p^2q}$

e. $\dfrac{2x - 4y}{6xy}$

f. $\dfrac{3c + 12}{c^2 - 16}$

5. Simplify.

a. $\dfrac{6 - m}{m^2 - m - 30}$

b. $\dfrac{r^2 - 7r - 8}{r^2 - 8r}$

c. $\dfrac{a^2 - 5a - 36}{a^2 - 7a - 18}$

d. $\dfrac{k^2 - 6k + 9}{k^2 + 2k - 15}$

6. The area of a square is given by the expression $(16x^2 + 8x + 1)$ cm². Find an expression for the length of one side of the square.

7. Simplify.

a. $\dfrac{4x^2 + 11x - 3}{4x^2 - 9x + 2}$

b. $\dfrac{10k^2 + 13k - 3}{4k^2 + 12k + 9}$

c. $\dfrac{12n^2 - 32n + 5}{36n^2 - 1}$

d. $\dfrac{5p^2 - 19p - 4}{3p^2 - 14p + 8}$

e. $\dfrac{4y^2 - 5y - 3}{2y^2 + 11y + 5}$

f. $\dfrac{8u^2 - 10u}{16u^2 - 40u + 25}$

g. $\dfrac{15 + 7a - 2a^2}{2a^2 - 13a + 15}$

h. $\dfrac{16r^2 - 2r - 3}{2r^2 + 5r - 3}$

8. A car travels distances of $(10t^2 - 17t - 33)$ km and $(8t^2 - 4t - 27)$ km. If the total travel time is $(3t + 4)$ h, then determine the average rate of travel.

9. The area for a triangle is given by the expression $(2x^2 + 5x - 7)$ square units, and the length of the base is given by the expression $(6x^2 + 13x - 28)$ units.

a. Can x have a value of 0.75 units? Explain.

b. Find an expression for the height of the triangle.

10. Factor the sum and difference of cubes and divide the common factors.

a. $\dfrac{4x^2 - 1}{8x^3 - 1}$

b. $\dfrac{a^3 + 27}{a^2 - 3a + 9}$

c. $\dfrac{125p^3 + 1}{10p^2 - 3p - 1}$

d. $\dfrac{a^3 - 8b^3}{a^2 - 4ab + 4b^2}$

e. $\dfrac{4t^2 - 9s^2}{27s^3 - 8t^3}$

f. $\dfrac{k^3 - 216m^3}{2k^2 - 11km - 6m^2}$

11. The volume of a rectangular prism is $125x^3 + 8$ cm³. If the height of the prism is $(5x + 2)$ cm, then find the area of the base.

12. If the total value of $3n - 4$ coins is given by the expression $6n^2 + 22n - 40$ dollars, then find the average value of each coin.

2·15 Multiplication and Division

When multiplying or dividing rational expressions, we follow the same process as multiplying and dividing rational numbers. The process often can be made easier by factoring and then dividing common factors. Remember to state the restrictions on all the variables **before** multiplying or dividing the rational expressions.

Example 1

Find the product.

$$\frac{x^2 - 4x + 3}{x^2 - 9} \times \frac{x^2 + 3x}{3x}$$

$$= \frac{(x-3)(x-1)}{(x+3)(x-3)} \times \frac{x(x+3)}{3x}$$

Factor if possible and state the restrictions.
$x \neq -3$, $x \neq 3$, and $x \neq 0$

$$= \frac{(x-3)(x-1)(x)(x+3)}{(x+3)(x-3)(3x)}$$

Divide the common factors.

$$= \frac{x-1}{3}$$

To divide by a rational expression, multiply by the reciprocal of the divisor.

Example 2

Divide.

$$\frac{x^2 - 4}{x^2 - 5x + 6} \div \frac{3x^2 - 5x - 2}{6x^2 + 2x}$$

$$= \frac{(x-2)(x+2)}{(x-2)(x-3)} \div \frac{(3x+1)(x-2)}{2x(3x+1)}$$

$$= \frac{(x-2)(x+2)}{(x-2)(x-3)} \times \frac{2x(3x+1)}{(3x+1)(x-2)}$$

Neither the numerator nor the denominator of the divisor can equal zero.
$x \neq 0$, $x \neq 2$, $x \neq 3$, and $x \neq -\dfrac{1}{3}$

$$= \frac{2x(x-2)(x+2)(3x+1)}{(x-2)(x-3)(x-2)(3x+1)}$$

$$= \frac{2x(x+2)}{(x-3)(x-2)}$$

All the factoring processes should be checked when multiplying and dividing rational expressions.

Example 3

Multiply.

$$\frac{2xz + 8x - yz - 4y}{2x^2 - 7xy + 3y^2} \times \frac{2x^2 - 9xy + 9y^2}{z^2 - 16}$$

$$= \frac{(2xz + 8x) - (yz + 4y)}{(2x - y)(x - 3y)} \times \frac{(2x - 3y)(x - 3y)}{(z + 4)(z - 4)}$$

$$= \frac{2x(z + 4) - y(z + 4)}{(2x - y)(x - 3y)} \times \frac{(2x - 3y)(x - 3y)}{(z + 4)(z - 4)}$$

$x \neq \dfrac{1}{2}y$, $x \neq \dfrac{1}{3}y$, and $z \neq \pm 4$

$$= \frac{(z + 4)(2x - y)(2x - 3y)(x - 3y)}{(2x - y)(x - 3y)(z + 4)(z - 4)}$$

$$= \frac{2x - 3y}{z - 4}$$

Exercises

1. In Example 1 of this display, why were the restrictions stated before simplifying the expression?

2. State the restrictions on the variables.

a. $\dfrac{a^2}{a+1} \times 4$ **b.** $\dfrac{a^2}{a+1} \times \dfrac{a^2-1}{a^3+a^2}$

c. $\dfrac{k^2-9}{k^2-3k} \times \dfrac{5k^2}{4k^2+13k+3}$

d. $\dfrac{m^3+8}{m+2} \times \dfrac{8m-4m^2}{3m^2-16m+20}$

For the remainder of the exercises, state the restrictions on all variables.

3. Multiply. Simplify your answer.

a. $\dfrac{3}{5} \times \dfrac{5}{9}$ **b.** $\dfrac{1}{2} \times \dfrac{2}{3} \times \dfrac{3}{4}$

c. $\dfrac{5x}{x^2} \times \dfrac{2x+6}{x+3}$ **d.** $\dfrac{4x}{6x} \times \dfrac{7y}{y^2}$

4. Simplify by dividing.

a. $\dfrac{3x}{15xy} \div \dfrac{7x^2}{14x}$ **b.** $\dfrac{-5a^2}{4b} \div \dfrac{10a}{2b^2}$

c. $\dfrac{8m^2n^3}{4mn} \div m^5$ **d.** $\dfrac{3ab^2}{8b^3} \div \dfrac{7a}{2b}$

5. The simple interest paid by a bank on money in an account is given by the formula $I = prt$, where p is the principal amount, r is the interest rate, and t is the time period. Find an expression for the interest earned on $\$\left(\dfrac{2x^2+4x+2}{x^2-1}\right)$ for $\left(\dfrac{3x^2+2x-5}{2x^2-4x-6}\right)$ years at a rate of $\left(\dfrac{1}{3x+5}\right)\%$.

6. Why must the restrictions be stated for the numerator and the denominator of the divisor when dividing two rational expressions?

7. The height of a triangle is represented by $(6x^2 - 22x - 8)$ cm and the area is $\left(\dfrac{3x+1}{x}\right)$ cm². Find an expression for the length of the base.

8. If the diameter of a circle is given by the expression $(8m - 5)$ cm, then find an expression for the area of the circle.

9. Multiply. Simplify your answer.

a. $\dfrac{b^2-b-6}{b^2-4} \times \dfrac{5b^2-11b+2}{10b^2+18b-4}$

b. $\dfrac{8m^3-1}{2m-6} \times \dfrac{6m^2-13m-15}{12m^2+4m-5}$

c. $\dfrac{8ac+4ad}{3a^2-2ab+b^2} \times \dfrac{2ac-ad-2bc+bd}{d^2-4c^2}$

d. $\dfrac{2k^2-6k+18}{k^3+27} \times \dfrac{4k^2+14k+6}{6k}$

e. $\dfrac{4p^2+pq-3q^2}{32p^2-18q^2} \times \dfrac{4p^2-21pq-18q^2}{p^3+q^3}$

f. $\dfrac{3y^2+24yz+48z^2}{xy+4xz-3y-12z} \times \dfrac{2x^2-18}{20}$

g. $\dfrac{9a^2-6ab+b^2-16c^2}{4a^3+32b^3} \times \dfrac{a^2+2ab+4b^2}{3a-b+4c}$

10. While shopping in Lethbridge, Kara spends three quarters of her money. The taxi fare home requires one third of what she had left. How much money did Kara start with if she spent a total of $\$70$?

11. The volume of a cube is given by the expression $\dfrac{x^9+y^9}{x^3+y^3}$ m³. Write this expression in simplified form.

12. Divide. Simplify your answer.

a. $\dfrac{m+1}{m^2} \div \dfrac{m^2+m}{m^3-m^2}$

b. $\dfrac{8x^2-4x-40}{8x^2-50} \div \dfrac{12+6x}{8x^3+125}$

c. $\dfrac{3ac+5c+9ad+15d}{10c-5d+6ac-3ad} \div \dfrac{5c^2-45d^2}{2c^2+cd-d^2}$

d. $\dfrac{15-m-2m^2}{4m^2-20m+25} \div \dfrac{mn+3n-2m-6}{2mn-5n-4m+10}$

e. $\dfrac{20p^2-5q^2}{2p^2-6p+pq-3q} \div \dfrac{-q+10p^2-2p+5pq}{25p^2-70p-15}$

13. Divide the product of $\dfrac{8x^3-125}{12x^2-75}$ and $\dfrac{4x^2-28x+45}{6xy-27y}$ by $4x^2+10x+25$.

2·16 Addition and Subtraction I

In order to add or subtract rational expressions, all the expressions must have common denominators. The common denominator is the Least Common Multiple of all the denominators in the expression.

Example 1

Find the Least Common Multiple (LCM) of each.

a. $3x$, $5xy$, $15x^2$

b. $2(x+1)$, $4x(x+1)$, $(x+1)^2$

LCM of 3, 5, and 15 is 15.
LCM of x, x, and x^2 is x^2.
LCM of y is y.
$\therefore$ LCM of $3x$, $5xy$, $15x^2$ is $15x^2y$.

LCM of 2, 4, and 1 is 4.
LCM of $(x+1)$, $(x+1)$, and $(x+1)^2$ is $(x+1)^2$.
$\therefore$ LCM of $2(x+1)$, $4x(x+1)$, $(x+1)^2$ is $4(x+1)^2$.

Example 2

Add or subtract.

a. $\dfrac{2x}{3} - \dfrac{5y}{7}$

$= \dfrac{14x - 15y}{21}$

b. $\dfrac{3}{2a} + \dfrac{8}{5a^2}$

$= \dfrac{(3 \times 5)a}{10a^2} + \dfrac{8 \times 2}{10a^2}$

$= \dfrac{15a + 16}{10a^2}$

> State the restrictions on the variable. $a \neq 0$

Example 3

Simplify by adding or subtracting.

$\dfrac{x^2 + 2x}{x+5} + \dfrac{5x + 10}{x+5}$

Since the two rational expressions have the same denominator, the expression can be added directly.

$= \dfrac{x^2 + 7x + 10}{x+5}$

$= \dfrac{(x+5)(x+2)}{x+5}$

$= x + 2$

> $x \neq -5$

Notice how the numerator in the rational expression was factored and the common factor divided. In general, a rational expression is in simplified form when **all** common factors have been found and divided.

Example 4

Simplify. $\dfrac{a^2 - 5}{a+2} - \dfrac{2a}{4(a+2)} = \dfrac{4(a^2 - 5)}{4(a+2)} - \dfrac{2a}{4(a+2)}$

> $a \neq -2$

$= \dfrac{4a^2 - 2a - 20}{4(a+2)}$

$= \dfrac{2(2a - 5)(a+2)}{4(a+2)}$

$= \dfrac{2a - 5}{2}$

Exercises

1. Find the LCM of each.

a. 3, 6   **b.** 25, 45

c. $18x$, $22xy$ **d.** $2x$, $4x^2$, $3xyz$

e. $3(x-4)$, $2x-8$ **f.** a, ab, bc

2. Write each expression with a denominator of $4ab$.

a. $7c$ **b.** $\dfrac{4ac}{5}$

c. $2a+3c$ **d.** $a+b+c-9$

3. State the restrictions on the variables of Exercise 2, part **a**. Are they the same for all parts of Exercise 2?

4. Add.

a. $\dfrac{4}{3ac}+\dfrac{7}{3ac}$ **b.** $\dfrac{5}{x+2}+\dfrac{8}{x+2}$

c. $\dfrac{3}{4x}+\dfrac{5}{4x}$ **d.** $\dfrac{2t}{t-3}-\dfrac{3}{t-3}$

e. $\dfrac{6m}{m+5}+\dfrac{5m}{m+5}$ **f.** $\dfrac{2s}{s-3}+\dfrac{6}{s-3}$

5. Subtract.

a. $\dfrac{5}{3xy}-\dfrac{2}{3xy}$ **b.** $\dfrac{12}{5x}-\dfrac{8}{5x}$

c. $\dfrac{7y}{y-1}-\dfrac{6}{y-1}$ **d.** $\dfrac{b-3}{b+4}-\dfrac{3b+2}{b+4}$

e. $\dfrac{a+b}{ab}-\dfrac{a-b}{ab}$ **f.** $\dfrac{3x^2}{x^2}-\dfrac{5x-4}{x^2}$

6. Simplify by addition or subtraction.

a. $\dfrac{3}{4x}+\dfrac{5}{2x}$ **b.** $\dfrac{a+6}{2}-\dfrac{3a-1}{5}$

c. $\dfrac{1}{ab}-\dfrac{3}{abc}$ **d.** $\dfrac{2s}{s-1}+\dfrac{s-5}{2(s-1)}$

e. $\dfrac{7y}{y^2}+\dfrac{3xy}{xy}$ **f.** $\dfrac{9}{5ab^2}-\dfrac{2}{a^2b}$

g. $\dfrac{9}{2(y+3)}-\dfrac{4}{(y+3)^2}+\dfrac{1}{y+3}$

7. If $xy=12$ and $x-y=-3$, then find the value of the expression $\dfrac{2}{x}-\dfrac{2}{y}$. (*Hint*: Do not evaluate x and y.)

8. Find the perimeter.

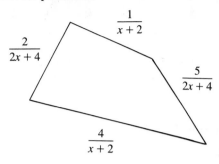

9. The perimeter of a triangle is given by the expression $\dfrac{2x+5}{x+3}$ cm. Find an expression for the length of the third side if the other two sides have a sum of $\dfrac{3x-1}{2x+6}$ cm.

10. Add $\dfrac{2x^2+8x+15}{2x^2-x-15}$ to the sum of $\dfrac{4x^2}{2x^2-x-15}$ and $\dfrac{17x+10}{(2x+5)(x-3)}$.

11. Wooden window stripping is to be placed inside a window frame as shown. If the window measures 75 cm by 50 cm, and the area of the space left is 900 cm², then find the width of the strip.

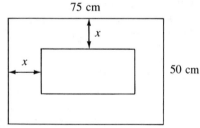

12. Add or subtract.

a. $\dfrac{x}{5x+1}-\dfrac{4}{3x-2}$

b. $\dfrac{2}{5}+\dfrac{2m}{m+1}-\dfrac{3}{m+1}$

c. $\dfrac{2x}{(x-3)(x+3)}+\dfrac{x+1}{(x-6)(x+3)}$

d. $\dfrac{5}{m+3}+4-\dfrac{8m}{2m-1}$

e. $\dfrac{4p^2q}{6p}+\dfrac{27q^3r}{15pq^2r}$

2·17 Addition and Subtraction II

In the previous section, rational expressions were added and subtracted after finding a common denominator. However, in most rational expressions it is often easier to find a common denominator if the original expression is factored first.

Example 1

Add.

$$\frac{5}{t-4} + \frac{6}{t^2-16}$$

$$= \frac{5(t+4)}{(t-4)(t+4)} + \frac{6}{(t-4)(t+4)} \qquad \left\{ \text{Factor the denominator. } t \neq \pm 4 \right\}$$

$$= \frac{5t+20+6}{(t-4)(t+4)}$$

$$= \frac{5t+26}{(t-4)(t+4)}$$

Sometimes, when the numerator and the denominator of a rational expression are factored, there are common factors that can be divided.

Example 2

The perimeter of an object is given by the expression $\dfrac{x^2+3x+9}{x^3-27}$ cm. The sum of all the sides but one is given by the expression $\dfrac{2x^2-9x+4}{2x^2-2x-24}$ cm. Find the length of the unknown side.

$$\frac{x^2+3x+9}{x^3-27} - \frac{2x^2-9x+4}{2x^2-2x-24}$$

$$= \frac{x^2+3x+9}{(x-3)(x^2+3x+9)} - \frac{(2x-1)(x-4)}{2(x+3)(x-4)} \qquad \left\{ \begin{array}{l} \text{Divide the common factors and state} \\ \text{the restrictions. } x \neq -3, 3, 4 \end{array} \right.$$

$$= \frac{1}{x-3} - \frac{2x-1}{2(x+3)}$$

$$= \frac{2(x+3)}{2(x-3)(x+3)} - \frac{(2x-1)(x-3)}{2(x-3)(x+3)}$$

$$= \frac{2(x+3) - (2x-1)(x-3)}{2(x-3)(x+3)} \qquad \left\{ \text{Be aware of the negative sign.} \right\}$$

$$= \frac{2x+6 - 2x^2 + 7x - 3}{2(x-3)(x+3)}$$

$$= \frac{-2x^2+9x+3}{2(x-3)(x+3)}$$

The length of the remaining side is $\dfrac{-2x^2+9x+3}{2(x-3)(x+3)}$ cm.

Exercises

1. State the restrictions on the variables.

a. $\dfrac{3x + 8}{5x - 4} + \dfrac{-6}{2y + 3}$

b. $\dfrac{a^2 - 8a + 12}{4a^2 - 11a - 3} - \dfrac{3p^2 + p - 9}{12p^2 - 75}$

c. $\dfrac{5x^2 - 2xy}{x^2 - 2xy - 8y^2} - \dfrac{m^3 - n^3}{6m^2 - 27mn - 15n^2}$

2. Is it necessary to state the restrictions on the variables in the numerator when adding or subtracting rational expressions? Explain.

For the remainder of the exercises, state the restrictions on all variables.

3. Find the sum or difference.

a. $\dfrac{x + 2}{3} + \dfrac{x^2}{x - 4}$

b. $\dfrac{4}{a + 3} + \dfrac{a + 1}{a - 5}$

c. $\dfrac{12k}{6k - 2} - \dfrac{15k + 5}{9k^2 - 1}$

d. $\dfrac{3m^2 - 2m}{6m^2 - m - 2} + \dfrac{3m - 12}{2m^2 - 32}$

e. $\dfrac{p^3 - 1}{2p^2 - 2} - \dfrac{2p^2 - 7p + 6}{10p - 15}$

f. $\dfrac{4}{2x - 6} - \dfrac{5x}{x^3 - 27}$

4. Find the perimeter.

a.

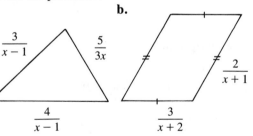

b.

5. Add or subtract.

a. $\dfrac{9x^2}{12x^2 - 3} + \dfrac{3}{2x - 1}$

b. $\dfrac{6s^2 - 27s - 15}{2s^2 - 11s + 5} + \dfrac{3st - 6s - t + 2}{5t - 10}$

c. $\dfrac{(x - y)^2 - 4}{x - y + 2} + \dfrac{x^2 - 2y - 2x + xy}{4 - x^2}$

d. $\dfrac{3a - 5}{a + 1} + \dfrac{5a}{2} - \dfrac{2a + 3}{a - 2}$

e. $\dfrac{p^2 - 9}{2p^2 + 6p} - \dfrac{2p^2 - 7p - 8}{p^2 - 8p + 16} - \dfrac{6}{3p - 12}$

6. Find an expression for the length of the unknown side.

a.

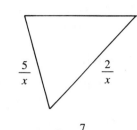

$$P = \dfrac{24}{3x^2 - 3x}$$

b.

$$P = \dfrac{7}{x^2}$$

7. In Exercise 3, part **f**, if a third term added is 1, predict how this would change the simplification of the expression. Simplify the expression to check your prediction.

8. Find the sum of $\dfrac{3a^3 + 5a^2b - 2ab^2}{4a^2 + 7ab - 2b^2}$ and $\dfrac{2c - 4d}{ac - 2ad + 3bc - 6bd}$.

9. State the steps you used to simplify the expression in Exercise 8.

10. List expressions for the perimeter and the area.

a.

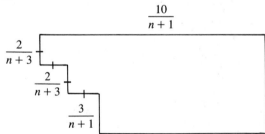

b.

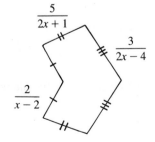

59

2·18 Equations with Rationals

Solving equations with rational expressions will require finding a common denominator for all the expressions in the equation.

Example 1

Find three consecutive even integers such that when one quarter of the largest integer is subtracted from the sum of one third of the smallest integer and one half of the middle integer, the result is 7.

Let $2x$ represent the first even integer. Therefore, the second even integer is $2x + 2$ and the third even integer is $2x + 4$.

$$\frac{1}{3}(2x) + \frac{1}{2}(2x + 2) - \frac{1}{4}(2x + 4) = 7$$

Multiply both sides of the equation by the least common multiple of the denominators.

$$12\left\{\frac{2x}{3} + \frac{2x + 2}{2} - \frac{2x + 4}{4}\right\} = 12(7)$$
$$4(2x) + 6(2x + 2) - 3(2x + 4) = 84$$
$$8x + 12x + 12 - 6x - 12 = 84$$
$$14x = 84$$
$$x = 6$$

If $x = 6$, then $2x = 12$, $2x + 2 = 14$, and $2x + 4 = 16$. Therefore, the three consecutive even integers are 12, 14, and 16. All solutions to equations involving rational expressions should be checked by substituting into the **original** equation.
$$\left[\frac{1}{3}(12) + \frac{1}{2}(14)\right] - \frac{1}{4}(16) = 7$$

Sometimes, there is no solution to an equation.

Example 2

Solve.
$$\frac{3x + 1}{x + 3} - \frac{x - 5}{x + 3} = 0$$

The value for x cannot be -3. Why?
$$\frac{3x - x + 1 - (-5)}{x + 3} = 0$$
$$\frac{2x + 6}{x + 3} = 0$$
$$(x + 3)\left(\frac{2x + 6}{x + 3}\right) = (x + 3)(0)$$
$$2x + 6 = 0$$
$$x = -3$$

Since $x \neq -3$, the equation has no solution.

Example 3

Solve.
$$\frac{8t^2 + 13t - 6}{4t + 8} - 5 = \frac{6t^3 + 2t^2}{3t^2 - 2t - 1}$$
$$\frac{(8t - 3)(t + 2)}{4(t + 2)} - 5 = \frac{2t^2(3t + 1)}{(3t + 1)(t - 1)}$$

The values for t cannot be -2, $-\frac{1}{3}$, or 1. Why?
$$\frac{(8t - 3)}{4} - 5 = \frac{2t^2}{t - 1}$$
$$(8t - 3)(t - 1) - 4(5)(t - 1) = 8t^2$$
$$8t^2 - 11t + 3 - 20t + 20 = 8t^2$$
$$\frac{23}{31} = t$$

Since the value of t is not a restricted value, and it makes the original equation true, $t = \frac{23}{31}$.

Exercises

1. Explain why the restrictions on the variables are found before solving for the variables in Examples 2 and 3 of the display.

2. Find the Least Common Multiple of each.
a. 12, 8
b. $15a, 20ab^2$
c. $2c - 3, 2c$
d. $x + 1, 3x - 5$
e. $8k, 2k^2 + 6k$
f. $y^2 - 9, y - 3$
g. $3x, 6xy, 15y^2$
h. $2m^2, 5mn, 3n^2$

3. Solve these equations. Verify your solutions.
a. $\dfrac{x + 2}{3} + \dfrac{x - 5}{2} = 1$
b. $\dfrac{3m + 5}{4} = \dfrac{2m - 1}{6}$
c. $\dfrac{p - 6}{15} - \dfrac{2 + 3p}{9} = 2$
d. $\dfrac{5t + 2}{8} + 3 = \dfrac{t + 4}{2}$
e. $\dfrac{1}{3}(4a - 1) = \dfrac{1}{2} + \dfrac{1}{4}(a + 6)$
f. $\dfrac{2}{5}(k + 3) - \dfrac{3}{2}(2k + 1) = 3$

4. Solve. State all the restrictions on the variables.
a. $\dfrac{8}{x} - 4 = \dfrac{3}{x}$
b. $6 - \dfrac{2}{c + 1} = \dfrac{5c}{c + 1}$
c. $\dfrac{-5}{3x - 2} = \dfrac{2}{x + 6}$
d. $\dfrac{3}{a} - \dfrac{2}{5} = \dfrac{1}{2a}$
e. $\dfrac{3}{2y} = \dfrac{5}{y - 2}$
f. $\dfrac{5}{2m} - \dfrac{1}{4} = \dfrac{8}{3m}$

5. Solve these equations.
a. $\dfrac{3}{p} - \dfrac{5p}{2 - 5p} = 1$
b. $\dfrac{x - 5}{x + 1} + 5 = \dfrac{6x - 6}{x + 2}$
c. $\dfrac{2a - 5}{3 - a} = \dfrac{3}{4}$
d. $\dfrac{2}{2x - 3} = \dfrac{5}{3x + 1}$
e. $2 - \dfrac{4}{3t} = \dfrac{2t}{t + 4}$
f. $\dfrac{2y + 3}{2y} + 6 = \dfrac{7y}{y + 1}$
g. $\dfrac{2x + \dfrac{x - 3}{x + 2}}{3 - \dfrac{7x + 3}{x^2 - 1}} = -2$
h. $\dfrac{3x - \dfrac{7x + 8}{x - 1}}{\dfrac{9x^2 - 10}{3x - 7} + x} = 4$

6. Ryan starts jogging at a rate of 6 km/h. After reaching Harbourfront, he begins jogging back home. Due to fatigue, the trip home takes 1 h longer. On his return trip, his speed decreases to 4.5 km/h. Determine the total distance Ryan jogged.

7. Solve these equations. State all the restrictions on the variables.
a. $\dfrac{2x}{x^2 + 3x} = \dfrac{x - 3}{2x^2 - 13x + 21}$
b. $\dfrac{2p^2 + 5p - 3}{6p + 18} - \dfrac{p^2 - 3p}{5p} = 0$
c. $\dfrac{k^2 + 6k + 9}{k^2 + k - 6} = \dfrac{2k^2 + 5k}{2k^2}$
d. $\dfrac{4n}{n^2 - 1} - \dfrac{6}{n + 1} = \dfrac{3}{n - 1}$
e. $\dfrac{8a^2 - 10a - 3}{4a^2 + a} = \dfrac{20a^2 + 3a - 2}{10a^2 - a - 2}$

8. The total resistance, R, when two resistors, p ohms and q ohms, are connected in a parallel circuit is given by the relation $\dfrac{1}{R} = \dfrac{1}{p} + \dfrac{1}{q}$.
a. If one of the parallel resistances is 5 ohms, and it is necessary to have a total resistance of 2 ohms, then find the measure of the other resistance.
b. If a total resistance of 4 ohms is needed, and the two parallel resistors are in the ratio of 2:1, then find the measure of the two resistors.

9. A parallelogram has a base length of 12 cm. In order to increase the area of the parallelogram by 54 cm² , the length of the base is increased by 2 cm and the height is increased by 3 cm. Find the area of the original parallelogram.

10. There are three numbers such that the second is 10 more than the first and the third is 5 times the first. Find the numbers if the sum of one half of the first, two thirds of the second, and one quarter of the third is equal to 26.

11. The area of an isosceles triangle is given by the expression $6x^2 - x - 2$ square units. The height of the triangle is given by the expression $3x^2 - x - 4$ units. If the perimeter of the triangle is $\dfrac{x^2 - 2}{x - 1}$ units, find the lengths of the two congruent sides.

2·19 Computer Application— The Golden Ratio

Many problems that do not have an apparent solution can be solved with the help of a computer. For example, find a number that is one less than its square. An equation can be set up to find the number. It is either $x^2 - x = 1$ or $x^2 - x - 1 = 0$. Since neither equation factors easily, the zero of the polynomial can be found using this computer program. Note that the computer cannot compare the equality of two values. Therefore, when the value of $x^2 - x - 1$ goes from negative to positive, the computer will print that value of x. This is an approximation of the solution.

```
10 REM A PROGRAM TO SET UP A TABLE OF VALUES FOR
20 REM THE EQUATION X ^ 2 - X - 1
30 FOR X = 1 TO 2 STEP 0.001
40 LET Y = X ^ 2 - X - 1
50 IF Y > 0 THEN 70
60 NEXT X
70 PRINT "THE NUMBER THAT IS ONE LESS THAN ITS SQUARE IS
APPROXIMATELY "; X
80 END
```

Exercises

1. In the program in the display, which line defines the polynomial?

2. Why is the value of x from 1 to 2 in steps of 0.001?

3. When will the value of the polynomial be printed?

4. What is the purpose of line 70 in the program?

5. Run the program and record the output.
a. Evaluate this expression correct to four decimal places. $\dfrac{1 + \sqrt{5}}{2}$
b. Compare the value of the expression in part **a** to the output from the program in the display. Are they the same?
c. Both the program in the display and the expression in part **a** approximate one of the more famous ratios. What ratio is being approximated?

6. What may be the result if too large an increment is chosen for the values of x?

7. Modify the program in the display to find the number that is one greater than its reciprocal. In other words, have the computer approximate a zero for the equation $x - \dfrac{1}{x} = 1$. Is this an approximation of the Golden Ratio?

8. Piracy of computer programs is a problem for all software developers. This happens when a person buys software and then makes free copies for friends. Write a short essay on the question of whether the laws against piracy should be extremely harsh. Take into account the viewpoint of both the user and the developer of the software.

2·20 Chapter Review

1. Determine the product of the factors.
a. $(5a - 3)(2a - 9)$ **b.** $3(4p + 3)(p - 5)$
c. $(2s + 1)^2$ **d.** $2(2k - 6)^2$
e. $(4x + 3y)(x^2 - 2xy - y^2)$
f. $[(a + 3b) + 4c][(a + 3b) - 4c]$

2. Simplify by collecting like terms.
a. $(3 - 2x)(4 + x) + (3x + 1)^2$
b. $5(t - 2)^2 - (5t + 6)(t - 3)$
c. $4(2m + 3)(2m + 5) + 2(3m)(4m - 7)$
d. $(5s - 1)(s + 8) - 5(s + 2)(s - 2)$

3. Factor completely. (*Hint*: Group common factors.)
a. $2a^2 - 3ab + 10ad - 15bd$
b. $8xy - 12xz - 2y^2 + 3yz$
c. $6m^2n - 25 + 15n - 10m^2$
d. $12a^2 - 4ab + 3a - b$

4. Factor completely.
a. $x^2 - y^2 + 10x + 25$
b. $4ab + 9 - 4a^2 - b^2$
c. $9n^2 + 4m^2 - 4p^2 + 12mn$
d. $x^2 + 9 - y^2 - z^2 - 6x - 2yz$

5. Factor the sum and difference of cubes.
a. $x^3 - 27y^3$ **b.** $125a^3 + 1$
c. $8p^3 - 27q^6$ **d.** $250m^3 + 16n^3$
e. $(x + 2)^3 - y^3$ **f.** $64 + (a - 3b)^3$

6. A circle has an area represented by $\pi(4x^2 - 4x + 1)$ square units. Find the radius of the circle.

7. Factor completely.
a. $8(k^2 - 4) + j^3(k^2 - 4)$
b. $2x^3y - 5x^3 + 2y - 5$
c. $4x^2y^2 - y^2 - 16x^2 + 4$
d. $y^2(x^2 + 3x + 2) - 4(x^2 + 3x + 2)$

8. Factor by completing the square.
a. $p^4 + 2p^2q^2 + 9q^4$
b. $4c^4 - 20c^2d^2$
c. $25x^4 - 9x^2y^2 + 16y^4$
d. $9a^4 - 10a^2b^2c^4 + b^4c^8$

9. Which binomials are factors of $x^3 + 3x^2 - 10x - 24$?
a. $x - 2$ **b.** $x - 3$ **c.** $x - 4$
d. $x + 2$ **e.** $x + 3$ **f.** $x + 4$

10. Determine which values are zeros of $x^3 - 7x - 6$ and write the three factors of the polynomial.
a. ± 1 **b.** ± 2 **c.** ± 3

11. If $x = 4$ is a zero of the polynomial $2x^4 - x^3 - 35x^2 + kx + 48$, then find the value of k.

12. State the restrictions on the variable and explain why the restrictions are necessary.
a. $\dfrac{5x - 8}{2x}$ **b.** $\dfrac{16}{2x^2 - x - 15}$

13. Simplify.
a. $\dfrac{24m^2n}{18mn^4}$ **b.** $\dfrac{-15xy^2}{20x^6y}$
c. $\dfrac{2t - 8}{3t^2 - 12t}$ **d.** $\dfrac{m^2 + 7m + 6}{m^2 + m - 30}$
e. $\dfrac{4a^2 + 7ab - 2b^2}{2a^2 + 5ab + 2b^2}$ **f.** $\dfrac{8c^2 - 13cd - 6d^2}{c^3 - 8d^3}$
g. $\dfrac{4p^2 - 16pq + 15q^2}{4p^2 - 20pq + 25q^2}$ **h.** $\dfrac{2y - 6x - 2}{(3x + 1)^2 - y^2}$

14. What is the remainder when $x^3 - 3x^2 + 2x + 4$ is divided by $x + 2$?

15. Perform the indicated operations and simplify.
a. $\dfrac{4x + 16}{x^2 + 2x - 8} \times \dfrac{x^2 - 4}{12x}$
b. $\dfrac{2x^2 + 11x - 6}{x^2 - 36} \div \dfrac{6x^2 + 7x - 5}{2x^2 - 12x}$
c. $\dfrac{4ac + 3bd - 6bc - 2ad}{4c^2 - 4cd + d^2} \times \dfrac{4c^2 - d^2}{8a^3 - 27b^3}$
d. $\dfrac{4m^2 - 11mn - 3n^2}{3mnp - 9m^2p} \times \dfrac{15m^2n}{4m^2 - 3mn - n^2}$

16. Perform the indicated operations.
a. $\dfrac{5a + 2}{6} + \dfrac{3 - a}{8}$ **b.** $\dfrac{7}{4x} + \dfrac{2}{x - 3}$
c. $\dfrac{x - 2}{3x + 1} - \dfrac{2x}{x - 4}$ **d.** $\dfrac{4x - 3}{10x^2 + 5x} + \dfrac{6}{2x + 1}$

2·21 Chapter Test

1. Determine the product of the factors.
a. $(m - 4n)(3m - 2n)$
b. $3(x + 5y)(2x - y)$
c. $(4a + 5b)(a^2 - 3ab - 2b^2)$
d. $(p - q + 5r)^2$

2. Factor completely.
a. $4ac + 6bc + 2ad + 3bd$
b. $125b^6 + 1$ **c.** $2x^3 - 18xy^2$
d. $(x - 2y)^2 - z^2$ **e.** $2k^3 + 16$
f. $3y(x^2 + 3x - 4) + 2(x^2 + 3x - 4)$
g. $4x^2 - y^2 + 9 - 12x$
h. $108s^4 - 4s$
i. $4a^2b^2 + 16ab^2 - 9b^2$
j. $50m^2p - 75m^2q - 2p + 3q$

3. Why is it possible to check the factors of a polynomial by multiplication?

4. Factor by completing the square.
a. $16x^4 + 7x^2 + 1$
b. $4a^4 - 16a^2b^2 + 9b^4$
c. $m^4 - 23m^2n^4 + n^8$
d. $4r^4 - r^2t^2 + 4t^4$

5. If a polynomial in x has zeros of 1, -2, and 4, then what are its factors? Explain why you chose these factors.

6. Find the zeros of $3x(2x - 5)(x + 6)$.

7. State the value of k if the binomial is a factor of the given polynomial.
a. $kx^3 + 19x^2 + 9x - 6; (x + 2)$
b. $2x^4 - 7x^3 - 15x^2 + 34x + k; (x - 4)$
c. $3x^4 + 5x^3 + kx^2 - 25x - 10; (x + 1)$

8. Using the formula for kinetic energy, $K = \frac{1}{2}mv^2$, determine the total kinetic energy, K, if the mass of the object in motion is $(4a + 8b)$ kg and it is moving with a velocity of $(a - 2b)$ m/s.

9. State the restrictions on the variable.
a. $\dfrac{8x^2 + 1}{-3x}$ **b.** $\dfrac{5x^2 - 3x + 1}{x^2 - 4}$

10. Add or subtract.
a. $\dfrac{a + 3}{-2} + \dfrac{a + 3}{5}$
b. $\dfrac{4}{k - 2} - \dfrac{5 - 3k}{k}$
c. $\dfrac{1}{2x^2 + 11x - 6} - \dfrac{2}{x^2 + 2x - 24}$
d. $\dfrac{4p^2 + 11p - 3}{8p^2 + 18p - 5} - \dfrac{6p - 18}{p^2 - 9}$
e. $\dfrac{12y^2 - 11y - 5}{9y^2 + 1} - \dfrac{5y^2 + 28y - 12}{10y^2 - 4y}$

11. From the sum of $\dfrac{b^3 + 8}{b^2 - 2b + 4}$ and $\dfrac{4b^2 - 16b - 9}{4b^2 - 81}$, subtract $\dfrac{4b^2 - 9b + 2}{12b - 3}$.

12. By long division find the quotient and remainder when $2x^3 + 3x^2 - 48$ is divided by $x - 4$.

13. Determine the interest earned if $(m + 5n)$ dollars is invested at a rate of $(3m - 2n)\%$/a simple interest for a period of 10 a.

14. A car has travelled a distance of $(9x^3 + 36x^2 - x - 4)$ km in $(3x + 1)$ h. Find the expression which represents the rate of travel.

15. Simplify.
a. $\dfrac{42a^2b^3c}{-14ab^5c}$ **b.** $\dfrac{2x - 1}{3 - 6x}$
c. $\dfrac{4p^2 - 9}{12p^2 + 16p - 3}$ **d.** $\dfrac{3x^2 + 23x - 8}{x^2 + 16x + 64}$
e. $\dfrac{4a^2 + 7ab - 2b^2}{3a^2 + 7ab + 2b^2}$ **f.** $\dfrac{27m^3 + n^3}{3m^2 - 15m + mn - 5n}$
g. $\dfrac{x^2 + 4x + 4 - 9y^2}{2x + 4 - 6y}$ **h.** $\dfrac{x^3 - 4x + x^2y - 4y}{x^2 - 2y - 2x + xy}$

16. Use the formula for energy, $E = Fd$, to determine d, the distance an object moves, if $E = 8p^3 + 125q^3$ joules and $F = (2p^2 + 3pq - 5q^2)$ N.

RATIO AND PROPORTION

Tune Up

1. Express the rational expressions in lowest terms. State the restrictions on the variables.

a. $\dfrac{464}{824}$ **b.** $\dfrac{45x^2}{9y^2}$ **c.** $\dfrac{3x(x-2)}{9x^2-36}$

d. $\dfrac{-121+x^2}{-11+x}$ **e.** $\dfrac{21t}{7}$ **f.** $\dfrac{z^2+7z+6}{(z+6)(z+1)}$

g. $\dfrac{17s}{31t}$ **h.** $\dfrac{x^5+x^2}{x^2}$ **i.** $\dfrac{a^2b^3-4t^2b}{ab^2+2tb}$

j. $\dfrac{\sqrt{28}}{\sqrt{252}}$ **k.** $\dfrac{x+y}{x^2-y^2}$ **l.** $\dfrac{\pi r^2}{2\pi r}$

2. Simplify these fractional expressions. Check your simplification for $x=3$ and $t=2$.

a. $\dfrac{11}{\left(\dfrac{33}{3}\right)}$ **b.** $\dfrac{8x}{\left(\dfrac{8x^2}{16}\right)}$ **c.** $\dfrac{4t(x-2)}{\left(\dfrac{16t^2}{x-2}\right)}$

3. What process is used when evaluating a rational expression where both the numerator and the denominator are rational expressions?

4. Express the equation(s) in terms of $\dfrac{y}{x}$. The first one is done as an example.

$$\dfrac{3x}{16}=\dfrac{2y}{\sqrt{3}}$$

$$\dfrac{3\sqrt{3}}{32}=\dfrac{y}{x}$$

a. Outline the process used in the example.
b. $8x=3\pi y$ **c.** $-2x+5y=0$
d. $\dfrac{1}{2}x=\dfrac{3}{7}y$ **e.** $\dfrac{x}{y}=\dfrac{3t}{8}+\dfrac{5s}{30}$

5. Solve for x.

a. $\dfrac{3x+6}{4}=\dfrac{x-2}{2}$ **b.** $\dfrac{2x-7}{x-2}=\dfrac{13}{5}$

c. $\dfrac{5x+3}{x-3}=\dfrac{1}{2}$ **d.** $\dfrac{2x+6}{x+3}=3$

e. Explain why part **d** is impossible.

6. A box contains x tennis balls, and all but 8 are green. Write an expression for the fraction of tennis balls which are green. If there were 14 tennis balls altogether, then what fraction would be green?

7. For each equation, prepare a table of values and graph the function.

a. $y=2x-4$ **b.** $2x-3y=0$
c. $xy=4$ **d.** $y=x^2+2$
e. $\dfrac{3}{2}x-\dfrac{7}{4}y=1$ **f.** $y-1=3x$

g. Which of these functions are linear?
h. Which of these functions do not have an x-intercept? a y-intercept?

8. In your own words, define the x-intercept and the y-intercept of a graph.

9. A frog stands on one end of a log and starts to hop. It jumps $\dfrac{1}{2}$ the distance to the other end of the log every time. Will the frog ever reach the other end? Explain.

3·1 Ratio

The relationship between two or more different items can be stated in terms of a common unit of measure. For instance, a brick and a golf club are two different items, but we can say that the mass of a brick is four times the mass of a golf club. We also can say that the number of teeth on the front sprocket of a bicycle is 1.5 times the number of teeth on the back sprocket. The comparison of two or more different items in terms of a common numerical property is a **ratio**.

The relationship between the mass of the golf club and the mass of the brick can be written in fraction form, $\dfrac{\text{mass of brick}}{\text{mass of club}} = \dfrac{4}{1}$, or as mass of brick:mass of golf club = 4:1 (read as "4 to 1"). The fractional expression of a ratio is usually written in lowest terms, and the units of measurement are not included in the ratio. Multiplying or dividing both sides of a ratio by the same nonzero number will not alter the value of the ratio. In the two-term ratio $a:b$, a is the **first term** and b is the **second term**. In a ratio, $a:b$, $b \neq 0$.

> If two quantities are in the ratio $a:b$, where a and $b \in R$ and $b \neq 0$, then $a:b$ can be written as $\dfrac{a}{b}$ and there exists a nonzero constant, k, such that $\dfrac{a}{b} = \dfrac{ka}{kb}$.

Example 1

Write the ratio $36:12$ as a fraction in lowest terms.

$$\frac{36}{12} = \frac{36 \div 12}{12 \div 12}$$
$$= \frac{3}{1}$$

Example 2

Write $x^2 - 4 : x^2 + x - 2$ as a fraction in lowest terms.

$$\frac{x^2 - 4}{x^2 + x - 2} = \frac{(x - 2)(x + 2)}{(x + 2)(x - 1)} \quad \{x \neq 1, \ -2\}$$
$$= \frac{(x - 2)}{(x - 1)}$$

Ratios also can be used to help predict future events.

Example 3

At the midway point of the regular 80-game hockey season, the Soo Peewee team had a win:loss ratio of 9:7. If 45 wins are necessary to make the playoffs, can the Soo Peewee team expect to make the playoffs?

In order to predict whether the team will make the playoffs, it is necessary for us to predict how many wins they will achieve.

Let the number of wins and losses be represented by $9k$ and $7k$ respectively, where k is a nonzero constant. Therefore, there are $16k$ games played.

Since there is an 80-game season, $16k = 80$ and $k = 5$.

Therefore, $9k = 45$, and the Soo Peewee team can expect to make the playoffs.

Example 4

In his will, a man wished to leave $98 000 to one charity and $56 000 to a second charity. However, when the man died, his estate was valued at only $92 400. His lawyers decided to use ratios to divide the estate.

a. In the will, what is the ratio of the first charity's amount to the second charity's amount?
b. If the estate is divided according to the ratio in the will, then how much money will each charity receive?

a. Express the original amounts as a ratio in lowest terms.

$$\frac{98\ 000}{56\ 000} = \frac{7}{4}$$

Therefore, the charities will receive money in the ratio of 7:4.

b. Let the amounts received be represented by $7k$ and $4k$ respectively.

Therefore, $7k + 4k = 92\ 400$ Why $7k$ and $4k$?
$$11k = 92\ 400$$
$$k = 8400$$

The charities will receive 7×8400 or $58 800 and 4×8400 or $33 600 respectively.

In some cases, we compare three or more terms in a ratio. For example, the fertilizer that is used on a lawn is often in the form 20-16-8. This means that the fertilizer contains 20% nitrogen, 16% phosphoric oxide, and 8% potash available by mass. On the fertilizer bag, the ratio of the percentages is separated by a hyphen. Mathematically, this could be done using colons—20:16:8—and this is read as "20 to 16 to 8". This means that for every 20 units of nitrogen, there are 16 units of phosphoric oxide and 8 units of potash.

Example 5

Express the ratio 20:16:8 in lowest terms and find how many kilograms of each nutrient will be in a 22 kg bag of fertilizer.

As is the case with "two-term" ratios, the "three-term" ratios also can be expressed in lowest terms by dividing each term by the same nonzero number. In this case, the ratio in lowest terms is 5:4:2.

Use the ratio expressed in lowest terms to find the number of nutrients in a 22 kg bag.
Let the mass of nitrogen, phosphoric oxide, and potash be represented by $5k$, $4k$, and $2k$ respectively.
The total mass is represented by the equation $5k + 4k + 2k = 22$, or $11k = 22$.
Therefore, $k = 2$ and there will be 10 kg of nitrogen, 8 kg of phosphoric oxide, and 4 kg of potash in the 22 kg bag.

Exercises

1. Write the ratio in lowest whole-number terms.
a. 17:51 **b.** $2\frac{1}{4}$:3 **c.** 36:64
d. $3a$:$6a$ **e.** 32:16:64 **f.** 8.5:4.25:6.5

2. Write the ratio in lowest terms.
a. $27xy$:$9x$:$81xyz$ **b.** 2.5:6.5:8:10.5
c. $x-1$:x^2-1 **d.** $15y^3$:$20y^2$
e. x^2-4x:x^2-16
f. $x^2-3x-10$:$2x^2-7x-15$:x^2-25
g. $4a^2-1$:$4a^2+4a-3$:$2a^2-a$

3. In the display, it states that any ratio in the form a:b cannot have a value of b that is equal to zero. Explain why this is true.

4. Express as a ratio in lowest terms. (*Hint*: The terms must have the same unit of measure.)
a. 10 m to 8 cm
b. five years to twelve weeks
c. 24 mm to 6.4 dm
d. $2.50 to 75¢

5. If 2 out of every 7 office workers can type, then find the ratio of the number of people who can type to the number of people who cannot type.

6. A batting average for a baseball player is the ratio of the number of hits to the number of times at bat.
a. Express Mary's average, 0.375, as a ratio in lowest terms.
b. Why can 0.375 be expressed as a ratio?
c. If Mary was at bat 64 times, then how many hits did she get?

7. In an experiment involving transistors, it was found that the number of transistors rejected to the number of transistors accepted is in the ratio 35:400. How many transistors would you expect to reject in a sample of 500 transistors?

8. Two people win a lottery with a prize worth $650 000. If the proceeds are to be split in the ratio 4:11, then how much did each person receive?

9. The ratio of wins to losses for a hockey team is 7:9.
a. If there are 80 regular season games, then how many wins and losses did the team record?
b. If there were 16 games in the playoffs, and the ratio remained the same, then how many games were won and lost?
c. What is the relationship between the number of games won and lost in part **b** and the total number of games played in the playoffs?

10. Express the ratio of the areas of pairs of circles having these radii.
a. 2 cm and 4 cm **b.** 1 m and 10 cm

11. Express the ratio of the volumes of spheres having these radii. (*Hint*: $V = \frac{4}{3}\pi r^3$.)
a. 1 cm and 3 cm **b.** 10 dm, 10 cm, and 1 m

12. A circular helicopter landing pad, with a radius of 13 m, costs $50 000 to pave. If the cost of paving is based on the area, then find the cost of paving a landing pad that has a radius of 18 m. (*Hint*: Find the cost per square metre.)

13. The roster of a football team has 16 players listed on defence, 22 players on offence, and 4 special team players. Express the roster as a ratio in lowest terms.

14. Find three numbers in the ratio of 3:6:11 that have a sum of 100.

15. The velocities of three radioactive particles are in the ratio of 9:7:3. If the second particle has a velocity of 48.3 m/s, then find the velocity of the other particles.

16. The ratio of the speed of light in air to its velocity in water is 4:3. If the speed of light in air is 299 796 km/s, then find the speed of light in water.

17. A boxcar has dimensions in the ratio of 8:3:2. What are the dimensions of the boxcar if the total surface area is 368 m²?

18. The *n*th number in the Fibonacci sequence is obtained by adding the $(n-1)$th and the $(n-2)$th numbers. The first few terms of the Fibonacci sequence are 1, 1, 2, 3, 5, 8, ... After the first four numbers, the ratio between the *n*th and the $(n-1)$th number approximates the **Golden Ratio**.
a. Find an approximation for the Golden Ratio.
b. Compare this approximation to the actual Golden Ratio. If necessary, use the library.

19. A class contains boys and girls in a ratio of 4:3. If the class size is 28, then how many girls are in the class?

20. A rectangle has a length to width ratio of 5:2. The perimeter of the rectangle is 84 cm.
a. Find the ratio of length to perimeter.
b. Find the area of the rectangle.
c. Find the ratio of the area to the perimeter.
d. Which is the larger ratio, part **a** or part **c**? Explain.

21. Golf balls are sold in boxes of three. The balls are stacked vertically. The first ball touches the top of the box and the third ball touches the bottom of the box. Which is the greater value, the height of the box, or the perimeter of the top of the box?

22. Find the ratio of the area of a circle with radius *r* to the area of a circle with a radius of 0.5*r*.

23. A cooling system requires a 5:1 ratio of antifreeze to water. If there is 12 L of coolant in the system, then how many litres are antifreeze?

24. A rich relative left A.T. and three cousins $25 369.90. The will stated that the money should be divided in the ratio 8:7:6:5. How much would A.T. receive if A.T. was to receive the most money?

25. Two triangles are similar if the ratios of corresponding sides are congruent. Draw two triangles that are similar, give the lengths of the three sides, and challenge a classmate to prove that they are similar.

26. Three triangles are similar if the ratio of corresponding sides are congruent. Add a third triangle to the ones drawn in Exercise 25 and show that they are similar.

27. Triangle *ABC* and triangle *DEF* are similar.

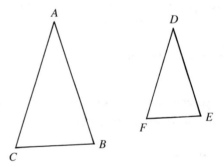

a. Find $\overline{CB}$ if $\overline{AC} = 5$ cm, $\overline{DF} = 8$ cm, and $\overline{FE} = 9$ cm.
b. Find $\overline{DF}$ if $\overline{AC} = 4$ m, $\overline{AB} = 12$ m, and $\overline{DE} = 16$ m.
c. Find $\overline{EF}$ if $\overline{AC} = 12$ mm, $\overline{BC} = 1$ cm, and $\overline{DF} = 4$ cm.

Using the Library

Find the percentages of nutrients suitable for fertilizer to be applied during the summer on a hot day and during the fall on a cooler day with leaves falling from the trees. Report on why the two mixtures are suited to the particular season and why the ratios on the bags are not expressed as ratios in lowest terms.

3·2 Proportion

In the previous section, it was stated that if two values are in the ratio $a:b$, then there exists a constant c, such that $a:b = ac:bc$. In fractional form, this can be written as $\dfrac{a}{b} = \dfrac{ac}{bc}$. A statement in which two or more ratios are equivalent is a **proportion**. As is the case with ratios, a proportion can also be written either in fractional form, $\dfrac{a}{b} = \dfrac{c}{d}$, or in ratio form, $a:b = c:d$.

Example 1

Solve for x. $x:2 = 21:7$

Set up the ratio in the form $\dfrac{x}{2} = \dfrac{21}{7}$, find the lowest common denominator of both sides, and multiply both sides of the equation by the lowest common denominator. In this case, the lowest common denominator is 14.

$$14\left(\frac{x}{2}\right) = 14\left(\frac{21}{7}\right)$$
$$7x = 42$$

Notice that this result is the same as writing $7x = 21 \times 2$ through the "short cut" of cross multiplication. Both processes will yield $x = 6$.

> In a ratio of the form $\dfrac{a}{b} = \dfrac{c}{d}$, $ad = bc$, where $b \neq 0$ and $d \neq 0$.

This generalization implies that we can solve $\dfrac{a}{x} = \dfrac{x}{d}$ so that $ad = x^2$ or that $x = \pm\sqrt{ad}$. In this case, x is the **mean proportional** between a and d.

Example 2

The tax payable on property is based on its assessed value. The tax payable on property assessed at $85 000 is $950. Find the tax payable on property assessed at $75 000 and the assessed value of property if the tax payable is $902.50.

Understand the Problem
A proportion must be set up equating the known and the unknown values.

Develop a Plan
Set up a proportion with three ratios.
Separate the entire proportion into two proportions that are solved using $ad = bc$.

Carry Out the Plan
Let t represent the tax.
Let v represent the value of the property.
Therefore, $\dfrac{85\ 000}{950} = \dfrac{75\ 000}{t} = \dfrac{v}{902.50}$.
The two ratios to be solved are:
$\dfrac{85\ 000}{950} = \dfrac{75\ 000}{t}$ and $\dfrac{85\ 000}{950} = \dfrac{v}{902.50}$.
Solving both proportions gives a property value of $80 750 and tax payable of $838.24.

Look Back
By substituting the values found into the original proportion, and dividing the numerator by the denominator, the same decimal equivalent will result. This is the **constant of proportionality**. The constant value of the ratio of two quantities can be expressed as $y = kx$.
We can solve for v using this calculator key sequence: 85000 $\boxed{\times}$ 902.5 $\boxed{\div}$ 950 $\boxed{=}$.

Exercises

1. In your own words, explain the terms "proportional" and "constant of proportionality".

2. Copy and complete to form a proportion.
a. $60:\blacksquare = 25:180$
b. $8:\blacksquare:17 = 28:52.5:\blacksquare$
c. $10:14:\blacksquare = 2\frac{1}{2}:\blacksquare:4\frac{1}{2}$
d. $\dfrac{5}{7} = \dfrac{\blacksquare}{21} = \dfrac{5x}{\blacksquare} = \dfrac{\blacksquare}{3.5}$
e. $\dfrac{51}{\blacksquare} = \dfrac{3}{\blacksquare} = \dfrac{\blacksquare}{85} = \dfrac{a}{\dfrac{a}{3}}$
f. $c:b:\blacksquare = c^2:\blacksquare:cs$

3. Use Example 2 of the display to find the tax on properties having these assessed values.
a. \$110 000   **b.** \$90 000   **c.** \$65 500

4. Find the number that must be added to each term of the ratio $\frac{2}{3}$ so that the ratio becomes $\frac{5}{7}$. The solution is started for you. Explain the reason for each line that you use in your solution.
Let x represent the number that must be added.
$$\dfrac{2+x}{3+x} = \dfrac{5}{7}$$

5. Solve these proportions for the unknown value.
a. $\dfrac{15}{8} = \dfrac{y}{9}$ **b.** $\dfrac{21}{y} = \dfrac{7}{3}$
c. $\dfrac{12}{x} = \dfrac{x}{6}$ **d.** $8:m = m:32$

6. Find the mean proportional if these are the known values in the proportion.
a. 125 and 5   **b.** 3 and 27   **c.** x and y

7. One half is to six as x is to twenty-two. What is the value of x?

8. The air pressure outside a jetliner at an altitude of 10 km is 25 kPa. If the inside:outside pressure ratio must not exceed 7:2, then find the maximum inside pressure allowed.

9. For these specific examples, give the corresponding general form using the variables a, b, c, and d.
a. $\dfrac{3}{4} = \dfrac{12}{16}$ then $\dfrac{3}{12} = \dfrac{4}{16}$
b. $\dfrac{3}{4} = \dfrac{12}{16}$ then $\dfrac{4}{3} = \dfrac{16}{12}$
c. $\dfrac{3}{4} = \dfrac{12}{16}$ then $\dfrac{3+4}{4} = \dfrac{12+16}{16}$
d. $\dfrac{3}{4} = \dfrac{12}{16}$ then $\dfrac{3+2\times4}{4} = \dfrac{12+2\times16}{16}$

10. Two specific properties of proportions are given. Use specific examples to verify them.
i) If $\dfrac{a}{b} = \dfrac{c}{d}$ then $\dfrac{a+b}{a-b} = \dfrac{c+d}{c-d}$.
ii) If $\dfrac{a}{b} = \dfrac{c}{d}$ and $\dfrac{e}{f} = \dfrac{g}{h}$ then $\dfrac{ae}{bf} = \dfrac{cg}{dh}$.

11. Decide which equations are proportions. Explain your reasoning.
a. $\dfrac{12a}{11a} = \dfrac{12}{11}$ **b.** $\dfrac{t}{s} = \dfrac{sr}{tr}$
c. $\dfrac{1}{a} - \dfrac{1}{b} = \dfrac{a-b}{ab}$ **d.** $\dfrac{a-b}{1} = \dfrac{a^2-b^2}{a+b}$
e. $\dfrac{a^2+2ab+b^2}{a+b} = \dfrac{a+b}{1} = \dfrac{a^2+b^2}{a+b}$

12. If $a:b = 4:5$ and $b:c = 5:6$, then find $a:c$.

13. The ratio of hockey players to football players in a school is 2:3. If five hockey players become football players, the ratio will be 3:7. How many hockey players and how many football players are there in the school?

Using the Library

Although Sir Isaac Newton was perhaps the greatest mathematician of the modern era, he also was said to be one of the most absent-minded of people. Legend has it that while giving a dinner party, he left the table for a bottle of wine, and while on this errand, forgot his guests and went to church instead.

Write a short paragraph describing Newton's dislike of controversy.

3·3 Application of Proportions

To aid in wildlife management, biologists, conservation experts, and government conservation ministries require approximate figures for the number of wildlife in a particular area or the number of fish in a particular lake or stream. As a result, a method is needed to approximate these population sizes.

A proportion can be used to approximate the total population in a particular area. The procedure is the **capture-recapture** process. A sample of the members of a population are captured, tagged, and released back into the population. After a period of time, a second sample is taken and the tagged members are compared to the total number in the second sample. On the assumption that the second sample is a typical representation of the total population, this proportion is used to approximate the total population:

$$\frac{\text{Number tagged in 1st sample}}{\text{Total population}} = \frac{\text{Number found tagged in 2nd sample}}{\text{Total number in 2nd sample}}.$$

Example 1

Every year a small lake in Fundy National Park is stocked with trout. The lake can support a maximum of 3450 trout. The conservation officer for the park must determine how many trout she must add to increase the population to its maximum. She captured a sample of 150 trout, tagged them, and released them back into the lake. She then returned in twenty days, captured a sample of 320 trout, and found that 20 had been tagged previously. Approximate how many trout are needed to restock the lake to its maximum population.

She used the capture-recapture proportion described above to approximate the number of trout currently in the lake.

Let p represent the total trout population currently in the lake.

$$\frac{150}{p} = \frac{20}{320}$$
$$p = \frac{(150)(320)}{20} \qquad \left\{ \text{Solve the proportion for } p. \right.$$
$$p = 2400$$

The lake has about 2400 trout. Therefore, she will need to add about 1050 trout to the lake.

Example 2

The average human-male blood carries about 16 g of hemoglobin for every 100 mL of blood. Find the mass of hemoglobin that would be found in an average male who has about 15 L of blood in his body.

A proportion can be set up by comparing the masses of hemoglobin in the bloodstream to the known amounts of blood. In this case, the known amounts are 100 mL and 15 000 mL.

Let m represent the total amount of hemoglobin in the bloodstream.

$$\frac{\text{Known mass}}{\text{Known sample}} = \frac{\text{Unknown mass}}{\text{Total in body}}$$
$$\frac{16}{100} = \frac{m}{15\ 000}$$
$$240\ 000 = 100m$$
$$2400 = m$$

There are about 2400 g of hemoglobin in the average male's bloodstream.

Exercises

1. Why does the capture-recapture method yield only an approximation of the total population?

2. Calculate the population of trout if the total number of fish recaptured is 320 and the number in the tagged sample is given as follows.
a. 5   **b.** 1   **c.** 25
d. 15   **e.** 75   **f.** 90

3. In Example 1 in the display, why did the conservation officer wait twenty days before recapturing a sample of the population?

4. Ontario once had a population density of about 9.4 persons per square kilometre.
a. If the population was uniformly distributed across the province, then how many people would you expect there to be in a district 15 km by 30 km?
b. Why would this approximation be less accurate if the population was not uniformly distributed?

5. A crane exerts a force of 1 kN to lift a 1000 kg mass. What force would the same crane exert to lift a 100 t locomotive if the force is proportional to the mass?

6. A mass of oxygen occupies 10.5 L^3 at 12°C. What volume will the same gas occupy at 30°C assuming constant pressure and that volume and temperature are proportional?

7. A seafood salad dressing contains 125 g of sour cream for every 75 mL of salad oil and 37 mL of mild vinegar. How many millilitres of salad oil and mild vinegar should be mixed with 40 kg of sour cream?

8. A.T., the "Mathematics Wizard", said that the capture-recapture model would be more accurate if the total members in the second sample was the same as the number originally marked. Do you agree with A.T.? Explain.

9. The Take It or Leave It clothing store had 17 items returned after a sale of 142 items. How many items would you expect to be returned if 750 items have been sold?

10. Find the length of the missing sides in the triangles.
a.

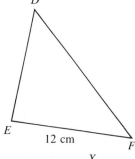

b.

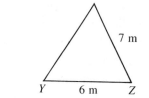

11. A rocket engine uses liquid oxygen at the rate of 3.9 kg/s to oxidize alcohol fuel at the rate of 1.04 kg/s.
a. Find the rate of consumption of liquid oxygen when fuel consumption is increased to 8.7 kg/s.
b. What assumptions were made to find the solution in part **a**?

12. How much water must freeze in order to form 763 cm³ of ice, if water expands 9% of its volume when it freezes?

13. A wildlife officer in the Yukon captures and tags 8 deer with colourful ear tags. The deer are released back into the population. After one month, 30 deer are viewed with binoculars and 3 are identified with the ear tags.
a. Is this an accurate way of approximating the deer population? Explain.
b. Is there a better way to approximate the deer population?
c. How many deer would the officer claim are in this territory?

3·4 Direct and Joint Variation

A gas station sells unleaded gasoline at \$0.50/L. The amount of money spent on gasoline is related to the number of litres bought.

Number of Litres (N)	Cost (C)
1	\$0.50
2	\$1.00
3	\$1.50
5	\$2.50
10	\$5.00

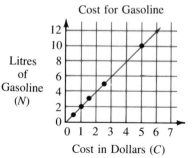

Cost for Gasoline

Litres of Gasoline (N)

Cost in Dollars (C)

From the graph and the table of values, we see that the origin, (0, 0), satisfies the relation because if no litres are purchased, then there is no cost to the consumer. Also notice that an increase in the number of litres purchased, N, results in a proportional increase in the amount paid, C. For instance, if N is doubled, then C is doubled; if N is tripled, then C is tripled; and so on. The ratio of number of litres purchased to cost is constant and is written as $\dfrac{N}{C} = k$ or $N = kC$. We also can write $\dfrac{N_1}{C_1} = \dfrac{N_2}{C_2}$. Since these three conditions exist, the cost is **directly proportional** to the number of litres purchased, and can be written as $N \propto C$. This is read as: "N **varies directly** as C".

If two quantities, a and b, vary directly, then $\dfrac{a_1}{b_1} = \dfrac{a_2}{b_2}$, $a \propto b$ and $a = kb$.

The graph of $a = kb$ is a line that passes through the origin, (0, 0).

$\propto$ means "proportional to".

The k in the equation $a = kb$ is a constant, called the **constant of proportionality**.

Example 1

The first space shuttle travelled approximately 102 000 km in 3.2 h while moving at a constant speed. If the distance varies directly as the time, then how far will the space shuttle travel in 54 h?

Let s represent the distance travelled.
Let t represent the time.
Writing the given information in the form of an equation will produce $s = kt$. By substituting the known information into the equation, we can solve for the constant of proportionality, k.

$102\ 000 = 3.2k$
$31\ 875 = k$
When $t = 54$,
$\quad s = 31\ 875(54)$
$\quad\ \ = 1\ 721\ 250$

The space shuttle will travel 1 721 250 km.

A proportion also can be set up to help in the solution of problems.

Example 2

The amount of water passing through a turbine is directly proportional to the time the water is running. At a power station, a water meter records 500 000 L passing through every 3.5 min. At this rate, how much water will pass through the turbine in 5.5 min?

Understand the Problem
We are to determine the amount of water that will pass through the turbine in 5.5 min given that 500 000 L passes through in 3.5 min.

Carry Out the Plan
Let x represent the amount of water flowing through the turbine in 5.5 min.

$$\frac{\text{Water at Time 1}}{\text{Time 1}} = \frac{\text{Water at Time 2}}{\text{Time 2}}$$

$$\frac{500\ 000}{3.5} = \frac{x}{5.5}$$

$$x = 785\ 714$$

Develop a Plan
Since the amount of water passing through the turbine is directly proportional to the time, a proportion can be set up and solved.

Look Back
Therefore, 785 714 L of water passes through the turbines in 5.5 min. Can this problem be solved another way?

Sometimes, a direct variation can involve exponents, radicals, or even the product of two or more variables. A direct variation that involves two or more variables is a **joint variation**. For example, the area of a rectangle varies directly as the product of the length, ℓ, and the width, w, of the rectangle. This is expressed symbolically as $A \propto \ell w$. Similarly, the cost, C, of painting the sides of a cylindrical silo is directly proportional to the product of the square of the radius, r, and the height, h, of the silo. This can be written as $C \propto r^2 h$.

Example 3

A car, starting from rest, travels a distance that is directly proportional to the acceleration and the square of the time travelled. The car accelerates at a rate of 4 m/s² and travels a distance of 200 m in 10 s. How far will a car accelerating at 7.5 m/s² travel in 15 s?

Since the distance travelled, s, varies directly as the product of the acceleration, a, and the square of the time, t^2, then the proportion can be set up as $\dfrac{s_1}{a_1 t_1^2} = \dfrac{s_2}{a_2 t_2^2}$.

$s_1 = 200 \quad s_2$ is unknown
$a_1 = 4 \quad\quad a_2 = 7.5$
$t_1 = 10 \quad\quad t_2 = 15$

Substitute the known values into the proportion.

$$\frac{200}{4(10)^2} = \frac{s_2}{7.5(15)^2}$$

$$s_2 = 843.75$$

Therefore, the second car will travel 843.75 m.

Exercises

1. In the display, find the constant value of $\frac{N}{C}$ and explain why it is a constant.

2. Solve Examples 1 and 2 of the display in a different way. Which process do you prefer?

3. Graph the relation between s and at^2 in Example 3 of the display. Is it a direct variation? Explain.

4. Translate these phrases into two different mathematical expressions. The first one is done as an example.

x varies directly as y
$x \propto y$ and $x = ky$

a. a varies directly as b
b. x varies directly as the square of y
c. the mass of an object varies directly with the product of its density and its volume

5. In your own words, explain the meaning of the terms "direct variation", "directly proportional to", and "joint variation".

6. What are two things you should look for to determine if a graph is a direct variation?

7. In the relation between F and a, F varies directly as a. If F is 64 when a is 16, then find the value of F for the given value of a.
a. 10   **b.** 27   **c.** 0.75   **d.** -22

8. In Exercise 7, what happens to the value of F if the value of a is doubled? when the value of a is halved?

9. The power, in kilowatts, that a shaft can transmit varies directly as the speed of rotation of the shaft. If a shaft turning at a rate of 20 rev/s transmits 26 kW of power, then calculate the kilowatts of power transmitted by a shaft rotating at 6 rev/s, 60 rev/s, and 100 rev/s.

10. The rate of water flowing, under constant pressure, from the end of a circular pipe is directly proportional to the area of the end of the pipe. If a pipe end with an area of 16 cm² releases water at the rate of 13 500 cm³/s, then at what rate will a pipe having an area of 25 cm² release water under the same pressure?

11. The shadow length of a vertical object varies directly with the height of the object. A tree 10 m high casts a shadow 22 m long. If the shadow of a building is 235 m at the same time of day, then how tall is the building?

12. The distance a freely falling object travels from rest is directly proportional to the square of the time it falls. An object fell a distance of 29.4 m after 2.7 s.
a. Graph the relation between the distance an object falls and the square of the time it falls.
b. Is this a direct variation, a joint variation, or both?
c. How far will an object fall after 12 s?

13. The time it takes to "fire" a pot in a kiln is directly proportional to the square root of its mass. A 3 kg pot requires 2.5 h in the kiln.
a. Graph the relation between the time in the kiln and the square root of the mass of the pot.
b. What type of variation is this?
c. What happens to the time a pot takes in the kiln if the mass of the pot is doubled? if the mass of the pot is halved?

14. The kinetic energy of a moving object varies directly as the mass of the object and square of the velocity of the object. An object moving at 15 m/s, and having a mass of 10 kg, will have a kinetic energy of 750 J.
a. Graph the relation between kinetic energy and the product of the square of the velocity and the mass of the object.
b. What type of variation is this?
c. What will happen to the kinetic energy of the object if the velocity is doubled?
d. Find the kinetic energy of an object if it is moving at 10 m/s and has a mass of 12 kg.

3·5 Inverse Variation

The length of time required to cook a dinner is related to the constant temperature of the oven. The greater the temperature, the less time required to cook the dinner. The table of values and the graph show various average temperatures and the corresponding cooking times for a chicken dinner.

Temperature (t)	Time (h)
75°C	15 h
100°C	11.25 h
150°C	7.5 h
300°C	3.75 h
450°C	2.5 h

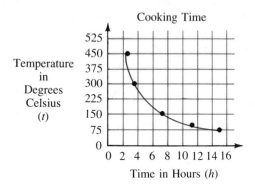

The table of values and the graph show a relationship that is different from the direct variation relationship. Notice that the graph is **not** a straight line and that it does **not** pass through the origin. The relationship between the variables shows that when one is doubled, the other is halved; when one is tripled, the other is divided by three; and so on. This implies that the product of the two variables is a constant. In this example, the constant is 1125, and the temperature, t, is inversely proportional to the time, h.

In this case, h **varies inversely** as t. This can be written as $h \propto \dfrac{1}{t}$. In equation form, $h = \dfrac{k}{t}$ or $ht = k$.

Example 1

A roast cooks in a pressure cooker in 55 min when the cooker is set at a constant pressure of 150 kPa. How long will it take to cook the same roast at 250 kPa if the cooking time varies inversely as the pressure?

Let t represent the cooking time in minutes.
Let p represent the pressure of the cooker in kilopascals.

Since the pressure and time are inversely proportional, there exists a **constant of proportionality**, k, that is equal to the product of the time, t, and the pressure, p. If 55 min are required to cook a roast at a pressure of 150 kPa, then the constant of proportionality is 55×150 or 8250.

$$t = \frac{k}{p}$$

{ The product pt is a constant, denoted by k, and has no units.

$$= \frac{8250}{250}$$
$$= 33$$

The roast will cook in 33 min if the pressure is 250 kPa.

Inverse variations also can occur with respect to the product of two or more variables or the square of the variables.

Example 2

The illumination per square metre over an object is inversely proportional to the square of the distance of the object from the light source. If the illumination is 4000 lm/m² from a distance of 10 m, then find the illumination when the same object is 5 m from the light source.

Understand the Problem

The relation is an inverse variation.
The fact that illumination is 4000 lm/m² from a distance of 10 m is given. We are to find the illumination from a distance of 5 m.

Develop a Plan

Since it is given that this is an inverse relation, a proportion can be set up after finding the constant of proportionality.

Carry Out the Plan

Let l represent the illumination in lumens per square metre.
Let d represent the distance of the object from the light source in metres.

Therefore, $l = \dfrac{k}{d^2}$, where k is the constant of proportionality.

Therefore, k equals 4000×10^2 or $400\ 000$.

$$l = \frac{400\ 000}{d^2}$$
$$= \frac{400\ 000}{5^2}$$
$$= 16\ 000$$

Look Back

The illumination from 5 m will be 16 000 lm/m².

The problem can be verified using the relationship that $l_1 d_1^2 = l_2 d_2^2$, where l_1 and l_2 represent the two illuminations, and d_1 and d_2 represent the respective distances from the light source.

Therefore, $4000 \times 10^2 = l_2 \times 5^2$

$$\frac{400\ 000}{25} = l_2$$
$$16\ 000 = l_2$$

This type of problem can be extended to include a combination of direct and inverse variations.

Example 3

The density of an object varies directly as the mass of the object and inversely as the volume of the object. The density of a 2 kg object with a volume of 4 cm³ is 0.5 kg/cm³. Find the density of an 8 kg object made from the same material that has a volume of 5 cm³.

Let m represent the mass of the object.
Let d represent the density of the object.
Let v represent the volume of the object.

Density is directly proportional to mass and inversely proportional to volume. The relation can be written as $d = \dfrac{km}{v}$. Solving for k, which will be common in the proportion, gives $k = \dfrac{dv}{m}$.
If $m = 2$, $v = 4$, and $d = 0.5$, then $k = 1$. To find the density when $k = 1$, $m = 8$, and $v = 5$, substitute into the equation $d = \dfrac{km}{v}$.

$$d = \frac{(1)(8)}{5}$$
$$= 1.6$$

Therefore, the density of the second object is 1.6 kg/cm³.

Exercises

1. In your own words;
a. explain what is meant by an inverse variation.
b. explain how the equation in Example 3 of the display was found.

2. In an inverse variation, can the constant of proportionality ever be zero? Explain your answer.

3. Write as a mathematical statement.
a. x is inversely proportional to y.
b. x is directly proportional to y and inversely proportional to z^2.
c. x is inversely proportional to the product of y and z.
d. a is directly proportional to y^2 and inversely proportional to the product of x and z.

4. If V varies inversely as A, and V is 125 when A is 35, then find the value of V when A has these values.
a. A is 100.   **b.** A is 42.
c. $A = 250$ **d.** $A = 10$

5. If x varies inversely as y, and x is $\frac{3}{4}$ when y is $\frac{8}{27}$, then find the value of y when x is 14.

6. Find a value for r such that each ordered pair belongs to the same inverse variation.
a. $(100, 12)$, $(r, 2.4)$ **b.** $(r, 35)$, $(35, 6)$
c. $\left(\frac{1}{5}, r\right)$, $\left(\frac{2}{3}, \frac{3}{7}\right)$ **d.** $(5x, 11x)$, (x, r)

7. If x varies inversely as the square of y, then how does the value of y change when x is doubled?

8. If a is inversely proportional to b, then is it true that b is inversely proportional to a? Explain.

9. Travel time is inversely proportional to average velocity. If it takes 3.75 h to travel from Edmonton to Calgary at an average velocity of 80 km/h, then how long will it take for the same trip at an average velocity of 95 km/h? Use a calculator if one is available.

10. The unit cost of producing computers varies inversely as the number of computers produced. If the unit cost of producing 1000 computers is $1850, then what is the unit cost of producing 6250 computers?

11. Boyle's Law states that the volume of a gas varies inversely as the pressure at a constant temperature. The volume of a gas is 25 L at 135 kPa.
a. Graph this relation.
b. Find the volume of the same gas at 360 kPa.

12. Two meshed gear wheels have 27 and 81 teeth respectively. If the gear speeds vary inversely as the number of teeth, then find the speed the first gear must turn to drive the second gear at 60 revolutions per second.

13. Radiant heat varies inversely as the square of the distance from the heat source. If a body 4 m from a radiant source receives 81 W/m², then at what distance must the body be placed to receive radiant heat of 144 W/m²?

14. A cashier in the local supermarket claimed she gave a customer $1.77 that included sixty pennies. Was the cashier correct? Explain.

15. The force of attraction varies directly as the product of the two masses and inversely as the square of the distance between the two masses. Two marbles, one with a mass of one gram, and the other with a mass of three grams, have a force of attraction of approximately 10^{-11} when they are 1 m apart.
a. State this relationship as a mathematical equation.
b. Find the force of attraction between two different marbles, one having a mass of 0.5 g, and the other having a mass of 2 g, if they are 0.5 m apart.
c. Explain, in some detail, how you arrived at the answer for part **b**.

16. A construction project can be completed in 30 months by 375 workers. How many workers must a contractor hire to complete the project in two years?

3·6 Partial Variation

The value of a relation may be composed of two parts. One part may vary directly as a given variable and the second part may be a constant value. This type of relation is a **partial variation**.

Consider a professional portrait photographer who charges a basic fee for each "sitting" and an additional charge for each portrait ordered. There is a fixed (constant) price and a cost that varies directly with the number of portraits ordered. If the fixed fee for each "sitting" is $75 and the price for each portrait is $12.50, then we can find an equation that will relate price and the number of portraits ordered, as well as draw a graph of this relation.

The cost to the purchaser depends on the number of portraits ordered. For every portrait, the cost increases by $12.50. Therefore, if C represents the cost to the purchaser, and n the number of portraits that are ordered, the equation is $C = 75 + 12.5n$, and C is said to **vary partially** with n.

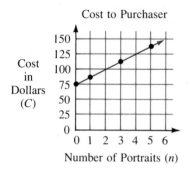

Cost to Purchaser

Number Ordered	0	1	3	5
Total Cost ($)	75.00	87.50	112.50	137.50

> Any equation of the form $y = mx + b$, where b is a nonzero constant, represents a partial variation.

Example

On October 1, a sales representative rented a car to make sales calls throughout the province. She had to leave a deposit of $500 and pay $450 per month for the car. Find an equation that will show how much money she owes for the car based on the monthly rental.

The sales representative's payment schedule is shown in the table. In the chart, A represents the amount paid and n represents the number of months for which payments were made.

Payment Date	Number of Monthly Payments Made (n)	Amount Paid (A)
Oct. 1	0	$500
Nov. 1	1	$950
Dec. 1	2	$1400
Jan. 1	3	$1850

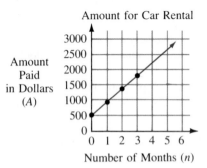

Amount for Car Rental

There is an initial payment of $500 and monthly payments of $450. Therefore, the equation is $A = 500 + 450n$.

Partial variation may also involve a fixed amount which is reduced in direct relation with a given variable. For example, the value of a car over a period of time. It is initially worth a fixed amount, and its present value reduces each year.

80

Exercises

1. How does partial variation differ from direct variation?

2. Find the cost for these numbers of photographs purchased from the photographer in the display.
a. 10   **b.** 15   **c.** 20   **d.** 30

3. A taxi has a basic fare of $2.25 and a variable rate of $0.90/km.
a. Write a partial variation equation for this relation.
b. Find the total fare for a trip of 35.7 km.
c. Graph the relation without the aid of a table of values.

4. The cost charged for a ferry in British Columbia for a commercial vehicle is $43 for the vehicle, the driver, and a trailer that measures up to 6 m in length. For each additional metre of trailer length, there is an extra charge of $7.38/m.
a. Sketch a graph of this relation.
b. Write a partial variation equation for this relationship.
c. Find the fare for a trailer whose length is 8.5 m.
d. Graph the relation and check whether your sketch is correct.

5. The income from ticket sales for a hockey game consists of two parts, the fixed income from pre-sold season tickets and the variable income from the sale of single game tickets. The fixed income is $110 000 per game. Single game tickets sell for $10 for a green seat, $12 for a red seat, and $16 for a blue seat.
a. Write an equation showing income from a single game.
b. Find the income for one game if the following tickets were sold for the single game: 2450 green seats, 3760 red seats, and 1910 blue seats.
c. If possible, graph this relation.

6. The cost of printing an advertising brochure is the sum of a fixed cost of $10 000 and a variable cost of $0.045 for each brochure printed.
a. Write an equation for this relation.
b. Find the cost of producing 500 000 brochures.

7. The normal rate at which air temperature decreases with altitude is a 2°C drop for every 300 m increase in altitude.
a. What is the air temperature at 8000 m if the air temperature is 15°C at sea level?
b. What is the air temperature at sea level if the air temperature is −10°C at 3045 m?
c. A pilot announced that the outside air temperature was −34°C. What was the altitude of the aircraft if the air temperature was 10°C at sea level?

8. In your own words, state the similarities and the differences between a direct variation, an inverse variation, and a partial variation. Use graphs to help with your explanations.

9. A travel agent offered three plans for a resort holiday. Plan A charged $600 airfare plus $25/d; Plan B charged $300 airfare plus $50/d; and Plan C charged $100/d with airfare included.
a. Write equations and sketch the graphs showing the relation between cost and number of days for each plan.
b. Which plan is the most economical? Explain.
c. Which plan does not show a partial variation between cost and days? Why?

Historical Note

Isaac Barrow (1630-1677)
Isaac Barrow was born in London, England, in 1630. It is said that he was so troublesome in his early school days that his father would pray that if God decided to take one of his children, he could best spare Isaac. Eventually, Isaac reached high academic standards at Cambridge University. He is well known for his ability in mathematics, physics, astronomy, theology, and he was one of the top scholars of ancient Greece of his time. He was the first to occupy the Lucasian chair at Cambridge. He later resigned the chair in favour of his most prized student—Sir Isaac Newton.

Research Barrow's greatest work and record the theorem to which his work led.

3·7 Applications

The force of gravitational attraction between bodies is inversely proportional to the square of the distance between the bodies. The momentum of an object is directly proportional to the product of its mass and its velocity. These are just two examples of the many problems that can be solved using ratios, proportions, or variations. In this section, we will look at some of the situations that can be solved, or simplified, using the four-step problem-solving model, and ratios, proportions, and variations. You will also be introduced to some of the terminology generally used for situations that have been encountered previously.

Example 1

The gravitational force of attraction between two bodies is inversely proportional to the square of the distance between the two bodies. The gravitational force between two bodies 2 m apart is 6 N. Find the gravitational force of attraction between the same two bodies when they are 3 m apart.

Understand the Problem

This situation is an **inverse variation** where the square of the distance between the bodies is the varying factor. Given the new distance, we must find the new gravitational force of attraction.

Develop a Plan

Use the fact that the gravitational force, F, is inversely proportional to the square of the distance, x^2, between the bodies. In this case, $F \propto \dfrac{1}{x^2}$. This is an **inverse square variation**.

Carry Out the Plan

The equation for the inverse variation can be written as $F = \dfrac{k}{x^2}$, where k is the constant of proportionality. To solve for k, substitute the known values into the equation.

$6 = \dfrac{k}{2^2}$

$k = 24$

Now use the constant of proportionality and the fact that the bodies are now 3 m apart to find the new force of attraction.

$F = \dfrac{24}{3^2}$

$\quad \doteq 2.67$

Look Back

The force of attraction between the same two bodies 3 m apart is about 2.67 N. Why is this an inverse square variation? Can this problem be solved another way?

This model also can be extended to include problems where there is more than one type of variation. Recall that any variable that changes in value directly, according to the product of two or more variables, is called a **joint variation**. Any variation that includes both a joint and inverse variation is called a **combined variation**.

Example 2

The centripetal force acting on an object is directly proportional to the square of the velocity along a circular path and inversely proportional to the radius of the circular path. An object moving with a velocity of 6 m/s in a circular path with a radius of 3 m has a centripetal force of 180 N. Find the centripetal force acting on the same object when the object moves at a velocity of 12 m/s in a circular path with a radius of 5 m.

Understand the Problem
Centripetal force is a force that is directed towards the centre of a circular path. It is sometimes described as a "centre-seeking" force. The given facts include a force of 180 N when an object moves in a circular path of radius 3 m at a velocity of 6 m/s. Find the force when the path has a radius of 5 m and the velocity is 12 m/s.

Develop a Plan
Write the information in the form of an equation. In this case, let F represent the force, v represent the velocity, and r represent the radius. Therefore, $F = \frac{kv^2}{r}$. Solve for k using the given information, and then use k to find the missing value.

Carry Out the Plan
$$F = \frac{kv^2}{r}$$
$$180 = \frac{k(6)^2}{3}$$
$$k = 15$$
For $r = 5$ and $v = 12$, $F = \frac{15 \times 12^2}{5}$ or 432.

Look Back
The centripetal force for the new situation is 432 N. What type of variation is shown? Is there another way to solve the problem?

Example 3

The time required to produce a school newspaper varies directly with the number of pages and inversely as the number of students on the job. If it takes 13 h for 5 students to produce a 10-page edition, then how long will it take 10 students to produce a 15-page newspaper?

Understand the Problem
The given facts include a time of 13 h for 5 students to produce a 10-page newspaper. Find the time it takes 10 students to produce a 15-page edition of the paper.

Develop a Plan
Write the information in the form of an equation. In this case, let t represent the time, s the number of students, and p the number of pages in the edition. Therefore, $t = \frac{kp}{s}$. Solve for k using the given information, and then use k to find the missing value.

Carry Out the Plan
$$t = \frac{kp}{s}$$
$$13 = \frac{k(10)}{5}$$
$$k = 6.5$$
For $p = 15$ and $s = 10$, $t = \frac{6.5(15)}{10}$ or 9.75.

Look Back
The length of time needed for 10 students to produce a 15-page edition is 9 h 45 min. Does this situation assume that each student works as hard as every other student?

Exercises

1. Answer the questions posed in the Look Back section of Examples 1, 2, and 3 in the display.

2. Example 1 in the display is an example of an inverse square variation. If the force between the objects had been directly proportional to the square of the distance, then what would the variation be called?

3. Find the intensity of light, l, needed to photograph the dark side of the Moon if a power source of 90 000 cd is required to produce 100 lm of illumination, E, at a distance of 30 m. (*Hint*: $E = \dfrac{l}{d^2}$ and the distance to the Moon is 384 400 km.)

4. Five students, in a school project, raised $10 in 1 h shovelling snow off sidewalks. If the time varies directly as the money raised and inversely as the number of students shovelling, then how long would it take 75 students to raise $1000 shovelling snow?

5. In Example 3 in the display, why must we assume that every student works as hard as every other student? Is this the same assumption that is used in Exercise 4?

6. A banquet has been arranged to raise money for a local charity. The banquet will cost the organizers $300 plus $6.50 per person in attendance. The banquet hall can hold a maximum of 75 people.
a. What type of variation is described?
b. Sketch a graph of the cost versus the number of people attending the banquet.
c. Set up an equation to describe the relation.

7. Write sentences that describe these proportions and identify the type of relation.
a. $t \propto \dfrac{P}{k}$ **b.** $x \propto py$ **c.** $T \propto \dfrac{x^2}{y}$

8. A $200 profit was produced when 325 students attended a dance at which a 6-piece band played. If the profit from the dance varies directly as the number of students attending and inversely as the number of musicians in the band, then how many students would have to attend a dance to make a $350 profit when an 8-piece band played?

9. The distance a freely falling object travels is directly proportional to the square of the time it falls. A booster stage breaks loose from a rocket and falls 44 m in 3 s.
a. Draw a graph of distance versus the square of the time the object falls.
b. Explain what type of variation this is.
c. How far will a tile fall in 3 min?

10. The power needed to drive a new style of boat through the water to the landing site of a spacecraft varies inversely as the cube of its velocity. If 745 kW of power are needed to drive the ship, then how many kilowatts of power are needed to double its velocity?

11. The variable C varies directly as m and inversely as d^2.
a. What type of variation is this? Explain.
b. What is the change in C when m and d are both tripled?

12. The variable P varies directly as v and inversely as r^2.
a. Describe this variation both mathematically and in your own words.
b. What type of variation is it? Explain.
c. What will be the change in P when both v and r are quartered?

13. The cost of operating an airplane varies directly as the flying time and inversely as the number of passengers carried and the average fare. The cost of a 4 h flight carrying 400 passengers at an average fare of $150 is $80 000. Find the operating cost when the same plane flies for 2 h, carrying 350 passengers at an average fare of $300.

14. List all the types of variation that have been introduced in this chapter. Give a brief explanation of each type, listing the similarities and differences among them. Use graphs to help with your explanations where applicable.

15. Kaori deposits $1500 on January first and is paid simple monthly interest based on a rate of 15%/a.
a. What type of relation is this?
b. Sketch a graph of the amount of money Kaori will have at the end of each month.

16. Is it possible to solve all proportions through the use of a constant of proportionality? Explain.

17. The angles in a triangle are in the ratio of 7:9:2. Find the measure of the angles in the triangle. (*Hint*: Recall the sum of the measures of the angles of a triangle.)

18. Two numbers are in the ratio 3:4. Together their sum is 42. What are the two numbers?

19. What number must be added to each term of the ratio 5:8 to arrive at a ratio of 9:11?

20. One of the properties of proportions is if $\frac{a}{b} = \frac{c}{d}$, then $\frac{a+b}{a-b} = \frac{c+d}{c-d}$.
a. Prove this statement.
b. Extend this property to include $a^2:b^2 = c^2:d^2$.

21. The ratio of $a:b$ is 3:4. Find these ratios.
a. $b:a$ **b.** $(a+b):a$
c. $(a+b):(a-b)$ **d.** $(2b-a):b$

22. The variables m and n are inversely proportional.
a. Write this statement as a proportion statement.
b. Is the product mn a constant? Explain.
c. Are $m + n$ and $m \div n$ also constants? Explain.
d. If m is multiplied by -4 in this inverse proportion, what will happen to the value of n?

23. The size of the largest load a beam can support safely varies jointly as its width and the square of its depth, and inversely as the length between supporting ends. A beam 10 cm wide, 20 cm deep, and 10 m long supports a 10 t load. What is the maximum load that this beam can safely support if it is turned on its side and doubled in length?

24. The resistance to bloodflow in vessels varies jointly as the length of the vessel and the fluid viscosity of the blood. Resistance varies inversely as the fourth power of the diameter of the vessel. The resistance is 3.5 units in a vessel of diameter 1 unit and length 3 units when the blood viscosity is 3 units. Find the resistance in a blood vessel with a diameter of 4 units, length 2 units, and a viscosity of 1.5 units. (*Hint*: Assume a constant pressure gradient.)

25. The time required to close a water valve to avoid the "water hammer effect" varies jointly with the length of the pipe and the velocity of flow, and inversely as the difference in pressure when there is no flow and when there is full flow. The time is 2.4 s when the flow is 10 m/s in a 30 m pipe which has a no-flow pressure of 450 kPa and a full-flow pressure of 200 kPa. Find the time to safely close a water valve in a 100 m pipe in which water travels 20 m/s and which has a no-flow pressure of 610 kPa and a full-flow pressure of 550 kPa.

26. Centripetal acceleration varies directly as the square of the velocity of a revolving body and inversely as the radius of its circular path. A force of 480 N is produced by an object revolving at 5.5 m/s in a circular path of radius 1 m. Find the force produced by an object revolving at 12 m/s in a circular path 3 m in radius.

Braintickler

If the radius of a circle is increased by one unit, then what is the ratio of the new circumference to the new diameter? Can you generalize this relation with a formula? (*Hint*: Increase the diameter by one unit, then two units, and so on, to determine if a pattern emerges.)

3·8 Computer Application— Solving Ratios

Solving ratios and proportions can be time consuming when there are many terms to be considered. The computer can often help to make the calculations easier. This program will solve for x and y in a ratio of the form $x:y:q = a:b:c$, where q, a, b, and c are known variables.

```
10  REM A PROGRAM TO FIND A TRIPLE RATIO
20  REM OF THE FORM X:Y:Q=A:B:C,
30  REM WHERE Q, A, B, C ARE GIVEN.
40  INPUT "ENTER CONSTANTS, Q, A, B, C"; Q, A, B, C
50  IF C = 0 THEN GOTO 100
60  LET X = Q / C * A
70  LET Y = Q / C * B
80  PRINT "THE RATIO IS "; X; ":"; Y; ":"; Q; "="; A; ":"; B;
    ":"; C
90  GOTO 120
100 PRINT "RATIO IS UNDEFINED. ENTER NEW DATA"
110 GOTO 40
120 END
```

Exercises

1. Explain the purpose of lines 60 and 70 in the program in the display.

2. What is the purpose of line 50 of the program in the display?

3. "Computers have become necessary tools in our daily lives and in many cases have replaced people in performing certain jobs. However, there are some professions, such as medicine or law, in which computers may never be useful." Write a brief report either defending or rejecting this statement.

4. Solve these ratios using the program in the display.
a. $x:y:3 = 4:5:11$
b. $x:y:-5 = -1:-3:9$
c. $x:y:0 = 1:2:3$
d. $x:y:21 = 42:45:0$
e. $x:y:4 = 100:101:102$

5. Rewrite the program in the display using these modifications.

```
40 INPUT "ENTER THE NUMERATOR
AND THE DENOMINATOR OF EACH
CONSTANT "; Q1, Q2, A1, A2, B1,
B2, C1, C2
45 LET Q = Q1 / Q2
46 LET A = A1 / A2
47 LET B = B1 / B2
48 LET C = C1 / C2
```

a. What does this modification instruct the computer to do?
b. Solve the ratio $x:y:\dfrac{4}{5} = \dfrac{3}{5}:\dfrac{2}{10}:\dfrac{7}{15}$.

6. Modify the program in Exercise 5 to solve a ratio of the form $x:y:z:q = a:b:c:d$ where a, y, and z are unknowns and the rest of the variables are known. Pick your own ratios and use the program to check whether your program works.

3·9 Chapter Review

1. Write the ratio in lowest terms.
a. $15:30$
b. $27:81$
c. $\dfrac{9}{2}:\dfrac{5}{4}$
d. $3(x-2):12(x-2)$
e. $3x^2y^3:51xy^2$
f. $45:100:215$
g. $x^3-27:3x^2+9x+27$
h. $8z(x-1):16z^2(x^2-1):24z$

2. A triangle has a base that is 3 cm, a height that is 4 cm, and third side that is 5 cm.
a. Accurately draw the triangle.
b. What type of triangle is it?
c. A second triangle is similar to the one described and has a base of 5 cm. Find the length of the other two sides.

3. In your own words, explain the meaning of the terms "ratio" and "proportion".

4. The ratio of height to base in triangle T_1 is $4:3$. If the height:base ratio is the same in triangle T_2 but the base is four times the length of the base in T_1, then find the ratio of the areas of $T_1:T_2$.

5. Victoria has $1000 to invest. After talking to an investment expert, she finds the best way of dividing the money is in a $6:5:4$ ratio between savings bonds, guaranteed interest certificates, and simple stocks.
a. Find, to the nearest dollar, how much money went into each type of investment.
b. If she made $110 on her investments the first year, then how should she divide the new total so it is also in a $6:5:4$ ratio?

6. Solve the proportions for x.
a. $15:12 = x:45$
b. $1:x = x:8$
c. $9x:13 = 17:30$
d. $100:x = x:200$
e. $\dfrac{3}{x} = \dfrac{102}{104}$
f. $a:b = bx:b$

7. In your own words, explain the mean proportional. What parts of Exercise 5 find the mean proportional?

8. If a volleyball team has a win to tie ratio of $6:2$ and a tie to loss ratio of $2:3$, then find the win to loss ratio.

9. Sugar is being added to a vat of cola mixture that has no sugar. A quantity is removed from the storage tanks and 0.5 L of sugar is added. The cola is replaced and a second sample is tested. One hundred and twenty litres are found to contain 0.1 L of sugar. Find the total amount of cola in the vat.

10. The momentum, p, of a particle varies directly as the mass, m, and the velocity, v. A 45 kg mass moving at 23 m/s has momentum of 1035 kg·m/s.
a. Graph the relation between velocity and momentum.
b. What type of variation is this?

11. Coulomb's Law states that the electric force between two objects varies directly as the product of the charges of the objects and inversely as the square of the distance between them. If two particles have charges of 5 C and 10 C and the force between them is 6.0×10^9 N, then find the distance between the particles.

12. If A is inversely proportional to B and B is inversely proportional to C, is A inversely proportional to C? Explain.

13. A customized T-shirt company charges $45 for preparing the silk-screen and then a variable cost of $8.55 per shirt printed.
a. Write an equation for this relation and sketch its graph.
b. What kind of relation is it?
c. What would be the cost of producing 113 T-shirts?

14. If $a:3 = b:4$ then find these ratios.
a. $a:b$
b. $(a+b):ab$
c. $a^2:b^2$
d. $(a-b):\dfrac{a}{b}$
e. $b:a$
f. $(b-a):(a-b)$

3·10 Chapter Test

1. Write the ratio in lowest terms.
a. $23:96$
b. $x^2 + 1:x^4 + 2x^2 + 1$
c. $mnp:pqr$
d. $24xy^2:8x^2y^2$
e. $x^3 - 27:4(x - 3)$
f. $3x:8xy:16xyz$

2. Solve the ratio.
a. $x:y:4 = 5:6:7\frac{1}{4}$
b. $x:3:13 = 12:y:169$

3. The volume of a sphere is $\frac{4}{3}\pi r^3$ and the circumference of a circle is $2\pi r$.
a. Find the ratio of the volume of a sphere to the circumference of a circle.
b. If the radius of the sphere is doubled, then what is the increase in the volume?

4. In your own words, explain what is meant by the term "constant of proportionality".

5. Solve for x in the proportion.
a. $\dfrac{4 + x}{5 + x} = \dfrac{21}{8}$
b. $4.5:x = 13:26$
c. $2:x = x:128$
d. $(x^2 + 3x + 2):(x + 2) = 2:3$
e. $x:27 = 81:x$

6. If a ratio is given as $a:b$, then explain why b cannot equal 0. Illustrate your answer with an example.

7. Julie found that if she studied three times as much for chemistry as for math, and spent twice as much time studying for math as for physics, she could maintain her current average.
a. If Julie has 8 h available for studying, then how much time should she spend on each subject?
b. Express the studying time as a ratio in lowest terms.

8. How much of each ingredient is needed to make 1 kg of trail mix if the ratio of nuts to raisins to dried fruits is $4:7:3$?

9. A study is done to determine the number of deer in a provincial park. One hundred deer are tagged and released into the park. Several months later, 300 deer are found and 18 of these had been tagged previously. Estimate how many deer are in the park.

10. A competitor wants to improve the trail mix in Exercise 8 by adding 2 parts granola. To make 2.5 kg of the new mixture, how much of each ingredient is needed?

11. Hooke's Law for springs states that the force the object at the end of the spring exerts on the spring is proportional to the length of the extension of the spring. The force on the spring is 17 N when it is extended 0.1 m.
a. Find an expression for the spring constant k.
b. Graph the relation.
c. What kind of variation is Hooke's Law? Explain.

12. The cost of printing a local newspaper is determined by adding fixed and variable costs. For one issue, renting the press and paying the employees cost $4500, and the publisher charges $500 for every four pages printed.
a. What kind of variation is this?
b. Write an equation for the relation and sketch its graph.
c. The newspaper's revenue comes from advertising. If $15 000 worth of advertising is sold, then how many pages can be printed?

13. A frog stands at one end of a diving board. The frog jumps to the middle of the board. Then it jumps to the middle of the remaining half of the diving board, then half of that remaining section, and so on. After one hop, the ratio of distance travelled to distance remaining is $1:1$; after two hops, $3:1$.
a. Find the ratios for the next three hops.
b. Identify a general expression for the ratio after n hops.

Cumulative Review   Chapters 1–3

1. Perform the operations indicated and simplify.
a. $2(3x + 2) + 5(x - 3) + 6$
b. $5x - 3(2x - 3) + 4(2x + 3)$
c. $2a(4a + b) + (a + 4b)(3a - 2b)$
d. $(m + 2n)(m + 4n) - 2(2m - n)(m + 3n)$

2. State the nonpermissible values of x and simplify the expressions.

a. $\dfrac{12}{-3x}$
b. $\dfrac{8}{2x - 8}$
c. $\dfrac{x^2 - x - 2}{2x^2 - 8}$
d. $\dfrac{4x^2 + 20x + 25}{2x^2 - x - 15}$

3. Perform the operations and simplify the rational expressions.

a. $\dfrac{3x - 15}{2x^2 - 9x - 5} \times \dfrac{2x^2 - 7x - 4}{x^2 - 9x + 20}$
b. $\dfrac{x^2 - 4}{4x^2 - 12x + 9} \div \dfrac{10x^2 + 20x}{10x - 15}$
c. $\dfrac{5}{a + 6} + \dfrac{3}{2a}$
d. $\dfrac{8}{m^2 - 2m - 3} - \dfrac{2}{2m^2 + m - 1}$

4. Solve.
a. $5(a - 2) + 4 = 3(3a + 1)$
b. $(2p - 9)(2p - 1) - 4(p + 3)(p - 6) = 0$
c. $3(p + 3)(2p + 1) = 10 + 2p(3p - 2)$
d. $4(x - 3) + 2 \le 2(3x + 1)$
e. $6 - 3(2x + 5) > 2(3 - 4x) - 5$
f. $\dfrac{m + 8}{3} = \dfrac{2m + 1}{2} + 4$
g. $\dfrac{3}{a + 3} = \dfrac{2}{a - 2} + \dfrac{5}{a^2 + a - 6}$

5. The perimeter of a rectangle is 44 cm. If the length is 2 cm less than 5 times the width, find the dimensions of the rectangle.

6. Find the perimeter of the quadrilateral.

7. Find the product of the factors and simplify.
a. $(4a - 5b)(2a - 3b)$
b. $2(m + 8n)(2m - n)$
c. $(3x^2 - 4)(2x + 5)$
d. $(p + 2)(3p^2 - 4p - 1)$

8. Factor completely.
a. $4x + 6xy - 15y - 10$
b. $12x^2 - 3$
c. $12a^2 - 4a - 5$
d. $p^2(p + 3) - 4(p + 3)$
e. $9 - m^2 - 4mn - 4n^2$
f. $8x^3 - 27$

9. Factor by completing the square.
a. $x^4 - 8x^2 + 4$
b. $p^4 - 7p^2q^2 + q^4$

10. Determine the value of k given the binomial is a factor of the polynomial.
a. $2x^3 - 13x^2 + 23x + k$; $(x - 1)$
b. $kx^3 + 8x^2 - 15x - 9$; $(x + 3)$

11. Simplify by reducing the common factors.
a. $\dfrac{a^3 - b^3}{a^2 - b^2} \times \dfrac{ac + 2ad + bc + 2bd}{c^2 + 2cd}$
b. $\dfrac{4x + 8y - 4z}{(x + 2y)^2 - z^2} \div \dfrac{x^3 + xy^2 - x^2y - y^3}{x^4 - y^4}$

12. Perform the indicated operations and write in simplest form.
a. $\dfrac{2x}{x + 2} + \dfrac{8}{x - 5}$
b. $\dfrac{6}{3x^2 + 5x - 2} + \dfrac{2}{3x^2 - 5x + 2}$
c. $\dfrac{8a + 28}{2a^2 + 3a - 14} - \dfrac{a^2 - 9}{a^2 + 6a + 9}$
d. $\dfrac{2m^2 + 7mn - 4n^2}{2m^2 - 7mn + 3n^2} + \dfrac{4m^2 - 2mn + n^2}{8m^3 + n^3}$

13. Find the expressions for the area of a triangle if its base is given by $(6x - 4)$ cm and its altitude is $(2x^2 + 5x - 1)$ cm.

14. Write the ratio in lowest terms.
a. $10:35$
b. $9:45:21$
c. $24\pi r^2 : 16\pi r^2$
d. $2x - 6 : x^2 - 4x + 3$

Cumulative Review   Chapters 1–3

15. The ratio of the length to the width of a rectangle is 8:5. If the length of the rectangle is 40 cm, find the width.

16. In Exercise 15, if a rectangle's sides are in the same ratio, find its length for a width of 12 cm.

17. The ratio of dimes to quarters is 2:7. If there are 108 dimes and quarters, how many of each coin would there be?

18. The ratio of an angle and its supplement is 7:8. Find the measures of the two angles.

19. Determine the mean proportional between the values given.
a. 4 and 16   **b.** 8 and 12

20. Solve for n.
a. $5:n = 9:20$ **b.** $8:3 = n:25$
c. $12:n = n:30$ **d.** $4n:15 = 12:35$

21. If the rate of travel is constant, the distance travelled varies directly as the time of travel. If a distance of 68 km is travelled in 2.5 h, determine how long it will take to travel 100 km at the same rate.

22. The intensity of a light varies inversely as the square of the distance from the source. If the distance from the light source is tripled, how would the intensity of light compare at this point?

23. The total cost of silk screening a company logo on T-shirts is partly a constant and partly varies directly as the number of T-shirts silk screened. The total cost of silk screening 20 T-shirts is $132.50 and the cost for 50 T-shirts is $237.50. Determine the cost of silk screening 180 T-shirts.

24. Each of the letters in this multiplication represents a digit. Find the digits.

$$\begin{array}{r} H\,I\,S \\ I\,S \\ \hline R\,O\,B\,S \end{array}$$

25. A man gave 17 cattle to his three children. The oldest gets half of them, the second one third, and the youngest one ninth. Obviously there is a problem. The man's brother donates one. So now there are 18 cattle. The oldest gets 9, the second gets 6, and the youngest gets 2. This gives us a total of 17 cattle so the brother can take his back. What went wrong?

26. Describe the similarities and differences between the graphs of a direct and a partial variation.

27. Assume $x = y$
Therefore, $xy = y^2$
$$x^2 - y^2 = x^2 - xy$$
$$(x - y)(x + y) = x(x - y)$$
$$x + y = x \qquad \text{But } x = y$$
$$x + x = x$$
$$2x = x$$
Therefore $2 = 1$
What went wrong?

28. The area of the washer is equal to the area of the hole. Determine the ratio of the radius of the hole to the radius of the outer edge of the washer.

29. What is the product of the first 612 whole numbers?

30. Find the product.
$$\left(1 - \tfrac{1}{4}\right)\left(1 - \tfrac{1}{5}\right)\left(1 - \tfrac{1}{6}\right)\cdots\left(1 - \tfrac{1}{52}\right)$$

31. The school lunchroom has two sets of tables; one set which will seat 6 at each table and another which will seat 10 at each table. If fewer than 10 tables are used and each chair is filled, how many of each type of table will be used to seat 78 people?

REAL NUMBERS AND RADICALS

Tune Up

1. List ten elements of each set of numbers.
a. natural numbers
b. whole numbers
c. integers

2. Which sets of numbers make up the set of real numbers?

3. Solve.
a. $4x - 3 = x - 45$
b. $\dfrac{a}{3} - \dfrac{a}{4} = \dfrac{1}{2}$
c. $\dfrac{3-y}{4} - \dfrac{y+1}{3} = \dfrac{y-2}{2}$
d. $4(2x - 1) - (x - 5) = 11$
e. $3(y - 4) - 5y = -6$
f. $0.2(x - 2) = 1.2(2x - 1)$
g. $2(x + 1) + 3(2x - 3) = 5x + 8$

4. Expand.
a. $5xy(7x + 8y)$
b. $x^3y^2(x - 3y)$
c. $3x(2x - 5y + 3z)$
d. $(x - 3y)(x + 5y)$
e. $(2x - 7y)^2$
f. $(5x - 9y)(5x + 9y)$

5. Factor.
a. $x^2 + 6x + 5$
b. $x^2 + 2x - 80$
c. $6(x - 3) - 7x(x - 3)$
d. $x^2 - 2x - 15$
e. $9x^2 - 4$
f. $x^2 + 0.1x - 0.2$
g. $6x^2 + 11x + 3$
h. $10x^2 - 35x + 15$

6. Solve for x.
a. $x^2 - 9x + 20 = 0$
b. $3x^2 + 4x - 7 = 0$
c. $x^2 - 16 = 0$
d. $5x^2 - 6x - 8 = 0$
e. $8x^2 - 29x - 12 = 0$
f. $28x^2 + 48x + 9 = 0$
g. $16x^2 - 25 = 0$
h. $2x^2 - 8 = 0$

7. Simplify.
a. $\dfrac{12x^2y - 16xy^2}{4xy}$
b. $\dfrac{72x^3y^4 + 54x^2y^2 - 6x^2y}{6x^2y}$

8. If $x = -2$, $y = 5$, and $z = 0.5$, then evaluate these expressions.
a. $x^y + y^x + z^x$
b. $5x - 7y + 12$
c. $\dfrac{x^3 + y^2}{z^2}$
d. $\dfrac{z^3 + 5y^2 - x}{x^{-z}}$

9. Calculate the amount \$38 500 will be after being invested for 3 a at an interest rate of 14.75%/a compounded quarterly. (*Hint*: $A = P(1 + i)^n$.)

10. Solve for x.
a. $2^x = 16$
b. $3^{x+1} = 81$
c. $5^x = 1$

11. The velocity of a projectile fired at a 45° angle is determined by the formula $V = \sqrt{Sg}$, where S is the range of the projectile in metres and $g = 9.8\,\text{m/s}^2$. Calculate the velocity required to fire the projectile 1600 m.

4·1 The Real Number System

The **real number system** was described initially in 1872 by Richard Dedekind, a German mathematician. Dedekind separated all numbers into those that can be expressed as fractions and those that cannot. These are called **rational** and **irrational** numbers respectively. Together, they form the set of real numbers.

A rational number, Q, can be expressed either as a **terminating** decimal or as a **periodic** decimal. In a periodic decimal, a finite set of numbers repeats indefinitely. The block of repeating digits is the length of the period. For example, in the periodic decimal $0.\overline{142\ 857}$, 142 857 is the period and the length of the period is 6.

A terminating decimal with n digits after the decimal is converted to a fraction by making a fraction with the period as the numerator and 10^n as the denominator. For example, the terminating decimal 0.4375 can be written as $\dfrac{4375}{10^4}$ or $\dfrac{7}{16}$ when reduced to lowest terms.

Any fraction can be expressed as a decimal equivalent. Therefore, any terminating or periodic decimal can be expressed as a fraction.

Example

A new type of playground swing has a seat attached to a spring. The seat initially stretches the spring to $\dfrac{8}{10}$ of its original length, and due to continual use, the spring will stretch another $\dfrac{1}{100}$ of its original length the first day, $\dfrac{1}{1000}$ of its original length the second day, and so on. If the swing is to be left in the park indefinitely, then what fraction will represent the total length of the spring?

$$\frac{8}{10} + \frac{1}{100} + \frac{1}{1000} + \ldots = 0.8 + 0.01 + 0.001 + \ldots$$

$$= 0.8\dot{1} \qquad \text{A bar or a dot indicates the repeating decimals.}$$

$$\text{Let } n = 0.8\dot{1}$$

$$100n = 81.\dot{1} \qquad \text{Multiply by 100 to place the decimal at the end of the first period.}$$

$$-\ 10n = \ \ 8.\dot{1}$$

$$90n = 73 \qquad \text{Subtract to eliminate the repeating decimals.}$$

$$n = \frac{73}{90}$$

The spring will stretch to $\dfrac{73}{90}$ of its original length.

Although irrational numbers cannot be expressed exactly as a fraction, they can be displayed accurately on a graph. For example, $\sqrt{2}$ neither repeats nor terminates. However, using the Pythagorean Theorem, the relative length of $\sqrt{2}$ can be displayed.

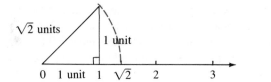

$\sqrt{2}$ units   1 unit

0   1 unit   1 $\sqrt{2}$ 2   3

Can you draw a line $\sqrt{3}$ units long?

Exercises

1. Identify each as a rational or irrational number. Explain your answers.

a. $\sqrt{7}$ **b.** $0.\overline{123\ 456}$

c. $\sqrt{16}$ **d.** $4.\overline{123}$

e. $0.151\ 151\ 115\ \ldots$ **f.** $\dfrac{\pi}{3}$

g. $\dfrac{1}{6.\dot{6}}$ **h.** -13

i. π **j.** $\dfrac{1.917}{\pi}$

2. Using the diagram from the display, draw a line having a relative length of $\sqrt{3}$ units.

3. State the period and the length of the period.

a. $0.\overline{763}$ **b.** $3.5\dot{5}\dot{5}$

c. $-120.\overline{56}$ **d.** $0.212\ 221\ 22\overline{2\ 122}$

4. Express these fractions as decimals. Use a calculator if one is available. The first one is done for you using the calculator keying sequence.

$$\dfrac{7}{11}$$

$$7 \boxed{\div}\ 11\ \boxed{=}\ \mathtt{0.6363636}$$

$$\therefore \dfrac{7}{11} = 0.\overline{63}$$

a. $\dfrac{3}{8}$ **b.** $\dfrac{7}{9}$ **c.** $-3\dfrac{1}{2}$

d. $\dfrac{12}{13}$ **e.** $\dfrac{1}{7}$ **f.** $\dfrac{5}{8}$

5. Express these decimals in the form $\dfrac{a}{b}$.

a. 0.71 **b.** 0.3 **c.** 0.625

d. $0.\dot{7}$ **e.** $0.123\ \overline{123}$ **f.** $0.\overline{4512}$

g. $0.66\dot{6}$ **h.** $0.\overline{47}$ **i.** $0.\overline{2957}$

6. Each year, the runoff from the melting snow on Bear Mountain deposits sand in Lake Michiboom in a decreasing rate. The recorded amounts over four years were 0.4 t, 0.04 t, 0.004 t, and 0.0004 t. What will be the total deposit of sand in the lake if this uniform rate continues indefinitely? Express the answer as a rational number in lowest terms.

7. Use a hockey puck with a 4 cm diameter to find a piece of string π cm long.

8. An experiment was conducted in the Space Lab to determine the loss of muscle strength in a gravity-free environment. Marshall's daily decrease in strength over a five-day period was 0.1, 0.08, 0.008, 0.0008, and 0.000 08 of his original strength. If he were to spend an indefinite period of time in space, then what fraction would be the total decrease in strength?

9. The sides of the square bases and the heights of the pyramids at Giza are constructed in the ratio of 11:7. Thus, the ratio of the perimeter of the base to twice the height approximates the value of π. Find this approximate value of π correct to six decimal places.

10. Find a decimal equivalent for $\dfrac{1}{7}, \dfrac{2}{7}, \dfrac{3}{7}$.

a. Predict a decimal equivalent for $\dfrac{4}{7}, \dfrac{5}{7}, \dfrac{6}{7}$.

b. Check your predictions by calculating $\dfrac{4}{7}, \dfrac{5}{7},$ and $\dfrac{6}{7}$. Use a calculator if one is available.

11. Express each in the form of $\dfrac{a}{b}$, where $a, b \in N$.

a. $0.3\dot{2}$ **b.** $0.7\dot{6}$ **c.** $0.9\dot{3}$

d. $2.\overline{79}$ **e.** $0.58\dot{6}$ **f.** $0.1\overline{87}$

g. $0.3\overline{81}$ **h.** $0.1\overline{573}$ **i.** $0.02\overline{19}$

12. Rikki decides to give away some money every day. On the first day, she gives away 0.16 of her money to the fifth person she sees. On the second day, she gives away 0.006 of the original amount to the eighth person she sees. On the third day, she gives away 0.0006 of the original amount to the thirtieth person she sees.

a. Find a decimal equivalent for the total amount of money she will give away.

b. Can you predict what numbered person will receive some money on the fifteenth day? Explain.

Using the Library

Use a dictionary to find the early meaning of the words "rational" and "irrational". Provide an explanation as to why these two words were used to describe the two sets.

4·2 Properties of Real Numbers

For many years, mathematicians throughout the world used only whole numbers. Legend has it, that a member of the secret Pythagorean group was drowned for revealing that $\sqrt{2}$ could not be written as a rational number. Such numbers were considered "absurd" and ignored. Eventually, a need was discovered for numbers other than whole numbers, and this led to the recognition of the set called the real numbers. In this section, many of the properties of real numbers will be introduced or discovered in the exercises.

The set of real numbers is said to be **dense** as there is always another real number between any two real numbers. For instance, if a and b are real numbers, then a real number between them is $\frac{a+b}{2}$. The term "dense" also has a secondary meaning. The graph of $x \geq -2$ on a real number line is a continuous solid line that has no "gaps" or breaks. In other words, a dense set of numbers has no points that are not identifiable by a number in the set.

These properties of real numbers allow us to solve equations. They are the properties that permit the rearrangement and substitution of terms and are the **axioms of equality** usually characterized by the phrase "is equal to".

i) Reflexive Property—anything that *is equal to* itself. For example, "Meegan is as tall as Meegan" is reflexive. Mathematically, this is written as "if $a = a$, then $a = a$."

ii) Symmetric Property—if the first *is equal to* the second, then the second *is equal to* the first. For example, if Jim is the brother of John, then John is the brother of Jim. Mathematically, this is written as "if $x = y$, then $y = x$."

iii) Transitive Property—if the first *is equal to* the second, and the second *is equal to* the third, then the first *is equal to* the third. For example, if Bob is the same age as Bill, and Bill is the same age as Ben, then Bob is the same age as Ben. Mathematically, this is written as "if $a = b$ and $b = c$, then $a = c$."

Exercises

1. In your own words, explain the reflexive property, the symmetric property, and the transitive property. Determine whether these sentences are reflexive, symmetric, or transitive.
a. Lee is the same age as Lee.
b. Mike is the brother of Bruce and Bruce is the brother of Lynn. Therefore, Mike is the brother of Lynn.

2. Is the phrase "a is a factor of b" symmetric?
a. Explain your reasoning.
b. How could you use the phrase "is a factor of" to make a symmetric sentence?

For the remainder of the exercises, assume that all variables are members of the real numbers.

3. Copy and complete the table to summarize some of the fundamental properties of real numbers. Use a mathematics dictionary if necessary.

Property	Addition	Multiplication
Closure	$a + b \in R$	$ab \in R$
Commutative		
Associative		
Identity		
Inverse		
Distributive		

4. Copy and complete to summarize the order properties.

a. Trichotomy property

If $a>b$, then $a-b>0$.

If $a=b$, then $a-$ ▮▮▮▮

If $a<b$, then $a-$ ▮▮▮▮

b. Addition property

If $a>b$, then $a+c>b+c$.

If $a=b$, then $a+$ ▮▮▮▮

If $a<b$, then $a+$ ▮▮▮▮

c. Multiplication property for $c>0$

If $a>b$, then $ac>bc$.

If $a=b$, then ac ▮▮▮▮

If $a<b$, then ac ▮▮▮▮

d. Multiplication property for $c<0$

If $a>b$, then $ac<bc$.

If $a=b$, then ▮▮▮▮

If $a<b$, then ac ▮▮▮▮

5. A.T., the "Mathematics Wizard", stated that if $-3x \leq 21$, then $x \geq 7$.

a. Is A.T. correct? Explain.

b. What property is A.T. using?

6. Identify the property of real numbers illustrated by each statement.

a. $(m)(1) = m$

b. $a + (-a) = 0$

c. $x - 11 \epsilon R$

d. $p = p$

e. $(3 - x) + 4 = 4 + (3 - x)$

f. $5(x - y) = 5x - 5y$

g. $12m - 9n = 3(4m - 3n)$

h. If $x = y$ and $y = -3$, then $x = -3$.

i. $5 > \sqrt{3}$ or $5 = \sqrt{3}$ or $5 < \sqrt{3}$.

j. If $a - b < 5$ and $5 < c$, then $a - b < c$.

k. If $a + b > c$ and $c > -13$, then $a + b > -13$.

l. $c < 0$. If $a < 9$, then $ac > 9c$.

7. Apply the properties of real numbers to copy and complete the statements.

a. If $x + 5 > 7$ and $7 > 2x - 5$, then ...

b. If $-3 < a + 6$ and $a + 6 < m$, then ...

c. $(p + q) = ...$

d. If $y < 3$ and $3 < w$, then ...

e. If $m > n$, then $-3m$ ...

f. If $p \neq q$, and $p \nless q$, then ...

8. Solve the inequality. (*Hint*: If $-x < 7$, then $x > -7$.)

a. $x - 3 < 5$

b. $m + 4 > -8$

c. $y + 1 > -2$

d. $6 > p - 11$

e. $5x < -20$

f. $-4x > 28$

g. $\frac{1}{2}x > -13$

h. $-\frac{2}{3}x < 12$

i. $\frac{5}{6}x > 0$

j. $-9x < 0$

k. $-12y \leq -36$

l. $-\frac{1}{5}d \geq -5$

9. Explain, and give a numeric example, of each property in Exercise 3.

10. Mentally calculate these expressions. Name the property that made the calculation easier.

a. $(48 + 52) + 27(100)$

b. $22.7(78 - 52) + 27.3(50 - 26)$

c. $0.17(25) - 0.23(25) + 0.06(25)$

Historical Note

The Moscow and Rhind papyri date back to approximately 1800 B.C. and 1600 B.C. respectively. They show their practical origin by dealing with questions regarding the strength of beer and bread, feed mixtures for cattle and domestic fowl, and the storage of grain. Many of these problems can be solved using a linear equation. For example, the solution to $\frac{x}{7} + x = 24$ can be found using the **rule of false position**. To solve the equation, substitute a convenient value for x, such as 7, into the equation. Since the solution is 8 and not 24, and $8 \times 3 = 24$, the solution to the equation is 7×3 or 21.

1. In your own words, explain the rule of false position.

2. Solve these equations using the rule of false position.

a. $\frac{2x}{6} + 3x = 30$

b. $\frac{x}{4} + 3x - x = 54$

4·3 Natural Number Exponents

An exponent is used to indicate how many times a given base is used as a factor. In this section, the laws of natural number exponents will be reviewed.

Number Bases	Variable Bases	Exponent Law ($m, n \in N$)
$(7^3)(7^2) = [(7)(7)(7)][(7)(7)]$ $= 7^{3+2}$ $= 7^5$	$(x^2)(x^4) = [(x)(x)][(x)(x)(x)(x)]$ $= x^{2+4}$ $= x^6$	Product Law $(x^m)(x^n) = x^{m+n}$
$(2^5) \div (2^2) = \dfrac{(2)(2)(2)(2)(2)}{(2)(2)}$ $= 2^{5-2}$ $= 2^3$	$x^5 \div x^3 = \dfrac{(x)(x)(x)(x)(x)}{(x)(x)(x)}$ $= x^{5-3}$ $= x^2$	Quotient Law $x^m \div x^n = x^{m-n}$ $(x \neq 0, \ m > n)$
$(5^3)^2 = [(5)(5)(5)][(5)(5)(5)]$ $= 5^{(3 \times 2)}$ $= 5^6$	$(x^2)^3 = [(x)(x)][(x)(x)][(x)(x)]$ $= x^{2 \times 3}$ $= x^6$	Power of a Power $(x^m)^n = x^{mn}$
$[(6)(7)]^3 = [(6)(7)][(6)(7)][(6)(7)]$ $= (6)(6)(6)(7)(7)(7)$ $= 6^3 \times 7^3$	$(xy)^4 = (xy)(xy)(xy)(xy)$ $= [(x)(x)(x)(x)][(y)(y)(y)(y)]$ $= x^4 y^4$	Power of a Product $(xy)^m = x^m y^m$
$\left(\dfrac{2}{9}\right)^5 = \left(\dfrac{2}{9}\right)\left(\dfrac{2}{9}\right)\left(\dfrac{2}{9}\right)\left(\dfrac{2}{9}\right)\left(\dfrac{2}{9}\right)$ $= \dfrac{2^5}{9^5}$	$\left(\dfrac{x}{y}\right)^4 = \left(\dfrac{x}{y}\right)\left(\dfrac{x}{y}\right)\left(\dfrac{x}{y}\right)\left(\dfrac{x}{y}\right)$ $= \dfrac{x^4}{y^4}$	Power of a Quotient $\left(\dfrac{x}{y}\right)^m = \dfrac{x^m}{y^m}$ $(y \neq 0)$

When simplifying an expression with exponents, use the laws to "reduce" the number of bases in the expression. Also remember to use the order of operations to simplify the expression.

Example 1

Simplify. $\left(\dfrac{21a^6 b^3 c^9}{7a^3 b^2 c^5}\right)^5$

$= \left[\left(\dfrac{21}{7}\right)\left(\dfrac{a^6}{a^3}\right)\left(\dfrac{b^3}{b^2}\right)\left(\dfrac{c^9}{c^5}\right)\right]^5$ { Group like bases and divide.

$= (3a^3 b c^4)^5$

$= (3)^5 (a^3)^5 (b)^5 (c^4)^5$

$= 243 a^{15} b^5 c^{20}$

Sometimes, an expression can be simplified, or an equation solved, by changing the bases.

Example 2

Express each exponent as a power with a base of 3 and simplify. $\dfrac{3^{2x+1} \times 9^{3x-1} \times 27^{5x}}{81^{2x}}$

$= \dfrac{3^{2x+1} \times (3^2)^{3x-1} \times (3^3)^{5x}}{(3^4)^{2x}}$

$= \dfrac{3^{2x+1} \times 3^{6x-2} \times 3^{15x}}{3^{8x}}$

$= \dfrac{3^{23x-1}}{3^{8x}}$

$= 3^{15x-1}$

Exercises

1. Simplify.

a. $(x^5)(x^3)$ **b.** $(m^4)(m)$

c. $q^{21} \div q^2$ **d.** $p^{20} \div p^7$

e. $(y^6)^8$ **f.** $(s^{11})^3$

g. $(cd)^5$ **h.** $(2x)^5$

i. $(a^3b^8)^2$ **j.** $(p^5q^7)^5$

2. Find the volume of a metal sphere with a diameter of 8 cm. Find its mass if 1 cm³ of metal has a mass of 0.72 g. (*Hint:* $V = \frac{4}{3}\pi r^3$.)

3. Evaluate the expression $3 + \frac{4^2}{7^2 + 8^2}$. Is this a good approximation for π? Explain.

4. The formula for calculating the amount of an investment when the interest is compounded is $A = P(1 + i)^n$ where P is the initial amount of money invested, n is the number of interest periods, and i is the interest rate, expressed as a decimal for each period. If $P = \$1000$, $i = 0.12$, and $n = 6$, then find the amount after the six interest periods.

5. Simplify. (*Hint:* Simplify the numerator and denominator separately where applicable.)

a. $(-3x^3)^5$ **b.** $(-2p^3q^2)^4$

c. $(p^{2x}q^y)^4$ **d.** $(k^{2n+1}m^{2n})^{5n}$

e. $\dfrac{(3x^5)(2x^3)}{28x^9 \div (-7x^5)}$ **f.** $\dfrac{144a^{16} \div (-48a^3)}{(56a^{10})(3a^1)}$

g. $(5m^6n^3)^2(4m^2n^7)^3$ **h.** $(a^5b^3c^7)^5(a^4bc^2)^3$

i. $\left(\dfrac{a^5b^6c^7}{a^4b^3c^2}\right)^3$ **j.** $\left(\dfrac{d^{2m}f^{3m}g^{5m}}{d^mf^{2m}g^{4m}}\right)^4$

k. $(-5m^6n^3)(-6mn^5) \div (2m^4n^2)(-5m^7n^9)$

6. Compare the values of $(3^2)^4$ and $3^{(2^4)}$.

a. Which do you think is larger?

b. Evaluate each.

c. Is it what you expected? Explain.

7. Evaluate. Use a calculator if one is available. The calculator key sequence for part **a** is given.

a. $(3.167)^5$

3.167 $\boxed{y^x}$ 5 $\boxed{=}$ ▬▬▬▬

b. 6^4 **c.** 5^5 **d.** 4^7

e. $(1.9)^8$ **f.** $(1.035)^{10}$ **g.** $(1.0083)^6$

8. A robot on an assembly line can perform a task $(x^5)^6$ times, where x is the number of tasks performed in a shift. If each task requires 2 h to be completed, the plant is open 16 h each day, and the robot is known to last 6 months, then how many times will the robot perform its task?

9. Simplify.

a. $2^{x+1} \times 2^{3x-5}$

b. $7^{2x-3} \times 7^{x+5} \div 7^{4x}$

c. $32^{x-1} \times 256x^{2x+3} \div 16^{4x+7}$

d. $81^{2x+3} \div 27^{5x} \times 9^{5+x}$

e. $(2.5)^{3x} \times (6.25)^{2x-1} \div (15.625)^{x-4}$

10. Solve for x.

a. $2^{x+3} \div 4^{x-1} = 16$

b. $27^{5x-9} \times 3^{x+6} \div 243^{3x} = 729$

c. $1 \times 5^{3x} \times 25^{2x} = 125$

11. Using the formula $n = n_0(3)^{0.27}$, evaluate n for these values of n_0.

a. 50   **b.** 100   **c.** 35

12. Copy and complete. Use a calculator if one is available.

$2^1 = 2$	$3^1 = 3$
$2^{0.9} =$ ▬▬▬	$3^{0.6} =$ ▬▬▬
$2^{0.5} =$ ▬▬▬	$3^{0.2} =$ ▬▬▬
$2^{0.1} =$ ▬▬▬	$3^{0.05} =$ ▬▬▬

a. What value does the power approach as the exponent decreases?

b. Use different bases and the exponents 1, 0.6, 0.2, and 0.05 to determine whether all bases approach the value in part **a** as the exponent approaches zero.

13. Evaluate if $a = 2$, $b = 3$, and $c = 5$.

a. $b^b - a^a$ **b.** $c^b + b^a - c^a$

c. $(a^a)(a^b)(a^c)$ **d.** $5^b \div (5^a)(5^c)$

e. $(7bc)^a$ **f.** $\left(\dfrac{-15a}{5c}\right)^b$

14. Using only a calculator, find the repeating digits in $\frac{7}{23}$.

4·4 Integral Exponents

In the previous section, the exponent laws were reviewed for natural number exponents. However, special meaning is given to exponents that are members of the integers. For example,

$$\frac{(x)(x)(x)(x)}{(x)(x)(x)(x)(x)(x)} = \frac{1}{x^2} \quad \text{also} \quad \frac{x^4}{x^6} = x^{4-6}$$

$$= x^{-2}$$

$$\boxed{x^{-a} = \frac{1}{x^a} \text{ or } \frac{1}{x^{-a}} = x^a, \ x \neq 0.}$$

In a similar manner, we can show that x^0 has a value of 1 for all $x \neq 0$.

Using these general forms, the exponent laws can be extended to include the set of integers. In your notebooks, redraw the chart in the display of Section 4·3 to include integral exponents.

Example 1

Evaluate.

a. 5^{-3}

$5^{-3} = \frac{1}{5^3}$

$= \frac{1}{125}$

b. -12^0

$-12^0 = -(12)^0$

$= -1$

Note the negative signs.

c. $(-12)^0$

$(-12)^0 = 1$

For this text, an answer is simplified when it is written with positive exponents only and without brackets.

Example 2

Simplify. Evaluate where possible.

a. $\left(\frac{5xy^{-1}}{2w^2}\right)^{-1} = \frac{5^{-1}x^{-1}y}{2^{-1}w^{-2}}$

$$= \frac{\left(\frac{1}{5}\right)\left(\frac{1}{x}\right)y}{\left(\frac{1}{2}\right)\left(\frac{1}{w^2}\right)}$$

$$= \frac{2yw^2}{5x}$$

b. $\left(\frac{1}{2}\right)^{-2} \times \left(\frac{3}{2}\right)^{-1} + \left(\frac{2}{3}\right)^2$

$$= \left(\frac{2}{1}\right)^2 \times \left(\frac{2}{3}\right) + \left(\frac{2}{3}\right)^2$$

$$= \frac{8}{3} + \frac{4}{9}$$

$$= \frac{28}{9}$$

The restrictions on the variables must be determined **before** the equation is simplified. In this case, x, y, and $w \neq 0$.

Exercises

1. Why do the restrictions on the variables have to be identified before the expression is simplified? Use Example 2, part **a**, of the display to help with your explanation.

2. Explain why -12^0 is evaluated as -1, while $(-12)^0$ is evaluated as 1.

3. Evaluate $\left(\frac{1}{7}\right)^{-3}$. Use a calculator if one is available and record the keying sequence.

For the remainder of the exercises, use a calculator if one is available.

4. Evaluate.

a. 2^{-3} **b.** $(-5)^0$ **c.** -7^0
d. $(-3)^{-3}$ **e.** $(2^2)^{-3}$ **f.** $(-7)^{-2}$
g. $\left(\dfrac{0}{3}\right)^0$ **h.** $\left(\dfrac{1}{2}\right)^{-3}$ **i.** $\left(\dfrac{3}{5}\right)^{-2}$
j. $(-0.01)^{-1}$ **k.** $(0.5)^{-4}$ **l.** $(-0.3)^0$

5. Express using positive exponents only.

a. $x^{-1}y^{-1}$ **b.** $\dfrac{1}{x^{-5}}$ **c.** $5m^{-5}$
d. $\dfrac{1}{3x^{-3}}$ **e.** $\dfrac{2x^{-2}}{5y^{-3}}$ **f.** $\dfrac{ab^{-5}}{c^{-3}d^{-1}}$

6. Explain why 0^0 is undefined.

7. Does 0^{-n} exist? Explain.

8. The length of one edge of a cube is $2x$ cm. Find its
a. surface area,
b. volume,
c. longest diagonal.

9. Simplify.

a. $(x^{12})(x^{-3})$ **b.** $(m^{-2})(m^{-5})$
c. $(p^{-11})(p^{13})$ **d.** $x^9 \div x^{10}$
e. $c^{-3} \div c^{-5}$ **f.** $d^{25} \div d^{-25}$

10. Estimate the values of $((2^{-2})^{-4})^0$ and $2^{(-2^{-4})^0}$.
a. Calculate each value.
b. How good were your estimations?

11. Simplify.

a. $(2x)^{-1}$ **b.** $(-5y)^{-2}$
c. $(15p^9)^0$ **d.** $(6r^{-7})^{-3}$
e. $\left(\dfrac{m^2}{n^3}\right)^{-4}$ **f.** $\left(\dfrac{5x^{-2}}{y^3}\right)^0$

12. Simplify. Write the answers with positive exponents and without brackets.

a. $(a^{-2}b^{-3})^3$ **b.** $(7x^{-3}y^{-5})(xy^{-1})(5x^4y^8)$
c. $\left(\dfrac{x^{-3}y^{-2}}{x^{-2}y^3}\right)^{-2}$ **d.** $\dfrac{(-3m^2n^3)^{-1}}{(2m^3n^2)^{-2}}$

13. The volume of a cube is given by the expression $64x^6y^3$ cm^3.
a. Find an expression for the area of one of its faces.
b. Find an expression for the length of its longest diagonal.

14. Evaluate if $x = -3$ and $y = 2$.

a. x^{-1} **b.** x^2y^{-1}
c. $\left(\dfrac{y^3}{x}\right)^{-2}$ **d.** $x^2 + y^{-2}$
e. $x^{-3} - y^{-1}$ **f.** $x^y \div y^x$

15. Estimate the value of the expression for $x = 62$ and $y = -73$. $(8x - 7(9x + (3y - (x - 5y))))^0$
a. Evaluate the expression.
b. Is your estimation reasonable? Explain.
c. What conclusions can be made about expressions where the exponent is zero?

16. Calculate the amount, A, of a \$100 000 investment, P, after 10 a if the interest rate is 9.75%/a, compounded annually. (*Hint:* $A = P(1 + i)^n$.)

17. Solve for x.

a. $\left(\dfrac{3}{5}\right)^x = \dfrac{9}{25}$ **b.** $\left(\dfrac{3}{5}\right)^x = \dfrac{25}{9}$

18. Evaluate each correct to five decimal places.
a. $(1.035)^{-10}$ **b.** $(1.125)^{-10}$
c. $(1.07)^{-15}$ **d.** $(1.105)^{-25}$

19. What amount, P, invested today will accumulate to \$10 000 three years from now if the interest rate is 10.5%/a compounded annually?

20. Simplify.

a. $(4m^{-2}n^{-3})^{-3}(2m^{-5}n^{-1})^2$
b. $\left(\dfrac{m}{n}\right)^{-2} \div \left(\dfrac{n}{r}\right)^{-1} \div \left(\dfrac{r}{m}\right)^{-3}$
c. $\left(\dfrac{7x^3y^5}{z^3}\right)^{-2} \div \left(\dfrac{x^{-2}y^3}{z^{-2}}\right)^{-1}$
d. $(-3a^2b^{-3}c^5)^2 \div (9a^{-1}b^2)^{-1}(6a^5b^2)$
e. $\left(\dfrac{5p^{-2}q^{-1}r^{-3}}{p^{-3}q^{-5}r^8}\right)^{-2}$
f. $\dfrac{(2a^2b)^{-2}}{(3ab)^{-3}} \times \dfrac{(4ab^2)^2}{(6a^3b^{-2})}$
g. $\dfrac{3x^{-5}y^{-7}}{z} \div \dfrac{9x^3yz^2}{z} \div \dfrac{27x^{-3}y}{z^{-2}}$

4·5 Introduction to Radicals

The Pythagoreans were the first to discover that there is no rational number corresponding to the length of the diagonal of a square with side lengths of one unit. Numbers, such as $\sqrt{2}$, are called **irrational** numbers. Irrational numbers are often written in **radical** form; for example, $\sqrt[3]{14}$ or $\sqrt[5]{4}$. Since radicals such as $\sqrt{4}$ have two roots, ± 2, the value of $\sqrt{4}$ is generally designated as the **principal** (positive) square root. All radicals are expressed either as a **mixed** radical, such as $5\sqrt{3}$, or a **pure** radical, such as $\sqrt{23}$.

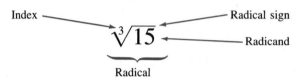

Index — Radical sign

$$\sqrt[3]{15}$$

Radicand

Radical

Some radicals can be evaluated exactly. However, the majority of radicals can only be approximated.

Example 1

Evaluate.

a. $\sqrt{81}$

Since $9 \times 9 = 81$, $\sqrt{81} = 9$.

b. $\sqrt[3]{343}$

Since $7 \times 7 \times 7 = 343$, $\sqrt[3]{343} = 7$.

The radicands in Example 1 were either a perfect square or a perfect cube. However, most radicals do not evaluate as easily. A calculator can be used to approximate these radicals.

Example 2

Evaluate. $\sqrt[4]{27}$

27 $\boxed{\text{INV}}$ $\boxed{y^x}$ 4 $\boxed{=}$ $\mathsf{2.2795070}$

$\sqrt[4]{27} \doteq 2.3$

Example 3

Find a real number that represents the product.
$\sqrt{16} \times \sqrt{36}$

$$\sqrt{16} \times \sqrt{36} = 4 \times 6 \qquad \sqrt{16} \times \sqrt{36} = \sqrt{576}$$
$$= 24 \qquad\qquad\qquad = 24$$

$$\boxed{\sqrt{ab} = \sqrt{a} \times \sqrt{b},\ a \geq 0,\ b \geq 0,\ \text{and } a,\ b \epsilon R.}$$

Generally, when a radical is rounded using a calculator, the approximation is rounded to one decimal place. However, the number of places to which the approximation is rounded will be left to the student.

Example 4

Convert to a pure radical. $5\sqrt{7}$

$$5\sqrt{7} = \sqrt{25} \times \sqrt{7}$$
$$= \sqrt{175}$$

Example 5

Express as a mixed radical. $\sqrt[3]{x^5 y^6}$

$$\sqrt[3]{x^5 y^6} = (\sqrt[3]{x^5})(\sqrt[3]{y^6})$$
$$= (\sqrt[3]{(x^3)(x^2)})(\sqrt[3]{(y^2)(y^2)(y^2)})$$
$$= (x)(\sqrt[3]{x^2})(y^2)$$
$$= xy^2\sqrt[3]{x^2}$$

Exercises

For all exercises, use a calculator if one is available.

1. Define the terms "mixed radical", "pure radical", and "principal root".

2. Express each as a mixed radical and pure radical.
a. $\sqrt{25} \times \sqrt{7}$ **b.** $\sqrt{16} \times \sqrt{6}$
c. $\sqrt{36} \times \sqrt{3}$ **d.** $\sqrt{5} \times \sqrt{49}$
e. $\sqrt{7} \times \sqrt{81}$ **f.** $\sqrt{64} \times \sqrt{5}$

3. Express as a pure radical.
a. $2\sqrt{7}$ **b.** $5\sqrt{3}$ **c.** $11\sqrt{5}$
d. $6\sqrt{13}$ **e.** $15\sqrt{2}$ **f.** $10\sqrt{7}$
g. $9\sqrt{5}$ **h.** $8\sqrt{3}$ **i.** $7\sqrt{15}$

4. Evaluate.
a. $\sqrt{3} \times \sqrt{16}$ **b.** $\sqrt{8} \times \sqrt{8}$ **c.** $\sqrt{12} \times \sqrt{3}$
d. $\sqrt{6} \times \sqrt{24}$ **e.** $\sqrt{9} \times \sqrt{25}$ **f.** $\sqrt{36} \times \sqrt{3}$

5. Evaluate correct to one decimal place.
a. $\sqrt{0.25}$ **b.** $\sqrt{0.144}$ **c.** $\sqrt{225}$
d. $\sqrt{55}$ **e.** $\sqrt{34}$ **f.** $\sqrt{0.0009}$
g. $\sqrt{0.0025}$ **h.** $\sqrt{91.46}$ **i.** $\sqrt{43.287}$

6. Express as a mixed radical in simplest form. (*Hint*: A mixed radical in simplest form has a radicand that is a prime number.)
a. $\sqrt{125}$ **b.** $\sqrt{98}$
c. $\sqrt{32}$ **d.** $\sqrt{72}$
e. $\sqrt{48}$ **f.** $\sqrt{450}$
g. $\sqrt{180}$ **h.** $\sqrt{192}$

7. Express as a mixed radical in simplest form.
a. $\sqrt{x^2 y}$ **b.** $\sqrt{a^3 b}$
c. $\sqrt[3]{x^3 y^2}$ **d.** $\sqrt[3]{m^5 n^4}$
e. $\sqrt{p^5 q^3}$ **f.** $\sqrt[3]{c^7 d^2}$
g. $\sqrt[3]{f^{12} g^8}$ **h.** $\sqrt{w^{11} x^{15}}$

8. Verify that these are true statements.
a. $\sqrt{6} \times \sqrt{2} = \sqrt{12}$ **b.** $\sqrt{7} \times \sqrt{13} = \sqrt{91}$
c. $\sqrt{15} \times \sqrt{6} = \sqrt{90}$ **d.** $\sqrt{8} \times \sqrt{4} = 4\sqrt{2}$
e. $\sqrt{17} \times \sqrt{6} = \sqrt{102}$
f. $4\sqrt{2} \times 3\sqrt{5} = 12\sqrt{10}$

9. Verify that $4\sqrt{2} > 3\sqrt{3}$.

10. Show that these expressions are equivalent.
$12\sqrt{2} - 8\sqrt{5} + 8\sqrt{7}$
$3\sqrt{32} - 4\sqrt{20} + 2\sqrt{112}$
$4\sqrt{18} + 4\sqrt{28} - 2\sqrt{80}$

11. Express as a mixed radical in simplest form.
a. $\sqrt{16x^5 y^8}$ **b.** $\sqrt{27m^3 n^2}$
c. $\sqrt[3]{81p^7 q^6}$ **d.** $\sqrt{4c^3 d}$
e. $\sqrt{49a^2 b^3}$ **f.** $\sqrt[3]{8r^9 t^{12}}$
g. $\sqrt[3]{m^3 n^6 p^2}$ **h.** $\sqrt{a^{10} b^7 c^{14}}$

12. A cable suspended from the CN Tower acts as a pendulum. If the length of the cable is 490 m, calculate the period of the pendulum. The equation for the period, T, is $T = 2\pi \sqrt{\dfrac{\ell}{g}}$, where $g = 9.8$ m/s^2.

13. On a clear day, the distance you can see to the horizon is given by $d = \sqrt{13h}$, where d is the distance measured in kilometres, and h is the height above ground level a person is standing in metres. If a person is at the top of a 1000 m mountain, how far can that person see?

14. Calculate the length of the diagonal of a square whose side is 5 m.

15. The area of a triangle can be found using Heron's formula: $A = \sqrt{s(s-a)(s-b)(s-c)}$, where a, b, and c are the lengths of the sides and $s = \dfrac{a+b+c}{2}$. Find the area of a triangle whose sides are 10 cm, 16 cm, and 20 cm respectively.

16. The time for an object to fall a distance d, is given by the formula $t = \sqrt{\dfrac{2d}{g}}$, where $g = 9.8$ m/s^2. Calculate the time required to fall 980 m.

17. The length of one side of a rectangle is $\sqrt{5}$ cm, while the other side is $3\sqrt{5}$ cm. Without using a calculator, find the area of the rectangle.

4·6 Adding and Subtracting Radicals

The distributive property of addition can be used to add and subtract "like" terms in an algebraic expression. The same concept is used to add and subtract like radicals.

$$3x + 7x - 4x = (3 + 7 - 4)x$$
$$= 6x$$

$$3\sqrt[3]{11} + 7\sqrt[3]{11} - 4\sqrt[3]{11} = (3 + 7 - 4)\sqrt[3]{11}$$
$$= 6\sqrt[3]{11}$$

Radicals with the same radicand and the same index are called "like" radicals. Just as $4x + 3y$ cannot be combined because they are not "like" terms, $4\sqrt{3}$ cannot be combined with $3\sqrt{7}$ because they are not "like" radicals. A radical expression is simplified when all "like" radicals are combined.

> In order to combine radicals using addition and subtraction, they must have the same index and be expressed using the same radicand.

Example 1

Add. $\sqrt[4]{3} + 4\sqrt[4]{3}$
$$= (1 + 4)\sqrt[4]{3}$$
$$= 5\sqrt[4]{3}$$

Example 2

Simplify. $5\sqrt{7} + 3\sqrt{3} - 2\sqrt{3} - \sqrt{7}$
$$= (5 - 1)\sqrt{7} + (3 - 2)\sqrt{3}$$
$$= 4\sqrt{7} + \sqrt{3}$$

Example 3

A rectangular parking lot has dimensions of $75\sqrt{2}$ m and $25\sqrt{2}$ m. How much fencing is needed so that a fence can be placed around the entire parking lot?

Understand the Problem
Since a fence is going to be placed around the entire parking lot, the perimeter will be needed. In this case, the length of the parking lot is $75\sqrt{2}$ m and the width is $25\sqrt{2}$ m.

Develop a Plan
The formula for finding the perimeter of an object is $P = 2\ell + 2w$ or $P = \ell + \ell + w + w$.

Carry Out the Plan
$$P = \ell + \ell + w + w$$
$$= 75\sqrt{2} + 75\sqrt{2} + 25\sqrt{2} + 25\sqrt{2}$$
$$= (75 + 75 + 25 + 25)\sqrt{2}$$
$$= 200\sqrt{2}$$

Look Back
Therefore, $200\sqrt{2}$ m, or about 283 m, of fencing will be needed. Is this answer reasonable?

Sometimes radicals have different radicands that can be simplified to allow for addition and subtraction.

Example 4

Subtract. $\sqrt{54} - \sqrt{24}$
$$= \sqrt{9 \times 6} - \sqrt{4 \times 6}$$
$$= 3\sqrt{6} - 2\sqrt{6}$$
$$= (3 - 2)\sqrt{6}$$
$$= \sqrt{6}$$

Example 5

Simplify. $5\sqrt[3]{a^3b^2c^5} + 2ac\sqrt[3]{b^2c^2}$
$$= 5ac\sqrt[3]{b^2c^2} + 2ac\sqrt[3]{b^2c^2}$$
$$= 7ac\sqrt[3]{b^2c^2}$$

Exercises

1. Add or subtract.
a. $2\sqrt{3} + 5\sqrt{3}$ **b.** $13\sqrt{7} - 8\sqrt{7}$
c. $7\sqrt{2} + 11\sqrt{2}$ **d.** $15\sqrt{3} + 5\sqrt{3}$
e. $12\sqrt{5} - \sqrt{5}$ **f.** $25\sqrt{2} - 18\sqrt{2}$

2. Maki needed wood to frame a square picture. However, upon arriving at the hardware store, he could not remember the dimensions of the picture; only the area. If he buys $3\sqrt{2}$ m of wood to frame a picture that has an area of 1 m², did he buy enough? Use a calculator if one is available.

3. Simplify. A radical is expressed in simplest form when all perfect squares have been removed from the radical.
a. a stack of books $\sqrt{8}$ m high
b. the distance of a $\sqrt{70\ 000}$ m race
c. a building $2\sqrt{300}$ m long
d. Jack's height of $\frac{1}{2}\sqrt{12}$ m

4. Add or subtract.
a. $\sqrt{12} + \sqrt{27}$ **b.** $\sqrt{75} - \sqrt{12}$
c. $\sqrt{32} - \sqrt{8}$ **d.** $\sqrt{300} + \sqrt{27}$
e. $\sqrt{20} + \sqrt{80}$ **f.** $\sqrt{98} + \sqrt{8}$

5. Add or subtract.
a. $2\sqrt{3} + 5\sqrt{12}$ **b.** $7\sqrt{8} - 3\sqrt{2}$
c. $7\sqrt{18} - \sqrt{2}$ **d.** $3\sqrt{48} + 5\sqrt{3}$
e. $15\sqrt{50} + 7\sqrt{2}$ **f.** $6\sqrt{300} - 10\sqrt{3}$
g. $8\sqrt{2} - \sqrt{98}$ **h.** $9\sqrt{7} + 5\sqrt{28}$

6. Mai-Lee wants to build a snug-fitting cabinet for a square television she plans to buy. The diagonal of the television screen is 50 cm in length. What should be the inside perimeter of the cabinet? Express your answer as a mixed radical first; then as a decimal. Use a calculator if one is available.

7. Show that $2\sqrt{5} + 1$ is a root of the equation $x^2 - 2x - 19 = 0$.

8. Simplify by addition or subtraction.
a. $5\sqrt{x^2y} - x\sqrt{y}$ **b.** $3a^2b\sqrt{b} - \sqrt{a^4b^3}$
c. $3\sqrt{x^3y^2} + 4xy\sqrt{x}$ **d.** $\sqrt[7]{p^3q^3} + 9pq\sqrt{pq}$

9. Add or subtract.
a. $5\sqrt{27} + 7\sqrt{48}$ **b.** $12\sqrt{8} - 3\sqrt{50}$
c. $6\sqrt{18} + 9\sqrt{32}$ **d.** $3\sqrt{125} + 8\sqrt{80}$
e. $7\sqrt{200} - 3\sqrt{98}$ **f.** $7\sqrt{54} - 5\sqrt{24}$
g. $8\sqrt{45} + 3\sqrt{24}$ **h.** $6\sqrt{96} - 2\sqrt{175}$

10. Find the difference between $15\sqrt{8}$ and the sum of $20\sqrt{2}$ and $25\sqrt{27}$.

11. Express as a mixed radical in simplest form.
a. $\frac{1}{2}\sqrt{8} + \frac{3}{4}\sqrt{32} - \frac{2}{5}\sqrt{50}$
b. $\frac{5}{6}\sqrt{72} - \frac{1}{4}\sqrt{32} + \frac{3}{7}\sqrt{98}$
c. $\frac{1}{2}\sqrt{12} - \frac{2}{3}\sqrt{27} + \frac{3}{4}\sqrt{48}$
d. $\frac{1}{3}\sqrt{45} + \frac{3}{4}\sqrt{20} + \frac{1}{5}\sqrt{300}$
e. $\frac{3}{5}\sqrt{700} - \frac{2}{3}\sqrt{63} + \frac{1}{2}\sqrt{28}$
f. $\frac{1}{4}\sqrt{24} + \frac{2}{3}\sqrt{54} - \frac{3}{2}\sqrt{108}$

12. Find the largest radical in each pair of radicals. Do not use a calculator and explain your reasoning.
a. $\sqrt{7}, \sqrt{5}$ **b.** $3\sqrt{16}, 13$
c. $5\sqrt{2}, 4\sqrt{3}$ **d.** $6\sqrt{7}, 7\sqrt{6}$
e. $3\sqrt{2}, 2\sqrt{3}$ **f.** $10\sqrt{12}, 20\sqrt{2}$

13. A tank of amoebas double in population every minute. If there are originally 17 amoebas in the tank, and the tank is full in 2 h, then how long will it take for the tank to be half full of amoebas?

14. The perimeter of a square is given by the expression $(8\sqrt{3} + 12\sqrt{5})$ m.
a. Draw a square with these dimensions.
b. Find the length of one side of the square.
c. If a second square with the same side length was drawn on one side of the square, then find the perimeter of the new shape.

15. Find the sum.
$400\sqrt{3} - 399\sqrt{3} + 398\sqrt{3} - 397\sqrt{3} + \dots$
$2\sqrt{3} - \sqrt{3}$

4·7 Multiplication of Radicals

In Section 4·5, multiplication of radicals was defined as $\sqrt{ab} = \sqrt{a} \times \sqrt{b}$, where $a \geq 0$, $b \geq 0$, and $a, b \in R$. The multiplication of radicals does not depend on having "like" radicals, but does depend on the radicals having the same index. Just as $3x$ and $2y$ can be multiplied to give a product of $6xy$, $3\sqrt{3}$ and $2\sqrt{2}$ can be multiplied to give a product of $(3 \times 2)(\sqrt{3} \times \sqrt{2})$ or $6\sqrt{6}$.

Example

Find the product.

a. $2\sqrt{5}(4\sqrt{7} - 3)$

b. $(\sqrt{3} - \sqrt{5})(\sqrt{3} + \sqrt{5})$

The properties of real numbers summarized in Exercise 3 of Section 4·2 are used when multiplying radical expressions. In this case, the distributive property of multiplication is used.

$$= (2\sqrt{5} \times 4\sqrt{7}) - (2\sqrt{5} \times 3)$$
$$= (2 \times 4)\sqrt{35} - 6\sqrt{5}$$
$$= 8\sqrt{35} - 6\sqrt{5}$$

$$= \sqrt{3} \times \sqrt{3} + \sqrt{3} \times \sqrt{5} - \sqrt{5} \times \sqrt{3} - \sqrt{5} \times \sqrt{5}$$
$$= 3 - 5$$
$$= -2$$

Remember, when multiplying a mixed radical by a mixed radical where the indices are the same, multiply both the real numbers outside the radical and also the radicands.

Exercises

1. Find the product.

a. $\sqrt{3} \times \sqrt{3}$ **b.** $\sqrt{7} \times \sqrt{7}$
c. $\sqrt{5} \times \sqrt{5}$ **d.** $\sqrt{11} \times \sqrt{11}$
e. $(\sqrt{12})^2$ **f.** $(\sqrt{15})^2$
g. $(\sqrt{133})^2$ **h.** $(\sqrt{17})^2$

2. The term $(\sqrt{a} - \sqrt{b})$ is the **conjugate radical** of $(\sqrt{a} + \sqrt{b})$.
a. What is the product of $(\sqrt{a} - \sqrt{b})$ and $(\sqrt{a} + \sqrt{b})$?
b. State the conjugate radical of $(\sqrt{a} + \sqrt{b})$.
c. What is the product of $(\sqrt{a} + \sqrt{b})$ and its conjugate?
d. Write a generalized statement for the product of a two-term radical and its conjugate.

3. Find the product.

a. $(\sqrt{3a})^2$ **b.** $(3\sqrt{2a})^2$
c. $(\sqrt{a+b})^2$ **d.** $(\sqrt{2a-b})^2$
e. $(2\sqrt{3a-b})^2$ **f.** $(3\sqrt{2x-4})^2$
g. $(2 + \sqrt{3+b})^2$ **h.** $(2 + \sqrt{3a+b})^2$

4. Which has the greatest volume: a cube with side lengths of $\sqrt{3}$ m or a rectangular prism with lengths and widths of $\sqrt{2}$ m and a height of $2\sqrt{2}$ m?

5. Find the product.
a. $2\sqrt{3} \times 5\sqrt{7}$ **b.** $6\sqrt{2} \times 12\sqrt{3}$
c. $10\sqrt{2} \times 7\sqrt{2}$ **d.** $3\sqrt{10} \times 2\sqrt{5}$
e. $\sqrt{7}(\sqrt{14} - 5)$ **f.** $\sqrt{5}(\sqrt{20} + \sqrt{3})$
g. $\sqrt{15}(\sqrt{3} - \sqrt{5})$ **h.** $\sqrt{17}(\sqrt{17} + \sqrt{6})$

6. The top of Ken's new desk is $(\sqrt{3} - 1)$ m wide and $\sqrt{5}$ m long. Find the area of the top of his desk.

7. A rectangular picture frame has outside measurements of $(2\sqrt{5} + 1)$ cm by $2\sqrt{5}$ cm. Find the area enclosed by the frame.

8. Find the product of these conjugates.
a. $(\sqrt{7} + 1)(\sqrt{7} - 1)$
b. $(2\sqrt{3} + \sqrt{5})(2\sqrt{3} - \sqrt{5})$
c. $(7\sqrt{5} + \sqrt{2})(7\sqrt{5} - \sqrt{2})$
d. $(8\sqrt{6} - 2\sqrt{3})(8\sqrt{6} + 2\sqrt{3})$
e. $(9\sqrt{11} - 3\sqrt{6})(9\sqrt{11} + 3\sqrt{6})$

4·8 Division of Radicals

Just as multiplication of radicals does not depend on having "like" radicals, neither does the division of radicals. The single requirement for division, like multiplication, is that the radicals have the same index.

$$\frac{\sqrt{100}}{\sqrt{4}} = \frac{10}{2} \qquad \text{also} \qquad \frac{\sqrt{100}}{\sqrt{4}} = \sqrt{\frac{100}{4}}$$
$$= 5 \qquad\qquad\qquad\qquad = \sqrt{25}$$
$$\qquad\qquad\qquad\qquad\qquad = 5$$

$$\boxed{\frac{\sqrt{a}}{\sqrt{b}} = \sqrt{\frac{a}{b}}\,, \ a \geq 0,\ b > 0, \text{ and } a,\ b \in R.}$$

A radical expression is in simplified form when it is written without radicals in the denominator. This is called **rationalizing the denominator**. This can be done when the denominator is not a factor of the numerator.

Example

Rationalize the denominator.

a. $\dfrac{5\sqrt{3} - 6}{7\sqrt{2}}$

$= \dfrac{5\sqrt{3} - 6}{7\sqrt{2}} \times \dfrac{\sqrt{2}}{\sqrt{2}} \qquad \left\{ \dfrac{\sqrt{2}}{\sqrt{2}} = 1 \right\}$

$= \dfrac{5\sqrt{6} - 6\sqrt{2}}{14}$

b. $\dfrac{2\sqrt{5}}{\sqrt{5} - 1}$

$= \dfrac{2\sqrt{5}}{\sqrt{5} - 1} \times \dfrac{\sqrt{5} + 1}{\sqrt{5} + 1} \quad \left\{ \begin{array}{l} \text{Multiply the denominator} \\ \text{by the conjugate.} \end{array} \right.$

$= \dfrac{10 + 2\sqrt{5}}{4}$

$= \dfrac{5 + \sqrt{5}}{2} \qquad \left\{ \text{Factor and divide.} \right.$

Exercises

1. A.T., the "Mathematics Wizard", stated that "to rationalize a denominator, multiply the numerator and denominator by the same conjugate radical to eliminate all radical signs". Is A.T. correct? Explain.

2. Why is it necessary that $a \geq 0$ and $b > 0$ when dividing radicals?

3. Divide.

a. $\dfrac{\sqrt{18}}{\sqrt{2}}$
b. $\dfrac{\sqrt[3]{27}}{\sqrt[3]{125}}$
c. $\dfrac{\sqrt{30}}{\sqrt{5}}$

d. $\sqrt{\dfrac{36}{49}}$
e. $\sqrt{\dfrac{49}{7}}$
f. $\dfrac{\sqrt[4]{243}}{\sqrt[4]{3}}$

4. State the product. $(a\sqrt{b} + c\sqrt{d})(a\sqrt{b} - c\sqrt{d})$

5. Rationalize the denominator.

a. $\dfrac{\sqrt{7} + 1}{3\sqrt{7}}$
b. $\dfrac{4 - 2\sqrt{10}}{\sqrt{50}}$

c. $\dfrac{9 - 3\sqrt{15}}{8\sqrt{5}}$
d. $\dfrac{5\sqrt{26} - 2}{2\sqrt{13}}$

e. $\dfrac{\sqrt{2}}{\sqrt{5} + \sqrt{2}}$
f. $\dfrac{\sqrt{3}}{\sqrt{3} - \sqrt{2}}$

g. $\dfrac{2\sqrt{3}}{2\sqrt{3} - 1}$
h. $\dfrac{5\sqrt{7}}{5\sqrt{7} - 6}$

6. Find the smallest value of a that will make the product an integer.

a. $2\sqrt{3} \times \sqrt{a}$
b. $5\sqrt{7} \times \sqrt{a}$
c. $7\sqrt{5} \times \sqrt{a}$
d. $-3\sqrt{11} \times \sqrt{a}$
e. $15\sqrt{3} \times \sqrt{a}$
f. $4\sqrt{12} \times \sqrt{a}$

7. The base area of a cylindrical water tank is $(3\sqrt{5} - 2)$ m². What height would be necessary for the tank to contain a volume of 80 m³? Express your answer as a radical.

4·9 Radical Equations

An equation, where the variable is part of the radicand, is a **radical equation**. You will be asked to solve three types of radical equations: an equation with one radical, an equation with two like radicals, and an equation with two unlike radicals.

Example 1

Solve. $\sqrt{x} - 4 = 0$

As is the case when solving any equation, isolate the variable using known algebraic properties.

$$\sqrt{x} - 4 = 0$$
$$\sqrt{x} = 4$$
$$(\sqrt{x})^2 = 4^2 \quad \text{Square both sides once the radical has been isolated}$$
$$x = 16$$

Using the **original** equation, $x = 16$ can be verified.
$$\sqrt{16} - 4 = 0$$
$$4 - 4 = 0$$

Verification of an answer is an important step in the solution of a radical equation. Because of the "squaring" step that is necessary, some roots that do not satisfy the equation (**extraneous roots**), may appear. Extraneous roots can be identified when the value(s) of the variables are substituted into the original equation.

Example 2

The area of a square is x cm², while the length of one side of an equilateral triangle is $\sqrt{x}$ cm. The perimeter of the triangle plus 8 cm is equal to the side of the square plus 12 cm. Calculate the perimeter of the triangle.

Understand the Problem

The given information is summarized on the diagrams.

The side length of the square is $\sqrt{x}$ cm and the length of one side of the triangle is $\sqrt{x}$ cm.

Develop a Plan

Since we must solve for x, set up an equation using the perimeter of the triangle and the length of one side of the square.

Carry Out the Plan
$$3\sqrt{x} + 8 = \sqrt{x} + 12$$
$$2\sqrt{x} = 4$$
$$\sqrt{x} = 2$$
$$(\sqrt{x})^2 = (2)^2$$
$$x = 4$$

Look Back

If $x = 4$, then the left side of the equation becomes 14 and the right side becomes 14. Since both sides of the equation are equal, the solution is verified.

Example 3

Solve for x. $\sqrt{3x+1} + 2\sqrt{x} = 0$

$$\sqrt{3x+1} = -2\sqrt{x}$$
$$(\sqrt{3x+1})^2 = (-2\sqrt{x})^2$$

> Square the number not in the radical as well as the radical.

$$3x + 1 = 4x$$
$$1 = x$$

Substituting $x = 1$ into the original equation will give a value on the left side of 4. Since this does not equal zero, the root is extraneous and there is no solution.

The process of isolating the radical and squaring both sides of the equation may have to be repeated more than once before all radicals have been "removed" from the equation.

Example 4

Solve. $\sqrt{2x+9} - \sqrt{x+1} = 2$

When the sum or difference of two radicals equals a nonzero number, it is often easier to isolate the more complicated radical first.

$$\sqrt{2x+9} - \sqrt{x+1} = 2$$
$$\sqrt{2x+9} = 2 + \sqrt{x+1}$$
$$(\sqrt{2x+9})^2 = (2 + \sqrt{x+1})^2$$
$$2x + 9 = 4 + 4\sqrt{x+1} + (x+1)$$
$$2x - x + 9 - 4 - 1 = 4\sqrt{x+1}$$

> Isolate the radical term again.

$$x + 4 = 4\sqrt{x+1}$$
$$(x+4)^2 = (4\sqrt{x+1})^2$$
$$x^2 + 8x + 16 = 16(x+1)$$
$$x^2 - 8x = 0$$
$$x(x-8) = 0$$
$$\therefore x = 8, \text{ or } x = 0$$

As always, verify the solution by substituting into the original equation.

For $x = 0$;

$$\sqrt{2(0)+9} - \sqrt{0+1} = 2$$
$$\sqrt{9} - \sqrt{1} = 2$$
$$2 = 2$$

For $x = 8$;

$$\sqrt{2(8)+9} - \sqrt{8+1} = 2$$
$$\sqrt{25} - \sqrt{9} = 2$$
$$2 = 2$$

Since the equality holds for both $x = 0$ and $x = 8$, they are both solutions to the equation.

Exercises

1. A.T., the "Mathematics Wizard", stated that "no matter what value for x is found for a radical equation, it must be verified." Is A.T. correct? Explain.

2. The solutions to $x - 2 = \sqrt{x-1} + 1$ are found to be $x = 5$ and $x = 2$.

a. Substitute both values into the equation.

b. Which solution is a root of the equation?

c. The other solution is an extraneous root. In your own words, explain the term "extraneous root".

107

3. Solve.

a. $\sqrt{x} = 5$ **b.** $\sqrt{x} = -6$

c. $\sqrt{x} = 3$ **d.** $\sqrt{x} - 5 = 2$

e. $\sqrt{x} + 2 = -5$ **f.** $\sqrt{x} - 7 = 8$

4. Explain why there is no real solution for the equation $\sqrt{x} = -5$.

5. Expand by removing the brackets.

a. $(\sqrt{x} + 3)^2$ **b.** $(x - 5)^2$

c. $(a + 1)^2$ **d.** $(\sqrt{x^2 + 6x + 9})^2$

e. $(\sqrt{x + 6} - 3)^2$ **f.** $(7 - \sqrt{2 - x})^2$

6. Find the solution.

a. $\sqrt{x + 3} = 5$ **b.** $\sqrt{y - 9} = -2$

c. $7 = \sqrt{x + 8}$ **d.** $\sqrt{y - 3} = 1$

e. $\sqrt{x + 8} = 1$ **f.** $\sqrt{x + 10} = -3$

7. Is there a solution for the equation $\sqrt{x - 7} = \sqrt{x - 5}$? Explain.

8. Use a dictionary to determine the meaning of the word "extraneous".

a. Which meaning best fits the use of the word in this section?

b. Compare the definition to your definition in Exercise 2.

9. Solve.

a. $\sqrt{7 - 2x} = \sqrt{x + 3}$ **b.** $\sqrt{3x - 5} = \sqrt{x + 7}$

c. $\sqrt{2x + 3} = \sqrt{5x + 7}$ **d.** $\sqrt{4x - 1} = \sqrt{2x + 7}$

10. Solve.

a. $\sqrt{3x - 5} = \sqrt{3x + 7}$

b. $3\sqrt{x} - 5 = 7\sqrt{x} - 13$

c. $x\sqrt{16} + 7\sqrt{9} = x\sqrt{64} - 3$

11. The square root of three times a number is 18. Find the number.

12. Find the hypotenuse of a right triangle if the two sides measure $(6 - \sqrt{5})$ cm and $(6 + \sqrt{5})$ cm respectively.

13. The area of a circle is given by the equation $A = \pi r^2$.

a. Solve for r in terms of A.

b. If $A = 150$ cm², then find the radius of the circle.

14. The distance, s, travelled by a free-falling body is determined by the equation $s = \frac{1}{2}gt^2$.

a. Solve this equation for the time, t, in terms of s.

b. If $g = 9.8$ m/s² and $s = 490$ m, then calculate the time elapsed.

15. The formula $t = 2\sqrt{\dfrac{d^3}{216}}$ gives the duration of a hurricane or tornado where t is the time in hours and d is the diameter of the storm in kilometres.

a. Solve the formula for d in terms of t.

b. If a hurricane lasts 30 min, what is the diameter of the storm?

16. Solve.

a. $\sqrt{x} + 7 = 12 - 2\sqrt{x}$

b. $3\sqrt{x} - 1 = \sqrt{x} + 7$

c. $10 - \sqrt{x} = 5\sqrt{x} + 1$

d. $3 + 7\sqrt{x} = 12\sqrt{x} - 12$

e. $18 - 12\sqrt{x} = 6\sqrt{x} + 12$

f. $2\sqrt{x} - 1 = 9\sqrt{x} + 15$

17. Solve.

a. $\sqrt{x + 4} = 1 + \sqrt{x - 1}$

b. $\sqrt{x} - \sqrt{2x} = 5$

c. $\sqrt{2x^2 - 7} = 5$

d. $\sqrt{3x - 2} - \sqrt{2x - 3} = 1$

e. $\sqrt{2x + 5} - \sqrt{x - 2} = 3$

f. $\sqrt{2x^2 - 49} = x$

18. The difference in lengths of the hypotenuses in these right triangles is 1 cm. Calculate the dimensions of each triangle.

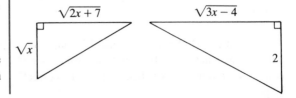

4·10 Applications

The Toronto Parks Commission decided to build a circular pool in Rennie Park. The pool will cover an area of 5000 m², and due to the number of people that will use it, they decided to put a 20 m cement walkway around the pool. The commissioners needed to know how much additional area the walkway will take up.

A mathematics student was hired to help with the problem. She drew this diagram and proceeded to find the radius of the pool, the total area taken by the pool and the walkway, and then the area of the walkway.

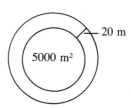

1. Find the radius of the pool. $A = \pi r^2$

$r = \sqrt{\dfrac{A}{\pi}}$

$\doteq 40$

The pool has a radius of about 40 m.

2. Find the area of the pool and walkway.

$A = \pi(r + 20)^2$

$\doteq \pi(40 + 20)^2$

$\doteq 11\ 304$

The total area is about 11 304 m².

3. Find the total area of the walkway.

Walkway Area = Total Area − Pool Area

$\doteq 6304$

The area of the walkway will be about 6304 m².

Exercises

1. The velocity of a projectile fired at a 45° angle is given by the equation $V = \sqrt{Sg}$, where S is the range or the distance the projectile is fired, V is the velocity, and $g = 9.8$ m/s².
a. Solve for S.
b. Calculate S if $V = 2500$ m/s.

2. The duration, t, measured in hours, of a hurricane or tornado is given by $t = 2\sqrt{\dfrac{d^3}{216}}$, where d is the diameter of the storm measured in kilometres.
a. Solve the formula for d.
b. Calculate the diameter of a tornado that lasts 8 min.

3. The period of a pendulum is given by the formula $T = 2\pi\sqrt{\dfrac{\ell}{g}}$, where $g = 9.8$ m/s² and ℓ is the length of the pendulum measured in metres.
a. Find an equation for ℓ.
b. Calculate ℓ if T is 2 s.

4. The speed at which a car is moving when it starts to skid can be determined by the length of the skid mark and the coefficient of friction of the road. The formula used is $s = \sqrt{254df}$, where s is the speed in kilometres per hour, d is the length of the skid mark in metres, and f is the coefficient of friction for the road. How long will a skid mark be if the coefficient of friction on the road is 0.8 and the car is travelling at 55 km/h?

5. On a clear day, from a height of h metres, a person can see a distance d, measured in metres, to the horizon according to the formula $d = \sqrt{13h}$.
a. Find an equation for h.
b. At what height can one see a distance of 12 km?

6. The time, t, to fall a distance, d, is given by the equation $t = \sqrt{\dfrac{2d}{g}}$. How far can an object fall in 20 s?

4·11 Rational Exponents

The laws of exponents can be extended to include rational number exponents. Exponents that are rational have a special meaning that is consistent with our understanding of rational numbers.

Example 1

a. $(\sqrt{5})(\sqrt{5})$

$(\sqrt{5})(\sqrt{5}) = 5$

b. $(5^{\frac{1}{2}})(5^{\frac{1}{2}})$

$$(5^{\frac{1}{2}})(5^{\frac{1}{2}}) = 5^{\frac{1}{2}+\frac{1}{2}}$$
$$= 5^1$$

Since both products have the same answer, $\sqrt{5} = 5^{\frac{1}{2}}$.

Example 2

Evaluate.

a. $(5^{\frac{2}{3}})(5^{\frac{2}{3}})(5^{\frac{2}{3}})$

$$(5^{\frac{2}{3}})(5^{\frac{2}{3}})(5^{\frac{2}{3}}) = 5^{\frac{2}{3}+\frac{2}{3}+\frac{2}{3}}$$
$$= 5^2$$
$$= 25$$

b. $(\sqrt[3]{25})(\sqrt[3]{25})(\sqrt[3]{25})$

$$(\sqrt[3]{25})(\sqrt[3]{25})(\sqrt[3]{25}) = \sqrt[3]{(25)(25)(25)}$$
$$= \sqrt[3]{15\ 625}$$
$$= 25$$

Therefore, $5^{\frac{2}{3}}$ is the same as $\sqrt[3]{25}$, $\sqrt[3]{5^2}$, or $(\sqrt[3]{5})^2$.

$$\boxed{x^{\frac{a}{b}} = \sqrt[b]{x^a} = (\sqrt[b]{x})^a, \text{ where } x \geq 0 \text{ if } b \text{ is even, } b \neq 0, \text{ and } a \text{ and } b \text{ are integers.}}$$

Example 3

Evaluate.
a. $16^{\frac{3}{4}}$

$$16^{\frac{3}{4}} = (\sqrt[4]{16})^3$$
$$= (2)^3$$
$$= 8$$

b. $(-27^5)^{\frac{1}{3}}$

$$(-27^5)^{\frac{1}{3}} = (-27^{\frac{1}{3}})^5$$
$$= (-3)^5$$
$$= -243$$

Generally, $25^{\frac{1}{2}}$ is referred to as the **principal root** of 25. It is important that the principal root is taken when working with many problems. Also, note that the laws of exponents that are true for integral exponents are true for rational exponents.

Example 4

Find the current, I, in amperes, running through a hair dryer requiring 1200 W of power, P, and having a resistance, R, of 90 Ω using the formula $I = \sqrt{\dfrac{P}{R}}$.

$$I = \left(\frac{P}{R}\right)^{0.5}$$

$0.5 = \dfrac{1}{2}$ and indicates the principal root.

$$= \left(\frac{1200}{90}\right)^{0.5}$$
$$\doteq 3.65$$

Therefore, the current is approximately 3.65 A.

Exercises

1. Write in radical form.

a. $5^{\frac{1}{2}}$ **b.** $15^{\frac{1}{4}}$

c. $259^{\frac{1}{6}}$ **d.** $12^{\frac{1}{3}}$

e. $100^{\frac{1}{5}}$ **f.** $1000^{\frac{1}{2}}$

2. Write in radical form.

a. $x^{\frac{3}{2}}$ **b.** $(-y)^{\frac{4}{3}}$

c. $56^{\frac{3}{5}}$ **d.** $m^{\frac{5}{6}}$

e. $p^{\frac{5}{2}}$ **f.** $(-111)^{\frac{7}{3}}$

3. Write in exponential form.

a. $\sqrt{3^4}$ **b.** $\sqrt[3]{9^2}$ **c.** $\sqrt[3]{-9^2}$

d. $(\sqrt[5]{y})^3$ **e.** $\sqrt[4]{xy}$ **f.** $(\sqrt[3]{xy^2})^2$

4. Explain why x must be positive or zero when b is an even number in $\sqrt[b]{x}$, but can be either positive, negative, or zero when b is odd.

5. Evaluate. Use a calculator if one is available. The first one is done for you.

$-125^{\frac{1}{3}}$

$125 \boxed{+/-} \boxed{y^x} \boxed{(\!(} 1 \boxed{\div} 3 \boxed{)\!)} \boxed{=} -5$

a. $8^{\frac{1}{3}}$ **b.** $256^{\frac{1}{8}}$

c. $(-27)^{\frac{1}{3}}$ **d.** $25^{\frac{1}{2}}$

e. $16^{\frac{1}{4}}$ **f.** $64^{\frac{1}{6}}$

6. Evaluate.

a. $8^{\frac{2}{3}}$ **b.** $256^{\frac{5}{8}}$

c. $27^{\frac{5}{3}}$ **d.** $64^{-\frac{5}{6}}$

e. $16^{\frac{3}{4}}$ **f.** $81^{0.25}$

g. $(-8)^{\frac{2}{3}}$ **h.** $(-8)^{-\frac{2}{3}}$

i. $625^{0.75}$ **j.** $16^{0.75}$

7. An experiment began with 500 kg of a radioactive substance. It disintegrated almost entirely over a period of 14 d. The half-life of the substance was found to be 2 d. Calculate the mass of the substance after 8 d using the formula $x = x_o(2^{-\frac{t}{H}})$, where x is the mass remaining after time t, x_o is the initial amount, and H is the half-life of the substance.

8. A culture initially containing 3000 bacteria doubles every 3 h. Find the number of bacteria in the culture after 24 h. Use the formula $n = n_o(2^{\frac{t}{D}})$, where n is the number after time t, n_o is the initial number of bacteria, and D is the doubling period.

9. After a period of 4 d, $\frac{1}{16}$ of a quantity of radioactive matter remains. Calculate the half-life of this radioactive matter. (*Hint*: Use the formula of Exercise 7.)

10. Simplify.

a. $(a^{-6}b^3)^{-\frac{2}{3}}$ **b.** $(-27p^6)^{\frac{5}{3}}$

c. $(x^6y^{-4})^{-\frac{1}{2}}$ **d.** $(k^{\frac{3}{4}})^{\frac{1}{3}}$

11. Evaluate.

a. $\left(\frac{4}{9}\right)^{\frac{1}{2}}$ **b.** $\left(\frac{27}{8}\right)^{-\frac{2}{3}}$

c. $\left(\frac{100}{9}\right)^{-\frac{5}{2}}$ **d.** $\left(\frac{-32}{243}\right)^{\frac{3}{5}}$

12. Different calculators require different keying sequences to evaluate expressions such as $8^{\frac{2}{3}}$. Experiment with several types and record the keying sequence for each.

13. Between 14:00 and 16:00, a bacteria population triples. When will the population be 27 times what it was at 14:00?

14. A certain radioactive substance has a half-life of 54 h. How long does it take for 75% of the radioactivity to dissipate?

Brainticker

Karim must travel from Elmira to Oakville but must meet his friend Pierre somewhere on the road between Waterloo and Guelph. Find the shortest distance Karim can travel.

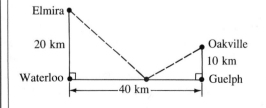

4·12 Applications

The laws of exponents can be applied to a variety of equations relating to both business and science. One of the more common applications is the Guaranteed Investment Certificate. It offers a compound interest rate if money is left on deposit for a specified period of time.

Example

The Saskatoon Trust Company offers an annual rate of interest of 9.75%, compounded semiannually, for $25 000 investments left on deposit five years. A local bank offers a simple annual interest rate of 10.25% on the same $25 000 and does not require that the money be left on deposit for five years. Which is the best investment for $25 000?

Understand the Problem

The trust company offers a semiannual compound rate of 9.75% on a $25 000 investment for five years. The bank offers a higher interest rate of 10.25%/a; however, it is a simple interest which is not compounded. It does not require the money to be left for five years. Which is the better investment?

Develop a Plan

The compound-interest formula is $A = P(1 + i)^n$. For simple-interest investments, the amount, A, is found using the formula $A = p + I$, where $I = prt$. In this case, I is the total interest, r is the rate of interest payable, and t is the length of time the investment is left. Calculate each to find the best rate of return.

Carry Out the Plan

For compound interest:
$$A = P(1 + i)^n$$
$$= 25\ 000(1 + 0.048\ 75)^{10}$$
$$= 40\ 240.16$$

The compound-interest rate would yield approximately $40 240.16 over the five years.

For simple interest:
$$A = p + prt$$
$$= 25\ 000 + (25\ 000)(0.1025)(5)$$
$$= 37\ 812.50$$

The simple-interest rate would yield $37 812.50 over five years.

Look Back

If the investor has the opportunity to invest money for five years, the compound-interest rate would be preferable over the simple-interest rate as it produces a higher return. However, the money is tied up for five years and there may be a substantial penalty in interest paid if the money is withdrawn before the end of the period. The simple-interest rate investment allows the investor to retrieve the money at any time.

Exercises

1. For the example in the display, after what interest period would the compound-interest account have more money than the simple-interest account?

2. Joyce invests $10 000 at the rate of 10.5%/a compounded annually for a period of three years. What amount does she receive after three years?

3. A nonreflecting glass absorbs sunlight according to the formula $x = x_0(1 - 0.2)^n$, where x, measured in lumens, is the intensity of the light absorbed by the glass, x_0 is the original intensity of the light, and n is the number of sheets of nonreflecting glass. If the original intensity of light is 10 lm, then find the intensity of light absorbed by 4 sheets of glass.

4. Once a bacteria culture is established, the number of bacteria after t seconds is given by the formula $N = 1000\left(\frac{27}{10}\right)^t$. How many bacteria are present after 1 s? after 3 s?

5. Mothballs evaporate according to the formula $V_t = V_o\left(\frac{7}{5}\right)^{-t}$, where t is the time measured in weeks, V_o is the initial volume, and V_t is the volume after t weeks. Find the volume remaining after 4 weeks if the initial volume of mothballs is 4 cm³.

6. Show that the area of the semicircle on the hypotenuse of a right triangle equals the sum of the areas of the semicircles on the other two sides.

7. If the population of the world increases at the rate of 2%/a, we can calculate the expected population after n years using the formula $P_t = P_o(1 + 0.02)^t$, where P_t is the population in the future, P_o is the original population, and t is the number of years elapsed. If the population in 1988 was 4 500 000 000, find the expected population in the year 2000.

8. Jerry's new car costs $17 600, but it depreciates a certain percent every year. Its resale value after n years is given by the expression $17\ 600\left(1 - \frac{1}{5}\right)^n$. Find the car's value after three years.

9. To determine how long an amount of money must be invested, when interest is paid yearly at a compound rate, we can use the rule of 72. This rule states that the time to double, in years, is calculated using the expression $\frac{72}{\text{Interest Rate}}$.

a. Using several different interest rates, verify the rule of 72.

b. A.T., the "Mathematics Wizard", stated that this rule could help justify the $40 240.16 found in the example in the display. Is A.T. correct? Explain.

10. Find a number, which, when added to $15\frac{1}{2}$ gives $3\frac{1}{2}$.

11. In five years, James wishes to have $20 000 as a down payment on a house. How much should he invest now if his investment has an interest rate of 10%/a compounded semiannually?

12. Gina invests her money at an interest rate of 9%/a compounded monthly. How long must she wait for her money to triple? (*Hint:* Find n from the formula $A = P(1 + i)^n$, where $\frac{A}{P} = 3$.)

13. The population of Canada has been increasing at a steady rate of 2%/a. If the population in 1988 was 25 000 000, what was the population 10 a earlier?

14. Ralph invests the $10 000 legacy left by his grandfather in a guaranteed account which compounds interest yearly at 8%. He plans to leave the money there until he finishes high school and university in 5 a time. What amount can he withdraw after 5 a?

Braintickler

If $3 \bullet 6 \bullet 12 = 12$,
$2 \bullet 5 \bullet 12 = 60$, and
$6 \bullet 7 \bullet 14 = 42$, then find
$5 \bullet 2 \bullet \ \ 7$.

4·13 Variable Exponents

Equations that contain exponents do not always readily appear to have an answer. For example, the solution to $3^x = 27$ can be found using the process of trial and error and you will find that x equals 3. However, this process may not be successful for equations like $2^x = \frac{1}{128}$. For such equations, note that both sides of the equation can be written as powers of the same base and then the exponents equated.

$$2^x = \frac{1}{128}$$
$$= \frac{1}{2^7}$$
$$= 2^{-7}$$
$$x = -7$$

Equate the exponents when the powers are written using the same base.

Therefore, the value of the exponent is -7.

Example 1

Solve. $64^{-y} = 2$
$$(2^6)^{-y} = 2$$
$$2^{-6y} = 2^1$$
$$-6y = 1$$
$$y = -\frac{1}{6}$$

Why does $-6y = 1$?

Example 2

Solve. $4^{x+3} = 16^{2x}$
$$4^{x+3} = (4^2)^{2x}$$
$$= 4^{4x}$$
$$x + 3 = 4x$$
$$x = 1$$

Why does $x + 3 = 4x$?

The solution can be verified by substituting the value of the variable into the original equation. In Example 2, substituting $x = 1$ into $4^{x+3} = 16^{2x}$ will give $4^4 = 16^2$. Since both sides of this equation equal 256, the solution is verified.

Example 3

The students at Fowler High School made a snow sculpture for the winter carnival competition. In warm sunshine, the sculpture will melt to $\frac{1}{256}$ of its original mass in 24 h. If the judging starts 3 h after the sculpture is completed, how much of the sculpture will remain if it melts at a rate of $(2)^{-\frac{24}{H}}$, where H is the time for half of the sculpture to melt?

Understand the Problem
Solve for H to find the half-life of the snow sculpture using the fact that only $\frac{1}{256}$ of it remains after 24 h.

Develop a Plan
$\frac{1}{256} = 2^{-\frac{24}{H}}$ is the equation to be solved. Since 256 can be written with a base of 2, both sides of the equation can be related and a solution found for H.

Carry Out the Plan
$$2^{-8} = 2^{-\frac{24}{H}}$$
$$-8 = -\frac{24}{H}$$
$$3 = H$$

Look Back
Since the half-life of the sculpture is 3 h, only half of the sculpture will remain when the judging starts.

Exercises

1. Solve.

a. $2^x = 2^5$

b. $3^x = 3^7$

c. $7^{\frac{3}{4}} = 7^x$

d. $\left(\frac{2}{3}\right)^9 = \left(\frac{2}{3}\right)^x$

e. $9^x = 9^0$

f. $8^x = 8^{-4}$

g. $\left(\frac{1}{2}\right)^x = \left(\frac{1}{2}\right)^{-5}$

h. $2^{x+3} = 2^4$

i. $5^{2x+1} = 5^3$

j. $3^{5x-1} = 81$

2. Copy and complete the solution for x.

$\left(\frac{4}{7}\right)^x = \frac{343}{64}$

$\quad = \left(\frac{7}{4}\right)^{\blacksquare}$

$\quad = \left(\frac{4}{7}\right)^{-\blacksquare}$ Why?

$\left(\frac{4}{7}\right)^x = \left(\frac{4}{7}\right)^{-\blacksquare}$

$\therefore x = -\blacksquare.$

3. Solve. Verify your solution.

a. $2^x = 8$

b. $3^x = 81$

c. $\left(\frac{1}{2}\right)^x = \frac{1}{16}$

d. $\left(\frac{2}{3}\right)^x = \frac{8}{27}$

e. $7^x = 49$

f. $5^x = \frac{1}{5}$

g. $15^x = 1$

h. $6^x = \frac{1}{216}$

i. $\left(\frac{1}{3}\right)^x = \frac{1}{27}$

j. $\left(\frac{1}{49}\right) = 7^x$

k. $2^x = \frac{1}{64}$

l. $7^x = \frac{1}{343}$

4. The doubling period of a bacteria is 6 h. How much time is required for the number of bacteria to increase to 512 times the original number?

5. Scientists at the Chalk River nuclear testing facility found that after 45 d a radioactive material had decomposed to $\frac{1}{1024}$ of its original mass. Calculate the half-life of this substance.

6. Let p represent any prime number that is greater than 3.

a. Select four different prime numbers and square them.

b. Divide each of the products by 12.

c. What is the remainder for each division in part b?

d. What conclusion can you make?

7. A ball bounces and returns to 70% of its previous height with each bounce. If dropped initially from a height of 100 m, the formula to represent the height on the nth bounce is $x = 100(1 - 0.3)^n$. Which bounce returns the ball to a height of 24.01 m? (*Hint*: Use trial and error as a problem-solving method.)

8. Solve. Verify your solution.

a. $4^{x-2} = 8$

b. $2^{2d+1} = 8$

c. $8^{5a-2} = 64$

d. $27^{2f-1} = 9$

e. $3^{5-k} = 9^{-1}$

f. $3^{12} = 81^{2m+3}$

g. $5^{p-3} = 1$

h. $\left(\frac{1}{2}\right)^y = 0.125$

i. $\left(\frac{1}{4}\right)^{2+n} = \left(\frac{1}{8}\right)^{n-1}$

j. $32^{\frac{r}{5}} = 4^{-1}$

k. $\left(\frac{2}{3}\right)^d = \frac{27}{8}$

l. $16^{-h} = 2$

9. Describe the set of all possible solutions for x in the equation $1^x = 1$.

10. Solve.

a. $\left(\frac{2}{3}\right)^x = \frac{9}{4}$

b. $\left(\frac{5}{8}\right)^y = \frac{25}{64}$

c. $\left(\frac{25}{64}\right)^h = \frac{5}{8}$

d. $\left(\frac{49}{81}\right)^d = \frac{9}{7}$

e. $\left(\frac{27}{64}\right)^x = \frac{3}{4}$

f. $\left(\frac{125}{343}\right)^k = 1$

g. $\left(\frac{625}{1000}\right)^a = 1$

h. $81^{-m} = 3$

i. $32^{-c} = 2$

j. $27^{-p} = 3$

11. An investment of $5000 is made in the stock of a company that loses its value at a rate of 26% compounded monthly. At this rate, how long will it take for the original investment to be worth only $500? Use a calculator if one is available.

12. A certain radioactive substance has a half-life of 60 d. How long will it take for the substance to decompose to approximately 0.1% of its original mass?

13. If money can be invested at 9.5%/a compounded quarterly, then how long would it take an investment to double?

4·14 Computer Application— Exponential Equations

Computers can be used to evaluate exponential expressions and equations. Finding the unknown variable in an exponential equation also can be done on a computer using a table of values. Finding the solution to $5.2^x = 731.1616$ can be difficult because a common base is not readily apparent. This program will evaluate the expression 5.2^x for various integral values of x and display the results on the screen. You will have to scan the output to find the value for x that makes the equation true. The program will check values between 1 and 20 because 5.2^1 is less than 731 and 5.2^{20} is greater than 731. For these types of programs, it is important that the user estimate the range for the variable before writing the program.

```
10  REM A PROGRAM TO EVALUATE THE EXPRESSION 5.2 ∧ X
20  PRINT "X", "5.2 ∧ X ="
30  FOR X = 1 TO 20
40  LET ANS = 5.2 ∧ X
50  PRINT X, ANS
60  NEXT X
70  END
```

Exercises

1. Run the program in the display and record the output. What is the value of x in the expression $5.2^x = 731.1616$?

2. What is the purpose of lines 30 through 60 of the program in the display?

3. Modify the program in the display to find the value of these equations. All equations have integral solutions. Estimate an answer before writing the program.

a. $3^x = 243$ **b.** $5^x = 3125$
c. $9^x = 1$ **d.** $4^x = 0.25$
e. $5^x = 0.04$ **f.** $0.3^x = 0.000\ 729$
g. $3.2^x = 0.3125$ **h.** $1.7^x = 24.137\ 569$

4. If the value of x in an equation is known to be correct to one decimal place, then how could the program be modified to check values of x correct to one decimal place?

5. Modify the program in the display as in Exercise 4. Use the modified program to solve for the variable in these equations. All answers are known to be correct to one decimal place.

a. $4^x = 8$ **b.** $32^x = 2048$
c. $32^x = 2$ **d.** $16^x = 12\ 416.75$
e. $25^x = 78\ 125$ **f.** $0.25^x = 0.125$
g. $81^x = 59\ 049$ **h.** $161\ 051^x = 11$

6. A radar gun is a kind of computer used by the police to determine how fast a car is moving.
a. Use the library to learn more about the accuracy of this type of computer.
b. Write a short essay on the use of the radar gun in traffic-court evidence.

7. The doubling period for a bacteria culture is known to be 10 h. Write a program to find how long it will take for the culture to be 100 times its original number. (*Hint*: $n = n_0 2^{\frac{t}{b}}$.)

4·15 Chapter Review

1. Identify the numbers as belonging to the set of rational (Q) or irrational numbers ($\bar{Q}$).
a. $\sqrt{13}$　　　　　　　**b.** 0.121 211 12 ...
c. $\sqrt{36}$　　　　　　　**d.** 6.923 692 269 ...

2. Express in decimal form. State the period and the length of the period.
a. $\frac{2}{7}$　　　**b.** $\frac{13}{15}$　　　**c.** $\frac{-5}{8}$

3. Express in fractional form.
a. 5.623　　**b.** $0.\overline{71}$　　**c.** $3.\dot{2}$　　　**d.** $0.5\dot{3}$

4. Illustrate each with an example.
a. the distributive property of multiplication over addition
b. the transitive property of order

5. Simplify by performing the indicated operations.
a. $\dfrac{2^{5x} \times 2^{3x-1} \times 2^5}{2^{4x}}$　　　**b.** $\dfrac{3 \times 9 \times 81}{27^2}$

6. Evaluate the expression $a^b + b^c + c^a$ if $a = 2$, $b = 1$, and $c = 3$.

7. Simplify. Express your answer with positive exponents only.
a. $(x^5)(x^8)$　　　　　　**b.** $y^9 \div y^{12}$
c. $(m^7)^3$　　　　　　　**d.** $(pq)^5$
e. $\left(\dfrac{r}{t}\right)^8$　　　　　　**f.** $(2x^3y^2)^0$
g. $(3x^2)(-2x^{-3})$　　　**h.** $12x^3y^2 \div 36x^5y$
i. $(5a^3b^2)^3$　　　　　**j.** $\left(\dfrac{25c^5d^2}{15c^6d^7}\right)^{-1}$
k. $(64a^{12}b^6)^{\frac{1}{6}}$　　　**l.** $(a^{\frac{1}{3}}b^{\frac{1}{4}})^{-12}$

8. Evaluate. Use a calculator if one is available.
a. $27^{\frac{1}{3}}$　　**b.** 5^0　　　**c.** $81^{\frac{1}{4}}$
d. $64^{\frac{1}{3}}$　　**e.** $8^{\frac{2}{3}}$　　　**f.** 2^{-1}
g. 5^{-3}　　**h.** $16^{\frac{-3}{4}}$　　**i.** $4^{\frac{3}{2}}$

9. Evaluate.
a. $(1.075)^3$　　　　　　**b.** $(1.015)^{-12}$
c. $(0.52)^{\frac{1}{8}}$　　　　　　**d.** $7^{\frac{1}{3}}$
e. $2^{\frac{3}{5}}$　　　　　　　　**f.** $5^{\frac{5}{6}}$

10. Solve. Verify the solution.
a. $\sqrt{x+1} = 9$　　　　**b.** $\sqrt{x-3} - 8 = 10$
c. $\sqrt{5x^2 - 48} = x$　　　**d.** $7\sqrt{x} + 5 = 2\sqrt{x} + 9$
e. $\sqrt{4x-5} - \sqrt{2x-6} = 3$

11. A population of seagulls is increasing according to the formula $n = 40(2^{\frac{t}{0.5}})$, where n is the number after t years. Find the population after a period of 4 a.

12. What investment must one make today, at an interest rate of 9.75%/a compounded semi-annually, to obtain an accumulated amount of $5000 after a period of 3 a? (*Hint:* Use the formula $P = A(1 + i)^{-n}$.)

13. Express as a mixed radical in simplest form.
a. $\sqrt{18}$　　　　**b.** $5\sqrt{32}$　　　　**c.** $7\sqrt{300}$
d. $\sqrt{x^2y^4}$　　　**e.** $\sqrt[3]{n^3m^5}$　　　**f.** $\sqrt[3]{27x^4y^6}$

14. Add or subtract.
a. $5\sqrt[4]{3} + 7\sqrt[4]{3} - 2\sqrt[4]{3}$
b. $12 - 6\sqrt{7} + 2\sqrt{7}$
c. $\sqrt{12} + \sqrt{18} + \sqrt{24}$
d. $2\sqrt{8} + 5\sqrt{32}$
e. $-3\sqrt{45} + 6\sqrt{20} - \sqrt{5}$
f. $\frac{1}{3}\sqrt{63} - \frac{3}{2}\sqrt{28} + \sqrt{52}$
g. $5\sqrt[3]{x} + 7\sqrt[3]{x} - \sqrt{x}$
h. $2x\sqrt{x^3y^5} + 3\sqrt{x^5y^5}$

15. Multiply.
a. $\sqrt{3}(\sqrt{7} - 2\sqrt{3})$　　　**b.** $7\sqrt{5}(3\sqrt{5} + 8)$
c. $(2\sqrt{6} + 7)(2\sqrt{6} - 3)$　　**d.** $(5\sqrt{7} + 3\sqrt{21})^2$

16. Multiply each by its conjugate.
a. $\sqrt{11} - \sqrt{5}$　　　　**b.** $3\sqrt{2} + 4\sqrt{3}$

17. Rationalize the denominator.
a. $\dfrac{3\sqrt{5}}{7\sqrt{15}}$　　　　　**b.** $\dfrac{2\sqrt{7} + 4\sqrt{2}}{3\sqrt{14}}$
c. $\dfrac{6\sqrt{6}}{4\sqrt{7} + 5}$　　　　**d.** $\dfrac{5\sqrt{3} + 3\sqrt{7}}{5\sqrt{3} - 2\sqrt{7}}$

117

4·16 Chapter Test

1. Identify the numbers as rational (Q) or irrational numbers ($\bar{Q}$).

a. $\sqrt{21}$ **b.** 0.1765

c. $0.123\ 412\ 341$ **d.** π

2. Calculate the decimal equivalent for each fraction, and state the period and length of period for each.

a. $\frac{5}{7}$ **b.** $\frac{6}{19}$ **c.** $\frac{1}{121}$

3. A burro walks 0.85 km on his first birthday. On the day after, he walks 0.005 km further; on the following day, he increases the distance by 0.0005 km, and continues this pattern each day. Calculate the total distance he walks in a day after many years.

4. Simplify. Express your answer with positive exponents only.

a. $(m^2)(m^9)$ **b.** $a^6 \div a^8$

c. $(m^3)^5$ **d.** $(3h)^3$

e. $\left(\frac{5}{p}\right)^4$ **f.** $(-17m^9n^2)^0$

g. $(7k^7)(13k^8)^2$ **h.** $48f^{-2}g^6 \div 8f^3k^2$

i. $(6r^4s^7)^3$ **j.** $\left(\frac{30w^8x^3}{10w^4x^5}\right)^{-3}$

k. $(81m^{12}n^8)^{\frac{1}{4}}$ **l.** $(2^{\frac{1}{3}}p^{\frac{1}{5}})^{-15}$

5. Evaluate the expression $x^y - y^w + (xyw)^x$ if $x = 3$, $y = 2$, and $w = 0$.

6. Evaluate. Use a calculator if one is available.

a. $(1.025)^5$ **b.** $(1.085)^{-25}$

c. $(0.45)^{\frac{1}{6}}$ **d.** $6^{\frac{3}{5}}$

7. Solve for x.

a. $3^x = 243$ **b.** $2^{x+3} = 64$ **c.** $\left(\frac{1}{5}\right)^x = 625$

8. Evaluate.

a. $125^{\frac{1}{3}}$ **b.** 23^0 **c.** $16^{\frac{1}{4}}$

d. $27^{\frac{2}{3}}$ **e.** $8^{\frac{2}{3}}$ **f.** 5^{-1}

g. 6^{-3} **h.** $81^{\frac{-3}{4}}$ **i.** $9^{\frac{3}{2}}$

9. Solve. Verify the solution.

a. $\sqrt{a+1} + 9 = 12$ **b.** $\sqrt{x-3} = 18$

c. $\sqrt{3x^2 - 36} = x$ **d.** $8\sqrt{x} - 5 = 5\sqrt{x} + 2$

e. $2 - \sqrt{2x+10} - 2\sqrt{x+6} = 0$

10. The percent of colour left in a pair of blue jeans is determined by the formula $C_1 = C_0(1 - 0.05)^n$, where C_1 is the amount of colour after washing, C_0 is the original colour, and n is the number of washings. Calculate the percent of colour remaining after 20 washings.

11. Express as a mixed radical in simplest form.

a. $\sqrt{48}$ **b.** $3\sqrt{98}$ **c.** $\sqrt[3]{8a^5b^9}$

12. Determine whether $2\sqrt{5} - 3$ is a root of the equation $x^2 - 5x + 1 = 0$.

13. Add or subtract.

a. $2\sqrt{7} - 5\sqrt{7} + \sqrt{3}$ **b.** $\sqrt[3]{2} + 3\sqrt[3]{2} - 4\sqrt[3]{2}$

c. $\sqrt{32} - \sqrt{24} + \sqrt{44}$ **d.** $7\sqrt{27} + 4\sqrt{63}$

e. $-5\sqrt{75} + 6\sqrt{125} - 2\sqrt{3}$

f. $\frac{1}{2}\sqrt{72} - \frac{5}{7}\sqrt{98} + \sqrt{150}$

g. $3\sqrt{y} - 4\sqrt{y} + \sqrt[4]{x}$

h. $3a\sqrt{a^4b^7} + 3\sqrt{a^6b^7}$

14. Multiply.

a. $\sqrt{5}(\sqrt{6} - 7\sqrt{5})$ **b.** $3\sqrt{6}(3\sqrt{6} - 7)$

c. $(4\sqrt{3} + 7)(5\sqrt{3} - 2)$ **d.** $(8\sqrt{2} - 6\sqrt{15})^2$

15. Multiply by the smallest expression that will produce an integer.

a. $\sqrt{13} - \sqrt{12}$ **b.** $9\sqrt{3} - 7\sqrt{2}$

16. Express in simplest form by rationalizing the denominator.

a. $\frac{6\sqrt{2}}{3\sqrt{21}}$ **b.** $\frac{3\sqrt{6} - 2\sqrt{5}}{5\sqrt{30}}$

c. $\frac{2\sqrt{3}}{3\sqrt{5} - 7}$ **d.** $\frac{8\sqrt{5} + 6\sqrt{2}}{3\sqrt{5} - 2\sqrt{2}}$

DEDUCTIVE PROOF AND PLANE GEOMETRY

Tune Up

1. Illustrate with the aid of a diagram. Label and name each part of the diagram.
a. a point
b. a line
c. a plane
d. a line segment
e. a ray
f. two rays with a common endpoint

2. What is the minimum number of points needed to determine each?
a. a line
b. a plane
c. space

3. Define these terms.
a. complementary angles
b. supplementary angles
c. a linear pair of angles
d. congruent angles

4. Find the supplement of the angle.
a. $47°$
b. $75°$
c. $137°$
d. $99°$
e. $169°$
f. $a°$
g. $5x°$
h. $(25 + x)°$

5. Find the complement of the angle.
a. $37°$
b. $1°$
c. $85°$
d. $86°$
e. $53°$
f. $k°$
g. $2a°$
h. $(75 - 3x)°$

6. Draw and label a diagram to illustrate.
a. opposite rays
b. a half-line
c. a half-plane
d. two parallel lines

7. Give a classification of triangles according to the lengths of their sides.

8. Give a classification of triangles according to the size of their angles.

9. Solve the equation.
a. $(2x - 15) + (3x + 10) = 180$
b. $\dfrac{3x - 4}{2} = \dfrac{5x - 2}{3}$
c. $(4x - 7) + (3x - 5) = 3(4x - 9)$

10. Explain why redrawing the length of a line segment using compasses and a straightedge is more accurate than using just a ruler.

11. Draw and label a diagram to illustrate.
a. congruent triangles
b. similar triangles

12. Write a definition for each type of triangle with reference to its angles. Use a diagram to reinforce your definition.
a. an acute triangle
b. a right triangle
c. an obtuse triangle
d. an isosceles triangle
e. an oblique triangle
f. What do all triangles have in commmon?

13. A triangle has angles of $x°$, $3x + 20°$, and $2x - 20°$. Find the measure of each angle.

5·1 Introduction to Geometry

Geometry was originally developed as a process for measuring land area. Today, its meaning has been expanded to include the study of straight lines, circles, triangles, and other regular shapes.

The basis of geometry is postulates, theorems, and definitions. Before playing a game, a set of rules must be established that are accepted by anyone playing the game. Geometry has a similar set of rules or assumptions called **postulates** and they are accepted as true without proof. Postulates are the building stones of geometry. A **theorem**, on the other hand, must be proved before it is accepted as true. **Definitions** must mean the same thing to all who use them. Terms and definitions form the basis for any discussion of geometric principles, although not every term must be defined. Some, such as a point, line, and plane are understood intuitively. Some of these "intuitive" terms and definitions are shown.

Term	Picture	Symbol	Read as ...
Point	$\bullet B$	B	point B
Line	$M \quad N$	$\overleftrightarrow{MN}$	line MN
Segment	$X \quad Y$	$\overline{XY}$	segment XY
Ray	$K \quad R$	$\overrightarrow{KR}$	ray KR
Plane	β		plane β

Collinear points are on the same line, while **coplanar points** are in the same plane. **Congruent segments** have the same length and an **angle** is formed by two rays with a common endpoint. Other terms shall be defined as they are encountered throughout the chapter.

Various types of proofs will be discussed throughout the chapter. Writing a deductive proof is a form of problem solving and as such will follow the four basic steps used to solve any problem: Understand the Problem, Develop a Plan, Carry Out the Plan, and Look Back.

To **Understand the Problem**, it is important to understand the meaning of all the terms in the problem. Drawing and labelling diagrams, or using an existing diagram, can help in understanding the problem. You should also check for key words, restate the problem in your own words, identify any extraneous information, and know what has been given and what you are required to prove in this step.

Developing and **Carrying Out the Plan** are closely related. Using geometrical tools such as definitions, theorems, and postulates, as well as the algebraic properties you have studied in other grades, will help in developing and carrying out a plan to write a proof to a problem. To write a proof, recall strategies such as systematic trial, working backwards toward a solution, breaking the proof or the problem into parts, or dealing with a simpler problem.

Looking Back is necessary to check that you have proven correctly what was required. Also check if any facts could be used later or if another process could be used to complete the proof.

The chart shows how the four steps in the process are related. You may move back and forth among the four steps until the proof is discovered. If one plan doesn't work, don't be discouraged, but start over and develop a new plan. While carrying out the plan, you may have to check to see if you understand the problem. When looking back you should look back at all the steps.

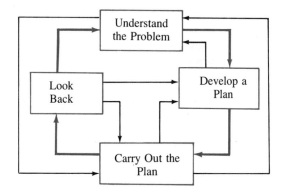

A deductive proof requires a series of statements in which each statement follows logically from the statements preceding it. Information will be given which is accepted as true and a conclusion must be reached. In general, a deductive proof begins with undefined terms, proceeds to defined terms, uses postulates that are accepted as true, and then draws conclusions.

Theorems and postulates are written in an "if ... then" form. For example, "If two points are given, then a line can be drawn through the points." The "if" is the **hypothesis** and is the given part of the statement, while the "then" is the **conclusion** and is the part of the statement **required** to be proven.

Example 1

State the hypothesis, the conclusion, and the given and required parts of this statement.
If students study each night, then they will receive high marks.

The hypothesis for the statement is, "if students study each night". This would also be the given part of the statement or what is accepted as true. The conclusion is, "they will receive high marks." This is what is required to be proven.

If a statement is not written in "if ... then" form, then it can be written in that form for easier use. For instance, the statement, "All parrots are birds", can be written as "If it is a parrot, then it is a bird."

Example 2

Write the statement in the "if ... then" form.
a. All Grade 11 students in Canada study mathematics.
b. The capital of British Columbia is Victoria.

a. If you are a Grade 11 student in Canada, then you will study mathematics.
b. If it is the capital of British Columbia, then it is Victoria.

Exercises

1. The terms "point", "line", and "plane" are terms in geometry.
a. In your own words, explain these terms.
b. Name some object which could be used as a physical representation of each of the three undefined terms in part **a.**

2. In your own words, define the terms "line segment" and "ray". Use diagrams if necessary to help with your explanations. Compare your definitions with those given in the glossary. Are they similar?

3. A ray and a half-line have different definitions.
a. State what you think the similarities and the differences between the two are.
b. Define half-line and ray using either the glossary to this text or a mathematics dictionary.
c. Predict a definition for a half-plane. Check your prediction with three others in your class to see if they agree with your definition.

4. Research the meaning of the word "postulate" using a dictionary. Does the dictionary definition agree with the definition given in the display?

5. Write each in the "if ... then" form.
a. All salmon are fish.
b. All Grade 11 students are brilliant mathematicians.
c. The sum of the measures of the angles of a triangle is 180°.
d. A person who lives in Dartmouth lives in Nova Scotia.
e. Anyone driving in Ontario must wear a seat belt.
f. Two parallel planes never meet.
g. The Sun never sets on the British Empire.
h. A person living in Saskatchewan knows how to drive in Waskesiu.
i. The 1988 Winter Olympics were held in Calgary.
j. A person who drives in North Bay drives in the snow.

6. State the hypothesis and conclusion of each "if ... then" statement.
a. If a school has good mathematics students, then it will win the mathematics competition.
b. If an angle is a right angle, then its measure is 90°.
c. If a figure is a square, then all its sides are congruent.
d. If you live in British Columbia, then you have seen the Rocky Mountains.
e. If you pass the final examination in the Grade 11 mathematics course, then you will study mathematics in Grade 12.
f. If you lived through the Depression, then you know the value of a dollar.

7. Write the given and required parts of each statement.
a. If a triangle is isosceles, then it has two congruent angles.
b. If two lines are parallel, then they will never intersect.
c. If a figure is a rectangle, then it has two congruent diagonals.
d. If there are six rows of five desks each in the classroom, then there are thirty desks in all in the classroom.

8. The area of an equilateral triangle is 20 cm². Find the perimeter of the triangle.

Using the Library

The Greek mathematician Euclid (about 330-275 B.C.) organized the concepts of geometry in his most famous work called *The Elements*. Modern plane geometry is based largely on the work of Euclid. In his book, Euclid described ten postulates. Five of these postulates were algebraic and the other five were geometric. Use the library to research Euclid's five postulates for geometry and summarize them in your own words.

5·2 Parallel Lines

Two lines are **parallel** if and only if they are in the same plane and never intersect. For example, railway tracks are in the same plane, never intersect, and can be extended indefinitely without ever crossing. The symbol for "is parallel to" is $\|$. We write $\ell_1 \| \ell_2$ for line 1 is parallel to line 2 or $\overleftrightarrow{AB} \| \overleftrightarrow{CD}$ for line AB is parallel to line CD.

A **transversal** is a line or line segment which intersects two or more lines at unique points. In this section, we will discuss the special case of a transversal, t, intersecting two parallel lines, ℓ_1 and ℓ_2, in two distinct points. This situation is illustrated in this diagram.

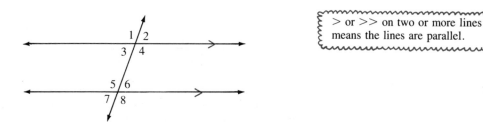

> or >> on two or more lines means the lines are parallel.

Eight angles are formed by a transversal and two lines, and are named according to their relative positions. Angles 3, 4, 5, and 6 are **interior angles** since they are "between" the two lines. Angles 1, 2, 7, and 8 are **exterior angles** as they are "outside" the two lines.

Alternate interior angles are pairs of angles that are interior and on opposite sides of the transversal. In the diagram, $\angle 3$ and $\angle 6$, and $\angle 4$ and $\angle 5$ are pairs of alternate interior angles.

Corresponding angles are pairs of angles where one is an interior angle and one is an exterior angle and they are both on the same side of the transversal. In the diagram, $\angle 2$ and $\angle 6$, $\angle 4$ and $\angle 8$, $\angle 1$ and $\angle 5$, and $\angle 3$ and $\angle 7$ are pairs of corresponding angles.

Consecutive interior angles are interior angles which are on the same side of the transversal. In this case, $\angle 4$ and $\angle 6$, and $\angle 3$ and $\angle 5$ are pairs of consecutive interior angles.

There are relationships between angles that will be needed when proving some deductions.

Two **congruent angles** are the same size.

Two **adjacent angles** share a common side.

Two **complementary angles** have a sum of 90°.

Two **supplementary angles** have a sum of 180°.

Vertically opposite angles are the nonadjacent congruent angles formed by two intersecting lines. Identify these angles on the diagram.

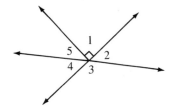

Theorem—O.A.T. The vertically opposite angles formed by two lines are congruent.

A theorem must be proven before it can be used in other proofs. The proof of the Opposite Angle Theorem will be left as an exercise.

Postulate If two parallel lines are cut by a transversal, then the alternate interior angles are congruent.

Example 1

Prove the theorem that if two parallel lines are cut by a transversal, then the corresponding angles formed are congruent.

An intuitive approach could be used to verify this theorem by measuring the angles or by cutting them out and comparing their size. However, a deductive proof will be shown using the four-step problem-solving model.

To **Understand the Problem**, ensure that the given and required information is identified, and draw and label a suitable diagram to help summarize the information.

$\ell_1 \parallel \ell_2$ and t is a transversal.
What do we wish to prove?
$\angle 3 \cong \angle 7$

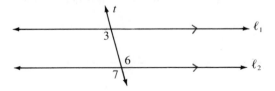

To **Develop a Plan**, review the knowledge we have about parallel lines. Besides knowing the various names for the angles formed when a transversal meets parallel lines, there is also a postulate which gives us information about alternate angles and parallel lines. Therefore, $\angle 3 \cong \angle 6$, and we can relate $\angle 3$ and $\angle 6$, $\angle 6$ and $\angle 7$, and $\angle 3$ and $\angle 7$.

To **Carry Out the Plan**, write the proof based on the information. A reason must be given for each statement presented.

Statement	Reason
1. $\ell_1 \parallel \ell_2$	1. Given
2. $\angle 3 \cong \angle 6$	2. Alternate angles are congruent in parallel lines. (Postulate)
3. $\angle 6 \cong \angle 7$	3. Vertically opposite angles are congruent. (Proof in Exercise 6)
4. $\therefore \angle 3 \cong \angle 7$	4. **Transitive** property—if $a = b$ and $b = c$, then $a = c$.

To **Look Back**, state the conclusion. Ensure you have proved what you started out to do. Check if there are any similar proofs to prove other properties of parallel lines.

> **Theorem**   If two parallel lines are cut by a transversal, then the corresponding angles formed are congruent.

Example 2

Find the measure of $\angle ABC$.

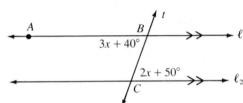

Since ℓ_1 and ℓ_2 are parallel, the alternate interior angles are congruent.

$3x + 40 = 2x + 50$
$\qquad x = 10$

Therefore, $\angle ABC = 70°$.

Exercises

1. Find an example of each in the diagram.

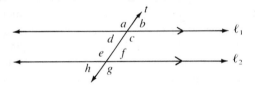

a. alternate interior angles
b. vertically opposite angles
c. corresponding angles
d. Find the measure of all angles if $\angle d$ is 54°.

2. A.T., the "Mathematics Wizard", stated that "with two parallel lines intersected by a transversal, the alternate interior angles and the corresponding angles are always congruent." Is A.T. correct? Explain.

3. Calculate the measure of the indicated angles. In your own words, explain how you arrived at each angle.

a. **b.**

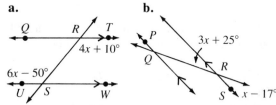

4. Find the measure of $\angle QRS$. (*Hint*: Write an equation and solve for x.)

a. **b.**

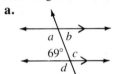
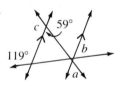

5. Calculate the measure of each indicated angle. Provide a reason for your solution.

a. **b.**

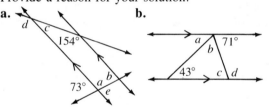

6. Copy and complete the proof to show that vertically opposite angles are congruent.

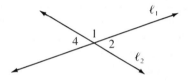

GIVEN: Two lines ℓ_1 and ℓ_2 that intersect.
REQUIRED: To prove that $\angle 1 \cong \angle 3$.
PROOF:

Statement	Reason
1. $\angle 1 + \angle 2 = 180°$	1. $\angle 1$ and $\angle 2$ form a line.
2. $\angle 3 + \angle 2 = 180°$	2. ■■■■■
3. $\angle \blacksquare + \angle \blacksquare = \angle \blacksquare + \angle \blacksquare$	3. ■■■■■
4. $\therefore \angle 1 \cong \angle 3$	4. Subtraction property

7. Two parallel lines are cut by a transversal.

> **Theorem** If a transversal cuts two parallel lines, then the consecutive interior angles are supplementary.

Follow these steps to prove this theorem.
a. Draw a diagram to illustrate the situation.
b. Identify the consecutive interior angles.
c. Identify supplementary angles.
d. Identify the given part of the theorem.
e. Identify the required part of the theorem.
f. If two lines are parallel and cut by a transversal, which pairs of angles are congruent?
g. Write a proof for this theorem. Provide reasons for each statement. (*Hint*: Use the fact that if $a + b = c$ and $b = d$, then $a + d = c$. This is the **substitution property**.)

8. In the figure below, $\overline{AD} \parallel \overline{BC}$ and $\overline{AB} \parallel \overline{DC}$.

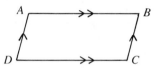

a. Prove that $\angle A \cong \angle C$. (*Hint*: Use the theorem in Exercise 7.)
b. What is the name for the figure $ABCD$?
c. Write a general statement to summarize the proof.

5·3 Congruent Angles

A **converse** statement is created if the "if" phrase and the "then" phrase are switched in the statement. For example, the statement, "If two lines are parallel, then the alternate interior angles are congruent" has a converse. It can be found by switching the "if" and "then" phrases. In this case, the "if" phrase is "two lines are parallel", and the "then" phrase is "the alternate interior angles are congruent." Therefore, the converse statement is, "If the alternate interior angles are congruent, then two lines are parallel."

Even if the original statement is true, the converse is not necessarily true. For example, "If one lives in Winnipeg, then one lives in Canada", is a true statement. However, the converse of the statement, "If one lives in Canada, then one lives in Winnipeg", is false. We shall accept as true the converse of the alternate interior angles postulate of Section 5·2.

> **Postulate** If two lines are intersected by a transversal so that two alternate interior angles are congruent, then the lines are parallel.

Example 1

Which lines are parallel?

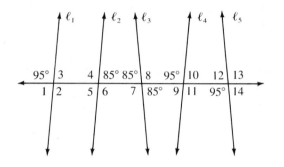

From the diagram $\angle 2 \cong \angle 4 = 95°$.
Therefore, $\ell_1 \parallel \ell_2$.
It will be left as an exercise to show that
$\angle 11 \cong \angle 12 \cong \angle 4$. Similarly, $\angle 8 = 95°$ and $\ell_3 \parallel \ell_5$.

Example 2

Prove that if two lines are intersected by a transversal so that corresponding angles are congruent, then the two lines are parallel.

Draw and label an appropriate diagram indicating the corresponding angles which are congruent and state what is given and what must be proved. Use the postulate above as the basis for the proof.

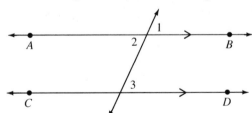

GIVEN: $\angle 1 \cong \angle 3$
REQUIRED: To prove that $\overleftrightarrow{AB} \parallel \overleftrightarrow{CD}$.
PROOF:

Reason	Statement
1. $\angle 1 \cong \angle 3$	1. Given
2. $\angle 1 \cong \angle 2$	2. Vertically opposite angles
3. $\angle 2 \cong \angle 3$	3. Transitive property
4. $\therefore \overleftrightarrow{AB} \parallel \overleftrightarrow{CD}$	4. Alternate angles are congruent.

> **Theorem** If two lines are intersected by a transversal so that corresponding angles are congruent, then the two lines are parallel.

Exercises

1. Find all parallel lines in Example 1 of the display. Explain your answers.

2. Write the converse of the statement.
a. If it is an airplane, then it flies.
b. If you discover gold, then you are a prospector.
c. If one competed in the 1988 Winter Olympics, then one competed in Alberta.
d. If you are a swimmer, then you swim for a swim team.
e. If blings blong, then krings krong.
f. If it is a bird, then it has feathers.

3. Write two statements which are true but have false converses.

4. Write two statements which are true and have true converses.

5. Write two statements which are false but have true converses.

6. In which case is ℓ_1 parallel to ℓ_2? Explain your answer.

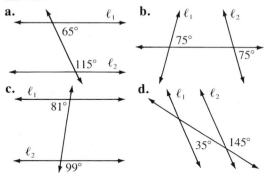

7. List the pairs of angles which would have to be congruent in order to prove these lines parallel. Justify your selections.

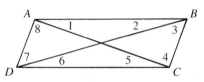

a. $\overline{AB} \parallel \overline{CD}$ **b.** $\overline{AD} \parallel \overline{BC}$

8. List the pairs of angles which would have to be congruent in order to prove that line m is parallel to line n.

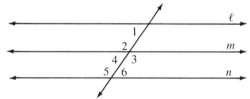

9. In the diagram, $\angle 1$ and $\angle 4$ are supplementary angles.

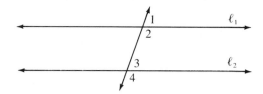

a. Name another angle which is supplementary to $\angle 4$.
b. What do you know about $\angle 1$ and $\angle 3$? Explain.
c. What name is given to $\angle 1$ and $\angle 3$?
d. Prove that $\ell_1 \parallel \ell_2$.

10. Recall the theorem that states: if a transversal cuts two parallel lines, the consecutive interior angles are supplementary.
a. State the converse of this theorem.
b. Draw a diagram and clearly show the given information.
c. State what you are trying to prove in the converse.
d. What is the sum of the measures of two angles which form a straight line?
e. What types of angles must be congruent to prove that two lines are parallel?
f. Prove the converse of the theorem stated.

11. Three planes are found in space. None of the planes are parallel. They do not meet at a single point. They do not all pass through the same line. Describe, or create a model, to show how the planes must be situated with respect to each other.

12. Which postulates or theorems can be used to prove lines parallel?

5·4 Constructions

Basic constructions can be done using only a straightedge and compasses. This is the most accurate way to produce drawings. A Mira also can be used in place of compasses and a straightedge.

1. Construct an angle congruent to a known angle.

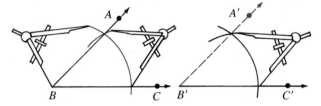

2. Bisect a known angle.

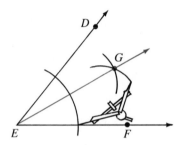

3. Construct the perpendicular bisector of a known line segment.

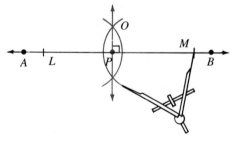

4. Construct a line perpendicular to a known line through any point, P, not on the line.

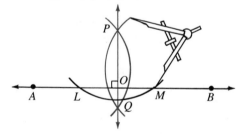

5. Construct a line perpendicular to a known line through a point, P, on the line.

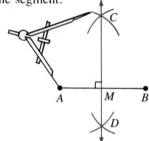

6. Construct a line parallel to a known line through a point, P, not on the line.

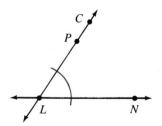 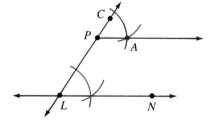 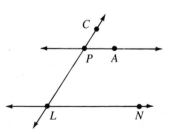

Exercises

1. In Construction 6 of the display, why is $\overrightarrow{PA} \parallel \overleftrightarrow{LN}$?

2. Use a straightedge and compasses, or a Mira, for these constructions. Verify your constructions using compasses and a protractor.
a. Draw a segment PQ. Construct the perpendicular bisector of $\overline{PQ}$.
b. Draw $\angle PQR$ as an obtuse angle. Construct the bisector of the angle.
c. Draw any $\angle XYZ$. Construct an angle congruent to $\angle XYZ$.
d. Draw a line AB with a point P on the line. Construct the perpendicular to $\overleftrightarrow{AB}$ through the point, P.
e. Repeat part **d** where P is not on the line.
f. Suggest an alternate method for constructing a line parallel to a given line through any point not on the line.

3. Complete the proof for Construction 6 in the display.
GIVEN: $\overleftrightarrow{LN}$ and point P not on the line.
REQUIRED: To prove that $\overleftrightarrow{LN} \parallel \overrightarrow{PA}$.
PROOF:

Statement	Reason
Construct $\angle PLN$ and $\angle CPA$.	
1. $\angle PLN = $ ■■■	**1.** Construction
2. $\overleftrightarrow{LN} \parallel \overrightarrow{PA}$	**2.** ■■■

4. Construct triangle ABC using a straightedge, compasses, and a protractor.
a. $\overline{AB} = 5$ cm, $\overline{BC} = 4.5$ cm, $\overline{AC} = 6.5$ cm
b. $\overline{AB} = 3.5$ cm, $\overline{BC} = 6$ cm, $\angle B = 73°$
c. $\angle C = 50°$, $\angle A = 35°$, $\overline{AC} = 5.5$ cm
d. $\overline{AB} = 5$ cm, $\overline{BC} = 5.5$ cm, $\angle A = 40°$

5. Draw an isosceles triangle using only a straightedge and compasses. Construct the perpendicular bisector of the noncongruent side. What relationship exists between this perpendicular bisector and the vertex opposite this side?

6. Attempt to construct triangles from the information given and explain why such constructions are impossible.
a. $\triangle XYZ$: $\overline{XY} = 3$ cm, $\overline{YZ} = 4$ cm, $\overline{XZ} = 8$ cm
b. $\triangle JCD$: $\overline{JC} = 6$ cm, $\overline{CD} = 3$ cm, $\angle J = 40°$

For Exercises 7 and 8, copy the diagram before completing the exercise.

7. Construct a ray TX through point T so that $\angle SRT$ and $\angle RTX$ are congruent.

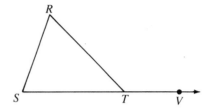

a. Explain why $\overline{SR}$ is parallel to $\overline{TX}$.
b. Explain why $\angle RST$ and $\angle XTV$ are congruent.

8. Find the midpoint, A, of $\overline{PQ}$. Construct $\overline{AX}$ parallel to $\overline{QR}$ such that X is located on $\overline{PR}$.

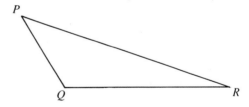

a. Use compasses to compare the lengths of $\overline{PX}$ and $\overline{XR}$. What can you conclude about X? $\overline{AX}$ is called the **midpoint line** of the triangle.
b. Explain why $\angle PAX$ and $\angle PQR$ are congruent.
c. Name another pair of congruent angles in the diagram.
d. Measure the lengths of $\overline{AX}$ and $\overline{QR}$. Compare the lengths.
e. Construct triangles of various shapes and find their midpoint lines. Compare the length of the midpoint line to the length of the third side in the triangle. Write a general statement of your results. Is this generalization inconclusive?

5·5 Angles of a Triangle

You are familiar with the fact that the sum of the angles of a triangle is 180°. Intuitively, this can be confirmed by drawing a triangle, cutting out the angles, and seeing that they form a straight line which has a measure of 180°. A protractor also could be used to measure the angles and find their sum. However, this may not produce a sum of exactly 180° due to either human error or the error of the protractor.

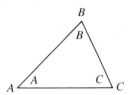 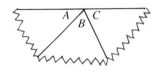 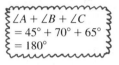

These processes do not prove **beyond doubt** that the sum of the angles of a triangle is 180°. By using the theorems and postulates developed in this chapter, as well as the four-step problem-solving model, it is possible to write a deductive proof to show that any triangle has an angle sum of 180°.

Example 1

Prove that the sum of the measures of the angles in a triangle is 180°.

Understand the Problem

Draw a diagram and summarize the given information. We are required to prove that the sum of the angles in a triangle is 180°.

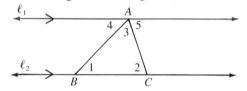

Develop a Plan

By constructing a line parallel to $\overline{BC}$ through vertex A, the sum of angles 3, 4, and 5 can be related to the sum of angles 1, 2, and 3. The relationships will be found using known postulates and theorems for parallel lines. A series of logical statements, as well as the reasons for the statements, will constitute the deductive proof.

Carry Out the Plan

Construct ℓ_1 parallel to $\overline{BC}$ through vertex A.

PROOF:

Statement	Reason
1. $\angle 3 + \angle 4 + \angle 5 = 180°$	1. Angles forming a straight line equal 180°.
2. $\angle 5 \cong \angle 2$	2. Alternate angles
3. $\angle 4 \cong \angle 1$	3. Alternate angles
4. $\therefore \angle 1 + \angle 2 + \angle 3 = 180°$	4. Substitution property

Look Back

State the conclusion as a theorem. You may wish to check your proof by attempting to use it with a different triangle.

Theorem	The sum of the measures of the angles in a triangle is 180°.

Example 2

Find the measure of each angle in this triangle.

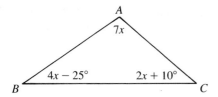

$\angle A + \angle B + \angle C = 180°$ (sum of the angles of a triangle)
$7x + (4x - 25) + (2x + 10) = 180$
$x = 15$

Therefore, $\angle A = 105°$, $\angle B = 35°$, and $\angle C = 40°$.

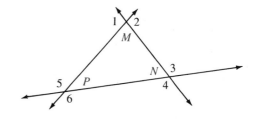

The **exterior angle** of a triangle is an angle which is adjacent and supplementary to an angle in the triangle. For instance, in the diagram to the right, $\angle 1$ is adjacent and supplementary to $\angle M$. Therefore, $\angle 1$ is an exterior angle to $\triangle MNP$. You will notice that there are six exterior angles for each triangle and they are numbered. The angle that is not an exterior angle, although it is "outside" the triangle, is an opposite angle and is equal in measure to the interior angle. There also exists a relationship between the measure of the exterior angle and the sum of the opposite interior angles.

Example 3

Prove that the measure of an exterior angle of a triangle is the sum of the measures of the interior opposite angles.

GIVEN: $\triangle ABC$ with $\overline{BC}$ extended to D.
REQUIRED: To prove that $\angle 1 + \angle 2 = \angle 4$.
PLAN: Use the fact that $\angle 1 + \angle 2 + \angle 3 = 180°$
and $\angle 3 + \angle 4 = 180°$.

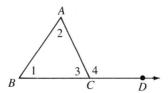

PROOF:

Statement	Reason
1. $\angle 1 + \angle 2 + \angle 3 = 180°$	1. Sum of interior angles
2. $\angle 3 + \angle 4 = 180°$	2. Supplementary angles
3. $\angle 3 = 180° - \angle 4$	3. Subtraction property
4. $\angle 1 + \angle 2 + 180° - \angle 4 = 180°$	4. Substitution property
5. $\therefore \angle 1 + \angle 2 = \angle 4$	5. Simplify statement 4.

Theorem The measure of an exterior angle of a triangle is the sum of the measures of the interior opposite angles.

Exercises

1. Find the measure of the unknown angle. Construct the triangle and use a calculator if one is available.

a. the third interior angle if the other two interior angles are 87° and 36°

b. the measure of two interior angles if they are equal and the third interior angle is 35°

c. the exterior angle if the two opposite interior angles are 48° and 56°

2. Find the measure of the unknown angles. Use a calculator if one is available.

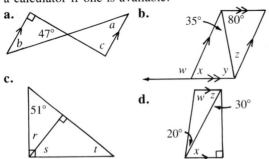

a.

b.

c.

d.

3. Find the measure of the third angle of the triangle. Use a calculator if one is available.

a. 37°, 66°   **b.** 119°, 43°
c. 28.4°, 109.5°   **d.** $r°$, $t°$
e. If you used a calculator, record your keying procedure if the two given angles are a and b.
f. Will this procedure work? Explain.

a [+] b [=] [+M] 180 [−] [MR] [=]

4. Calculate the measure of each angle.

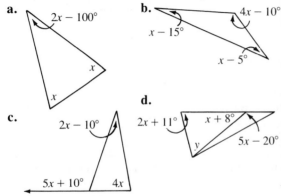

a. $2x - 100°$, x, x

b. $4x - 10°$, $x - 15°$, $x - 5°$

c. $2x - 10°$, $5x + 10°$, $4x$

d. $2x + 11°$, $x + 8°$, $5x - 20°$, y

5. In your own words, define the exterior angle of any polygon. Use a diagram if necessary.

6. Copy and complete to find the measure of $\angle ACD$. State the given and required information.

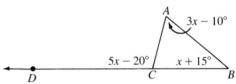

PROOF:

Statement	Reason
1. $\angle A + \angle B \cong \angle ACD$	**1.** ▬▬
2. $3x - 10 +$ ▬ = ▬	**2.** ▬▬
3. $x =$ ▬	**3.** ▬▬
4. $5x - 20 =$ ▬	**4.** ▬▬
5. Therefore, ▬	

7. Explain why the measure of an exterior angle of a triangle must be greater than any opposite interior angle.

8. In $\triangle ABC$, $\angle B \cong \angle C$ and $\overline{AD} \perp \overline{BC}$.
a. Draw the diagram.
b. Prove that $\angle BAD \cong \angle CAD$.

9. In the diagram, $\overline{DE} \perp \overline{AB}$ and $\overline{AC} \perp \overline{BD}$. Prove that $\angle A \cong \angle D$. (*Hint:* Separate $\triangle ABC$ and $\triangle DEB$ into two diagrams.)

10. Find the sum of the measures of the interior angles in each by drawing all the possible diagonals from one vertex.

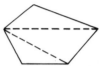

a. a quadrilateral   **b.** a pentagon
c. an octagon   **d.** a decagon
e. Construct a chart to generalize the number of sides in a polygon and the sum of the interior angles.

5·6 Congruent Triangles

Two line segments are congruent if they have the same length. Two angles are congruent if they have the same measure. Two triangles are congruent if they have the same size and shape. The size of a triangle is determined by its sides, while the shape of a triangle is determined by its angles.

These two triangles are congruent.

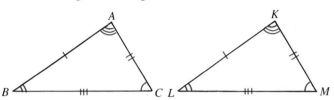

> Note the symbols for congruent sides and angles.

The corresponding sides are congruent.
$$\overline{AB} \cong \overline{KL}$$
$$\overline{AC} \cong \overline{KM}$$
$$\overline{BC} \cong \overline{LM}$$

The corresponding angles are congruent.
$$\angle A \cong \angle K$$
$$\angle B \cong \angle L$$
$$\angle C \cong \angle M$$

$$\triangle ABC \cong \triangle KLM$$

The order of the letters in the congruence statement determines the correspondence of the angles. If corresponding angles and corresponding sides in a triangle are congruent, then the two triangles are congruent. Conversely, if two triangles are congruent, then the corresponding sides and the corresponding angles are congruent.

Exercises

1. List the congruent sides and the congruent angles. Then state the congruence between the two triangles.

a.

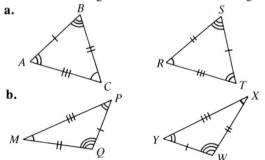

b.

2. If $\triangle RST \cong \triangle VWX$, state which sides and angles are congruent.

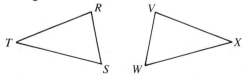

3. Draw each pair of congruent triangles and indicate the congruent parts on the diagram.
a. $\triangle EFG \cong \triangle RMN$
b. $\triangle QRS \cong \triangle CBA$
c. $\triangle XYZ \cong \triangle XZY$

4. Draw and label a diagram to illustrate each and then find the indicated angle or side.
a. $\triangle HIJ \cong \triangle PEN$, $\overline{HI} = 5x - 3$ and $\overline{PE} = 3x + 12$. Find the length of $\overline{PE}$.
b. $\triangle ZAP \cong \triangle BAM$, $\angle Z = 2x + 25°$ and $\angle B = 6x - 55°$. Find the measure of $\angle Z$.

5. A.T., the "Mathematics Wizard", stated that if the corresponding angles in a triangle are congruent, then the triangles are not necessarily congruent. Is A.T. correct? Explain.

6. If two angles of a triangle are congruent to two angles in a second triangle, what can we conclude about the third angle in each of the triangles?

133

5·7 Congruence Postulates

In the last section, it was noted that triangles are congruent if the corresponding angles and the corresponding sides are equal in magnitude. In this section, the minimum requirements for triangles to be congruent will be examined.

Investigation 1

Use the three segments to construct a triangle with only compasses and a straightedge. Comparing your construction with three of your classmates will show that all the triangles will be the same size and shape, although the sides may be in a different order. Turning the triangles will fit one triangle directly on top of the other.

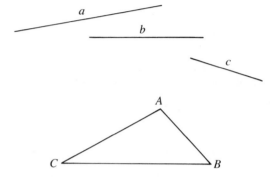

> **Congruence Postulate—S.S.S.** If three sides of one triangle are congruent to three sides of a second triangle, then the two triangles are congruent.

Investigation 2

Use the two segments and the angle to construct a triangle with only compasses and a straightedge. Compare your construction with the construction of three of your classmates. All the triangles will be the same size and shape, although you may have to "turn" one to make it fit directly on top of the other.

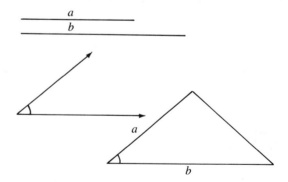

> **Congruence Postulate—S.A.S.** If two sides and a contained angle of one triangle are congruent to two sides and the contained angle of another triangle, then the two triangles are congruent.

Investigation 3

Choose two angles and a contained segment of your own to construct a triangle. Ask three classmates to use your angles and the contained segment for their constructions and compare the constructions. Notice that the triangles can be placed directly on top of each other.

> **Congruence Postulate—A.S.A.**   If two angles and the contained side of one triangle are congruent to two angles and a contained side of another triangle, then the two triangles are congruent.

Example

Two line segments, $\overline{AB}$ and $\overline{RS}$, intersect at X where X is the midpoint of $\overline{AB}$ and $\overline{RS}$. Prove that $\triangle ARX \cong \triangle BSX$.

Understand the Problem
Draw a diagram and label the given information. For ease in recognizing the given information, use the symbols for congruence of sides and angles.

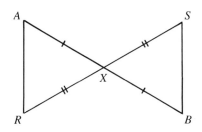

Develop a Plan
Since two triangles are to be proven congruent, one of the congruence postulates will be needed. In this case, if X is the midpoint of $\overline{AB}$, then $\overline{AX} \cong \overline{BX}$. Similarly, $\overline{RX} \cong \overline{SX}$. This gives two congruent sides in each of the triangles. Therefore, another side or the contained angle is needed. The only other piece of information that can be found is the fact that $\angle AXR$ and $\angle SXB$ are vertically opposite angles.

Carry Out the Plan
GIVEN: X is the midpoint of $\overline{AB}$ and $\overline{RS}$.
REQUIRED: To prove that $\triangle ARX \cong \triangle BSX$.
PROOF:

Statement	Reason
1. X is the midpoint of $\overline{AB}$.	**1.** Given
2. $\overline{AX} \cong \overline{BX}$	**2.** Definition of midpoint
3. X is the midpoint of $\overline{RS}$.	**3.** Given
4. $\overline{RX} \cong \overline{SX}$	**4.** Definition of midpoint
5. $\angle AXR \cong \angle BXS$	**5.** Vertically opposite angles
6. $\therefore \triangle ARX \cong \triangle BSX$	**6.** S.A.S.

Look Back
Therefore, $\triangle ARX \cong \triangle BSX$. This also implies that $\overline{RA} \cong \overline{SB}$, $\angle A \cong \angle B$, and $\angle R \cong \angle S$. This is the converse of the S.A.S. congruence postulate and shall be designated as **corresponding parts of congruent triangles** and abbreviated as C.P.C.T.

Exercises

1. Explain the term "contained angle" in the S.A.S. congruence postulate.

2. Explain the term "contained side" in the A.S.A. congruence postulate.

3. In $\triangle RKP$, state which side is contained between each pair of angles.

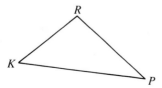

4. Write the converse of the three congruence postulates. Are the converses true? Explain.

5. Which pairs of sides must be congruent to use the S.A.S. postulate to prove congruence?

a. **b.**

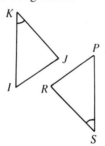

6. Which pairs of angles must be congruent to use the A.S.A. postulate to prove congruence?

a. **b.**

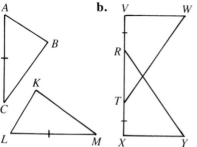

7. A.T., the "Mathematics Wizard", stated that in order to use the A.S.A. congruence postulate, the side must be contained between the two angles. Is A.T. correct? Explain.

8. State which congruent triangle postulate will prove each pair of triangles congruent. If there is more than one postulate which applies, state both of them. If no postulate applies, indicate this. Explain your reasoning in each case.

a. 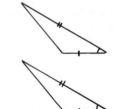 **b.**

c. 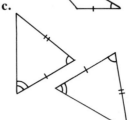 **d.**

e.  **f.**

9. Write a formal proof to show that each pair of triangles is congruent.

a.

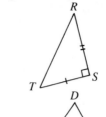

b.

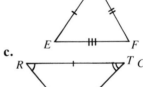

c.

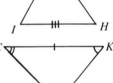

10. In △ABC, $\overline{AB} \cong \overline{AC}$, ∠B ≅ ∠C, and $\overline{AM}$ bisects $\overline{BC}$. Copy the diagram, mark the given information on the diagram, and give a formal proof to show that △ABM ≅ △ACM.

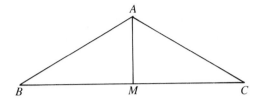

11. In △KQS, $\overline{KR}$ is the perpendicular bisector of $\overline{QS}$. Copy the diagram and mark the given information on the diagram.

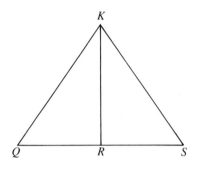

a. Copy and complete the proof.
GIVEN: $\overline{KR}$ is the perpendicular bisector of $\overline{QS}$.
REQUIRED: To prove that $\overline{KQ} \cong \overline{KS}$.
PROOF:

Statement	Reason
In △KRQ and △KRS,	
1. $\overline{KR}$ bisects $\overline{QS}$.	1. ▆▆▆▆▆
2. ▆▆▆▆▆	2. Perpendicular bisector
3. $\overline{KR} \perp \overline{QS}$	3. ▆▆▆▆▆
4. ∠KRQ ≅ ∠KRS	4. Perpendicular bisector
5. $\overline{KR} \cong \overline{KR}$	5. Reflexive property
6. △▆▆ ≅ △▆▆	6. ▆▆▆ postulate
7. ∴▆▆ ≅ ▆	7. C.P.C.T.

The **reflexive property** states that any segment or any angle is congruent to itself.
b. List the other parts of △KRQ and △KRS that are now known to be congruent.

12. Quadrilateral ABCD is a parallelogram.

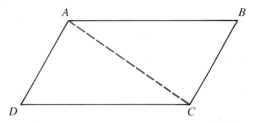

a. Copy and complete this proof to show that $\overline{AB} \cong \overline{CD}$.
GIVEN: ABCD is a parallelogram.
REQUIRED: To prove that $\overline{AB} \cong \overline{CD}$.
CONSTRUCTION: Draw $\overline{AC}$ as a diagonal of parallelogram ABCD.
PLAN: Use the A.S.A. congruence postulate.
PROOF:

Statement	Reason
In △ABC and △CDA,	
1. $\overline{AB} \parallel \overline{CD}$	1. Definition of a parallelogram
2. ∠▆▆ ≅ ∠▆▆	2. Alternate angles congruent
3. $\overline{AD} \parallel \overline{CB}$	3. ▆▆▆▆
4. ∠▆▆ ≅ ∠▆▆	4. ▆▆▆▆
5. ▆▆▆	5. Reflexive property
6. △▆▆ ≅ △▆▆	6. ▆▆▆ postulate
7. $\overline{AB} \cong \overline{CD}$	7. C.P.C.T.

b. Is $\overline{AD} \cong \overline{CB}$? Explain.
c. From the above proof write a general statement about parallelograms.

13. In the diagram, ∠M ≅ ∠P and $\overline{KM} \cong \overline{KP}$.

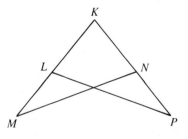

a. Prove that △KMN ≅ △KPL. (*Hint:* Separate the triangles.)
b. Prove that $\overline{KL} \cong \overline{KN}$. (*Hint:* Modify the proof of part **a**.)

5·8 Triangles

Triangles can be classified according to their sides or according to their angles.

Scalene triangle—no congruent sides
Isosceles triangle—two congruent sides
Equilateral triangle—all sides congruent

Acute triangle—all angles are acute
Right triangle—one right angle
Obtuse triangle—one angle is obtuse

The **altitude** of a triangle is a segment drawn from one vertex perpendicular to the opposite side of the triangle, or the opposite side extended.
The **median** of a triangle is a segment drawn from one vertex to the midpoint of the opposite side.

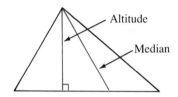

Theorem In an isosceles triangle, the angles opposite the congruent sides are congruent.

The completed proof will be done as an exercise.

GIVEN: $\overline{AB} \cong \overline{AC}$
PROVE: $\angle B \cong \angle C$
PLAN: Construct $\overline{AD}$ as the bisector of $\angle BAC$. Use the S.A.S. congruence postulate to prove $\triangle ABD \cong \triangle ACD$.

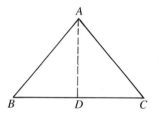

Exercises

1. Write the theorem in the display in the form of an "if … then" statement.

2. Copy and complete the proof in the display. By constructing $\overline{BD} \cong \overline{CD}$, complete a second proof of the theorem in the display.

3. Using compasses, a ruler, and a protractor, construct $\triangle ABC$, where $\angle A = 53°$, $\angle B = 74°$, and $\overline{AC} = 4.5$ cm.
a. Find the measure of $\angle C$.
b. Which congruence postulate would justify that all the triangles constructed in part **a** are congruent? Call this the S.A.A. congruence corollary.
c. Prove the S.A.A. congruence corollary.
d. Use a dictionary and explain why this is called a corollary and not a definition or theorem.

4. Each triangle is isosceles. Calculate the measure of each angle in the triangle.

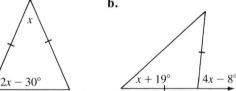

5. Write the converse of the theorem in the display. Write a proof for the converse. (*Hint*: Use the S.A.A. congruence corollary.)

6. In the diagram, $\overleftrightarrow{QT} \parallel \overline{RX}$ and $\angle 1 \cong \angle 2$. Prove that $\triangle QRX$ is isosceles.

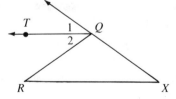

5·9 Quadrilaterals

A **quadrilateral** is a simple closed figure which is formed by four segments joining four points in a plane; no three of which are collinear. The four points form the vertices of the quadrilateral. The four segments which join the points may intersect only at the vertices of the quadrilateral. All quadrilaterals share these common properties.

Adjacent (consecutive) angles share a common side.
Adjacent (consecutive) vertices are endpoints of the same side.
Adjacent (consecutive) sides have a common endpoint.
Angles, sides, and vertices which are not consecutive are called **opposite angles, opposite sides**, and **opposite vertices**, respectively.
A **diagonal** is a line segment which joins opposite or nonconsecutive vertices.

Quadrilaterals are classified according to the properties they possess.
A **trapezoid** is a quadrilateral with **exactly** one pair of parallel sides.
A **parallelogram** is a quadrilateral with each pair of opposite sides congruent and parallel.
A **rectangle** is a parallelogram whose vertices all form 90° angles.
A **rhombus** is a parallelogram with all sides congruent.
A **square** is a rectangle with all sides congruent.

These definitions are purely arbitrary. As long as definitions do not contradict each other, are sufficient, and are consistent, they can be considered good definitions.

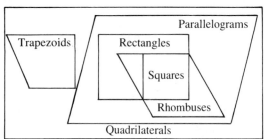

Example

Prove that a quadrilateral is a parallelogram if opposite sides are both parallel and congruent.

GIVEN: Quadrilateral $ABCD$ with $\overline{AB} \parallel \overline{DC}$ and $\overline{AB} \cong \overline{CD}$
PROVE: Quadrilateral $ABCD$ is a parallelogram.
PLAN: Draw the diagonal $\overline{BD}$ and prove the two triangles congruent to find a pair of alternate angles congruent.
PROOF:

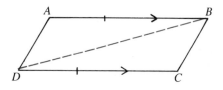

Statement	Reason
In △ABD and △CDB,	
1. $\overline{AB} \parallel \overline{DC}$	1. Given
2. $\angle ABD \cong \angle CDB$	2. Parallel segments form congruent alternate angles.
3. $\overline{AB} \cong \overline{CD}$	3. Given
4. $\overline{BD} \cong \overline{DB}$	4. Reflexive
5. △$ABD \cong$ △CDB	5. S.A.S.
6. $\angle ADB \cong \angle CBD$	6. C.P.C.T.
7. $\overline{AD} \parallel \overline{BC}$	7. Congruent alternate angles are formed by parallel lines.
8. ∴$ABCD$ is a parallelogram.	8. Pairs of opposite sides are congruent and parallel.

139

Exercises

1. Are the pairs of angles or sides adjacent or opposite?

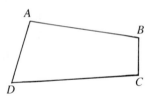

a. ∠A and ∠B

b. ∠B and ∠D

c. ∠B and ∠C

d. ∠A and ∠C

e. $\overline{AD}$ and $\overline{AB}$

f. $\overline{AD}$ and $\overline{BC}$

2. In your own words, state a definition of a quadrilateral. Why is it necessary to have the condition that the four segments which join the points may intersect **only** at the vertices of the quadrilateral?

3. Suggest other definitions for the special quadrilaterals. For example, a square could be defined as a rhombus whose vertices are right angles.

4. A rectangle is a parallelogram with one right angle. Explain why this implies that all the angles are right angles.

5. For each sentence, if the statement is always true, then write true. If the statement is not always true, then replace the underlined word to make it always true.

a. Consecutive angles of a <u>square</u> are congruent.

b. A <u>parallelogram</u> is a rectangle.

c. A <u>rhombus</u> is a parallelogram.

d. A rectangle is <u>equilateral</u>.

e. Each angle of a <u>square</u> is a right angle.

f. A square is a <u>rhombus</u>.

g. A <u>rhombus</u> is equiangular.

h. The angles of a <u>parallelogram</u> are congruent.

i. A parallelogram with congruent sides and angles is a <u>square</u>.

j. A <u>rectangle</u> has exactly one pair of parallel sides.

6. A rhombus is a parallelogram with one pair of adjacent sides congruent. Explain why this implies that all the sides are congruent.

7. Make an accurate drawing of a parallelogram, a trapezoid, a rectangle, a square, a rhombus, and a nonregular quadrilateral using a ruler and a protractor. Ensure that your quadrilateral is not one of the other figures you have drawn, and draw the diagonals in each figure.

a. In which figure(s) are the diagonals congruent?

b. In which figure(s) do the diagonals bisect each other?

c. In which figure(s) are the diagonals perpendicular to each other?

d. In which figure(s) are consecutive angles congruent?

e. In which figure(s) are opposite angles congruent?

f. In which figure(s) are consecutive angles supplementary?

g. In which figure(s) are opposite sides congruent?

h. In which figure(s) are consecutive sides congruent?

8. If you redrew your figures in Exercise 7 with different dimensions and angles, would your answers differ from those already found?

9. Explain why the sum of the interior angles of any quadrilateral is 360°.

10. Explain why the sum of the exterior angles of any quadrilateral is 360°.

For the theorems in Exercises 11 to 16,

a. write the theorem in an ''if ... then'' form.

b. ensure that you are familiar with the definitions of all terms in each statement.

c. draw a suitable diagram and label it.

d. write the given information and what is required to prove.

e. develop a plan and carry it out for proving the statement.

f. look back at your proof and be prepared to use the results in any of the succeeding theorems.

11. The opposite sides of a parallelogram are congruent.

12. Consecutive angles of a parallelogram are supplementary.

140

13. The diagonals of a parallelogram bisect each other.

14. The diagonals of a rectangle are congruent.

15. The diagonals of a rhombus are perpendicular to each other.

16. The diagonals of a rhombus bisect the vertices of the rhombus.

17. Is it necessary to prove that the opposite sides of a rectangle are congruent after you have completed the proof of Exercise 11? Explain.

18. For each proof in Exercises 11 to 16, state to which special quadrilaterals the proof applies.

19. Write the converse of each theorem in Exercises 11 to 16. State which converses are true.

For Exercises 20 to 22, use any of the proofs, theorems, or definitions from this section.

20. Given parallelogram *RSTV*.

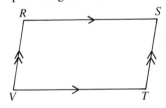

a. If $\overline{RS} = 5m - 10$ units, $\overline{ST} = 2m - 1$ units, and $\overline{VT} = 2m + 8$ units, then find the perimeter of the parallelogram.
b. If $\angle R = 3k - 25°$ and $\angle S = 2k - 20°$, then find the measures of $\angle T$ and $\angle V$.

21. In rhombus *CDEF*, the diagonals bisect each other at *O*.

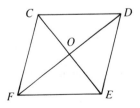

a. If $\angle CDE = 64°$, then find the measures of $\angle DCF$, $\angle CDO$, and $\angle DCO$.
b. If $\overline{FD} = 20$ units and $\overline{CE} = 14$ units, then find the lengths of $\overline{OD}$ and $\overline{OE}$.
c. If $\overline{FD} = 16$ units and $\overline{CE} = 12$ units, then find the length of $\overline{DE}$.

22. In rectangle *QRST*, the diagonals meet at *X*.

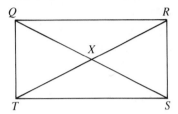

a. If $\overline{RX} = 4x + 7$ units and $\overline{SX} = 7x - 5$ units, then find the lengths of $\overline{QS}$ and $\overline{RT}$.
b. If $\overline{TS} = 24$ units and $\overline{RS} = 10$ units, then find the length of $\overline{QS}$.

> **Historical Note**
>
> **Sophie Germain** (1776-1831)
> Sophie Germain was born in Paris in 1776. Although her parents tried to keep her from gaining an education because they believed that "girls should not be straining their minds on such nonsense", she managed to become one of the more gifted mathematicians of her time. It is said that her interest in mathematics peaked in 1789, when, at the age of thirteen, she read a story about Archimedes' death. The story is that during the Roman invasion of Greece, he was so absorbed in the study of a geometric figure, that he ignored the questioning of a Roman soldier and was killed.
>   Sophie Germain worked mainly in the field of number theory. She developed the "modulus" system to describe remainders. For example, $x^3 \equiv 2 \pmod{p}$ means x^3 has a remainder of 2 when divided by p. Find a value for x and p that will make this statement true.

5·10 Triangles and Trapezoids

There are many interesting properties that appear in both triangles and trapezoids. Some of these will be discovered in this section.

Investigation 1

Construct $\triangle ABC$, with D and F the midpoints of $\overline{AB}$ and $\overline{AC}$ respectively.
a. Measure the length of $\overline{BC}$ and $\overline{DF}$.
b. Measure $\angle ADF$ and $\angle ABC$.
c. Are $\overline{BC}$ and $\overline{DF}$ parallel?

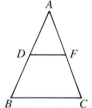

> **Theorem**   The segment joining the midpoints of two sides of a triangle is parallel and half the length of the third side.

Example

In $\triangle KLM$, S, T, and U are the midpoints of $\overline{KL}$, $\overline{KM}$, and $\overline{LM}$ respectively. If $\overline{KL} = 9$ cm, $\overline{KM} = 12$ cm, and $\overline{LM} = 17$ cm, find the lengths of $\overline{ST}$, $\overline{TU}$, and $\overline{SU}$.

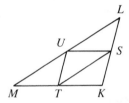

$\overline{ST}$ is half of $\overline{LM}$ or 8.5 cm, $\overline{TU}$ is half of $\overline{KL}$ or 4.5 cm, and $\overline{SU}$ is half of $\overline{KM}$ or 6 cm.

The **bases** of a trapezoid are the two parallel sides. The **median** of a trapezoid is the segment which joins the midpoints of the nonparallel sides. Are the properties of trapezoids similar to those of triangles? Investigation 2 will examine this question.

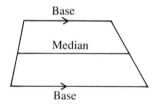

Investigation 2

Construct trapezoid $FGHI$, where $\overline{XY}$ is the median.
a. Find the lengths of $\overline{FG}$, $\overline{XY}$, and $\overline{IH}$.
b. Find the measures of $\angle FXY$ and $\angle XIH$.
c. Is the median of the trapezoid parallel to its base?
d. Is the length of the median equal to the average of the lengths of the bases?

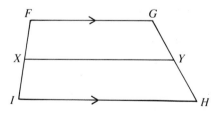

> **Theorem**   The median of a trapezoid is parallel to its bases, and its length is the average of the lengths of the bases.

Exercises

1. In Investigation 1, explain why $\overline{BC} \parallel \overline{DF}$.

2. In Investigation 2, explain why the median is parallel to the bases.

3. Identify the bases and the median in each trapezoid.

a.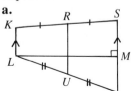

b.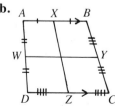

4. In $\triangle RST$, Q is the midpoint of $\overline{RS}$ and X is the midpoint of $\overline{RT}$.

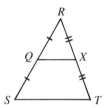

a. If $\overline{ST} = 24$ units, find $\overline{QX}$.
b. If $\overline{ST} = 25.2$ units, find $\overline{QX}$.
c. If $\overline{QX} = 14$ units, find $\overline{ST}$.
d. If $\overline{QX} = 19.6$ units, find $\overline{ST}$.

5. Use the trapezoid to find the indicated lengths.

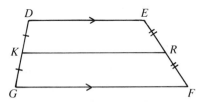

a. If $\overline{DE} = 16$ units and $\overline{GF} = 22$ units, find $\overline{KR}$.
b. If $\overline{DE} = 27$ units and $\overline{GF} = 39$ units, find $\overline{KR}$.
c. If $\overline{DE} = 15.2$ units and $\overline{GF} = 12.8$ units, find $\overline{KR}$.
d. If $\overline{DE} = 2x - 3$ units, $\overline{GF} = 4x + 5$ units, and $\overline{KR} = 4x - 5$ units, find the length of the median.
e. If $\overline{DE} = 7x + 2$ units, $\overline{GF} = 2x + 9$ units, and $\overline{KR} = 5x + 1$ units, find the length of the median.

6. Prove the first theorem in the display. (*Hint*: Use similar triangles.)

7. A.T., the "Mathematics Wizard", defined a trapezoid in which one of the bases has a length of zero as a triangle. Is A.T. correct? Explain.

8. In trapezoid $KXRT$, M is the midpoint of $\overline{KT}$ and N is the midpoint of $\overline{XR}$.

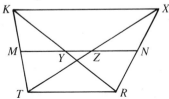

a. If $\overline{KX} = 18$ units and $\overline{TR} = 10$ units, find the lengths of $\overline{MY}$, $\overline{NZ}$, and $\overline{YZ}$.
b. If $\overline{TR} = 14$ units and $\overline{MZ} = 10$ units, find the lengths of $\overline{KX}$, $\overline{NZ}$, and $\overline{YZ}$.
c. If $\overline{MN} = 25$ units and $\overline{TR} = 16$ units, find the lengths of $\overline{KX}$, $\overline{NY}$, and $\overline{YZ}$.

9. Find the area of each trapezoid in Exercise 8 if the height of the trapezoid is 12 units in all cases.

10. If X, Y, and Z are the midpoints of the sides of $\triangle ABC$, prove that the perimeter of $\triangle XYZ$ is one half of the perimeter of $\triangle ABC$.

11. An **isosceles trapezoid** is a trapezoid which is symmetric about a line through the midpoints of its bases. In other words, folding the trapezoid through the midpoint of the bases has one half of the trapezoid falling on the other half.
a. Draw an isosceles trapezoid showing its line of symmetry.
b. Prove that the diagonals of an isosceles trapezoid are congruent.

12. An isosceles trapezoid has bases of lengths 10 units and 6 units. The altitude of the trapezoid is 8 units. The two diagonals are drawn, and a line perpendicular to the two bases is drawn through their point of intersection. Find the lengths of the parts into which the altitude is divided by the point of intersection of the diagonals.

5·11 Indirect Proof

Bob is accused of entering a grocery store on July 7, taking the money from the cash register, and running away before the police arrived. Bob's lawyer presents the case saying, "Either my client is guilty or he isn't. If my client is guilty, then he must have been able to run on July 7. However, I have a report from Bob's doctor which states that on July 3, Bob broke his leg in a football game, and an immobilizing cast was placed on his leg for six weeks. Therefore, Bob could not have been the man who robbed the store, and he is not guilty of the charge."

The lawyer followed the basic steps of **indirect reasoning** by making an assumption and then using the facts available to disprove the assumption. There are four basic steps to follow when using indirect reasoning.

1. State the only two possibilities (either Bob is guilty or he isn't).

2. Assume one of the possibilities (assume that he is guilty).

3. Show by deductive reasoning that this leads to a contradiction of at least one known fact (if he could run—but he couldn't).

4. State that the only remaining possibility must be true (Bob is not guilty).

Example

Prove that if $\angle A$ of $\triangle ABC$ is obtuse, then neither $\angle A$ nor $\angle B$ is obtuse.

Understand the Problem
We are given $\triangle ABC$ where $\angle A$ is greater than $90°$.

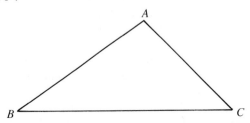

Develop a Plan
Assume that either $\angle B$ or $\angle C$ is greater than $90°$, and use the fact that the sum of the angles in a triangle is $180°$ to show a contradiction.

Carry Out the Plan
Assume that $\angle B$ is greater than $90°$. Therefore, $\angle A + \angle B > 180°$ and the sum of the interior angles of $\triangle ABC$ is greater than $180°$. However, this is impossible as the sum of the interior angles of a triangle is $180°$. Therefore, $\angle B$ cannot be obtuse. The same reasoning can be used to show that $\angle C$ cannot be obtuse.

Look Back
If one angle of a triangle is greater than $90°$, then neither of the other two angles can be greater than $90°$. Indirect proof has a unique format and strategy. If we want to prove that something is true, then we prove that it cannot be false. This is different than the deductive proof as it leads to a contradiction. However, you must use known facts to lead to your contradiction, as well as give reasons for each of your facts.

Exercises

1. Assume you are to use indirect reasoning to prove each statement below. State two possibilities and the initial assumption that you would make.

a. Ducks have webbed feet.
b. In $\triangle XYZ$, $\angle X$ is not congruent to $\angle Y$.
c. In $\triangle HIG$, $\angle G$ is a right angle.
d. Variables a and b are not equal.
e. $\ell_3 \parallel \ell_4$.
f. Triangle RST is equilateral.
g. Quadrilateral $ABCD$ is a square.
h. In $\triangle ABC$, $\angle 3$ is not an exterior angle.

2. Prove that if two lines are cut by a transversal so that alternate interior angles are congruent, then the two lines are parallel. (*Hint*: Assume the two lines are not parallel.)

3. You arrive in your mathematics class but have left your homework at home. There are two possibilities with respect to your homework assignment.
 i) You did all of your homework.
ii) You did not do all of your homework.
Give a form of indirect reasoning to show your teacher that you did do all of your homework.

4. In $\triangle PQR$, $\angle Q = 55°$ and $\angle R = 75°$. Copy and complete the proof to prove that $\angle P \neq 40°$.
GIVEN: ▮▮▮▮▮▮▮▮▮▮
REQUIRED: ▮▮▮▮▮▮▮▮▮▮▮
PLAN: ▮▮▮▮▮▮▮▮
PROOF:

Statement	Reason
1. Either $\angle P = 40°$ or $\angle P \neq 40°$.	**1.** ▮▮▮▮▮▮
2. Assume that $\angle P = 40°$.	**2.** ▮▮▮▮▮
3. $\angle Q + \angle R + \angle P = 180°$.	**3.** ▮▮▮▮▮
4. $55° + 75° + 40° = $ ▮▮▮	**4.** ▮▮▮▮▮
5. Therefore, ▮▮▮▮▮▮	**5.** ▮▮▮▮

5. In $\triangle ABC$, prove that $\angle B$ and $\angle C$ cannot both be right angles.

6. Prove that a triangle cannot have two sides which are parallel.

7. In $\triangle ABC$, D is not the midpoint of $\overline{BC}$, and $\overline{AD}$ bisects $\angle A$. Copy and complete to prove that $\overline{AB} \not\cong \overline{AC}$.

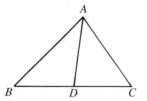

GIVEN: ▮▮▮▮▮▮▮▮
REQUIRED: ▮▮▮▮▮▮▮▮
PLAN: ▮▮▮▮▮▮▮▮
PROOF:

Statement	Reason
1. Either $\overline{AB} \cong \overline{AC}$ or $\overline{AB} \not\cong \overline{AC}$.	**1.** ▮▮▮▮▮
2. Assume that $\overline{AB} \cong \overline{AC}$.	**2.** ▮▮▮▮
In $\triangle ABD$ and $\triangle ACD$,	
3. $\overline{AB} \cong \overline{AC}$	**3.** Assumption
4. $\overline{AD}$ bisects $\angle A$.	**4.** ▮▮▮▮▮
5. $\angle BAD \cong \angle CAD$	**5.** ▮▮▮▮
6. $\overline{AD} \cong \overline{AD}$	**6.** ▮▮▮
7. ▮▮▮▮▮▮▮	**7.** ▮▮▮▮

8. If n is a natural number which is prime, then copy and complete to prove that $2n$ is not prime.

Statement	Reason
1. Either $2n$ is prime or it isn't.	**1.** ▮▮▮▮▮
2. Assume that $2n$ is prime.	**2.** ▮▮▮▮
3. n is a natural number which is prime.	**3.** ▮▮▮▮
4. Then, $2n$ is an even number.	**4.** ▮▮▮▮
5. Every even natural number greater than 2 is not prime.	**5.**
6. ▮▮▮▮▮▮	**6.** ▮▮▮▮

Braintickler

Four girls decided to switch clothes for school the next day. No one wore their own skirt or sweater. Joan borrowed the sweater belonging to the girl whose skirt was borrowed by Doreen, and Doreen's sweater was borrowed by the girl who took Joan's skirt. Ellen borrowed Simone's skirt. Whose skirt and whose sweater did Joan and Doreen borrow?

145

5·12 Computer Application— Congruent Triangles

Anna had not done her homework on proving triangles congruent using the S.S.S. congruence postulate. However, she remembered that the length of the sides of the first triangle must be congruent to the corresponding length of sides of the second triangle. She was asked to prove whether the triangle with coordinates at (1, 4), (4, 5), and (3, 7) is congruent to the triangle with coordinates (2, 5), (5, 7), and (4, 8). Since the computer room was open, she ran this program to help her decide.

```
10 REM A PROGRAM TO TEST THE S.S.S. CONGRUENCE POSTULATE
20 INPUT "THE COORDINATES OF THE FIRST TRIANGLE";
X1, Y1, X2, Y2, X3, Y3
30 INPUT "THE COORDINATES OF THE SECOND TRIANGLE";
A1, B1, A2, B2, A3, B3
40 REM CHECK THE LENGTHS OF THE CORRESPONDING SIDES
50 IF SQR((Y2 - Y1) ∧ 2 + (X2 - X1) ∧ 2) <> SQR((B2 - B1) ∧ 2
+ (A2 - A1) ∧ 2) THEN 90
60 IF SQR ((Y3 - Y1) ∧ 2 + (X3 - X1) ∧ 2) <> SQR((B3 - B1) ∧ 2
+ (A3 - A1) ∧ 2) THEN 90
70 IF SQR((Y3 - Y2) ∧ 2 + (X3 - X2) ∧ 2) <> SQR((B3 - B2) ∧ 2
+ (A3 - A2) ∧ 2) THEN 90
80 PRINT "THE TRIANGLES ARE CONGRUENT"
85 GOTO 99
90 PRINT "THE TRIANGLES ARE NOT CONGRUENT"
99 END
```

Exercises

1. Run the program in the display to determine if the triangles are congruent. Verify the computer output by drawing the triangles on a coordinate grid.

2. What is the purpose of lines 50, 60, and 70 of the program in the display?

3. Run the program for these triangles.
a. Triangle 1: (2,2), (3,3), (4,5)
  Triangle 2: (3,3), (4,4), (5,6)
b. Triangle 1: (0,0), (5,0), (0,4)
  Triangle 2: (1,1), (6,1), (1,5)
c. Triangle 1: (3,2), (5,6), (8,8)
  Triangle 2: (3,5), (5,7), (8,10)

4. Modify the program in the display so that it prints the lengths of the sides of the triangles as they are calculated.

5. Verify the program in Exercise 4 by running it using the triangles of Exercise 3.

6. Elementary students often spend weeks learning the multiplication and division tables. Write a short essay on whether children should be allowed to use calculators or computers to eliminate the classroom time spent this way.

7. Modify the program in the display so that it prints the slopes of the sides of a triangle instead of the lengths. Verify your program using the triangles of Exercise 3.

5·13 Chapter Review

1. Calculate the measures of the indicated angles.

a.

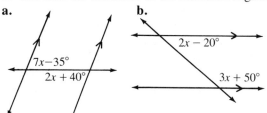

$7x - 35°$
$2x + 40°$

b.

$2x - 20°$
$3x + 50°$

2. Calculate the measures of the angles in the triangles.

a.

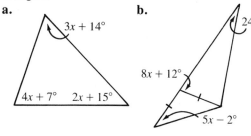

$3x + 14°$
$4x + 7°$ $2x + 15°$

b.

$24°$
$8x + 12°$
$5x - 2°$

3. Sketch a scalene triangle and find the perpendicular bisector of each of the sides.

4. In the triangles, what other information would have to be given in order to prove the triangles congruent using the congruence postulate shown?

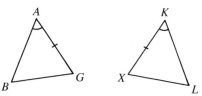

A *G* *B*   *K* *X* *L*

a. A.S.A. postulate   **b.** S.A.S. postulate

5. If $\overline{AB} \parallel \overline{MN}$ and $\overline{AX} \cong \overline{NX}$, then prove that $\triangle ABX \cong \triangle NMX$.

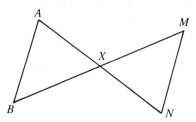

6. Prove that the bisector of the angle between the congruent sides in an isosceles triangle also bisects the side opposite that angle.

7. In quadrilateral *PQRS*, the diagonals bisect each other. Prove that *PQRS* is a parallelogram.

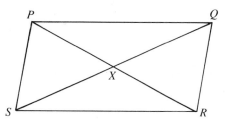

8. In your own words, explain the terms "postulate", "theorem", and "definition".

9. If the statement is always true, then write true. If the statement is not always true, then replace the underlined word to make it true.

a. A trapezoid is a <u>parallelogram</u>.

b. Consecutive angles of a <u>parallelogram</u> are supplementary.

c. A <u>square</u> is a parallelogram with a pair of adjacent sides congruent.

d. The diagonals of a <u>rectangle</u> are both congruent and perpendicular to each other.

e. One pair of opposite sides in a <u>trapezoid</u> is parallel.

10. In $\triangle JKR$, $\overline{JM} \cong \overline{JN}$ and $\angle KJM$ is not congruent to $\angle RJN$. Use an indirect proof to prove that $\overline{KM}$ is not congruent to $\overline{RN}$.

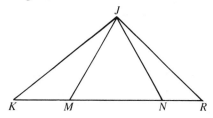

K *M* *N* *R*

11. Akim had 9 straws that had lengths of 2, 3, 4, 5, 6, 7, 8, 9, and 10 cm. How many triangles could Akim form if he used exactly 3 straws each time?

5·14 Chapter Test

1. From the diagram, choose the following pairs of angles.

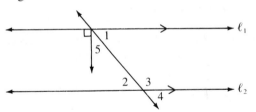

a. supplementary   **b.** alternate
c. consecutive interior   **d.** corresponding
e. complementary

2. Refer to the diagram in Exercise 1.
a. Name three different pairs of angles which could be used to prove that $\ell_1 \parallel \ell_2$.
b. State the reason for selecting each pair in part **a**.

3. Write an "if ... then" statement where
a. both the statement and its converse are true.
b. the statement is true and its converse is false.
c. both the statement and its converse are false.

4. Calculate the measure of $\angle a$.
a.

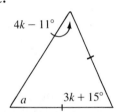

b.

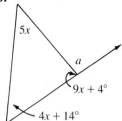

c.

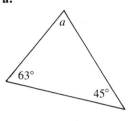

d.

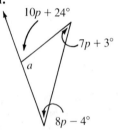

5. Name the quadrilateral(s) with these properties.
a. The diagonals are congruent.
b. Consecutive angles are congruent.
c. The figure is equilateral.
d. The diagonals meet at right angles.
e. Exactly one pair of opposite sides is parallel.
f. Every pair of consecutive angles is supplementary.
g. The diagonals bisect the vertices of the figure.

6. Triangle ACD is isosceles with $\overline{AC} \cong \overline{AD}$ and $\overline{BC} \cong \overline{ED}$. Prove that $\angle BAC \cong \angle EAD$.

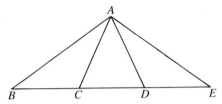

7. Refer to the diagram in Exercise 6. It is given that $\angle B \cong \angle E$ and $\overline{BC} \cong \overline{ED}$. Prove that $\triangle ADB \cong \triangle ACE$.

8. Given that $\overline{KM}$ and $\overline{NP}$ intersect at L with $\overline{NL} \cong \overline{PL}$ and $\overline{KL} \cong \overline{ML}$. Prove that $\overline{KN} \parallel \overline{PM}$.

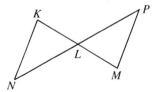

9. Use an indirect proof to prove that if n is an integer such that n^2 is odd, then n is also odd.

10. Find the total number of triangles in the figure having the given points as vertices and any of the given line segments as sides.

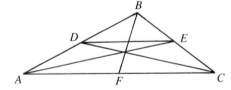

148

CHAPTER SIX

ANALYTIC GEOMETRY

Tune Up

1. Divide $5000 in a ratio of 3:5.

2. Solve the proportion.

a. $\dfrac{8}{p} = \dfrac{4}{12}$

b. $\dfrac{r-6}{r+1} = \dfrac{3}{5}$

3. This grid shows the numbering of the four quadrants on the Cartesian coordinate grid. Name the quadrant in which the ordered pair (x, y) is located.

a. $x>0$ and $y<0$ **b.** $x<0$ and $y>0$

c. $x<0$ and $y<0$ **d.** $x>0$ and $y>0$

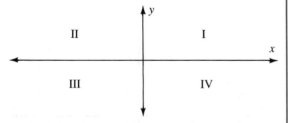

4. Where does the point (u, v) lie on the Cartesian coordinate grid?

a. $u<0$ and $v=0$ **b.** $v>0$ and $u=0$

5. Describe the coordinates of all ordered pairs (x, y) for each condition.

a. on the x-axis

b. on the y-axis

c. two units to the right of the y-axis

d. five units below the x-axis

e. symmetric about the x-axis

f. symmetric about the origin

6. Copy and complete the table of values. Graph the relation. Is this the graph of $y = 5$?

x	-3	-2	-1		1	
y	5	5	5	5		5

7. In many applications, the scales on the two axes of a graph are not the same. This graph shows pairs of points representing the distance, d, in kilometres and the time, t, in hours. Estimate the coordinates for each point.

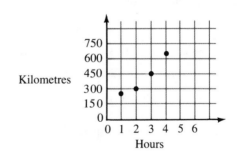

8. Describe the difference between the median and the altitude of a triangle. When is the median and the altitude the same line segment?

9. List the properties of each geometric shape.

a. a rhombus   **b.** a parallelogram

c. a trapezoid   **d.** an isosceles triangle

6·1 Slope

One of the main concerns of a skier going down a ski hill or a builder putting a roof on a house is the steepness or slope of the hill or roof. In mathematics, we use the term "**slope**" to mean the ratio of the vertical height (rise) to the horizontal length (run). For example, the Ptarmigan ski hill at Lake Louise has a vertical rise of 390 m and a horizontal run of 920 m. The slope of the ski hill is

$$\frac{rise}{run} = \frac{390}{920}$$
$$\doteq 0.42$$

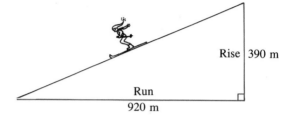

On a Cartesian coordinate grid, the slope ratio can be found by using the coordinates of two known points on the line. The rise, often denoted by Δy and read "delta y", is the difference between the y-values of the two points. The run, often denoted by Δx and read "delta x", is the difference between the x-values of the two points.

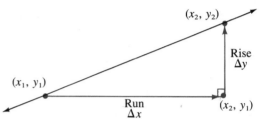

Slope $= \dfrac{\Delta y}{\Delta x}$ or $\dfrac{y_2 - y_1}{x_2 - x_1}$ for any two points (x_1, y_1) and (x_2, y_2) on the line.

Example

Calculate the slope of the line.

a.

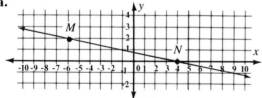

b.

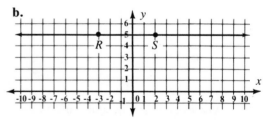

Two points on the graph can be identified as $M(-6, 2)$ and $N(4, 0)$.

Slope $= \dfrac{0 - 2}{4 - (-6)}$

$= \dfrac{-1}{5}$

The value for slope has no units.

This slope describes a line where a decrease of 1 unit in the y-values results in an increase of 5 units in the x-values. For example, starting at $N(4, 0)$ and moving 1 unit down and 5 units to the right gives another point on the line of $(9, -1)$.

Any horizontal line will have the same y-values. In this case, two points on the line are $(-3, 5)$ and $(2, 5)$.

Slope $= \dfrac{5 - 5}{2 - (-3)}$

$= 0$

Since the common y-values of any vertical line will result in a numerator of zero when calculating slope, all horizontal lines will have a slope of 0.

Exercises

1. In your own words, explain the meaning of the term "slope".

2. Determine Δx and Δy for each pair of points.
a. $(-3, 1)$, $(7, -5)$ **b.** $(2, -5)$, $(-4, -6)$
c. $(4x, -2y)$, $(x, 3y)$ **d.** (x_1, y_1), (x_2, y_2)

3. A.T., the "Mathematics Wizard", stated that the slope of a vertical line is **undefined**. Is A.T. correct? Explain. Use examples to support your answer.

4. Calculate the slope of a line passing through each pair of points.
a. $(0, 0)$, $(6, 3)$ **b.** $(-5, 5)$, $(2, 0)$
c. $(-3, 0)$, $(0, 7)$ **d.** $(-4, -3)$, $(4, 3)$
e. $(-1, -8)$, $(5, -8)$ **f.** $(2, 5)$, $(2, -1)$

5. Plot each pair of points in Exercise 4 on a co-ordinate grid and draw the line joining the two points. What general statement can you make about the direction of a line with a positive slope and the direction of a line with a negative slope?

6. Write an expression for the slope, if defined, of a line passing through each pair of points.
a. $(2a, b)$, $(-5a, 3b)$ **b.** (p, p^2), $(1, p)$
c. $(2, a + 2)$, $(1, 2)$ **d.** $(5r, 10s)$, $(15, 30)$
e. $(12v, 6v)$, $(-8v, 6v)$
f. $(m^2, -2m - 3)$, $(m + 6, -m^2)$
g. $(t^2 + 7t - 1, t^2 - 6t)$, $(-1 + 7t + t^2, 3 + t^2)$

7. What does the expression for the slope in Exercise 6, part **g**, indicate about the two given points? Substitute several values for t and graph the resulting points to support your answer.

8. The Nakiska ski hill at Mount Alan in Alberta has a vertical rise of 918 m and a horizontal run of 210 m. Calculate the slope to two decimal places.

9. A ramp leading up to a platform has a slope of $\frac{2}{3}$. If its horizontal run is 24 m, then find its vertical height.

10. A construction firm built a roof with a rise of 2.7 m on a house with a width of 14.5 m. What is the slope of the roof correct to one decimal place?

11. Determine the value of a such that the line joining the two points will have the indicated slope.
a. $(-6, a)$, $(3, -6)$; slope of $\frac{2}{5}$
b. $(-3, 5)$, $(2, a)$; slope of 0
c. $(a, -4)$, $(1, 5)$; slope is undefined
d. $(4, 3)$, $(a, -1)$; slope of -4

12. Determine the slope of each side of the figure.

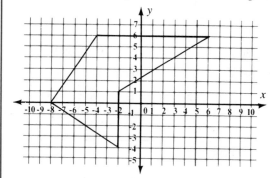

13. Use the coordinates of the vertices of these quadrilaterals to compare the slopes of opposite sides. What can you conclude about the slopes of opposite sides of each figure?
a. a rectangle   **b.** a square

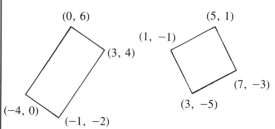

c. a rhombus   **d.** a parallelogram

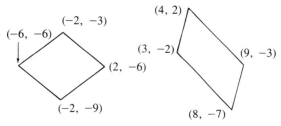

6·2 Sketching Linear Graphs

The visual representation of information is an important part of mathematics. Sketching graphs can be used as an aid when solving problems, presenting solutions, or analyzing relations. This section relates the concepts of slope and linear graphs.

Example

Sketch a line with a slope of $\frac{5}{3}$ and passing through the point $A(2, 1)$.

1. Plot the point $A(2, 1)$ on the grid.
2. From A, count 3 units to the right (a run of 3) and mark the point B.
3. From B, count 5 units straight up (a rise of 5) and mark the point C.
4. Draw a line through A and C. This line has a slope of $\frac{5}{3}$ and contains the point $(2, 1)$.

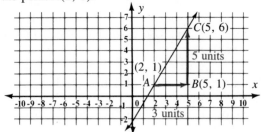

The example shows how to sketch a linear graph from the slope of the line and a point on the line. If you are given the slope of a line and a point on the line, any other point on the line can be found using the slope ratio.

Exercises

1. Sketch the graph of each special case.
a. $y = 3$ **b.** $x = -5$
c. $-y = \frac{3}{2}$ **d.** $-x = -\frac{5}{6}$

2. Sketch the line through each pair of points. Use the slope to identify three other points on the line.
a. $(-5, 2)$ and $(2, -4)$ **b.** $(-4, -3)$ and $(6, 1)$
c. $(-7, 4)$ and $(3, 2)$ **d.** $(3, 5)$ and $(-1, 0)$

3. Sketch the graph of each line.
a. Contains the point $(-3, 5)$ with a slope of $\frac{8}{3}$.
b. Has a slope of 4 and passes through $(0, -4)$.
c. Passes through $(-3, 5)$ and has a slope of 0.
d. Has a slope of $\frac{-3}{2}$ and passes through $(-5, -2)$.
e. Passes through $(2, 5)$ and the slope is undefined.

4. Sketch a line through $(0, 0)$ with each slope.
a. $\frac{4}{5}$ **b.** $\frac{-5}{2}$ **c.** $\frac{3}{-4}$ **d.** 0

5. Does the point $(-2, 5)$ lie on the line which passes through the points $(4, -1)$ and $(6, -3)$? Explain.

6. Use units of rise and run to sketch the lines passing through $(2, 1)$ with each slope.
a. -5 **b.** -1 **c.** $\frac{-1}{5}$
d. 0   **e.** $\frac{1}{5}$ **f.** undefined

7. Make a table of values to sketch the graph of $3x + 2y = 12$.

Historical Note

Thomas Harriot (1560-1621)
Harriot is considered the founder of the English school of Algebraists. His book, *Artis analyticae praxis*, dealt with the theory of equations and includes a treatment of equations in the first, second, third, and fourth degree. He was the first mathematician to use lower-case letters instead of capital letters for variables.

How would Harriot have written these expressions?
a. $AX^2 + BX + C$ **b.** $2X^2 - 7X^3 - 42X$
c. $3A^2 - 12A^3B^2$ **d.** $-8M - 24M^2X$

6·3 Collinear Points

The points in a set are **collinear** if they lie on the same straight line. In analytic geometry, there are three methods of checking collinearity: calculating the slopes between all points in the set, determining if there is an equation of a line through the points, or finding the distance between the points. The first method is discussed in this section.

Example

Use the slopes to determine if the points $M(-3, -2)$, $N(1, 2)$, and $P(5, 6)$ are collinear.

In order for the points to be collinear, the slope between the points must be the same.

The slope of $\overline{MN}$ is $\frac{2 - (-2)}{1 - (-3)} = \frac{4}{4} = 1$.

The slope of $\overline{NP}$ is $\frac{6 - 2}{5 - 1} = \frac{4}{4} = 1$.

The slope of $\overline{MP}$ is $\frac{6 - (-2)}{5 - (-3)} = \frac{8}{8} = 1$.

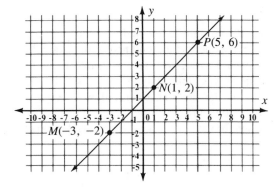

Since the slopes are the same, the points are collinear. By plotting the three points on a coordinate grid, and joining them, we can see that the points lie on the same straight line. Once again, other points on the line can be found by using the slope and any known point on the line.

Exercises

1. In your own words, explain the phrase "collinear points".

2. A.T., the "Mathematics Wizard", stated that the points $(-6.4, -2.1)$, $(-1, -3)$, and $(5, -4)$ are collinear. Is A.T. correct? Explain.

3. Determine which set of points are collinear.
a. $(4, 3)$, $(3, 4)$, $(2, 5)$
b. $(-3, 1)$, $(0, 0)$, $(1, -3)$
c. $(-5, 4)$, $(-1, 4)$, $(4, 4)$
d. $(1.5, 3)$, $(2.2, 4.5)$, $(3.1, 6.2)$
e. Is it necessary to calculate the slopes of all three segments? Explain.

4. Determine the coordinates of two other points collinear with each pair of points.
a. $(1, -1)$, $(3, 0)$ **b.** $(-2, -8)$, $(0, 0)$
c. $(6.2, -4)$, $(-3, 5.8)$ **d.** $(-3, r)$, $(4, 2r)$

5. Three ships at sea have grid references of $(-390, 50)$, $(60, 40)$, and $(-550, 150)$. Do the ships lie in a straight line? Explain.

6. Determine two other points on each line.
a. a y-intercept of -4; slope of $\frac{5}{7}$
b. an x-intercept of 5; slope of $\frac{-3}{2}$
c. through the point $(-2, -1)$; slope of 0
d. through the point $(4, -2)$; slope is undefined

7. Three fire lookout towers have grid references of $(-9, -5)$, $(1, 1)$ and $(17, 9)$. Determine whether the towers form a straight line.

8. List two other points collinear with the points (a, b) and $(-3a, 3b)$. Is $(0, 0)$ collinear with the given points? Explain.

9. A circle is cut by six straight lines. What is the maximum number of sections that can be produced?

6·4 Writing Linear Equations

Every set of collinear points can be defined by a linear equation that relates each abscissa with each ordinate.

Example 1

In a biology experiment, it was found that the relationship between the temperature, t, and the mass, g, of a microbe colony was linear. The graph of the relation shows that the line passes through the point $(-2, 5)$ and its slope is $\frac{\Delta g}{\Delta t} = 2$. Sketch the line on a coordinate grid and write an equation for the line.

Since a point on the line and the slope are given, we can use the method outlined in the example of Section 6·2 to locate a second point on the line. An equation for this relationship will satisfy all the points on the line. Therefore, if we choose any general point $P(t, g)$ on the line, we can write an equation for the slope using this point and the known point $(-2, 5)$.

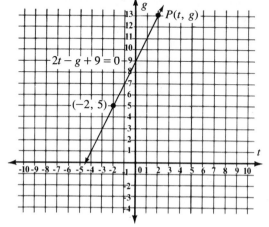

$$\text{Slope} = \frac{g_2 - g_1}{t_2 - t_1}$$
$$2 = \frac{g - 5}{t - (-2)}$$
$$2t + 4 = g - 5$$
$$2t - g + 9 = 0$$

The equation for the line is $2t - g + 9 = 0$. We verify the equation by substituting -2 for t and 5 for g. We get $2(-2) - 5 + 9 = 0$. The equation is verified.

The equation of a linear graph also can be determined by using two known points on the line.

Example 2

Sketch the graph of the line passing through $A(-3, 5)$ and $C(6, 1)$. Write an equation for this line.

Consider $B(x, y)$ as a general point on the line. Since A, B, and C are collinear, the slopes between them must be constant.

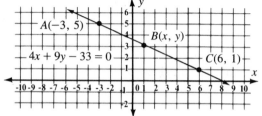

$$\therefore \text{Slope } \overline{AB} = \text{Slope } \overline{AC}$$
$$\frac{y - 5}{x - (-3)} = \frac{1 - 5}{6 - (-3)}$$
$$\frac{y - 5}{x + 3} = \frac{-4}{9}$$
$$9y - 45 = -4x - 12$$
$$4x + 9y - 33 = 0$$

The equation of the line is $4x + 9y - 33 = 0$. We verify the equation by using the ordered pairs $(-3, 5)$ and $(6, 1)$. Substituting, we get $4(-3) + 9(5) - 33 = 0$ and $4(6) + 9(1) - 33 = 0$. Since the original ordered pairs satisfy our equation, the equation is verified.

Exercises

1. Refer to Example 1.
a. The ordered pair was used, first to derive the equation and then to verify it. Explain why.
b. Explain what would happen if the variable g and t were reversed on the axes.

2. According to the graph in Example 1 of the display, the mass of the microbe is 9 g when the temperature is 0°C. Verify this by using the equation.

3. Sketch the graph of each line and write an equation for the line.
a. Passes through $(-7, 8)$ with a slope of -6.
b. Has a slope of $-\frac{5}{3}$ and contains the point $(0, 4)$.
c. Has a slope of 4 and passes through $(7, -3)$.
d. Passes through $(-2, -4)$ with a slope of $\frac{3}{7}$.
e. Passes through $(2, -1)$ with a slope of $-\frac{1}{4}$.

4. Graph the line through each pair of points and write an equation for the line.
a. $(1, 5), (7, 2)$ **b.** $(-2, 0), (4, 4)$
c. $(-4, -3), (2, -1)$ **d.** $(0, 7), (7, 0)$

5. Collinearity can be checked by determining an equation of the line joining the points.
a. Sketch the graph of the line through $A(-3, 11)$ and $B(3, 3)$.
b. Write an equation for the line.
c. Does the point $D(6, -1)$ lie on the line?
d. What conclusion can you make about the three points?

6. In a sailing regatta, the finish line was designated on a grid by two buoys located at $A(-20, 30)$ and $B(50, -20)$. Two sailboats are located at $R(20, 0)$ and $S(0, 22)$. Which sailboat is located on the finish line? Explain.

7. Set up a table of five ordered pairs that satisfy each equation and graph the points to verify that the equation describes a straight line.
a. $t = 3s + 1$ **b.** $p + q = 12$
c. $y - 6 = 2(x - 1)$ **d.** $4x - 2y + 10 = 0$

8. Write an equation of a horizontal line through each point.
a. $(2, 4)$ **b.** $(-5, 1)$ **c.** $(0, 3)$ **d.** $(-1, 0)$

9. Equations of vertical lines cannot be determined by the process used in Example 1. Sketch the vertical line through each point and write an equation of the line. Verify the equation by substituting points on the line.
a. $(2, 4)$ **b.** $(-5, 1)$ **c.** $(0, 3)$ **d.** $(-1, 0)$

10. Sketch the graph of each line and write an equation of the line.
a. Passes through $(3, 1)$ parallel to the x-axis.
b. Has a slope of $\frac{-5}{2}$ and a y-intercept of 3.
c. Has an x-intercept at 4 and a y-intercept at -1.
d. Passes through $(4, -2)$ parallel to the y-axis.
e. Has a slope of 3 and an x-intercept of -6.
f. Perpendicular to the x-axis and has an x-intercept of 5.

11. The length, L, of a spring and the attached mass, k, are related by a linear equation. When the length of the spring is 117 cm, there is a 6 kg mass attached to it. When the spring is 225 cm long, a 15 kg mass is attached to it.
a. Write a linear equation that describes this relation between the variables k and L.
b. How long is the spring when no mass is attached?

12. Write equations of the lines containing the sides of each geometric figure.
a.   **b.**

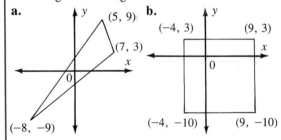

13. Determine equations for the diagonals of rhombus $JKLM$ with vertices at $J(-3, 0), K(0, 4), L(5, 4)$, and $M(2, 0)$.

14. In your own words, explain the steps required to write an equation of a line given its slope and one point on the line.

6·5 Graphing Linear Equations I

Information can be obtained from a linear equation which can be used to help sketch a graph of the set of points. For example, the linear equation $y - 5 = 4(x - 1)$ is written in a convenient form for graphing.

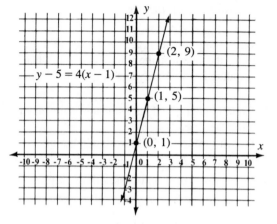

Since only two points are needed to form a line, any two ordered pairs that satisfy the equation can be used. In this case, plot the points $(0, 1)$ and $(2, 9)$, and draw a line through them.

The slope of the line can be determined by using the same two points. Therefore, the slope is $\frac{9-1}{2-0}$ or 4.

By substituting the point $(1, 5)$ into the equation, we can check if it is on the line.

$$y - 5 = 4(x - 1)$$
$$5 - 5 = 4(1 - 1)$$
$$0 = 0$$

Therefore, $(1, 5)$ is a point on the line. Note the relationship between the slope, the point $(1, 5)$, and the equation of the line. The equation $y - 5 = 4(x - 1)$ is said to be in **point-slope** form since the slope and a point on the line can be identified easily.

> The point-slope form of a linear equation is $y - y_1 = m(x - x_1)$ where m is the slope and (x_1, y_1) is a point on the line.

Example 1

Sketch the graph of the equation $y - 3 = -2(x + 5)$.

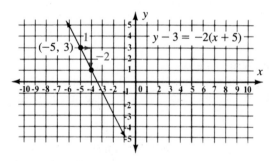

The equation is in the point-slope form. Therefore, the slope is -2 and $(-5, 3)$ is a point on the line. By using the method outlined in the previous sections, we can sketch the graph using the slope and the point.

The point-slope form can be used to write linear equations when two points on the line are given, or when a point and the slope are given.

Example 2

Write an equation for the line in the point-slope form.
a. passing through $(-1, 4)$ and $(5, -2)$

The slope of the line passing through these points is -1. Using the point $(5, -2)$, the equation of the line is $y + 2 = -(x - 5)$.

b. containing $(-3, 2)$ with a slope of 5

Since $m = 5$, $x_1 = -3$, and $x_2 = 2$ the equation of the line in the point-slope form is $y - 2 = 5(x + 3)$.

156

The equation $y = 2x - 7$ also is written in a convenient form for graphing. Since only two points are needed to graph the line, it often is easiest to use the x- and y-intercepts. Recall that the x-intercept is the point where the line crosses the x-axis ($y = 0$), and the y-intercept is the point where the line crosses the y-axis ($x = 0$). A table of values is set up with the x-intercept, the y-intercept, and a third point on the line.

x	y
$\frac{7}{2}$	0
0	-7
3	-1

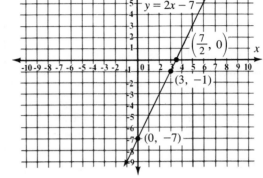

Using the points $(0, -7)$ and $(3, -1)$, the slope of the line can be found.

$$m = \frac{-1 - (-7)}{3 - 0}$$
$$= 2$$

m represents slope.

Notice the relationship between the slope, the y-intercept, and the equation of the line. The equation $y = 2x - 7$ is in the **slope y-intercept** form, where the slope is 2 and the y-intercept is -7.

> The slope y-intercept form of a linear equation is $y = mx + b$, where m is the slope and b is the y-intercept.

Example 3

Sketch the graph of $y = -4x + 5$.

Since the equation is in the slope y-intercept form, the slope is -4 and the y-intercept is 5. In order to graph the line, plot the point $(0, 5)$ on the graph and, using the slope, find another point on the graph. Now that we have two points on the line, we can sketch the graph of $y = -4x + 5$.

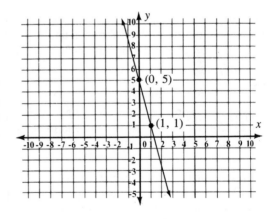

The slope y-intercept form can be used to write linear equations when the slope and the y-intercept of a line is known.

Example 4

Use the slope y-intercept form to write an equation of a line through the point $(0, -3)$ with a slope of 6.

The point $(0, -3)$ indicates that the y-intercept of the line is -3. Therefore, $b = -3$. Since the slope is 6, $m = 6$, and the equation of the line is $y = 6x - 3$.

157

Exercises

1. In your own words, explain the meaning of each term. Use examples if necessary.
a. the point-slope form of a linear equation
b. the slope y-intercept form of a linear equation
c. the y-intercept
d. the x-intercept

2. Identify the slope and one point on the line. Sketch the graph of each equation. If necessary, rewrite the equation in the point-slope form.
a. $y - 3 = 5(x - 2)$ **b.** $y + 6 = -2(x - 1)$
c. $y + 12 = 0.5(x + 4)$ **d.** $y - 1 = 6x + 18$
e. $-2(y + 4) = -x + 1$ **f.** $-3y - 6 = 5x + 30$

3. Write an equation of each line in the point-slope form and sketch the graph.
a. passing through $(0, 5)$ and $(2, -3)$
b. containing $(-3, 4)$ with a slope of -1
c. passing through $(-2, -5)$ with a slope of $\frac{5}{3}$
d. passing through $(-1, 6)$ and $(3, 2)$
e. passing through $(0, 3)$ and $(-4, 0)$
f. containing $(0, 0)$ with a slope of $\frac{-7}{9}$

4. Show how the point-slope form of the linear equation can be obtained from the definition of slope. (*Hint*: Use $m = \frac{y_2 - y_1}{x_2 - x_1}$.)

5. In your own words, explain why a linear equation in the form $y + 3 = -2(x + 1)$ is said to be in the point-slope form.

6. On a coordinate grid, a submarine sails from $(7, -8)$ to $(-9, 6)$. Write a linear equation in the point-slope form for the submarine's course.

7. On his telephone bill, Ernie was charged $6.74 for an 8 min call to Halifax and $9.94 for a 13 min call to Halifax.
a. Write a linear equation in the form $c = mt + b$ describing the relation between the charge, c, for the phone calls and the length, t, of the call.
b. Sketch the graph of the equation.
c. What would be the charge for a 22 min call?

8. Identify the slope and the y-intercept of each line and sketch the graph of the equation. If necessary, rewrite the equation in the slope y-intercept form.
a. $y = -x + 4$ **b.** $y = -\frac{7}{3}x + \frac{5}{2}$
c. $y = 2(x + 1)$ **d.** $3y = 6x - 5$
e. $-5y = 2x - 4$ **f.** $2y - 5x = 8$

9. Write the equation of each line in the slope y-intercept form and sketch the graph.
a. a y-intercept of 4 and a slope of -2
b. $m = \frac{6}{7}$ and $b = 7$
c. a slope of $\frac{-3}{4}$ and a y-intercept of $-\frac{4}{5}$
d. through $(0, -5)$ with slope of 8
e. $b = \frac{-1}{3}$ and $m = -1$

10. Write each equation in the slope y-intercept form and sketch the graph.
a. $y - 2 = 3x + 5$ **b.** $2x - 3 = 4y + 6$
c. $y - 5 = 4(x + 2)$ **d.** $3y = 5x + 4$
e. $6y + 3 = 4x - 1$ **f.** $5x - 3y - 18 = 0$

11. Write each equation in the point-slope form.
a. $y = 5x - 2$ **b.** $2y = -3x + 4$
c. $-3y + 5 = x - 1$ **d.** $2(y + 5) = -x + 2$

12. Show how the slope y-intercept form of the linear equation can be derived from the definition of slope. (*Hint*: Use $m = \frac{y_2 - y_1}{x_2 - x_1}$.)

13. Su-tai hopes to buy a used car for $1700. She starts a savings account with $200 and each week she plans to add $55.
a. Write a linear equation in the form $a = mw + b$ which relates the amount of money, a, with the number of weeks, w. Use the horizontal axis for weeks.
b. Find the slope and the point of intersection with the vertical axis.
c. Sketch the graph of the equation.
d. How much money will she have in 15 weeks?
e. How long will it take her before she has enough money to buy the car?

6·6 Graphing Linear Equations II

In this section, you will be introduced to the standard form of a linear equation (any equation in the form $Ax + By + C = 0$), and its relationship to the point-slope form of a linear equation and the slope y-intercept form of a linear equation.

Example 1

Determine the slope and the y-intercept of the equation $4x - 5y + 2 = 0$. Sketch the graph of the line.

In order to find the slope and the y-intercept, it is easiest to write the equation in the slope y-intercept form by solving for y.

Therefore, $4x - 5y + 2 = 0$.

$$y = \frac{4}{5}x + \frac{2}{5}$$

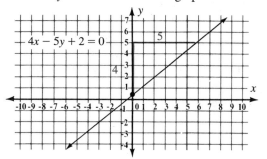

The graph of the line now can be sketched using the y-intercept of $\frac{2}{5}$ and the slope of $\frac{4}{5}$.

The equation $4x - 5y + 2 = 0$ is written in standard form, where $A = 4$, $B = -5$, and $C = 2$. The slope of the line is $\frac{4}{5}\left(-\frac{A}{B}\right)$ and the y-intercept is $\frac{2}{5}\left(-\frac{C}{B}\right)$. The slope and the x-intercept also can be determined from the standard form in order to graph it.

Example 2

Determine the slope and the x-intercept of the equation $-2x + 3y - 4 = 0$. Sketch the graph of the line.

From Example 1, we know that the slope is
$$-\frac{A}{B} = -\frac{(-2)}{3} = \frac{2}{3}.$$

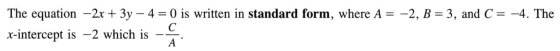

The x-intercept is evaluated at $y = 0$. By substituting $y = 0$ into the equation we get,
$-2x + 3(0) - 4 = 0$
$\qquad -2x = 4$
$\qquad\quad x = -2$

Therefore, the x-intercept is -2. By using the point $(-2, 0)$ and the slope $\frac{2}{3}$, we can sketch the graph of the equation.

The equation $-2x + 3y - 4 = 0$ is written in **standard form**, where $A = -2$, $B = 3$, and $C = -4$. The x-intercept is -2 which is $-\frac{C}{A}$.

The standard form of a linear equation is $Ax + By + C = 0$. The x-intercept is $-\frac{C}{A}$, the y-intercept is $-\frac{C}{B}$, and the slope is $-\frac{A}{B}$.

159

Exercises

1. Express each equation in standard form.
a. $3x - 5y = 16$ **b.** $y = 2x + 1$
c. $y - 3 = 2(x + 1)$ **d.** $y = \frac{3}{10}x - \frac{2}{5}$

2. Use the y-intercept and the slope to sketch the graph of these lines.
a. $2x - 3y - 1 = 0$ **b.** $-x + y + 5 = 0$
c. $3x - 2y + 5 = 0$ **d.** $4x + 7y - 28 = 0$
e. $-5x + y - 15 = 0$ **f.** $8x - 5y + 16 = 0$

3. Rewrite the equation in standard form and use the x-intercept and the slope to sketch the graph of these lines.
a. $y - 3 = -(x + 2)$
b. $2y - 5x - 3 = 0$
c. $-7y + 4 = -5(x - 1)$
d. $y = \frac{3}{2}x + 4$
e. $-y + 4 = 3x + 5$
f. $5 = 3x + 7y$

4. Rewrite the equation in standard form and sketch the graph of the equation using the x-intercept and the y-intercept.
a. $x - 3y = 2$ **b.** $6y - 2 = -x$
c. $-\frac{4}{5}y - 3 = \frac{2}{7}x + 3$ **d.** $y - 2 = (x + 6)$

5. Write the equation of each line in standard form.
a. a slope of -2; a y-intercept of 3
b. an x-intercept of $-\frac{5}{2}$; a y-intercept of $\frac{5}{3}$
c. a slope of $\frac{4}{3}$; an x-intercept of $\frac{-3}{2}$
d. a y-intercept of 0; a slope of 0

6. Special cases occur when A or B are equal to 0. Graph each and explain what is special.
a. $0x + 6y + 12 = 0$ **b.** $0x - 4y - 9 = 0$
c. $3x + 0y + 9 = 0$ **d.** $-8x + 0y - 6 = 0$

7. The slope y-intercept form of the equation is extremely useful when information about the slope or the y-intercept is either given or required. Is the standard form more useful when graphing the equation? Explain.

8. Write an equation of the line for each graph in standard form.
a. 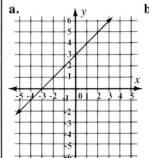   **b.**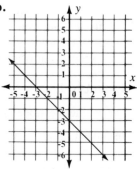

9. Sketch the graph of each line and write an equation for the line in standard form.
a. Passes through $(-5, -1)$ and $(5, 1)$.
b. Passes through $(-3, 4)$ with a slope of $\frac{-7}{5}$.
c. Has a y-intercept of 3 and a slope of 0.5.
d. Has an x-intercept and a y-intercept at 7 and -1 respectively.
e. Has a slope of -3 and an x-intercept of 1.

10. This table lists the taxi fares, f, in dollars for the various distances, d, in kilometres travelled.

d	0	8	14	25
f	\$3.10	\$7.90	\$11.50	\$18.10

a. Plot the points on a Cartesian coordinate grid.
b. Write an equation describing the relation between f and d in standard form.
c. What does the ordered pair $(0, 3.10)$ tell us about hiring a taxi?
d. What is the cost per kilometre after the initial cost?

11. On a grid reference, a bulldozer plows a straight road from $(-12, 15)$ to a distant point. The slope of the line is $\frac{6}{5}$. Write an equation for its course in standard form.

12. Determine an equation for a line through $(a, 9)$ and $(4, -1)$.
a. For what value of a is the slope of the line undefined?
b. For what value of a is the slope positive? negative?

160

13. The Student Council for East Hill Collegiate was investigating the cost of dinner for their spring formal. The caterer's brochure showed the cost of $2520 for 150 people. This cost included a fixed cost and a cost per person. If 250 people went to the formal, the cost would be $4120.

a. Write a linear equation describing the relation between the total cost, c, and the number of people, p.

b. Sketch the graph of the line.

c. What is the fixed cost?

d. What is the cost per person after the basic cost?

e. What is the cost for 100 people? for 375 people?

14. Identify the form of each equation and find the x-intercept, the y-intercept, and the slope.

a. $y - 3 = -5(x + 1)$ **b.** $4x - y + 7 = 0$

c. $y = 7x - 2$ **d.** $mx - ny - p = 0$

e. $y + e = -f(x - g)$ **f.** $y = px - q$

g. $-3(x + a) + 4(y - b) = c$

h. $(a + b)x + (c + d)y + (e + f) = 0$

15. Write linear equations for the lines forming each geometric figure.

a.

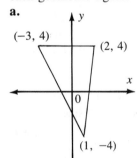

b.

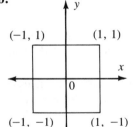

c.

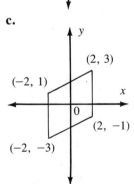

d.

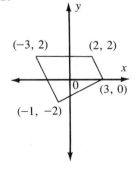

16. For what value of p will the given point lie on the given line?

a. $(7, -13)$; $3x - (5 + p)y + 5 = 0$

b. $(0, 5)$; $y - 4 = (1 - p)x + 1$

c. $(-5, 7)$; $(9 - p)x + (4 + p)y = 19$

d. $\left(\frac{17}{8}, 0\right)$; $y - (2p + 1) = px$

17. For what values of h will the given points lie on the line $5x - 8y + 37 = 0$?

a. $(4, h)$ **b.** $(-h, 12)$ **c.** $(h, 0)$

d. $\left(-\frac{h}{2}, -7\right)$ **e.** $(4h, 17)$ **f.** $(-23, h)$

18. The monthly electrical bill for an office building in Fredericton is determined by a basic charge and an additional charge per kilowatt hour used. The electrical bill for May was $82.93 for 869 kWh; while the bill for March was $94.69 for 1052 kWh.

a. Write a linear equation relating the total charge, c, to the total number of kilowatt hours, h, and sketch the graph of the equation.

b. What is the basic charge?

c. What is the cost per kilowatt hour after the basic charge?

19. Explain how each graph differs from that of $y = 3x + 4$.

a. $y = -3x + 4$ **b.** $y = x + 4$

c. $y = 3x - 2$ **d.** $y = 3x$

20. Explain how the graph of the equation differs from that of $y - 3 = 2(x + 4)$.

a. $y - 5 = 2(x + 4)$ **b.** $y - 3 = 2(x - 4)$

c. $y - 3 = (x + 4)$ **d.** $y - 3 = -2(x + 4)$

21. Explain how the graph of the equation differs from that of $4x - 5y - 2 = 0$.

a. $2x - 5y + 2 = 0$ **b.** $4x + 3y + 2 = 0$

c. $4x - 5y - 3 = 0$ **d.** $x - y = 0$

Braintickler

If $5^{\blacksquare} \bullet 7^{\blacksquare} \bullet 6^{\blacksquare} = 44$,

       $1^{\blacksquare} \bullet 3^{\blacksquare} \bullet 2^{\blacksquare} = 8$,

and $3^{\blacksquare} \bullet 5^{\blacksquare} \bullet 4^{\blacksquare} = 22$,

then $7^{\blacksquare} \bullet 9^{\blacksquare} \bullet 8^{\blacksquare} = \blacksquare\blacksquare$.

6·7 Families of Lines

The next two sections examine the mathematical properties of special types of lines. A set of linear equations that have either one point or a slope in common is called a **family of lines**.

Example

Write an equation for the family of lines that pass through the point $(-1, 4)$. Before writing an equation, plot the point on a coordinate grid and draw several lines through the point $(-1, 4)$. Notice that the slopes of these lines are all different. Let (x, y) represent a point on any of the family of lines. The definition of slope can be used to obtain an equation for the family of lines through the point $(-1, 4)$.

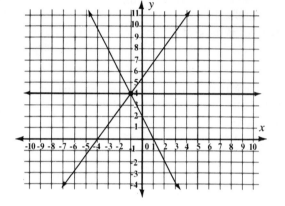

Therefore, $m = \dfrac{y - 4}{x + 1}$

$m(x + 1) = y - 4$

$y = m(x + 1) + 4$

The parameter in this case is m and it represents the changing slopes of the lines. A **parameter** can be assigned any value to identify one particular member of the family.

> The equation for the family of lines through the point (x_1, y_1) is $y = m(x - x_1) + y_1$.

Exercises

1. Find the slope of each line in the example. Substitute the slope for m in $y = m(x + 1) + 4$ and simplify.

2. Write an equation for the family of lines that share the common point.
a. $(4, -2)$ **b.** $(-1, 5)$ **c.** $(-3, -7)$
d. $(0, -8)$ **e.** $(2, 0)$ **f.** $(6, -9)$

3. Identify the common point and graph four members from these families of lines.
a. $y = m(x - 3) - 2$ **b.** $y = m(x + 1) + 6$
c. $y = m(x + 4)$ **d.** $y = mx - 3$

4. Write the equation of the line with a slope of -3 and passing through each point. Sketch the graph.
a. $(2, 4)$ **b.** $(-1, 5)$ **c.** $(-3, -1)$ **d.** $(0, -3)$
e. What do you notice about the equations and the graphs of these lines?

5. Can a family of lines for a slope of -3 be described by $y = -3x + b$? Explain. What is the parameter in this case? What effect does a change in the value of the parameter have?

6. Graph three members from each of the family of lines. Write the equation of each line.
a. $y = -x + b$ **b.** $y = 2x + b$ **c.** $y = -\dfrac{1}{4}x + b$

7. Write a general equation for the family of lines.
a. $m = -\dfrac{1}{2}$ **b.** y-intercept of -6

8. Write an equation describing each family of lines.
a. **b.**

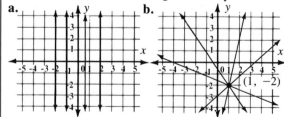

6·8 Parallel and Perpendicular Lines

Recall that the slopes of two parallel lines are equal and that the slopes of two perpendicular lines are negative reciprocals.

Example 1

Write an equation for the line passing through $(-2, 7)$ which is parallel to the line $7x + 6y + 24 = 0$.
The two lines are parallel if they have the same slope. In this case, the slope of the lines is $-\frac{7}{6}$.

$$(y - 7) = -\frac{7}{6}(x + 2)$$

$$6(y - 7) = -7(x + 2)$$

$$7x + 6y - 28 = 0$$

In both equations, the numerical coefficients of x and y remained the same and the constant term changed.

Example 2

Write an equation for the line through $(3, -2)$ which is perpendicular to the line $-2x + 5y - 9 = 0$.
The slopes must be negative reciprocals in order for the lines to be perpendicular. Since the slope of the given line is $\frac{2}{5}$, the slope of the required line is $-\frac{5}{2}$.

$$(y + 2) = -\frac{5}{2}(x - 3)$$

$$2(y + 2) = -5(x - 3)$$

$$2y + 4 = -5x + 15$$

$$5x + 2y - 11 = 0$$

Exercises

1. In your own words, explain the meaning of "parallel lines" and "perpendicular lines". Graph the lines in Examples 1 and 2 to help with your explanation.

2. Write an equation for each line through the given point. Sketch the graphs.
a. $(-7, 3)$, parallel to $2x - y + 4 = 0$
b. $(2, -1)$, perpendicular to $6x - y + 10 = 0$
c. $\left(-7, \frac{1}{4}\right)$, parallel to a line with slope $-\frac{4}{3}$
d. $\left(-7, \frac{1}{4}\right)$, perpendicular to a line with slope $-\frac{4}{3}$

3. If $a\Delta b = (a + b) + (ab) + b$, evaluate $(2\Delta3)\Delta6$.

4. Sketch the graph of each pair of equations and state the relation between the two lines.
a. $y = 2x + 4$ **b.** $y - 2 = 3(x + 1)$
$\quad y = -\frac{1}{2}x + 4$ $\quad y - 3 = 3(x + 4)$

5. Explain how the graph of each line is related to the graph of $-3x + y - 4 = 0$.
a. $-3x + y + 6 = 0$ **b.** $-x + 3y - 4 = 0$
c. $x - 3y + 6 = 0$ **d.** $-3x + y + 5 = 0$

6. Which pairs of equations describe parallel or perpendicular lines. Verify your answers by sketching the graphs of the lines.
a. $y = 7x + 1$ **b.** $y - 3 = 2(x + 5)$
c. $4x - 2y - 3 = 0$ **d.** $7y = -x + 2$
e. $x = 6$ **f.** $7x - y + 5 = 0$
g. $y = -1$ **h.** $x = 0$

6·9 Lengths and Midpoints

In analytic geometry, it is often necessary to find the distance between two points on a grid system. Although the distance sometimes can be estimated, it is desirable to have an algebraic solution to give more accurate results. The Pythagorean Theorem can be used.

The diagram shows the roof of a house with vertices at $A(5, 1)$, $B(-9, 1)$, and $C(-2, 7)$. An architect wants to find the length of one slant side of the roof.

Understand the Problem
What is the width of the house? What is the height of the roof peak above the ceiling?

Develop a Plan
If you know the lengths of the legs of a right triangle, the Pythagorean Theorem can be used to find the length of the hypotenuse (the slant side).

Carry Out the Plan
To find the length of the hypotenuse:
$$\overline{AC}^2 = \overline{AD}^2 + \overline{DC}^2$$
$$= [5 - (-2)]^2 + (7 - 1)^2$$
$$\overline{AC}^2 = 7^2 + 6^2$$
$$\overline{AC} \doteq 9.2$$

The length of the slant side is about 9.2 units.

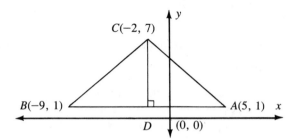

Look Back
State the method you used in a general formula for all analytic situations.

> The distance between two points $P(x_1, y_1)$ and $Q(x_2, y_2)$ is $|\overline{PQ}| = \sqrt{(x_2 - x_1)^2 + (y_2 - y_1)^2}$.

The architect wants to position vertical supports in the middle of each slanted portion of the roof (at points E and F). Two congruent triangles AHE and EGC are formed by the support on the right. Point E has the same x-coordinate as point H, and visually, this can be estimated as 1.5. Since H is the midpoint of the length from A to D, the x-coordinate can be calculated as:

$$x = \frac{5 + (-2)}{2}$$
$$= 1.5$$

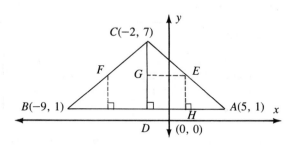

Also, E has the same y-coordinate as G, and the same method can be used to find the y-coordinate:

$$y = \frac{1 + 7}{2}$$
$$= 4$$

Hence, the coordinates of E are (1.5, 4). The coordinates for F are found in a similar manner.

> The midpoint of a line segment with endpoints at (x_1, y_1) and (x_2, y_2) is $P(x, y) = \left(\dfrac{x_1 + x_2}{2}, \dfrac{y_1 + y_2}{2}\right)$.

Example

Find the length and midpoint of the line segment between $T(-5, -3)$ and $V(7, 0)$.

To find the length, use the formula:

$|\overline{TV}| = \sqrt{(x_2 - x_1)^2 + (y_2 - y_1)^2}$
$= \sqrt{(7 - (-5))^2 + (0 - (-3))^2}$
$= \sqrt{(12)^2 + (3)^2}$
$= \sqrt{153}$
$\doteq 12.4$

To find the midpoint, use the formula:

$\text{Midpoint} = \left(\dfrac{x_1 + x_2}{2}, \dfrac{y_1 + y_2}{2}\right)$
$= \left(\dfrac{-5 + 7}{2}, \dfrac{-3 + 0}{2}\right)$
$= (1, -1.5)$

The line segment is approximately 12.4 units long and its midpoint is at $(1, -1.5)$.

Exercises

1. Find the coordinates of F on the roof shown in the display. Explain how you arrived at these coordinates.

2. In your own words, explain how to find the length of a line segment and the coordinates of the midpoint given the coordinates of its endpoints.

3. Calculate $|\overline{AB}|$ for $A(-4, 2)$ and $B(8, -3)$. Does it matter in which order we choose the x-coordinates? the y-coordinates? Explain.

4. Find the distance between each pair of points correct to one decimal place.
a. $(0, 0)$ and $(4, 3)$
b. $(-2, 6)$ and $(3, 1)$
c. $(-8, 0)$ and $(-1, 0)$
d. $(-6, -4)$ and $(2, 0)$
e. $(3, 5)$ and $(2, -1.4)$
f. $(-3.2, 6)$ and $(7, 1)$

5. Which of these points are exactly five units from the origin?
a. $(3, 4)$ **b.** $(0, 5)$ **c.** $(4, 4)$
d. $(1, 6)$ **e.** $(-5, 0)$ **f.** $(-3, 4)$

6. Find the midpoint of the line joining each pair of points.
a. $(1, 1)$ and $(7, 1)$
b. $(-5, 4)$ and $(3, -2)$
c. $(0, 3)$ and $(3, 0)$
d. $(-5, 6)$ and $(-5, -3)$
e. $(-6, -3)$ and $(7, 3)$
f. $(-7.1, 4.3)$ and $(5.2, -0.8)$

7. Show that quadrilateral $DEFG$ with vertices at $D(-1, 1)$, $E(-3, -4)$, $F(2, -2)$, and $G(4, 3)$ is a rhombus. (*Hint*: A rhombus has all sides equal in length.)

8. Triangle XYZ is a right triangle with vertices at $Y(-3, 6)$ and $Z(-3, 2)$. What are two possible sets of coordinates for the vertex X located on the y-axis?

9. A satellite determines the coordinates of two ships at sea as $(-12, 16)$ and $(9, -7)$. Determine the distance between the two ships and the coordinates of the midpoint between them.

10. Which of these points lie in the interior of a circle with centre at $(2, 3)$ and radius 3? Explain.
a. $(5, 1)$ **b.** $(0, 0)$ **c.** $(2, 0)$
d. $(0, 6)$ **e.** $(4, 5)$ **f.** $(3, 1)$

11. For a triangle with vertices at $A(0, 0)$, $B(10, 0)$ and $C(14, 10)$, find the equation of the line that contains the median from each vertex, the equation of the line that contains the altitude from each vertex, and the length of each median and altitude.

12. Graph quadrilateral $ABCD$ with coordinates at $A(-6, 1)$, $B(2, 7)$, $C(5, -2)$, and $D(-5, -3)$.
a. Label the coordinates of the midpoints of each side and join them.
b. What figure is formed?
c. Prove your answer to part **b** by using the slope and the length of the lines.

13. A circle passes through the vertices of $\triangle PQR$ with vertices at $P(-5, 7)$, $Q(6, 10)$, and $R(-2, -4)$.
a. If $\overline{QR}$ is a diameter of the circle, then find the coordinates of the centre of the circle.
b. Show that $\triangle PQR$ is a right triangle.

14. Two craters on the Earth's Moon are Plato and Copernicus. Their locations on a grid are $P(123, 165)$ and $C(-78, 210)$. The proposed landing site of a satellite probe is $(200, 0)$.
a. Calculate the distance between the two craters.
b. Calculate the coordinates of the midpoint between the craters.
c. Write an equation for the line from the landing site, perpendicular to the line connecting the two craters.
d. What is the distance from the landing site to each crater?

15. Points A, B, and C, in that order, are collinear if $|\overline{AB}| + |\overline{BC}| = |\overline{AC}|$. Use the lengths of the line segments joining points A, B, and C to find which points are collinear.
a. $A(-2, 4)$, $B(6, 10)$, $C(-10, -2)$
b. $A(4, -6)$, $B(2, -2)$, $C(11, 3)$
c. $A(3, 3)$, $B(10, -3)$, $C(-4, 9)$
d. $A(-5, -4)$, $B(5, 6)$, $C(-9, 3)$

16. A.T., the "Mathematics Wizard", plotted the points $M(12, 15)$, $N(4, 7)$ and $R(-8, -5)$ on a coordinate grid and stated that the triangle formed, with these points as the vertices, had an area of one square unit. Is A.T. correct? Explain.

17. If $\overline{TS}$ is parallel to the y-axis and its midpoint is on the x-axis, then find the coordinates of T in each case.
a. if S is at $(4, 5)$ **b.** if S is at $(-3, -1)$
c. if S is at (a, b) **d.** if S is at $(m + 2, n - 3)$

18. If $\overline{KL}$ is parallel to the x-axis and its midpoint is on the y-axis, then find the coordinates of K in each case.
a. if L is at $(3, -2)$ **b.** if L is at $(2, 4)$
c. if L is at (p, q) **d.** if L is at $(k + 2, k - 3)$

19. Write an expression for the distance between each pair of points and an expression for the midpoints.
a. $(2, a)$, $(5, a)$ **b.** $(p, -1)$, $(q, -1)$
c. (m, n), $(1, 1)$ **d.** (a, b), $(a - 2, b + 3)$
e. $(2p, 4q)$, $(3p, 6q)$ **f.** $(3, t + 1)$, $(2t, t - 1)$

20. In $\triangle EFG$, $\overline{EK}$ is both a median and an altitude.

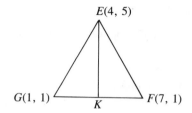

a. Determine the coordinates of K.
b. Compare the slopes of $\overline{EK}$ and $\overline{FG}$. What do you notice?
c. Calculate the area of $\triangle EFG$ using $\overline{FG}$ as a base and $\overline{EK}$ as the height.

21. Red Deer has a spherical water tank with a radius of 4 m. The town council decides to double the mass of water on reserve by replacing the tank with a new one. What should be the diameter of the new water tank?

Using the Library

In 1829, geometer Julius Plücker (1801-1868) made interesting contributions to the study of analytic geometry. He noted that the fundamental element in geometry need not be the point and that geometric entities such as straight lines or circles can be used instead.

a. Research Plücker's contribution to analytic geometry and write a short paper on his contributions.
b. The negative reciprocals, u and v, of the x- and y-intercepts of a line are known as the line's Plücker coordinates. Find the Plücker coordinates of the lines whose Cartesian equations are $5x + 3y - 6 = 0$ and $ax + by + 1 = 0$.
c. Write the Cartesian equation of the line having Plücker coordinates of $(1, 3)$.

6·10 Division of Line Segments

Any point on a line segment will divide the entire segment into two parts whose lengths form a ratio. For example, the line segment $\overline{PR}$, with endpoints at $P(1, 1)$ and $R(7, 4)$, is divided by the point $Q(3, 2)$. In what ratio does Q divide $\overline{PR}$?

First we draw a diagram. As is often the case in mathematics, there is more than one way to solve the problem. Two methods are shown.

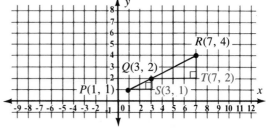

a. Calculate the lengths of each segment directly; then find the ratio.

$$|\overline{PQ}| = \sqrt{(3-1)^2 + (2-1)^2}$$
$$= \sqrt{5}$$
$$|\overline{QR}| = \sqrt{(7-3)^2 + (4-2)^2}$$
$$= \sqrt{20}$$
$$= 2\sqrt{5}$$
$$|\overline{PQ}| : |\overline{QR}| = \sqrt{5} : 2\sqrt{5}$$
$$= 1 : 2$$

b. Use the right triangles to set up a proportion; then find the ratio of the sides.

$$\triangle PSQ \sim \triangle QTR$$
$$\frac{\overline{PQ}}{\overline{QR}} = \frac{\overline{PS}}{\overline{QT}}$$
$$\frac{\overline{PQ}}{\overline{QR}} = \frac{2}{4}$$
$$= \frac{1}{2}$$

> Calculate the respective lengths.

Therefore, Q divides $\overline{PR}$ in a ratio of $1:2$ or $\frac{1}{2}$.

Sometimes a ratio is given and the coordinates of the point must be found.

Example

Find the coordinates of a point $D(x, y)$ that divides $\overline{AB}$ in a ratio of $3:4$, given $A(2, 5)$ and $B(9, 8)$.

Point D divides $\overline{AB}$ such that $|\overline{AD}| : |\overline{DB}| = 3:4$. Draw right triangles APD and DQB. The coordinates of P and Q are $(x, 5)$ and $(9, y)$ respectively. Since the triangles are similar, the corresponding sides are proportional. The ratio of the lengths of the corresponding sides of $\triangle APD$ and $\triangle DQB$ is $3:4$.

$$\frac{|\overline{AP}|}{|\overline{DQ}|} = \frac{3}{4}$$
$$\frac{\sqrt{(x-2)^2 + (5-5)^2}}{\sqrt{(9-x)^2 + (y-y)^2}} = \frac{3}{4}$$
$$\frac{x-2}{9-x} = \frac{3}{4}$$
$$4x - 8 = 27 - 3x$$
$$7x = 35$$
$$x = 5$$

$$\frac{|\overline{DP}|}{|\overline{BQ}|} = \frac{3}{4}$$
$$\frac{\sqrt{(x-x)^2 + (y-5)^2}}{\sqrt{(9-9)^2 + (8-y)^2}} = \frac{3}{4}$$
$$\frac{y-5}{8-y} = \frac{3}{4}$$
$$4y - 20 = 24 - 3y$$
$$7y = 44$$
$$y = \frac{44}{7}$$

Point $D\left(5, \frac{44}{7}\right)$ divides $\overline{AB}$ in a ratio of $3:4$.

Exercises

1. Find the ratio in which W divides $\overline{TV}$.
a. $W(-4, 3)$, $T(-6, 5)$, $V(1, -2)$
b. $W(5, 4)$, $T(2, 1)$, $V(7, 6)$
c. $W(-3, 3)$, $T(-10, 5)$, $V(4, 1)$
d. $W(0, 3)$, $T(-3, -6)$, $V(2, 9)$

2. Calculate lengths to verify that the corresponding sides of the two right triangles are proportional.

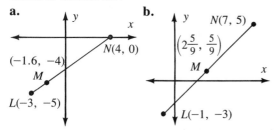

3. Use similar triangles to determine the ratio in which M divides $\overline{LN}$.

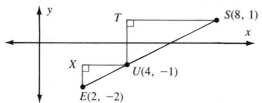

4. Use right triangles and proportional sides to determine the coordinates of the point D dividing $\overline{PQ}$ in a ratio of $2:3$.

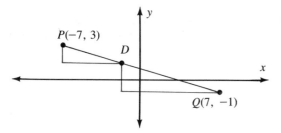

5. Use similar right triangles to determine the coordinates of the point that divides $\overline{AB}$ in a $1:1$ ratio for $A(-4, 1)$ and $B(6, 5)$.
a. Find the midpoint of $\overline{AB}$.
b. What do you notice about the two points?
c. In what ratio does the midpoint divide the line segment?

6. Find the coordinates of B such that B divides the line joining $A(-5, -7)$ and $C(6, 9)$ in the given ratios.
a. $\frac{3}{4}$ **b.** $\frac{2}{5}$ **c.** $\frac{1}{3}$ **d.** $4:7$
e. $\frac{5}{6}$ **f.** $\frac{p}{q}$ **g.** $a+1:a$ **h.** $s-a:1$

7. The point $P(5, 3.2)$ divides $\overline{AB}$ in the ratio $1:4$. Point $A(3, 2)$ is closer to point P. Find the coordinates of point B.

8. The coordinates of a point that divides the line segment joining (x_1, y_1) and (x_2, y_2) in a ratio, k, for $k \in Q$, are given by the formula $\left(\dfrac{x_1 + kx_2}{1+k}, \dfrac{y_1 + ky_2}{1+k}\right)$. Use this formula to calculate the coordinates of P given the endpoints and the ratio.
a. P divides $Q(3, 1)$ to $R(24, 15)$ in a ratio of $3:4$.
b. C divides $A(-5, 10)$ to $B(11, -5)$ in a ratio of $1:2$.
c. M divides $L(5, -8)$ to $N(-7, 10)$ in a ratio of $1:5$.

9. Refer to the formula in Exercise 8.
a. What value of k in the formula will determine a midpoint?
b. Use that value of k to show that the formula will determine the midpoint of a segment in general.
c. Use specific endpoints in the formula to determine a midpoint.

10. The coordinates of the vertices of a parallelogram are $A(-2, 4)$, $B(4, 4)$, $C(8, -2)$, and $D(2, -2)$. Points E and F are the midpoints of $\overline{AD}$ and $\overline{BC}$ respectively. Show that $\overline{EB}$ and $\overline{FD}$ trisect $\overline{AC}$.

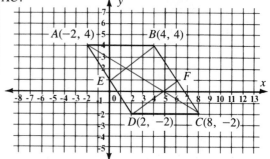

168

6·11 Analytic Investigations

Analytic geometry is combined with algebra to facilitate the investigations of properties of geometric figures.

Example 1

Show that $\triangle DEF$ with vertices at $D(2, 3)$, $E(-2, 0)$, and $F(5, -1)$ is a right triangle.

Understand the Problem
Given the coordinates of the vertices of $\triangle DEF$, we are to verify that the triangle is a right triangle.

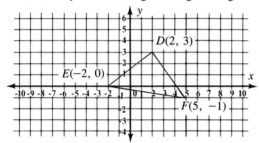

Develop a Plan
Draw the triangle and find the lengths of the three sides. Check whether the side lengths satisfy the Pythagorean Theorem.

Carry Out the Plan
$$|\overline{FD}| = \sqrt{16 + 9} = 5 \quad \text{Length formula}$$
$$|\overline{FE}| = \sqrt{1 + 49} = 5\sqrt{2}$$
$$|\overline{DE}| = \sqrt{9 + 16} = 5$$
$$|\overline{FD}|^2 + |\overline{DE}|^2 = |\overline{FE}|^2$$
$$5^2 + 5^2 = (5\sqrt{2})^2$$
$$50 = 50$$

Look Back
The side lengths satisfy the theorem so the $\triangle DEF$ is a right triangle. Is there any other way to solve the problem? (*Hint*: Use slopes.)

Example 2

For a given circle with centre at $C(0, 0)$ and a radius of a, show that any point $P(x, y)$ on the circle forms a right triangle with the diameter having endpoints of $A(-a, 0)$ and $B(a, 0)$.

To understand the problem, sketch a circle with all the data on a coordinate grid. We are to prove that $\overline{AP}$ is perpendicular to $\overline{BP}$.

Our plan consists of making two triangles by drawing a line from P perpendicular to the x-axis at $D(x, 0)$. We will show that the product of the slope of $\overline{AP}$ (m_{AP}) and the slope of $\overline{BP}$ (m_{BP}) is -1. We will need to draw in the radius $\overline{OP}$ to show that $y^2 = a^2 - x^2$.

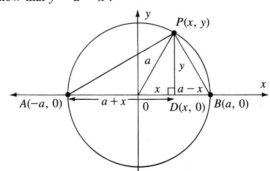

$$m_{AP} = \frac{\overline{PD}}{\overline{DA}}, \ m_{BP} = \frac{\overline{PD}}{\overline{DB}}$$
$$\therefore m_{AP} = \frac{y}{a + x} \text{ and } m_{BP} = \frac{-y}{a - x}$$
$$(m_{AP})(m_{BP}) = \left(\frac{y}{a + x}\right)\left(\frac{-y}{a - x}\right)$$
$$= \frac{-y^2}{a^2 - x^2}$$
$$= -1\left(\frac{a^2 - x^2}{a^2 - x^2}\right)$$
$$= -1$$

Since the product of m_{AP} and m_{BP} is -1, $\triangle APB$ is a right triangle.

169

The property that the endpoints of a diameter and any point on a circle form a right triangle has been proven in Example 2. Whenever a property is proven for a general case, the property can be assumed to be true in all cases. In this case, we proved the property for any point $P(x, y)$ and two endpoints that form the diameter of a circle.

Example 3

Prove that the line joining the midpoints of two sides of a triangle is equal to one half the length of the third side.

Understand the Problem

This requires a general proof which does not depend upon using specific coordinates. Draw the triangle on the coordinate grid in a convenient way to simplify the proof. In this case, one vertex at $W(0, 0)$ and one side along the x-axis. Let $V(a, b)$ represent the coordinates of the second vertex and $Z(c, 0)$ the coordinates of the third vertex. Note that moving this triangle around on the grid will not change any of its properties.

Develop a Plan

Use the midpoint formula to write the general coordinates of the midpoints of two sides of the triangle. Use the length formula to write an expression for the length of the line segment joining the midpoints and also an expression for the length of the third side. Compare these lengths.

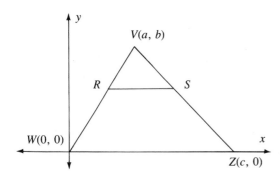

Carry Out the Plan

The midpoint, R, between $W(0, 0)$ and $V(a, b)$ is $\left(\dfrac{0+a}{2}, \dfrac{0+b}{2}\right)$ or $\left(\dfrac{a}{2}, \dfrac{b}{2}\right)$.

The midpoint, S, between $V(a, b)$ and $Z(c, 0)$ is $\left(\dfrac{a+c}{2}, \dfrac{b+0}{2}\right)$ or $\left(\dfrac{a+c}{2}, \dfrac{b}{2}\right)$.

The distance between the midpoints ($\overline{RS}$) is

$$\sqrt{(x_2 - x_1)^2 + (y_2 - y_1)^2} = \sqrt{\left(\dfrac{a+c}{2} - \dfrac{a}{2}\right)^2 + \left(\dfrac{b}{2} - \dfrac{b}{2}\right)^2}$$

$$= \sqrt{\dfrac{c^2}{4} + 0}$$

$$= \dfrac{c}{2}$$

Look Back

The length of the third side, $\overline{WZ}$, of the triangle is c units, which is twice the length of $\overline{RS}$. State the findings as a rule.

> The segment joining the midpoints of two sides of a triangle is equal to one half the length of the third side.

170

Exercises

1. For Example 1, provide an alternate solution using slope.

2. Find the length of the sides to verify that $\triangle PQR$ is an isosceles triangle.

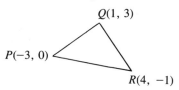

3. Use slopes to verify each statement.
a. *PQRS* is a trapezoid

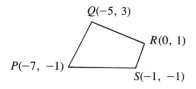

b. *MLNP* is a parallelogram

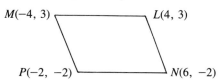

4. Verify each statement.
a. *QRST* is a rhombus

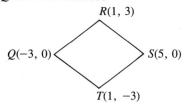

b. *WXYZ* is a square

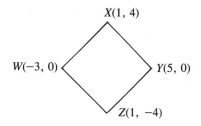

5. Verify each statement.
a. $\overline{PT}$ is a median of $\triangle PQR$

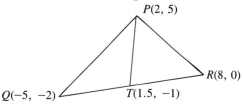

b. $\overline{AT}$ is an altitude

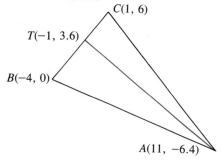

6. Verify that $\overline{DE}$ is parallel to $\overline{BC}$ and that $\dfrac{AD}{DB} = \dfrac{AE}{EC} = \dfrac{DE}{BC}$.

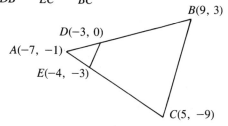

7. Verify that $\overline{ST}$ is parallel to $\overline{QR}$ and one half its length.

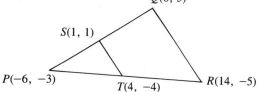

8. Prove these statements.
a. The diagonals of a rhombus are perpendicular.
b. The diagonals of a parallelogram bisect each other.
c. The diagonals of a rectangle are equal in length.
d. The line segments joining the midpoints of a rectangle in order form a rhombus.

171

6·12 Areas from Coordinates

The areas of various geometric figures can be found using analytic methods and the coordinates of the figure.

Example 1

Centre ice at a hockey rink is being painted with a team logo. The logo consists of two congruent scalene triangles and it is plotted on a grid with the centre of the ice surface at (0, 0) as illustrated in the diagram. Calculate the area of the triangular section with vertices at $A(2, 3)$, $B(4, 1)$, and $C(9, 5)$, measured in metres from the centre of the rink.

Understand the Problem

This problem involves determining the area of the logo which consists of two scalene triangles. The base length of the triangle can be calculated using the length formula, but the height is not readily available. Therefore, directly applying the area of a triangle formula, $A = \frac{1}{2}bh$, is not a possible strategy. However, the area can be determined using other known areas.

Develop a Plan

The scalene triangle is within a rectangular frame $KLMC$ with horizontal and vertical sides through A, B, and C as shown. The area of one triangle is equal to the area of the rectangle minus the sum of the areas of the three right triangles.

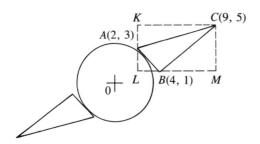

Carry Out the Plan

From the diagram, the coordinates of the rectangle are $K(2, 5)$, $L(2, 1)$, $M(9, 1)$ and $C(9, 5)$. Using the entire rectangle as a frame, the area of triangle ABC equals the area of rectangle $KLMC$ − area of $\triangle KAC$ − area of $\triangle ALB$ − area of $\triangle BMC$.

$$= (4 \times 7) - \frac{1}{2}(2 \times 7) - \frac{1}{2}(2 \times 2) - \frac{1}{2}(5 \times 4)$$
$$= 28 - 7 - 2 - 10$$
$$= 9$$

Look Back

The area of $\triangle ABC$ is 9 m². This seems to be a reasonable result since the triangle appears to be approximately one third the area of the rectangle in the diagram. The other triangle is congruent to it so the total area is 18 m². This method of framing the triangle with a rectangle can be used to develop a general formula for the area of a triangle. The proof of the general formula will be done as an exercise.

The area of a triangle with vertices at (x_1, y_1), (x_2, y_2), and (x_3, y_3), is
$$\frac{1}{2}\left|(x_1 y_2 + x_2 y_3 + x_3 y_1 - y_1 x_2 - y_2 x_3 - y_3 x_1)\right|.$$

Example 2

Use the coordinates of the vertices to calculate the area of the quadrilateral *JKMN* with vertices at $J(-4, 2)$, $K(-3, -5)$, $M(6, 1)$, and $N(0, 5)$.

Divide the figure into triangles by drawing a diagonal, as shown, and label the coordinates of one triangle in counterclockwise order. We can simplify the procedure of using the formula by following these steps for $\triangle JKN$.

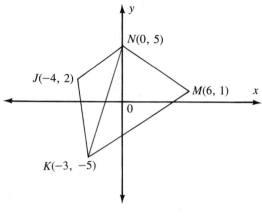

Step 1	Step 2	Step 3
List the vertices in counterclockwise order.	Calculate the products "down".	Calculate the products "up".
$(x_1, y_1) \rightarrow (-4, 2)$ $(x_2, y_2) \rightarrow (-3, -5)$ $(x_3, y_3) \rightarrow (0, 5)$ $(x_1, y_1) \rightarrow (-4, 2)$	$\begin{matrix} x_1 & y_1 \\ x_2 & y_2 \\ x_3 & y_3 \\ x_1 & y_1 \end{matrix}$	$\begin{matrix} x_1 & y_1 \\ x_2 & y_2 \\ x_3 & y_3 \\ x_1 & y_1 \end{matrix}$

Repeat the first line.

The area of $\triangle JKN$ is calculated by using the formula.

$$\triangle JKN = \frac{1}{2} \left| \text{(Sum of products down)} - \text{(Sum of products up)} \right|$$

$$= \frac{1}{2} \left| [(-4)(-5) + (-3)(5) + (0)(2)] - [(-3)(2) + (0)(-5) + (-4)(5)] \right|$$

$$= \frac{1}{2} |5 + 26|$$

$$= 15.5$$

The area of $\triangle JKN$ is 15.5 square units.

The area of $\triangle KMN$ is calculated in a similar manner.

$$\triangle KMN = \frac{1}{2} \left| [(-3)(1) + (6)(5) + (0)(-5)] - [(6)(-5) + (0)(1) + (-3)(5)] \right|$$

$$= 36.0$$

The area of $\triangle KMN$ is 36.0 square units.

The area of quadrilateral *JKMN* is $15.5 + 36.0$ or 51.5 square units.

The "vertices formula" can be used to determine the area of any closed convex polygon by drawing diagonals to divide the polygon into triangles.

Exercises

1. Label the coordinates of the vertices of the rectangle enclosing the triangle.

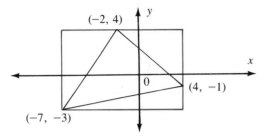

2. Use the method of Example 1 in the display to calculate the area of each triangle with the given vertices.
a. (1, 2), (2, 5), (5, 3)
b. (−1, 4), (3, 7), (6, −2)
c. (−5, 0), (0, 4), (5, 0)
d. (−2, 6), (−3, −5), (4, −1)

3. Use the general formula to determine the area of the triangle.

a.   **b.**

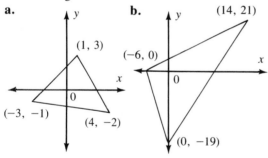

4. Calculate the area of the shaded figures.

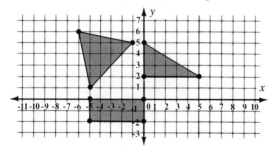

5. Calculate the area of quadrilateral *PQRS* with vertices at (0, 6), (0, 0), (3, 0), and (5, 4).

6. Use two different methods, the traditional area formula and the "vertex formula", to calculate the area of this triangle.

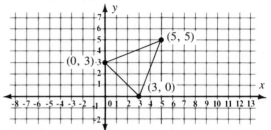

7. If all the coordinates of the vertices of a triangle are doubled, what happens to the area of the triangle? (*Hint:* Consider the location of the vertices and investigate specific cases.)

8. Use this diagram to derive the formula for the area of △*ART*.

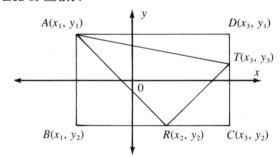

a. Why is the absolute value taken?
b. Explain why the procedure suggested in the display requires the vertices to be labelled counterclockwise.

9. The method for calculating area by using the coordinates of vertices can be extended to any convex polygon. Determine the area of this polygon by dividing it into triangles.

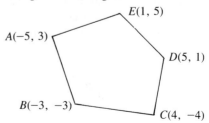

6·13 Distance from a Point to a Line

In this section, the formula for the perpendicular distance from a point to a line will be developed by using the analytic properties studied so far in this chapter. For example, determine the perpendicular distance from point $P(x_1, y_1)$ to the line $Ax + By + C = 0$.

Given the point $P(x_1, y_1)$ and the line $Ax + By + C = 0$, we are to determine the length of $\overline{PS}$, the perpendicular from $P(x_1, y_1)$ to the line. Assume that the line $Ax + By + C = 0$ intersects both axes at Q and R as illustrated in the diagram.

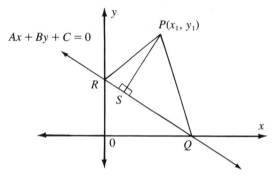

R is the y-intercept with coordinates at $\left(0, -\dfrac{C}{B}\right)$ and Q is the x-intercept with coordinates at $\left(-\dfrac{C}{A}, 0\right)$.

The area of $\triangle PQR = \frac{1}{2}|\overline{QR}| \times |\overline{PS}|$, where $\overline{QR}$ is the base and $\overline{PS}$ is the altitude. Using the formulas from the previous sections, we can find the area of $\triangle PQR$ and $|\overline{QR}|$.

$$\text{Area of } \triangle PQR = \frac{1}{2}\left| -\frac{C}{B}x_1 - \frac{C}{A}y_1 - \frac{C^2}{AB} \right|$$
$$= \frac{1}{2}\left|\frac{C}{AB}\right| |Ax_1 + By_1 + C|$$

$$|\overline{QR}| = \sqrt{\frac{C^2}{A^2} + \frac{C^2}{B^2}}$$
$$= \sqrt{\frac{(A^2 + B^2)C^2}{A^2 B^2}}$$
$$= \left|\frac{C}{AB}\right| \sqrt{A^2 + B^2}$$

By combining the two equations for the area of $\triangle PQR$ and solving for $|\overline{PS}|$, we get:

$$\frac{1}{2}\left|\frac{C}{AB}\right|\sqrt{A^2 + B^2} \times |\overline{PS}| = \frac{1}{2}\left|\frac{C}{AB}\right| |Ax_1 + By_1 + C|$$
$$|\overline{PS}| = \frac{|Ax_1 + By_1 + C|}{\sqrt{A^2 + B^2}}$$

The perpendicular distance from $P(x_1, y_1)$ to the line $Ax + By + C = 0$ is $\dfrac{|Ax_1 + By_1 + C|}{\sqrt{A^2 + B^2}}$.

Exercises

1. Determine the perpendicular distance from the point to the line.
a. $B(1, -3)$; the line $4x - 6y - 7 = 0$
b. $A(0, 0)$; the line through $(1, 2)$ and $(3, -1)$

2. Determine the length of the altitude $\overline{XA}$ in $\triangle XYZ$.
a. $X(-4, 4)$, $Y(-2, -5)$, and $Z(5, 3)$
b. $X(2, 8)$, $Y(-4, 1)$, and $Z(4, -4)$

3. Calculate the missing coordinates.
a. The area of a triangle with vertices at $(p, 0)$, $(4, 2)$, and $(-2, 4)$ is 8 square units.
b. The area of a triangle with vertices at $(0, q)$, $(-2, 2)$, and $(4, 6)$ is 14 square units.

4. Find the perpendicular distance from $(2, 3)$ to $3x - 5y + 9 = 0$. What conclusion can be made about the point and the line?

175

6·14 Vectors

Quantities such as mass, length, and cost involve only magnitude: 32 kg, 15 mm, and $36.84. These are **scalar** quantities. Force and velocity on the other hand, involve both a magnitude and a direction: 45 N downward, 32 km/h southeast. Such quantities are called **vectors**.

A vector has both **magnitude** and **direction**. Vectors are represented in diagrams by **directed line segments**. For example, a vector from point A to point B is represented by $\overrightarrow{AB}$, where point A is the **starting** point of the vector (called the **tail** or **initial point**) and point B is the finishing point of the vector (called the **head** or **terminal point**). The head of the vector shows the direction of the vector.

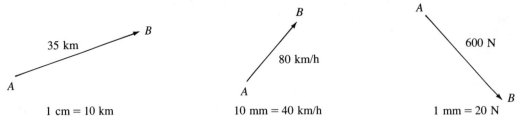

Example 1

Use a vector to represent each quantity.
a. a displacement of 40 km east

b. a velocity of 150 km/h northwest

Whenever you use vectors to represent a quantity, the scale that has been used to draw the vector, as well as a "north arrow", must be placed on the diagram.

Directions for vectors commonly are given in two ways.

In navigation, bearings are used. North is 000°. Moving clockwise, all other directions are given a three-digit number in degrees. For example, due west is 270°. In the diagram, $\overrightarrow{AB}$ is at 135°.

A second method is **standard** direction. Direction is measured from the north or the south and the number of degrees to the east or the west. For example, $\overrightarrow{AB}$ is at S60°E.

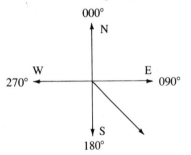

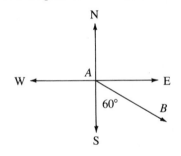

A vector [3, 1] describes a magnitude and a direction which is made up of two components: a **horizontal** component of 3 units and a **vertical** component of 1 unit. All the vectors shown are represented by [3, 1]. Often it is convenient to have a vector represented geometrically with its tail at the origin. We can translate any vector so that its initial point is on the origin. $\overrightarrow{AB}$, $\overrightarrow{CD}$, $\overrightarrow{EF}$, and $\overrightarrow{GH}$ are equal vectors with horizontal components of 3 and vertical components of 1. Each is a translation of the others.

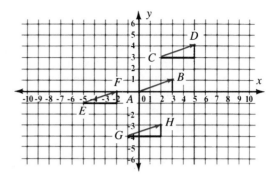

Example 2

Express $\overrightarrow{AB}$ algebraically using the points $A(-2, 5)$ and $B(3, 1)$ and find its magnitude.

In the vector $\overrightarrow{AB}$, A is the tail of the vector and B is the head. Since it is more convenient to have the tail of the vector at the origin, we **translate** the vector 2 units to the right and 5 units down. This will move the head of the vector to the point $(5, -4)$ and $\overrightarrow{AB}$ can be represented by [5, -4].

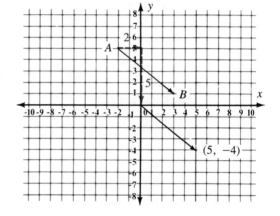

The magnitude of the vector can be found using the Pythagorean Theorem.

$$\overrightarrow{AB} = [5, -4]$$
$$|\overrightarrow{AB}| = \sqrt{5^2 + (-4)^2}$$
$$= \sqrt{41}$$

The magnitude of $\overrightarrow{AB}$ is $\sqrt{41}$ units.

Vectors can be represented both algebraically and geometrically. Vectors can be named by using two capital letters or one lower case letter. So far, we have shown vectors represented by two capital letters. The diagrams below show **equivalent** vectors. Note that equivalent vectors have the same magnitude and the same direction.

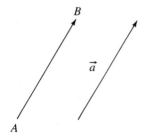

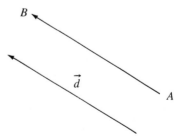

The magnitude of many vectors is expressed as $\vec{d}$ to represent a displacement vector. In this text, we will interchange the use of vector symbols and use both single, lower-case letters and two capital letters.

Exercises

1. In your own words, describe the difference between each.
a. a scalar quantity and a vector quantity
b. an algebraic vector and a geometric vector
c. a horizontal component and a vertical component

2. Identify those quantities that are best represented by a scalar and those that are best represented by a vector. Give an example of each.
a. time **b.** force
c. age **d.** class size
e. shoe size **f.** velocity
g. acceleration **h.** compass bearing

3. On a coordinate grid, draw the vector.
a. [2, 6]
b. [6, 2]
c. a velocity of 120 km/h on a bearing of 195°
d. a force of 75 N at S50°E

4. Identify the vectors that are equal.

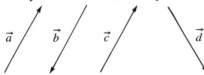

5. Plot the points $M(5, 2)$, $N(9, 6)$, $R(3, -1)$, $S(-1, 6)$, and $T(-3, -4)$ on a coordinate grid. Represent each vector in the form $[x, y]$.
a. $\overrightarrow{MN}$ **b.** $\overrightarrow{MR}$ **c.** $\overrightarrow{NS}$ **d.** $\overrightarrow{MS}$
e. $\overrightarrow{SN}$ **f.** $\overrightarrow{TM}$ **g.** $\overrightarrow{SR}$ **h.** $\overrightarrow{TR}$

6. In your own words, describe how each vector will appear.
a. [5, 3] **b.** [0, 5]
c. [-2, 0] **d.** [0, 0]

7. In your own words, explain the meaning of equivalent vectors and draw two equivalent vectors.

8. Find the magnitude of these vectors correct to one decimal place.
a. [4, 3] **b.** [-3, 4]
c. [0, 12] **d.** [-6, -7]
e. [15, -14] **f.** [-6, 0]

9. On a coordinate grid, draw [-1, -4]. Find the initial points of the equal vectors with these terminal points.
a. $F(3, 4)$ **b.** $A(-3, 6)$
c. $B(-7, 0)$ **d.** $D(0, 5)$
e. $Q(0, 0)$ **f.** $S(-3, 3)$

10. In this diagram of a parallelogram, $\vec{a}$ is equivalent to $\vec{d}$, and there are three other pairs of equal vectors. List the three pairs.

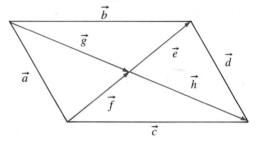

11. A vector is drawn with a slope of -2. What is the slope of an equivalent vector?

12. If the vector in Exercise 11 was rotated 90°, then what would be the new slope?

13. Name four pairs of equivalent vectors in trapezoid $ABCD$ with midpoints at E, F, G, and H.

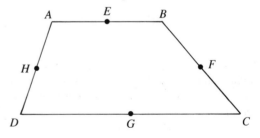

Braintickler

Two trains of equal length, each travelling in opposite directions at 90 km/h, pass each other. A conductor on one of the trains records that it took 5 s for the other train to pass. How long are the trains? An observer by the side of the tracks records that it took 10 s for the trains to pass. Why are the two times different?

6·15 Operations With Vectors

Vectors represent displacements in a certain direction. Vectors can be combined to find the net displacement from a fixed point. In this section, we will study the combined effect of both adding and subtracting vectors, as well as the result when a vector is multiplied by a scalar.

Example 1

A rally car drives 20 km due north and then 15 km due east. How far, and in what direction, is the car from its starting point?

Understand the Problem

This situation describes two displacements of 20 km due north and 15 km due east. The net or resultant displacement is required for both the magnitude and the direction.

Develop a Plan

Draw a vector diagram to represent the displacements. Use the Pythagorean Theorem to find the net displacement. Use a protractor or trigonometry to find the measure of the angle.

Carry Out the Plan

The net displacement of the car from the starting point is from the tail of the 20 km vector to the head of the 15 km vector. Since the angle formed by the vectors is 90°, the displacement can be found using the Pythagorean Theorem.

$$|\vec{d}|^2 = 20^2 + 15^2$$
$$= 625$$
$$\vec{d} = 25$$

The protractor shows the measure of angle BAC as 37°.

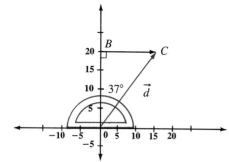

Look Back

The car is 25 km from its starting point at an angle of about N37°E. We can make this generalization: when finding the displacement of two vectors, the tail of the second vector is placed at the head of the first vector. The triangle was completed to find the displacement vector.

> The addition of vectors can be found by placing the tail of the second vector at the head of the first vector. This is the **triangle law** of addition. The sum or **resultant vector** is from the tail of the first vector to the head of the second vector.

The diagram shows $\overrightarrow{AB}$ and $\overrightarrow{AD}$ having a common tail A. The sum of two such vectors is $\overrightarrow{AC}$ which is found by completing the parallelogram $ABCD$. Notice $\overrightarrow{BC} = \overrightarrow{AD}$ and $\overrightarrow{DC} = \overrightarrow{AB}$. This is a vector model of the real-life situation in which two people (B and D) pull a toboggan (A). We know the resulting force should be greater than either of the single forces. This is seen in that $\overrightarrow{AC} > \overrightarrow{AD}$ and $\overrightarrow{AC} > \overrightarrow{AB}$. This is the **parallelogram law** of addition.

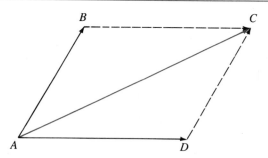

The subtraction of vectors is related to addition in the same way that subtraction is related to addition in the whole numbers: to subtract we "add the opposite". Hence, $p - q = p + (-q)$. Algebraically, if $\vec{q} = [4, 5]$, then $-\vec{q} = [-4, -5]$.

Example 2

Given the vectors $\vec{a} = [3, 2]$ and $\vec{b} = [4, 5]$, find
a. the sum $\vec{a} + \vec{b}$.　　**b.** the difference $\vec{a} - \vec{b}$.

a. We draw the vector $\vec{a} = [3, 2]$ and at its head put the tail of $\vec{b} = [4, 5]$. The resulting vector is $[7, 7]$. Algebraically: $[3, 2] + [4, 5] = [7, 7]$

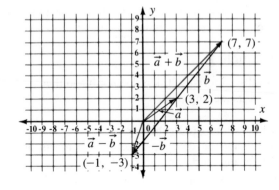

b. We want $[3, 2] - [4, 5]$ or $[3, 2] + [-4, -5]$. Draw the vector $[3, 2]$ and at its head we put the tail of $[-4, -5]$. The resulting vector is $[-1, -3]$.
Algebraically: $[3, 2] - [4, 5] = [3 - 4, 2 - 5]$
$$= [-1, -3]$$

In general, addition and subtraction is given by

For $\vec{p} = [a, b]$ and $\vec{q} = [c, d]$, then
$\vec{p} + \vec{q} = [a, b] + [c, d] = [a + c, b + d]$, and
$\vec{p} - \vec{q} = [a, b] - [c, d] = [a - c, b - d]$.

Scalar multiplication can be illustrated using the fact that $\vec{p} + \vec{p} + \vec{p} = 3\vec{p}$. Let $\vec{p} = [3, 1]$. On the coordinate grid, show $\vec{p} + \vec{p} + \vec{p}$ by plotting the three vectors, one attached to the other as shown. We see that $[3, 1] + [3, 1] + [3, 1] = [9, 3]$. Therefore, $3[3, 1] = [3 \times 3, 3 \times 1] = [9, 3]$.

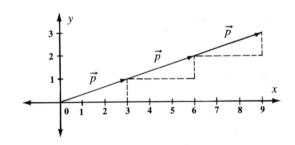

In general, scalar multiplication is given by

For $\vec{v} = [a, b]$, then $\vec{kv} = [ka, kb]$.

Example 3

The displacements of particles in physics are represented by the vectors $\vec{p} = [5, -2]$ and $\vec{g} = [7, 6]$. The path of one particle is $2\vec{p} - \vec{q}$.
Find the resultant vector, $\vec{r}$,
a. geometrically.　　**b.** algebraically.

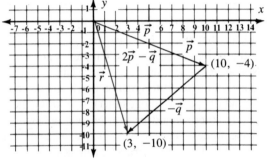

a. The diagram shows the result geometrically to be $[3, -10]$.

b. $2\vec{p} - \vec{q} = 2[5, -2] - [7, 6]$
$= [10, -4] - [7, 6]$
$= [10 - 7, -4 - 6]$
$= [3, -10]$

180

Exercises

1. In your own words, explain the "triangle law" and the "parallelogram law" for addition of vectors.

2. Trace these vectors into your notebook and find the sum.

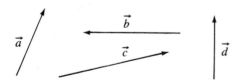

a. $\vec{a} + \vec{b}$　**b.** $\vec{b} + \vec{c}$　**c.** $\vec{c} + \vec{d}$　**d.** $\vec{a} + \vec{d}$

3. Graph each pair of vectors and find the sum.
a. [3, 1], [−5, 2]　**b.** [0, 7], [4, −4]
c. [1, −1], [−1, −1]　**d.** [−6, 0], [3, 0]

4. A boat steers due east from its dock at a velocity of 16 km/h. The tide carries the boat due south at 12 km/h. Draw a vector model to calculate the displacement of the boat from the dock and find the direction the boat is actually moving.

5. Draw the negative of each vector in Exercise 2.

6. A.T., the "Mathematics Wizard", stated that finding the negative of a vector is the same as multiplying the vector by a scalar of −1. Is A.T. correct? Explain.

7. Graph $\vec{m} = [−1, 7]$ and $\vec{n} = [3, −2]$.
a. Graph $−\vec{n}$.
b. Find $\vec{m} − \vec{n}$.
c. Graph $−\vec{m}$.
d. Find $−\vec{m} − \vec{n}$.
e. Graph $\vec{m} + \vec{n}$.
f. Graph $−(\vec{m} + \vec{n})$.
g. Is $−(\vec{m} + \vec{n})$ the same as $−\vec{m} − \vec{n}$?

8. If $\vec{m} = [2, 1]$, $\vec{n} = [a, b]$, $\vec{p} = [−1, −3]$, and $\vec{n} = \vec{m} + \vec{p}$ then find the values of a and b.

9. Describe the magnitude and the direction of each vector relative to $\vec{w}$.
a. $6\vec{w}$　　**b.** $−3\vec{w}$　　**c.** $0.5\vec{w}$

10. Find a single vector to represent each sum.

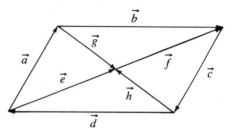

a. $\vec{a} + \vec{g}$　　**b.** $\vec{g} + \vec{e}$　　**c.** $\vec{b} + \vec{h}$
d. $\vec{e} + \vec{c}$　　**e.** $\vec{h} − \vec{e}$　　**f.** $\vec{b} − \vec{f}$

11. In this rectangular prism, $\vec{j} = \overrightarrow{PQ}$, $\vec{m} = \overrightarrow{QR}$, and $\vec{z} = \overrightarrow{PO}$. Use $\vec{j}$, $\vec{m}$, and $\vec{z}$, to find a single vector that will represent each.

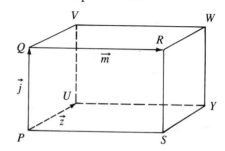

a. $\overrightarrow{UV}$　**b.** $\overrightarrow{SR}$　**c.** $\overrightarrow{WR}$　**d.** $\overrightarrow{QS}$
e. $\overrightarrow{PV}$　**f.** $\overrightarrow{QW}$　**g.** $\overrightarrow{PW}$　**h.** $\overrightarrow{VS}$

Historical Note

Josiah Willard Gibbs (1839-1903)
As a native of New Haven, Josiah Gibbs studied mathematics and physics at Yale University, receiving a doctorate in 1863. In 1871, he was appointed professor of mathematical physics at Yale. In 1881, he published *Vector Analysis* which introduced the idea that two vectors are equal if and only if they have the same length and direction; a concept that you have encountered in this chapter.

Another of Josiah Gibbs' vector theorems is that vector addition is commutative. Prove this theorem.

6·16 Applications

Vectors are applied in many situations in which magnitude and direction are both significant.

Example 1

A plane, flying with a velocity of 360 km/h due east, encounters a side wind with a velocity of 45 km/h due south. Find the direction that the plane is flying and its speed.

Understand the Problem
A plane, flying at 360 km/h due east, encounters a side wind of 45 km/h due south.

Develop a Plan
Because both direction and magnitude are involved with velocity, a vector scale drawing can be used to help solve the problem.

Carry Out the Plan

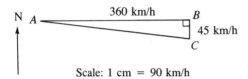

Scale: 1 cm = 90 km/h

Look Back
The plane will be flying at approximately 363 km/h on a bearing of about 97°. The value of 363 km/h can be verified by measuring the length of the displacement vector and then multiplying by 4.

The resultant vector can be found using the Pythagorean Theorem.

$$d^2 = 360^2 + 45^2$$
$$= 131\ 625$$
$$d \doteq 362.8$$

By measuring, $\angle BAC$ is about 7°.

Example 2

Two four-wheel jeeps are used to pull a truck out of a ditch. The first jeep pulls with a force of 7000 N at an angle of N20°W. The second jeep pulls with a force of 8500 N at an angle of N30°E. Calculate the net force and its direction.

Make a scale drawing. Measure and calculate the resultant vector. Measure the angle of the resultant from the North line.

$$\overrightarrow{AB} + \overrightarrow{AC} = \overrightarrow{AD}$$

By measuring the length of $\overrightarrow{AD}$, we can determine that the resultant force is about 14 400 N.

By using a protractor, we can determine that the angle DAN is about 9°.

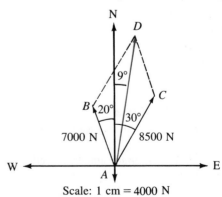

Scale: 1 cm = 4000 N

Exercises

1. A speedboat heads in a direction of N30°E at a velocity of 160 km/h. A north wind at a velocity of 45 km/h is blowing it off course. Use a vector diagram, drawn to scale, to show the two velocities as vectors and measure the resultant vector to determine the speed and the direction of the boat.

2. On a Cartesian coordinate grid, draw a vector diagram to show an object being pulled by two forces described by $\overrightarrow{AB} = [1, -5]$ and $\overrightarrow{AC} = [7, 3]$. Find a vector that describes the single force that has the combined effect of the two given forces.

3. An object is being pulled by two forces: one of 350 N in a direction due north and the other of 550 N in a direction due east. Illustrate, using a vector diagram, the resultant of the two forces and find its magnitude and direction.

4. Use these two velocity vectors to draw the resultant vector and find its magnitude.

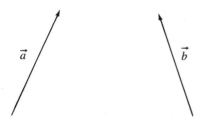

5. A parachutist is dropping with a vertical velocity of 60 km/h and is being blown by a horizontal wind of 45 km/h. Use a vector scale diagram to find the resultant direction and velocity relative to the ground. (*Hint*: The downward direction should have a positive velocity.)

6. Find the sum of each set of velocity vectors.
a. 3 km/h east and 15 km/h south
b. 10 km/h northwest and 10 km/h east
c. 12 km/h northwest and 25 km/h south
d. 16 km/h west and 20 km/h southwest
e. 20 km/h west, 5 km/h south, and 8 km/h southwest

7. A bird is flying with a velocity of 35.5 km/h in a direction due west. It is taken off course by a northwest wind with a velocity of 18 km/h. Draw a vector diagram to find the direction of the bird's flight and find its speed in relation to the land.

8. Use a scale diagram to show forces of 16 N and 8 N acting on an object directly upward and at 45° to the horizontal respectively. Use the parallelogram law to draw the resultant of these two forces and find its magnitude and direction.

9. A passenger at the front of a train moving forward with a velocity of 85 km/h is walking to the snack bar at the back of the train. The passenger moves with a velocity of 6 km/h. Find the passenger's velocity with respect to the ground.

10. A van is travelling at 80 km/h. If a ball is rolled directly across the van at 6 km/h, find the actual velocity of the ball relative to the road.

11. A toy boat in a river is moved downstream by an 8 km/h current. It is being blown by a wind of 10 km/h directly across the river. Draw a vector diagram to show the resulting direction of the boat and find its resultant velocity and direction.

12. A plane heading N45°W at 350 km/h encounters an 80 km/h wind from S30°E. Draw a vector diagram to show the direction and speed of the plane.

Braintickler

A boat is tied to a dock and floats so that 3 m of the boat is above the water. A five metre tide comes in and then almost completely leaves 4 h later. After 3 h, how much of the boat is above the water?

6·17 Vector Proofs

In the previous chapter, you were introduced to the Euclidean form of a deductive proof, as well as proofs by contradiction and indirect proofs. In this chapter, you have seen some of the methods of coordinate geometry used to prove certain hypotheses. Vectors also can be used to prove some deductions that otherwise cannot be proved or are difficult to prove using Euclidean or coordinate geometry methods.

Certain statements that are made using vectors have definite geometric implications.

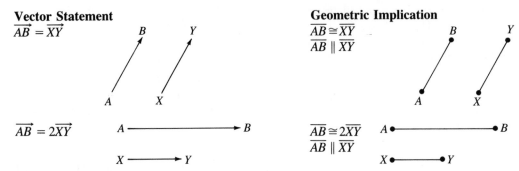

Vector Statement
$\overrightarrow{AB} = \overrightarrow{XY}$

$\overrightarrow{AB} = 2\overrightarrow{XY}$

Geometric Implication
$\overline{AB} \cong \overline{XY}$
$\overline{AB} \parallel \overline{XY}$

$\overline{AB} \cong 2\overline{XY}$
$\overline{AB} \parallel \overline{XY}$

Since the congruence of two vectors implies that they are scalar multiples of each other and/or parallel, vectors are useful for proving that one vector is parallel to another or that one vector is a scalar multiple of another.

In a general proof, which proves that a property holds in all cases, it is helpful to mark a diagram with vectors representing congruent segments or parallel segments.

Example

Prove that the line segments joining the midpoints of the sides of a quadrilateral form a parallelogram.

GIVEN: Quadrilateral $ABCD$ with P, Q, R, and S representing the midpoints of $\overrightarrow{BC}$, $\overrightarrow{CD}$, $\overrightarrow{DA}$, and $\overrightarrow{AB}$ respectively.
REQUIRED: To prove that quadrilateral $PQRS$ is a parallelogram.
PROOF: To simplify the procedure, the sides of quadrilateral $ABCD$ have been named by single letters. Construct diagonal $\overrightarrow{AC}$ and join P, Q, R, and S to form a quadrilateral.
From the diagram,
1. $2\vec{a} + 2\vec{b} = \overrightarrow{AC}$
2. $2\vec{d} + 2\vec{c} = \overrightarrow{AC}$
3. $2\vec{a} + 2\vec{b} = 2\vec{d} + 2\vec{c}$
4. $\vec{a} + \vec{b} = \vec{d} + \vec{c}$
$\therefore \overrightarrow{SP} = \overrightarrow{RQ}$
Similarly, $\overrightarrow{SR} = \overrightarrow{PQ}$.

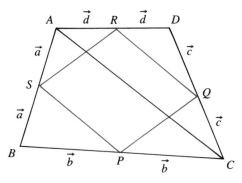

Because congruence of vectors implies that the lines also are parallel, quadrilateral $PQRS$ is a parallelogram.

184

Exercises

1. In the proof of the display, why is $\overrightarrow{AB}$ divided into two vectors of equal length?

2. Summarize the relationship between the vector statement and the geometric implications that are shown in the display.

3. Copy this trapezoid into your notebook and use the properties of a trapezoid and the given information to assign letter names to the six different congruent and/or parallel segments.

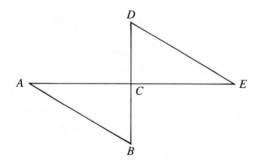

4. In this diagram, $\overline{AB} \parallel \overline{DE}$, $\overline{AB} \cong \overline{DE}$, and C is the midpoint of $\overline{AE}$. Use vectors to prove that C is the midpoint of $\overline{BD}$.

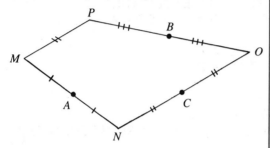

5. Draw any triangle DEF.
a. Place points G and H along $\overline{DE}$ and $\overline{DF}$ respectively so that the points divide the sides in the ratio of 1:2.
b. Prove that $\overline{GH} \parallel \overline{EF}$.
c. Use the proof of part **b** to show that $\overline{GH} = \frac{1}{3}\overline{EF}$.

6. The points A and B are the midpoints of $\overline{JM}$ and $\overline{KL}$ respectively in parallelogram $JKLM$.
a. Draw parallelogram $JKLM$ and midpoints A and B.
b. Use vectors to prove that $\overline{AK}$ and $\overline{MB}$ are congruent and parallel.

7. If P divides $\overline{AB}$ in a 1:2 ratio and Q divides $\overline{AC}$ in the same ratio, then prove that $\overline{PQ} \parallel \overline{BC}$.

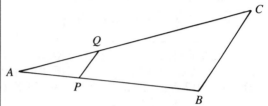

8. Prove that the line joining the midpoints of two sides of any triangle has half the magnitude of and is parallel to the third side.

9. Prove that if the diagonals of a quadrilateral bisect each other, the quadrilateral is a parallelogram.

10. In $\triangle DEF$, X, Y, and Z are the midpoints of sides $\overline{DE}$, $\overline{EF}$, and $\overline{DF}$ respectively. Prove that $\overline{DY} + \overline{EZ} + \overline{FX} = 0$.

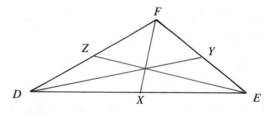

11. Line segments joining the midpoints of a parallelogram form a parallelogram.
a. Use vector geometry to prove this statement.
b. Prove the statement using a Euclidean proof.
c. Compare the two proofs and indicate which method of proof you consider to be most efficient in this case.

12. A.T., the "Mathematics Wizard", stated that when proving a hypothesis, one should be attempting to find equivalent sums of vectors. Is A.T. correct? Explain.

6·18 Computer Application— Areas of Polygons

Heron's formula for calculating the area of a triangle is often a most useful formula. This formula only relies on knowing the lengths of the sides of a triangle. In this section, you have been introduced to finding the lengths of lines using the coordinates of its vertices. This program will calculate the area of a triangle based on the coordinates of its vertices. Recall that Heron's formula is $\sqrt{s(s-a)(s-b)(s-c)}$ where $s = \dfrac{a+b+c}{2}$.

```
10  REM CALCULATE THE AREA OF A TRIANGLE FROM ITS VERTICES
20  REM BE CAREFUL OF THE ORDER THAT YOU ENTER THEM
30  INPUT "ENTER COORDINATES OF THE VERTICES "; X1, Y1,
X2, Y2, X3, Y3
40  LET A = SQR((Y2 − Y1) ∧ 2 + (X2 − X1) ∧ 2)
50  LET B = SQR((Y3 − Y1) ∧ 2 + (X3 − X1) ∧ 2)
60  LET C = SQR((Y3 − Y2) ∧ 2 + (X3 − X2) ∧ 2)
70  LET S = (A + B + C ) / 2
80  LET AR = SQR(S * (S − A) * (S − B) * (S − C))
90  PRINT "THE AREA OF THE TRIANGLE IS "; AR; " SQUARE UNITS"
99  END
```

Exercises

1. In your own words, summarize Heron's formula.

2. Explain the purpose of lines 40 to 80 of the program in the display.

3. How many times will the computer execute the lines in the program?

4. Run the program in the display to calculate the area of these triangles. Draw the triangle on a co-ordinate grid and check the reasonableness of the computer output for part **a** by calculating the area yourself.
a. (3, 2), (7, 1), (4, 4)
b. (−3, 2), (5, 6), (7, 5)
c. (−9, 0), (0, 4), (8, 6)
d. (−2, 5), (−5, −5), (−4, −12)
e. (6, 6), (−6, −6), (−9, −9)

5. Can you explain the output for Exercise 4, part **e**?

6. Modify the program in the display to find the area of a regular four-sided polygon.
a. On a coordinate grid, draw a regular polygon of your own.
b. Calculate the area of the polygon using a calculator.
c. Run the program that you have written using the coordinates of the polygon to verify the program.

7. Modify the program of Exercise 6 to calculate and print the perimeter of a regular polygon. Verify your program using the regular polygon of Exercise 6.

8. A school needs new software for its computer students but does not have the money to buy it. Jodi has the latest software in her possession because her uncle is a software developer and earns his living from the royalties of the sale of the software. Jodi refuses to copy the software and her best friend in the computer class will not speak to her. Write a short report either defending Jodi or her best friend.

186

6·19 Chapter Review

1. Calculate the slope of a line through each pair of points.
a. $(-3, 7), (4, 0)$ **b.** $(-9, 4), (1, 4)$
c. $(3, 6), (3, -6)$ **d.** $(1, 5), (-6, -1)$

2. Sketch the graphs.
a. $3x + 4y - 12 = 0$
b. $y = \frac{3}{4}x + 6$
c. $y - 3 = 4(x + 2)$

3. In your own words, describe the three methods used to determine if points are collinear.

4. List two points collinear with the given points.
a. $(5, -4)$ and $(2, 1)$ **b.** $(-3, -2)$ and $(8, 0)$

5. Determine the distance, correct to one decimal place, between each pair of points.
a. $(-3, 6)$ and $(2, 2)$ **b.** $(-5, -1)$ and $(12, 9)$

6. Determine the coordinates of the midpoint given the endpoints of each line segment.
a. $(3, 7), (9, -1)$ **b.** $(-5, 2), (10, 2)$
c. $(-1, 10), (1, -10)$ **d.** $(-3, -2), (8, -5)$

7. Write the equation of each line and draw the graph on a coordinate grid.
a. through the point $(1, -4)$ and with a slope of $-\frac{3}{2}$

b. with an x-intercept of 3 and with a slope of $\frac{1}{4}$
c. through the points $(-7, -3)$ and $(2, 0)$
d. through the point $(-1, 8)$ and parallel to the line $4x - 5y + 10 = 0$
e. through the point $(4, -4)$ and perpendicular to the line with a slope of $-\frac{5}{3}$

8. Identify the pairs of perpendicular lines.
a. $x + y = 10$ **b.** $x + 2y = 0$
c. $y = 2x + 1$ **d.** $3x + 2y = 4$
e. $2x - 3y - 6 = 0$ **f.** $x - y = 5$

9. For $\triangle ABC$ with vertices at $A(13, -7), B(-8, 1)$, and $C(2, -5)$, write an equation of the median from A to BC.

10. What are the coordinates of the point that divides PD into a ratio of 2:3 for $P(7, 1)$ and $D(-3, 3)$?

11. Calculate the area of each figure given the co-ordinates of the vertices.
a. triangle ABC for $A(-3, -6), B(5, 0)$, and $C(0, 4)$
b. pentagon $PQRST$ for $P(-5, 0)$, $Q(-3, -4)$, $R(1, -1)$, $S(0, 6)$, and $T(-2, 3)$
c. $E(-4, -7)$, $F(-1, -1)$, and $G(3, 7)$
d. What does the area calculation for part **c** indicate about the three vertices?

12. A submarine is spotted on a radar screen and is travelling along a course defined by the equation $3x - 4y = 5$. An island with coordinates $(4, 7)$ also is spotted on the screen. How far is the submarine from the island?

13. Prove that the midpoint of the hypotenuse of right triangle MNP with vertices at $M(-4, 0)$, $N(-2, -5)$ and $P(6, 4)$ is equidistant from each vertex.

14. If $\vec{r} = [5, 1], \vec{s} = [0, 6]$, and $\vec{t} = [-2, -5]$, draw the resultant vector on a coordinate grid and determine the magnitude of the vector.
a. $\vec{r} - \vec{s}$ **b.** $\vec{s} + 4\vec{t}$
c. $\vec{t} - 3\vec{r}$ **d.** $\vec{r} + \vec{t}$
e. $\vec{r} - \vec{s} + \vec{t}$ **f.** $\vec{r} + 2\vec{s} - 3\vec{t}$

15. An object is being pulled by two forces. One is 30 N in a vertically downward direction and the other is 50 N in a direction 45° to the horizontal.
a. Draw a scale diagram showing the object being pulled by the two forces.
b. What is the magnitude and direction of the resultant force?

16. In $\triangle ABC$, D is the midpoint of $\overline{AB}$. Then $\overline{CD}$ is extended to E such that $\overline{CD} = \overline{DE}$. Use vector methods to prove that $\overline{BE} \parallel \overline{CA}$ and $\overline{BE} \cong \overline{CA}$.

6·20 Chapter Test

1. Sketch the graph.

a. $y = \frac{5}{2}x - 2$ **b.** $y + 8 = -2(x + 1)$

2. Are these points collinear?
$A(2, 3)$, $B(8, 5)$, $C(-3, -1)$

3. Write an equation of each line and draw the graph on a coordinate grid.

a. a slope of $\frac{3}{5}$ and through the point $(2, -1)$

b. an x-intercept of -2 and a y-intercept of 5

c. a y-intercept of 7 with a slope of -5

d. a slope of $\frac{2}{3}$ and through the point $(4, -5)$

e. through point $(-2, 4)$ and parallel to $y = 3w + 4$

f. through point $(5, -5)$ and perpendicular to $y + 4 = 3(x + 5)$

4. Describe each family of lines.

a. $y = m(x - 2) + 4$, m is the parameter

b. $y = 3x + b$, b is the parameter

5. Write an equation of a line perpendicular to the line through the points $(7, -4)$ and $(-3, 0)$.

6. Calculate the distance between the points $(3, -9)$ and $(-5, 6)$.

7. Determine the midpoint of each line segment given the endpoints.

a. $(0, 8)$ and $(-6, -8)$ **b.** $(-3, 9)$ and $(6, -5)$

8. A.T., the "Mathematics Wizard", stated that figure $TVWN$ with vertices at $T(0, 7)$, $V(5, 4)$, $W(8, -2)$ and $N(3, 1)$ is a rhombus. Is A.T. correct? Explain.

9. Triangle GHK has vertices at $G(-1, 1)$, $H(0, 7)$, and $K(5, 3)$.

a. Determine an equation for the median from G to $\overline{HK}$.

b. Determine the coordinates of the point on that median that divides it in a 2:1 ratio.

10. Verify that the diagonals of quadrilateral $ABCD$ with vertices at $A(1, 2)$, $B(0, -4)$, $C(-1, -3)$, and $D(-2, 1)$ are equal.

11. Verify that $TPRV$ with vertices at $T(-6, 4)$, $P(-5, 0)$, $R(7, 3)$, and $V(10, 8)$ is a trapezoid. What is the distance between the parallel sides?

12. Write a general proof to show that there are two medians of an isosceles triangle equal in length.

13. Use the traditional area of a triangle formula and the coordinate formula to calculate the area of $\triangle MNP$ with vertices at $M(-5, 3)$, $N(0, -2)$, and $P(4, 4)$.

14. Consider the vectors $\vec{m} = [3, 7]$ and $\vec{n} = [-4, 1]$.

a. Draw $\vec{m} + \vec{n}$.

b. Calculate the magnitude of $\vec{m}$.

c. What vector is the opposite of $\vec{n}$?

d. What ordered pair describes $4\vec{m} - 3\vec{n}$?

e. Show that $\vec{m} - \vec{n} \neq \vec{n} - \vec{m}$.

15. In this scale diagram, two forces are acting on an object P.

(1 cm = 60 N)

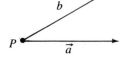

a. Sketch the vector diagram into your notebooks.

b. Use the parallelogram law to draw an accurate resultant of these two vectors.

c. Use the scale to determine the magnitude of the resultant?

16. In $\triangle ABC$, P divides $\overline{AB}$ in a 2:3 ratio and Q divides $\overline{AC}$ in the same ratio. Use vector methods to prove that $\overline{PQ} \parallel \overline{BC}$.

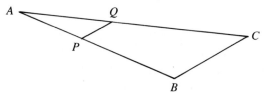

Cumulative Review   Chapters 4–6

1. Identify the numbers as belonging to the set of rational or irrational numbers.

a. $\sqrt[3]{27}$ **b.** $\dfrac{7}{9}$ **c.** 3.14

d. π **e.** $\sqrt{11}$ **f.** 0.232 232 223 …

2. Express $\dfrac{5}{11}$ in decimal form.

3. Express $4.\overline{53}$ in fractional form.

4. Simplify by expressing with positive exponents only.

a. $\dfrac{2m^{-5}}{m^2}$ **b.** $\dfrac{-3q^2 r^{-3}}{qr^{-4}}$

c. $(2x^5)(3x^4)$ **d.** $(2pq^2)^3$

e. $(4m^6) \div (-2m^3)$ **f.** $(27a^3b^9)^{-\frac{1}{3}}$

g. $\left(\dfrac{36a^{-2}b^3}{9a^{-1}b^{-1}}\right)^{-2}$ **h.** $\dfrac{(2k^{-1}m^2n^{-3})^{-2}}{(4k^{-2}mn^3)^{-1}}$

5. Evaluate.

a. $64^{\frac{2}{3}}$ **b.** $9^{\frac{1}{2}}$ **c.** $8^{-\frac{4}{3}}$ **d.** $625^{-\frac{3}{4}}$

6. Simplify.

a. $(3^{2x+1})(3^{5x-1})$ **b.** $7^{4x-1} \div 7^{x-3}$

7. Evaluate when $a = -1$, $b = 2$, and $c = -5$.

a. $2abc$ **b.** $a^b c^a$

c. $(a + b - c)^2$ **d.** $b^c \div b^a$

8. Express as a mixed radical.

a. $\sqrt{12a^4b^3}$ **b.** $\sqrt[3]{54k^7m^9}$

9. Add or subtract.

a. $5\sqrt{5} + 3\sqrt{5} - 7\sqrt{5}$

b. $\sqrt{75} - \sqrt{12} + \sqrt{147} - \sqrt{108}$

10. Multiply.

a. $3\sqrt{2}(\sqrt{6} - 2\sqrt{2})$ **b.** $(\sqrt{x} - 2\sqrt{y})^2$

11. Rationalize the denominator.

a. $\dfrac{2\sqrt{3}}{\sqrt{2}}$ **b.** $\dfrac{\sqrt{3} - 5\sqrt{2}}{\sqrt{2} + 3\sqrt{3}}$

12. Solve.

a. $\sqrt{4x - 1} = 7$ **b.** $\sqrt{3x - 2} = \sqrt{x + 1}$

13. Find the measures of the indicated angles.

a.

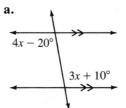

b.

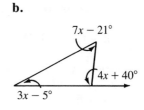

14. Construct a scalene triangle and find the bisectors of the angles of the triangles. Write a general statement concerning the three angle bisectors.

15. Explain the difference between a theorem and a postulate.

16. In $\triangle KZT$, $\overline{KR} \perp \overline{ZT}$ and $\overline{KZ} \cong \overline{KT}$. Prove that $\overline{ZR} \cong \overline{TR}$.

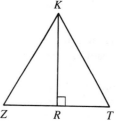

17. Write an "if … then" statement in which

a. both the statement and the converse are true.

b. the statement is false and the converse is true.

18. Explain the difference between each.

a. a square and a rhombus.

b. a rectangle and a parallelogram

c. a parallelogram and a trapezoid

19. In $\triangle QMN$, $\overline{QM} \cong \overline{QN}$ and $\angle SMN \cong \angle RNM$. Prove $\triangle QRN \cong \triangle QSM$.

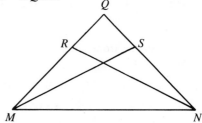

Cumulative Review   Chapters 4–6

20. Using the diagram in Exercise 19, if $\overline{RN} \cong \overline{SM}$ but $\overline{SN} \ncong \overline{RM}$, prove that $\triangle SMN \ncong \triangle RNM$.

21. Points A, B, and C have coordinates of $(-3, 1)$, $(-5, 2)$, and $(4, -3)$ respectively. Find each.
a. length of $\overline{AB}$
b. slope of $\overline{AC}$
c. midpoint of $\overline{BC}$
d. length of $\overline{AC}$
e. slope of $\overline{BC}$
f. midpoint of $\overline{AB}$

22. State which pairs of lines are parallel and which pairs are perpendicular.
a. $2x - 3y = 7$
b. $4y = 3 - 2x$
c. $3x - 2y - 5 = 0$
d. $y = 2x - 4$
e. $x = \frac{3}{2}y + \frac{1}{2}$
f. $y = -\frac{3}{2}x + 3$

23. Find the equation of a line with a slope of $-\frac{3}{5}$ and passing through $(4, -2)$.

24. Find the equation of a line which is parallel to $6x - 5y - 2 = 0$ and passing through $(-4, -1)$.

25. Find the equation of a line which is equidistant from the points $A(-2, 5)$ and $B(-4, -3)$.

26. Find the equation of a line with a slope of -4 and a y-intercept of -2.

27. Triangle XYZ has vertices at $X(-5, 2)$, $Y(3, -2)$, and $Z(1, 7)$.
a. Find the equation of the altitude from X.
b. Find the equation of the median from Z.
c. Find the point of intersection of the altitude from Y and the median from X.

28. Find the equation of a line containing points $A(-7, 2)$ and $B(-3, 1)$. Determine two other points on this line.

29. Find the distance from point $K(-6, 1)$ to the line $3x + 5y - 7 = 0$.

30. A quadrilateral with sides of 5, 7, and 12 is inscribed in a circle with a diameter of 13. Find the length of the fourth side.

31. Shown is the tiling of a floor in the recreation room of a house. Determine the fraction of the floor which is shaded.

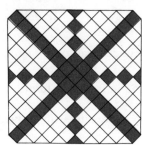

32. Find the remainder when (7 777 777 777)² is divided by 9.

33. A secret society with five directors gathers to exchange information they have collected from various sources. To avoid arousing suspicion, they meet only in a series of two-person exchanges. What is the minimum number of two-person exchanges required for all five directors to pass their information to each other?

34. The sum of n distinct positive integers is 150. Find the largest possible value of n.

35. If $\vec{k} = [3, 8]$, $\vec{m} = [-5, 1]$, and $\vec{n} = [-2, -5]$, draw the resultant vector on the Cartesian coordinate grid and determine the magnitude of the resultant vector.
a. $\vec{k} + \vec{m}$
b. $\vec{m} - \vec{n}$
c. $2\vec{m} - 3\vec{k}$
d. $\vec{n} - 3\vec{k} + 2\vec{m}$

36. If 3093 digits were used to number the pages of a book, how many pages are in the book?

37. Martha and Maurie sail out to a small cove where they intend to fish. They drop their anchor vertically in the still water and start fishing. Five hours later when they pull up anchor, they find that the tide has fallen 3 m and their boat has moved a horizontal distance of 15 m from its anchor. How long is the anchor chain which is in the water?

CHAPTER SEVEN

FUNCTIONS AND RELATIONS

Tune Up

1. Determine the slope of the line passing through these ordered pairs.
a. $(5, -4)$, $(-3, -4)$ **b.** $(15,6)$, $(20, -4)$
c. $(4, -2)$, $(4,3)$ **d.** (a,b), (c,d)

2. What do the variables m and b represent in the equation $y = mx + b$? Use a graph to help explain your answer.

3. In which quadrant are these points located?
a. $(-3,2)$ **b.** $(5,7)$ **c.** $(-3, -10)$
d. $(4, -2)$ **e.** $(-5,0)$ **f.** $(0,5)$
g. Plot the points on the same coordinate grid.
h. Identify the four quadrants on the coordinate grid of part **g**.

4. Solve.
a. $|x| - 7 = 0$ **b.** $10 + |-x| = 0$

5. State the degree of the equation.
a. $x + 3y = 2$ **b.** $x^2 - y^2 + 3xy = 5$
c. $xy = 1$ **d.** $4x^2 + 6y^2 = 12$

6. Graph the relation and describe the difference between the graphs of parts **a** and **b**.
a. $\{(x,y) \mid y = x, x \in R\}$
b. $\{(x,y) \mid y = -x, x \in R\}$
c. Will the mapping $(x,y) \rightarrow (x, -y)$ translate the graph of part **a** onto the graph of part **b**?

7. Graph the relation and describe the difference between the graphs of parts **a** and **b**.
a. $\{(x,y) \mid y = |x|, x \in R\}$
b. $\{(x,y) \mid x = |y|, x \in R\}$
c. Will the mapping $(x,y) \rightarrow (x, |y|)$ translate the graph of part **a** onto the graph of part **b**?

8. Sketch the line having a slope of 4 and passing through the point $(1, -2)$.
a. Estimate the x-intercept and the y-intercept.
b. Find an equation of the line.
c. Calculate the x-intercept and the y-intercept using the equation of part **b**.
d. Were your estimates in part **a** accurate? Explain.

9. Determine the equation for these lines.
a. passes through the point $(4,4)$ and has a slope of -1
b. has a slope of 4 and a y-intercept of -2

10. Graph. $x \in R$
a. $y \geq 3x$ **b.** $y > 3x + 4$

11. Graph the relation. Estimate the coordinates of either the maximum or minimum point using the graph.
a. $y = |x|$ **b.** $y = -|x| + 2$

191

7·1 Relations

A connection or relation between two people or objects occurs often in our daily lives. For instance, Norma is the daughter of Edna, or the number of cars sold is related to its popularity, are examples of relations. When two quantities or sets are related, the set of all possible pairings is called a **relation**.

> A relation is a set of ordered pairs which connects items in one set with items in another set.

A relation can be expressed in words, as a mapping, as a table of values, or as ordered pairs. The first set of items in any relation is the **domain**, while the second set of items in the relation is the **range**.

Example

A worker is paid a wage of $10.65/h.
a. Express the relation between the hours worked and the hourly wage.
b. State the domain and the range of the relation.

a.

In words	As a mapping		As a table of values		As ordered pairs
			Hours	Pay	
1 h earns $10.65	$1 \longrightarrow 10.65$		1	10.65	(1, 10.65)
2 h earns $21.30	$2 \longrightarrow 21.30$		2	21.30	(2, 21.30)
3 h earns $31.95	$3 \longrightarrow 31.95$		3	31.95	(3, 31.95)
n hours earns $10.65n$	$n \longrightarrow 10.65n$		n	10.65n	(n, 10.65n)

b. The first set of numbers representing the hours worked is the domain. The second set of numbers, representing the hourly wage, is the range. The domain is $D = \{x \mid x \geq 0,\ x \in R\}$ and the range is $R = \{y \mid y \geq 0,\ y \in R\}$.

The mapping notation of a relation such as $x \rightarrow 2x$ is read as "x is mapped onto $2x$". There are three different types of mappings for relations.

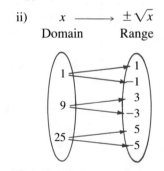

i) $\quad x \longrightarrow 5x - 2$
  Domain   Range

ii) $\quad x \longrightarrow \pm\sqrt{x}$
  Domain   Range

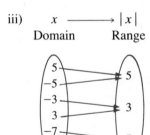

iii) $\quad x \longrightarrow |x|$
  Domain   Range

One-to-one mapping
For every member of the domain, there is exactly one member of the range.

One-to-many mapping
For every member of the domain, there is more than one member of the range.

Many-to-one mapping
For every member of the range, there is more than one member of the domain.

Exercises

1. In your own words, explain the meaning of the terms "relation", "domain", and "range".

2. State the domain and the range for these sets of ordered pairs.
a. {(−5, −4), (−1,0), (2,3), (4,5)}
b. {(0,0), (4,2), (9,3), (16,4)}
c. {(5, −3), (6, −3), (7, −3), (8, −3)}
d. {(−5,5), (−3,3), (0,0), (3,3), (5,5)}
e. {(−2, −8), (−1, −1), (0,0), (1,1), (2,8)}
f. {(2, −7), (2, −4), (2,0), (2,3), (2,7)}

3. A.T., the "Mathematics Wizard", stated that "a possible equation for Exercise 2, part **a**, is $y = x + 1$."
a. Is A.T. correct?
b. Find a possible equation for each part of Exercise 2.

4. In your own words, explain the phrases "one-to-one mapping", "many-to-one mapping", and "one-to-many mapping". Use examples to help in your explanations.

5. State the type of mapping the sets of ordered pairs in Exercise 2 represent.

6. State the domain and the range of these relations.
a. *D*   *R*   **b.** *D*   *R*

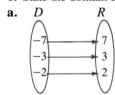
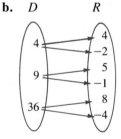

c. *D*   *R*   **d.** *D*   *R*

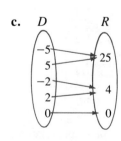
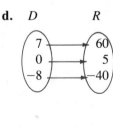

7. State the type of mapping the relations in Exercise 6 represent.

8. Refer to the example in the display to determine the ordered pair that describes the total pay for these hours worked.
a. 10 h   **b.** 24 h   **c.** 44 h

9. Using the mapping $x \rightarrow 5x - 1$, find the missing value in each ordered pair.
a. (5,■)   **b.** (−8,■)   **c.** (■, −6)
d. (■,1)   **e.** (−10,■)   **f.** (0,■)

10. Express these sets of ordered pairs as a mapping.
a. {(−2,5), (−1,7), (0,9), (1,11), (2,13)}
b. {(−3,0), (−1, −2), (0, −3), (1, −2), (3,0)}
c. {(−2,8), (−1,6), (0,4), (1,6), (−2,8)}

11. Using the mapping $x \rightarrow 2|x| - 3$, find the missing value in each ordered pair.
a. (3,■)   **b.** (■,5)   **c.** (−7,■)
d. (■,0)   **e.** $\left(\frac{3}{4}, ■\right)$ **f.** (−16,■)

12. A ticket for a concert costs $15.25.
a. Use a table of values to show the cost of 1 ticket, 2 tickets, 5 tickets, 8 tickets, and *n* tickets.
b. Express your answer to part **a** in words and as ordered pairs.

13. Given the domain and the range, express the relation as a mapping notation and as an arrow diagram.
a. $D = \{x \mid x = -4, -2, 0, 2, 4\}$
    $R = \{y \mid y = -7, -3, 1, 5, 9\}$
b. $D = \{x \mid x = -2, -1, 0, 1, 2\}$
    $R = \{y \mid y = 11, 7, 3, -1, -5\}$
c. $D = \{x \mid x = -5, -3, 0, 2, 4\}$
    $R = \{y \mid y = 37, 25, 7, -5, -17\}$

14. A photographer charges $4.00 for the first 5 pictures developed and $2.50 for each additional picture ordered. How much will it cost to buy 6 pictures, 9 pictures, 15 pictures, and *n* pictures? Express your answer in a table of values.

15. Express each mapping as a set of ordered pairs for the indicated values of *x*.
a. $x \rightarrow 4x - 2$ $D = \{x \mid x = -2, 0, 2\}$
b. $x \rightarrow |x| - 10$ $D = \{x \mid x = -10, 0, 10\}$
c. $x \rightarrow \frac{1}{2}x^2 + 1$ $D = \{x \mid x = -4, 0, 4\}$

193

7·2 Graphing Relations

Relations can be expressed as a graph, by plotting the ordered pairs of the relation on a coordinate system, or as an equation. Recall that the first coordinate of the ordered pair is called the **abscissa**, and the second coordinate is called the **ordinate**.

Example 1

The mass of a corn plant, measured in grams, was found at various times and a table of values was constructed. Graph the relation.

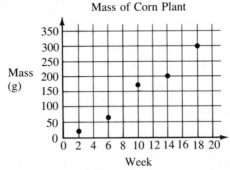

Mass of Corn Plant

Week	Mass (g)
2	20
6	60
10	170
14	200
18	300

In this relation, the set of weeks is the domain and the set of masses is the range. Since the mass of the corn plant was taken at specific times, the ordered pairs of the relation are represented on the graph as a set of **isolated** points.

$D = \{2, 6, 10, 14, 18\}$
$R = \{20, 60, 170, 200, 300\}$

Example 2

Graph the relation $y = |x| - 4$, where $x \in R$. State the domain and the range of the relation.

In order to graph this relation, various ordered pairs for the relation should be found. The table of values shows five such points.

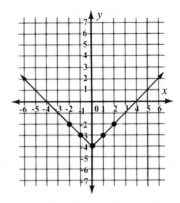

x	y
-2	-2
-1	-3
0	-4
1	-3
2	-2

Since there are an infinite number of points between the ones plotted on the graph, the relation is **continuous**.

Once the ordered pairs have been established, a pattern should emerge. From the graph of the relation, the domain and the range of the relation can be determined. The domain is $D = \{x \mid x \in R\}$. The range is $R = \{y \mid y \geq -4, y \in R\}$ because the lowest value that the y-coordinate will have is -4.

Exercises

1. Is Example 2 of the display a linear relation? Explain. What is necessary in order to have a linear relation?

2. A.T., the "Mathematics Wizard", claims that "the y-values of the relation $y = |x| - 16$ would be greater than or equal to -16." Is A.T. correct? Explain.

3. Explain why the graph in Example 1 of the display is a set of isolated points, whereas the graph in Example 2 is a set of continuous points.

4. How would the graph of the relation in Example 2 of the display look if the relation were defined over the set of integers.

5. State the domain and the range for these sets of ordered pairs.
a. $\{(2,2), (3,3), (4,4), (5,5), (6,6)\}$
b. $\{(0,0), (1,1), (2,4), (3,9), (4,16)\}$
c. $\{(10, -10), (7, -7), (4, -4), (3, -3), (1, -1)\}$
d. $\{(-5,8), (-10,6), (-15,4), (-20,2), (-25,0)\}$
e. $\{(-1,3), (0,3), (1,3), (2,3), (3,3)\}$
f. $\{(7,5), (7,4), (7,3), (7,2), (7,1)\}$

6. State the domain and the range of these graphs.
a.
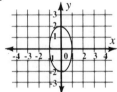
b.
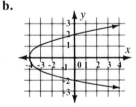

c.

d.

e. The graph of part **c** is often called a **step-function**. Why?

7. List the ways in which a relation can be expressed.

8. State the domain and the range for the relation over the set of real numbers. Explain how you arrived at your answer. The first one is done as an example.

$$\left\{ (x,y) \mid y = \frac{1}{x + 4} \right\}$$

Since $x + 4 \neq 0$, the domain of the relation is $D = \{x \mid x \neq -4, x \in R\}$.
Since the numerator is a constant, the expression can never have a value of 0. Therefore, the range is $R = \{y \mid y \neq 0, y \in R\}$.

a. $\left\{ (x,y) \mid y = \dfrac{3}{x - 9} \right\}$

b. $\left\{ (x,y) \mid y = \dfrac{x}{(x + 2)(x + 1)} \right\}$

c. $\left\{ (x,y) \mid y = \dfrac{12}{(x - 5)(x + 7)} \right\}$

9. Using a table of values, graph the relation and state the domain and range of the relation over the set of real numbers.
a. $\{(x,y) \mid y = 2x + 5\}$ **b.** $\left\{ (x,y) \mid y = 4 - \dfrac{1}{3}x \right\}$

c. $\{(x,y) \mid y = 3|x|\}$ **d.** $\{(x,y) \mid y = -3|x|\}$

e. $\{(x,y) \mid y = |6 - x|\}$ **f.** $\{(x,y) \mid y = 2^x\}$

10. In your own words, describe a continuous relation and a linear relation.
a. A relation which is not continuous is a **discontinuous relation**. State an equation of a discontinuous relation.
b. State an equation of a **non-linear relation**.

11. A freely falling body falls according to the equation $t = \sqrt{\dfrac{d}{4.9}}$, where t represents the time in seconds and d represents the distance in metres.
a. Using a table of values, graph the relation over the set of real numbers.
b. State the domain and the range for the relation.

12. In a science class, water was brought to a boil for 5 min and allowed to cool.
a. Sketch a possible graph for the time the water was boiling versus the temperature of the water.
b. State the domain and the range of the relation you have just sketched.

go to 198

195

7·3 Graphing Inequalities

In the previous section, linear graphs of relations were drawn using the ordered pairs which satisfied the equation. These ordered pairs were points on the line. In this section, we will graph linear inequalities. The process is very similar to that of graphing an equation. While equations describe the points on the line, inequalities describe points which may or may not be on the line, and lie either to the right of the line or to the left of the line.

Example 1

Graph the inequality. $2x + 5y \leq 10$, $x \in R$

In order to set up a table of values, it is often easier to express the inequality in terms of x by isolating the y-variable and determining the ordered pairs that satisfy the equation.

$$2x + 5y \leq 10$$
$$5y \leq 10 - 2x$$
$$y \leq 2 - \frac{2}{5}x$$

The equation form of the inequality is $y = \frac{-2}{5}x + 2$.

Since the domain, x, is defined over the set of real numbers, choose any convenient x-values for the table.

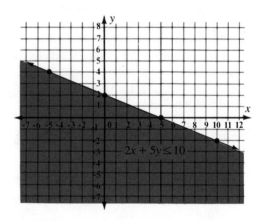

x	y
-5	4
0	2
5	0
10	-2

Notice that any coordinate in the shaded area of the graph satisfies the inequality. In Example 1, the inequality is expressed using a solid line. This is the case whenever the relation uses the symbols $\geq$ or $\leq$. If the inequality uses the symbols $>$ or $<$, then the line is dotted.

Example 2

Graph the inequality. $\frac{1}{2}(1 - y) < \frac{-2}{5}(10x - 5)$, $x \in R$

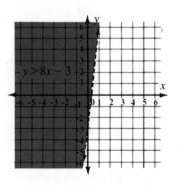

$$\frac{1}{2}(1 - y) < \frac{-2}{5}(10x - 5)$$
$$5(1 - y) < -4(10x - 5)$$
$$5 - 5y < -40x + 20$$
$$-5y < -40x + 15$$
$$y > 8x - 3$$

When multiplying or dividing by a negative, reverse the inequality.

Exercises

1. List three points for each example in the display that satisfy the inequality and three points that do not satisfy the inequality.

2. Explain why the inequality should be reversed when multiplying or dividing by a negative number. Use an example to support your explanation.

3. Does the given point satisfy the inequality?
a. $2y - x \geq 4$; $(3, 2)$
b. $|x| - |y| > 0$; $(-2, -3)$
c. $4a - 2b \geq 0$; $(-3, 1)$
d. $y \geq 7$; $(9, 12)$

4. Graph the relation. $x, y \in R$
a. $x \geq 0$ **b.** $y \leq 0$
c. $y < x$ **d.** $y > 0$

5. Isolate the y-variable, construct a table of values, and graph the inequality.
a. $x + y < 5$ **b.** $2x + 3y > 0$
c. $x - y < 4$ **d.** $x > 2y$
e. $|x| - y > 1$ **f.** $\frac{3}{4}x - \frac{1}{2}y \geq 3$

6. For the inequalities in Exercise 5, list three ordered pairs which satisfy the inequality and three ordered pairs which do not satisfy the inequality.

7. A football team needs 10 points to make the playoffs. A win is worth 2 points and a tie is worth 1 point. How many wins, w, and ties, t, will the team need to make the playoffs?
a. Write an equation describing this inequality.
b. Graph the inequality.

8. A bridge has a load limit of 30 t. If an average car has a mass of 1.5 t and an average truck has a mass of 5 t, then how many cars, c, and trucks, t, will cause this bridge to be overloaded?
a. Write an equation describing the inequality.
b. Graph the inequality.
c. Will 3 cars and 5 trucks overload the bridge? Explain.

9. Write an inequality to describe the graphs.
a. 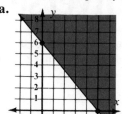   **b.**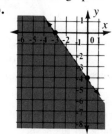

10. One gram of hamburger has 3 calories and one French fry has 14 calories. How much hamburger and how many French fries can a person have if they wish to have a meal that is less than 420 calories?
a. Write an equation describing this inequality.
b. Graph the inequality.

11. A shellfish farmer received \$20/kg for scallops and paid \$15/h in expenses. How many kilograms of scallops, and how many hours would be needed, to maintain a profit of more than \$3000?
a. Write an inequality describing this relation.
b. Would 300 kg of scallops in 200 h provide a profit for the farmer?

12. List the four inequalities which will describe the shaded region.

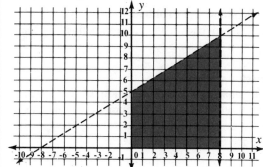

Using the Library

Determine whether the graph describing the equations $x \geq 0$ and $x > 0$ are the same. Answer the questions "will the x-axis remain solid or will it be dotted? What happens at the origin, $(0, 0)$?"

7·4 Inverse of a Relation

Every relation has a domain and a range. In this section, we will investigate the effect of interchanging the elements of the ordered pairs that make up a relation. In such cases, the resulting relation is the **inverse** of the relation.

The relation $L = \{(0,3), (1,5), (2,7), (3,9)\}$ describes the number of litres of water pumped into a tank in each successive second after the pump starts. An inverse relation, L^{-1} (read "L inverse"), can be obtained by interchanging the elements of the ordered pairs. In this case, $L^{-1} = \{(3,0), (5,1), (7,2), (9,3)\}$. The graph shows the relation L and its inverse L^{-1}. Notice that the inverse, L^{-1}, is the reflection of L in the line $y = x$, and that the line $y = x$ is the perpendicular bisector of any segment joining two corresponding points in the relation and its inverse. That is, $\overline{AC} \cong \overline{A'C}$

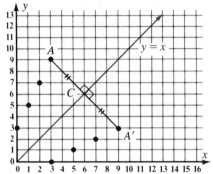

and $\overline{AC}$ is perpendicular to the line $y = x$. The domain and range of L is $D = \{x \mid x = 0,1,2,3\}$ and $R = \{y \mid y = 3,5,7,9\}$ respectively. The domain and range of L^{-1} is $D = \{x \mid x = 3,5,7,9\}$ and $R = \{y \mid y = 0,1,2,3\}$ respectively. How are the four sets related?

> The inverse of a relation is a reflection in the line $y = x$.

Example

Find an equation for the inverse of the relation $y = 3x + 5$, where $x \in R$.

Understand the Problem

Find the inverse of the relation defined by the equation $y = 3x + 5$.

Develop a Plan

Since an inverse is a reflection in the line $y = x$, then "interchanging" the numeric coefficients of the original equation and solving for y will give the equation of the inverse.

Carry Out the Plan

The original equation is $y = 3x + 5$.
Therefore, interchanging the variables x and y yields $x = 3y + 5$. Solving for y will give the standard form of the inverse relation. In this case, $y = \frac{1}{3}x - \frac{5}{3}$.

Look Back

The graph indicates that the inverse relation is a reflection in the line $y = x$.

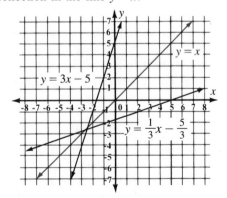

To verify numerically, determine an ordered pair in the original equation, find its inverse, and see if it satisfies the inverse equation.

Exercises

1. Determine an ordered pair which satisfies the original relation in the example of the display.
a. Interchange the x and y terms of the ordered pair.
b. Substitute the new ordered pair into the equation of the inverse relation.
c. Does the new ordered pair satisfy the inverse relation?
d. Explain why this method of checking the inverse of a relation is successful.

2. State the domain and the range of the relation and its inverse for the example of the display.

3. Estimate the point where the relation and its inverse intersect the line $y = x$ in the example of the display.

4. Write the inverse of each set of ordered pairs and state the domain and the range of both the relation and its inverse.
a. $\{(4,0), (4,-1), (4,1), (4,-2), (4,2)\}$
b. $\left\{\left(\sqrt{2},\frac{1}{\sqrt{2}}\right),\left(\sqrt{3},\frac{1}{\sqrt{3}}\right),\left(\sqrt{5},\frac{1}{\sqrt{5}}\right),\left(\sqrt{6},\frac{1}{\sqrt{6}}\right)\right\}$
c. $\{(a,V), (b,W), (c,X), (d,Y), (e,Z)\}$

5. Which of these graphs shows a relation and its inverse? Explain.

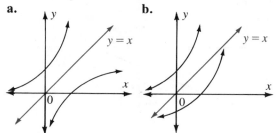

a.   **b.**

6. Given the relation $\frac{1}{2}x - 2$, where $x \in R$.

a. Graph the relation using the x- and y-intercepts.
b. Draw the line of reflection. $y = x$
c. Reflect the x- and y-intercepts in the line $y = x$.
d. Draw the inverse of the relation using the two new points.
e. Do the relation and its inverse intersect the line $y = x$? If so, estimate the point of intersection.

7. Is it possible for an inequality to have an inverse? Explain.

8. Given the relation $y = \sqrt{x}$, where $x \in R$,
a. state the domain and the range of the relation,
b. determine the domain and the range of the inverse relation. Explain the steps involved.
c. graph the relation and its inverse on the same set of axes.

9. State the inverse of each relation over the set of real numbers.
a. $\{(x,y) \mid y = 4x - 7\}$ **b.** $\left\{(x,y) \mid y = \frac{1}{2}x\right\}$
c. $\{(x,y) \mid y = x^{-1}\}$ **d.** $\left\{(x,y) \mid y = \frac{-1}{|x|}\right\}$
e. $\{(x,y) \mid y = 5 - |x|\}$ **f.** $\left\{(x,y) \mid y = x^{\frac{1}{3}}\right\}$

10. Draw a graph of the relation and its inverse over the set of real numbers. State the domain and the range of the relation and its inverse. Explain how you graphed the inverse.
a. $\{(x,y) \mid y = 2^x\}$ **b.** $\{(x,y) \mid y = 3x - 2\}$
c. $\{(x,y) \mid y = -|x|\}$ **d.** $\{(x,y) \mid y = x^x\}$

11. A.T., the ''Mathematics Wizard'', stated that ''the only relation that is its own inverse is the straight line $y = x$.'' Is A.T. correct? Explain.

12. For the relation $xy = 4$, state the domain and the range of the inverse function.
a. Using a table of values, graph the relation and its inverse.
b. Is this relation its own inverse? Explain.

13. Repeat Exercise 12 for the relation $xy = -4$.

14. Two brothers, Jim and Joe, cannot agree on what to plant in their garden. The garden's shape is a right triangle with sides of 30 m, 40 m, and 50 m. They decide to build a fence running from the right angle to the hypotenuse to separate the garden into two parts of equal perimeter. Jim says the fence will be 25 m in length. Joe says it will be closer to 27 m. Who is correct?

7·5 Functions

In Section 7·1, three types of relations were shown by means of a mapping: one-to-one mappings, one-to-many mappings, and many-to-one mappings. The one-to-one mapping and the many-to-one mapping are special in that each element in the domain is matched with exactly one element in the range. These special relations are called **functions**.

The word "function" is used to describe how one quantity depends on another. For example, the length of the shadow of a post is a function of the position of the sun. The only way that this sentence can be rewritten is to say that the length of the shadow of a post depends on the position of the sun. Since the shadow of the post cannot have two different shadow lengths at the same time, this is a special relation called a function.

> A function is a relation such that for every member of the domain, there is exactly one member of the range.

A function also can be said to be a relation in which no two ordered pairs have the same x-coordinate. As a result, the graph of any relation is easily identifiable as either a function or a relation using the **vertical line test**. This test states that if a straight vertical line intersects a graph in more than one point, then the graph is not a function. For the graphs shown, the graph to the left is a function, while the graph to the right is not a function.

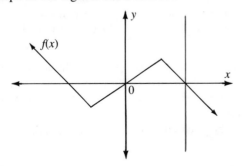

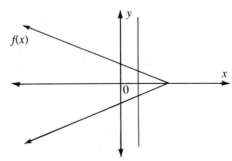

Example 1

Is the relation described a function?
a. {(9,0), (12,0), (8,10), (10,10)}
b. {(7,1), (7,2), (7,3), (7,4)}

a. Since the x-coordinate (domain) of the relation are all different, there is only one possible member of the range (y-coordinate). Therefore, the relation is a function.
b. Since all the x-coordinates are the same, there is more than one y-coordinate for each x-coordinate. Therefore, the relation is not a function.

The relations in Example 1 are shown graphically. Notice how a vertical line will pass through the relation of part **a** only once, but that it will intersect the graph of part **b** more than once when $x = 7$.

a.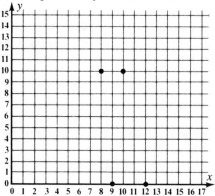

b.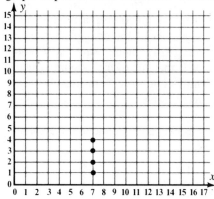

Example 2

Graph $y = x^2$. Determine whether the relation is a function.

The relation $y = x^2$ has a table of values as shown.

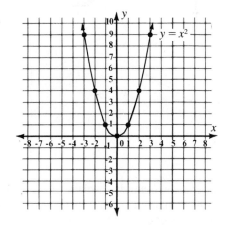

x	-3	-2	-1	0	1	2	3
$y = x^2$	9	4	1	0	1	4	9

From the graph, the relation $y = x^2$ is a function because a vertical line will touch the curve in exactly one spot. A function whose points cannot be joined by a single straight line is called a **non-linear** function.

Example 2 illustrates another test for a function. If a value for x can be found that will produce more than one value of y, the equation does not represent a function. This is the **equation test** for a function.

Example 3

Without graphing, determine which are functions.
a. $x = y^2$
b. $3x = y$

a. We must determine if there is any value for x that will produce more than one value for y. In this case, there are many values. For example, if $x = 4$, then $y^2 = 4$, and $y = \pm 2$. Therefore, the relation is not a function.
b. Every value for x will produce a unique value for y. Therefore, the relation is a function.

Exercises

1. a. A.T., the "Mathematics Wizard", stated that the sentences "a function is a relation such that for every member of the domain there is exactly one member of the range" and "a function is a relation such that for every x-coordinate there is exactly one y-coordinate" are interchangeable. Is A.T. correct? Explain.

2. Which relations are functions? Explain your selections.

a.
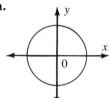

b.
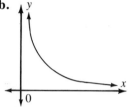

c.
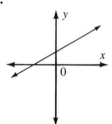

d.
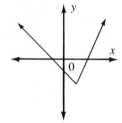

3. In your own words, explain each phrase. Give an example of each to help explain your definitions.
a. linear function
b. non-linear function
c. vertical line test for a function
d. equation test for a function

4. Graph the relation and determine whether it is a function.
a. $y = 3x + 2$ **b.** $y = 4x - 5$
c. $y = \frac{1}{2}x - \frac{2}{3}$ **d.** $x^2 + 4y^2 = 16$
e. $y = |x|$ **f.** $y = \sqrt{x}$

5. Sketch the graph of $xy = 1$.
a. How many distinct parts does the graph have?
b. Is it a function? Explain.
c. Does a graph have to be continuous (the parts connected) to be a function? Explain.

6. Can an inequality be a function? Explain.

7. Using a table of values, draw the graphs of $y = k^x$ for $k = 2, 3$, and 4, and $x \in R$. Are the relations also functions?

8. The equation $y = \dfrac{3}{x + 5}$ is undefined for $x = -5$.
a. Using the equation test for a function, predict whether the relation is a function.
b. Construct a table of values for the relation.
c. Graph the relation.
d. Using the vertical line test, verify your prediction from part **a**.

9. In Example 1 of the display, the graph was drawn with y along the vertical axis and x along the horizontal axis. In this case, we say that "y is a function of x". If the graph was drawn with x along the vertical axis and y along the horizontal axis, can we say that "x is a function of y"?

10. Are all linear relations functions? If not, find one that is not a function.

11. The rate at which a burning candle shortens is given by the relation $h = 0.1t + 20$.
a. State the range if the domain is $D = \{t \mid t = 0, 1, 2, 4\}$.
b. Graph the relation and determine whether it is a function.

12. The volume, V, of a gas varies directly as the distance, D, below the ocean's surface. The volume is half the original at 10 m, one quarter the original at 30 m, and one eighth the original at 70 m.
a. Write an equation expressing the relation between D and V.
b. Graph the relation.
c. Is it a function? Explain.

7·6 Function Notation

The word function was introduced by Leibniz in the seventeenth century and is derived from the Latin word *functio* which means "to perform". In mathematics, a relation that is also a function can be represented by symbols such as $f(x)$ or $g(x)$. For example, the notation for $y = x^2$ is $f(x) = x^2$ and is read "f of x equals x squared". The function is evaluated by substituting values for x into the expression. The function notation has the advantage of recording the particular x-value for which the expression is being evaluated. For example, instead of saying "evaluate $y = x^2$ for $x = 2$", function notation allows us to write $f(2) = x^2$. In this case, $f(2) = (2)^2$ or 4.

Example

If $f(x) = x^2 + 3$, then find $f(-2)$, $f(5)$, and $f(2a)$.

$$f(-2) = (-2)^2 + 3$$
$$= 4 + 3$$
$$= 7$$

$$f(5) = (5)^2 + 3$$
$$= 25 + 3$$
$$= 28$$

$$f(2a) = (2a)^2 + 3$$
$$= 4a^2 + 3$$

Exercises

1. If $g(x) = x + 3$, then evaluate each.
a. $g(0)$ **b.** $g(-3)$ **c.** $g\left(\frac{1}{2}\right)$

2. Write an expression for each if $g(x) = 3x^2 + 2$.
a. $g(\sqrt{5})$ **b.** $g(-x)$ **c.** $g(x^2)$

3. Evaluate each for $f(x) = (x + 1)^2$.
a. $f(3)$ **b.** $f(-0.5)$ **c.** $f(-1.5)$

4. If $g(x) = \dfrac{x}{x + 2}$, then evaluate each.
a. $g(4)$ **b.** $5[g(3)]$
c. $\dfrac{g(3)}{g(-1)}$ **d.** $g(0) + g(2)$
e. State the domain and the range of the function.

5. A.T., the "Mathematics Wizard", stated that he knew more about functions than most people in the class. He claimed that "it does not matter what the function is, $f(2) + f\left(\frac{1}{2}\right)$ is equivalent to $f\left(2 + \frac{1}{2}\right)$." Pick a series of functions and check whether A.T. is the wizard he claims to be.

6. Given $f(x) = x^2$ and $g(x) = 3x - 1$, find:
a. $f(3) + g(2)$ **b.** $f(4) - g(1)$
c. $f(6) \times g(8)$ **d.** $\dfrac{f(1)}{g(0.5)}$

7. Use the function $h(n) = \dfrac{-n}{1 - n^2}$ to answer these questions.
a. Find the domain and the range of the function.
b. For what value of n will $h(n)$ be zero?
c. For what value of n will $h(n)$ have no value?

8. For the function $f(x) = 2x$, does $f(ab) = f(a) \times f(b)$?

9. If $g(a) = a^2 + 3a$, find $\dfrac{g(x + h) - g(x)}{h}$.

10. For the function $P(x) = x^2 + 4x + 4$, evaluate each.
a. $P(2)$ **b.** $P(-2)$ **c.** $P(0)$
d. $P(y)$ **e.** $P(y^2)$ **f.** $P(y + 2)$
g. $P(y - 2)$ **h.** $P(\sqrt{3})$ **i.** $P(3x - 1)$

11. For the function $f(x) = 2^x$, evaluate each.
a. $f(0)$ **b.** $f(3)$ **c.** $f(-2)$
d. $\dfrac{f(2)}{f(-3)}$ **e.** $-2[f(5)]$ **f.** $f(-1) \times f(4)$
g. $[f(-1)]^2$ **h.** $[f(-2)]^{-2}$ **i.** $[f(2)]^2$

7·7 Inverse of a Function

The inverse of a relation is a reflection in the line $y = x$ and can be determined by interchanging the coordinates of the ordered pairs in the relation. Since a function is a special relation, the inverse of a function, written $f^{-1}(x)$ and read "the inverse of f at x", can be determined in the same manner.

Example 1

The number of bacteria in a colony doubles every four minutes. The equation relating the number of bacteria, N, to the time, t, in minutes is $N = 2^{0.25t}$. Find an equation for the inverse of this relation, and determine whether the equation and its inverse are functions.

Since $t \geq 0$, the table of values for $N = 2^{0.25t}$ can be produced.

t	0	4	8	12	16
N	1	2	4	8	16

Interchanging the values of t and N produces the table of values for the inverse $t = 2^{0.25N}$.

t	1	2	4	8	16
N	0	4	8	12	16

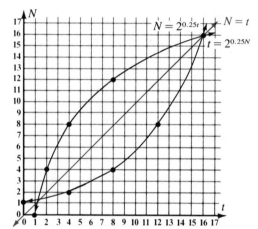

The inverse, $t = 2^{0.25N}$, is a reflection of $N = 2^{0.25t}$ in the line $N = t$. By applying the vertical line test to the graph, both the equation and its inverse are found to be functions. However, the inverse of a function is not always a function.

Example 2

A function is defined by $f(x) = x^2 - 3$, where $x \in R$. Find an equation for $f^{-1}(x)$ and determine whether it is a function.

The original function, $f(x) = x^2 - 3$, can be written as $y = x^2 - 3$. Interchanging x and y yields the equation $x = y^2 - 3$. Solving this new equation for y in terms of x will give the inverse $f^{-1}(x)$.

$$x = y^2 - 3$$
$$\pm \sqrt{x + 3} = y$$

Therefore, $f^{-1}(x) = \pm \sqrt{x + 3}$.

By using a table of values, we can determine whether $f^{-1}(x)$ is a function.

x	-2	-1	0	1	2
$f(x)$	1	-2	-3	-2	1
$f^{-1}(x)$	± 1	$\pm \sqrt{2}$	$\pm \sqrt{3}$	± 2	$\pm \sqrt{5}$

From the table of values for $f^{-1}(x)$, there are two possibilities for every x-value. Therefore, $f^{-1}(x)$ is not a function by the equation test for a function.

Exercises

1. Refer to Example 2 in the display.
a. State the domain and the range of the function and its inverse.
b. Graph the function and its inverse on the same set of axes.
c. Are they both continuous? Explain.
d. Is $f^{-1}(x)$ a reflection in the line $y = x$?
e. In your own words, explain why the inverse of the function is not a function.

2. Determine the inverse of the function $f(x) = x^2$, where $x \in R$.
a. State the domain and the range of the function and its inverse.
b. Construct a table of values and graph the function and its inverse on the same set of axes.
c. Is $f^{-1}(x)$ a function? Explain.

3. The inverse of the function $f(x) = x + 2$ is $f^{-1}(x) = x - 2$. Evaluate.
a. $f(-2)$ **b.** $f^{-1}(-2)$
c. $f(4)$ **d.** $f^{-1}(4)$
e. $f(x - 2)$ **f.** $f^{-1}(x + 2)$
g. What do you notice about parts **e** and **f**?
h. Can a general statement be made about what will happen when the expression for the inverse is substituted into the function and vice versa? Use other functions to support your conclusion and write your conclusion as a general statement.

4. Can a relation that is not a function have an inverse that is a function? Justify your answer with an example.

5. Construct a table of values and graph the function and its inverse on the same set of axes. State the restrictions, if any, on all variables and state which functions have inverses that are also functions. (*Hint*: Carefully label your axis.)
a. $f(x) = \dfrac{12}{x}$ **b.** $g(x) = 2x - 3$
c. $h(x) = \dfrac{1}{2}|x|$ **d.** $f(a) = -\dfrac{1}{12}a^2$
e. $f(t) = \sqrt{9 - t^2}$ **f.** $h(u) = -\dfrac{1}{2}\sqrt{u} + 2$

6. Edna invested money at 8% interest compounded annually. If $1000 was deposited, the amount of money accumulated, A, each year, n, is determined using the equation $A = 1000(1.08)^n$.
a. Is the equation a function?
b. State the inverse of this equation.
c. Is the inverse of the equation a function?

7. When light penetrates water, it is partially absorbed by the water at the rate of one percent per metre. The light intensity at a depth, m, is determined by the equation $I = 100(0.99)^m$.
a. Is the equation a function?
b. Is the inverse of the equation a function?
c. Explain the meaning of the inverse.

8. The equation describing the distance, d, in kilometres, a swimmer swam during a swimming competition is $d = -3|t - 0.5| + 1.5$, where t is the time in minutes.
a. Is the equation a function?
b. State the inverse of the function.
c. Is the inverse of the equation a function?

9. Verhulst's hypothesis regarding the rate of growth of a population is expressed by the formula $R = k_u N - k_c N^2$ where k_u and k_c are constants and N is the number of individuals in the population. If $k_u = 1.071$, $k_c = 0.001\,60$, and R is the number of yeast cells added to a population in a 2 h period, then find the total population at the end of 2 h, 4 h, 6 h, 8 h, and 10 h. Use a calculator if one is available.
a. Graph this growth curve.
b. Is the equation a function?
c. State the inverse of this equation.
d. Is the inverse a function?

10. Does $f^{-1}(x) = \dfrac{1}{f(x)}$? Explain.

Braintickler

The base of a right circular cylinder is inscribed in the base of a cube. The length of one side of the cube is 10 cm. Find the volume of the cube not in the cylinder.

7·8 Translating Functions

We often talk about a function in general terms without specific reference to the algebraic expression it represents. For instance, we can let $y = f(x)$, where $f(x)$ is any expression evaluated over the real numbers. In this section, the translations of $y = f(x)$ will be introduced.

Example 1

Consider the graph of the function $y = |x|$. How would the graph of the functions $y = |x| + 4$ and $y + 4 = |x|$ compare with the graph of $y = |x|$? By constructing a table of values, and graphing the functions, the graphs of $y = |x| + 4$ and $y + 4 = |x|$ can be compared to $y = |x|$. The function $y + 4 = |x|$ can be written as $y = |x| - 4$.

x	-2	-1	0	1	2
$|x|$	2	1	0	1	2
$|x| + 4$	6	5	4	5	6
$|x| - 4$	-2	-3	-4	-3	-2

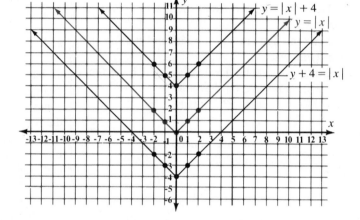

Using the table of values and the graphs, notice that the function $y = |x| + 4$ is the same as the graph of $y = |x|$ moved up 4 units. Since the function $y + 4 = |x|$ is equivalent to $y = |x| - 4$, the result is the graph of $y = |x|$ moved down 4 units. In fact, adding any constant, b, to a function will move the graph up b units, while subtracting a constant, b, will move the graph down b units.

> The graph of $y = f(x) + b$ is a **vertical translation** of $y = f(x)$ by b units, $b \in R$.

This approach can be used to graph any general function of the form $y = f(x)$.

Example 2

The graph of a general function $f(x)$ is in colour.
Sketch these graphs.

a. $y = f(x) + 4$ **b.** $y = f(x) - 5$

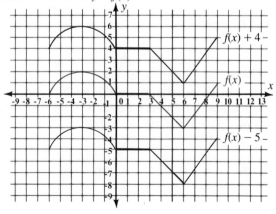

a. Since the constant 4 is **added** to the function $f(x)$, the result is a vertical translation of 4 units. That is, the graph of $f(x)$ is moved up 4 units.
b. Since the constant 5 is **subtracted** from the function $f(x)$, the result is a vertical translation of -5 units. That is, the graph of $f(x)$ is moved down 5 units.

Exercises

1. In your own words, explain how the graph of $y = |x| + 8$ differs from the graph of $y = |x|$.

2. If the graph of $f(x)$ in Example 2 of the display had been translated 9 units down, then what would have been the resulting general equation? Sketch the graph.

3. Given the graph of the function $f(x)$, copy and sketch the graph of the indicated translations.

a.

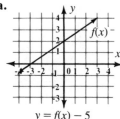

$y = f(x) - 5$

b.

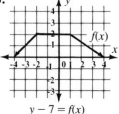

$y - 7 = f(x)$

c.

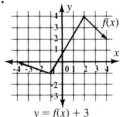

$y = f(x) + 3$

d.

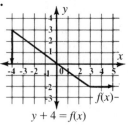

$y + 4 = f(x)$

4. Use a table of values to graph $f(x) - 2 = |x|$ and $f(x) = |x| - 2$.
a. State the domain and the range of the functions.
b. In your own words, explain the relationship between the two graphs and $f(x) = |x|$.

5. Graph the function $f(x) = 2^x$.
a. State the domain and the range for this function.
b. Is this a linear function? Explain.
c. Predict what the graph of $f(x) = 2^x + 3$ will look like. Verify your prediction.
d. Will the domain and the range of $f(x) = 2^x + 3$ be different from $f(x) = 2^x$?
e. Are both $f(x)$ and $f(x) + 3$ functions? Explain.

6. Use a table of values to graph the inverse of $f(x) = 2^x$. On the same set of axes, graph the inverse of $f(x) = 2^x + 3$. Are the inverses functions? Explain.

7. Copy the graphs. Draw the graphs of the related function.

a.

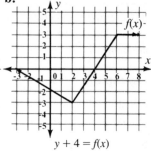

$y = f(x) + 5$

b.

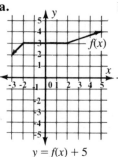

$y + 4 = f(x)$

8. Use a table of values to graph the function $f(x) = 3^x$.

a. On the same set of axes, graph $y = \dfrac{1}{f(x)}$ from a table of values.

b. State the domain and the range of $y = \dfrac{1}{f(x)}$.

c. Is $y = \dfrac{1}{f(x)}$ a function? Explain.

d. Sketch the graph of $y = \dfrac{1}{f(x)} + 3$.

9. If the graph of a function is reflected in the x-axis, will the resultant graph always be a function? Explain.

10. The function $f(p) = \dfrac{30}{p}$ describes the amount, in millions of barrels, of oil sold at price, p, where $f(p) \geq 0$ and $p > 0$.
a. Predict the effect on the price and the amount of oil sold if after a change in the market the equation of the function becomes $f(p) = \dfrac{30}{p - 5}$.
b. Graph the original relation and the new relation on the same set of axes to verify your prediction.
c. Is the graph of the new relation a function?
d. State the domain and the range of the function.

11. Graph x^x.
a. Construct a table of values for $(2x)^x$.
b. Sketch $(2x)^x$.
c. What restrictions are placed on x?

12. Solve $(3x^2 + 2x)^x = 1$. (*Hint*: State all restrictions on the variable.)

7·9 Graphing $y = f(x - a)$

In the previous section, we examined what happened to the graph of a function, $f(x)$, when a constant was added. In this section, we will examine what happens to the graph of the function when the x-value is changed.

Example 1

Construct a table of values and graph $f(x) = 2^x$, where $x \in R$. How are the graphs of $f(x - 2)$ and $f(x + 1)$ related to the graph of $f(x)$?

Since $f(x) = 2^x$, $f(x - 2) = 2^{x-2}$ and $f(x + 1) = 2^{x+1}$.

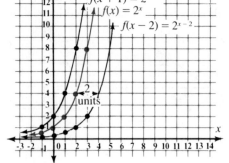

x	-1	0	1	2	3
2^x	$\dfrac{1}{2}$	1	2	4	8
2^{x-2}	$\dfrac{1}{8}$	$\dfrac{1}{4}$	$\dfrac{1}{2}$	1	2
2^{x+1}	1	2	4	8	16

From the graphs of the functions, notice that the function $f(x - 2)$ is the same as the graph of $f(x)$ moved horizontally 2 units to the right (that is, in the positive direction). The graph of $f(x + 1)$ is the same as the graph of $f(x)$ moved horizontally 1 unit to the left (that is, in the negative direction).

> The graph of $y = f(x - a)$ is a **horizontal translation** of $y = f(x)$.

Example 2

The graph of the general function $y = f(x)$ is in colour. Sketch these graphs.
a. $y = f(x + 3)$ **b.** $y = f(x - 1)$

a. Since the constant 3 is **added** inside the bracket, the result is a horizontal translation of -3 units. That is, the graph of $y = f(x)$ is moved 3 units to the right.
b. Since the constant 1 is **subtracted** from inside the brackets, the result is a horizontal translation of 1 unit. That is, the graph of $y = f(x)$ is moved 1 unit to the right.

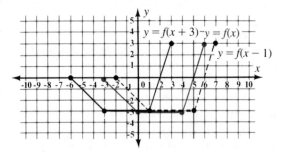

When translating a graph, ask yourself how much was each point in the original graph moved to get the new graph. For example, if each point in the graph was moved 8 units to the right, then the new equation would be $y = f(x - 8)$. Be careful with the negative sign in the horizontal translation.

Exercises

1. How do the graphs of $y = f(x) - 2$ and $y = f(x - 2)$ differ from the graph of $y = f(x)$?

2. If the graph of $f(x) = 2^x$ in Example 1 in the display was translated horizontally 8 units in the positive direction, then what would be the resulting equation? Draw the graph.

3. Given the graph of $f(x)$, sketch the graph of the indicated translation.

a.

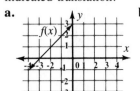

$$y = f(x - 2)$$

b.

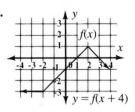

$$y = f(x + 4)$$

c.

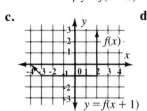

$$y = f(x + 1)$$

d.

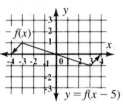

$$y = f(x - 5)$$

4. Construct a table of values and sketch the graph of $f(x) = 3^x$.
a. Sketch the graph of $f(x) = 3^{x+2}$.
b. Sketch the graph of $f(x) = 3^{x-3}$.
c. Describe how the graphs differ.
d. What conclusions can you draw from the graphs about the relationship between $f(x) = a^x$ and $f(x) = a^{x-p}$?

5. Sketch $f(x) = |x|$.
a. On the same axes, sketch the graphs of $f(x) = |x - 4|$ and $f(x) = |x + 3|$ without using a table of values.
b. Check various points on the graphs to verify your sketches.
c. In your own words, explain the relationships among the graphs.
d. On a different set of axes, sketch the graphs of the inverses.
e. How are the inverses related?
f. Are the inverses functions?

6. The number of bacteria, N, in a culture is a function of time, t, in minutes and is expressed by the equation $N = 2^t$. If a new culture is started five minutes after the first, then write an equation for the population of the second culture in terms of the first, and sketch the graph of the population curve for each culture.

7. The distance, d, a car travels at an average speed of 80 km/h is a function of time, t, and is described by the function $f(t) = 80t$. If two cars start 5 h apart, then write an equation describing the distance travelled by the second car and sketch the graph of distance versus time for each car on the same grid.

8. Construct a table of values and sketch the graph of $y = \sqrt{x}$ and $y = \sqrt{x + 3}$.
a. Explain how the graph of $y = \sqrt{x + 3}$ differs from $y = \sqrt{x}$.
b. Sketch the inverses and explain how they are related.

9. Sketch the graph of $f(x) = \dfrac{1}{x}$.
a. State the domain and the range of this function.
b. Predict how the sketch of $f(x) = \dfrac{1}{x + 3}$ will appear.
c. State the domain and the range of the function in part **b**.
d. In your own words, explain how the two graphs are related.
e. Repeat parts **a** to **d** for the function $f(x) = \dfrac{1}{x - 2}$.
f. What conclusions can you draw by comparing the graphs of $f(x)$ and $f(x) = \dfrac{1}{x - a}$?

10. Sketch the graph of $f(x) = \dfrac{1}{|x| + 1}$. From this graph, predict what the graph of $f(x) = \dfrac{1}{|x - 1| + 1}$ will be. Verify your prediction.

7·10 Graphing $y = kf(x)$

Any function can be translated, dilatated, or reflected about a point or a line. You have seen how functions can be translated and how a function can be reflected about the line $y = x$. In this section, you will discover what must be done to stretch or compress a function.

Example 1

Construct a table of values and graph the functions $y = |x|$, $y = 2|x|$, and $2y = |x|$. Explain how each graph is related. Notice that $2y = |x|$ also can be written as $y = \frac{1}{2}|x|$.

x	-2	-1	0	1	2
$y = |x|$	2	1	0	1	2
$y = 2|x|$	4	2	0	2	4
$y = \frac{1}{2}|x|$	1	$\frac{1}{2}$	0	$\frac{1}{2}$	1

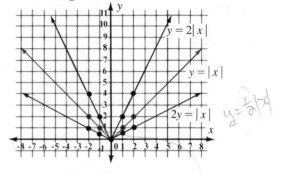

Using the table of values and the graphs, notice that the graph of the function $y = 2|x|$ is the same as the function $y = |x|$ compressed by a factor of 2. Similarly, the graph of $y = \frac{1}{2}|x|$ is the same as the graph of $y = |x|$ stretched by a factor of 2.

> The graph of $y = kf(x)$ is a **stretch** of the graph $y = f(x)$ by a factor of k when $0 < k < 1$ and a **compression** of the graph $y = f(x)$ when $k > 1$.

However, what happens to a function when it is multiplied by a factor that is less than 0? In the next example, the effect of $y = kf(x)$, where $k < 0$, will be examined.

Example 2

The graph of $y = x^2$ is shown in colour. Graph $y = -2x^2$ on the same axes.

x	-3	-2	-1	0	1	2	3
$y = x^2$	9	4	1	0	1	4	9
$y = -2x^2$	-18	-8	-2	0	-2	-8	-18

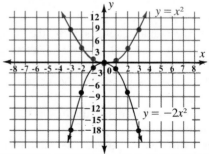

From the table of values and the graph, notice that the graph of $y = -2x^2$ is a reflection in the x-axis followed by a compression of 2 units. In fact, when a function is multiplied by a constant less than zero, a reflection in the x-axis results.

> The graph of $y = kf(x)$ where $k < 0$, is a **reflection** of the graph $y = f(x)$ in the x-axis, followed by either a stretch or compression by a factor of k.

Exercises

1. If the graph of $y = |x|$ from Example 1 of the display had been stretched vertically by a factor of 8, then what would have been the resulting equation?

2. How would the graph of $y = \frac{1}{3}|x|$ differ from the graph of $y = |x|$?

3. Copy each graph. Sketch the graph of $y = kf(x)$ if $k = -1, 2, -2,$ and $-\frac{1}{2}$.

a.

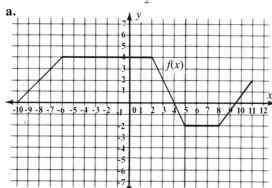

b.

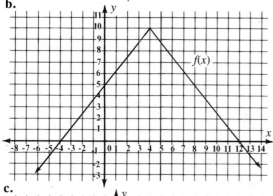

c.

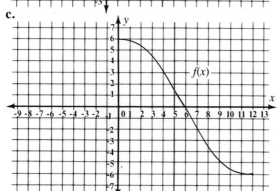

4. Write the equation of the graph resulting from the indicated stretch or compression.
a. $y = \sqrt{x}$ by a factor of 7
b. $y = 5x$ by a factor of $\frac{1}{10}$
c. $y = 4|x|$ by a factor of $\frac{1}{8}$
d. $y = 3^x$ by a factor of 4

5. In your own words, explain what effect each value of k would have on the graph of the equation.
a. $y = x;\ k = 4$ **b.** $y = \sqrt{x};\ k = \frac{1}{5}$
c. $y = |x|;\ k = 12$ **d.** $y = |x|;\ k = \frac{-1}{9}$
e. $y = |x|;\ k = -1$ **f.** $y = 2^x;\ k = 5$
g. $y = 7^x;\ k = \frac{1}{7}$ **h.** $y = 1^x;\ k = \frac{-3}{4}$

6. If $f(x)$ is the equation of any function, then describe how each of these functions are obtained from the graph of $f(x)$.
a. $y = 9f(x)$ **b.** $y = -f(x)$
c. $y = \frac{1}{6}f(x)$ **d.** $y = -2f(x)$

7. The graph of the function $p(x)$ describes the path of a ray of light as it strikes and reflects off a mirror. Sketch the changes in the path produced by each function. The mirror is placed along the x-axis.

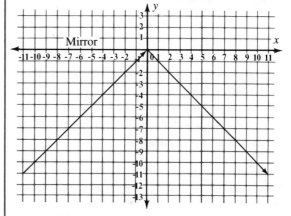

a. $y = -p(x)$ **b.** $4y = p(x)$
c. $\frac{1}{2}y = p(x)$ **d.** $y = -3p(x)$

8. In order to graph any function of the form $y = kf(x - a)$, the graph of $f(x)$ is initially sketched. Explain why this helps to sketch the new graph.

211

7·11 Graphing $y = kf(x - a) + b$

The previous sections investigated the individual effects that the constants a, b, and k had on the graphs of functions of the form $y = f(x)$. In this section, the combined effects of these variables on the graphs of functions will be investigated.

Example 1

For the function $y = \frac{1}{2}|x - 1| + 2$, identify the variables a, b, and k, and graph the function without using a table of values.

Understand the Problem

To graph the function, the values of a, b, and k must be known. In this case, $a = 1$, $b = 2$, and $k = \frac{1}{2}$.

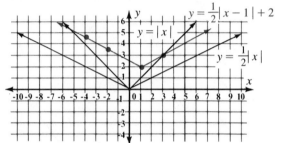

Develop a Plan

To graph the function, use the standard graph and translate it using a, b, and k. In this case, the standard graph is $y = |x|$.

Carry Out the Plan

1. Sketch $y = |x|$.

2. Sketch $y = \frac{1}{2}|x|$.

3. Translate all points on the graph 1 unit right and 2 units up. How do these transformations relate to the variables a, b, and k?

Look Back

The graph of $y = (x)$ is moved up and to the right due to the variables b and a respectively, while the compression of $f(x)$ is changed due to the variable k.

Some of the points on the graph $y = |x|$ and $y = \frac{1}{2}|x - 1| + 2$ are listed to show the effects of the transformation.

$(0,0) \rightarrow (1,2)$; $(2,2) \rightarrow (3,3)$; $(-5,5) \rightarrow (-4,4.5)$

Example 2

The graph of the function $N = 2^t$ shows the normal growth curve in the population of mosquitoes, N, as a function of time, t, in days. Due to a lack of moisture, the hatching of mosquitoes was delayed five days, and temperature conditions slowed the increase in numbers by a factor of 0.5. The function $N = 0.5(2)^{t-5}$ describes the new population curve.

Graph the new population curve.

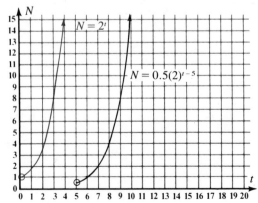

To graph the new curve, the values of a and k should be determined. Under the new conditions, $a = 5$ and $k = 0.5$. Transform the normal population curve function using the values of k and a. The normal population curve is the graph of $N = 2^t$. Vertically stretch it by a factor of $\frac{1}{2}$ and horizontally translate it 5 units in the positive direction to obtain the graph of $N = 0.5(2)^{t-5}$.

212

Exercises

1. Describe how the graph of each equation is achieved from the graph of the basic equation $f(x) = x$.

a. $f(x) = x + 1$ **b.** $f(x) = x - 2$

c. $f(x) = \frac{3}{4}x$ **d.** $f(x) = 4x$

e. $f(x) = -x + 3$ **f.** $f(x) = \frac{x - 3}{5}$

g. $-f(x) - 5 = x + 2$ **h.** $\frac{f(x) + 6}{2} = x + 5$

2. Sketch the graph of $y = \frac{-1}{3}f(x) + 4$ if $y = f(x)$ is shown.

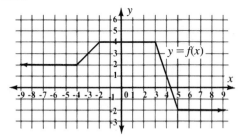

3. Describe how the graph of each equation is achieved from the graph of the basic equation $f(x) = |x|$.

a. $f(x) = -|x|$ **b.** $x = |f(x)|$

c. $f(x) = |x + 7| - 2$ **d.** $-2f(x) = |x - 3| + 5$

e. $f(x) = \left|\frac{x - 3}{2}\right|$ **f.** $\frac{f(x)}{4} = |x - 1|$

g. $\frac{f(x) - 1}{3} = |x - 3|$ **h.** $-x = \left|\frac{f(x)}{4}\right|$

i. $\frac{x - 10}{6} = |f(x)|$ **j.** $\frac{f(x) - 7}{3} = |x - 9|$

4. Sketch the graph of the equations in Exercise 3.

5. The equation describing profit, in thousands of dollars, for a T-shirt manufacturer is a function of time, t, measured in months. $f(t) = |t - 6| + 1$

a. State the domain and the range of this function.

b. Graph the function.

c. Find the minimum profit the company will achieve.

d. Is the inverse of this function a function?

e. State the meaning, if any, of the inverse of this function.

6. In your own words, describe the effects of a, b, and k in the equation $y = kf(x - a) + b$ on the standard graph of $y = f(x)$.

7. The distance, d, in metres that a chair is from the bottom of an operating chairlift is given by the equation $d = -100|t - 10| + 1000$ where time, t, is measured in minutes.

a. Graph this function.

b. Find the maximum distance, in metres, that the chairlift can go.

c. When is a chair at the bottom of the lift?

d. How many minutes after starting does a chair reach its maximum distance from the bottom?

e. Is the inverse of this function a function?

f. State the meaning, if any, of the inverse of this function.

8. Express the surface area of a sphere, S, as a relation of its radius.

a. Is this relation a function?

b. Is this relation a linear function? Explain.

213

7·12 Computer Application— Testing for a Function

The straight line test for a function can be done on the computer. Enter the program shown, run it, and check whether the vertical line eliminates two dots at the same time. If it does, the relation is not a function. This program uses high resolution graphics to plot the points.

```
10  REM A PROGRAM THAT CHECKS FOR A FUNCTION
20  HGR
30  HCOLOR = 7
40  FOR X = 0 TO 279
50  LET Y = 0.005 * X ∧ 2
60  IF Y > = 159 THEN 90
70  HPLOT X, Y
80  NEXT X
90  FOR K = 0 TO 279
100 HCOLOR = 5
110 HPLOT K, 0 TO K, 159
120 HCOLOR = 0
130 FOR P = 1 TO 100: NEXT P
140 HPLOT K, 1 TO K, 159
150 FOR P = 1 TO 100: NEXT P
160 NEXT K
170 END
```

Exercises

1. What is the relation that is being tested? Is it a function?

2. Modify the program so that the relation $y = x + 2$ is tested. Is it a function?

3. The high resolution screen is divided into 280 columns and 160 rows. Using this fact, what is the purpose of line 60 in the program?

4. Why are the y-values plotted restricted to less than 279?

5. Modify the program to test whether the relation $y = x^2 - 2x + 3$ is a function.

6. Modify the program in the display to input the values of a, b, and c for the equation $y = ax^2 + bx + c$. Have the computer print the function so that you can decide whether the relation is a function based on the straight line test.

7. Computers have become an intricate part of the business world of today. Most people that enter business will be using computer software systems. As a result, computer proficiency is a must in to-day's world. Write a short paragraph explaining whether it is the responsibility of the education system, or the responsibility of the company that hires you, to ensure that you are proficient on a microcomputer.

7·13 Chapter Review

1. State the domain and the range of these sets.
a. $\{(1,0), (4,5), (7,10), (10,15), (13,20)\}$
b. $\{(x,y) \mid y = -4x + 6, x, y \in R\}$
c. $\left\{(x,y) \mid y = \dfrac{\sqrt{9 - x^2}}{(x - 3)(x + 1)}, x, y \in R\right\}$
d. $\{(x,y) \mid y < |x| + 3, x, y \in R\}$

2. In your own words, explain the meaning of the term "relation".

3. Find the domain and the range of the relation $f(x) = 3|x| + 9$ and its inverse. How do these sets compare with each other?

4. Find the inverse of the relation, its domain and range, and graph both the original and the inverse on the same set of axes.
a. $\{(x,y) \mid g(x) = x^3, x, y \in R\}$
b. $\{(x,y) \mid f(x) = (3\pi)^{2x}, x, y \in R\}$
c. $\{(x,y) \mid 8xy - 5 = 0, x, y \in R\}$

5. Show that $x^2 + y^2 = 4$ is its own inverse. Verify your result by sketching the graph of the relation and its inverse.

6. Explain how the vertical line test shows if a relation is a function.

7. Light intensity, I, varies as the square of the inverse of the distance, D, from the source of light. The intensity of a flashlight is 4 units at a distance of 4 m, and 64 units at a distance of 1 m.
a. Write an equation expressing the relation between I and D.
b. Graph the relation.
c. Is this relation a function? Explain.

8. If $h(x) = x^4 - x^3 + 0.1$, then find each.
a. $h(3)$ **b.** $h(0)$ **c.** $h(y)$
d. $h(0.5)$ **e.** $h(3w)$ **f.** $h\left(\dfrac{2}{3}\right)$

9. Describe how the graph of each equation is achieved from the graph of the basic equation $f(x) = x^2$.
a. $f(x) = x^2 - 2$ **b.** $f(x) = -(x + 1)^2$
c. $f(x) = 3x^2$ **d.** $3f(x) = -2x^2 - 5$
e. $\dfrac{-f(x) - 6}{5} = x^2 + 3$ **f.** $5 - f(x) = 7(x + 3)^2$

10. Find the inverse of the function. State whether the inverse is a function.
a. $f(x) = x^3 - 3x^2 + 9x$ **b.** $y = 3$
c. $4x + 9y = -11$ **d.** $g(x) = \sqrt{1 - 3x^2}$

11. Construct a table of values and graph the inverse equations for Exercise 10.

12. Is it true that $f^{-1}(x) = \dfrac{1}{f(x)}$? Explain.

13. Express the circumference of a circle in terms of its diameter. Is this relation a function?

14. When a movie theatre box office opens, there is $150 in the cash register. Every patron who enters the theatre pays $5 to see the movie.
a. Express the amount of money in the register in terms of the number of people who view the movie.
b. Is this relation a function?
c. Is it a linear function?
d. If there is less than $750 in the register at the end of the evening, the theatre will be in debt to the film distributor. How many people must enter the theatre each night so this won't happen?

15. Sketch the graph.
a. $f(x) = 3|x| - 5$ **b.** $g(x) = |x - 4|$
c. $h(x) = -5x + 1$ **d.** $k(x) = -|3x|$

16. For a function $f(x)$, $y = kf(x - a) + b$ is the general form of the transformation. For what values of a, b, and k will the function remain unchanged?

7·14 Chapter Test

1. State the domain and the range of the relation.
a. $\{(x,y) \mid x + y = 11, x, y \in R\}$
b. $\{(1,2), (2,5), (3,10), (0,1), (-1,0)\}$
c. $\{(x,y) \mid y = |x|, x \in R\}$
d. $\left\{(x,y) \mid y = \dfrac{3x}{x - \pi}, x, y \in R\right\}$

2. State the domain and the range of these graphs.

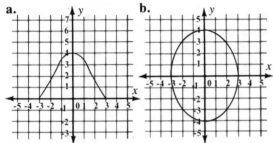

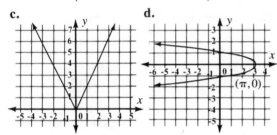

3. In your own words, explain an inverse relation and an inverse function. Carefully discuss the differences between the two terms.

4. Find a relation which is its own inverse.

5. State the inverse relation.
a. $\{(x,y) \mid y = -0.5x + 4, x, y \in R\}$
b. $\{(x,y) \mid y = 4x^5, x, y \in R\}$
c. $\{(x,y) \mid y = 10^{2x}, x, y \in R\}$
d. $\{(x,y) \mid y = \sqrt{x^2 + 3x - 1}, x, y \in R\}$

6. Given $f(x) = x + 1$ and $g(x) = \dfrac{3}{x - 2}$, evaluate these expressions.
a. $f(3)$ **b.** $g(-1)$ **c.** $f(3a + 1)$
d. $g(2)$ **e.** $\dfrac{f(a + 1)}{g(a + 1)}$ **f.** $g\left(\dfrac{3}{2}\right)$

7. The distance travelled by a car, M, and its resale value, V, are found to be inversely proportional. A dealer found that for a particular make of car, if the odometer read 75 000 km, then the resale value was one eighth of the original price, while if the odometer read 50 000 km, its resale value was one quarter of the original price.
a. Write an expression relating V and M.
b. If the original value of the car was \$15 000, then find its resale value after 45 000 km.
c. Graph the relation. Is it a function?

8. Using the functions in Exercise 6, what value of x will make $f(x)$ equal $g(x)$?

9. Find a function which will satisfy the condition.
a. $f(ab) = f(a)f(b)$
b. $f(a + b) = f(a) + f(b)$
c. $f\left(\dfrac{a}{b}\right) = \dfrac{f(a)}{f(b)}$

10. A fisherman in New Brunswick earns \$7/kg for oysters and \$6/kg for clams. How many kilograms of clams and oysters need to be sold to earn more than \$420?
a. Write an inequality describing this relation.
b. Graph this relation.
c. Is this relation a function?

11. Sketch the graph of these functions.
a. $g(x) = |x + 3|$ **b.** $H(x) = -3x + 1$

12. If $H(x) = -3x + 1$ is reflected in the x-axis, then what is the equation of the new function?

13. If $H(x) = -3x + 1$ is transformed so that $H(x) = x$, then describe the transformation in your own words.

14. State one general form of a linear function. In this form, express these functions, given the slope and y-intercept.
a. slope 4, y-intercept -3
b slope -1, y-intercept 10
c. slope $\dfrac{2}{3}$, y-intercept $\dfrac{1}{2}$

CHAPTER EIGHT

QUADRATIC FUNCTIONS

Tune Up

1. State the degree of each expression.
a. $2x^2$ **b.** $a + b$
c. 5 **d.** $7a^3 - 3b$

2. In your own words, explain the meaning of the terms "relation" and "function".

3. Determine which relation is a function. Explain your answer.
a. $y = x + 2$ **b.** $y^2 = 3x - 5$
c. $y = |x| - 1$ **d.** $-y = \sqrt{x} + 6$
e. $-2x = -3|y - 1| + 9$ **f.** $-2y = \frac{3}{5}x - 4$

4. Expand.
a. $2(x + 3)$ **b.** $(x - 2)(x + 5)$
c. $3x(y - 3)(y + 3)$ **d.** $-5(4x + 3y)^2$
e. $(a + b)(a^2 - ab + b^2)$ **f.** $(4 - ab)(5 - a)$

5. Factor.
a. $2x - 4x^2$ **b.** $25x^2 - 10x + 1$
c. $3ax^2 - 4ax^4$ **d.** $8a^3 - 64b^3$

6. Sketch the graph of each and determine if it is a function. Use a table of values if necessary.
a. $y = -3|x| - 1$ **b.** $y = 2x + 3$
c. $-4y = 5|x + 3|$ **d.** $y = -2|x - 1| + 3$
e. $-y = \sqrt{x} - 4 + 1$ **f.** $y = x^2 - 2$

7. Determine the zeros of each polynomial.
a. $8y^2 + 8y + 2$ **b.** $(x - 2)(x^2 - 4)$
c. $(y + 3)(y^2)$ **d.** $a^2x^2 - 2abx + b^2$

8. If the area of a triangle is given by the expression $\dfrac{8x^3 - 58x^2 - 13x + 7}{3x^3 - 7x^2 - 11x + 3}$ and the height by the expression $\dfrac{x - 7}{3x - 1}$, determine the expression for the base of the triangle.

9. Identify the functions. Explain your answers.

a.

b.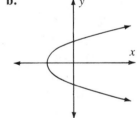

c.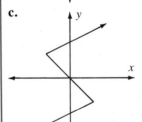

d.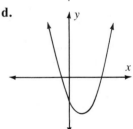

10. State the restrictions and solve.
$$\frac{6x^2 - 11x - 2}{3x - 6} + 4 = \frac{2x^3 + 4x^2}{x^2 + 3x + 2}$$

11. Is $(x - 3)$ a factor of the expression $35x^3 + 53x^2 - 32x + 4$?

8·1 The Quadratic Function

There are numerous examples of curves which can be associated with the graph of a second degree or quadratic function. For example, the path of a projectile, the reflective mirror in a flashlight, and the arches in some buildings can be described by quadratic functions.

> A **quadratic function** can be written in the form $y = ax^2 + bx + c$ or $f(x) = ax^2 + bx + c$ where a, b, and c are constants and $a \neq 0$. The graph of a quadratic function is a **parabola**.

Example 1

Determine whether the function is a quadratic function.

a. $y = 5(x^2 + 3x)$

$f(x) = 5x^2 + 15x$
This is a quadratic function since the function can be written in the form
$f(x) = ax^2 + bx + c$, where $c = 0$.

b. $y = \dfrac{3}{x^2} + 4x$

This function cannot be written in the form $f(x) = ax^2 + bx + c$ because the degree of this function is -2. All quadratic functions are of degree 2.

Example 2

Write in the form $y = ax^2 + bx + c$ and give the values of a, b, and c.

a. $y = 4(x - 2)^2$

$y = 4(x^2 - 4x + 4)$
$y = 4x^2 - 16x + 16$
$a = 4,\ b = -16,\ c = 16$

b. $y = -3x(x - 6) + 4x$

$y = -3x^2 + 18x + 4x$
$y = -3x^2 + 22x$
$a = -3,\ b = 22,\ c = 0$

Exercises

1. Indicate whether these are quadratic functions. Explain your answer.

a. $y = 4x^2 - 1$ **b.** $y = 5 - 8x^3$

c. $y = \dfrac{3}{2}x^2 + x + 10$ **d.** $y^2 = x^2 + 6$

e. $y = x^2 - \dfrac{1}{x^2}$ **f.** $y = -3(x^2 - 2)^2 + 7x$

2. Write the function in the form $f(x) = ax^2 + bx + c$ and state the values of a, b, and c.

a. $y = 2(x^2 - 5x + 12)$ **b.** $y = -3(x + 2)^2$
c. $y = 4x + (x - 3)^2$ **d.** $y = -(3x + 5)^2$
e. $y = 3(x^2 + 1) + 2(x - 8)^2$
f. $y = -6(2x^2 - 5x) + 4(3x + 1)$

3. A.T., the "Mathematics Wizard", stated that an equation of the form $y = \dfrac{1}{2x^2 - 4x + 1}$ is a quadratic function. Is A.T. correct? Explain.

4. A circle of radius r is placed inside a square so that the four sides of the square touch the circle. Sketch a diagram, and write an expression, as a function of r, for the area that is outside the circle and inside the square.

Using the Library

Write a report on a catenary. Describe the shape of a catenary and how it compares to a parabola. Describe places where one might see a catenary.

8·2 Graphing Quadratic Functions

A diver springs upward off a diving board and plunges into the pool below. A baseball flies into the air and lands in the outfield. A support cable is attached to towers at each end of a bridge and to the roadway between the towers. These are three examples of parabolas.

The graph of a quadratic function can be sketched by constructing a table of values, plotting the points, and drawing a smooth curve through the points. Since the graph is a curve, it is necessary to plot several points to obtain a suitable graph. Later in this chapter, the curve will be sketched by using certain properties of the quadratic function.

Example 1

The graph of a support cable on a bridge can be approximated by the quadratic function $f(x) = x^2 + 2x + 1$. The value of the function, $f(x)$, represents the height of the cable above the roadway, and x represents the position along the road. Construct a table of values and sketch the function where $-3 \le x \le 3$. Estimate the point at which the cable is attached to the road (at the cable's lowest point). Analyse the graph.

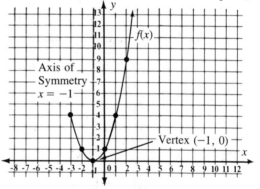

x	-3	-2	-1	0	1	2	3
$f(x)$	4	1	0	1	4	9	16

Point $A(-1, 0)$ is the **vertex** of the parabola, where the cable is at its lowest point. This is the **minimum** value of the function. The domain of the function is $\{x \mid -3 \le x \le 3, x \in R\}$. The range of the function is $\{y \mid 0 \le y \le 16, y \in R\}$. The line of symmetry is defined by the equation $x = -1$. The graph of a parabola which opens upward is **concave upward**.

Example 2

The flight of a baseball is defined by the equation $h(t) = -4t^2 + 80t$, where $h(t)$ is the height in metres and t is the time of flight, in seconds. Sketch the path followed by the ball and find its maximum height. Analyse the graph.

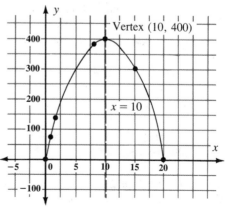

t	0	1	2	8	10	15	20
$h(t)$	0	76	144	384	400	300	0

The **maximum** height the ball reaches is about 400 m, which is at $t = 10$ s. The line of symmetry is the line defined by the equation $x = 10$. The graph is a parabola that opens downward (is **concave downward**). The domain is $\{x \mid 0 \le x \le 20, x \in R\}$, and the range is $\{y \mid 0 \le y \le 400, y \in R\}$. The **zeros of the function**, 0 and 20, are the values of x for which the function equals zero. These are the **x-intercepts** of the graph. The values for $h(t)$ are graphed onto the y-axis. The values for t are graphed onto the x-axis.

Exercises

1. How are the vertex and the line of symmetry related in the graph of a quadratic function?

2. A.T., the "Mathematics Wizard", was quoted as saying, "All quadratic functions are quadratic relations, but not all quadratic relations are quadratic functions." Using graphs, determine whether A.T. is correct. Explain.

3. Analyse each graph. Estimate the coordinates of the vertex, state the zeros of the function, write the equation of the axis of symmetry, and describe the curve.

a.

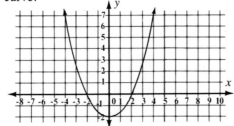

b.

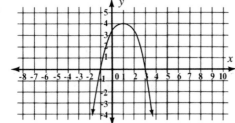

4. Using a table of values, sketch each quadratic function. Analyse by giving the domain and range, the maximum and/or minimum points, the axis of symmetry, and the direction of opening. Estimate the zeros of each function if there are any.

a. $f(x) = x^2$ **b.** $f(x) = -x^2$

c. $f(x) = x^2 - 9$ **d.** $f(x) = -(x^2 - 9)$

e. $f(x) = x^2 - 16$ **f.** $f(x) = -(x^2 - 16)$

g. $f(x) = 2(x^2 + 3x) + 3$

5. Sketch the graph of $f(x) = x^2 - 2x + 5$.

a. Predict how the graph of $f(x) = -(x^2 - 2x + 5)$ will look.

b. Using a table of values, sketch the graph to check your prediction. How are the graphs related?

6. State whether the vertex of the graph of each function is a maximum or minimum point.

a. $f(x) = x^2 + 2x - 3$ **b.** $f(x) = -x^2 + 2x - 3$

c. $f(x) = 2x - x^2 - 3$ **d.** $f(x) = -2(x - 1)^2$

7. If $f(x) = 3x^2 - x - 9$, state the value of each.

a. $f(0)$ **b.** $f(2)$ **c.** $f(-2)$ **d.** $f(5)$

8. Determine which of the points belong to the graph of the function in each of the following.

	i)	ii)	iii)
a. $x^2 - x - 2$	$(-1, 0)$	$(5, 18)$	$(0, 0)$
b. $-x^2 + 2x$	$(0, 0)$	$(-2, 0)$	$(-1, -3)$
c. $2 - x^2$	$(-5, 27)$	$(3, 7)$	$(0, -2)$

9. The height of a bullet fired upward is given by $h(t) = -4.9t^2 + 245t$, where h is the height in metres and t is the elapsed time in seconds.

a. Use a table of values to sketch the graph. State the domain and the range of the function.

b. What is the maximum height the bullet will reach?

c. At what height will the bullet be after 10 min? Explain your answer.

d. Can the graph ever go below the x-axis? Explain.

10. The yearly profit for a company is defined by the function $p(x) = -0.4x^2 + 29.6x - 256$, where $p(x)$ is the profit, in dollars, and x is the number of units sold. The company can only produce and sell a maximum of 85 units each year.

a. Sketch the function.

b. At what point does the company break even?

c. How many units must be sold to make the maximum profit? Estimate the maximum profit.

11. What shape would be obtained if a parabola was "spun" around its axis of symmetry?

12. The velocity a "free-falling" marble will reach is given by the function $v(t) = 4.9t^2$, where $v(t)$ is the velocity in metres per second and t is the elapsed time in seconds.

a. Construct a graph for $0 \leq t \leq 10$.

b. State the domain and the range for the function.

c. Describe the effect on the velocity if the time is doubled.

8·3 Graphing $f(x) = ax^2$

In the previous chapter, the graph of $f(x) = x^2$ was introduced. In this chapter, the graph of $f(x) = ax^2$, where $a \neq 0$, will be introduced. We will develop a process for sketching any quadratic function using the graph of $f(x) = x^2$.

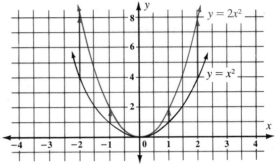

Consider the graphs of $f(x) = x^2$ and $f(x) = 2x^2$. The graph of $f(x) = 2x^2$ differs from the first graph in that it is "stretched" in the vertical direction. Every value of the second function is twice that of the first. For both graphs, the vertex is at $(0, 0)$, the axis of symmetry is the y-axis or $x = 0$, the domain is $\{x | x \in R\}$, the range is $\{y | y \geq 0, y \in R\}$, and they are concave upwards.

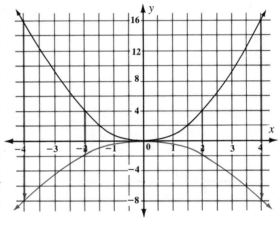

Now consider the graphs of $f(x) = x^2$ and $f(x) = -0.5x^2$. How do they differ? The original graph is concave upwards, while the new graph is concave downwards. The negative coefficient causes the graph to be concave downward. Also, the second graph is "compressed" in the vertical direction so that it appears to be spread out more. This is caused by the absolute value of a being less than 1. All values of the function $f(x) = x^2$ are multiplied by -0.5, while the x-values stay the same. For both, the axis of symmetry is $x = 0$, the domain is $\{x | x \in R\}$, and the vertex is at $(0, 0)$. However, they differ in their range: $f(x) = x^2$ has a range of $\{y | y \geq 0, y \in R\}$, while the reflected graph has a range of $\{y | y \leq 0, y \in R\}$.

Example 1

Sketch the graph of $y = -2x^2$.

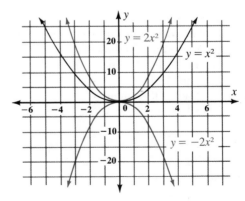

Understand the Problem
We are to sketch the graph of $y = -2x^2$.
We know the shape of the graph of $y = x^2$.

Develop and Carry Out a Plan
Sketch the graph of $y = x^2$. Apply a stretch of factor 2. Then reflect it in the x-axis.

Look Back
A table of values can be used to verify the relationships. We can analyse the two graphs by comparing: the direction they open, the axes of symmetry, the coordinates of the vertices, the type and amount of stretch (if any), and the domains and ranges.

221

Example 2

Determine the equation of a parabola in the form $f(x) = ax^2$ which passes through the points $(-2, 8)$ and $(3, 18)$.

The values given must satisfy the function.

For $(-2, 8)$ $8 = a(-2)^2$

             $a = 2$

Check:

For $(3, 18)$ $18 = a(3)^2$

             $a = 2$ ✓

The function is $f(x) = 2x^2$.

Exercises

1. Analyse the graphs in Example 1 as indicated in the Look Back section.

2. When asked to analyse graphs or functions, what features does one describe?

3. Sketch the graphs of each pair of quadratics on the same set of axes. Analyse each pair.
a. $f(x) = x^2$; $f(x) = 4x^2$
b. $y = x^2$; $y = -x^2$
c. $y = x^2$; $y = -3x^2$
d. $y = 2x^2$; $y = -0.1x^2$

4. For the graph of $y = ax^2$, write a statement which relates the direction of the opening and the sign of the coefficient a. State the axis of symmetry.

5. Without sketching the graphs, analyse the graphs. Then sketch each to check your predictions.
a. $y = -x^2$ **b.** $y = 0.3x^2$
c. $y = 6x^2$ **d.** $y = -4x^2$

6. Find the function of the form $f(x) = ax^2$ in which the graph passes through these points.
a. $(0, 0)$ and $(1, 3)$
b. $(-1, 5)$ and $(1, 5)$
c. $(-3, -27)$ and the origin
d. $(-1, -0.5)$ and $(3, -4.5)$

7. Write a general set of rules about the graphs of $y = ax^2$ and the coefficient a with respect to each of the features in an analysis.

8. How would you explain the difference between the graphs of $y = 3x^2$ and $y = 0.3x^2$ to a friend on the telephone?

9. The function of each curve shown takes the form of $y = ax^2$. Write a statement about the relative value of the coefficient a for each parabola.

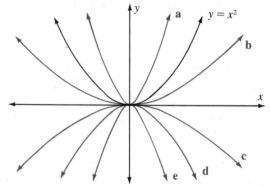

10. What does the general graph of the parabola $y = ax^2$ approach as the coefficient a takes on values closer to zero? Explain your answer using sketches.

11. How do the graphs $f(x) = 3x^2$ and $f(x) = |-3x^2|$ relate? In your explanation, refer to the direction of opening, the domain and range, and the axis of symmetry. Expand the explanation to include the general case of $f(x) = ax^2$ and $f(x) = |-ax^2|$.

Using the Library

The fields of force between two magnets can be shown using curves resembling parabolas. Research the magnetic patterns of two "like" magnets and two "unlike" magnets. Draw a sketch to show the fields of force and comment on why the fields of force react in this manner. Use iron filings on a blank piece of paper to show what you know about how the fields of force behave. Do you think all the lines are parabolas? Explain.

8·4 Graphing $f(x) = x^2 + q$

You can now graph functions of the form $y = ax^2$. In this section, you will learn to sketch and describe graphs of the translated parabolas of the form $y = ax^2 + q$.

Consider the graph of $y = x^2$ when a constant is added. The graphs of $f(x) = x^2$ and $f(x) = x^2 + 3$ are shown. The difference between the graphs is that the second graph has been translated up 3 units. All points on the first graph have been translated up by 3 units. The new vertex is (0, 3). The axis of symmetry is still $x = 0$ (the y-axis). The direction of opening is concave upwards. The domain for both is $\{x|x\epsilon R\}$. However, the range has changed to $\{y|y \geq 3, y\epsilon R\}$. Notice that there are no x-intercepts in the translated graph. The graph of $y = x^2 - 4$ also is shown. It has been translated down 4 units and it has two x-intercepts: $x = -4$ and $x = 4$.

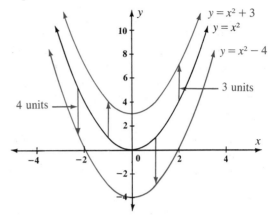

The graph of a quadratic function of the form $f(x) = x^2 + q$ is congruent to that of $f(x) = x^2$ and has the same axis of symmetry and direction of opening as $f(x) = x^2$. Its vertex is at (0, q).

Exercises

1. In analysing the graph of $y = x^2 + q$, what other features should you consider in addition to those considered in the display above?

2. Use a table of values to graph these functions on one set of axes. Analyse the graphs.
a. $y = x^2$ **b.** $y = x^2 + 5$ **c.** $y = x^2 - 8$

3. Sketch the basic graph $y = x^2$. Without tables, sketch the following. Identify the steps you used in sketching the graphs. Analyse the graphs.
a. $y = x^2 + 6$ **b.** $y = x^2 - 9$ **c.** $y = x^2 - 6$

4. Sketch the graphs. The first one is partially done for you.

a. $y = -2x^2 + 4$
Plan: Sketch the graph of $y = x^2$.
     Stretch it with a factor of 2.
     Reflect this in the x-axis.
     Translate the result 4 units up.

b. $y = 3x^2 - 5$ **c.** $y = -0.5x^2 - 4$

5. Write a function that would match each parabola.

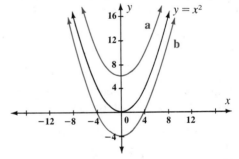

6. A sky diver jumps from an airplane at an altitude of 2440 m. The function relating the height (y) and the elapsed time in seconds (x) is $y = -4.9x^2 + 2440$.
a. Sketch the graph of the function.
b. Approximate the elapsed time of the fall for the diver to be at an altitude of 1000 m.
c. The parachute automatically opens at 500 m. Approximately how long has the diver been in free fall when the chute opens?

7. What are the conditions on q for a parabola to intercept the x-axis at more than one point if $a > 0$? $a < 0$?

8·5 Graphing $f(x) = (x - p)^2$

In this section, we will translate the basic function $f(x) = x^2$ horizontally to reflect functions of the form $f(x) = (x - p)^2$.

Two of the graphs shown to the right are those of $y = x^2$ and $y = (x - 4)^2$. The graph has been translated to the right 4 units. The vertex of the translated graph is $(4, 0)$. The axis of symmetry is $x = 4$. The direction of opening is concave upwards. The domain and range for both is $\{x | x \in R\}$ and $\{y | y \geq 0,\ y \in R\}$.

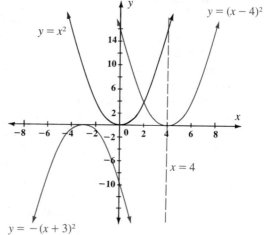

The graph of $y = -(x + 3)^2$ also is shown. Analyse this parabola. What new feature is introduced in the analysis of this form of the quadratic function?

> Any quadratic function of the form $f(x) = (x - p)^2$ has a line of symmetry at $x - p = 0$ and a vertex at $(p, 0)$.

Exercises

1. A.T., the "Mathematics Wizard", stated, "To find the x-coordinate of the vertex of any parabola, simply solve $x - p = 0$". Is A.T. correct? Explain.

2. Use a table of values to graph these functions on one set of axes. Analyse the graphs.
a. $y = x^2$ **b.** $f(x) = (x + 3)^2$ **c.** $y = (x - 5)^2$

3. Outline the steps required to sketch the graph of $y = (x + 8)^2$ using transformations.

4. Write a function that matches each parabola.

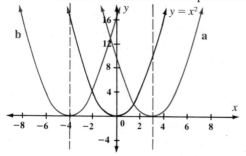

5. In the function $y = (x - p)^2 + q$, what are the conditions on p and q such that the axis of symmetry is on the positive side of the y-axis and there are two zeros of the function?

6. Sketch the graphs. The first one is partially done for you.
a. $y = -2(x - 3)^2$
Plan: Sketch the graph of $y = x^2$.
    Stretch it with a factor of 2.
    Reflect the graph in the x-axis.
    Translate the graph to the right 3 units.

b. $y = 3(x + 6)^2$ **c.** $y = -0.5(x + 8)^2$

7. Without sketching the parabolas, state the direction of opening, the location of the vertex, the equation of the line of symmetry, the x- and y-intercepts (if they exist), and the domain and range. Sketch to check.
a. $f(x) = x^2 + 2$ **b.** $f(x) = (x - 4)^2$
c. $y = -(x + 2)^2$ **d.** $y = x^2 - 5$
e. $y = 2(x - 4)^2$ **f.** $y = -0.5(x - 4)^2$

8. The speed in metres per second (y) of a projectile is given by $y = (x - 25)^2$, where x is the elapsed time in seconds after firing. Sketch the graph of the function.
a. Approximate the speed of the projectile at firing and after 10 s.
b. How much time elapses before the projectile has a speed of 0 m/s?

8·6 Graphing $f(x) = a(x - p)^2 + q$

In this section, we will sketch graphs involving all of the previous transformations: stretches, reflections in the x-axis, and horizontal and vertical translations.

Consider the graph of $y = 2(x + 3)^2 - 4$ and its relationship to $y = x^2$. Convert it to this form.

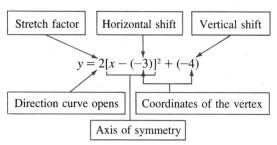

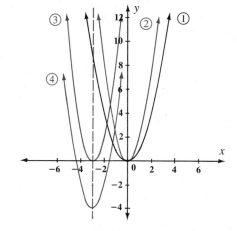

The graph of $y = x^2$ ① has been vertically stretched by a factor of 2 ②. The curve opens upward. The graph has been translated 3 units to the left ③ and 4 units down ④. In graph ④, the axis of symmetry is $x = -3$. The vertex of the parabola is $(-3, -4)$. The domain is $\{x | x \in R\}$, and the range is $\{y | y \geq -4, y \in R\}$.

Example 1

Analyse the graph of $y = -2(x - 1)^2 + 4$.

Since $a < 0$, the graph opens downward. Since $p = 1$ and $q = 4$, the maximum value is 4. Solving $x - 1 = 0$ for x gives the axis of symmetry as $x = 1$. Since the graph opens downwards and the vertex is above the x-axis, there are two x-intercepts; which means there are two zeros of the function. Using this information we can sketch the graph.

Example 2

Determine the quadratic function of the form $f(x) = a(x - p)^2 + q$ if the coordinates of the parabola are $(1, 4)$ for the vertex and $f(3) = 16$.

Since the vertex is located at the point $(1, 4)$, then $p = 1$ and $q = 4$. Therefore, $y = a(x - 1)^2 + 4$. Also, since $f(3) = 16$, then $16 = a(3 - 1)^2 + 4$. Hence, $a = 3$. The function is $y = 3(x - 1)^2 + 4$.

Example 3

Determine the x- and y-intercepts of $y = (x + 5)^2 - 3$.

To determine the y-intercept,
let $x = 0$. $\quad y = (0 + 5)^2 - 3$
$\qquad\qquad = 22$

To determine the x-intercept,
let $y = 0$. $\quad 0 = (x + 5)^2 - 3$
$\qquad\qquad \pm\sqrt{3} = x + 5$
$\qquad\qquad\quad x = -5 \pm \sqrt{3}$

The y-intercept is 22 and the x-intercepts are $-5 \pm \sqrt{3}$.

Exercises

1. Identify the features to be considered in an analysis of the graph of $y = a(x - p)^2 + q$.

2. Using a table of values and the graph of $f(x) = -2(x + 3)^2 - 4$, demonstrate and list the effects of the -2, the 3, and the -4 on the basic graph of $f(x) = x^2$.

3. Write an equation in the form $y = a(x - p)^2 + q$ for each parabola.

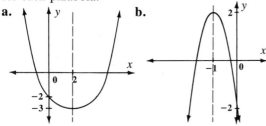

a. **b.**

4. For each parabola, state the direction of opening, the location of the vertex, the equation of the line of symmetry, the x- and y-intercepts (if they exist), and the domain and range.
a. $f(x) = (x - 3)^2 + 2$ **b.** $f(x) = (x - 4)^2 - 8$
c. $y = -0.7(x + 2)^2 - 3$ **d.** $y = x^2 - 5$
e. $f(x) = 3(x - 4)^2 - 2$ **f.** $y = -5(x - 4)^2 - 5$

5. Sketch the graph of the parabolas in Exercise 4 using the information found.

6. Sketch the graph of $y = x^2$ after it has been reflected in the x-axis and translated to the right 5 units and upward 2 units. Write a function satisfying these conditions.

7. Sketch the graph of $y = 2(x + 3)^2 - 2$. Translate the graph to the right 4 units. Write the new equation of the function after the translation.

8. Describe how each graph would be different from the graph of $y = x^2$.
a. $y = x^2 + 5$ **b.** $y = x^2 - 3$
c. $y = (x + 4)^2$ **d.** $y = (x - 8)^2$
e. $y = -4x^2$ **f.** $y = \frac{1}{2}x^2$
g. $y = 2(x + 1)^2$ **h.** $y = -3(x - 2)^2$
i. $y = (x + 2)^2 + 10$ **j.** $y = (x + 3)^2 - 4$

9. Find an equation of each parabola.
a. has a vertex at $(0, 4)$ and is congruent with the graph of $f(x) = x^2$
b. has a vertex at $(4, -2)$ and zeros at 2 and 6
c. has the y-axis as an axis of symmetry and passes through $(1, -1)$ and $(-2, 5)$

10. Describe the change in the graphs of $f(x) = 3(x - p)^2 - 2$ as p varies from -3 to 3.

11. Describe the change in the graphs of $y = -3(x - 4)^2 + q$ as q varies from -4 to 4.

12. Sketch and describe each function.
a. $y = 2(x + 5)^2$ **b.** $y = -4x^2$
c. $y = (x + 2)^2 - 2$ **d.** $y = 3x^2 - 9$
e. $y = -2(x - 3)^2$ **f.** $y = 5(x + 1)^2 - 4$

13. Write a quadratic function in the form $y = a(x - p)^2 + q$ which fits the given description for each. Assume that $a = \pm 1$.
a. opens downward; vertex at $(3, 0)$
b. opens upward; vertex at $(-5, 2)$
c. opens upward; vertex at $(2, 6)$
d. opens downward; vertex at $(-1, -1)$
e. opens upward; equation of the axis of symmetry is $x = 4$; and $y = 10$ when $x = 4$
f. opens upward; vertex lies on the x-axis; equation of the axis of symmetry is $x = -3$
g. opens downward; vertex is on the y-axis; maximum value of the function is 2

14. The cable supporting a bridge forms the shape of a parabola. The cable is connected to the towers at each end of the bridge. The towers are 160 m above the roadway of the bridge. The road is 1400 m long. Determine an equation for the parabola.

15. Solve for $x - 1$. $\dfrac{1}{2 - \dfrac{x-1}{x}} = \dfrac{1}{2}$

Braintickler

Copy and complete the sequence.
a. J, F, M, A, M, J, ■, ■, ■, ■, ■, ■
b. 121, 441, 961, 691, ▄▄ , ▄▄ , ▄▄

8·7 Completing the Square

In the previous sections, we developed a method of sketching the graphs of quadratic equations of the **standard form** $y = a(x - p)^2 + q$ using values and the meanings of the constants a, p, and q. While other forms of the quadratic can be graphed using tables of values, tables are sometimes tedious to produce and are prone to calculation errors. Hence, when we are required to sketch a graph given the more common **general form** $y = ax^2 + bx + c$, often it is desirable to convert the equation to the standard form. To do this, a process called **completing the square** is used.

Recall that $(x + 3)^2 = x^2 + 2(3)x + 3^2$
and $(x - 5)^2 = x^2 + 2(-5)x + (-5)^2$

> The constant term in the expression is the square of half the coefficient of x.

Example 1

Write $y = x^2 + 8x + 3$ in the standard form $y = a(x - p)^2 + q$.

$y = x^2 + 8x + 3$
$y = (x^2 + 8x) + 3$
$y = (x^2 + 8x + 4^2 - 4^2) + 3$ $\frac{1}{2}(8) = 4$ Add 4^2 and subtract 4^2.
$y = (x^2 + 8x + 4^2) - 4^2 + 3$
$\qquad\qquad\underbrace{\qquad\qquad}$ Perfect Square
$y = (x + 4)^2 - 13$ Factor the square and simplify the constants.
$y = [x - (-4)]^2 + (-13)$ Complete the standard form.

We can now graph this function using the techniques of the previous sections.

In Example 1, the coefficient of x^2 was 1. The next example illustrates completing the square of a quadratic function when the coefficient is not equal to 1.

Example 2

Complete the square for $f(x) = -3x^2 + 2x + 2$.

$f(x) = -3x^2 + 2x + 2$
$\quad = -3\left(x^2 - \frac{2}{3}x\right) + 2$ Factor the coefficient -3.
$\quad = -3\left(x^2 - \frac{2}{3}x + \frac{1}{9} - \frac{1}{9}\right) + 2$ Half of $\frac{2}{3}$ squared is $\frac{1}{9}$; add and subtract $\frac{1}{9}$.
$\quad = -3\left(x^2 - \frac{2}{3}x + \frac{1}{9}\right) + \frac{1}{3} + 2$ $-3\left(\frac{-1}{9}\right) = \frac{1}{3}$
$\quad = -3\left(x - \frac{1}{3}\right)^2 + \frac{7}{3}$

Now we can analyse the graph of this function.

$$y = -3\left(x - \frac{1}{3}\right)^2 + \frac{7}{3}$$

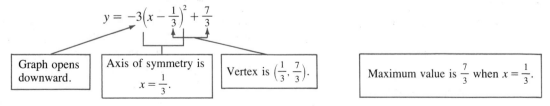

| Graph opens downward. | Axis of symmetry is $x = \frac{1}{3}$. | Vertex is $\left(\frac{1}{3}, \frac{7}{3}\right)$. | Maximum value is $\frac{7}{3}$ when $x = \frac{1}{3}$. |

227

Exercises

1. What constant term must be added to complete the square?

a. $x^2 + 6x$ **b.** $x^2 + 4x$
c. $x^2 + 12x$ **d.** $x^2 + 9x$
e. $x^2 + 5x$ **f.** $x^2 + x$

2. Copy and complete to complete the square.

a. $y = x^2 + 6x + 10$
$= [x^2 + 6x + \blacksquare - \blacksquare] + 10$
$= [x^2 + 6x + \blacksquare] - \blacksquare + 10$
$= (x + \blacksquare)^2 + \blacksquare$
$= (x - \blacksquare)^2 + \blacksquare$

b. $y = x^2 + 5x + 3$
$= [x^2 + 5x + \blacksquare - \blacksquare] + 3$
$= [x^2 + 5x + \blacksquare] - \blacksquare + 3$
$= (x + \blacksquare)^2 - \blacksquare$
$= (x - \blacksquare)^2 + \blacksquare$

3. Complete the square and write each function in the form $y = a(x - p)^2 + q$. Analyse each function by stating the domain and range, the coordinates of the vertex, the axis of symmetry, the direction of opening, the maximum or minimum value of the function, and the value of x at which this occurs. Sketch the parabolas.

a. $y = x^2 - 8x + 4$
b. $y = x^2 + 10x - 3$
c. $y = x^2 + 6x$
d. $y = x^2 + 7x - 5$
e. $y = x^2 - 3x + 12$
f. $y = x^2 - x + 9$

4. Copy and complete to complete the square.

a. $y = 3x^2 - 12x + 5$
$= 3[x^2 - 4x + \blacksquare - \blacksquare] + 5$
$= 3[x^2 - 4x + \blacksquare] - \blacksquare + 5$
$= 3(x - \blacksquare)^2 + \blacksquare$

b. $y = -2x^2 - 5x - 1$
$= -2[x^2 + \frac{5}{2}x + \blacksquare - \blacksquare] - 1$
$= -2[x^2 + \frac{5}{2}x + \blacksquare] - \blacksquare - 1$
$= -2(x + \blacksquare)^2 + \blacksquare$
$= -2(x - \blacksquare)^2 + \blacksquare$

5. Complete the square and write each function in the form $y = a(x - p)^2 + q$. Graph and analyse each.

a. $y = 3x^2 + 6x + 8$ **b.** $y = 2x^2 + x + 4$
c. $y = 5x^2 - 3x + 2$ **d.** $y = -2x^2 + 3x + 1$
e. $y = -4x^2 - 5x + 8$ **f.** $y = \frac{1}{2}x^2 - 3x - 6$

6. Complete the square. Sketch the graph. Show the coordinates of the vertex and the axis of symmetry.

a. $y = x^2 - 7x + 5$ **b.** $y = 4x^2 + x - 2$
c. $y = -3x^2 + 2x + 2$ **d.** $y = 5x^2 + 12x - 1$
e. $y = x^2 + 2x$ **f.** $y = -2x^2 + \frac{1}{2}x + 3$

7. Complete the square. Sketch the graph. Explain how each differs from the graph of $f(x) = x^2$.

a. $y = \frac{1}{5}x^2 + 6x + 1$ **b.** $y = \frac{2}{3}x^2 - 6x$

c. $y = \frac{-3}{4}x^2 + 9x + 2$ **d.** $y = \frac{2}{3}x^2 - x + \frac{1}{2}$

8. A rental agent uses this function to approximate the monthly profit (y) in dollars from the rental of a building with x apartments: $y = -20x^2 + 640x$. Complete the square and sketch the profit curve. Identify the maximum profit and the number of apartments yielding this profit.

Historical Note

In Bagdad, in the ninth century, there were many scholars. One of particular note was Mohammed ibn Mûsâ al-Khowârizmî, a great mathematician and astronomer. He wrote the book *Hisâb al-jabr w' al-mugabâlah*, which translates to *The Science of Reduction and Comparison*. When the Moors moved to Spain, this book went with them. In the twelfth century, the book was translated into Latin, which was the common language of scholars in Europe. The word "al-jabr" or "al-ge-bra" became synonymous with equation solving.

A major centre of the Moors in Spain was Granada where they built the famous palace, the Alhambra. Use the library to find pictures of the Alhambra and draw sketches of some of the courtyard arches which are parabolic in shape.

8·8 The General Case

Practical applications can be found for the maximum or minimum points, and the axis of symmetry for real situations expressed by means of a general quadratic function. It is not always convenient, nor is it always an efficient use of time, to complete the square of a general quadratic function in order to find maximum or minimum values. Sometimes it is more efficient to use formulas to calculate the maximum or minimum and the value of x at which this occurs.

In this section, we develop these formulas.

Compare completing the square of the general case with that of a specific case.

$y = ax^2 + bx + c$

$\qquad = a\left(x^2 + \dfrac{bx}{a}\right) + c$

$\qquad = a\left(x^2 + \dfrac{bx}{a} + \dfrac{b^2}{4a^2} - \dfrac{b^2}{4a^2}\right) + c$

$\qquad = a\left(x^2 + \dfrac{bx}{a} + \dfrac{b^2}{4a^2}\right) - \dfrac{b^2}{4a} + c$

$\qquad = a\left(x + \dfrac{b}{2a}\right)^2 - \dfrac{b^2}{4a} + \dfrac{4ac}{4a}$

$\qquad = a\left(x + \dfrac{b}{2a}\right)^2 + \dfrac{4ac - b^2}{4a}$

$y = 2x^2 + 12x + 4$

$\qquad = 2(x^2 + 6x) + 4$

$\qquad = 2(x^2 + 6x + 3^2 - 3^2) + 4$

$\qquad = 2(x^2 + 6x + 3^2) - 2(3^2) + 4$

$\qquad = 2(x + 3)^2 - 2(3)^2 + 4$

$\qquad = 2(x + 3)^2 - 14$

If $a<0$, then maximum. If $a>0$, then minimum.	Maximum/minimum occurs when $x = \dfrac{-b}{2a}$.	Maximum/minimum value is $\dfrac{4ac - b^2}{4a}$.

Example

For the function $y = 3x^2 - 4x + 2$, find
a. the maximum or minimum value.
b. the value of x when the maximum or minimum occurs.

Identify the values of a, b, and c for use in the formulas.
$a = 3$, $b = -4$, $c = 2$

a. Since $a>0$, then the function is concave upward.
The minimum value is $y = \dfrac{4ac - b^2}{4a}$ or $\dfrac{4(3)(2) - (-4)^2}{4(3)} = \dfrac{2}{3}$.
b. The minimum occurs when $x = \dfrac{-b}{2a}$ or when $x = \dfrac{2}{3}$.

Exercises

1. For $y = -6x^2 + 8x - 5$, identify the values of a, b, and c. Then determine whether the function has a maximum or minimum value. Calculate the value and the corresponding x-value.

2. Use the formulas to find the maximum or minimum values and the corresponding values of x.
a. $y = 4x^2 + 8x + 12$ **b.** $y = 12x^2 + 36x + 56$
c. $y = -3x^2 + 5x + 6$ **d.** $y = -2x^2 + 3x + 9$
e. $y = 12 - 7x - 4x^2$ **f.** $y = x - 7 - 5x^2$
g. $y = -x^2 + 7x + 9$ **h.** $y = 9x^2 + 6x + 1$
i. $y = 4x^2 + 7x$ **j.** $y = 8x - 3x^2$

3. Use the formulas to find the maximum or minimum values and the corresponding values of x. Sketch each and approximate the zeros of the functions (if there are any).
a. $y = 3x^2 + 6x - 4$ **b.** $y = -x^2 + 6x + 9$
c. $y = 5x - 2 - 2x^2$ **d.** $y = 4x^2 - 8x$
e. $y = -x^2 + x - 1$ **f.** $y = -x^2 - 4$
g. $y = (x - 6)(x - 4)$ **h.** $y = (x - 7)^2$
i. $y = (2x - 3)(4x + 3)$ **j.** $y = (3x - 5)^2$

4. A hockey arena manager in Flin Flon determined that the formula for the dollar revenue (y) from ticket sales is $y = -100x^2 + 500x + 5000$ where x is the number of dollars increase over $5 per ticket. What is the greatest revenue and at what price per ticket does the maximum occur?

5. A gable end of a roof is in the shape of an isosceles triangle with a length base of 6 m and a height of 2 m. The owner wishes to put in the largest rectangular window possible for the maximum amount of light. Find the dimensions and the area of the window.

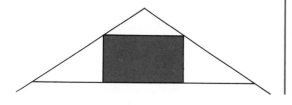

6. A light-rail transit line in Calgary has 100 000 customers daily. Each ticket costs 40¢. A study shows that for each 5¢ increase in tickets, 500 customers are lost. Should the transit line increase its ticket price? Explain.

7. An apartment rental manager in Hull knows that if there are too many suites in the building, not all can be rented and the net profit drops. The function used to approximate the profit (y dollars) from renting a building with x number of suites is $y = -100x^2 + 2800x$. Calculate the number of suites that yields the maximum profit and the corresponding profit.

8. The Singhs are planning to fence several garden plots. They have 400 m of fencing material to use on each. Calculate the maximum area and the dimensions of each garden plot.

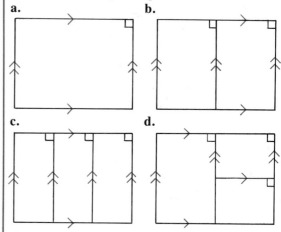

9. Solve for $x + 5$. $(x + 2)^{x+5} = 1$

10. Solve for $x - 2$. $(x - 2)^{x-2} = 1$

Braintickler

A checkerboard consists of 32 red and 32 black squares. Two squares are removed from opposite corners of the board leaving 62 squares. Can the checkerboard be covered with 31 dominoes, each domino covering two adjacent squares? Explain.

8·9 Maxima and Minima

The graphs of quadratic functions are parabolas. A graph that is concave upward has a vertex whose y-value is the minimum value of the function. A graph that is concave downward has a vertex whose y-value is the maximum value of the function. By writing a quadratic function in the form $f(x) = a(x - p)^2 + q$, the a-value indicates whether there is a maximum or minimum and the corresponding value is q.

These two examples illustrate the use of the a-value and of the p- and q-values.

Example 1

The function $f(x) = 2(x - 4)^2 + 6$ has a vertex at (p, q) or $(4, 6)$. Since $a > 0$, it opens upward. The function has a minimum value of q or 6. Its axis of symmetry is $x - p = 0$ or $x = 4$. From this data, we can sketch the graph.

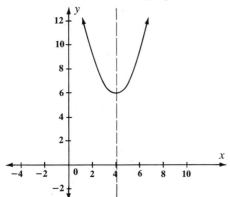

Example 2

The function $f(x) = -[x - (-5)]^2 + 1$ has a vertex at (p, q) or $(-5, 1)$. Since $a < 0$, it opens downward. The function has a maximum value of q or 1. Its axis of symmetry is $x - p = 0$ or $x = -5$. From this data we can sketch the graph. Notice that this graph yields two zeros of the function: $x = -4$ and $x = -6$.

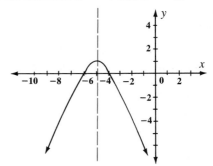

In summary:

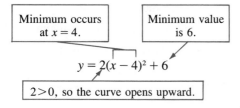

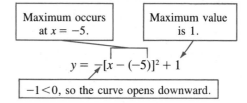

Example 3

Weather balloons can be tracked on radar with a coordinate grid. Find the maximum height $(h(t))$ a balloon will reach if it follows a path determined by the function $h(t) = -100t^2 + 800t + 300$, where t is the time in minutes. Transform the function into the standard form by completing the square.

$$h(t) = -100t^2 + 800t + 300$$
$$= -100(t^2 - 8t + 16) + 1600 + 300$$
$$= -100(t - 4)^2 + 1900$$

The maximum height of the balloon is 1900 m. It takes 4 min to reach its maximum height.

231

Example 4

Find two numbers that differ by 6 and whose product is a minimum. State the product.

For any problem where the answer is not immediately known, the four-step problem-solving model is often useful.

Understand the Problem
We are looking for two numbers whose product is a minimum and differ by 6. Once they are found, the product of the two numbers will be the solution.

Develop a Plan
Set up an algebraic equation to find the two numbers.

Carry Out the Plan
Let n and $n - 6$ be the two numbers.
Product $p = n(n - 6)$
$$= n^2 - 6n$$
$$= (n^2 - 6n + 9) - 9$$
$$= (n - 3)^2 - 9$$

Look Back
Since $a > 0$, the vertex of the function will produce a minimum value. There will be a minimum value of -9 when the numbers are 3 and -3. A graph will verify this solution.

Exercises

1. State whether the function has a maximum or minimum, determine this value, and state the value of x for which it occurs.
a. $f(x) = (x - 3)^2$
b. $f(x) = 4x^2 - 5$
c. $f(x) = -3(x + 1)^2 + 2$
d. $f(x) = x^2 - 6x + 2$
e. $f(x) = -3x^2 + 4x + 1$

2. Graph the function in Example 4. Does it graphically represent the solution reached? Explain.

3. In general, how can the maximum or minimum value of $f(x) = ax^2 + bx + c$ be found?

4. The steps used to solve maximum or minimum problems are illustrated. Find two numbers whose sum is 22 and whose product is a maximum. Complete the solution.

Understand the Problem
a. Identify the quantity to be maximized or minimized. The product is to be a maximum.
b. Identify given information related to this quantity.
c. Two numbers are to be multiplied. The sum of the two is ■■.

Develop and Carry Out a Plan
a. Write expressions for quantities involving one variable.
b. Let one number be x. Let the other number be $22 - ■$.
c. Combine expressions into a quadratic function that represents the quantity to be maximized or minimized: $f(x) = x(■)$.
d. Express the function in the form you wish to use. $y = -x^2 + ■$
e. Calculate the maximum or minimum using $\frac{4ac - b^2}{4a}$. The maximum is ■.
f. Calculate the x-value for the maximum or minimum by using $\frac{-b}{2a}$. One number is ■.

Look Back
Answer the questions.

5. Find two numbers which differ by 7 and whose product is a minimum.

6. A rectangular enclosure for a dog is made using one wall of a barn. Find the dimensions of the largest possible enclosure if 400 m of fencing will be used for the three sides.

7. Compare each function to $y = 3(x - 8)^2 + 2$. With respect to the maximum or minimum value of the function, describe the effect of these changes to the respective function.
a. $y = -3(x + 8)^2 + 2$
b. $y = -3(x - 8)^2 - 2$
c. $y = 3(x - 8)^2 - 2$

8. A rectangular garden is to be enclosed using 500 m of fencing material. Determine the dimensions of the garden with the largest area possible.

9. A garden plot in the shape of a rectangle is divided into three sections by constructing two fences parallel to the width of the garden. A total of 100 m of fencing are available to enclose the entire garden as well as to divide it into the three sections. Find the dimensions of the garden which will enclose the largest area.

10. Natalie runs a lemonade stand at the end of her driveway. She sells an average of 12 drinks each hour at 25¢ a glass. For each 2¢ decrease in the price, her sales increase by 3 drinks per hour. At what price per drink will she make the most money? How much will she receive?

11. A marketing expert determines that sales of television sets can be increased by 3 sets per week for each $20 decrease in price. Weekly sales average 18 sets at $440 each. At what price per television set will the most money be made? How much money will be received?

12. The sum of the length and the width of a rectangle is 10 cm. Find the dimensions of the rectangle such that a triangle whose base lies along the length of the rectangle and whose altitude is the width, has a maximum area. (*Hint:* Find the area of this triangle using this diagram.)

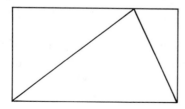

13. One number is 3 more than another number. Find the two numbers such that the difference between the square of the larger number and twice the square of the smaller number is a maximum. Graph all possible combinations of numbers.

14. A total of 800 m of fencing material is used to enclose a rectangular field and to divide the field into four portions by fences parallel to one of the sides of the field. Find the maximum area which can be enclosed in this rectangle and its dimensions.

15. A two-digit number has a "2" for one of its digits. The digits are reversed so that the unit's digit now becomes the ten's digit. If the square of the smaller number is subtracted from the larger number, then find the larger number which will divide into this difference.

16. A freight trucking company sends transports between Vancouver and Toronto. At 08:00 each morning, a truck leaves both cities destined for the other city. The entire trip takes four 24 h periods. How many eastbound company trucks will each westbound truck driver meet?

17. Two fractions $\dfrac{A}{M}$ and $\dfrac{B}{M}$ are added and the result is $\dfrac{3}{2M}$. What is the value of $A + B$?

18. A designer found that a series of problems fell into one type that could be solved using the general function $y = ax^2 + bx + c$. Transform this to the standard form $y = a(x - p)^2 + q$.
a. What are the conditions on the value of a such that the function has a maximum value?
b. In terms of a, b, and c, what is the maximum/minimum value and what is the value of x when this occurs?

19. Solve for x given that
$(x^2 - 5x + 5)^{x^2 - 9x + 20} = 1$.

8·10 The Inverse of Quadratics

In a previous chapter we reflected functions in the line $y = x$ to produce the inverse. We will do the same with quadratic functions. Recall that the inverse of a function ($f^{-1}(x)$) is obtained by interchanging the x and y in the original function.

Example

Given the function $f(x) = (x - 3)^2 + 4$,
a. find its inverse $f^{-1}(x)$; and
b. sketch the original and its inverse on the same axes.
c. Is $f^{-1}(x)$ a function?

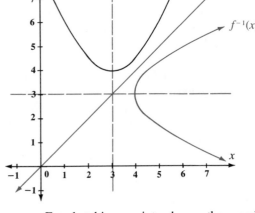

a. Interchange x and y in the function and solve for y.
$$y = (x - 3)^2 + 4 \to x = (y - 3)^2 + 4$$
$$\pm \sqrt{x - 4} = y - 3$$
$$f^{-1}(x) = 3 \pm \sqrt{x - 4}$$

b. $f(x)$ has an axis of symmetry at $x = 3$. The vertex is at (3, 4), and the curve opens upward.
The inverse is graphed by reflecting $y = (x - 3)^2 + 4$ in $y = x$. For sketching we interchange the x and y for the critical points: the axis of symmetry is $y = 3$ and the vertex is (4, 3). The curve opens to the right (in the positive x-direction).

c. Since the graph of the inverse does not pass the vertical line test, $f^{-1}(x)$ is not a function.

Exercises

1. On the same axes, sketch the graphs of $y = x^2$ and $y = -x^2$.
a. Sketch the inverses of the two functions. Use reflections of a table of values.
b. State the domain and the range of each relation.
c. State the direction of opening of each graph.
d. State the equation of the axis of symmetry and the coordinates of the vertex of each graph.
e. In general, what functions will yield a graph that opens to the left? opens to the right?

2. Identify which are inverses.

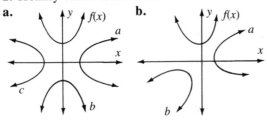

3. Find the inverse of each.
a. $y = x^2 + 5$ **b.** $y = x^2 - 4$
c. $y = (x - 4)^2 - 8$ **d.** $y = (x + 6)^2 + 2$
e. $y = 3(x - 4)^2 - 6$ **f.** $y = -2(x + 3)^2 + 8$

4. Copy each and graph the inverse on the same axes. Which inverses are functions?

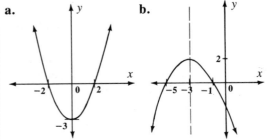

5. Sketch each. Then sketch the inverse. Determine whether the inverse is also a function.
a. $y = x^2$, $x \geq 0$ **b.** $y = (x - 4)^2$, $x \leq 8$
c. $y = x^2 - 4$, $x \geq 0$ **d.** $y = 2(x - 4)^2$, $x \leq 8$

8·11 Quadratic Inequalities

The quadratic function $y = ax^2 + bx + c$ represents the set of points (x, y) which satisfies the function, and the graph is a parabola. However, when the equality is replaced by an inequality, we no longer have a function. The inequalities expressed as $y < ax^2 + bx + c$ and $y > ax^2 + bx + c$ are relations.

Example

Sketch the region defined by $y < x^2 + 10x + 14$.

Understand the Problem
The parabola is broken if the relation is expressed with a ">" or a "<" symbol, and it is solid if the relation is expressed with a "≤" or a "≥" symbol. The broken line indicates that the points on the curve are not included, while the solid line indicates that they are included.

Develop a Plan
Complete the square or use the formulas to sketch the curve for $y = x^2 + 10x + 14$. Then check any point inside the parabola. If it gives a true inequality, then shade inside the parabola; otherwise, shade outside the parabola. In this case, the parabola is indicated by a broken line.

Carry Out the Plan
By completing the square, the relation is $y < (x + 5)^2 - 11$. Since $a > 0$, the parabola opens upward, the vertex is at $(-5, -11)$, and the axis of symmetry is $x = -5$. By checking the point $(-5, 0)$, which lies inside the parabola, the relation is evaluated as $0 < -11$. This is false. Therefore, the point $(-5, -11)$ does not lie in the required region, and so the region outside the parabola is shaded.

Look Back

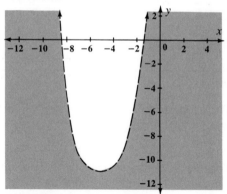

Exercises

1. Graph each to illustrate the different regions in a Cartesian plane.
a. $y = 2(x - 3)^2 + 5$ **b.** $y < 2(x - 3)^2 + 5$
c. $y > 2(x - 3)^2 + 5$ **d.** $y \leq 2(x - 3)^2 + 5$
e. $y \geq 2(x - 3)^2 + 5$ **f.** $y \geq 3(x - 3)^2 + 5$

2. Sketch these graphs. Identify the vertex. Is it included in the relation?
a. $y > x^2$ **b.** $y < 2(x - 3)^2 + 3$
c. $y > -3x^2 + 2$ **d.** $y < -(x + 4)^2 + 5$
e. $y < (x + 2)^2 - 6$ **f.** $y > (x - 5)^2 + 1$
g. $y \leq x^2 - 3x + 4$ **h.** $y \geq -2x^2 + 9$

3. Sketch the graphs.
a. $y \geq x^2 - 4$ **b.** $y \leq 2x^2$
c. $y \leq (x + 1)^2 + 3$ **d.** $y \geq (x - 2)^2 + 1$
e. $y \leq -(x + 4)^2 + 3$ **f.** $y \leq 2(x - 3)^2 - 2$

4. Shade the region which will satisfy both relations.
a. $y \geq (x + 2)^2 - 3$ and $y \leq x^2 - 6x$
b. $y < -x^2 + 8x - 10$ and $y > -x^2 + 8x - 16$

Braintickler

What is the next number?
77, 49, 36, 18, ■

235

8·12 Computer Application—Extrema

In Section 8·8, it was shown that any quadratic function of the form $y = ax^2 + bx + c$ can be written as $y = a\left(x + \dfrac{b}{2a}\right)^2 + \dfrac{4ac - b^2}{4a}$. The following program uses this standard form to evaluate the maximum or minimum values of any quadratic function in the form $y = ax^2 + bx + c$. Recall that the maximum value of the function is $\dfrac{4ac - b^2}{4a}$. Use CTRL-C to exit from the program.

```
10 REM A PROGRAM TO FIND THE MAXIMUM OR MINIMUM VALUE
20 REM OF A QUADRATIC FUNCTION IN THE FORM Y = AX ∧ 2 + BX + C
30 INPUT "VALUE OF A, B, AND C "; A, B, C
40 IF A < 0 THEN 80
50 LET MIN = ((4 * A * C) − B ∧ 2) / (4 * A)
60 PRINT "Y = "; A; "X ∧ 2 + "; B; "X + "; C; " HAS A MINIMUM
VALUE OF "; MIN
70 GOTO 100
80 LET MAX = ((4 * A * C) − B ∧ 2) / (4 * A)
90 PRINT "Y = "; A; "X ∧ 2 + "; B; "X + "; C; " HAS A MAXIMUM
VALUE OF "; MAX
100 GOTO 30
```

Exercises

1. What is the purpose of lines 60 and 90 of the program in the display?

2. When does the program calculate the maximum or minimum value of the function?

3. How does the program determine whether the function has a maximum or minimum? Is this sound reasoning by the programmer? Explain.

4. Predict the output that would appear on the screen for the following values.
a. $A = 1$, $B = -3$, $C = 4$
b. $A = -2$, $B = 5$, $C = -6$
c. $A = 3$, $B = 0$, $C = -1$
d. $A = -1$, $B = 9$, $C = 5$
e. Enter the program on a computer to check your predictions. Is the computer output reasonable?

5. Use the program in the display to find the maximum or minimum values of these functions.
a. $y = 3x^2 + 8x - 2$ **b.** $y = -4x^2 + x + 6$
c. $y = 2x^2 - 15x + 12$ **d.** $y = x^2 + 3x - 6$
e. $y = -x^2 + 4x + 18$ **f.** $y = 9x^2 - 6x + 1$

6. Will the program work if $A = 0$? Explain.
a. Enter and run the program using $A = 0$ to check your prediction. What error does the computer give?
b. Modify the program to prevent the error signal. Run the program using $A = 0$ to check.

7. Modify the program in the display so that it gives the vertex of a function as well as the maximum value.

8. Computers are being used in many supermarkets, where prices are input and added so quickly that the customer cannot keep up with the addition. When mistakes are made, whose responsibility is it to detect and find the error? Write a short essay defending your point of view.

8·13 Chapter Review

1. Write each quadratic function in the form $y = ax^2 + bx + c$ and give the values of a, b, and c.
a. $y = 5x^2 - 3(2x - 1)$
b. $y = -2(x - 4)^2$
c. $y = 3(x + 2)^2 - 5$
d. $y = (x - 3)^2 + 2(3x - 4)$

2. Describe the graphs of the quadratic functions with respect to the direction of opening, the equation of the axis of symmetry, and the coordinates of the vertex.

a.
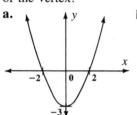
b.
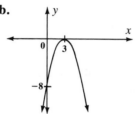

3. Sketch the graph of $y = -3x^2 + 5x + 1$. Analyse the graph.

4. Describe the graph of $y = 3x^2$ in comparison to the graph of $y = x^2$.

5. Describe the graph of $y = -2(x - 1)^2 + 8$ in comparison to the graph of $y = -x^2$.

6. Determine the direction of opening, the coordinates of the vertex, and the equation of the axis of symmetry.
a. $y = 3x^2 - 1$ **b.** $y = 2(x + 5)^2$
c. $y = -(x - 8)^2 - 3$ **d.** $y = \frac{-1}{2}(x - 1)^2 + 6$

7. Write the quadratic function $y = a(x - p)^2 + q$ described by these conditions. Assume $a = \pm 1$.
a. parabola opens upward; vertex at $(0, 4)$
b. parabola opens downward; vertex at $(3, -2)$
c. parabola opens upward; vertex on the x-axis at $x = -6$
d. parabola with equation of the axis of symmetry $x = 5$ and a minimum value of 2

8. Describe the domain and range of each function.
a. $y = -2x^2$ **b.** $y = 4(x + 10)^2 + 2$
c. $y = -5(x + 3)^2 + 2$ **d.** $y = (x - 4)^2 - 8$

9. Complete the square and write in the form $y = a(x - p)^2 + q$.
a. $y = x^2 - 10x + 3$ **b.** $y = -2x^2 + 6x + 5$
c. $y = 4x^2 + 3x$ **d.** $y = \frac{1}{2}x^2 - x + 3$

10. For the quadratic function $y = x^2 - 12x + 5$, find the value of the function for these values of x.
a. $x = 4$ **b.** $x = 0$
c. $x = \frac{1}{2}$ **d.** $x = \sqrt{2}$

11. Determine the maximum or minimum value of the function, indicate whether it is a maximum or minimum, and give the value of x when the function has a maximum or minimum.
a. $y = x^2 - 8x + 2$ **b.** $y = 4(x + 6)^2 - 5$
c. $y = 2x^2 - x - 5$ **d.** $y = -(x - 3)^2 + 1$

12. Determine two numbers whose sum is 30 and whose product is a maximum.

13. A cruise boat is chartered for an excursion. Its capacity is 200. The cost for each ticket is $30 if 100 or fewer people sign up. However, if more than 100 sign up, the price per ticket is reduced by 20¢ for each ticket sold in excess of 100. What number of tickets will produce the largest income?

14. Draw the graphs.
a. $y > (x - 3)^2 - 2$ **b.** $y \le x^2 + 1$
c. $y < -x^2 + 6x + 5$ **d.** $y > 2x^2 - 8x - 3$

15. For the function $y = ax^2 + bx + c$, give the value of the maximum or minimum and the corresponding value of x, in terms of a, b, and c.

16. Sketch the inverse of $y = -2(x + 4) - 5$ and explain whether it is a function.

8·14 Chapter Test

1. Indicate which of the following are quadratic functions. Explain your answers.

a. $y = 3x^2 - \frac{1}{4}x$ **b.** $y^2 = x^2 + 2x - 1$

c. $y = (x + 1)^2 + (x - 3)^2$

d. $y = x + \frac{1}{x^2}$

2. Write each function in the form $y = ax^2 + bx + c$.

a. $y = 4x(x - 2) + 1$

b. $y = -2(x - 5)^2$

c. $y = x(3x + 1) - 4(2x - 5)$

d. $y = (2x - 1)(x - 9)$

e. $2y = (4x - 3)(2x + 5)$

3. Sketch the graph of $y = -(x + 2)^2 + 3$. Analyse the graph.

4. Sketch the graphs without using a table of values. Label the coordinates of the vertices.

a. $y = x^2 - 8$

b. $y = -0.1x^2$

c. $y = -2(x - 1)^2$

d. $y = (x + 3)^2 - 4$

e. $y = 2x^2 - 5x$

5. For each parabola, write the quadratic function in the form $y = a(x - p)^2 + q$. Assume $a = \pm 1$.

a.

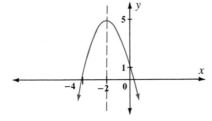

b.

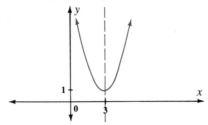

6. Given $y = x^2$, sketch the graph of the quadratic function described. Assume $a = \pm 1$ and write an equation for each.

a. a horizontal translation of 6 units to the left

b. a reflection in the x-axis

c. a vertical translation 3 units downward

d. a vertical translation 4 units upward and a horizontal translation 2 units to the left

e. a vertical translation 5 units upward, followed by a reflection in the x-axis.

7. Complete the square and write in the form $y = a(x - p)^2 + q$. Sketch the graphs. Label the coordinates of the vertices.

a. $y = -x^2 + 3x + 5$ **b.** $y = 2x^2 + 10x - 3$

8. Find the maximum value of the function.

a. $y = -2x^2 + 2x + 7$ **b.** $y = -x^2 - 3x + 6$

9. Find the value of x when the function $y = 3x^2 + 10x - 2$ has a minimum.

10. Two numbers differ by 16. If the sum of their squares is a minimum, find the numbers.

11. Grant's company is selling Dustin vacuum cleaners at \$80 per unit. A decrease of \$4 in the price will increase the weekly sales of 20 vacuums per week by 2. At what price per vacuum will his company make the most money? How much money will be received?

12. Draw the graphs.

a. $y \le 2(x - 1)^2 + 4$

b. $y > -(x + 2)^2 + 6$

c. $y \ge x^2 + 6x - 3$

13. Sketch the inverse of $y = 2(x - 3)^2 - 5$. Explain whether the inverse is also a function.

14. Use formulas to find the maximum or minimum and the corresponding value of x.

a. $y = 2x^2 - 3x + 4$

b. $y = 3x - 4x^2 - 6$

QUADRATIC EQUATIONS

Tune Up

1. Describe each set of numbers using examples.
a. integers **b.** rationals
c. irrationals **d.** real numbers

2. Simplify.
a. $\sqrt{49}$ **b.** $-\sqrt{225}$
c. $-2\sqrt{27}$ **d.** $5\sqrt{56}$
e. $7\sqrt{12} - \sqrt{75}$ **f.** $-4\sqrt{128} + 3\sqrt{288}$
g. $12\sqrt{72} - \sqrt{150}$
h. $8\sqrt{90} + 4\sqrt{135} - 5\sqrt{48}$

3. State the conjugate of each radical expression.
a. $\sqrt{3}$ **b.** $-\sqrt{6}$
c. $1 - \sqrt{5}$ **d.** $2 + \sqrt{37}$
e. $-\sqrt{162} - 5$ **f.** $8\sqrt{216} - 3$

4. Expand.
a. $x(2 - 3x)$ **b.** $(x + 3)(x - 5)$
c. $(x^2 + 1)(4 - 5x)$ **d.** $(-3x + 6y)(5y - x)$
e. $(3x - 2\sqrt{54})^2$ **f.** $(3 - \sqrt{21})(3 + \sqrt{21})$

5. Determine the product of each radical expression in Exercise 3 and its conjugate.

6. Simplify by rationalizing the denominator.
a. $\dfrac{1}{1 - \sqrt{3}}$ **b.** $\dfrac{\sqrt{2}}{5\sqrt{2} - 1}$
c. $\dfrac{-\sqrt{5} + 3\sqrt{16}}{4\sqrt{48}}$ **d.** $\dfrac{5y - 3\sqrt{x}}{\sqrt{x} - 2y}$
e. $\dfrac{x^2 + 4x\sqrt{23}}{x - \sqrt{y}}$ **f.** $\dfrac{-12y - 4\sqrt{252x}}{2 + \sqrt{5y}}$

7. Factor.
a. $2x - 4y$ **b.** $12x^2 + 4xy - 8y$
c. $-7x + 4y + 28xy$ **d.** $-5x^3 - 30x^2 + 10x$
e. $15x^3 + 34x^2 + 5x - 6$ **f.** $4x^2 - 56x + 196$
g. $16x^2 - 81y^2$ **h.** $64a^3 + 729b^3$

8. Determine the zeros of each function.
a. $y = 2x^2 - 7x$ **b.** $y = x^2 - x - 20$
c. $y = 6x^2 + 13x - 5$ **d.** $y = -4x^2 - 11x + 3$
e. $y = 24x^2 - 40x - 224$
f. $y = -120x^3 + 42x^2 + 36x$

9. Sketch the graph of each quadratic function.
a. $y = x^2 + 3x - 4$ **b.** $y = x^2 + 3$
c. $y = 3 - x^2$ **d.** $y = -x^2 - 4x - 5$
e. $y = x^2 - 10x - 25$ **f.** $y = -x^2 - 8x - 16$
g. $y = 7x^2 + 28x + 23$ **h.** $y = 48x - 185 - 3x^2$

10. Graph each function.
a. $y = (x - 4)^2$ **b.** $y = x^2$
c. $y = x^2 + 4$ **d.** $y = -2x^2$
e. $y = (x - 4)^2 + 5$ **f.** $y = -2(x + 3)^2 - 4$

11. Explain the role of each underlined part for the graph of $y = \underline{a}(x - \underline{p})^2 + \underline{q}$.

12. For the graph of $ax^2 + bx + c = y$, what does each represent?
a. $\dfrac{-b}{2a}$ **b.** $\dfrac{4ac - b^2}{4a}$ **c.** $\left(\dfrac{-b}{2a}, \dfrac{4ac - b^2}{4a}\right)$

239

9·1 Solving Quadratic Equations

The path of a ball that is kicked across a field is represented mathematically by the function $y = -10x + 70x$, where y is the height in metres and x is the elapsed time in seconds after it is kicked. An observer would like to know in advance when the ball will land. One way to solve this problem is to graph the function and approximate the x-intercepts. These values of x make the function equal to zero and are called the zeros of the function. We see from the graph that the zeros of the function appear to be at 0 and 7. From the graph, the ball will land 7 s after it is kicked.

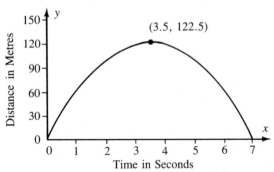

Note that the ball will land when the height is 0 m; that is, when $y = 0$. Substituting 0 in the function yields the equation $0 = -10x^2 + 70x$. This equation can be solved using methods learned earlier. Recall that if $P \times Q = 0$, then either $P = 0$, $Q = 0$, or both P and Q equal zero.

$0 = -10x^2 + 70x$
$0 = x^2 - 7x$ Divide each side by -10.
$0 = x(x - 7)$ Factor.

Hence, either $x = 0$, or $x - 7 = 0$
$$x = 7$$

Since the ball is kicked at 0 s, the time elapsed until the ball lands is 7 s.

Example 1

Find the roots of each.
a. $2x^2 - 2x - 12 = 0$ **b.** $x^2 + 16 = 0$

a. Solve for x by factoring.

$2x^2 - 2x - 12 = 0$
$2(x + 2)(x - 3) = 0$
$x + 2 = 0$ $x - 3 = 0$
$x = -2$ $x = 3$

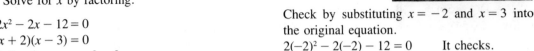

Check by substituting $x = -2$ and $x = 3$ into the original equation.
$2(-2)^2 - 2(-2) - 12 = 0$ It checks.
$2(3)^2 - 2(3) - 12 = 0$ It checks.

The roots of the equation are $x = -2$ and $x = 3$.

b. Since this equation will not factor readily, we solve for x directly.

$x^2 + 16 = 0$
$x^2 = -16$
$x = \sqrt{-16}$

Since there is no real number x such that $(x)(x) = -16$, there are no roots in the set of real numbers.

240

Example 2

Sketch these three graphs on one set of axes and find the zeros of each function.

a. $y = (x - 6)^2 - 4$ **b.** $y = (x - 1)^2$ **c.** $y = (x + 5)^2 + 1$

Analysis:

a. This function has two zeros since it intersects the x-axis in two places, namely $x = 4$ and $x = 8$.
b. This function only intersects the x-axis at one point. It has a zero at $x = 1$.
c. This function does not intersect the x-axis, so it has no zeros.

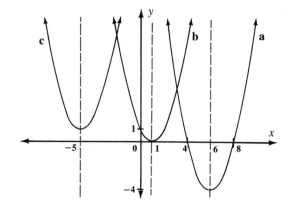

From the graph, we would predict that the three equations would have two roots, one root, and no real root, respectively. This can be checked by factoring, and then solving for x.

Solving for the function in part **a**,

$$(x - 6)^2 - 4 = 0$$
$$x^2 - 12x + 32 = 0$$
$$(x - 4)(x - 8) = 0$$

Hence,

$$x - 4 = 0 \qquad x - 8 = 0$$
$$x = 4 \qquad x = 8$$

The roots are $x = 4$ and $x = 8$. This agrees with our prediction.

The function in part **b** can be expanded to find the factors directly.

$$(x - 1)^2 = 0$$
$$(x - 1)(x - 1) = 0$$

There are two factors: $x - 1 = 0$ and $x - 1 = 0$. They yield the identical roots $x = 1$ and $x = 1$.

The third equation, $(x + 5)^2 + 1 = 0$, can be written as $x^2 + 10x + 26 = 0$. This cannot be factored using simple factoring techniques. Solving quadratic equations by simple factoring has limitations. In the next several sections, alternate methods of solving quadratics are introduced.

Example 3

What two numbers are related such that their sum is 96 and their product is 1728?

Develop and Carry Out a Plan

Use one unknown to express each number. Then write the product of the two as an equation and solve. Let x be the first number. Then $96 - x$ is the second number. The product is $x(96 - x)$. The equation is $x(96 - x) = 1728$. Write this in the general form, factor, and solve.

$$x^2 - 96x + 1728 = 0$$
$$(x - 24)(x - 72) = 0$$
$$x = 24 \text{ and } x = 72$$

Check: $24 + 72 = 96$
$24 \times 72 = 1728$ They check.

The two numbers are 24 and 72.

Exercises

1. Solve each by graphing. Analyse to find the roots of each.

a. $x^2 - 16 = 0$ (*Hint*: Let $y = x^2 - 16$.)
b. $x^2 - 7x = 0$ **c.** $36x^2 + 72x = 0$
d. $0 = 20 + x - x^2$ **e.** $2x^2 + 7x - 4 = 0$
f. $9x^2 = 0$ **g.** $-3x^2 + 12 = 0$
h. $(x - 2)^2 + 4 = 0$ **i.** $-2(x + 5)^2 - 5 = 0$

2. Solve these equations. Verify your results.

a. $x^2 + 16 = 10x$ **b.** $6p^2 = 11p + 7$
c. $144 - 4k^2 = 0$ **d.** $5d^2 - 12d = 0$
e. $4c^2 - 2c = 30$ **f.** $33x + 6x^2 = 0$
g. $16n^2 + 5 = 24n$ **h.** $3p^2 = 5p + 12$
i. $15m^2 + 26m = -8$ **j.** $x^2 - 25 = 0$
k. $4b^2 + 28b = -49$ **l.** $25x^2 = 100$

3. a. Find the x-intercepts of $y = 3x^2 - 15x - 18$.
b. Find the roots of $3x^2 - 15x - 18 = 0$.
c. Explain how and why the answers above are related.

4. The smaller integer is five less than the larger integer. If the sum of the square of the smaller integer plus four times the larger is equal to eighty, find the integers.

5. Find the roots of these equations.
a. $0 = a^2 - 2a - 15$ **b.** $2r^2 - 9r + 4 = 0$
c. $0 = 4k^2 + 7k - 2$ **d.** $9t^2 = 30t - 25$

6. The graphs of three functions are shown. Identify and explain the number of roots in each corresponding equation when $y = 0$.
a. $y = x^2 + 9$ **b.** $y = x^2 - 16$
c. $y = x^2 - 2x - 15$

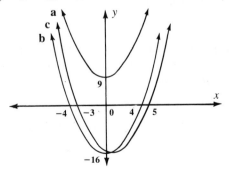

7. Graph these functions. From the graph, estimate the zeros of the function, verify your results algebraically, and state the domain and the range of the functions.
a. $f(x) = 6x^2 + 17x - 3$
b. $y = 6x^2 + 9x - 60$
c. $y = 8x^2 + 9x - 14$
d. $f(x) = 6x^2 - 32x - 24$
e. $f(x) = 5x^2 - 12x + 4$

8. Find three integers if the second is seven more than the first, the third is one less than three times the first, and the sum of the square of the first integer plus the product of the second and third integers is 193.

9. A cannonball is fired from ground level on an arc described by $h = -t^2 + 9t$, where h is the height in metres and t is the time in seconds. How many seconds after firing will it land?

10. Solve each.
a. $6(5x - 7) = 54$ for $\dfrac{5x + 7}{3}$

b. $x - y = -3$ for $\dfrac{y - x}{2}$

11. The small circle passes through the centre of the large circle. The area of the shaded portion is 27π square units. What is the radius of each circle? Account for both roots of the equation.

12. An arc of a circle is drawn in a square. Points P and Q are the midpoints of the sides. What portion of the square is shaded? (*Hint*: Find $\angle APB$.)

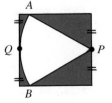

9·2 Completing the Square

In the previous section, the quadratic equation was factored to determine the roots. But what if the quadratic is not factorable over the set of rational numbers? Or what if the roots are from the set of irrational numbers?

Consider the solution to $x^2 - x - 1 = 0$ which cannot be factored over the set of rationals. We are able to approximate the roots using a calculator. By nesting, we have $(x - 1)x = 1$. Try $x = 1.7$.

$1.7 \rightarrow$ $\boxed{(}$ 1.7 $\boxed{-}$ 1 $\boxed{)}$ $\boxed{\times}$ 1.7 $\boxed{=}$ $\mathbf{1.19}$ Too large. Try 1.6.

$1.6 \rightarrow$ $\boxed{(}$ 1.6 $\boxed{-}$ 1 $\boxed{)}$ $\boxed{\times}$ 1.6 $\boxed{=}$ $\mathbf{0.96}$ Very close. The root is greater than 1.6.

For the other root, try $x = -0.7$.

$-0.7 \rightarrow 0.7$ $\boxed{+/-}$ $\boxed{-}$ 1 $\boxed{=}$ $\boxed{\times}$ 0.7 $\boxed{+/-}$ $\boxed{=}$ $\mathbf{1.19}$ Try -0.6

$-0.6 \rightarrow 0.6$ $\boxed{+/-}$ $\boxed{-}$ 1 $\boxed{=}$ $\boxed{\times}$ 0.6 $\boxed{+/-}$ 1 $\boxed{=}$ $\mathbf{0.96}$ Very close. The root is less than -0.6.

To one decimal place, the roots are $x = 1.6$ and $x = -0.6$. If this process was continued, we would find that there are no exact decimal numbers that satisfy this equation. It seems that the roots of $x^2 - x - 1 = 0$ are **not** from the set of **rational numbers**.

To find the exact roots, we will use the method of completing the square.

$$x^2 - x - 1 = 0$$
$$x^2 - x = 1$$
$$x^2 - x + 0.25 = 1 + 0.25$$
$$(x - 0.50)^2 = 1.25$$
$$x - 0.50 = \pm\sqrt{1.25}$$
$$x = 0.5 \pm \sqrt{1.25}$$

Using a calculator, we can check our earlier approximations:

$x = 0.5 \pm \sqrt{1.25}$

$x = 0.5 \pm 1.118\ 034$ (to 6 decimal places)

$x \doteq 0.618\ 034$ and $x \doteq 1.618\ 034$

This agrees with our earlier approximation.

This shows that the roots of $x^2 - x - 1 = 0$ are from the set of **real numbers**.

Example

The distance, in metres, a vehicle travels in s seconds is given by the equation $2s^2 + 5s - 8 = d$. How long does it take to go 4 m? Since the distance is 4 m, use $d = 4$.

$$2s^2 + 5s - 8 = 4$$
$$2s^2 + 5s = 12$$
$$s^2 + \frac{5}{2}s = 6 \qquad \text{Divide both sides by 2.}$$
$$s^2 + \frac{5}{2}s + \left(\frac{5}{4}\right)^2 = 6 + \left(\frac{5}{4}\right)^2 \qquad \text{Add } \left(\frac{5}{4}\right)^2 \text{ to each side.}$$
$$\left(s + \frac{5}{4}\right)^2 = \frac{96 + 25}{16}$$
$$s = -\frac{5}{4} \pm \frac{11}{4} \qquad \sqrt{\frac{121}{16}} = \pm\frac{11}{4}$$

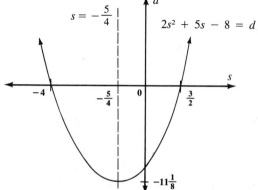

Since the time must be positive, the negative root is **extraneous** or **inadmissible**.

The object will have travelled 4 m in $\frac{-5}{4} + \frac{11}{4}$ s, or $\frac{3}{2}$ s.

Exercises

1. In the example of the display, explain why the negative root is considered extraneous or inadmissible.

2. Solve by factoring the trinomial square. Explain the number of roots.

a. $x^2 + 6x + 9 = 0$ **b.** $x^2 - 8x + 16 = 0$

c. $x^2 - x + \frac{1}{4} = 0$ **d.** $x^2 + 5x + \frac{25}{4} = 0$

e. $x^2 - \frac{2}{3}x + \frac{1}{9} = 0$ **f.** $x^2 + \frac{3}{4}x + \frac{9}{64} = 0$

3. Use a calculator to approximate both roots to one decimal place.

a. $x^2 - 5x - 2 = 0$ **b.** $x^2 + x - 5 = 0$
c. $15x = 9x^2 + 4$ **d.** $9x^2 - 60x + 100 = 0$
e. $x^2 - 7x + 3 = 0$ **f.** $8x^2 - 22x + 15 = 0$

4. Use a calculator to approximate both roots to two decimal places.

a. $x^2 - 7x + 3 = 0$ **b.** $x^2 - 7x - 3 = 0$
c. $6x^2 - x - 2 = 0$ **d.** $3x^2 + x - 1 = 0$
e. $5x^2 - 50x = 500$ **f.** $3x^2 - 11x = 7$

5. Determine the value of C such that the trinomial is a square of a binomial.

a. $x^2 + 8x + C$ **b.** $x^2 - 12x + C$
c. $x^2 - 9x + C$ **d.** $x^2 + 3x + C$
e. $x^2 - \frac{4}{5}x + C$ **f.** $x^2 + \frac{5}{3}x + C$

6. Determine the value of p that will make the equations equivalent.

a. $2x^2 + 6x = 1$; $x^2 + px = \frac{1}{2}$

b. $3x^2 - x = 2$; $x^2 + px = \frac{2}{3}$

c. $5x^2 + 4x = -5$; $x^2 + px = -1$

d. $\frac{2}{3}x^2 + 6x = -2$; $x^2 + px = -3$

e. $-x^2 + 5x = 2$; $x^2 + px = -2$

f. $\frac{-1}{4}x^2 - x = 3$; $x^2 + px = -12$

7. Complete the square for parts **a** and **b**. Discuss the similarities and the differences in the two processes.

a. $y = 2x^2 + 12x + 9$ **b.** $2x^2 + 7x + 3 = 0$
c. Explain what each tells us about the respective function or equation.

8. Solve the equations by completing the square.

a. $x^2 + 10x - 2 = 0$ **b.** $x^2 - 6x + 3 = 0$
c. $x^2 - 8x - 8 = 0$ **d.** $x^2 + 9x + 2 = 0$
e. $x^2 + 5x + 6 = 0$ **f.** $x^2 + 7x + 3 = 0$
g. $-x^2 + 6x + 3 = 0$ **h.** $-x^2 - 2x + 10 = 0$
i. $-x^2 + 5x - 1 = 0$ **j.** $-x^2 - 3x + 8 = 0$
k. $x^2 + 11x + 20 = 0$ **l.** $x^2 + 7x + 4 = 0$
m. $x^2 = -2x + 3$ **n.** $5x = -x^2 - 4$

9. Francis was having difficulty with his car so it took him 6 min longer to drive to school than usual. He estimated that his average speed over the 30 km was 10 km/h slower than when his car was working properly. How long did it normally take him to drive to school? (*Hint:* Speed is distance ÷ time.)

Understand the Problem
What information are you given? What are you to find? What information will you need that is not given?

Develop and Carry Out a Plan
Use t as his usual driving time, and express his usual speed and delayed speed. $\frac{30}{t}$ and $\frac{30}{t} - 10$

Write an expression for his delayed time.

$t + \frac{1}{10}$

Write another expression for his average delayed speed.

$\dfrac{30}{t + \dfrac{1}{10}}$

Write an equation for his average delayed speed and solve for t.

$$\frac{30}{t} - 10 = \frac{30}{t + \dfrac{1}{10}}$$

$10t^2 + t - 3 = 0$

Find the roots.

Look Back
Interpret the roots. Are both roots admissible? What is the answer to the question? What other information can you determine now that you know what t is? Write a similar problem to exchange with a classmate.

10. The product of a number and the number plus five is six. What is the number?

11. The width of a rectangle is three less than twice the length. The area is 4 m². What are the dimensions to one decimal place?

12. A local and an express train each travel 210 km to Regina. The local train takes 1 h longer than the express to make the run. The local train travels 20 km/h slower than the express. Find the speed to one decimal place for each train.

13. The altitude of a triangle is 2 m longer than the corresponding base. The area is 40 m². What are the dimensions of the altitude and the base?

14. A gardener wanted to have two square arrays of gladioli. One array was to have one more row than the other array. Altogether the gardener has 71 bulbs. Can the gardener plant the bulbs in this way? Explain.

15. An airplane flew 6240 km to Halifax. If the average speed had been 40 km/h less than it was, the airplane would have taken 1 h more to fly the distance. What was the speed of the plane?

16. Solve by completing the square.
a. $2x^2 + 16x - 1 = 0$ **b.** $3x^2 - 12x + 5 = 0$
c. $5x^2 + 10x - 3 = 0$ **d.** $2x^2 - 4x - 7 = 0$
e. $2x^2 - 3x - 4 = 0$ **f.** $3x^2 + 5x - 1 = 0$
g. $5x^2 - x - 2 = 0$ **h.** $4x^2 + 4x - 3 = 0$
i. $-2x^2 - 8x + 3 = 0$ **j.** $-3x^2 + 12x - 1 = 0$
k. $-5x^2 + 20x + 5 = 0$ **l.** $-2x^2 - 16x + 5 = 0$
m. $-2x^2 + x + 4 = 0$ **n.** $-12x = 45 - x^2$

17. A.T., the "Mathematics Wizard", stated that "the process of completing the square is actually factoring the equation." Is A.T. correct? Explain.

18. Solve by completing the square.
a. $\frac{1}{2}x^2 + x - 3 = 0$ **b.** $\frac{1}{3}x^2 - 2x - 4 = 0$

c. $\frac{2}{3}x^2 + 8x + 4 = 0$ **d.** $\frac{5}{2}x^2 - 10x - 15 = 0$

e. $\frac{1}{4}x^2 + 2x + 1 = 0$ **f.** $\frac{3}{5}x^2 - x - 1 = 0$

19. A daredevil jumps from an airplane. She descends so that her height above the ground is given by the formula $h = -4.9t^2 + \frac{1}{2}t + 5400$. What is the maximum time that she can free fall before she must open her parachute if she requires 25 s with her chute open fully?

20. Find the error.   Let $a = b$
$$a^2 = ab$$
$$a^2 - b^2 = ab - b^2$$
$$(a - b)(a + b) = b(a - b)$$
$$a + b = b$$
If $a = 1$, then $2 = 1$

Using the Library

Many ancient civilizations were intrigued by mathematics. While the Greeks are noted for their contributions to mathematics, other civilizations contributed also. Some notable contributions are outlined here.

1. An Egyptian mace dating back to 3100 B.C. has numbers in the millions and hundreds of thousands written on it in hieroglyphics. These numbers form a part of the records of military campaigns.

2. About 2900 B.C., the pyramid of Giza was constructed with incredible accuracy. The stone blocks were cut and put into place with such precision that it would match many modern engineering feats.

3. The Moscow papyrus (1850 B.C.) is a mathematical text containing many mathematical problems.

4. The Rhind papyrus (1650 B.C.) contains 85 problems. The Rollin papyrus (1350 B.C.) shows some practical uses of large numbers with business accounts. The Harris papyrus (1167 B.C.) prepared by Rameses IV, listed the wealth of his father.

One papyrus showed how to decompose any fraction except $\frac{2}{3}$ into two or more unit fractions.

For example, $\frac{3}{8} = \frac{1}{4} + \frac{1}{8}$.

Prepare a report on how this is done.

9·3 The Quadratic Formula

The roots of a quadratic equation can always be found by completing the square. However, completing the square of the general equation $ax^2 + bx + c = 0$, $a \neq 0$, yields a formula that can be used to solve for the roots of any quadratic equation.

$$ax^2 + bx + c = 0$$
$$x^2 + \frac{bx}{a} = -\frac{c}{a} \qquad \text{Divide by } a.$$
$$x^2 + \frac{bx}{a} + \left(\frac{b}{2a}\right)^2 = \left(\frac{b}{2a}\right)^2 - \frac{c}{a} \qquad \text{Complete the square.}$$
$$\left(x + \frac{b}{2a}\right)^2 = \frac{b^2 - 4ac}{4a^2} \qquad \text{Simplify.}$$
$$x + \frac{b}{2a} = \pm\frac{\sqrt{b^2 - 4ac}}{2a} \qquad \text{Take the square root of each side.}$$
$$x = \frac{-b \pm \sqrt{b^2 - 4ac}}{2a} \qquad \text{Solve for } x.$$

The formula, $x = \dfrac{-b \pm \sqrt{b^2 - 4ac}}{2a}$, is the **quadratic formula**. The quadratic formula is used generally when an equation is not factorable, or as an alternative to the process of completing the square. This formula should be memorized.

Example 1

Use the quadratic formula to find the roots, if any, in the set of real numbers.

a. $3x^2 - 4x - 3 = 0$

$a = 3$, $b = -4$, $c = -3$
The quadratic formula is:

$$x = \frac{-b \pm \sqrt{b^2 - 4ac}}{2a}$$
$$x = \frac{-(-4) \pm \sqrt{(-4)^2 - 4(3)(-3)}}{2(3)}$$
$$= \frac{4 \pm \sqrt{52}}{6}$$
$$= \frac{4 \pm 2\sqrt{13}}{6} \qquad \text{Reduce common factors.}$$
$$= \frac{2 \pm \sqrt{13}}{3}$$
$$= \frac{2 + \sqrt{13}}{3} \text{ or } \frac{2 - \sqrt{13}}{3}$$

This equation has two real roots.

b. $2m^2 + m + 5 = 0$

$a = 2$, $b = 1$, $c = 5$
The quadratic formula is:

$$m = \frac{-b \pm \sqrt{b^2 - 4ac}}{2a}$$
$$m = \frac{-1 \pm \sqrt{(1)^2 - 4(2)(5)}}{2(2)}$$
$$= \frac{-1 \pm \sqrt{-39}}{4}$$
$$= \frac{-1 + \sqrt{-39}}{4} \text{ or } \frac{-1 - \sqrt{-39}}{4}$$

Since $\sqrt{-39}$ is not a real number, this equation has no real roots.

If an equation is not in the form $ax^2 + bx + c = 0$, it can be solved using the quadratic formula once the conversion to that form is made.

Example 2

Transform the equation into the form $ax^2 + bx + c = 0$ and find its roots.

$$2 = \frac{2}{x+3} + \frac{3}{x}$$

Multiply by the common denominator of $x(x + 3)$. Note the restrictions on the variable: $x \neq 0$ and $x \neq -3$.

$$2x(x + 3) = 2x + 3(x + 3)$$
$$2x^2 + 6x = 5x + 9$$
$$2x^2 + x - 9 = 0$$

$$x = \frac{-1 \pm \sqrt{73}}{4}$$

$$x = \frac{-1 + \sqrt{73}}{4} \text{ or } x = \frac{-1 - \sqrt{73}}{4}$$

Example 3

A tennis ball is hit to an opponent. The height of the ball above the ground, in metres, is given by $h = -2t^2 + 8t + 1$, where t is the time the ball is in the air. For how long is the ball in the air?

Let $h = 0$, since the ball will not be in the air when the height is 0 m.

$$0 = -2t^2 + 8t + 1$$
$$a = -2, b = 8, c = 1$$

$$t = \frac{-b \pm \sqrt{b^2 - 4ac}}{2a}$$

$$= \frac{-8 \pm \sqrt{8^2 - 4(-2)(1)}}{2(-2)}$$

$$= \frac{-8 + \sqrt{72}}{-4} \text{ or } \frac{-8 - \sqrt{72}}{-4}$$

$$\doteq -0.1 \text{ or } 4.1 \text{ (rounded)}$$

Since time can only be positive, the ball is in the air for approximately 4.1 s.

Example 4

Use the quadratic formula to determine and interpret the roots of $x^2 - 10x + 25 = 0$.

$$a = 1, b = -10, c = 25$$
$$x = \frac{10 \pm \sqrt{(-10)^2 - 4(1)(25)}}{2}$$
$$= 10 + \sqrt{0} \text{ or } 10 - \sqrt{0}$$
$$= 5 \text{ or } 5$$

Since the value of the radicand is zero, the result is a single value: $x = 5$.

Exercises

1. In Example 2 of the display, why should one list the restrictions on the variables before finding the roots of the equation?

2. Write these equations in the form $ax^2 + bx + c = 0$. State the values of a, b, and c.
a. $3x + 2x^2 + 8 = 0$ **b.** $4 = 2x - 7x^2$
c. $-6x^2 + 5 = x$ **d.** $6 = 5x^2$
e. $x(x + 3) = 3x - 4$ **f.** $3(x - 1)^2 - 1 = 0$

3. Write these equations in the form $ax^2 + bx + c = 0$. State the values of a, b, and c.
a. $\dfrac{3}{x-2} - \dfrac{4}{x} = 6$ **b.** $\dfrac{2}{x^2-1} - 4 = \dfrac{1}{x-1}$
c. $\dfrac{6}{x-2} - \dfrac{x}{x-1} = 6$ **d.** $\dfrac{x}{x^2+2x+1} + 5 = \dfrac{2}{x+1}$

4. Solve the equations over the set of real numbers.
a. $x^2 - 8x - 8 = 0$ **b.** $n^2 + 6n + 2 = 0$
c. $p^2 + 5p - 2 = 0$ **d.** $m^2 - m - 3 = 0$
e. $2h^2 + 3h - 5 = 0$ **f.** $6y^2 - 10y + 1 = 0$
g. $2c^2 - 5c - 2 = 0$ **h.** $5k^2 - 6k + 1 = 0$

5. Solve the equations over the set of real numbers. If any roots are not real, explain why.

a. $k^2 + 3k + 5 = 0$ **b.** $r^2 - 9r + 1 = 0$
c. $3x^2 + 3x + 8 = 0$ **d.** $4s^2 - s - 2 = 0$
e. $3x^2 - 7x + 9 = 0$ **f.** $-4t^2 + 5t - 4 = 0$
g. $9p^2 + 30p + 25 = 0$ **h.** $-2x^2 + 9x + 3 = 0$

6. a. Solve for x. $(x^2 - 3x - 3)^{x^3 - 16x} = 1$
b. Solve for $x + y$ given that $x^2 + y^2 = 20$ and $xy = 16$.
c. How many ways can you solve each problem?

7. A rectangle has a length that is 9 cm longer than its width. If the area of the rectangle is 22 cm², then what are the dimensions of the rectangle?

8. Solve. Evaluate the real roots of the equations to one decimal place.

a. $x^2 + 3x - 1 = 0$ **b.** $p^2 - 9p + 12 = 0$
c. $4t^2 - t - 2 = 0$ **d.** $3m^2 + 7m + 5 = 0$

9. Solve. Evaluate the real roots to two decimal places.

a. $2k^2 - 3k - 5 = 0$ **b.** $5r^2 + 9r + 3 = 0$
c. $s^2 + 4s - 2 = 0$ **d.** $8x^2 - 13x + 4 = 0$
e. $-3t^2 + 7t + 1 = 0$ **f.** $-2p^2 - 5p + 7 = 0$

10. Write each equation in the quadratic form $ax^2 + bx + c = 0$ and find the real roots. State the restrictions on the variables where necessary.

a. $(2p - 1)(p + 4) + 3p^2 = 0$
b. $(x - 3)^2 = 4(x + 2) - 5$
c. $12 - (2s - 1)(s + 5) = 8 - 4s$
d. $(3k + 1)(k - 4) + 2(5k - 3) = 0$
e. $5x + \dfrac{2}{x + 1} = 3$
f. $\dfrac{4}{p + 2} = \dfrac{3}{p + 4} + 1$
g. $\dfrac{3}{2} - \dfrac{1}{4t + 1} = \dfrac{2}{t}$
h. $\dfrac{5x - 7}{x^2 - 4} + \dfrac{x - 6}{x + 2} = \dfrac{3x}{x - 2}$

11. Find the real roots of each by completing the square and by the quadratic formula. Which method do you prefer? Why?

a. $3x^2 + x - 10 = 0$ **b.** $\frac{1}{3}x^2 + \frac{3}{2}x = 3$

12. A.T., the "Mathematics Wizard", solved two equations, then forgot which answer went with which question. Match the questions and answers. In how many ways can you solve this problem?

a. $2r^2 - 8r + 3 = 0$ **i)** $4, -\dfrac{1}{3}$
b. $3w^2 - 11w = 4$ **ii)** $2 \pm \dfrac{\sqrt{10}}{2}$

13. These equations require a combination of skills in finding the roots.

a. $n^2(n^2 + 3n + 2) - 4(n^2 + 3n + 2) = 0$
b. $2x^4 - 5x^2 + 3 = 0$
c. $t^2(t + 3) - 4t(t + 3) - t - 3 = 0$
d. $3x(x - 1) - x^2(x + 2) + x^3 - 8 = 12$
e. $\sqrt{2}x^2 - x - 3\sqrt{2} = 0$
f. $\sqrt{2} + \sqrt{3}x = \sqrt{2}x^2$
g. $\dfrac{m^2}{4} + \dfrac{m}{3} = \dfrac{3}{4}$
h. $\dfrac{d - 1}{d - 1} - \dfrac{2d}{d + 1} = 6$

14. Solve for x. What information do you know about the graph of each?
a. $6x^2 + 7x - 3 = 0$ **b.** $x^2 - 6x + 12 = 0$

Historical Note

Hrosvitha, Opera (*c.* 935-1000)
Hrosvitha was a nun of the Benedictine abbey in Saxony. She is noted for her work in number theory, especially with **perfect numbers**. A perfect number is equal to the sum of its factors including 1, but excluding the number itself. For example, 6 is a perfect number since $1 + 2 + 3 = 6$. Hrosvitha was also an author of several plays. In one she tells of Emperor Hadrian demanding the ages of three daughters, namely Faith, Hope, and Charity. Their father, Wisdom, replies by referring to the three perfect numbers 28, 496, and 8128.

a. Show that the three numbers are perfect.
b. Develop a plan for a computer program to find all the factors of a natural number and to test whether the number is perfect.
c. Write the program and run it for the three perfect numbers mentioned by Hrosvitha.

9·4 The Nature of Roots

The quadratic formula $x = \dfrac{-b \pm \sqrt{b^2 - 4ac}}{2a}$ will give all the roots for a quadratic equation of the form $ax^2 + bx + c = 0$. The graph of a quadratic function will intersect the x-axis in either two points, one point, or zero points.

Let us analyse three different cases. The graphs illustrate the cases.

a. $2x^2 + 2x - 12 = 0$

$x = \dfrac{-2 \pm \sqrt{2^2 - 4(2)(-12)}}{2(2)}$

$x = -3$ or 2

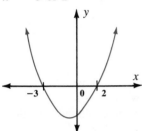

$b^2 - 4ac = 100$

Two real roots

b. $x^2 + 2x + 1 = 0$

$x = \dfrac{-2 \pm \sqrt{2^2 - 4(1)(1)}}{2(1)}$

$x = -1$ or -1

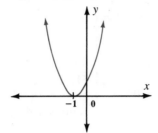

$b^2 - 4ac = 0$

Two equal real roots

c. $2x^2 - 3x + 8 = 0$

$x = \dfrac{-(-3) \pm \sqrt{(-3)^2 - 4(2)(8)}}{2(2)}$

$x = \dfrac{3 \pm \sqrt{-55}}{4}$

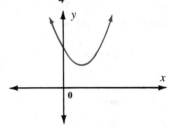

$b^2 - 4ac = -55$

No real roots

Note that the value of $b^2 - 4ac$ is the determining factor for how many points of intersection there are with the x-axis. The expression $b^2 - 4ac$ is called the **discriminant**.

> If $b^2 - 4ac > 0$, then there are two distinct real roots.
> If $b^2 - 4ac = 0$, then there are two equal real roots.
> If $b^2 - 4ac < 0$, then there are no real roots.

Example 1

Determine the nature of the roots.

a. $x^2 + 2x + 1$ **b.** $3x^2 - 3x + 8$ **c.** $3x^2 + 4x - 9$

Evaluate the discriminant for each.

$b^2 - 4ac \rightarrow 4 - 4 = 0$ $b^2 - 4ac \rightarrow 9 - 96 = -87$ $b^2 - 4ac \rightarrow 16 + 108 = 124$

There are two equal real roots.   There are no real roots.   There are two distinct real roots.

Example 2

Find a value for h such that $2x^2 - hx + 3 = 0$ has real roots, that is, $b^2 - 4ac \geq 0$.

$h^2 - 24 \geq 0$

$\quad h^2 \geq 24$

Therefore, $h \geq 2\sqrt{6}$ or $h \leq -2\sqrt{6}$. Note these are inequalities.

249

Exercises

1. Graph these three functions and find the roots using the quadratic formula. Evaluate the discriminant for each. What do you notice about the discriminants?

a. $y = x^2 + 4x + 4$ **b.** $y = x^2 + 4x + 3$
c. $y = x^2 + 4x + 12$

2. What must be the value of the discriminant so that the roots of an equation are rational?

3. In Example 2, $h^2 \geq 24$. Explain why this results in values of $h \leq -24$ and $h \geq 24$. Show these inequalities on a number line.

4. Find the value of the discriminant and determine the nature of the roots without solving for the roots.

a. $x^2 - 3x - 1 = 0$ **b.** $p^2 + 8p + 12 = 0$
c. $m^2 - 4m + 5 = 0$ **d.** $k^2 + 6k - 2 = 0$
e. $6s^2 + 8s + 1 = 0$ **f.** $-12t + 4t^2 = -9$

5. For each equation, find the values of m that will produce equations with no real roots, two equal real roots, and two distinct real roots.

a. $mx^2 - 3x + 4 = 0$ **b.** $2x^2 - mx + 13 = 0$
c. $x^2 - 4x + 3m = 0$ **d.** $mx^2 - 14 = 0$
e. $m(x^2 - 3) + 12x + 3m + 2 = 0$

6. For what values of k will the equation $x^2 - 3x + k + 1$ have real equal roots? (*Hint:* Assume that the constant term is $k + 1$.)

7. Copy and complete this chart.

Value of d: $d = b^2 - 4ac$	Nature of the Roots		
	Real or Not Real	Equal or Distinct	Rational or Irrational
$d > 0$			
$d = 0$			
$d < 0$			

8. What values of m will give this quadratic equation one real root? $4x^2 - mx + 3m - 4 = 0$

9. If $3 \bullet 4 = 12$, $4 \bullet 5 = 20$, and $3 \bullet 5 = 15$, then what is $5 \bullet 5$?

10. Match the three equations with the graphs. List the ways in which you can solve this problem.

a. $3x^2 - 6x + 8 = 0$
b. $6x^2 - 5x - 6 = 0$
c. $4x^2 - 12x + 9 = 0$

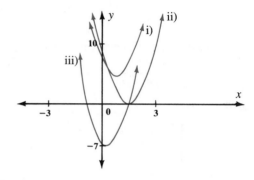

11. The height of a golf ball above the green is given by $h = 10t - 2t^2$, where h is in metres and t is in seconds. Is it possible to attain these heights?

a. 10 m   **b.** 12 m
c. 15 m   **d.** 20 m
e. List all the ways you can solve this problem.

12. Determine the nature of the roots and explain.

a. $x + \dfrac{1}{x} = \dfrac{13}{6}$ **b.** $\dfrac{4}{x-2} + \dfrac{1}{x+2} = 1$
c. $\dfrac{5}{h} = \dfrac{3}{h+1} + \dfrac{8}{7}$

13. A.T., the "Mathematics Wizard", had just watched the Olympics on television. A.T. claimed that "a diver followed a path defined by the function $h = 4.9t^2 + 13t$, where h is the height, in metres, above the water and t is the time in seconds." Does A.T.'s claim "hold water"? Explain.

Braintickler

The metric convention used in Canada for writing dates is to give the month first, then the date, as in 3-6 for March 6. In the United States, the convention is the reverse with the date followed by the month (3-6 would mean June 3). How many dates in the year are there that would have this ambiguous meaning in the two countries?

9·5 Sum and Product of Roots

Let us examine the sum and the product of the roots of quadratic equations. Are there relationships that will help us complete our study?

The roots of $3x^2 + 11x - 4 = 0$ are -4 and $\frac{1}{3}$.

Their sum is $-4 + \frac{1}{3} = -\frac{11}{3}$.

Is it accidental that this is $-\frac{b}{a}$?

Their product is $-4 \times \frac{1}{3} = -\frac{4}{3}$.

Is it accidental that this is $\frac{c}{a}$?

The roots of $2x^2 - 13x - 7 = 0$ are 7 and $-\frac{1}{2}$.

Their sum is $7 + \frac{-1}{2} = \frac{13}{2}$.

This is $-\frac{b}{a}$.

Their product is $7 \times \frac{-1}{2} = \frac{-7}{2}$.

This is $\frac{c}{a}$.

Can we show that these relationships hold for the general case? Let the two roots of the quadratic equation $ax^2 + bx + c = 0$ be $m = \frac{-b + \sqrt{b^2 - 4ac}}{2a}$ and $n = \frac{-b - \sqrt{b^2 - 4ac}}{2a}$.

The sum of the roots are:
$$m + n = \frac{-b + \sqrt{b^2 - 4ac}}{2a} + \frac{-b - \sqrt{b^2 - 4ac}}{2a}$$
$$= \frac{-2b}{2a} \text{ or } -\frac{b}{a}$$

The product of the roots are:
$$mn = \frac{-b + \sqrt{b^2 - 4ac}}{2a} \times \frac{-b - \sqrt{b^2 - 4ac}}{2a}$$
$$= \frac{4ac}{4a^2} \text{ or } \frac{c}{a}$$

Note that the general equation $ax^2 + bx + c = 0$ is equivalent to $x^2 + \frac{b}{a}x + \frac{c}{a} = 0$. By substitution, the quadratic equation becomes $x^2 - (m + n)x + mn = 0$.

Example 1

One of the roots of $2x^2 - 11x + 5 = 0$ is 5. Find the other root.

The sum of the roots is given as $-\frac{b}{a}$.

Let x represent the other root.

Then $x + 5 = \frac{11}{2}$

$\qquad x = \frac{1}{2}$

The second root of the equation is $\frac{1}{2}$.

Example 2

Write a quadratic equation given its roots as 4 and -3.

If m and n are the roots, then a form of the equation is $x^2 - (m + n)x + mn = 0$.

Then $m + n$ is $4 + (-3) = 1$
Then mn is $(4)(-3) = -12$

An equation is $x^2 - x - 12 = 0$.

Exercises

1. Copy and complete the chart.

Equation	a	b	c	Roots m and n	$m+n$	mn
$x^2 + 3x - 2 = 0$						
$x^2 - 3x - 4 = 0$						
$2x^2 + 7 = 0$						
$2x^2 - 5x + 3 = 0$						

Describe in words two relations between a, b, c, and the roots of the equation $ax^2 + bx + c = 0$.

2. For the equation $5x^2 - x - 4 = 0$, find the values of each, without factoring.

a. $-\dfrac{b}{a}$ **b.** $\dfrac{c}{a}$

3. For the equation $24x^2 - 14x - 5$, find the sum and the product of the roots.

4. Find the sum and the product of the roots of these equations.

a. $x^2 + 8x - 20 = 0$ **b.** $4x^2 - 5x + 1 = 0$
c. $3x^2 + x - 10 = 0$ **d.** $9x^2 - 4 = 0$
e. $5x^2 - 6x = 0$ **f.** $12x^2 - 17x + 6 = 0$
g. $\frac{1}{2}x^2 - 3x - 2 = 0$ **h.** $3x^2 - \frac{1}{2}x - 2 = 0$

5. Write a quadratic equation for the solution sets given. Verify your equation.

a. $\{2, -3\}$ **b.** $\{1, 4\}$
c. $\{0, 6\}$ **d.** $\left\{\frac{1}{2}, -5\right\}$
e. $\left\{-\frac{3}{4}, \frac{2}{5}\right\}$ **f.** $\{2 + \sqrt{3}, 2 - \sqrt{3}\}$

6. Let the roots of a quadratic be m and n. Then the product of the two factors equals zero. Hence $(x - m)(x - n) = 0$. By multiplying show that the equation is $x^2 - (m + n)x + mn = 0$.

7. Find k such that the product of the roots of $4x^2 + 7x + k = 0$ is equal to 12.

8. Let k and m represent the roots of the equation $3x^2 - 2x - 1 = 0$. The larger of the two roots is k. Find the value of these expressions.

a. $k - m$ **b.** $k^2 + m^2$ **c.** $(k + m)^2$
d. $\dfrac{k}{m} + \dfrac{m}{k}$ **e.** $k^2 - m^2$ **f.** $(k - m)^2$

9. One root of the equation is given. Find the other.

a. $5x^2 + 9x + 4 = 0$; $\dfrac{-4}{5}$

b. $-3z^2 + 7z - 4 = 0$; 1

c. $x + \dfrac{1}{x} = \dfrac{13}{6}$; $\dfrac{2}{3}$

10. Answer the following.
a. Find k such that the sum of the roots of $2kx^2 + (k - 3)x - 8 = 0$ is equal to 4.
b. Find k such that the product of the roots of $3x^2 + kx - 14 = 0$ is equal to the sum of the roots.
c. Find k such that the roots are reciprocals of each other. $-2x^2 + 5x + (k^2 + 3k) = 0$

11. In your own words, explain why a quadratic equation can be written in these forms.
a. $x^2 + (\text{sum of the roots})x + (\text{product of the roots}) = 0$
b. $(x - \text{one root})(x - \text{other root}) = 0$

12. Find k such that the roots are additive inverses. $6x^2 - (2k^2 - 7k + 5)x - 3 = 0$

13. $4x^2 + kx - 15 = 0$ has roots whose sum equals 0. Find k.

14. Given that m and n are the roots of the given equation, find $m^2 + n^2$.
a. $8x^2 - 22x + 15 = 0$ **b.** $x^2 + \frac{11}{3}x + 2 = 0$
c. $px^2 + qx + r = 0$

15. The roots of an equation are $\dfrac{(7 \pm \sqrt{13})}{6}$. Find the sum and the product of the roots and the equation with integral values of a, b, and c.

16. An **automorphic number** is one in which the tail of its square is the number itself. The number 76 is automorphic since $76^2 = 5776$. What are the automorphic numbers between 1 and 100?

9·6 Complex Numbers

We saw that if the discriminant $b^2 - 4ac > 0$, then a quadratic equation has no real roots since the square root of a negative number is not defined in the set of real numbers. For centuries, mathematicians dismissed negative discriminants when working with quadratic equations as being impossible. Then, in the middle of the seventeenth century, a number system was extended to include the square roots of negative numbers. Although $x^2 + 3 = 0$ has no solution in the real number system, it has a solution in the **complex number system**.

The real number system was extended by introducing the number i, called the **imaginary unit**, which has the property that $i^2 = -1$. The imaginary unit can be combined with real numbers resulting in such expressions as $3 + 4i$, $-5i$, and $1 - 2i$. These are called **complex numbers**.

> A complex number is a number of the form $a + bi$, where a, $b \in R$ and $i^2 = -1$.

Any real number can be expressed as a complex number since the real number system is a subset of the complex number system. Therefore, if $b = 0$, then $a + bi = a$, where $a \in R$ by definition. Also, if $a = 0$, then $a + bi = bi$. Since $b \in R$ and i is imaginary, then numbers of the form bi are called **pure imaginary numbers**. If $b = 0$, then $a + bi = a$ which is a real number (a subset of the complex numbers).

Example 1

Simplify.
a. $\sqrt{-144}$

b. $-\sqrt{-63}$

a. $\sqrt{-144} = \sqrt{144} \times \sqrt{-1}$
$= \sqrt{144} \times \sqrt{i^2}$ $\{ i^2 = -1 \}$
$= 12 \times i$
$= 12i$

b. $-\sqrt{-63} = -\sqrt{63} \times \sqrt{-1}$
$= -3\sqrt{7} \times i$ $\{ \sqrt{63} = \sqrt{9} \times \sqrt{7} \}$
$= -3i\sqrt{7}$

Many of the properties and laws used when performing operations with real numbers also apply to complex numbers.

Example 2

Simplify.
a. $(7 - 3i) + (2 + i) - (4 - 5i)$

b. $(2i)(3 - 2i)$

c. i^8

a. Add and subtract by collecting like real numbers and like imaginary numbers.
$(7 - 3i) + (2 + i) - (4 - 5i)$
$= (7 + 2 - 4) + [-3i + i - (-5i)]$
$= 5 + 3i$

b. By using the distributive property, we get
$(2i)(3 - 2i)$
$= (2i)(3) - (2i)(2i)$
$= 6i - 4(i^2)$
$= 6i - 4(-1)$
$= 4 + 6i$

c. By expanding the expression, we get
$i^8 = i^2 \times i^2 \times i^2 \times i^2$
$= -1 \times -1 \times -1 \times -1$
$= 1$

Example 3

Solve the equation $x^2 - 6x + 11 = 0$, $x \in C$.

The set of complex numbers is denoted by C.

This equation can be solved by using the quadratic formula.

$$\therefore x = \frac{-b \pm \sqrt{b^2 - 4ac}}{2a}$$

$$x = \frac{-(-6) \pm \sqrt{(-6)^2 - 4(1)(11)}}{2(1)}$$

$a = 1$, $b = -6$, $c = 11$

$$= \frac{6 \pm \sqrt{36 - 44}}{2}$$

$$= \frac{6 \pm \sqrt{-8}}{2}$$

$\sqrt{-8} = \sqrt{4} \times \sqrt{2} \times \sqrt{-1}$
$= 2i\sqrt{2}$

$$= \frac{6 \pm 2i\sqrt{2}}{2}$$

$$= 3 \pm i\sqrt{2}$$

The roots are $3 + i\sqrt{2}$ and $3 - i\sqrt{2}$. These can be verified by substituting them into the original equation. This will be left as an exercise.

Example 4

Sketch the graph of the equation $y = x^2 - 2x + 4$.

In order to determine the vertex of the graph, we can use $\left(\frac{-b}{2a}, \frac{4ac - b^2}{4a}\right)$.

$$\frac{-b}{2a} \rightarrow \frac{-(-2)}{2} = 1 \qquad \frac{4ac - b^2}{4a} \rightarrow \frac{4(1)(4) - (-2)^2}{4(1)} = 3$$

The vertex is at $(1, 3)$.

To determine the y-intercept, we let $x = 0$.
$\therefore y = (0)^2 - 2(0) + 4$
$y = 4$
The y-intercept is at 4.

To determine the x-intercepts, if they exist, we let $y = 0$.
$\therefore 0 = x^2 - 2x + 4$

Using the quadratic formula, we get

$$x = \frac{2 \pm \sqrt{4 - 16}}{2}$$

$$= \frac{2 \pm 2i\sqrt{3}}{2}$$

$$= 1 \pm i\sqrt{3}$$

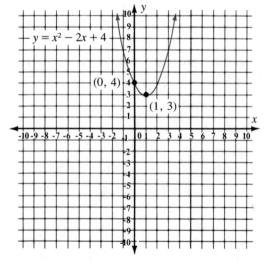

Since the equation has complex roots, there are no x-intercepts. That is, the graph does not cross the x-axis. This concurs with the fact that since $a > 0$, the graph is concave upwards.

Exercises

1. Simplify.
a. $\sqrt{-25}$ **b.** $\sqrt{-121}$ **c.** $\sqrt{-243}$
d. $2\sqrt{-100}$ **e.** $-3\sqrt{-338}$ **f.** $-\sqrt{-245}$
g. $(\sqrt{-3})^2$ **h.** $(-\sqrt{-24})^2$ **i.** $-5(\sqrt{-18})^2$
j. $(2\sqrt{-64})^2$ **k.** i^3 **l.** $4i^2$
m. $-i^5$ **n.** $(5i)^4$ **o.** $-(-3i^2)^3$

2. Simplify.
a. $(2-3i)+(1+i)$ **b.** $i-(5+6i)$
c. $(5-2i)-(7+3i)$ **d.** $(2i-3)+(6i+2)$
e. $(7+i)+(2+5i)$ **f.** $(8+5i)-(3+4i)$
g. $(a+bi)-(a+bi)$ **h.** $(a-bi)+(a-bi)$

3. Expand.
a. $(4i)(1-3i)$ **b.** $(-5)(7-5i)$
c. $(1-i)(2+i)$ **d.** $(8+5i)(3+4i)$
e. $(3-2i)(3+2i)$ **f.** $(5+4i)(5+4i)$
g. $(a-bi)(a+bi)$ **h.** $(a+bi)(a+bi)$

4. Verify the answer to Example 3 in the display. Also use another method to verify the roots.

5. Solve each equation and verify your answers. $x \in C$
a. $x^2-2x+6=0$ **b.** $x^2+8x+19=0$
c. $0=-x^2+4x-9$ **d.** $5x^2-30x+47=0$
e. $-x^2-4x-3=0$ **f.** $-4x^2-56x-201=0$
g. $0=3x^2-4x+6$ **h.** $0=-2x^2+7x-5$
i. $0=-15x^2+17x-9$ **j.** $17x^2-11x+2=0$
k. $11x^2-13x+7=0$ **l.** $-9x^2+5x-11=0$

6. Solve each equation. $x \in C$ (*Hint*: Multiply the equation by the least common denominator.)
a. $\dfrac{x}{x+2}+\dfrac{4}{x+3}=5$
b. $\dfrac{2x}{3x+1}-4=\dfrac{x-1}{x}$
c. $3-\dfrac{x-1}{2x-3}=\dfrac{6x}{x-2}$
d. $\dfrac{x-3}{x^2-9}-\dfrac{4}{x+2}=-1$

7. A.T., the "Mathematics Wizard", stated that "any real number can be written as a complex number." Is A.T. correct? Use examples to support your answer.

8. Sketch the graph of each equation.
a. $y=x^2+4$ **b.** $y=x^2+4x+9$
c. $y=-x^2-5$ **d.** $y=-x^2-8x-22$
e. $y=3x^2-30x+83$ **f.** $y=x^2+17$
g. $y=x^2-6x+16$ **h.** $y=-9x^2-36x-41$
i. $y=-5x^2+20x-29$ **j.** $y=4x^2-56x+168$

9. Multiply.
a. $(3+i)(3-i)$ **b.** $(4-2i)(4+2i)$
c. $(9-4i)(9+4i)$ **d.** $(p-qi)(p+qi)$

10. $a+bi$ and $a-bi$ are **conjugates**.
a. Determine the products of these pairs of conjugates. $(a+bi)(a-bi)$ and $(a-bi)(a+bi)$
b. If r and $s \in R$, find the product of $r+si$ and its conjugate.
c. What kind of number is the product of $r+si$ and its conjugate?
d. Write a general statement for the product of a complex number and its conjugate.

11. State the conjugate of each complex number.
a. $1-i$ **b.** $2+3i$
c. $15+2i$ **d.** $-5+4i$
e. $7i+3$ **f.** $8i-7$
g. 5 **h.** $-12i$

12. Determine the product of the complex number and its conjugate for each part of Exercise 11.

13. Simplifying the quotient of two complex numbers is similar to simplifying the quotient of radical expressions. Simplify each quotient. The first one is started as an example.

$\dfrac{1+i}{3-2i}=\dfrac{1+i}{3-2i}\times\dfrac{3+\blacksquare}{3+2i}$ $(3+2i)$ is the conjugate of $(3-2i)$.

$=\dfrac{3+2i+\blacksquare-\blacksquare}{9+4}$

$=\dfrac{1+\blacksquare}{\blacksquare}$

a. $\dfrac{i}{1-i}$ **b.** $\dfrac{2+5i}{3i}$ **c.** $\dfrac{5-4i}{2-9i}$

d. $\dfrac{i(4+7i)}{3+8i}$ **e.** $\dfrac{(3+2i)(1-4i)}{(2-3i)(5+i)}$ **f.** $\dfrac{(5-6i)^2}{2i(7-3i)}$

g. $\left[\dfrac{2+i}{6i-(1-2i)}\right]^2$ **h.** $\dfrac{(8+2i)-(1-i)}{(2+i)^2}$

255

14. Complex numbers can be plotted on a complex plane (the **Argand plane** named after Jean Argand). The horizontal axis is the real axis and the vertical axis is the imaginary axis. The complex number $2 + 3i$ is represented by a vector from the origin to the point $[2, 3]$ as shown in the diagram.

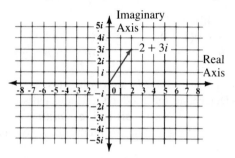

Plot these complex numbers on an Argand plane.
a. $1 - i$ **b.** $2 + 5i$ **c.** $-3 - 2i$
d. $6 + 7i$ **e.** 5 **f.** $4i$

15. Plot the conjugates of each complex number in Exercise 14 on an Argand plane.

16. Plot the complex number $2 - 5i$ on an Argand plane.
a. Multiply the number by i.
b. Plot the resulting number on the plane.
c. Determine the angle between the two vectors. What do you notice?
d. Repeat this process for the numbers $-3 + 4i$, $1 - i$, $7 + 2i$, $2 - 3i$, $-5i$, 4. Do you get the same result?
e. Write a general statement summarizing your findings.

17. A vector is defined by its direction and magnitude. Since complex numbers are represented by vectors, they also have a magnitude. For instance, the magnitude of $4 - 7i$ is $\sqrt{4^2 + 7^2}$ or $\sqrt{65}$. Determine the magnitude of these complex numbers.
a. $5 - 3i$ **b.** $2 + 5i$ **c.** $-3 + 4i$
d. 13 **e** $7i$ **f.** $8 - 9i$
g. $-13i$ **h.** $4 - i$ **i.** -34

18. Show that the points 1, $-\frac{1}{2} + i\frac{\sqrt{3}}{2}$, and $-\frac{1}{2} - i\frac{\sqrt{3}}{2}$ are the vertices of an equilateral triangle.

19. Show that the points $3 + i$, 6, and $4 + 4i$ are the vertices of a right triangle.

Historical Note

Abraham De Moivre (1667-1754)
De Moivre, who was born in France, spent most of his life in England where he became a friend of Isaac Newton. De Moivre is noted for his contributions to actuarial mathematics, the theory of probability, and analytic trigonometry. One of the more interesting stories about De Moivre is that of his death. According to the story, De Moivre noticed that each day he needed a quarter of an hour more sleep than the previous day. When the arithmetic progression reached twenty-four hours, he died.

De Moivre developed this familiar formula that has become the keystone of analytic trigonometry.
$(\cos x + i \sin x)^n = (\cos nx + i \sin nx)$,
$i^2 = -1$ and $n \in N$.

This relation, known as De Moivre's Theorem, is useful in deriving trigonometric identities and in finding the roots of a complex number.

Use De Moivre's formula to show each.
a. $i^n = \cos\left(n\frac{\pi}{2}\right) + i \sin\left(n\frac{\pi}{2}\right)$

b. $\sin 3\theta = 3\cos^2\theta \sin\theta - \sin^3\theta$
c. $(-1 - i)^{15} = -128 + 128i$

Using the Library

For his doctoral dissertation at the age of 20, Carl Friedrich Gauss proved the Fundamental Theorem of Algebra which states that a polynomial with complex coefficients and of degree n has at least one complex root. Research and explain Gauss' proof of this theorem.

256

9·7 Problem Solving

Many practical problems can be solved using quadratic equations and the processes discussed in Chapters 8 and 9. However, sometimes one or more of the solutions will not have meaning. Always check for extraneous roots, roots that do not satisfy the original quadratic equation, or solutions which do not have meaning. For example, if the solution to an equation representing a physical problem results in fractional numbers of people, negative time, or nonreal numbers for physical quantities, then these are inadmissible or extraneous roots.

Example 1

Find the dimensions of a rectangle with a width 7 cm less than its length and with an area of 98 cm².

Understand the Problem
We are given the area of the rectangle as 98 cm². Its length is 7 cm greater than its width. We are asked to find the dimensions of the rectangle.

Develop a Plan
Draw and label a diagram. Let x represent the width. Therefore, $x + 7$ represents the length. Set up a quadratic equation.

Carry Out the Plan

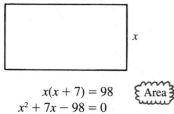

$$x(x + 7) = 98 \qquad \text{Area}$$
$$x^2 + 7x - 98 = 0$$
$$(x + 14)(x - 7) = 0$$
$$x = -14 \text{ or } x = 7$$

Look Back
Since length cannot be a negative quantity, the root -14 is rejected.

The width of the rectangle is 7 cm and its length is 14 cm.

A chart is often useful to organize information and to provide a hint as to how to proceed.

Example 2

Kelly drives 230 km in 5 h from his home to Whitehorse. For the last 150 km of the trip, Kelly increases his average speed by 10 km/h. What was his average speed during the first 80 km?

Let the speed for the first 80 km and the next 150 km be x and $x + 10$ respectively. As your plan, put the information in a chart and set up an equation.

Distance	Rate	Time
80 km	x km/h	$\dfrac{80}{x}$ h
150 km	$(x + 10)$ km/h	$\dfrac{150}{x + 10}$ h

Since the total time of the trip was 5 h,
$$\frac{80}{x} + \frac{150}{x + 10} = 5$$
$$80(x + 10) + 150x = 5x(x + 10)$$
$$x^2 - 36x - 160 = 0$$
$$(x - 40)(x + 4) = 0$$
$$x = 40 \text{ or } -4$$

The car averages 40 km/h during the first 80 km of the trip.

Exercises

1. In Example 2 of the display, why is it not necessary to record the restrictions on the original expression?

2. The length of a rectangle is 1 cm greater than twice the width. If the area of the rectangle is 91 cm², find its dimensions.

3. Find two numbers such that the larger is one more than twice the smaller and their product is 105.

4. The height, in metres, of a ball thrown upwards is given by $h = 50t - 5t^2$, where t is in seconds. Determine how high the ball goes when it reaches its maximum height, and how long the ball is in the air. Graph the function.

5. A freight train travels 600 km in 2 h more than a passenger train travels 900 km. The speed of the passenger train is 10 km less than twice that of the freight train. Find the speed of each train.

6. Find two consecutive even integers such that the sum of their squares is 1252.

7. Find three consecutive odd integers such that the sum of the square of the smallest integer and the product of the other two integers is 688.

8. One side of a square is increased by 3 cm while the other side is doubled. If the area of the rectangle is 72 cm² larger than the area of the square, find the dimensions of the rectangle.

9. Find the length of the diagonal of a square with an area of 72 cm².

10. The combined areas of two triangles is 288 cm². The altitude of the smaller triangle is 4 cm longer than its base. The base of the larger triangle is equal to the altitude of the smaller triangle, and the altitude of the larger triangle is twice the base of the smaller triangle. Find the base and altitude of the smaller triangle.

11. The length of one side of a right triangle is seven more than the shortest side, and the hypotenuse is one more than twice the shortest side. Find the lengths of the three sides of the triangle.

$a^2 + b^2 = c^2$

12. An open-topped box is constructed from a piece of cardboard with a length 2 cm longer than its width. A 6 cm square is cut from each corner and the flaps turned up to form the sides of the box. If the volume of the box is 4050 cm³, find the dimensions of the original piece of cardboard.

$x-$

13. A tinsmith makes an eaves trough for a playhouse by creasing a strip of aluminum 12 cm wide. Calculate the dimensions of the trough in order to have a maximum carrying capacity. (*Hint*: Maximum capacity results when the cross sectional area is at a maximum.)

$x(12-2x)$

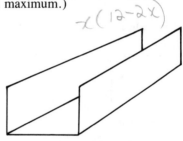

14. A plant physicist finds that a certain flowering plant grows to a height of 2.2 m and that its rate of growth varies jointly as its height and the difference between its height and 2.2 m.
a. For what height is its growth most rapid?
b. Does the plant ever have a growth rate of 2 m/unit of time? Explain.

$h(2.2-h)$

15. James rides his bicycle on a direct route to Lake Superior, a distance of 70 km. Ninety minutes later on his motor scooter, Wayne begins his trip along a different route to the lake and travels a distance of 120 km. Wayne arrives at the same time as James. If Wayne averages 40 km/h faster than James, determine their average speeds.

16. If a plane increased its average speed by 40 km/h, it could decrease the time required to fly a distance of 1440 km by 0.5 h. Find the speed of the plane.

17. A deck of uniform width is built around a rectangular pool 14 m by 22 m. If the area of the deck is 252 m², find the width of the deck.

18. The height of a projectile, propelled upward with an initial velocity of 40 m/s, after t s is given by $h = -4.9t^2 + 40t$. How long after launch will the object be 10 m above the ground?

19. Ayesha bought a number of portable cassette players for a total wholesale price of $2160. She decided to keep one for herself and give one to her friend. She was able to sell the remaining units at a retail price $15 per unit more than she paid and recovered her initial investment. What was the retail price of each unit?

20. The total cost of renting a tour bus is $1764. If 7 more people sign up for the tour, the cost per person will decrease by $21. Find the cost per person if 7 more people join the tour.

21. A photograph of the Handsworth Secondary graduating class of 192 students was taken with the students seated in the bleachers. After seating the students, it was found that the group was too wide to fit into the picture. The entire group could be included by increasing the number of rows by 4 and by decreasing the length of each row by 8 students. How many rows and how many students in each row would be needed? (*Hint*: Assume each row has the same number of students.)

22. Two pipes supply water for a fountain. The larger pipe can fill the holding tank in 4 min less than the smaller pipe by supplying water at a rate of 6 L/min faster than the smaller pipe. If the capacity of the tank is 480 L, how long will it take the larger pipe to fill the tank?

23. Given that w and v are two roots of the quadratic equation $ax^2 + bx + c = 0$, find the value of $\frac{w^2 + v^2}{w^2v^2}$.

24. Three pulleys are connected by a belt. The distance between the pulleys, each with a radius of 10 cm, is 8 cm. What is the belt length?

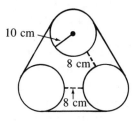

25. How many roots does $x^4 - 11x^2 - 80 = 0$ have? Solve for the roots.

26. Solve.
a. $x^4 - 8x^2 + 16 = 0$ **b.** $x^4 - 12x^2 + 27 = 0$
c. $d - 45 - 4\sqrt{d} = 0$ **d.** $9\sqrt{w} + w + 8 = 0$

27. Find the equations with the following roots.
a. $5 + 2i$ and $5 - 2i$ **b.** $\dfrac{-2 \pm i\sqrt{2}}{2}$

28. What property of complex numbers is shown by $(a + bi) - (c + di) = (a - c) + (b - d)i$.

Historical Note

Blaise Pascal (1623-1662)
Pascal, a French mathematician, devised a quick way to calculate the coefficients of the expansion of $(a + b)^n$.

Power	Coefficients of Expansion
$(a + b)^0 =$	1
$(a + b)^1 =$	1 1
$(a + b)^2 =$	1 2 1
$(a + b)^3 =$	1 3 3 1
$(a + b)^4 =$	1 4 6 4 1

1. Use the triangle to expand each.
a. $(a + b)^3$ **b.** $(a + b)^4$

2. Determine the coefficients of the expansion.
a. $(a + b)^5$ **b.** $(a + b)^7$

3. Give the expansion of each.
a. $(3m + 2n)^3$ **b.** $(3r - 2s)^4$
c. $(2a - 3b)^5$ **d.** $(-v + 2w)^7$

9·8 Computer Application— Factors of a Trinomial

A computer can be used to determine the roots of a quadratic equation. To find the roots, the programmer is asked to input the coefficients a, b, and c in the quadratic equation.

```
10 INPUT "THE COEFFICIENTS A, B, AND C ARE "; A, B, C
20 IF A = 0 THEN GOTO 10
30 PRINT "THE EQUATION BEING SOLVED IS "; A; "X ∧ 2 + "; B; "X
+ "; C; " = 0"
40 LET D = B ∧ 2 - 4 * A * C
50 IF D < 0 THEN 120
60 LET R1 = (-B + SQR(D)) / (2 * A)
70 LET X1 = INT(R1 * 100 + 0.5) / 100
80 LET R2 = (-B - SQR(D)) / (2 * A)
90 LET X2 = INT(R2 * 100 + 0.5) / 100
100 PRINT "THE ROOTS ARE "; X1; " AND "; X2
110 GOTO 130
120 PRINT "THERE ARE NO REAL ROOTS."
130 END
```

Exercises

1. Use the equation $2x^2 - 3x + 1 = 0$ and simulate the program to obtain its factors.

2. Explain the purpose of line 40.

3. Explain the purpose of line 120.

4. What is the purpose of the command SQR as found in lines 60 and 80?

5. What is the purpose of lines 70 and 90?

6. Modify the program to account for the cases where there are two real equal roots.

7. Does this program assume that all the coefficients are positive? Explain.

8. What will happen if the constant term is equal to zero?

9. Modify the program to print the factored form of the equation.

10. Find the factors of these expressions using the modified program from Exercise 9.
a. $12x^2 + 8x - 15$ **b.** $4x^2 - 5x - 6$
c. $6x^2 + 11x + 4$ **d.** $9x^2 - 27x + 8$
e. $12x^2 + 31x - 15$ **f.** $8x^2 - 11x - 10$

11. Modify the program in the display to print the complex roots, as well as the real roots, in the form $a + bi$.

12. Hand-held calculators have become increasingly popular. One of the reasons for this is the increased availability of calculators due to lower costs. Write a short essay explaining some of the reasons that hand-held calculators are common in most homes and businesses.

9·9 Chapter Review

1. Solve these equations by factoring.
a. $9x^2 - 30x + 25 = 0$ **b.** $x^2 - 25 = 0$

2. Solve each equation. Verify your solution.
a. $\dfrac{2x}{x-12} + \dfrac{1}{x+2} = 0$ **b.** $\dfrac{3}{x+4} + \dfrac{2}{5x} = 1$

3. By completing the square of $ax^2 + bx + c = 0$, show that $x = \dfrac{-b \pm \sqrt{b^2 - 4ac}}{2a}$.

4. Solve by completing the square. Verify your results using the sum and product of roots.
a. $x^2 - 6x - 2 = 0$ **b.** $2x^2 + 8x - 5 = 0$
c. $-2x^2 + x - 4 = 0$ **d.** $\frac{2}{3}x^2 - 6x - 1 = 0$

5. The surface area of a closed cylinder is given by $A = 2\pi r(r + h)$, where r is the base and h is the height of the cylinder. Find the radius if the height of the cylinder is 12 cm and the total surface area is 170π cm².

6. Explain how to determine the nature of roots. Find the value of the discriminant in each. Describe the nature of the roots.
a. $x^2 - 8x + 5 = 0$ **b.** $3x^2 + x + 2 = 0$
c. $5x^2 - 2x - 2 = 0$ **d.** $-2x^2 + 5x + 3 = 0$

7. Define the term "extraneous root" and give an example of a problem in which an extraneous root may occur.

8. Use the quadratic formula to solve. Leave your answer in radical form where appropriate.
a. $x^2 - 5x + 3 = 0$ **b.** $3x^2 + x - 8 = 0$
c. $2x^2 - 7x + 1 = 0$ **d.** $x^2 + 12x + 5 = 0$

9. Evaluate the roots to one decimal place.
a. $x^2 - 6x - 2 = 0$ **b.** $4x^2 + 9x + 1 = 0$
c. $2x^2 - 7x - 7 = 0$ **d.** $3x^2 + 4x - 6 = 0$

10. Without solving the equation, determine the sum and the product of the roots.
a. $3x^2 - 6x + 1 = 0$ **b.** $x^2 + 10x - 3 = 0$
c. $4x^2 - x - 5 = 0$ **d.** $2x^2 + 7x - 1 = 0$

11. The sum of the squares of two consecutive integers is 925. Find the integers.

12. Find a quadratic equation in the form $ax^2 + bx + c = 0$ for equations with these roots.
a. $\dfrac{-1}{3}, \dfrac{2}{5}$ **b.** $1 \pm \sqrt{5}$

13. Find k such that the sum of the roots of $(k - 3)x^2 + 6x - 15 = 0$ is equal to 12.

14. One side of a square is increased by 6 cm, and the adjacent side is increased by 3 cm. If the area of the newly-created rectangle is 304 cm², then find the original dimensions of the square.

15. A ball is thrown upward with an initial speed of 18 m/s. The height of the ball above the ground is given by $h = -4.9t^2 + 18t$.
a. How many seconds after the ball is released will it be 10 m above the ground?
b. How long will it take before the ball returns to ground level?
c. How high does the ball rise?

16. Forty metres of fencing material is available to enclose a rectangular garden. If the area of the garden is 91 m², find the dimensions of the garden.

17. Expand.
a. $(6 - 2i)(3 + 2i)$ **b.** $(3i - 2)(4 - 5i)$

18. Express the roots in the form $a + bi$.
a. $2x^2 - 5x + 4 = 0$ **b.** $x^2 - 3x + 1 = 0$

19. Find the quadratic equation whose roots are $2 + 3i$ and $2 - 3i$.

20. Show that $i^6 = -1$.

21. Use a square piece of paper to show that there are 360° in a circle.

22. Show that the product of the roots of the quadratic equation $ax^2 + bx + c = 0$ is $\dfrac{c}{a}$.

9·10 Chapter Test

1. Solve these equations by factoring.
a. $16x^2 - 9 = 0$ **b.** $4x^2 + 20x + 25 = 0$
c. $18x^2 - 9x - 2 = 0$

2. Solve each equation. Explain the steps as you perform them for part **b.**
a. $\dfrac{2x}{x+2} = \dfrac{6}{2x-1}$ **b.** $5 - \dfrac{x+4}{x+3} = \dfrac{3}{2x+5}$

3. Solve by completing the square.
a. $x^2 - 8x - 5 = 0$ **b.** $2x^2 + 12x + 3 = 0$

4. Determine the value of the discriminant and indicate what type of roots the equation has.
a. $x^2 - 9x + 3 = 0$ **b.** $5x^2 + 12x - 1 = 0$
c. $9x^2 - 6x + 1 = 0$ **d.** $3x^2 - 2x + 7 = 0$

5. Solve the equations. If the answer is irrational, write the answer using radicals.
a. $x^2 - 15x + 10 = 0$ **b.** $3x^2 + 2x - 2 = 0$
c. $2x^2 + 9x + 3 = 0$ **d.** $5x^2 - x - 3 = 0$

6. Find three consecutive integers such that twice the square of the middle integer is 65 more than the product of the other two integers.

7. Evaluate the roots of the equations to the nearest tenth.
a. $x^2 + 5x - 5 = 0$ **b.** $4x^2 - 9x + 2 = 0$
c. $3x^2 + 12x + 10 = 0$ **d.** $-2x^2 + 5x + 5 = 0$

8. Without solving the equation, determine the sum and the product of the roots.
a. $7x^2 - 4x + 10 = 0$ **b.** $x^2 + 15x - 12 = 0$
c. $-3x^2 - 5x + 14 = 0$ **d.** $2x^2 + 6x + 1 = 0$
e. Can you determine the roots using just their sum and their product? Use one of the equations to help with your explanation.

9. The length of the base of a rectangular box is 14 cm. The ends of the box are squares and the total surface area of the closed box is 666 cm². Find the dimensions of the ends.

10. Given the roots, write the quadratic equation in the form $ax^2 + bx + c = 0$.
a. $\dfrac{5}{4}, \dfrac{1}{2}$ **b.** $\dfrac{-2}{5}, 1$

11. Find k such that the product of the roots of $4x^2 - 8x + (k - 3) = 0$ is equal to $\dfrac{1}{2}$.

12. The sum of the first n consecutive positive even integers is $S = n(n + 1)$. Find the number of positive even integers needed to obtain 506 as the sum.

13. Find k such that the sum of the roots of $-3x^2 + (2k + 1)x - 11 = 0$ is equal to zero.

14. An object is thrown downward with a velocity of 10 m/s from the top of a tower 60 m above the ground. The height of the object above the ground after t seconds is given by $h = -4.9t^2 - 10t + 60$. Write your answers to one decimal place.
a. How long will it take to hit the ground?
b. For what value of t will the object be half the distance to the ground?
c. Graph the function and state its domain and range.

15. Expand.
a. $(6 + 2i)(3 - i)$ **b.** $(8 - 3i)(8 + 3i)$

16. Express the roots in the form $a + bi$.
a. $5m^2 - 2m + 6 = 0$ **b.** $2r^2 - 5r + 1 = 0$

17. Find the quadratic equation whose roots are $(4 - 3i)$ and $(4 + 3i)$.

18. Given $3x^2 + 4x + 5 = 0$, evaluate $m^2 + n^2$.

19. Show that the sum of the roots of a quadratic equation $ax^2 + bx + c = 0$ is $\dfrac{-b}{a}$.

Cumulative Review   Chapters 7–9

1. Describe the domain and the range of each relation.

a. 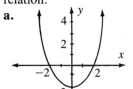   **b.**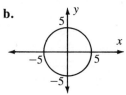

2. In a table of values, list five ordered pairs from the relation described by each equation. Then graph each relation over the real numbers.

a. $\{(x, y) \mid y = -\frac{3}{4}x + 5\}$ **b.** $\{(x, y) \mid y = |1 - 2x|\}$

3. Identify three ordered pairs that satisfy each inequality.

a. $3x - 2y < 0$ **b.** $\frac{x}{4} - \frac{2}{5}y \leq -1$

4. For the linear relation $y = -4x + 3$,
a. draw a graph.
b. use an inequality to describe the region below the line.
c. write ordered pairs for three points in the region below the line.
d. write an equation of the inverse.
e. draw a graph of the inverse.

5. Use your own words and a specific example to define ''a function''.

6. For $h(x) = x^2 - 3x + 2$, determine a value or an expression for each.
a. $h(-1)$ **b.** $h(0)$ **c.** $h(t)$ **d.** $h(a + 4)$

7. Use $g(x) = 3x - 2$ to show that the inverse of $g(x)$ and $\frac{1}{g(x)}$ are not the same.

8. Graph each pair of relations and describe a property that is common to each pair.
a. $y = x$ and $y = x + 3$ **b.** $y = 2^x$ and $y = 2^x + 3$
c. $y = |5x|$ and $y = |5x| + 3$
d. $y = \frac{1}{x}$ and $y = \frac{1}{x} + 3$
e. $y = \sqrt{x}$ and $y = \sqrt{x} + 3$

9. Use a graph to show the difference between $f(x) - 3$ and $f(x - 3)$ for each relation.
a. $f(x) = x^2$ **b.** $f(x) = \frac{1}{x}$
c. $f(x) = 2^x$ **d.** $f(x) = \sqrt{x}$

10. Draw a graph to illustrate the relationship between the given function $y = f(x)$ and $y = kf(x)$ for each k.
a. $y = 3x$; $k = 2$ **b.** $y = \sqrt{x}$; $k = \frac{1}{2}$

11. Use transformations of $y = |x|$ to graph $y = 4|x - 3| + 2$.

12. Rewrite these columns to match each equation from column I with a description from column II.

I	II
$y = 7x - 2$	second degree
$y = x^2 - 3x + 5$	linear
$4x + 9y - 3 = 0$	quadratic
$x^2 + y^2 = 6$	first degree

13. For each parabola identify the direction of opening, the coordinates of the vertex, and an equation of the axis of symmetry.
a. $y = -x^2$ **b.** $y = -\frac{1}{3}(x - 1)^2$

14. Sketch a graph of each parabola.
a. $y = x^2 - 3$ **b.** $y = (x + 4)^2 - 1$

15. Complete the square to determine the vertex of each parabola.
a. $y = x^2 + 8x + 3$ **b.** $y = x^2 - 7x + 1$

16. Identify the maximum and minimum value of each quadratic function.
a. $f(x) = x^2 - 10x - 5$
b. $h(n) = 0.5n^2 - 3n + 4.2$

17. Use transformations of $y = x^2$ to graph $y = -3(x - 4)^2 + 5$.

18. Sketch the graph of each inequality.
a. $y \geq 2x^2 + 2x + 2$ **b.** $x^2 + 3y \leq 5$

Cumulative Review   Chapters 7–9

19. Determine the roots of each quadratic equation.
a. $x^2 - 7x + 10 = 0$ **b.** $3a^2 - 10a - 8 = 0$

20. Solve each equation by completing the square.
a. $3t^2 - 12t - 15 = 0$ **b.** $-2x^2 + x + 4 = 0$

21. Use the quadratic formula to calculate real number solutions, to the nearest hundredth, for these equations.
a. $2x^2 - x - 1 = 0$ **b.** $p^2 = 4 - 2p$

22. Graph each quadratic function and describe how the discriminant in each case relates to the graph.
a. $y = x^2 - 5x + 6$ **b.** $y = x^2 + 5x + 11$

23. For what values of p will the equation $y = px^2 - 5x + 6$ have only one real root?

24. Use a, b, and c to describe how the sum of the roots and the product of the roots can be determined directly, from a quadratic equation in the form $ax^2 + bx + c = 0$.

25. This graph illustrates a relation between the price of gasoline and the total cost of a purchase. The relation is linear and includes the pairs (25, 13.35) and (40, 21.36).

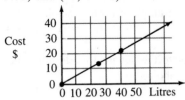

a. What is the price per litre?
b. What is the significance of the point (0, 0) on the graph?
c. How many litres will you get for $20?

26. A curious youngster, peeking through a crack in a fence, is trying to catch a glimpse of the horses and jockeys in their walk before the race. Fifty-four legs, of horses and jockeys, go by. How many horses are there?

27. A relation between the hours worked and the amount of a pay cheque is defined by the function $p(h) = 9.45h - 12.1$.
a. Explain the meaning of the symbol $p(h)$.
b. What is the value of $p(8)$ in this context?
c. Use function notation to determine the amount of a pay cheque for a forty-hour week.

28. The quadratic equation $s = -16t^2 + 100t$ describes the height of a certain object (in metres), t seconds after it was released.
a. Determine the maximum height of the object.
b. How long does it take to reach that maximum height?

29. Solve a quadratic equation to find two real numbers that have a sum of 23 and a product of -288.

30. The sum of the squares of three consecutive integers is 194. Use a quadratic equation to calculate the three integers.

31. A certain square is enlarged by adding 5 m to each side. If the area of the larger square is 39 m², what was the length, correct to one decimal place, of the original square?

32. A sign maker is designing a rectangular sign with a gold-braid border. Use a quadratic equation to determine the maximum area that can be enclosed by 25 m of the gold braid.

33. A developer is surrounding a parcel of land with 300 m of fencing to enclose two building lots, one square and one rectangular with length twice its width. What should be the dimensions of the two lots to provide the maximum area within the fencing?

34. A rectangular card is 6 cm by 8 cm. How much should be added to the shortest side to form a larger rectangular card with a diagonal 7 cm longer than the first?

SYSTEMS OF EQUATIONS

Tune Up

1. Solve the equation for x.
a. $-17x = 51$
b. $x^2 + 5 = 41$

2. Solve the inequality.
a. $-3y < 27$
b. $5x + 7 \geq -27$
c. In your own words, state a rule for multiplying or dividing both sides of an inequality by a negative number.
d. Does multiplying or dividing both sides of an equation effect the equality of the equation? Explain.

3. Find a table of values and the graph of the relation $y = 5x - 2$.
a. Calculate the slope of the graph from two points in the table.
b. Write the y-intercept of the line.
c. How does the y-intercept and the equation of the relation relate?

4. Find a table of values and graph the relation $x^2 + y^2 = 16$.
a. Find the x-intercepts and the y-intercepts of the relation.
b. What type of shape is this?

5. Solve these equations for the variable.
a. $x^2 - 64 = 0$
b. $m^2 - m - 2 = 0$
c. $y^2 + y - 156 = 0$
d. $3a^2 + 5a + 2 = 0$

6. State the y-intercepts, the x-intercepts, and graph the relation $3x^2 + 2y^2 = 72$.

7. Use the equation $\dfrac{x-1}{x} - \dfrac{3x+2}{4} = 5$ to answer these questions.
a. What are the restrictions on the variable?
b. Simplify the left side of the equation by finding a common denominator.
c. Are the restrictions still the same?
d. Solve for x.
e. Is the solution for x one of the restricted values?

8. In Exercise 7, if the solution to the equation had been a restricted value, would the answer be valid? Explain.

9. State the quadratic formula.
a. What would be the values of a, b, and c in the quadratic equation $-3x^2 + 48 = 0$?
b. Solve this equation using the quadratic formula and one other method.
c. Which method do you find most useful? Explain.

10. Use the quadratic formula to solve these equations.
a. $5y^2 + 11y - 12 = 0$
b. $9a^2 - 143 - 6a = 0$

11. Graph the relation $2x^2 + 3y^2 = 12$ using a table of values.

12. Graph each inequality.
a. $y \geq 4$
b. $3x^2 - y < 6$

10·1 Systems of Equations

A **system of linear equations** is a set of two (or more) equations. The solution to such a system involves finding the ordered pair(s) that satisfy these equations simultaneously.

Example 1

A plane flying from Vancouver travels a path defined by the equation $3x + 2y = 18$, at an altitude of 10 000 m. A second plane flying from Brandon travels a path defined by the equation $x + 2y = 10$, and has an altitude of 8000 m. At what point will the path of the plane from Vancouver be directly above the path of the plane flying from Brandon?

The two planes are flying on paths that are defined on the standard Cartesian coordinate grid. As a result, graphing the two paths will yield a point of intersection.

From the graph, the point of intersection is estimated as the ordered pair $(4,3)$. The point of intersection of the two equations always can be verified by substituting the values of x and y into the original equations.

$3(4) + 2(3) = 18$

$4 + 2(3) = 10$

Therefore, the paths will intersect at the point $(4,3)$ as this point satisfies both equations.

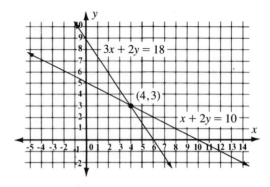

Example 2

A 4 g mixture of two different chemicals is being analysed. The less expensive chemical costs $1/g, while the second chemical costs $2/g. The difference between the total costs of the two chemicals is $5. Find the mass of each substance being analysed.

Understand the Problem

We are given that the total mass is 4 g, and that the cost of one chemical is $1/g, and the other is $2/g.

Carry Out the Plan

$x + y = 4$ and $2x - y = 5$.

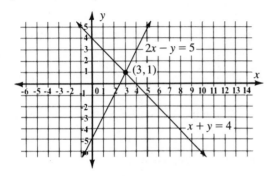

Develop a Plan

Two equations can be found and then graphed to find the point of intersection. For this system, let x represent the mass of the more expensive chemical, and let y represent the mass of the less expensive chemical.

Look Back

From the graph, the point of intersection is the ordered pair $(3,1)$. Therefore, there are 3 g of the more expensive chemical and 1 g of the less expensive chemical. This result can also be verified by substituting 3 for x and 1 for y in the equations found in the Carry Out the Plan section.

Exercises

1. A.T., the "Mathematics Wizard", stated that "when using the method of graphing, we estimate the solution to a system of equations." Is A.T. correct? Explain.

2. Graph each system to determine which has an intersection point of $(-3, 4)$.

a. $y = -2x - 2$
$y = 3x + 13$

b. $2y + x = 5$
$3y - 2x = 6$

c. $y = -3$
$x = 4$

d. $6x - 2y = -26$
$y = 4$

3. Graph these systems of equations and find the solution set. Verify your answers. If there is no point of intersection, explain why.

a. $x + y = 6$
$x - y = 2$

b. $y = x$
$2x + 3y = 10$

c. $x + y = 5$
$y = -3$

d. $x + 2y = 8$
$2x - y = 1$

e. $x + 2y = 0$
$5x + y = 18$

f. $2x + y = 1$
$x = 2y + 8$

g. $y = -x + 3$
$x + y = 6$

h. $x + y = -8$
$2x - 4y = 14$

4. Find the area of the triangle whose vertices are the points of intersection on the graphs of each system of equations.

a. $x = 7$
$y = -3$
$5y - 8x = -6$

b. $5x + 4y = 46$
$-5x + 6y = 44$
$y = 4$

5. Graph the system of equations to find the point of intersection. Explain why the solution is an estimation.

$4x = 3y$
$3y = 10 - 4x$

6. Find an equation for each line.

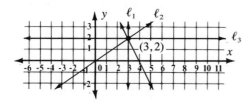

7. Two aircraft at different altitudes are flying courses described by the equations $x + 2y = 4$ and $x - y = 1$, where x is the distance in kilometres (east is positive and west is negative), and y is the distance in kilometres (north is positive and south is negative) from an airport. Will the paths of the aircraft cross? If so, at what point?

8. Write a system of equations that will intersect at these points.

a. $(3, 1)$ **b.** $(2, 4)$ **c.** $(0, 0)$ **d.** $(5, -2)$

9. Write the system of equations needed to solve each problem. Graph the system and state the solution set.

a. The sum of two numbers is 10 and their difference is 4. Find the numbers.

b. One number exceeds another number by 5 and together their sum is 1. Find the numbers.

c. The cost of 4 pens and 3 notebooks is $11. The cost of a pen is one dollar more than the cost of a notebook. Find the cost of each pen and each notebook.

d. A child has 60¢ in nickels and dimes. If the child has nine coins in all, then how many of each kind does the child have?

e. A man spent $13 on an order of hamburgers and French fries. If each hamburger cost $2, each order of fries cost $1, and a total of eight items were ordered, how many hamburgers and how many orders of fries were purchased?

10. The ABC manufacturing company makes fidgets. The manager wanted to know the break-even volume. This is the volume (number of fidgets) at which revenue (income from sales) equals cost. Revenue is described by the equation $y = 5x$, where x is the number of fidgets. Cost is described by the equation $y = 4x + 200$. Draw the graph of each equation and find the break-even volume and the total revenue at the break-even point.

11. Find an equation of a line that will intersect the line $3x + 4y = 16$ on the x-axis. State, in step form, how you found this equation.

10·2 Solution by Substitution

Solving systems of equations by graphing can produce points of intersection that cannot always be read accurately. Ordered pairs that do not fall exactly on the intersection points of a coordinate grid can be only estimated. To find an accurate point of intersection, a number of algebraic methods can be used. The four that will be studied in this chapter are solving by graphing, substitution, elimination, and comparison. This section will deal with the **method of substitution** in which the expression for one of the variables from one equation is substituted directly into the other equation.

Example 1

Solve this system of equations. $3x + 18y = 12$ ①
$$x - 5y = 15 \quad ②$$

The second equation can be solved for x in terms of y by adding $5y$ to both sides. We then substitute the expression for x into the first equation, solve for y, and then solve for x.

From equation ②, $x - 5y = 15$
$$x = 15 + 5y$$

Substitute this expression for x into the first equation and solve for y.
$$3x + 18y = 12$$
$$3(15 + 5y) + 18y = 12$$
$$y = -1$$

Substitute $y = -1$ into $x - 5y = 15$ to solve for x.
$$x - 5(-1) = 15$$
$$x = 10$$

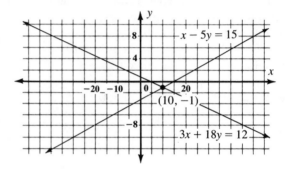

Therefore, the point of intersection of the two lines is the point $(10, -1)$.

When the solution to a system of equations has been found, either substitute the variables into the original equations to verify the results, or use a different method of solution to verify the point of intersection. Verifying is an important step in the solution to any system. Also note that either variable can be isolated and used to solve for the other.

Example 2

A 9% investment yielded $61 more than an 8% investment. The sum of the two investments was $2000. How much was invested at each rate?

Let x represent the amount invested at 9%.
Let y represent the amount invested at 8%.
Therefore, $x + y = 2000$, because the sum of the two investments is $2000. Also, $0.09x - 0.08y = 61$, because the difference of the return on the two investments is $61.
Solving the equation $x + y = 2000$, we get $y = 2000 - x$. The expression for y is substituted into the equation $0.09x - 0.08y = 61$ to solve for x.
$$0.09x - 0.08(2000 - x) = 61$$
$$0.17x = 221$$
$$x = 1300$$
Substituting 1300 for x into $y = 2000 - x$ will give a y-value of 700.

Therefore, $700 was invested at 8% and $1300 was invested at 9%.

Exercises

1. Verify the point of intersection for Example 2 by sketching the graphs of the lines.

2. Express x in terms of y in each equation.
a. $x - 6y = 7$ **b.** $2x - y = 10$
c. $3x + 5y = 17$ **d.** $5x - 7y = 19$

3. Express in the form $y = mx + b$.
a. $4x - y = 2$ **b.** $3y + x = 1$
c. $2x - 3y = 8$ **d.** $4x - 3y = 8$

4. When solving a pair of linear equations by the method of substitution, what are you finding?

5. In your own words, explain how the method of substitution works when solving a pair of linear equations.

6. In Exercise 1, you were asked to graph the two lines of Example 2 to verify the point of intersection. How else can the point of intersection be verified?

7. Solve each system of equations using the method of substitution. Verify your results.
a. $x + y = 18$ **b.** $x - 2y = -25$
$\quad\ x = 5y$ $\quad\ y = 3x$
c. $\quad\ a = 4b$ **d.** $\ m - n = 2$
$\quad b - 2a = 14$ $\quad 2n - m = 5$
e. $\ r - 6s = 7$ **f.** $\quad d - e = -1$
$\quad 12r - s = 13$ $\quad 3d - 5e = 21$
g. $5x + y = -3$ **h.** $\ 7x + y = 10$
$\quad x + 6y = 11$ $\quad 3x + 4y = 10$

8. Solve the system of equations using any method. Verify the results.
a. $-5m - 18n = 18$ **b.** $\ 4a - b = 5$
$\quad\ m + 22y = 1$ $\quad 2a + 3b = -1$
c. $8x - y = 2$ **d.** $\quad a + 2b = 7$
$\quad\ y - 2 = 4x$ $\quad 5a - 2b = 11$
e. $3x - 2y = 15$ **f.** $2a + 4b = 1$
$\quad x - \dfrac{y}{3} = 3$ $\quad a + 6b = 2.5$
g. $\quad\quad\ x + y = 700$ **h.** $\quad 2x - 7y = 21$
$\quad 0.01x + 0.05y = 27$ $\quad 0.07x + 17y = -51$

9. The masses of two blenders have a difference of 6. Together, their total mass is 28 kg. Find the mass of each blender.

10. One number exceeds another by 25. The difference between twice the larger and four times the smaller is 4. Find the numbers.

11. An investment manager invests $5000 for a client. Part is invested at 7% and the remainder at 12%. The total annual return on these investments is $425. Find the amount invested at each rate.

12. Tickets to a baseball game cost $5 for adults and $4 for students. If 1200 people attend the game and the receipts are $5150, how many students and how many adults paid admission?

13. Solve the system of equations. Verify the results.
a. $\dfrac{1}{2}x - \dfrac{2}{5}y = \dfrac{9}{10}$ **b.** $\dfrac{1}{3}x - \dfrac{1}{5}y = \dfrac{21}{5}$
$\quad \dfrac{1}{3}x - \dfrac{1}{4}y = \dfrac{2}{3}$ $\quad \dfrac{1}{5}x + \dfrac{1}{3}y = \dfrac{13}{3}$

14. A contractor paid 12 workers a total of $3680 for one week of work. Some of the workers were bricklayers who were paid $600 per week and the rest were general labourers who were paid $160 per week. How many workers were bricklayers and how many were general labourers?

15. Carlene bought a trail bike on sale for $276. She paid for the bike with $2 and $10 bills. If the number of $10 bills exceeded the number of $2 bills by six, then how many of each did she use?

16. Two compact disk players have a combined mass of 250 kg. Twice the mass of the heavier player exceeds three times the mass of the lighter by 55 kg. Find the mass of each compact disk player.

17. The average of two numbers is $\dfrac{29}{70}$. One half of their difference is $\dfrac{1}{70}$. Find the numbers.

10·3 Solution by Elimination

The **method of elimination** is a widely used method for solving systems of equations. This method makes use of equivalent systems formed by multiplying, dividing, adding, or subtracting the same quantity from each side of the equation. By adding or subtracting two equations, we will eliminate one of the variables and then solve for the other variable.

Example 1

Solve the system. $x + 2y = 5$ ①
$ x + y = 3$ ②

① − ② $\quad y = 2$
Substitute $y = 2$ into equation ②.

$x + 2 = 3$
$ x = 1$

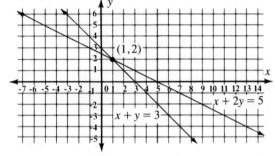

Therefore, the point of intersection of the two equations is $(1, 2)$.

Sometimes, neither of the variables can be "eliminated" directly, nor can we use the method of substitution as it involves fractions that are not easily substituted. Therefore, multiply one or both equations by the same nonzero number so that the numerical coefficients are the same.

Example 2

Solve the system. $4x - 3y = 5$
$ 3x - 2y = 8$

Understand the Problem
Find values for x and y to satisfy both equations simultaneously. To help with this method of solution, label the two original equations as equation ① and equation ②.

Carry Out the Plan
$4x - 3y = 5$ ①
$3x - 2y = 8$ ②
Multiply equation ① by 3 and equation ② by 4 to make each equation have a variable of $12x$.
① × 3 $\quad 12x - 9y = 15$ ③
② × 4 $\quad \underline{12x - 8y = 32}$ ④
④ − ③ $\qquad\qquad y = 17$
Substitute $y = 17$ into equation ① to solve for x.
$4x - 3(17) = 5$
$ x = 14$

Develop a Plan
Two basic properties are needed to solve a system by the method of elimination.

1. Any ordered pair that is the solution to the two equations simultaneously is also a solution to the sum or difference of the two equations.

2. The solution to two equations is not changed if both sides are multiplied by the same real, nonzero number.

Look Back
The point of intersection of the two lines is the ordered pair $(14, 17)$.

Verify.
$4(14) - 3(17) = 5$
$3(14) - 2(17) = 8$
Since the two equalities both are true, the solution to the system is verified.

Exercises

1. By what would you multiply the equations in Example 2 of the display if you were to "eliminate" the y-variable? Solve the system by eliminating the y-variable and compare the results. Are they the same?

2. The ordered pair $(8, 9)$ is a solution to the system $x + y = 17$ and $2x - 3y = -11$. Explain why $3x - 2y = 6$ also has a solution of $(8, 9)$.

3. Solve each system using the method of elimination. Verify the results. (*Hint*: Check for reasonableness by graphing.)

a. $x + y = 4$
$x - y = 16$

b. $x - 2y = 5$
$x + y = 8$

c. $5x + 3y = 14$
$2x - 3y = 0$

d. $2a + b = 3$
$3a - b = 7$

e. $3x + 4y = 11$
$3x - 5y = -16$

f. $2.5x + y = 7.5$
$-2.5x + 0.5y = 1.5$

4. When solving each system of equations,
  i) state the variable you would eliminate,
 ii) state the number by which you would multiply each term of the first equation,
iii) state the number by which you would multiply each term of the second equation, and
iv) solve the system of equations.

a. $2a - 4b = 6$
$3a - 2b = 13$

b. $5x + 3y = 14$
$2x + y = 6$

c. $3x + 7y = 27$
$5x + 2y = 16$

d. $5a + 6b = 17$
$6a + 5b = 12$

e. $15m + 7n = 29$
$9m + 15n = 39$

f. $14r - 3s = 29$
$6r + 17s = 35$

5. Solve by the method of elimination. (*Hint*: Find the Least Common Denominator of each pair of equations.)

$\frac{1}{2}x + \frac{1}{3}y = 4$ ①

$\frac{1}{4}x + \frac{1}{6}y = 4$ ②

6. Solve each system using the method of elimination. Verify your solution.

a. $2a + 3b = 20$
$3a + 2b = 15$

b. $x - y = 5$
$3x + 2y = 25$

7. Solve using elimination.

a. $5x + 2y = 24$
$3x - 4y = -22$

b. $3m - 2n = 5$
$m + 3n = 9$

c. $4a - 5b = 0$
$-5a + 6b = -2$

d. $4r - 3t = 36$
$2r + 5t = -8$

8. Solve the systems using any method.

a. $9d - 7e = 3$
$3d + 8e = -30$

b. $12x - 5y = -7$
$8x + 3y = -11$

c. $28x - 23y = 33$
$63x + 25y = 151$

d. $7a - 3b = 2$
$2a + 7b = 32$

e. $55m - 33n = 22$
$15m + 77n = 92$

f. $\frac{r}{5} + \frac{t}{2} = 5$
$r - t = 4$

9. Write the system of equations needed to solve each problem. Solve the system using the method of elimination.

a. Divide 63 into two parts whose difference is 19.

b. Marion cashed a cheque for $430 and asked the teller to give him only $20 and $50 bills. He received 20 bills. How many of each denomination did he receive?

c. During a school fund-raising campaign, Bill sold 10 toothbrush kits and 5 boxes of candles to raise $55 for the school. Elizabeth sold 15 toothbrush kits and 2 boxes of candles to raise $81 for the school. Find the price of one toothbrush kit and one box of candles.

10. Solve the system. $2x + 5y = 15$
$3x - 7y = 8$
Show that for every real number m and n, the solution satisfies the equation.
$m(2x + 5y - 15) + n(3x - 7y - 8) = 0$

11. Solve for x and y in terms of the other variables.

a. $x - y = p$
$2x + y = q$

b. $ax = by$
$bx + ay = v$

12. Solve.

a. $\frac{1}{4}a + \frac{1}{5}b = 6$
$\frac{1}{3}a + \frac{1}{6}b = 2$

b. $\frac{1}{2}m - \frac{1}{5}n = 4$
$\frac{1}{7}m + \frac{1}{15}n = 3$

c. $\frac{2}{3}a - \frac{1}{6}b = 0$
$\frac{1}{2}a + \frac{1}{4}b = 9$

d. $0.5x + 0.2y = -2.9$
$0.3x + 0.7y = -2.9$

10·4 Solution by Comparison

Three methods for solving systems of equations have been introduced so far: the methods of graphing to estimate a point of intersection, substitution, and elimination. In this section, a third algebraic method will be introduced, the **method of comparison**. This method allows you to compare two expressions that are equated to the same variable.

Example

Solve. $3x + 4y = 9$
$\qquad$ $2x - 3y = 6$

Understand the Problem
To solve the system, find the point of intersection of the two lines. Once again, label the equations as ① and ② respectively.

Develop a Plan
Both equations can be written in the form $y = mx + b$. Using the transitive property, the two expressions for y can be compared to solve for x. The value for x is then substituted into one of the equations to find the value for y.

Carry Out the Plan
$3x + 4y = 9$ ①
$2x - 3y = 6$ ②

From equation ①, $y = \dfrac{9 - 3x}{4}$.   ③

From equation ②, $y = \dfrac{2x - 6}{3}$.   ④

Comparing equations ③ and ④,
$$\frac{9 - 3x}{4} = \frac{2x - 6}{3}$$
$27 - 9x = 8x - 24$
$\qquad x = 3$
Substitute $x = 3$ into equation ④ to obtain $y = 0$.

Look Back
The solution to the system is the point $(3,0)$.

Verify.
$3(3) + 4(0) = 9$
$2(3) - 3(0) = 6$

Since both of these equations are true, the ordered pair $(3,0)$ is a solution to the system of equations.

The choice of which method to use is left to the individual. The choice might be based on the form in which the system of equations is written. There are no general rules that suggest one method should be used over another. It is important, regardless of which method you decide to use, to verify the solution either by solving the same system in a different manner, or by substituting the value of the variables into the original system of equations.

Exercises

1. In your own words, outline the method of comparison.

2. Why is it important to verify your solutions?

3. Solve these systems using the method of comparison.

a. $y = 3x + 2$
$\quad\ y = 7x - 10$

b. $y = 5x - 9$
$\quad\ y = 3x - 8$

c. $y = x - 6$
$\quad\ y = 3x + 2$

d. $y = 5x - 4$
$\quad\ y = 7x + 22$

4. Solve using the method of comparison. Verify your results.

a. $3x + 2y = 12$
$x - 2y = -4$

b. $m + n = 3$
$m - n = 5$

c. $a + 3b = -5$
$2a - b = -3$

d. $x + 2y = 6$
$y - 2x = 8$

e. $3x = 4 - 2y$
$3y = -4 - 2x$

f. $\frac{1}{2}p + 2q = 14$
$p - \frac{1}{4}q = -6$

5. Solve these systems using any method. Explain why you chose this method of solution over another method. Verify your results.

a. $4r - 5t = -2$
$3r - 2t = 0$

b. $2a = \frac{1}{2}(b - 3)$
$2b = 3 + a$

c. $5x + 3y = 6$
$6y - 12 = -10x$

d. $a + 3b = 3.5$
$2a + 4b = 3$

e. $2x - 3y = 1$
$6x - 5 = 9y$

f. $2m - n = 5$
$3m + 2n = -4$

6. A.T., the "Mathematics Wizard", claimed that "the method of comparison is superior because we are always comparing two quantities that are identical." Do you agree with A.T.? Explain.

Write the system of equations needed to solve each problem in Exercises 7 to 10. Solve each system and verify the results.

7. The difference between two numbers is 12. One eighth of their sum is 9. What are the numbers?

8. The cost of renting a car from Company A is $18/d plus $0.12/km, while from Company B the cost is $14/d plus $0.15/km. Find the number of kilometres driven for which the cost of renting the cars will be the same.

9. A bookstore receives a shipment of 60 paperback and hardbound copies of the latest mathematics text. The total value of the shipment was $380. The paperbacks cost $2.25 each and the hardbound texts cost $14.50 each. Find the number of paperbacks and hardbound texts in the shipment.

10. A photo technician has a 7% and a 15% developer solution. Twenty-four litres of a 10% solution are needed for a job. How much of each should be mixed?

11. Solve each system.

a. $2x + 3y = 17$
$3x - 5y = 12$

b. $x - y = 9$
$7x + 3y = 17$

c. $0.5x - 6.2y = 12.8$
$3.5x - 7.8y = 19.2$

d. $4.4x - 2.1y = -0.2$
$0.3x - 2.1y = 5.5$

e. $x + y = 8$
$x - y = 7$

f. $3x - y = 17$
$5x - 1.8y = 12$

12. Use the method of comparison to show that the system of equations $2x + 2y = -4$ and $-x - y = -2$ has no solution.
a. Graph the two straight lines.
b. How are these two graphs related?
c. State a general rule for systems of equations that are related in this manner.

13. The coffee machine dispenses coffee without cream and sugar for $0.50 per cup and coffee with cream and sugar for $0.55 per cup. At the end of a day, 25 cups had been used and $13.35 was in the machine. How many cups of coffee with cream and sugar had been sold?

14. Solve each system for x and y.

a. $x - y = n$
$x + y = m$

b. $x - y = a$
$x + 2y = b$

c. $ax + 2by = 4$
$ax - by = 6$

d. $ax + by = a^2$
$bx + ay = b^2$

15. The sum of the digits of a two-digit number is 9. If the digits are reversed, the resulting number is 9 more than four times the original number. Find the number.

Braintickler

The sum of the angles in a triangle is 180°. This can be proven deductively using parallel lines. Intuitively this can be done by cutting out a triangle from a piece of paper and folding the angles. Cut out a triangle and fold the angles in such a manner so that they obviously total 180°.

10·5 Systems in Three Variables

The method of elimination can be extended to solve three equations in three unknowns. This method requires the elimination of a variable using a pair of equations, and then eliminating the same variable using a different pair of equations. This will leave a linear system of two equations in two unknowns. Then, one of the methods studied can be used to solve this system of two equations.

Example

Solve.
$$x + 2y + z = 8 \quad ①$$
$$2x - y + 5z = 4 \quad ②$$
$$x + 4y - z = 12 \quad ③$$

Eliminate the x-terms from equations ① and ②.

① × 2	$2x + 4y + 2z = 16$	④
②	$2x - y + 5z = 4$	②
④ − ②	$5y - 3z = 12$	⑤

Eliminate the y-terms from equations ⑤ and ⑥.

	$5y - 3z = 12$	⑤
	$2y - 2z = 4$	⑥
⑤ × 2	$10y - 6z = 24$	⑦
⑥ × 5	$10y - 10z = 20$	⑧
⑦ − ⑧	$4z = 4$	
	$z = 1$	

Eliminate the x-terms from equations ① and ③.

③	$x + 4y - z = 12$	
①	$x + 2y - z = 8$	
③ − ①	$2y - 2z = 4$	⑥

Substitute $z = 1$ in ⑥.
$$2y - 2(1) = 4$$
$$y = 3$$
Substitute in ①.
$$x + 2(3) + 1 = 8$$
$$x = 1$$

The solution is $(1, 3, 1)$. The verification should be done by the student by substituting $x = 1$, $y = 3$, and $z = 1$ into each of the original equations.

Exercises

1. Could a different variable, other than x, be "eliminated" in the example in the display? Explain.

2. Solve each system of equations and verify the solution.

a. $a + 2b + c = 16$
$2a - b = 2$
$b + c = 6$

b. $x + y = 1$
$2x + 2y + z = 7$
$3y - z = 1$

c. $x + 3y + z = -13$
$5x - y = 15$
$3x + 4z = 6$

d. $3a + c = 16$
$-3b + 2c = 5$
$4a - 2b - 3c = -5$

3. In your own words, outline the method used to solve a system of three equations and three unknowns.

4. Solve each system of equations. In part **a**, explain each step as it is completed. Verify all results.

a. $2a - b + 4c = 17$
$3a + 4b - c = -1$
$4a + 3b + 2c = 11$

b. $6a + 2b - 5c = 13$
$3a + 3b - 2c = 13$
$a + 5b - 3c = 26$

c. $x + y - z = -5$
$x + y + z = 9$
$x - y + z = -1$

d. $2m - n + p = 5$
$m + 2n + p = 12$
$3m + n - 2p = 1$

e. $2a - 5c = -18$
$7b - 8c = -65$
$3a - 2b = 2$

f. $m - n = -3$
$n - p = -2$
$m + n = -1$

5. Eighteen tonnes of steel is to be made from three types of ingots, A, B, and C. The final product must contain 990 units of iron and 1080 units of carbon. The number of units of iron and carbon per tonne is given by the ordered pairs: A(30, 60), B(20, 80), C(80, 50). Find the number of tonnes of each ingot that must be used to make the steel.

10·6 Classifying Systems

You have been studying linear systems of equations that have unique solutions. Such a system of equations is classified as **independent and consistent**. However, some linear systems have no solution. The graphs of **inconsistent** systems show two parallel lines. Still other systems have an infinite number of solutions. Such systems are **dependent and consistent**. Graphs of these show the lines are coincident; that is, they lie one on top of the other. The three types of systems are illustrated.

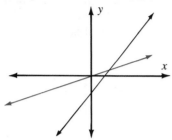

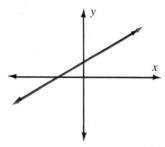

Independent and consistent
One point of intersection

Inconsistent
No points of intersection

Dependent and consistent
All points of intersection

Exercises

1. Identify the graph as either independent and consistent, dependent and consistent, or inconsistent. Explain your choice.

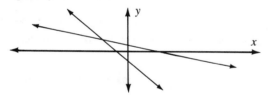

2. State whether each will result in an independent and consistent, inconsistent, or dependent and consistent solution.

a. a system of equations having at least two solutions
b. a system of equations having exactly one solution
c. a system of equations where the equations have the same slope and a different y-intercept

3. State whether these systems of equations are independent and consistent, inconsistent, or dependent and consistent.

a. $x + y = 6$
  $x - y = 2$
b. $x - 4y = 9$
  $-x + 4y = 9$
c. $3x - 2y = 7$
  $6x - 4y = 14$
d. $y = -x + 3$
  $y = -x + 1$

4. Classify each system as independent and consistent, inconsistent, or dependent and consistent. Solve where possible.

a. $x + 5y = 0$
  $3x - 2y = 4$
b. $2x - 3y = 5$
  $4x + y = 6$
c. $x + 2y = 3$
  $2x - y = 2$
d. $x + 2y = 8$
  $3x + 6y = 24$

5. In a system of two linear equations, what is the relationship between the y-intercepts, the x-intercepts, and the slopes of the two lines if they are independent and consistent, inconsistent, or dependent and consistent?

6. A.T., the "Mathematics Wizard", stated that "one type of system is classified as dependent and consistent because the value of y depends on the value of x and vice versa." Is A.T. correct? Explain.

Using the Library

Systems of equations that are dependent and consistent or independent and consistent often are labelled as dependent and independent. Explain why this is true.

10·7 Non-Linear Systems I

We have seen four methods that enable us to solve systems of linear equations. These same methods can be used to solve systems of equations where one of the equations is linear and the other is a quadratic equation. Such a system is called a **linear-quadratic system**. To visualize such a system, it is necessary to sketch the graphs of the standard quadratics.

In Chapters 8 and 9, you graphed the quadratic equation that produced parabolas: equations of the form $y = ax^2 + bx + c$. You also have been introduced to hyperbolas of the form $xy = c$, where the parabola does not touch either axis. For graphical solutions of linear-quadratic systems, you will be required to sketch the graph of ellipses, circles, and hyperbolas. These have the general form of $ax^2 + by^2 = c^2$, $x^2 + y^2 = c^2$, and $ax^2 - by^2 = c^2$ respectively.

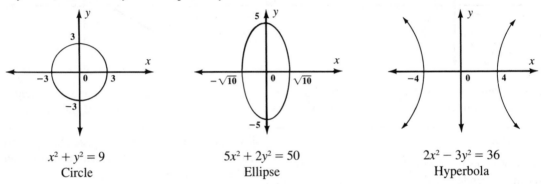

$x^2 + y^2 = 9$	$5x^2 + 2y^2 = 50$	$2x^2 - 3y^2 = 36$
Circle	Ellipse	Hyperbola

Example

A spacecraft on a linear trajectory, defined by the equation $2x + 5y = 20$, intercepts the elliptical orbit of a comet, defined by the equation $16x^2 + 100y^2 = 1600$. Find the point(s) of intersection of the spacecraft and the comet.

The method of comparison will not yield a solution because the two expressions are not of the same degree. As a result, the method of substitution will be used.

$$2x + 5y = 20 \quad ①$$
$$16x^2 + 100y^2 = 1600 \quad ②$$

From equation ①, $y = \dfrac{20 - 2x}{5}$.

Substitute $\dfrac{20 - 2x}{5}$ for y in equation ②.

$$16x^2 + 100\left(\frac{20 - 2x}{5}\right)^2 = 1600$$
$$x^2 - 10x = 0$$
$$x(x - 10) = 0$$
$$x = 0 \text{ or } x = 10$$

Substitute each value for x into $2x - 5y = 20$, the linear equation, and solve for y; $y = 4$ and $y = 0$. The points of intersection are $(0,4)$ and $(10,0)$.

Exercises

1. Explain why the method of elimination cannot be used when solving the equation in the example.

2. A straight line may intersect a curve of a quadratic in one point, more than one point, or not at all. Estimate the solution to each system and verify your estimate by substituting into the two equations.

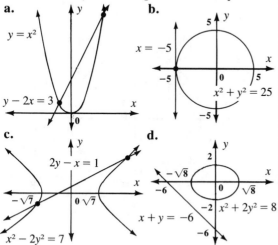

a. $y = x^2$; $y - 2x = 3$

b. $x = -5$; $x^2 + y^2 = 25$

c. $2y - x = 1$; $x^2 - 2y^2 = 7$

d. $x + y = -6$; $x^2 + 2y^2 = 8$

3. For each system,
  i) copy the appropriate graph from Exercise 2 on a Cartesian coordinate grid,
  ii) draw the line represented by the linear equation,
  iii) estimate the points of intersection, and
  iv) verify your calculations.

a. $x^2 + y^2 = 25$
   $x + 7y = 25$

b. $x^2 - 2y^2 = 7$
   $y = 3$

c. $x^2 + 2y^2 = 8$
   $x - y = 2$

d. $x^2 + 2y^2 = 8$
   $4x - 3y = 12$

4. Solve each system of equations algebraically and graphically check the reasonableness of the results.

a. $y = x^2$
   $2x - y = -3$

b. $3x^2 + 7x = 5$
   $x + 3 = 0$

c. $xy = 10$
   $y = 4x + 5$

d. $xy = 10$
   $y = 3x + 1$

5. The orbit of a weather satellite approximates a circle with an equation of $x^2 + y^2 = 17$. In the same plane is a space probe on a path with an equation of $x + y = 3$. Will the two paths cross? If so, at what point?

6. Solve the system of equations algebraically. Verify your solution by copying the appropriate diagram on a coordinate grid, sketching the linear equation, and estimating the points of intersection.

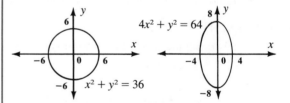

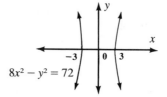

a. $4x^2 + y^2 = 64$
   $2x - 3y = 24$

b. $x^2 + y^2 = 36$
   $x + y = 6$

c. $y = x + 2$
   $x^2 + y^2 = 36$

d. $8x^2 - y^2 = 72$
   $x + y = 3$

e. $y = 8$
   $4x^2 + y^2 = 64$

f. $x - y = -6$
   $8x^2 - y^2 = 72$

Historical Note

Dr. Ursula M. Franklin (1921-   )
Dr. Franklin was born in Munich, Germany, on September 16, 1921. She was educated at the Technical University of Berlin and did post-doctoral studies at the University of Toronto. In 1967, she was the first woman to be appointed to the University of Toronto's Department of Metallurgy and Materials Science.

Dr. Franklin has been involved with studies on the effect of Strontium 90 on the teeth of children, has assisted in the development of the science policy for the Science Council of Canada and the Natural Sciences and Engineering Research Council of Canada, and has been a leader in the field of Archaeometry.

Research the field of Archaeometry and write a short essay describing the subjects which are studied.

10·8 Non-Linear Systems II

In this section, you will learn how to solve the **quadratic-quadratic system** of equations. Notice that there are no linear equations. We will use the methods from the previous sections.

Example 1

Graph this quadratic-quadratic system over the set of real numbers and find the points of intersection.

$6x^2 - 2y^2 = 4$ ①
$x^2 + y^2 = 34$ ②

Since the degrees of x (and y) are the same for both equations, the method of elimination can be used to find the value(s) of x and y.

② × 2 $2x^2 + 2y^2 = 68$ ③
         $6x^2 - 2y^2 = 4$ ①

③ + ① $8x^2 = 72$
             $x^2 = 9$

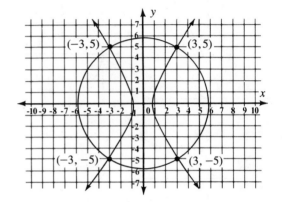

Therefore, $x = \pm 3$.

Substitute -3 and 3 for x into equation ② to find the value(s) of y.

For $x = -3$,   For $x = 3$,
$9 + y^2 = 34$ $9 + y^2 = 34$
   $y = \pm 5$ $y = \pm 5$

Therefore, the points of intersection are at $(-3, -5)$, $(-3, 5)$, $(3, -5)$, and $(3, 5)$.

Example 2

Leigh purchased a number of practise golf balls for $25. If they had cost $0.25 a piece less, she could have purchased 5 more golf balls for the same price. Find the cost of each golf ball.

Let n represent the number of golf balls purchased.
Let c represent the cost of one golf ball in cents.

$$nc = 2500 \quad ①$$
$$(n + 5)(c - 25) = 2500 \quad ②$$

From equation ①, solve for one variable in terms of the other and then substitute into equation ② to find the value of the isolated variable.

From equation ①, $n = \dfrac{2500}{c}$.   Substitute $\dfrac{2500}{c}$ into equation ②.

$\left(\dfrac{2500}{c} + 5\right)(c - 25) = 2500$ ⟨ Remove the brackets. Recall the FOIL method. ⟩

$2500 - \dfrac{62\,500}{c} + 5c - 125 = 2500$ ⟨ Multiply every term by c and simplify. ⟩

$5c^2 - 125c - 62\,500 = 0$
$c^2 - 25c - 12\,500 = 0$
$(c - 125)(c + 100) = 0$
$\therefore c = 125$ or $c = -100$

Each golf ball costs either $1.25 or $-$1.00. Since the price of an object cannot be negative, the negative solution is rejected, and each golf ball costs $1.25.

278

Exercises

1. Estimate the solution set in each diagram. Verify by substituting into both equations.

a.

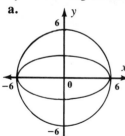

$$x^2 + y^2 = 36$$
$$x^2 + 5y^2 = 36$$

b.

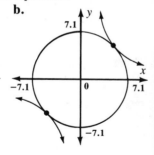

$$x^2 + y^2 = 50$$
$$xy = 25$$

2. Which method, substitution or elimination, would you use to solve each system? Explain your choice, outline the procedure of your solution, and solve the system.

a. $5x - y = 17$
 $xy = 12$

b. $2a^2 + 3b = 30$
 $a^2 + 3b = 21$

c. $2x^2 + y^2 = 32$
 $y^2 - x^2 = 5$

d. $x^2 + y^2 = 8$
 $xy = 4$

e. $3x^2 - y^2 = 5$
 $x^2 + 2y^2 = 3$

f. $x^2 + y^2 = 16$
 $y = x^2 - 4$

3. Sketch the graphs of a system of quadratic equations to illustrate the intersection of an ellipse and a circle with

a. 4 intersection points.
b. 3 intersection points.
c. 2 intersection points.
d. 0 intersection points.

4. A produce manager paid $120 for a shipment of oranges. The shipment contained 8 spoiled oranges which were discarded. The remaining oranges were sold for $236 which produced a profit of $0.25 on each orange. How many oranges were in the original shipment?

5. Two crop-dusting planes were used to spray a field. Plane A sprays a tract 22 m wider than Plane B, but it flys 30 m/s slower. Each plane sprays 1320 m²/s. Find the width of the tract each plane sprays.

6. If $xy = 17$ and $-x - y = -12$, then find $\dfrac{1}{x} + \dfrac{1}{y}$.

7. A student saved $600 for a vacation. His plan was to spend the same amount each day of the vacation. A last-minute change of plans reduced the vacation time by 4 d and increased the amount spent each day by $25, thus spending all $600. How many vacation days did he take?

8. A customer pays $640 interest on a loan each year. If the rate of interest was increased by 2% and the loan reduced by $1600, the interest would be the same. What is the amount of the loan and the rate of interest?

9. Solve these systems of equations. Verify your results graphically.

a. $y = x^2$
 $y = 3x^2 + 13x - 7$

b. $y = 3x^2 + 2x + 1$
 $y = 7x^2 - 2x + 2$

10. The orbit of a meteor is approximated by the curve $y^2 = 9 - 3x$. Two spacecraft, on the same plane, are on each of the arms of the curve $xy = 1$. One spacecraft has a better opportunity of intersecting the meteor than the other. Why?

11. It is known that a rational number raised to an exponent that also is a rational number is a rational number. Is it possible for an irrational number raised to an exponent that also is irrational to have a rational value?

12. Find two numbers whose sum is 8 and the sum of the reciprocals is $\dfrac{8}{15}$.

Using the Library

It is important in mathematics to be able to draw diagrams. Albrecht Dürer was a mathematician and an artist. Prepare a brief report outlining some of the points that tie art and mathematics together. If possible, refer to a copy of Dürer's engraving "Melencholia I".

279

10·9 Inequalities

A plane can be divided into three distinct regions by a curve. For example, the graph of $y = x^2$ is shown. The plane is divided into three distinct regions by the graph. There is the shaded part, $y > x^2$, the curve itself, $y = x^2$, and the nonshaded part, $y < x^2$.

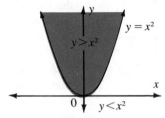

Example

A ship's radar scans an area defined by the inequality $x^2 + y^2 \le 81$. The ocean, not including the straight stretch of coastline, is represented by the inequality $3x - y < 12$. Graph the inequalities and shade the region of the ocean scanned by the radar.

Understand the Problem

A radar scans a circular area defined at its limits by $x^2 + y^2 = 81$. The coastline starts with the equation $3x - y = 12$. Recall that a dotted line is used for $<$ and $>$; while a solid line is used for $\le$ and $\ge$ in an inequality.

Develop a Plan

Graph and shade the inequality that represents the circular inequality scanned by the radar. Then graph and shade the region representing the ocean. The area that is common to both regions is the region of the ocean that is covered by the radar.

Carry Out the Plan

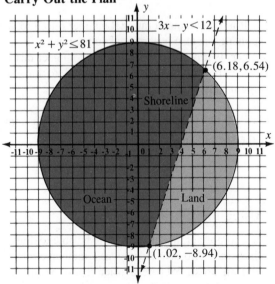

Look Back

The double-shaded area, including the solid line, is the region of ocean covered by the radar. This question requires you to interpret what is being asked and to represent it on the graph. Be careful to ensure that you read the question and understand it before a solution is attempted. Did we include the shoreline? Did we include the boundary of the circular region?

Notice on the graph that the points of intersection of the radar and the coastline have been included. When graphing any two systems of equations, it is important to place all points of intersection of the curves on the graph.

Exercises

1. State whether the boundary line will be solid or dotted on the graph for each inequality.

a. $x + y \geq 2$ **b.** $x^2 + y^2 > 4$
c. $y < 3x + 1$ **d.** $y \leq x^2 + 3$
e. $4x^2 + y^2 < 36$ **f.** $5x + 7y \geq 10$

2. Graph each inequality on a separate axis.

a. $x + y \leq 1$ **b.** $x < y$
c. $y \geq 5$ **d.** $x \geq -3$
e. $y < -2$ **f.** $x - 2y \leq 0$
g. $2x - y > 5$ **h.** $3x + 4y < 12$

3. A.T., the "Mathematics Wizard", stated that "the intersection of $x \geq 2$ and $x < y$ is the area shaded in the diagram. This is because we show
  i) the solid line $x = 2$,
  ii) the region defined by $x > 2$,
  iii) the dotted line $x = y$,
  iv) the shaded region $x < y$, and
  v) the intersection of the two shaded regions as the solution set." Is A.T. correct? Explain.

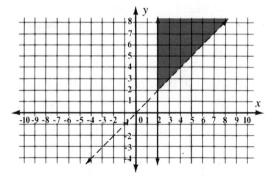

4. Graph the intersection of these regions. (*Hint*: The symbol "∩" means intersection.)

a. $\{(x,y) | x > y \ \cap \ x \leq 2\}$
b. $\{(x,y) | 2x < y \ \cap \ 4x + y \leq 8\}$
c. $\{(x,y) | 4x + 2y \leq 12 \ \cap \ 2x + 4y \leq 12\}$
d. $\{(x,y) | 5x + 2y \leq 10 \ \cap \ 2x - 4y \geq 8\}$

5. A submarine's sonar covers an area described by $x^2 + y^2 \leq 25$. The sonar of a second ship covers an area described by $y > x^2 - 9$ and $y < 4$. Graph the inequality and show the region covered by both sonars.

6. Graph each quadratic inequality on a separate grid.

a. $y \geq x^2 + 2$ **b.** $x < y^2$
c. $x^2 + y^2 \leq 16$ **d.** $x^2 + y^2 > 25$
e. $9x^2 + 4y^2 \leq 36$ **f.** $xy \geq 8$

7. Graph.

a. $x^2 + y^2 < 81$ **b.** $3x^2 + y^2 > 48$
  $2x^2 + y^2 \geq 90$ $y^2 < 4x$

8. A searchlight illuminates a region bounded by the inequality $y \leq \frac{1}{2}x^2 + 2$. A fence, the same height as the searchlight and described by the equation $x - 2y = -12$, cuts across this region. Shade the region in which the shadow of the fence is cast.

9. A radar scans a region defined by $x^2 + y^2 \leq 25$. A jet flies a path described by $4y + x^2 = 25$. Sketch the graphs to show the part of the jet's route that is picked up on radar.

10. A plane is on a path described by $y = x^2 - 4$. Restricted airspace is defined by the equation $y \leq -2x - 1$. Show the portion of the plane's flight that is in restricted airspace and find the coordinates at which the plane enters and leaves this restricted space.

11. Two dangerous coral reefs are defined by the equation $x^2 - 2y^2 \leq 7$. A ship is on a course defined by the equation $5y - 4x = 10$. Is the ship's course dangerous? Explain.

12. Sketch the graph of these inequalities.

a. $\{(x,y) | 3x - 4y \leq 6 \ \cap \ y \leq -x + 3\}$
b. $\{(x,y) | x - y \geq 3 \ \cap \ x^2 + y^2 < 36\}$
c. $\{(x,y) | y^2 > x - 2 \ \cap \ x^2 + y^2 \geq 4\}$
d. $\{(x,y) | y \geq x^2 - 4 \ \cap \ y^2 \leq x - 4\}$
e. $\{(x,y) | 4x^2 + 25y^2 \leq 100 \ \cap \ y > x^2 - 8\}$
f. $\{(x,y) | x^2 + y^2 \leq 9 \ \cap \ 25x^2 + 9y^2 \leq 225\}$

10·10 Linear Programming

Problems arise daily in industry, trade, commerce, and business in which decisions are made that will maximize profits while at the same time minimizing costs. The branch of mathematics that will help make these decisions is **linear programming**.

Example

A manufacturer has two plants making stereo systems and video recorders. In the Red Deer plant, workers must work 5 d on each stereo system and 2 d on each video recorder. In the Lethbridge plant, workers must work 3 d on each stereo system or video system produced. The Red Deer plant has 180 employee work days per week available, while the Lethbridge plant has 135 employee work days per week available. If the manufacturer makes $300 profit on each stereo system and $200 profit on each video recorder, then how many of each should be produced per week to maximize profit?

Understand the Problem

Set up a table showing the relevant data. In linear programming, this is often the best way to summarize data.

	Stereo	Video	Time Constraints
Red Deer	5 d	2 d	180 work d/week
Lethbridge	3 d	3 d	135 work d/week
Profit	$300	$200	/////////

Carry Out the Plan

The quantity to be maximized is the profit.
$P = 300x + 200y$
Because it is impossible to produce negative numbers of stereo and video systems, $x \geq 0$ and $y \geq 0$.
The time spent working at Red Deer and Lethbridge cannot exceed 180 d and 135 d respectively. Therefore, the other restrictions are $5x + 2y \leq 180$ and $3x + 3y \leq 135$.

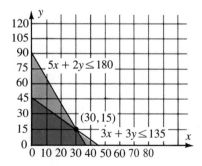

Number of Video Systems

Number of Stereo Systems

Develop a Plan

Identify two variables that will represent the number of stereos produced each week and the number of video systems produced each week. Set up a profit equation, graph the equations of the constraints, and check the vertices to find the maximum profit.

Let x represent the number of stereo systems.
Let y represent the number of video systems.

Look Back

Any point in the double-shaded area of the graph will satisfy all these restrictions. However, we must maximize profit. Therefore, only the extremes need to be checked for maximum profit. Set up a chart to show the profit at each vertex.

Vertex	Profit: $P = 300x + 200y$
(0,0)	$300(0) + 200(0) = 0$
(0,45)	$300(0) + 200(45) = 9000$
(30,15)	$300(30) + 200(15) = 12\ 000$
(36,0)	$300(36) + 200(0) = 10\ 800$

The maximum profit will be $12 000 per week if there are 30 stereo systems and 15 video systems produced.

Exercises

1. In your own words, outline the process of linear programming.

2. For these four inequalities: $x \geq 0$, $y \geq 0$, $5x + y \leq 20$, and $3x + 2y - 30 \leq 0$,
a. graph the single region described by these inequalities,
b. identify each vertex of the region,
c. check each vertex to determine the values of x and y that will give a maximum profit if profit is defined by the equation $P = 18x + 3y$.

3. A company makes an unknown number of Type A alarm clocks and an unknown number of Type B alarm clocks. Each Type A clock must be processed on Machine 1 for 4 h and Machine 2 for 2 h. Each Type B clock must be processed on Machine 1 for 2 h and Machine 2 for $4\frac{2}{3}$ h. Neither machine is to be used more than 22 h.
a. Find all the possibilities for the maximum number of each type of alarm clock that could be made within these restrictions.
b. Find the maximum profit if $5 is made on each Type A clock and $3 is made on each Type B clock.
c. Find the maximum profit if $6.50 is made on each Type A clock and $7.25 is made on each Type B clock.

4. An airline has a sum of money with which to purchase aircraft. The board of directors gave the following restrictions on the purchase.
 i) At least twenty million dollars is to be spent on single or twin engine aircraft.
ii) The airline needs at least 14 new single and/or twin engine aircraft.
Each single engine aircraft costs one million dollars and each twin engine craft costs two million dollars.
a. Write four inequalities that express the restrictions on the purchase.
b. Graph the solution set of the inequalities. State the coordinates of the vertices.

5. A small business in Victoria produces stained glass designs. In order to stay in business, they must produce at least 25 designs each day. The most they are able to sell in a day is 32. The work is done by a combination of skilled artists and part-time student help. An artist can produce five pieces per day and a student three pieces per day. There are always at least three skilled workers on the job and the employer is committed to having at least one student on the job as well. If the skilled employees earn $75/d and the students earn $45/d, then how many of each should be working in order to keep the labour costs to a minimum?

6. A school band plans to raise funds by selling 250 g bags of a mixture of peanuts and cashews. They save up $1000 to purchase the nuts. Peanuts cost $1/kg and cashews $3/kg. An acceptable mix must contain no more than 5 times as much peanuts as cashews. They must also produce a total of not less than 500 kg of nuts.
a. Draw a graph showing the possible amounts of each kind of nut they can buy.
b. If the mix they plan to sell costs them 50¢ per bag, what is the amount of each kind of nut they should buy to maximize their receipts?

7. Edna is organizing a Run and Ride event involving 75 runners and 33 riders with the entry fees being donated to charity. The entry fee for a rider must be at least as much as that for the runners; the most it can be is $2 more than the runner's fee. The total of the two fees cannot exceed $9 and the fee for each must be at least $3. What fee for each runner and each rider will produce the most money for the charity?

8. Set up your own linear programming question. Challenge one of your classmates to answer this question. If they fail to give a correct answer, then demonstrate where they went wrong.

10·11 Computer Application— Solving Pairs of Equations

A computer can be used to solve pairs of equations. This program will solve a quadratic-quadratic system of equations for x and then for y. The equations solved by this program are of the form $Ax^2 + By^2 = C$ and $Dx^2 + Ey^2 = F$.

```
10 REM A PROGRAM TO SOLVE A QUADRATIC-QUADRATIC SYSTEM
20 INPUT "THE COEFFICIENTS OF THE FIRST EQUATION ARE ";
A, B, C
30 INPUT "THE COEFFICIENTS OF THE SECOND EQUATION ARE ";
D, E, F
40 PRINT "EQUATION 1 IS "; A; "X ∧ 2 + "; B; "Y ∧ 2 = "; C
50 PRINT "EQUATION 2 IS "; D; "X ∧ 2 + "; E; "Y ∧ 2 = "; F
60 IF B * D - E * A = 0 THEN 120
70 LET S1 = SQR(ABS((F * B - C * E) / (B * D - E * A)))
80 LET S2 = SQR(ABS((D * C - A * F) / (B * D - E * A)))
90 PRINT "THE POINTS OF INTERSECTION ARE "
100 PRINT "("; S1; ", "; S2; "), ("; S1; ", "; -S2; "),
("; -S1; ", "; S2; "), ("; -S1; ", "; -S2; ")"
110 GOTO 130
120 PRINT "NO SOLUTION"
130 END
```

Exercises

1. Explain the purpose of these lines from the program.
a. line 60   **b.** line 70
c. line 80   **d.** line 100

2. Why is it important to have line 60 in the program?

3. Show how S1 and S2 are arrived at by solving these equations for x and y. (*Hint*: Use the method of elimination.)
$$Ax^2 + By^2 = C$$
$$Dx^2 + Ey^2 = F$$

4. Run the program in the display to solve these quadratic-quadratic systems of equations.
a. $3x^2 + 2y^2 = 49$ **b.** $2x^2 + 3y^2 = 26$
$\ x^2 + y^2 = 12$ $\ 2x^2 + 2y^2 = 22$
c. Verify the computer output algebraically.
d. Why does the computer take a few seconds to run the program?

5. Predict what the computer will print if $3x^2 + 2y^2 = 12$ and $3x^2 + 2y^2 = 20$ are input.
a. Explain your prediction.
b. Run the program using these equations to verify your prediction.

6. For the program in Exercise 5, part **b**, what would happen if line 60 was deleted? Explain after running the program with line 60 deleted.

7. Run the program in the display to solve these quadratic-quadratic systems of equations.
a. $9x^2 + y^2 = 9$ **b.** $x^2 + 16y^2 = 16$
$\ x^2 + y^2 = 1$ $\ x^2 + y^2 = 4$

8. A student decided to do all homework on a computer disk because it saved on storage space for notes, time in searching for information, and study time for all examinations. Write a short essay stating whether homework for all classes should be done on computer disks.

10·12 Chapter Review

1. Write each equation in the form $y = mx + b$. State the slope and y-intercept of the equation.
a. $3x - y = 6$
b. $y = -8$
c. $2x + 4y = 16$
d. $7x + 5y = 35$

2. Graph each system of equations and estimate the solution set.
a. $x + y = 10$
$x - y = 4$
b. $3x + y = 11$
$x = -2y - 3$

3. In your own words, describe the methods of comparison, elimination, and substitution for solving a system of linear equations.

4. State the value of m which makes each system inconsistent.
a. $y = mx - 3$
$4y = -4x + 3$
b. $4x + 5y = -10$
$y - mx = 0$

5. Ralph rented seven different video cassettes for $67. One type of cassette had a rental cost of $11 and the other had a rental cost of $9. How many of each type did Ralph purchase?

6. Solve each system of equations by the method of substitution. Verify the results.
a. $8x - 2y = 16$
$y - x = -2$
b. $3x - 4y = 16$
$-6x + 8y = -32$
c. $x + y = 2$
$x - y = 2$
d. $3x + 4y = 5$
$6x = 8y$

7. Tickets to a football game cost $19 for preferred seating and $12 for general admission. If 20 000 fans attend the game, and the total receipts for the game are $317 000, then how many $12 tickets were sold?

8. Solve each system of equations.
a. $a + 2b = 17$
$2a - 2b = 16$
b. $3x - 5y = -49$
$-15x + 35y = -55$
c. $\dfrac{x}{3} + \dfrac{y}{2} = 10$
$\dfrac{y}{4} + \dfrac{x}{2} = 7$
d. $\dfrac{3}{x} - \dfrac{8}{y} = -3$
$\dfrac{6}{x} + \dfrac{16}{y} = 2$

9. Solve each system of equations. State whether the system is dependent and consistent, independent and consistent, or inconsistent.
a. $a + 2b + 3c = 0$
$a - 2c - 3 = 0$
$b + c - 1 = 0$
b. $4x + 3y + z = -12$
$2x + y - z = -6$
$x + 5y + 3z = 7$

10. Graph each system of equations. Estimate the points of intersection of the graphs.
a. $x^2 + y^2 = 10$
$xy = 4$
b. $y = x^2 - 4$
$x + y = 16$

11. Verify your points of intersection for Exercise 10 by solving each system algebraically.

12. Solve.
a. $y = x - 5$
$x^2 + y = 7$
b. $y = 4$
$y = -x^2 - 3$

13. Steel bridge girders are assembled in the shape of a right triangle having a hypotenuse of 32.5 m. If the perimeter of a single girder is 75 m, then find the length of each leg of the girder.

14. Bill purchased a number of pens for $6.00. If the pens were $0.10 a piece less, Bill could have purchased 2 more for the same price. Find the cost of each pen.

15. Graph the intersection of the two regions.
a. $\{(x,y) \mid x + y \geq 2 \ \cap \ x - y < 0\}$
b. $\{(x,y) \mid y \leq -x^2 + 5 \ \cap \ y \geq 0\}$

16. When maximizing profit and minimizing cost using the process of linear programming, you are finding the points of intersection and substituting these values into the profit equation. Why do we substitute only these vertices and not every point from the shaded region?

17. Graph the inequality. $x^2 - 25 < 0$

285

10·13 Chapter Test

1. In your own words, state the difference between a dependent and consistent system of equations, an independent and consistent system of equations, and an inconsistent system of equations. Use graphs to help with your explanations.

2. When solving a system of equations using the method of sketching a graph, why is the solution only estimated and not an exact solution? In other words, why is an algebraic solution more accurate than a graphed solution?

3. Find the slope, the y-intercept, and the x-intercept of $4x - 2y = -5$.

4. Classify this system of equations. Verify your classification by sketching the graph of the system.
$$x + 3y = -17$$
$$-2x - y = 19$$

5. The sum of two integers is -7. The difference of the same two integers is 17. What are the two integers?

6. Solve each system of equations. Verify the results.
a. $5y + 2x = 23$
$3x + 4y = 24$
b. $m + 2n = 13$
$3m + n = 14$
c. $\dfrac{a}{5} + \dfrac{b}{2} = 5$
$a - b = 4$
d. $\dfrac{8}{r} - \dfrac{9}{s} = 1$
$\dfrac{10}{r} + \dfrac{6}{s} = 7$
e. $5c + 2d = 14$
$d - 6c = -15$
f. $5a - 3b = 16$
$6b - 7a = 21$

7. Solve. Verify the results.
$$2m + n + p = 16$$
$$m + 2n + p = 9$$
$$m + n + 2p = 3$$

8. A shoe store had a sale on two styles of sandals. One style sold for $25 a pair and the other sold for $30 a pair. In one day, the receipts for the sale of 18 pairs of sandals amounted to $490. How many of each style of sandal were sold that day?

9. Solve the system of equations for x and y.
$$x + y = c$$
$$x - y = 2d$$

10. Graph the system of equations. Estimate the points of intersection. Verify your estimate algebraically.
$$x^2 + y^2 = 25$$
$$4x + 3y = 0$$

11. A wire 264 mm long was bent into the shape of a right triangle. If the hypotenuse of the triangle is 122 mm long, then find the lengths of each leg of the triangle.

12. An aircraft aided by a tail wind of 50 km/h makes a 300 km trip in four minutes less time than it takes to make the trip in still air. Find the speed of the aircraft in still air.

13. The graph of $x^2 + y^2 = 10$ is a circle centred at the origin and having a radius of $\sqrt{10}$. Graph and solve this system of equations.
$$x^2 + y^2 = 10$$
$$xy = 2$$

14. A computer chip manufacturer produces computer chips in standard and deluxe models. A standard computer chip takes 4 h to produce and a deluxe computer chip takes 8 h. The manufacturer is just getting started and has a small factory that can employ no more than 20 people. The factory runs 8 h/d for 5 d each week. The materials to produce the computer chip cost $100 for both a standard chip and a deluxe chip. The factory must produce 50 standard chips and 40 deluxe chips every week to fill standing orders. A standard chip gives the factory a profit of $12, and a deluxe chip gives the factory a profit of $17. How many of each should the factory produce each week?

15. Graph the intersection of the regions. Find all points of intersection.
$$\{x, y \,|\, x - y > 0 \ \cap \ x \geq y^2 - 10\}$$

TRIGONOMETRY

Tune Up

1. Find the value of x correct to one decimal place.

a.

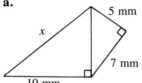

b.

2. If $x = a + 2$, then find the value of these expressions in terms of a.

a. $x^2 - 2x$ **b.** $(x - 2)^2$

c. $3x^2 - 5x + 2$ **d.** $\dfrac{5x - 3}{2x + 5}$

3. Factor completely.

a. $5y^2 - 5y$ **b.** $3xy - 2x$

c. $ax + 2x - 2a - 4$ **d.** $x^2 - 7x - 8$

e. $15x^2 - 14x - 8$ **f.** $9y^2 - 16$

g. $6a^2 - 5a - 6$ **h.** $16 - (3x - 1)^2$

i. $5a(x^2 + y^2) - b(x^2 + y^2)$

j. $x^2a^2 + 3x^2 - 4a^2 - 12$

4. Solve. State all restrictions on the variables.

a. $5x - 7 = 8$ **b.** $\dfrac{x}{5} = 11$

c. $\dfrac{18}{x} = 0.3$ **d.** $\dfrac{15}{26} = \dfrac{8}{(x - 2)}$

5. Solve for x by factoring.

a. $x^2 - 4x + 3 = 0$ **b.** $2x^2 + x - 3 = 0$

c. $x^2 + 3ax = 4a^2$ **d.** $\dfrac{3}{x - 2} = x$

6. Solve for x. Use a calculator if one is available and record your keying sequence.

a. $\dfrac{x - 7}{3} = 6$ **b.** $\dfrac{5 - x^2}{-12} = 3^2$

c. $\dfrac{15}{x} = \dfrac{23}{17}$ **d.** $\dfrac{42 - 23}{-9} = \dfrac{-27}{x^2}$

e. $x^2 = 5^2 + 4^2 - 2(5)(4)(0.23)$

7. State the corresponding sides for these similar triangles.

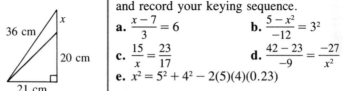

8. To name the sides in a triangle, either two capital letters may be used or one small letter. For example, in $\triangle ABC$, one of the sides is $\overline{AB}$ or c, since $\overline{AB}$ is the side opposite angle C. Draw each triangle and state another name for the side in the triangle.

a. $\triangle KLM$, $\overline{KL}$ **b.** $\triangle RST$, $\overline{RT}$

c. $\triangle PQR$, q **d.** $\triangle WKV$, v

9. Find the intersection point of these relations. Verify the point by drawing a graph.

a. $3x + y = 5$ **b.** $y = x^2 - 4$

     $x - y = 3$ $2x - y = 1$

11·1 Similar Triangles

Two figures that have the same shape and proportions, but not necessarily the same size, are **similar** figures. If two triangles *ABC* and *DEF* are similar, then

$$\frac{AB}{DE} = \frac{AC}{DF} = \frac{BC}{EF}, \angle A \cong \angle D, \angle B \cong \angle E, \text{ and } \angle C \cong \angle F.$$

The two similar triangles are written as $\triangle ABC \sim \triangle DEF$ and this is read as "triangle *ABC* is similar to triangle *DEF*."

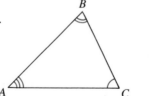

Similar triangles can be used to calculate distances which cannot be measured directly.

Example

At the same time as a building casts a shadow of 250 m, a tourist 2.0 m tall casts a shadow 2.3 m long. Find the height of the building.

Let *x* represent the height of the building.

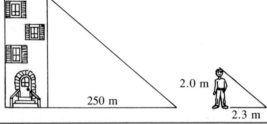

Therefore, $\dfrac{x}{250} = \dfrac{2.0}{2.3}$.

2.0 ⊠ 250 ⊟ 2.3 ⊟ **217.39130**

The building is approximately 217 m tall.

Exercises

For all exercises, use a calculator if one is available and round all answers to one decimal place.

1. Triangle *KLM* is similar to triangle *PQR*. Find the length of the unknown sides. (*Hint*: Side *k* is opposite angle *K*.)

a. $p = 6, q = 7, r = 8, k = 18$
b. $p = 15, q = 21, k = 40, m = 32$
c. $k = 12.3, l = 7.8, m = 9.6, q = 2.6$

2. At Silver Star Mountain, the Summit Chairlift and the Aberdeen Chairlift have the same slope. The Summit Chairlift has a length of 1220 m and a vertical rise of 305 m. If the Aberdeen Chairlift has a vertical rise of 335 m, then find its length.

3. A model car is 32.8 cm long and 16.2 cm wide. If the actual car is 2.3 m wide, then find the length of the car.

4. Identify the similar ratios in this diagram. Solve for $\overline{CB}$.

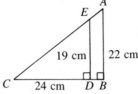

5. On a sunny day, a flagpole 6 m tall casts a shadow 7.2 m long. How tall is a second flagpole if its shadow is 8.4 m long at the same time?

Braintickler

The number 8 549 176 320 is unique. What makes it different from any other possible number?

11·2 The Tangent Ratio

A 100 m tower is supported by a cable which makes an angle of 48° with the ground. Three flags are tied to the cable along its span. The first flag is 90 m above the ground and 81 m from the foot of the cable measured along the ground; the second flag is 70 m above the ground and 63 m from the foot of the cable; the third flag is 30 m above the ground and 27 m from the foot of the cable.

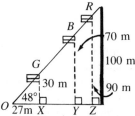

The four triangles formed by a perpendicular dropped from the cable at each flag to the ground are similar. Therefore, these ratios are congruent in each triangle formed. $\dfrac{GX}{XO} = \dfrac{BY}{YO} = \dfrac{RZ}{ZO} = \dfrac{10}{9}$

In all right triangles, the sides are given special names according to their relationship to an angle called the **reference** angle. In $\triangle OGX$ above, $\overline{GX}$ is the **opposite** side since it is opposite the 48° angle, $\overline{GO}$ is the **hypotenuse** because it is opposite the right angle, and $\overline{XO}$ is the **adjacent** side and is next to the 48° angle. In any right triangle, the ratio of the side opposite angle θ to the side adjacent to angle θ is called the **tangent** of the angle θ (abbreviated "tan θ").

In any triangle, $\tan \theta = \dfrac{\text{length of side opposite angle } \theta}{\text{length of side adjacent to angle } \theta}.$

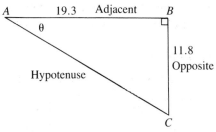

In this triangle, $\tan \theta = \dfrac{BC}{BA}$

$= \dfrac{11.8}{19.3}$

$\doteq 0.6114$ (rounded to 4 decimal places)

Every angle has its own tangent value. At the back of the book is a table containing the tangent ratios for angles between 0° and 90°.

Example 1

Find tan θ correct to four decimal places.

a.   **b.**   **c.**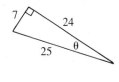

Label the sides of the triangle as opposite, hypotenuse, and adjacent before attempting a solution.

a. $\tan \theta = \dfrac{4}{3}$

$\doteq 1.3333$

b. $\tan \theta = \dfrac{5}{12}$

$\doteq 0.4167$

c. $\tan \theta = \dfrac{7}{24}$

$\doteq 0.2917$

289

A calculator can be used to find the tangent ratio. For example, to find tan 37°, ensure the calculator is in the "degree mode", enter 37, and press the tangent function $\boxed{\text{TAN}}$. The display shows 0.75355405.

Example 2

Find the tangent ratio for these angles correct to four decimal places.

a. 35°
tan 35° ≐ 0.7002

b. 56°
tan 56° ≐ 1.4826

c. 86°
tan 86° ≐ 14.3007

If the tangent ratio in a right triangle is known, the measure of the reference angle can be calculated. For example, if tan θ = 1.5392, scan the table to find the ratio closest to 1.5392. In this case, the ratio closest to 1.5392 is 1.5399, and θ is approximately 57°. When using a calculator, enter 1.5392 $\boxed{\text{INV}}$ $\boxed{\text{TAN}}$. The display shows 56.988695. Rounded to the nearest degree, θ will be 57°. Some calculators have a $\boxed{\text{MODE}}$, $\boxed{\text{2nd}}$, or $\boxed{\text{ARC}}$ key rather than the $\boxed{\text{INV}}$ key. These allow the same calculator key to have two functions.

Example 3

Find angle θ to the nearest degree.

a. tan θ = 0.4877
θ ≐ 26°

b. tan θ = 1.1923
θ ≐ 50°

c. tan θ = 2.4519
θ ≐ 68°

The tangent ratio is known for every angle θ, where 0° ≤ θ < 90°. Therefore, an unknown side in a right triangle can be found if the other side and one of the acute angles are known.

Example 4

Find the length of the indicated side correct to one decimal place.

a. $\tan 48° = \dfrac{x}{24.1}$

Using the tables;
24.1(tan 48°) = x
24.1(1.1106) = x
26.8 ≐ x

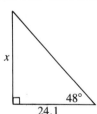

The unknown side is about 26.8 units.

b. $\tan 62° = \dfrac{19.3}{y}$

Using a calculator;
19.3 $\boxed{÷}$ 62 $\boxed{\text{TAN}}$ $\boxed{=}$
y ≐ 10.3

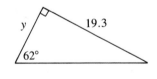

The unknown side is about 10.3 units.

Example 5

Find the measures of angles θ and β correct to the nearest degree.

$\tan \theta = \dfrac{7.5}{13.7}$
θ ≐ 29°

$\tan \beta = \dfrac{13.7}{7.5}$
β ≐ 61°

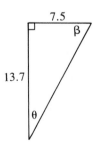

The two angles, θ and β, are complementary. Why?

Exercises

For all exercises, use a calculator if one is available.

1. Use the tangent tables to find a pattern in the values of the tangent ratios as the angle increases from
a. 0° to 45°.
b. 45° to 90°.
c. Explain why tan 45° is 1 and tan 0° is 0.

2. Find the value correct to four decimal places.
a. tan 23°　　　　　**b.** tan 50°
c. tan 73°　　　　　**d.** tan 89°

3. Find the measure of the angle to the nearest degree.
a. tan θ = 0.2867　　　**b.** tan β = 0.8693
c. tan θ = 2.6051　　　**d.** tan A = 0.5386
e. tan C = 1.4591　　　**f.** tan K = 5.6981

4. Find the value of these expressions.
a. tan 45° + 5　　　　**b.** tan 50°
c. tan 50° − tan 40°　　**d.** tan(50° − 40°)
e. 2tan 35°　　　　　**f.** tan 70°
g. (tan 8°)²　　　　　**h.** tan 64°

5. Enter 90 $\boxed{\text{TAN}}$ on a calculator. Why does it give an "Error"?

6. A set of stairs makes an angle of 25° with the horizontal. How wide is the step if it rises 14.8 cm?

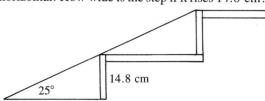

14.8 cm

25°

7. Find the tan K and tan L ratios correct to four decimal places.
a.

b.

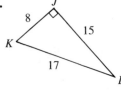

8. A ladder, leaning against the side of a house, reaches 3.2 m up the wall. If the ladder makes an angle of 59° with the ground, how far is the base of the house?

9. Find x correct to one decimal place.
a.

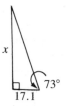

b.

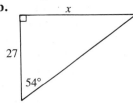

10. Find θ to the nearest degree.
a.

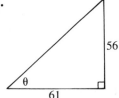

b.

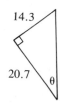

11. Triangle *ABC* has a right angle at *A*. Find the value of the indicated sides or angles correct to one decimal place or to the nearest degree. (*Hint*: Side *b* is opposite ∠*B*.)
a. *b* if ∠*B* = 34° and *c* = 8.0.
b. *c* if ∠*C* = 57° and *b* = 18.2.
c. *b* if ∠*C* = 69° and *c* = 23.5.
d. ∠*B* if *b* = 12.3 and *c* = 17.4.
e. ∠*C* if *b* = 9.7 and *c* = 15.4.

12. A 15.4 m flagpole casts a 22.3 m shadow. At what angle do the rays of the sun strike the ground?

13. Find the total number of nets which will form a cube if each net is made up of six congruent squares. One example is given.

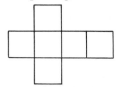

14. Two lines are drawn on a coordinate grid from the origin to (1,4) and from the origin to (−3,2). Find the angle between the two lines.

11·3 Sine and Cosine Ratios

The tangent ratio cannot always be used to find an unknown side or angle in a right triangle. For example, an electric company wishes to find the length of a supporting wire for a tower 14.7 m tall. The wire makes an angle of 59° with the ground. It will be difficult to get an accurate measurement if the tangent ratio is used to solve for the unknown side and then the Pythagorean Theorem is used to find the length of the hypotenuse. Therefore, it is necessary to define two other trigonometric ratios that involve the hypotenuse of a right triangle and one of the sides. These are the **sine** (sin) and **cosine** (cos) ratios.

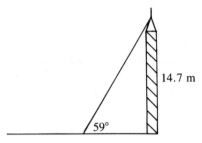

14.7 m

59°

$$\sin \theta = \frac{\text{side opposite angle } \theta}{\text{hypotenuse}}$$

$$\cos \theta = \frac{\text{side adjacent to angle } \theta}{\text{hypotenuse}}$$

Example 1

Given $\triangle ABC$ with a right angle at C, find the sine, cosine, and tangent ratios of angle A and angle B.

In $\triangle ABC$, the sides are labelled as opposite and adjacent depending on which reference angle is being used. In this case, if the reference angle is $\angle A$, then $\overline{AC}$ is the adjacent side and $\overline{BC}$ is the opposite side. However, if $\angle B$ is the reference angle, then $\overline{AC}$ is the opposite side and $\overline{BC}$ is the adjacent side.

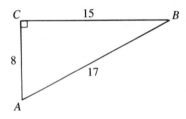

$\cos A = \frac{8}{17}$, $\sin A = \frac{15}{17}$, and $\tan A = \frac{15}{8}$. $\cos B = \frac{15}{17}$, $\sin B = \frac{8}{17}$, and $\tan B = \frac{8}{15}$.

Calculators with trigonometric functions contain a sine key, $\boxed{\text{SIN}}$, and a cosine key, $\boxed{\text{COS}}$. To find cos 53°, first make sure the calculator is in the degree mode, enter 53, and press $\boxed{\text{COS}}$. The display reads $0.6018150\mathrm{2}$. The table for the sine and cosine ratios is at the back of the book. Verify the calculator by checking cos 53° in the table.

Example 2

Evaluate each to four decimal places.

a. cos 12°   **b.** sin 71°   **c.** cos 89°
= 0.9781   = 0.9455   = 0.0175

It also is possible to find the angle of a trigonometric ratio when the ratio is known. For example, to find θ when $\sin \theta = 0.4685$, enter 0.4685 and press $\boxed{\text{INV}}$ $\boxed{\text{SIN}}$. The display will read 27.936972 or about 28°. When using the tables, find the ratio closest to 0.4685. In this case, it is 0.4695 which is the sine ratio for an angle of 28°.

Example 3

Find the value of θ correct to the nearest degree.

a. sin θ = 0.5299
    θ ≐ 32°

b. cos θ = 0.7193
    θ ≐ 44°

c. sin θ = 0.9762
    θ ≐ 77°

These ratios can be used to find the lengths of unknown sides or the magnitude of unknown angles. For all trigonometric problems, draw and label a diagram, and decide on the appropriate trigonometric ratio before attempting to solve the problem.

Example 4

Find the length of the unknown side x in the triangle.

Since 38° is the measure of the reference angle, 31 is the length of the hypotenuse and x is the opposite side. Therefore, the sine ratio should be used.

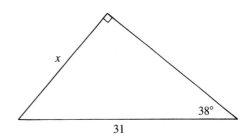

$$\sin 38° = \frac{x}{31}$$
$$31(\sin 38°) = x$$
$$31(0.6157) \doteq x$$
$$x \doteq 19.1$$

Therefore, the length of side x is approximately 19.1 units.

The length of x can also be found using this calculator keying sequence.
38 [SIN] [×] 31 [=] **19.085506**

Example 5

A 28.4 m ladder reaches up to the top window of a house, 17.1 m from the ground. The local safety commission says that a ladder is stable if it makes no more than a 60° angle with the ground. Is this ladder safe to climb?

In order to answer the question, we must find the angle the ladder makes with the ground. Therefore, that angle is the reference angle and is labelled as β. Since the side opposite β and the hypotenuse are known, the sine ratio can be used.

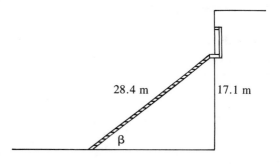

$$\sin β = \frac{17.1}{28.4}$$
$$= 0.6021$$
$$\therefore \angle β \doteq 37°$$

The ladder makes an angle of 37° with the ground and is safe to climb.

Exercises

1. Find the value correct to four decimal places. Use a calculator if one is available.
a. sin 57°   **b.** cos 18°   **c.** cos 77°
d. sin 38°   **e.** tan 75°   **f.** sin 90°

2. Use the trigonometric tables. Explain why neither the sine nor cosine ratios exceed 1.

3. At what angle are the sine and cosine ratios equal? Sketch a triangle in which the sine ratio equals the cosine ratio. Use the triangle to explain why this is true.

4. Find the ratio of sin A, cos A, tan A, sin B, cos B, and tan B in each triangle.

a. 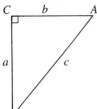   **b.**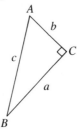

5. Find the value of the angle correct to the nearest degree. Use a calculator if one is available.
a. sin $\theta = 0.5592$ **b.** cos $\theta = 0.9336$
c. sin $A = 0.6553$ **d.** cos $B = 2.4561$
e. tan $X = 1.2764$ **f.** cos $\theta = 0.3333$
g. sin $\theta = \dfrac{3}{4}$ **h.** cos $\theta = \dfrac{3}{11}$

6. In Smokey Tent, the sun rises at precisely 06:00 and sets at 18:00. What time is it when the sun is 20° above the horizon?

7. Find the value of x correct to one decimal place. Use a calculator if one is available.

a. 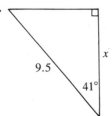   **b.**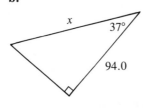

8. Find the value of θ correct to the nearest degree.

a. 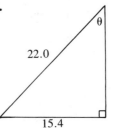   **b.**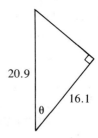

9. The main line of the Canadian Pacific Railway travels through the Kickinghorse Pass between Field, British Columbia, and Lake Louise, Alberta. Before the Spiral Tunnels were completed in 1909, the grade of the railway line was 4.5% (the railway rose 4.5 m for every 100 m of railway line). Find the angle the railway made with the horizontal.

10. Triangle XYZ has a right angle at Z. Find the measure of the unknown angle or side correct to one decimal place.
a. If $\angle Y = 37°$ and $z = 5.7$, find y.
b. If $\angle X = 51°$ and $y = 13.9$, find x.
c. If $y = 19.8$ and $z = 27.2$, find $\angle Y$.
d. If $z = 46.3$ and $y = 37.4$, find $\angle X$.

11. Find x correct to one decimal place.

a. 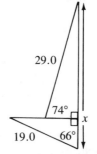   **b.**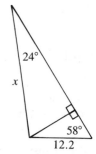

12. A rectangle measures 5 cm by 6 cm. It is rotated a full turn about the midpoint of the 5 cm edge and then rotated a full turn about the midpoint of the 6 cm edge. Which of the two rotations will produce the larger area?

13. Janet and Sanji are climbing up a hill which is inclined at 13° to the horizontal. After they have climbed 780 m up the slope, find their height above the horizontal.

11·4 Solving Right Triangles

Solving a right triangle means finding the measure of any unknown sides or angles. This can be done using the sine, cosine, and tangent ratios. To solve the triangle, it is necessary to know the lengths of two sides or the length of one side and the measure of one acute angle.

Example

Solve $\triangle XYZ$, where $\angle Z = 63°$, $\angle X = 90°$, and $z = 13.8$ units.

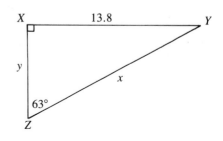

Before solving the triangle, draw a diagram and label it appropriately.
Since $\angle Z$ and $\angle Y$ are complementary, $\angle Y = 27°$.

Solving for side x: $\sin 63° = \dfrac{13.8}{x}$

$$x = \dfrac{13.8}{\sin 63°}$$
$$x \doteq 15.5$$

Using the trigonometric ratios and the given information, y is about 7 units. Therefore, the solution to the triangle is $x \doteq 15.5$, $y \doteq 7.0$, and $\angle Y = 27°$.

Exercises

1. Verify the lengths of the sides in the example in the display using the Pythagorean Theorem.
a. Are they the same?
b. Can you account for any difference?

2. Solve the right triangles.

a.

b.

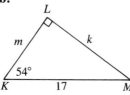

c.

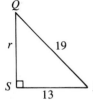

d.

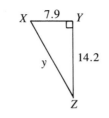

3. Solve $\triangle ABC$ with a right angle at B using these conditions.

a. $a = 6.9$, $\angle A = 35°$ **b.** $b = 17.0$, $\angle A = 47°$
c. $c = 19.3$, $b = 25.1$ **d.** $\angle C = 15°$, $c = 37$
e. $\angle C = 39°$, $b = 123$ **f.** $a = 65.1$, $c = 36.4$

4. Solve triangle ABC.

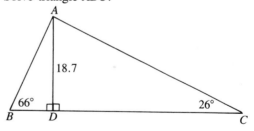

5. Two ladders lean against the opposite sides of a vertical wall 3.6 m high. Both ladders just reach the top of the wall and are exactly in line with each other. One ladder makes an angle of 52° with the ground, while the second ladder makes an angle of 71°.
a. Find the length of each ladder.
b. If the wall is 0.2 m thick, how far apart are the feet of the ladders?

Braintickler

In this six-point star, the area of the shaded portion is 2 cm². Find the area of the entire star.

11·5 Applications of Trigonometry

Trigonometry is used in many areas such as architecture, astronomy, electronics, physics, and space exploration. Two mathematical terms used when describing problems with angles are **angle of elevation** and **angle of depression**.

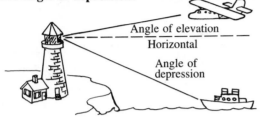

Example 1

An acceleration ramp for a highway has an angle of elevation of 5°. If the ramp is 240 m long, then find the increase in elevation for a car accelerating onto the highway.

Understand the Problem
Draw and label a suitable diagram to summarize the situation. We are required to find the vertical distance the car rises.

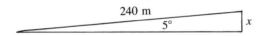

Develop a Plan
The angle of 5° is the reference angle, the ramp is the hypotenuse, and the height of the ramp, x, is the opposite side. Use the sine ratio to find the vertical distance the car travels. Remember, the angle of elevation is the angle the road rises above the horizontal.

Carry Out the Plan
$$\sin 5° = \frac{x}{240}$$
$$x \doteq 21$$

Look Back
The ramp rises approximately 21 m.
Verify the solution using another ratio.

Example 2

A climber, working her way up a vertical cliff, stops for a rest on a ledge. The ledge where she rests is 13 m wide. The angle of depression from the ledge to the bottom of the cliff is 73° and the angle of elevation to the top of the cliff is 87°. Find the height of the cliff.

Draw a diagram and consider the two right triangles separately. Let x and y represent the distance to the top of the cliff and the bottom of the cliff respectively.

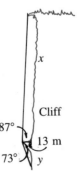

$$\tan 87° = \frac{x}{13} \qquad \tan 73° = \frac{y}{13}$$
$$13(\tan 87°) = x \qquad 13(\tan 73°) = y$$
$$x \doteq 248 \qquad y \doteq 43$$

The height of the cliff is about 291 m.

Exercises

1. A.T., the "Mathematics Wizard", stated that "the tangent ratio in Example 2 of the display was used to find both distances because a more accurate approximation cannot be found using the sine or cosine ratio." Is A.T. correct? Explain.

2. Find the horizontal length of the ramp in Example 1 of the display.

3. A forest ranger at the top of a fire tower spots a hiker in the woods. The angle of depression to the hiker is 29°. At the same instant, the hiker sees the top of the tower.
a. What is the angle of elevation for the hiker viewing the top of the tower?
b. How are the two angles related?

For the remaining exercises, draw a diagram and solve the problem using a calculator if one is available.

4. A kite is flying from a 250 m string and makes an angle of 42° with the ground. Find the height of the kite above the ground.

5. The shadow of a flagpole is 8.6 m long when the angle of elevation of the sun is 37°. How tall is the flagpole?

6. One of the steepest streets in the world is Russian Hill in San Francisco. It has a slope of 31.5% so that the street rises 31.5 m for every 100 m along the street. Find the angle of elevation of the street.

7. A ladder, 3.2 m long, leans against a wall and makes an angle of 58° with the ground. Find the distance from the foot of the ladder to the wall and the distance the ladder reaches up the wall.

8. The angle of depression of a diving submarine is 11°. The submarine travels 750 m while in its dive. If it started 150 m below the surface, then how deep does it go?

9. Find the width of the river.

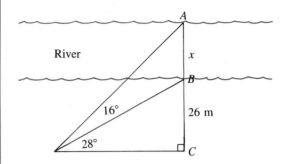

10. The Annacis Island-Surrey Bridge across the Fraser River was opened in 1986. It is the longest cable-supported bridge in the world. From a point 118 m directly above one end of the bridge, the angle of depression to the opposite end of the bridge is 3°. Find the length of the bridge.

11. A radio tower 138 m tall is supported by a guy wire. The wire makes an angle of 71° with the ground. The company maintaining the tower wishes to move the base of the guy wire an additional 8 m from the base.
a. How much additional wire will be needed?
b. What angle will the new wire make with the ground?

12. An isosceles triangle has two congruent sides of 21.3 cm and congruent angles of 54°. Find the length of the third side of the triangle, the perimeter of the triangle, and the area of the triangle.

13. A rectangle measures 23 cm by 15 cm.
a. Find the angle between the shortest side and the diagonal.
b. Find the length of the diagonal.
c. Use the Pythagorean Theorem to verify your results.

14. A ranger in a lookout station 75 m high spots two hikers in the woods below. The first hiker is seen at an angle of depression of 15°, while the second is seen at an angle of depression of 24°. Assuming the lookout and hikers are on level ground, find the closest and the farthest distance the hikers could be with respect to each other.

11·6 Trigonometric Definitions

The Cartesian coordinate system is used to study trigonometric ratios of angles larger than 90°. If the angle is placed on the coordinate grid with the vertex at the origin and one side, the **initial arm**, of the angle along the positive x-axis, the angle is in **standard position**. An arrow indicates the direction of rotation of the angle until it reaches the **terminal arm**. A rotation counterclockwise is a positive angle; while a rotation clockwise is a negative angle.

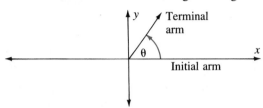
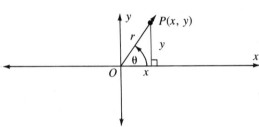

If any point $P(x,y)$ is taken on the terminal arm of an angle, a line perpendicular to the x-axis from $P(x,y)$ produces a right triangle. Therefore, $\overline{OP}$, which is generally referred to as r, can be found using the Pythagorean Theorem $r^2 = x^2 + y^2$ or $r = \sqrt{x^2 + y^2}$.

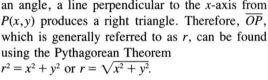

The point $P(x,y)$ may be located in any quadrant of the coordinate system and the three **primary trigonometric ratios** can be defined in terms of x, y, and r.

$$\sin \theta = \frac{y}{r} \qquad\qquad \cos \theta = \frac{x}{r} \qquad\qquad \tan \theta = \frac{y}{x}$$

The reciprocal of the primary trigonometric ratios gives the **reciprocal trigonometric ratios**.

$$\text{cosecant } \theta = \csc \theta = \frac{r}{y} \qquad \text{secant } \theta = \sec \theta = \frac{r}{x} \qquad \text{cotangent } \theta = \cot \theta = \frac{x}{y}$$

Example

If $\cos \beta = \frac{4}{\sqrt{41}}$ and β terminates in the fourth quadrant, find the value of all the trigonometric ratios.

Sketch and label an appropriate diagram. Since the cosine ratio is defined as $\frac{x}{r}$, then $x = 4$ and $r = \sqrt{41}$.

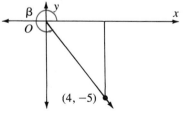

Using the Pythagorean Theorem, $y = \pm 5$, but since β is in the fourth quadrant, $y = -5$.

$$\sin \beta = \frac{y}{r} = \frac{-5}{\sqrt{41}} \qquad\qquad \cos \beta = \frac{x}{r} = \frac{4}{\sqrt{41}} \qquad\qquad \tan \beta = \frac{y}{x} = \frac{-5}{4}$$

$$\csc \beta = \frac{r}{y} = \frac{\sqrt{41}}{-5} \qquad\qquad \sec \beta = \frac{r}{x} = \frac{\sqrt{41}}{4} \qquad\qquad \cot \beta = \frac{x}{y} = \frac{4}{-5}$$

Exercises

1. In your own words, state the meaning of the reciprocal trigonometric ratios and show that $\sin \theta = \dfrac{1}{\csc \theta}$.

2. Find the value of these ratios using the tables at the back of the book.

a. $\sin 37°$ **b.** $\cos 79°$ **c.** $\tan 46°$
d. $\sin 69°$ **e.** $\cos 23°$ **f.** $\tan 0°$

i) Find the reciprocal of each using the $\boxed{1/x}$ key on a calculator.
ii) Compare your answer to the value of the corresponding reciprocal ratio from the tables.

3. Show how the primary trigonometric ratio can be used to find m. Explain why it may be easier to use a reciprocal trigonometric ratio.

a.   **b.**

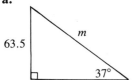

4. Solve for m in the triangles of Exercise 3 using a reciprocal trigonometric ratio. Use a calculator if one is available. The first one is done for you to show the keying sequence.

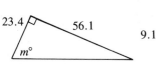

5. Find the measure of the indicated angle using a primary ratio.

a.   **b.**

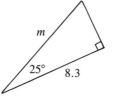

i) Find the value of the indicated angle using a reciprocal ratio.
ii) Show the calculator keying sequence to determine the solution of each triangle.
iii) Is there an advantage in using a reciprocal ratio rather than a primary ratio?

6. Find the value of the three primary trigonometric ratios.

a.   **b.**

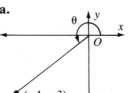

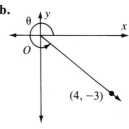

7. Find the value of the three reciprocal trigonometric ratios.

a.   **b.**

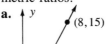

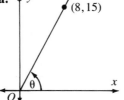

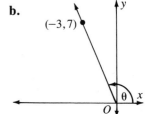

8. Find the value of all the trigonometric ratios.

a.   **b.**

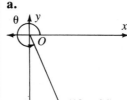

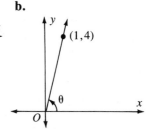

9. Draw a diagram of each angle in standard position. Find the value of the six trigonometric ratios.

a. $P(5, 12)$ **b.** $R(-4, -3)$
c. $K(-8, 15)$ **d.** $Q(9, -12)$

10. The angle θ terminates in the first quadrant and $\sin \theta = \dfrac{3}{5}$.

a. Draw a diagram of the angle in standard position.
b. Find the value of θ in the diagram.
c. Give a point on the terminal arm of angle θ.
d. Find the value of all trigonometric ratios.

11. Tan $\theta = \dfrac{8}{15}$ and θ terminates in the third quadrant. Find the value of $\sin^2 \theta + \cos^2 \theta$. (*Hint*: $\sin^2 \theta$ means $(\sin \theta)^2$.)

11·7 Ratios of Any Angle

The sign of a primary trigonometric ratio depends on the sign of x and y. For example, a point $P(x,y)$ in quadrant II has a negative x-value and a positive y-value. Therefore, the sine and cosecant ratios will be positive in quadrant II. The diagram illustrates the sign of the trigonometric ratios in each quadrant and is generally referred to as the **CAST** rule. It describes where each angle has a positive trigonometric ratio. In this case, all ratios are positive in quadrant I, the sine and cosecant ratios are positive in quadrant II, the tangent and cotangent ratios are positive in quadrant III, and the cosine and secant ratios are positive in quadrant IV.

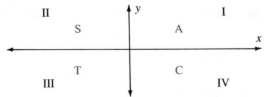

All trigonometric functions can be found on the calculator. The reciprocal ratios will require the use of the $\boxed{1/x}$ key on a calculator because the reciprocal ratios are not built-in functions.

Example 1

Find the value of csc 238°.

Draw and label an appropriate diagram. Determine the reference angle. Recall that it is the angle between the terminal arm and the x-axis. In this case, the reference angle is 58°. From the tables, csc 58° is 1.1792. Since the terminal arm is in quadrant III, we know that the ratio is negative. Therefore, csc 238° = -1.1792. Using a calculator, enter 238 $\boxed{SIN}$ $\boxed{1/x}$ -1.1792.

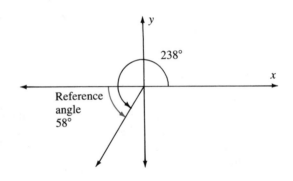

Example 2

If cot θ = -2.3559, then find the measure of θ where $0° \le θ \le 360°$.

The cotangent ratio is negative in quadrant II and quadrant IV. Therefore, there will be two angles that give cot θ = -2.3559. Using the tables, find 2.3559 under the cotangent column. The corresponding angle is approximately 23° and is the reference angle. Once the reference angle is found, draw and label an appropriate diagram. Notice where the terminal is drawn, angle θ is either 157° or 337°.

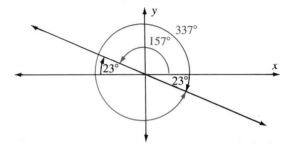

Using a calculator, the display will show about $-23°$. The calculator will always give the smaller of the two reference angles. Once it is found, draw and label an appropriate diagram to find the other possible angle.

300

Exercises

1. Explain the difference between the effect of the two keys, $\boxed{\text{INV}}$ and $\boxed{1/x}$, when used with the $\boxed{\text{TAN}}$, $\boxed{\text{SIN}}$, and $\boxed{\text{COS}}$ keys. Explain specifically how each is used.

2. State the measure of any positive angle in standard position where $0° \le \theta < 360°$, if the terminal arm of the angle is the
a. positive x-axis
b. positive y-axis
c. negative x-axis
d. negative y-axis.

3. State the quadrant(s) which meet these conditions.
a. Sine is positive and secant is negative.
b. Tangent is negative and cosine is positive. .
c. Both secant and cotangent are negative.

4. State the quadrant where each angle would have its terminal arm, if the angle is in standard position. State the reference angle. (*Hint*: A negative angle is a clockwise rotation.)
a. $73°$ **b.** $191°$ **c.** $327°$
d. $-115°$ **e.** $217°$ **f.** $-315°$

5. Explain what is being found using these calculator key sequences.
a. $\boxed{\text{INV}}$ $\boxed{\text{SIN}}$ **b.** $\boxed{\text{SIN}}$ $\boxed{1/x}$
c. $\boxed{1/x}$ $\boxed{\text{INV}}$ $\boxed{\text{TAN}}$ **d.** $\boxed{\pm}$ $\boxed{1/x}$ $\boxed{\text{INV}}$ $\boxed{\text{COS}}$

6. Find the value of each ratio. Use a calculator if one is available.
a. sec $137°$ **b.** cot $198°$ **c.** cos $323°$
d. csc $129°$ **e.** sec $75°$ **f.** sin $218°$
g. tan $131°$ **h.** csc $(-283°)$ **i.** cot $(-65°)$

7. Find θ where $0° \le \theta < 360°$.
a. sec $\theta = 1.4562$ **b.** cot $\theta = -1.1132$
c. cos $\theta = 0.4561$ **d.** sin $\theta = -0.3276$
e. tan $\theta = 1.4200$ **f.** csc $\theta = -2.3431$
g. cot $\theta = -0.6582$ **h.** sec $\theta = 0.5123$
i. cos $\theta = \dfrac{1}{2}$ **j.** cot $\theta = -1\dfrac{3}{4}$

8. If $P(x,y)$ is on the terminal arm of θ, then find θ to the nearest degree.
a. $P(5,2)$ **b.** $P(-3,1)$ **c.** $P(-1,-2)$

9. A computer in a fire tower indicates the direction of fires in terms of the tangent ratio. The direction of a fire is given by tan $\theta = -1.5492$.
a. State the direction of the fire if $0°$ is due east.
b. The fire tower has an east-to-west road running past it. If the fire is 4.2 km from the road, how far is the fire from the fire tower?

10. Find the new angle under the reflection defined by the mapping $(\theta,y) \rightarrow (-\theta,y)$. The first one is done as an example.

$\theta = 37°$
If $\theta = 37°$, then the angle is in quadrant I. Under the mapping, the angle is reflected in the y-axis so that the resulting angle is in quadrant II. Therefore, the angle is $(180 - 37°)$ or $143°$.

a. $\theta = 49°$ **b.** $\theta = 90°$
c. $\theta = 128°$ **d.** $\theta = 180°$
e. $\theta = 247°$ **f.** $\theta = 328°$

11. Find the new angle under the reflection defined by the mapping $(\theta,y) \rightarrow (-\theta, -y)$.
a. $\theta = 37°$ **b.** $\theta = 112°$ **c.** $\theta = 146°$
d. $\theta = 270°$ **e.** $\theta = 289°$ **f.** $\theta = 360°$

12. If θ is an angle in quadrant I, how do the trigonometric ratios change as θ increases?

13. If $\theta = 153°$ and $P(-5,k)$ is on the terminal arm, then find k.

14. If $P(x,y)$ is on the terminal arm of θ, then find $P'(x,y)$ and θ', to the nearest degree, under the mapping $(x,y) \rightarrow (x,-y)$.
a. $P(3,5)$ **b.** $P(-4,1)$
c. $P(-2,-5)$ **d.** $P(1,-7)$

15. Copy and complete the table showing the signs of the ratios in each quadrant.

Quadrant	sin	cos	tan	sec	csc	cot
First	+					
Second						
Third						
Fourth						−

301

11·8 Special Ratios

The trigonometric ratios can be calculated for any angle regardless of its size. With the availability of the computer and the calculator, calculating these ratios is no longer a long process.

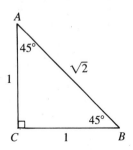

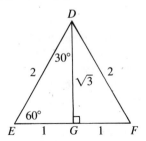

Triangle ABC is a 45°-45°-90° isosceles triangle. If the legs have a relative length of 1 unit, the hypotenuse, $\overline{AB}$, is $\sqrt{2}$.

Triangle DEF is an equilateral triangle with side lengths of 2 units. The length of altitude, $\overline{DG}$, is $\sqrt{3}$.

These special ratios for angles in the first quadrant are summarized in the chart.

Angle (θ)	sin θ	cos θ	tan θ	csc θ	sec θ	cot θ
30°	$\frac{1}{2}$	$\frac{\sqrt{3}}{2}$	$\frac{1}{\sqrt{3}}$	2	$\frac{2}{\sqrt{3}}$	$\sqrt{3}$
45°	$\frac{1}{\sqrt{2}}$	$\frac{1}{\sqrt{2}}$	1	$\sqrt{2}$	$\sqrt{2}$	1
60°	$\frac{\sqrt{3}}{2}$	$\frac{1}{2}$	$\sqrt{3}$	$\frac{2}{\sqrt{3}}$	2	$\frac{1}{\sqrt{3}}$

Example

Find the values of these ratios.

a. sin 240°

b. csc (−210°)

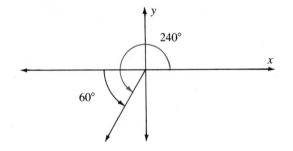

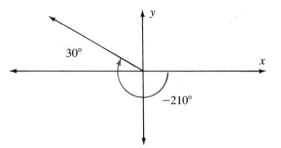

240° is in quadrant **III** where the sine ratio is negative. Therefore, the reference angle is 60° and sin 240° = −sin 60°
$$= \frac{-\sqrt{3}}{2}$$

−210° is in quadrant **II** where the cosecant ratio is positive. The reference angle is 30° and csc (−210°) = csc 30°
$$= 2$$

302

Exercises

1. Copy and complete the chart to include angles of 120°, 135°, 150°, 210°, 225°, 240°, 300°, 315°, and 330° for all six trigonometric ratios.

Angle (θ)	30°	45°	60°	90°	120°	135° ...
Sine						
Cosine						
Tangent			$\sqrt{3}$			-1
Secant						
Cosecant						
Cotangent						

2. Define the secant, cosecant, and cotangent ratios in terms of the adjacent side, the opposite side, and the hypotenuse of a right triangle.

3. Use a 30°-60°-90° triangle with sides of 5, 10, and $5\sqrt{3}$ units, to show that the trigonometric ratios of 30° and 60° remain unchanged from Exercise 1. Explain why this is so.

4. Find the exact measures of the unknown sides in each triangle. Express the length as a radical.

a.
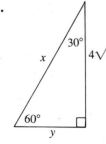

b.
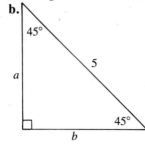

5. Find the exact value using radicals.
a. $\sin (-60°)$ **b.** $\cos (-210°)$
c. $\tan (-330°)$ **d.** $\sin (-135°)$
e. $\csc (-150°)$ **f.** $\cot (-225°)$
g. $\sec (-240°)$ **h.** $\csc (-45°)$

6. Are these statements true or false? If they are incorrect, correct them.
a. $\sin (-\theta) = -\sin \theta$ **b.** $\cos (-\theta) = -\cos \theta$
c. $\tan (-\theta) = -\tan \theta$ **d.** $\sec (-\theta) = -\sec \theta$
e. $\csc (-\theta) = -\csc \theta$ **f.** $\cot (-\theta) = -\cot \theta$

7. Find the measure of θ if $0° \le \theta < 360°$.
a. $\cos \theta = \frac{-1}{2}$ **b.** $\sin \theta = \frac{\sqrt{3}}{2}$

c. $\tan \theta = 1$ **d.** $\sec \theta = \frac{-2}{\sqrt{3}}$

e. $\csc \theta = \frac{1}{\sqrt{2}}$ **f.** $\cot \theta = -\sqrt{3}$

8. Show that $\tan \theta = \frac{\sin \theta}{\cos \theta}$ using values of θ in each of the four quadrants.

9. Find the exact value of each.
a. $\sin 45° \sec 225° - \cos 150° \cot 60°$
b. $\cos 240° \tan 315° + \cos 330° \cot 210°$
c. $\tan 135° \sec 225° - \csc 150° \cot 330°$
d. $\sec 60° \cos 300° \tan 120° \csc 240°$

10. An equilateral triangle with sides of 12 cm is circumscribed by a circle. Find the exact value of the area of the shaded portion.

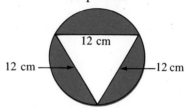

11. Evaluate. Leave your answer as a rational number.
a. $(\csc 260°)(\sin 360°)(\tan 51°)$
b. $(\sec 50°)(\cos 50°)(\tan 135°)$

Using the Library

There are many situations, often called **paradoxes**, where a statement is self contradictory. One such paradox is given by Bertrand Russell and has since been named the "Barber Paradox". The barber of a certain village claims that he shaves all people, and only people, who do not shave themselves. However, does this mean that the barber shaves himself? Use the library to find other paradoxes and attempt to write one of your own. Two other mathematicians that have worked with paradoxes are Georg Cantor and C. Burali-Forti.

11·9 Trigonometric Equations

The skills you have learned are used repeatedly in all branches of mathematics. In this section, we will use the skills that you have developed to help solve some trigonometric equations.

Example 1

Solve. $0° \leq \theta \leq 360°$

a. $\cos \theta = 0.5$

In this case, θ must be between $0°$ and $360°$. Therefore, θ is either in quadrant I or quadrant IV.

$\therefore \theta = 60°$ or $300°$

b. $\sin \theta + 1 = 0.5$

Isolate the trigonometric ratio.

$\sin \theta = -0.5$

$\therefore \theta = 210°$ or $330°$

Example 2

Solve this expression. $0° \leq \theta \leq 360°$

$4\cos^2 \theta + 4\cos \theta - 3 = 0$
$= 4(\cos \theta)^2 + 4\cos \theta - 3 = 0$
$= (2\cos \theta - 1)(2\cos \theta + 3) = 0$

$\left\{ \cos^2 \theta = (\cos \theta)^2 \right\}$

As is the case when solving a quadratic equation by factoring, both factors are equated to zero and a solution found:

$2\cos \theta - 1 = 0$

$\cos \theta = \frac{1}{2}$

$\theta = 60°$ or $300°$

$2\cos \theta + 3 = 0$

$\cos \theta = -\frac{3}{2}$

Since the minimum value for cosine is -1, there are no values of θ that satisfy this equation. Therefore, $\theta = 60°$ or $300°$ only.

Exercises

1. Why is it necessary to observe the restrictions on the variable before solving the equation?

2. Solve. $-360° \leq \theta \leq 360°$
a. $\sin \theta = 0.5$ **b.** $\sin \theta = 0.8660$
c. $\cos \theta = \frac{1}{\sqrt{2}}$ **d.** $\sin \theta = \frac{\sqrt{3}}{2}$
e. $\cos \theta = -1$ **f.** $\tan \theta = -1$

3. Solve. $0° \leq \theta \leq 360°$
a. $(\sin \theta - 1)(\sin \theta + 1) = 0$
b. $(\cos \theta + 3)(\cos \theta - \frac{1}{2}) = 0$
c. $(\tan \theta - 4)(2\tan \theta + 3) = 0$

For Exercises 4 and 5, use a calculator if one is available.

4. Solve for θ. $0° \leq \theta \leq 360°$
a. $\sqrt{2}\cos \theta = 1$
b. $\sin^2 \theta - 2\sin \theta - 3 = 0$
c. $\tan^2 \theta - 9 = 0$
d. $\cos^2 \theta - 4 = 0$
e. If any of parts **a** to **d** do not have a solution, explain why.

5. Solve. $-360° \leq \theta \leq 360°$
a. $2\sin^2 \theta + 3\sin \theta = -1$
b. $8\cos^2 \theta + 7\cos \theta - 1 = 0$
c. $2\tan^2 \theta - 5\tan \theta - 12 = 0$

6. Can the quadratic formula be used to help solve trigonometric equations? If so, use it to solve this equation.
$\frac{1}{2}\sin^2\theta - 5\sin \theta + 3 = 2$

11·10 The Law of Sines I

Not all triangles that we can solve are right triangles. Triangles that do not contain a right angle are **oblique** triangles. The **Law of Sines** can be used to solve some oblique triangles.

GIVEN: Triangle ABC is an oblique triangle.

REQUIRED: To prove $\dfrac{\sin A}{a} = \dfrac{\sin B}{b} = \dfrac{\sin C}{c}$.

PROOF: Construct the perpendicular to $\triangle ABC$ from vertex A.

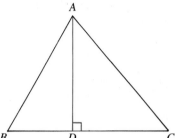

Statement	**Reason**
1. In $\triangle ACD$, $\sin C = \dfrac{h}{b}$	**1.** Primary trigonometric ratio
2. In $\triangle ABD$, $\sin B = \dfrac{h}{c}$	**2.** Primary trigonometric ratio
3. $h = (b)(\sin C)$	**3.** Multiplication Property
4. $h = (c)(\sin B)$	**4.** Multiplication Property
5. $(b)(\sin C) = (c)(\sin B)$	**5.** Transitive Property
$\therefore \dfrac{\sin C}{c} = \dfrac{\sin B}{b}$	

In a similar manner, if the perpendicular was drawn from vertex C, then $\dfrac{\sin A}{a} = \dfrac{\sin B}{b}$.

> The **Law of Sines** states that $\dfrac{\sin A}{a} = \dfrac{\sin B}{b} = \dfrac{\sin C}{c}$.

The Law of Sines can be used to solve any triangle if one side and two angles are known, or if two sides and an angle "opposite" one of the sides is known. Recall the meaning of an opposite side.

Example 1

Find the distance from Town A to Town C if Towns A, B, and C are on the opposite shores of the lake.

$\angle A = 180° - (56 + 41)°$ or $83°$

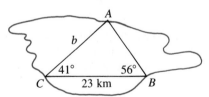

$\dfrac{\sin A}{a} = \dfrac{\sin B}{b}$

$b = \dfrac{23 \sin 56°}{\sin 83°}$

The distance from Town A to Town C is about 19 km.

Example 2

In triangle ABC, $\angle B = 73°$, side c is 12 cm long, and side b is 16 cm long. Solve the triangle. Sketch and label an appropriate diagram and find the magnitude of $\angle C$.

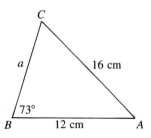

$\dfrac{\sin 73°}{16} = \dfrac{\sin C}{12}$

$\sin C = 0.7172$

Angle C is about 45.8°.

305

Exercises

1. A.T., the "Mathematics Wizard", stated that "in Example 2 of the display, angle C measured about 40° and side a measured about 15 cm." Is A.T. correct? Explain.

2. Prove the Law of Sines for any triangle that has an angle greater than 90°. (*Hint*: Construct the perpendicular from one of the angles less than 90° and use $\sin(180° - C) = \frac{h}{b}$.)

3. In oblique triangle ABC of the proof in the display, express the altitude of the triangle from each vertex in terms of the sine of an angle.

4. Find the measure of the indicated side or angle.

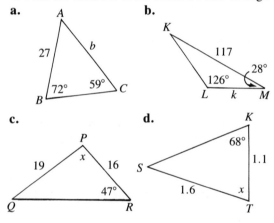

a.

b.

c.

d.

5. Three towns, Zing, Zang, and Zot, are located so that Zing is 15 km from Zang and 19 km from Zot. If the angle at Zang is 84°, then how far is Zang from Zot?

6. Find the measure of the indicated part.
a. In $\triangle ABC$, $\angle A = 47°$, $\angle B = 59°$, $b = 17$; find a.
b. In $\triangle KRM$, $\angle K = 73°$, $\angle M = 23°$, $k = 83$; find r.
c. In $\triangle PQR$, $\angle P = 94°$, $p = 19.3$, $q = 12.4$; find $\angle Q$.

7. Under what conditions may the Law of Sines be used to solve a triangle? Use a diagram to support your answer.

8. Prove the Law of Sines if the altitude in the triangle in the proof of the display is drawn from C.

9. Solve.
a. $\triangle RST$, $r = 35$, $s = 51$, $\angle S = 73°$
b. $\triangle FGH$, $\angle F = 123°$, $\angle G = 29°$, $h = 14.9$
c. $\triangle PKD$, $p = 8.1$, $k = 10.4$, $\angle K = 63°$

For the remaining exercises, draw and label an appropriate diagram before solving the problem.

10. Two lighthouses, one at Rock Port and one at Pirates' Cove, are 35 km apart. Rock Port is due north of Pirates' Cove. The lighthouse keeper at Rock Port spots a ship S35°E. At the same instant the lighthouse keeper at Pirates' Cove spots the ship at N57°E. How far is the ship from each lighthouse?

11. On her first shot, a golfer hits the ball 250 m but it slices 12° off a direct line to the hole. Her second shot is 92 m and it lands in the hole. How long was the hole?

12. A flagpole is tilted at an angle of 7° from the vertical and toward the sun. It casts a shadow of 14.3 m when the angle of elevation of the sun is 32°. Find the length of the flagpole.

Historical Note

François Viète (1540–1603)
François Viète was one of the more gifted mathematicians of the sixteenth century. One story has it that an ambassador claimed that France had no mathematicians capable of solving an equation to the 45th power. Viète was summoned and, realizing that the equation had an underlying trigonometric connection, was able to arrive at 23 roots.

Viète studied trigonometry and did much for the advancement of symbolic algebra. He once obtained rational expressions for $\cos n\theta$ as a function of $\cos \theta$ where n is a natural number. Using $\cos n\theta$, find its value when $n = 1, 2, 3, ..., 9$. How does it relate to $\cos \theta$?

11·11 The Law of Sines II

When two sides and the non-contained angle of a triangle are given, the triangle that is constructed is not unique. For example, in $\triangle ABC$, side a, side b, and $\angle B$ are known, and side a is longer than side b. The two possible triangles are constructed. From the construction, we may conclude that if two sides and a non-contained angle of a triangle are given, and the angle defined is opposite the smaller of the two sides, then a unique solution does not exist. This is the **ambiguous case**.

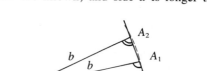

Example

In $\triangle ABC$, $\angle B = 53°$, b is 17 units, and a is 20 units. Find the measure of $\angle A$ and $\angle C$.

Since the non-contained angle is known, there are two possible triangles that can be constructed. Therefore, there will be two possibilities for both $\angle A$ and $\angle C$.

$$\frac{\sin 53°}{17} = \frac{\sin A_1}{20}$$
$$\sin A_1 = 0.9396$$
$$\angle A_1 = 70°$$

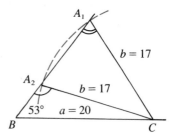

Since the Law of Sines will produce the same ratio for $\angle A_2$, the measure of $\angle A_2$ can be found using the fact that angles A_1 and A_2 are supplementary. Therefore, $\angle A_2 = 110°$ and $\angle C$ measures either 17° or 57°.

Exercises

1. Construct triangles with these dimensions. Draw two triangles if they exist.
a. $\triangle ABC$, $\angle A = 35°$, $b = 6$ cm, $a = 4$ cm
b. $\triangle ABC$, $\angle B = 57°$, $b = 7.5$ cm, $a = 6$ cm
c. $\triangle KRF$, $k = 7$ cm, $r = 4.5$ cm, $\angle R = 45°$

2. Find the length of c in the example of the display.

3. How many triangles can be constructed from the information given? Explain.
a. $\triangle ABC$, $\angle A = 48°$, $a = 13$, $b = 16$
b. $\triangle ABC$, $\angle A = 74°$, $a = 13$, $b = 16$
c. $\triangle ABC$, $\angle A = 30°$, $a = 6$, $b = 12$
d. $\triangle DEF$, $\angle E = 124°$, $e = 8$, $f = 7$
e. $\triangle DEF$, $\angle E = 36°$, $e = 8.0$, $f = 10.0$

4. Solve the triangles in Exercise 3. If a triangle cannot be solved, explain why.

5. In your own words, state the conditions for the ambiguous case to exist in a triangle.

6. Solve.
a. $\triangle ABC$, $a = 5.4$, $b = 4.6$, $\angle B = 57°$
b. $\triangle KXY$, $k = 76$, $x = 64$, $\angle X = 32°$
c. $\triangle DRM$, $m = 23.4$, $d = 15.2$, $\angle D = 29°$

7. Martha must take her sick son to the doctor by walking due east along a trail. At N63°E and 7.0 m from her house sleeps Andy. Andy has a reputation for tripping people with a rope that can spin around a radius of 4.0 m. How much of the distance along the trail is Martha in danger of being tripped if Andy doesn't move?

8. Explain whether Exercise 11 in Section 11·10 is an example of the ambiguous case.

11·12 The Law of Cosines

If we know two sides and a contained angle, or if three sides are known, a different process known as the **Law of Cosines** can be used to solve triangles.

> For any triangle, ABC, the Law of Cosines states that
> $$a^2 = b^2 + c^2 - 2bc \cos A$$
> $$b^2 = a^2 + c^2 - 2ac \cos B$$
> $$c^2 = a^2 + b^2 - 2ab \cos C$$
> where A, B, and C are the measures of the angles, and a, b, and c are the lengths of the sides opposite $\angle A$, $\angle B$, and $\angle C$ respectively.

To prove the Law of Cosines, it will be necessary to look at the two possibilities for the triangles; when the triangle has all acute angles and when the triangle has one obtuse angle. It also is necessary that one side be expressed in terms of the other sides and the contained angle.

GIVEN: Triangle ABC is an oblique triangle with $\overline{AD}$ perpendicular to $\overline{BC}$ (Case 1) or $\overline{BC}$ extended (Case 2).

REQUIRED: To prove that $a^2 = b^2 + c^2 - 2bc \cos A$, $b^2 = a^2 + c^2 - 2ac \cos B$, and $c^2 = a^2 + b^2 - 2ab \cos C$.

PROOF:

Case 1

Triangle ABC is acute.

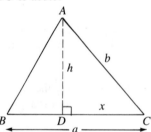

In $\triangle ADC$, $\cos C = \dfrac{x}{b}$.

$b \cos C = x$

also, $b^2 = h^2 + x^2$

In $\triangle ABD$, $c^2 = h^2 + (a - x)^2$

$c^2 = h^2 + a^2 - 2ax + x^2$

$c^2 = a^2 + (h^2 + x^2) - 2ax$

$c^2 = a^2 + b^2 - 2ab \cos C$

Case 2

Triangle ABC is obtuse.

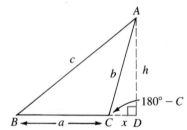

In $\triangle ADC$, $\cos(180° - C) = \dfrac{x}{b}$.

Since $\cos(180° - C) = \cos C$,

$b \cos(180° - C) = x$

$-b \cos C = x$

also, $b^2 = h^2 + x^2$

In $\triangle ABD$, $\quad c^2 = h^2 + (a + x)^2$

$c^2 = h^2 + a^2 + 2ax + x^2$

$c^2 = a^2 + (h^2 + x^2) + 2ax$

Substituting $\quad c^2 = a^2 + b^2 + 2a(-b \cos C)$

Therefore, $c^2 = a^2 + b^2 - 2ab \cos C$.

Similarly, the other two forms of the law can be proven by constructing a perpendicular from $\angle B$ or $\angle C$.

Example 1

Tam and Joshi began swimming from the shore of Lake Ontario. They swam at an angle of 43° to each other. When they stopped to rest, Tam had gone 230 m while Joshi had gone 150 m. How far apart were they?

Draw and label an appropriate diagram. The Law of Cosines can be used to find the distance, b.

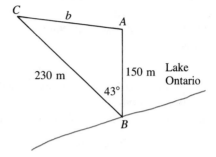

$b^2 = a^2 + c^2 - 2ac \cos B$
$b^2 = 230^2 + 150^2 - 2(230)(150)\cos 43°$
$b^2 = 52\ 900 + 22\ 500 - 69\ 000 \cos 43°$
$b^2 \doteq 24\ 937$
$b \doteq 157.9$

They are approximately 158 m apart.

Here is the calculator keying sequence that could be used to solve the equation.

230 $\boxed{x^2}$ $\boxed{+}$ 150 $\boxed{x^2}$ $\boxed{-}$ $\boxed{(}$ 2 $\boxed{\times}$ 230 $\boxed{\times}$ 150 $\boxed{\times}$ 43 $\boxed{\text{COS}}$ $\boxed{)}$ $\boxed{=}$ $\boxed{\sqrt{x}}$ **157.91325**

Example 2

In triangle ABC, a is 43 cm, b is 38 cm, and c is 61 cm. Solve the triangle.

Understand the Problem
Draw and label an appropriate diagram. We are required to find all unknown angles in the triangle.

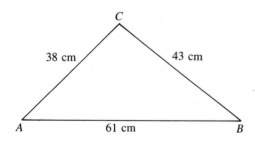

Develop a Plan
When solving for the angles of a triangle given three sides, find the measure of the largest angle first. The largest angle is opposite the largest side so $\angle C$ should be found first. The Law of Cosines can be rearranged so that the angle is solved. Here are the formulas for the angles.

$$\cos C = \frac{a^2 + b^2 - c^2}{2ab}$$
$$\cos B = \frac{a^2 + c^2 - b^2}{2ac}$$
$$\cos A = \frac{b^2 + c^2 - a^2}{2bc}$$

Carry Out the Plan
$$\cos C = \frac{a^2 + b^2 - c^2}{2ab}$$
$$= \frac{43^2 + 38^2 - 61^2}{2(43)(38)}$$
$$\doteq -0.1310$$
$$\angle C \doteq 97.5°$$

Look Back
The other two angles can be found using the Law of Sines. The angles of the triangle are approximately 98°, 44°, and 38°. You now have two methods for solving triangles.

Exercises

1. Refer to Example 2 in the display.
a. Why is ∠C an obtuse angle?
b. Why is the Sine Law suggested to find ∠A and ∠B rather than the Cosine Law? Verify that the angles found are correct.
c. Show the calculator keying sequence you would use to find ∠C.

2. In the proof of the Law of Cosines in the display it states that $\cos(180° - C) = -\cos C$. Give reasons for each step in the proof of this statement.

$$\cos(180° - C) = \cos[-(C - 180°)]$$
$$= \cos(C - 180°)$$
$$= -\cos C$$

3. Find the unknown side or angle in these triangles.
a.
b.

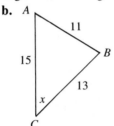

4. Three towns, Nim, Boom, and Raj, are joined by straight roads. The distance from Nim to Boom is 18 km. The distance from Nim to Raj is 7 km. If the distance from Boom to Raj is 13 km, then find the angle formed by the roads which meet at Raj.

5. Find the measure of the indicated part after constructing each triangle.
a. In △ABC, $a = 18$, $b = 21$, $c = 25$; find ∠A.
b. In △XYZ, $x = 96$, $y = 73$, ∠Z = 29°; find z.
c. In △PQR, $p = 4.3$, $q = 3.7$, $r = 4.1$; find ∠R.

6. Prove the Law of Cosines for both obtuse and acute triangles if the perpendicular is drawn from ∠B.

7. Solve each triangle.
a. △ABC, $a = 5$, $b = 12$, $c = 13$
b. △KRS, $k = 57$, $r = 49$, $s = 107$
c. △UVW, ∠U = 74°, $v = 8$, $w = 11$
d. △PRT, ∠T = 55°, $p = r = 18.1$

8. A raquetball player hits the ball 2.1 m to the side wall. The ball rebounds at an angle of 140° and travels 4.4 m to the front wall. How far is the ball from the player when it hits the front wall?

9. A plane is flying from Calgary to Edmonton, a distance of 300 km. A navigational error was discovered and it was determined that the plane had flown 17° off course for 250 km. How far was the plane from Edmonton when the error was discovered?

10. Colin is an avid golfer. On a 180 m hole, he hits his tee shot 170 m and then sinks his 30 m chip shot. At what angle did he slice his tee shot?

11. The goal posts in a football game are 4 m apart. A kicker attempts to score a field goal by kicking the ball from a point 25 m from the top of one goal post and 28 m from the top of the other goal post. Within what angle must the kick be made?

12. How many grooves does a record have that is played at a speed of 45 rpm?

13. Toeh has a pool table in the basement of his home. He discovered that if he hits a shot from one corner pocket to the opposite bank, that the ball hits the middle of the table at an angle of 60° to the bank and goes into the corner pocket on the same side of the table from which the ball was originally shot. If the ball travels 3 m until it hits the bank, then how long is the pool table?

14. A hockey player is attempting to score a goal by sliding the puck along the ice. If a line is drawn from each goal post to the point where the shot is taken, the angle formed will be 26°. If the goal is 2.5 m wide, then how far away is the player?

11·13 Area of a Triangle

The most common formula for the area of a triangle requires the length of the base and the height or altitude of the triangle. The height of the triangle is not always known. However, the height can be calculated using one of the trigonometric ratios, and a formula for the area of a triangle can be developed.

There are two possible cases for $\triangle ABC$: an acute triangle or an obtuse triangle. Segment AD is the perpendicular to $\overline{BC}$, or $\overline{BC}$ extended, and it is the height of the triangle.

Case 1

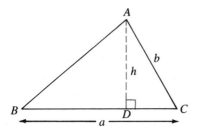

In $\triangle ACD$, $\sin C = \dfrac{h}{b}$.

$b \sin C = h$

Case 2

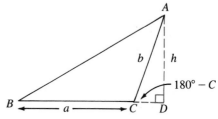

In $\triangle ACD$ $\sin (180° - C) = \dfrac{h}{b}$.

$b \sin (180° - C) = h$
Since $\sin (180° - C) = \sin C$
$b \sin C = h$

For both cases, in $\triangle ABC$, Area $= \dfrac{1}{2}$(base)(height)

$$= \dfrac{1}{2}ab \sin C$$

For any triangle ABC, where two sides and a contained angle are known, the area is found using $\dfrac{1}{2}ab \sin C$, $\dfrac{1}{2}ac \sin B$, or $\dfrac{1}{2}bc \sin A$.

If one side and two angles of $\triangle ABC$ are known, the area of a triangle can be found depending upon which angles and sides are known.

$$\text{Area} = \dfrac{c^2 \sin A \sin B}{2 \sin C} \quad \text{or} \quad \text{Area} = \dfrac{b^2 \sin A \sin C}{2 \sin B} \quad \text{or} \quad \text{Area} = \dfrac{a^2 \sin B \sin C}{2 \sin A}$$

Example

Find the area using the appropriate formula.

a. $\triangle ABC$, $\angle A = 67°$, $\angle B = 42°$, $a = 12.3$ cm, $\angle C = 71°$

$\text{Area} = \dfrac{a^2 \sin B \sin C}{2 \sin A}$

$= \dfrac{(12.3)^2(\sin 42°)(\sin 71°)}{2 \sin 67°}$

$\doteq 51.0$

The area is approximately 51.0 cm².

b. $\triangle ABC$, $a = 12$ cm, $b = 9$ cm, $\angle C = 56°$

$\text{Area} = \dfrac{1}{2}ab \sin C$

$= \dfrac{1}{2}(12)(9)\sin 56°$

$\doteq 44.8$

The area is approximately 44.8 cm².

Exercises

1. Construct $\triangle ABC$ with $a = 4$ cm, $b = 5$ cm, and $c = 6$ cm.

a. Calculate s where $s = \dfrac{a + b + c}{2}$.

b. Calculate A where $A = \sqrt{s(s - a)(s - b)(s - c)}$, and A represents the area of the triangle. Parts **a** and **b** are the calculations necessary for finding the area of a triangle when all three sides are known. This is called **Heron's Formula.**

2. In your own words, summarize how to find the area of a triangle using Heron's Formula.

3. Which formula would be used to find the area of the triangle? Justify your selection by constructing the triangle.

a. $a = 12$, $b = 13$, $\angle C = 43°$
b. $a = 3$, $b = 4$, $c = 6$
c. $\angle A = 56°$, $\angle B = 76°$, $b = 34$

4. Find the area of these triangles. Construct the triangle where necessary.

a. 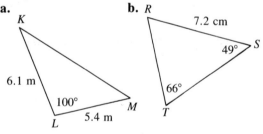 **b.** R

c. $\triangle JSM$, $j = 5.3$, $s = 5.1$, $\angle J = 72°$
d. $\triangle ABC$, $\angle A = 67°$, $\angle B = 89°$, $a = 12$
e. $\triangle ABC$, $a = 3.4$, $b = 2.1$, $c = 4.3$
f. $\triangle RST$, $r = 45$ cm, $s = 56$ cm, $t = 58$ cm

5. Using the Law of Sines, prove that the area of any triangle ABC can be found using the formula $\dfrac{a^2 \sin B \sin C}{2 \sin A}$.

6. A parallelogram has sides of 13 cm and 15 cm. The angle between the sides is 71°. Find the area of the parallelogram.

7. The volume of a regular solid can be found by multiplying the area of its base by its height. Find the volume of these solids.

a. 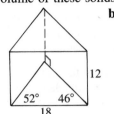 **b.**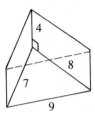

8. Find the area of these figures. Construct the figure before attempting the solution.

a. a regular pentagon with sides of 8 cm (*Hint:* Divide it into 5 congruent triangles from its centre.)
b. a regular octagon with sides of 15 cm

9. Find the area of the triangle. Account for all possibilities.

a. $\triangle ABC$, $a = 12$ cm, $b = 10$ cm, $\angle B = 35°$
b. $\triangle DEF$, $d = 17$ cm, $f = 11$ cm, $\angle F = 57°$
c. $\triangle JKM$, $k = 35$ m, $m = 42$ m, $\angle K = 19°$

10. The volume of a pyramid is found by multiplying the area of its base by the height and taking one third of the product. Find the volume and surface area of these solids.

a. 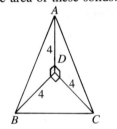 **b.**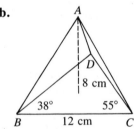

11. A farmer has a farm in the shape shown in the diagram. What is the area of the land that the farmer owns?

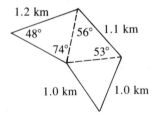

11·14 Applications

Trigonometric laws have many practical applications. Approach each question as a problem to be solved using the four-step model. Remember, most trigonometric applications can be simplified by drawing and labelling a suitable diagram.

Example

Two airplanes fly from the same airport. The first leaves the airport at 08:00 flying N43°W at 120 km/h. The second leaves the airport at 08:30 flying N27°E at 150 km/h. How far apart are the two airplanes at 11:00?

Understand the Problem

Draw a diagram showing the direction of the two airplanes and the distances each have travelled by 11:00.

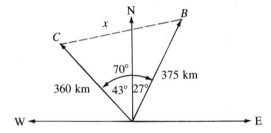

Develop a Plan

Since two sides and the contained angle are known, the Cosine Law should be used. This is not a possibility for the ambiguous case.

Carry Out the Plan

$$a^2 = b^2 + c^2 - 2bc \cos A$$
$$x^2 = 360^2 + 375^2 - 2(360)(375)\cos 70°$$
$$x \doteq 421.7$$

Look Back

The airplanes are approximately 422 km apart at 11:00. The answer appears reasonable.

Exercises

1. A wheelchair ramp is to be installed at a train station. The height of the platform above ground level is 1.7 m. The angle of inclination of the ramp is to be 6°. Find the length of the ramp, and how far from the edge of the platform the ramp should start.

2. Mount Allan has a vertical rise of 865 m. The face of the mountain covers a distance of 3196 m. Find the angle of elevation.

3. Two tracking stations 175 km apart spot a rocket at the same time. The angles of elevation to the rocket are 27° and 59°. If the rocket is overhead and between the two stations, find the height of the rocket above the Earth's surface.

4. Canada's highest waterfall is Della Falls on Vancouver Island. An observer standing at the same level as the base of the falls views the top of the falls at an angle of elevation of 58°. When the observer moves 31 m closer to the base of the falls, the angle of elevation increases to 61°. Find the height of Della Falls.

5. A farmer has a field in the shape of a triangle. Standing at one corner, it is 530 m to the second corner and 750 m to the third corner. The angle between the lines of sight to the two corners is 53°. Find the perimeter and area of the field.

6. A sailboat leaves the dock at Gibson's Landing on a bearing of S57°W. After sailing for 8 km, the ship tacks and travels S31°E for 5 km.
a. How far is the sailboat from Gibson's Landing?
b. What direction would it have to sail to return to the dock at Gibson's Landing?

11·15 Computer Application—
Law of Sines

The most successful computer programs can be used with minor revisions to solve different problems and ease the task of calculating. This program will solve for one side of any triangle using the Law of Sines if two angles and a non-contained side are known. In this case, it will solve for side b, given side a as well as the measures of $\angle A$ and $\angle B$.

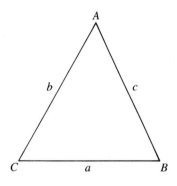

```
10  REM APPLICATION OF THE LAW OF SINES
20  INPUT "ANGLES IN DEGREES ARE ";A, B
30  INPUT "LENGTH OF SIDE A "; A1
40  LET PI = 3.14159
50  LET A = PI / 180 * A
60  LET B = PI / 180 * B
70  LET B1 = A1 * SIN(B) / SIN(A)
80  PRINT "SIDE OPPOSITE ANGLE B IS ";
    B1; " CM"
90  END
```

Exercises

1. Run the program in the display and record the output if $a = 8$ cm, $\angle A = 35°$, and $\angle B = 45°$.

2. Explain the purpose of lines 20, 30, and 70 of the program in the display.

3. Using the program in the display, evaluate side b of $\triangle ABC$ given these measures for side a, $\angle A$, and $\angle B$.
a. $a = 8$ cm, $\angle A = 22°$, $\angle B = 44°$
b. $a = 4.6$ cm, $\angle A = 22.1°$, $\angle B = 33.7°$
c. $a = 12$ cm, $\angle A = 108°$, $\angle B = 51.2°$
d. $a = 33.245$ cm, $\angle A = 12.9°$, $\angle B = 121.5°$
e. Verify the computer's output for parts **a** and **b** by calculating the areas using the Law of Sines. Is the computer output reasonable? Explain.

4. For the program in the display, what do you think the computer output will be if $\angle A = 100°$ and $\angle B = 85°$? Run the program to test and help explain your hypothesis.

5. Write a program to find the area of a triangle given the length of the three sides. Enter your program on a computer and test it using these lengths of sides.
a. 3 cm, 4 cm, 5 cm
b. 2 cm, 3.5 cm, 4.2 cm
c. 5.2 cm, 2.7 cm, 6.3 cm
d. 4 cm, 5 cm, 10 cm
e. Check your output for part **d**. Does it give you an error?
f. Explain why the program will not work for the triangle in part **d**.
g. Check the computer's output for parts **a** to **c** using Heron's Formula for the area of a triangle. Is the computer output reasonable?

6. Calculators and computers have become so much a part of everyday life that critical thinking in mathematics is no longer necessary. Write a short essay either defending or rejecting this statement.

11·16 Chapter Review

1. Solve for x.

a.

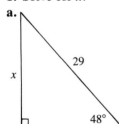

29

x

48°

b.

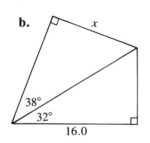

x

38°

32°

16.0

2. The Leaning Tower of Pisa tilts at an angle of about 5° from the vertical. The top of the tower is 54.0 m above the ground. If an apple is dropped from the top of the tower at its leaning edge, how far from the base of the tower would it land?

3. The tangent function is an **increasing function**, while the cotangent function is a **decreasing function**. Explain this statement. (*Hint*: Use the tables at the back of the book.)

4. Find the value of the other five trigonometric ratios if $\cos \theta = -\dfrac{\sqrt{5}}{3}$ and θ is in the second quadrant.

5. Evaluate. Use a calculator if one is available.
a. $\cot 97°$ **b.** $\sec 346°$
c. $\csc 268°$ **d.** $\tan 139°$

6. Find θ where $0° \le \theta < 360°$.
a. $\cos \theta = 0.3519$ **b.** $\csc \theta = 1.6732$
c. $\tan \theta = -2.4765$ **d.** $\sec \theta = \dfrac{-5}{3}$
e. $\sin \theta = \dfrac{2}{9}$ **f.** $\cot \theta = -\dfrac{4}{3}$

7. Find θ where $0° \le \theta < 360°$.
a. $\sin \theta + \sqrt{3} = \dfrac{\sqrt{3}}{2}$
b. $\tan^2 \theta - 9 = 0$
c. $\cos^2 \theta - \dfrac{1}{6}\cos \theta - \dfrac{1}{6} = 0$
d. $\sin^2 \theta + 2\sin \theta = 3$

8. Express in terms of $\sin \theta$, $\cos \theta$, or both.
a. $\sec^2 \theta - 1$ **b.** $\cot \theta \sec \theta$
c. $\dfrac{\tan x}{\sec x}$ **d.** $\dfrac{\sec t}{\csc t}$

9. The top of a vertical cliff in the Rocky Mountains is inaccessible to surveyors who must find its height. One of the surveyors draws the scale diagram shown. Find the height of the cliff.

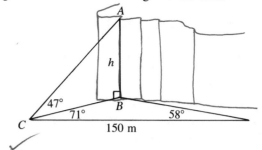

A

h

47°

71°

B

58°

C

150 m

10. Solve the equation if $0° \le \theta < 360°$.
a. $2\sin^2 \theta = \sin \theta + 1$ **b.** $3\sin \theta = 2\sin \theta$
c. $2\sin^2 \theta = 1 + \sin \theta$ **d.** $\sin^2 \theta = \dfrac{1}{4}$

11. Solve the triangle and find its area.
a. $\triangle ABC$, $\angle B = 77°$, $\angle C = 84°$, $c = 31$ units
b. $\triangle CJR$, $c = 2$ units, $j = 3.0$, $r = 4$ units
c. $\triangle UVW$, $\angle V = 38°$, $v = 19$ units, $w = 22$ units

12. Two planes leave Halifax at the same time. One travels at 400 km/h in a direction N72°E. The other travels at 500 km/h in a direction N23°W. They both fly at an altitude of 500 m. How far apart are the planes after 3 h?

13. A tree 26 m high, which has been growing at an angle, is to be cut down. A 40 m rope is tied to the top of the tree. The rope makes an angle of 39° with the ground. What angle does the tree lean from the vertical?

14. Explain how to use a calculator to find the solution of $\sin 38° = \dfrac{14.3}{x}$ if the division key is broken.

315

11·17 Chapter Test

1. The Ridge Chair ski lift at Big White Ski Village has a length of 1780 m with a vertical rise of 420 m. The Village Chair at the same resort has approximately the same slope.
a. If the vertical rise of the Village Chair is 260 m, calculate the length of the Village Chair to the nearest 10 m.
b. What assumptions are made in finding this length?

2. Solve the triangle. Angle A is a right angle.
a. $\triangle ABC$ with $b = 8.7$ units, $\angle B = 35°$
b. $\triangle ABC$ with $a = 19$ units, $c = 12$ units

3. Two trees are 100 m apart. From a point halfway between the two trees, the angle of elevation of their tops is 12° and 18°.
a. How much taller is one tree than the other?
b. Where would a person have to stand in order to have the same angles of elevation to the top of each tree?

4. If $\tan \theta = -\dfrac{7}{4}$ and θ is in quadrant IV, then find the value of the other five trigonometric ratios.

5. In which quadrant is the terminal arm if the angle is in standard position?
a. 173°   **b.** 715°   **c.** −271°
d. 198°   **e.** −87°   **f.** −532°

6. Write one positive and one negative angle coterminal with the angles in Exercise 5.

7. Solve for θ where $0° \le \theta < 360°$. Use a calculator if one is available.
a. $\sin \theta = -\dfrac{1}{2}$ **b.** $\cot \theta = \sqrt{3}$
c. $\cos \theta = 1$ **d.** $\sec \theta = -\sqrt{2}$
e. $\tan \theta = 0$ **f.** $\csc \theta = 0$

8. Solve the equation if $0° \le \theta < 360°$.
a. $\cos \theta = \dfrac{1}{\sqrt{2}}$ **b.** $\cos \theta = \dfrac{1}{4}\sec \theta$
c. $\sin^2 \theta = \sqrt{3} \sin \theta$
d. $1 - 2\cos^2 \theta = -1$
e. $\sin^2 \theta + \sin \theta = 0$
f. $\cos \theta + 2(1 - \cos^2 \theta) = 1$

9. Solve the triangle and find its area.
a. $\triangle ABC$, $\angle A = 79°$, $\angle B = 37°$, $c = 6.4$ units
b. $\triangle CDE$, $c = 13$ units, $d = 15$ units, $\angle D = 64°$
c. $\triangle PQR$, $p = 30$ units, $q = 40$ units, $r = 50$ units

10. Two lifeguards, Doran and Kim, are stationed 250 m apart on the shore of Lake Ontario. They both spot a swimmer in distress. Who is closer to the swimmer and by how much?

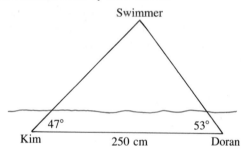

11. At Exhibition Stadium in Toronto, the distance from home plate to "dead centre" field is 119 m. A fly ball is hit to the centre fielder at the wall. He throws out a runner trying to steal third base. How far did he throw the ball if the distance from home plate to third base is 27.4 m? (*Hint*: Draw and label a diagram of a baseball diamond.)

12. A tree growing vertically on the side of a hill is hit by lightning. The top of the tree falls on the downhill side so that it touches the ground without completely breaking off from the tree. The angle of elevation of the hill is 13° and the tip of the tree makes an angle of 16° with the ground. If the tip of the tree lands 19 m from the base of the trunk, then how tall was the tree before being hit by lightning?

GEOMETRY OF THE CIRCLE

Tune Up

1. Copy and complete this proof to show that $\overline{AB} \cong \overline{CD}$.

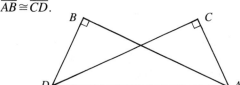

GIVEN: $\angle ABD \cong \angle ACD = 90°$
REQUIRED: To prove that $\overline{AB} \cong \overline{CD}$.
PROOF:

Statement	Reason
In $\triangle ABD$ and $\triangle ACD$,	
1. $\angle ABD \cong \angle ACD$	**1.** ▬▬▬▬
2. $\overline{DA} \cong \overline{AD}$	**2.** ▬▬▬▬
3. $\triangle ABD \cong \triangle$▬▬	**3.** Hypotenuse-side
4. $\overline{AB} \cong$ ▬▬	**4.** C.P.C.T.

a. Explain the hypotenuse-side theorem in words.
b. Explain the meaning of C.P.C.T.

2. What is the sum of the measures of the angles in each?
a. triangle   **b.** quadrilateral

3. Find the length of $\overline{TP}$ and the coordinates of its midpoint.

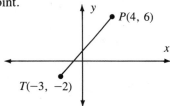

4. Solve for r.

5. Given $2x - 3y = 10$ and $x = y$, solve for x and y.

6. Calculate the diameter of a circle with a circumference of 10 cm.

7. For every circle, the real number π is the ratio of the circumference of the circle to its diameter.
a. Write the first five digits in the decimal representation of π.
b. What does it mean to say that π is an irrational number?

8. Write the coordinates of the point that is symmetric, as indicated, with the point $(4, -7)$.
a. about the y-axis   **b.** about the x-axis
c. about the origin   **d.** about the line $y = x$

9. Verify that the line represented by the equation $3x - 7y + 5 = 0$ passes through the point $(10, 5)$.

10. Write an equation of a line passing through $(4, 5)$ and perpendicular to a line through the points $(0, 0)$ and $(4, 5)$.

317

12·1 Angles in a Circle

In order to understand circle geometry, it is necessary to understand certain terminology and to recognize patterns associated with circular figures. Several circle-related terms, with specific focus on angles, will be discussed in this section.

A **sector or central angle** is formed by two radii and has its vertex at the centre of the circle. $\angle AOB$ is a central angle.

An **inscribed angle** has its vertex on the circle and its sides intersect the circle at two other points. $\angle XTZ$ and $\angle XYZ$ are inscribed angles.

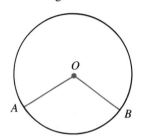

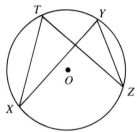

The intersection of the sides of these angles with the circles defines **arcs**. $\angle AOB$ defines a **minor arc** AB and a **major arc** AB. The minor arc AB is the shorter path along the circle from A to B, and the major arc AB is the longer path. We say that $\angle AOB$ is **subtended** by arc AB.

Example

Identify the indicated angles in this circle.
a. the inscribed angle subtended by minor arc TV
b. the central angle subtended by major arc VS

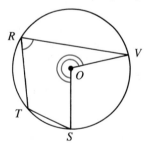

a. Minor arc TV subtends the inscribed angle $\angle TRV$.
b. Major arc VS subtends the central angle $\angle VOS$.

Since a **chord** is defined by the end points of an arc, it is common to refer to an angle subtended by a chord. In this diagram, chord GH subtends the central angle $\angle GOH$, and chord KL subtends the inscribed angle $\angle KML$.

318

Exercises

1. In your own words, define each term.
a. sector angle **b.** minor arc
c. chord **d.** major arc
e. inscribed angle **f.** subtends

2. Draw a circle to illustrate each of the following.
a. a sector angle ∠MON with M and N on a circle
b. an inscribed angle ∠PQR subtended by minor arc PR
c. an inscribed angle ∠PTR subtended by major arc PR

3. Sketch the circle shown and use it to indicate these angles.
a. a central angle subtended by major arc BC
b. an inscribed angle subtended by minor arc BC
c. an inscribed angle subtended by chord DE

4. Name the angles subtended by minor arc PT in this circle.

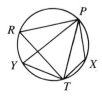

5. Sketch this diagram and identify each of the following.
a. an inscribed angle subtended by chord DE
b. an inscribed angle subtended by chord DF

6. Use the properties of isosceles triangles and the sum of angles in a triangle to determine the values of the variables representing the measures of angles in each circle.

a.

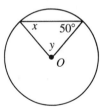

b.

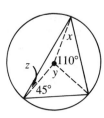

7. Use compasses to draw a large circle with centre O and with any two points A and B on the circle.
a. Draw a sector angle ∠AOB.
b. Use a protractor to measure ∠AOB subtended by the minor arc AB.
c. Draw an inscribed angle ∠ACB subtended by the minor arc AB.
d. Use a protractor to measure ∠ACB.
e. Compare the measures of the two angles. What do you notice?
f. Write a conclusion about the relationship between sector angles and inscribed angles subtended by the same arc. If necessary, repeat steps **a** to **e**.

8. Use the circle in Exercise 7 to complete the following steps.
a. Draw and measure two other inscribed angles subtended by the same minor arc.
b. Compare the measures of each of the inscribed angles. What do you notice about the measures of the angles?
c. Write a conclusion about the relationship between inscribed angles subtended by the same arc.

9. Determine the measure of an inscribed angle subtended by the diameter of a circle. Is this true for all such angles? Try several examples.

319

12·2 Angle Relationships

Angles in circles form a fascinating study of patterns and relationships. Many of the angles formed by radii and arcs of circles are related.

Example 1

Show that the measure of a central angle is twice the measure of an inscribed angle subtended by the same arc.

Understand the Problem

Using a diagram of a circle with centre at O, minor arc AC, central angle $\angle AOC$, and inscribed angle $\angle ABC$, we are required to show that the measure of $\angle AOC$, subtended by minor arc AC, is twice the measure of $\angle ABC$.

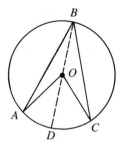

Develop a Plan

Draw a diameter through B and O to establish a connection between the two angles. Then use $\triangle AOB$ and $\triangle BOC$, and their exterior angles at O, to relate the angles in a proof. Use the fact that $\triangle AOB$ and $\triangle BOC$ are isosceles triangles.

Carry Out the Plan

We will write a two-column proof.

Statement	Reason
1. $\overline{OA} \cong \overline{OB} \cong \overline{OC}$	1. Radii of the same circle
2. $\angle AOD \cong \angle ABO + \angle OAB$	2. Exterior angle equal to sum of opposite interior angles
3. $\angle ABO \cong \angle OAB$	3. $\triangle AOB$ is isosceles.
4. $\angle AOD \cong 2\angle ABO$	4. Substitution property
Similarly, it can be shown that	
5. $\angle COD \cong 2\angle OBC$	5. Substitution property
6. $\angle AOD + \angle COD \cong 2\angle ABO + 2\angle OBC$	6. Addition of Statements 4 and 5
7. $\therefore \angle AOC \cong 2\angle ABC$	7. Simplify Statement 6.

Look Back

Using the properties of radii and triangles, we have proven that the measure of a central angle is twice the measure of an inscribed angle if they are both subtended by the same arc.

> **Theorem** If an inscribed angle and a central angle are subtended by the same arc, then the inscribed angle is one half the measure of the central angle.

This theorem leads directly to the two following properties of inscribed angles.

320

Example 2

Show that an inscribed angle subtended by a diameter of a circle is a right angle.

Let $\overline{AC}$ be any diameter and B be any point on the circle. Arc AC subtends the central angle $\angle AOC$ which has a measure of 180°. Also, arc AC subtends the inscribed angle $\angle ABC$. As was shown in Example 1, the measure of an inscribed angle is one half the measure of the central angle subtended by the same arc. Therefore, the measure of $\angle ABC$ is one half the measure of $\angle AOC$ or 90°.

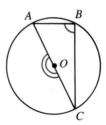

Theorem An inscribed angle subtended by a diameter of a circle is a right angle.

Example 3

Show that the measures of two inscribed angles subtended by the same arc are equal.

An arc may subtend an infinite number of inscribed angles. In this diagram, minor arc XY subtends two inscribed angles. Each inscribed angle is equal to one half the central angle $\angle XOY$. If the central angle has a measure of $2a°$, then each inscribed angle has a measure of $a°$. Therefore, the two inscribed angles subtended by the same arc are equal in measure.

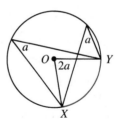

Theorem Inscribed angles subtended by the same arc are congruent.

Exercises

1. If the inscribed angle $\angle A$ is subtended by the same arc as the central angle, determine the measure of $\angle A$.

a.

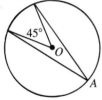

b.

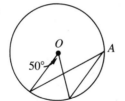

2. Determine the measures of the indicated angles.

a.

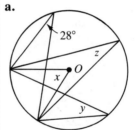

b.

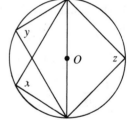

3. Determine the measures of the indicated angles.

a.

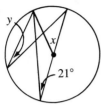

b.

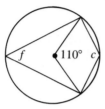

c.

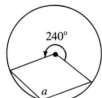

d.

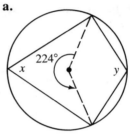

4. Copy this diagram and complete the following steps to show that the measure of a central angle is twice the measure of an inscribed angle subtended by the same arc.

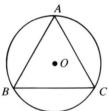

a. Join A, B, and C to the centre O.
b. Show that $\triangle AOB$, $\triangle BOC$, and $\triangle AOC$ are isosceles and indicate the congruent angles in each triangle by the variables x, y, and z respectively.
c. Express the central angle in $\triangle BOC$ in terms of y.
d. Write an equation for the sum of the angles in $\triangle ABC$ in terms of x, y, and z.
e. Use the equation from part **d** to solve for $(x + z)$ and relate it to the expression for the central angle in part **c**.
f. What conclusion can you make from this proof?

5. Determine the measures of the indicated angles.

a.

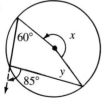

b.

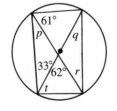

6. A.T., the "Mathematics Wizard", stated that "the longer the chord, the greater the measure of an inscribed angle subtended by that chord". Is A.T. correct? Explain. Use a diagram to support your answer.

7. Determine the value in degrees of $(x + y)$ in each circle.

a.

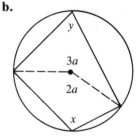

b.

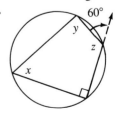

8. An **inscribed quadrilateral** has vertices on the circumference of the circle.

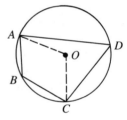

Use the relationship between sector angles and inscribed angles subtended by the same chords to prove that the opposite angles in a cyclic quadrilateral are supplementary.

9. Determine the value of the indicated angles.

a.

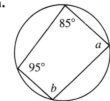

b.

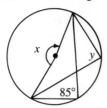

322

12·3 Properties of Chords

In this section, some of the interesting properties of chords and their lengths will be developed.

Example 1

Show that a line through the centre of a circle and the midpoint of a chord is perpendicular to the chord.

GIVEN: Circle with centre at O and a line passing through the midpoint of chord AC and O. B is the midpoint of chord AC.

REQUIRED: To prove that $\overline{OB} \perp \overline{AC}$.

PROOF:

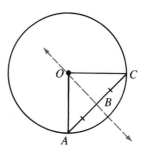

Statement	Reason
1. $\overline{OA} \cong \overline{OC}$	1. Radii of same circle
2. $\overline{AB} \cong \overline{BC}$	2. Midpoint
3. $\overline{OB} \cong \overline{OB}$	3. Reflexive property
4. $\therefore \triangle AOB \cong \triangle COB$	4. S.S.S.
5. $\angle OBA \cong \angle OBC$	5. C.P.C.T.
6. Since, $\angle ABC = 180°$	6. Straight line
7. Then, $\angle OBA \cong \angle OBC = 90°$	
$\therefore \overline{OB} \perp \overline{AC}$	

> **Theorem** A line through the centre of a circle and the midpoint of a chord is perpendicular to the chord.

The lengths of intersecting chords result in another intersecting property.

Example 2

Show that the products of the lengths of the segments of two intersecting chords are equal.

GIVEN: Circle with centre at O, and two chords, AB and CD, intersecting at E.

REQUIRED: To prove that $|\overline{AE}| \times |\overline{EB}| = |\overline{CE}| \times |\overline{ED}|$.

PROOF:

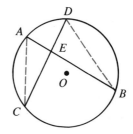

Statement	Reason
In $\triangle AEC$ and $\triangle BED$,	
1. $\angle AEC \cong \angle BED$	1. Opposite angles
2. $\angle CAE \cong \angle BDE$	2. Inscribed angles subtended by minor arc CB
3. $\angle ACE \cong \angle DBE$	3. Inscribed angles subtended by minor arc AD
4. $\therefore \triangle AEC \cong \triangle BED$	4. A.A.A.
5. $\therefore \dfrac{\overline{AE}}{\overline{DE}} = \dfrac{\overline{CE}}{\overline{BE}}$	5. Ratio of similar sides in $\triangle AEC$ and $\triangle BED$
6. $\therefore \overline{AE} \times \overline{BE} = \overline{CE} \times \overline{DE}$	

> **Theorem** If two chords of a circle intersect, the products of the lengths of the two segments of each chord are equal.

Exercises

1. Show that a line segment from the centre of a circle and perpendicular to a chord bisects the chord.

2. Show that the perpendicular bisector of a chord of a circle passes through the centre of the circle.

3. Calculate the length of the indicated side in each circle.

a.

b.

c.

d.

4. Determine the length of each side of the square bracing used to support a circular table with a 2.6 m diameter.

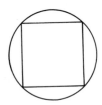

5. Describe how the centre of the circle can be located using these two chords, compasses, and a straightedge, or using a Mira.

6. A circular mirror, with a 26 cm radius, is mounted on a triangular backing as shown.

a. How far from the centre of the mirror are the bracings if each bracing is 45 cm in length?
b. Calculate the area of the triangular enclosure.

7. Given equal chords AB and CD, prove that $\overline{AC} \cong \overline{DB}$.

8. $\overline{PQ}$ and $\overline{ST}$ are two chords of a circle that intersect at R so that $\overline{PR} \cong \overline{SR}$. Prove that $\overline{QR} \cong \overline{TR}$.

9. Determine the lengths of the indicated segments of two intersecting chords.

a.

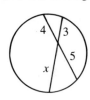

b.

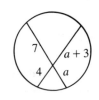

10. In this diagram, $\triangle PQR$ is equilateral and $\overline{QY} \cong \overline{XR}$.

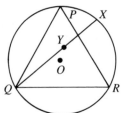

a. Prove $\triangle PQY \cong \triangle PXR$.
b. Prove $\triangle PYX$ is equilateral.

12·4 Properties of Tangents

A straight line can intersect a circle either at two points, one point, or no points. A straight line which intersects a circle at two points is called a **secant**. A straight line which intersects a circle at only one point is called a **tangent**. The point at which the tangent touches the circle is called the **point of tangency**. This section will examine properties involving circles and tangents.

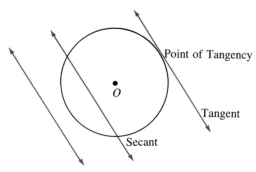

Example 1

Show that a radius to a point of tangency is perpendicular to the tangent.

One way to approach this problem is to use an indirect proof. Recall that in an indirect proof, an assumption is made which leads to a contradiction and indirectly proves that the opposite is true.

GIVEN: Circle with centre at O, tangent $\overline{ST}$ with the point of tangency at A, and radius $\overline{OA}$.
REQUIRED: To prove $\overline{OA} \perp \overline{ST}$.
ASSUMPTION: Assume $\angle OAT \neq 90°$. Let C represent a point on the tangent such that $\overline{OC} \perp \overline{ST}$ and let D represent another point on the tangent such that $\overline{AC} \cong \overline{DC}$.
PROOF:

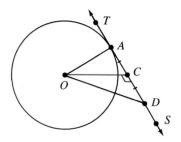

Statement	Reason
In $\triangle OAC$ and $\triangle ODC$,	
1. $\overline{AC} \cong \overline{DC}$	**1.** Given
2. $\angle OCA \cong \angle OCD$	**2.** Both are 90°.
3. $\overline{OC} \cong \overline{OC}$	**3.** Reflexive property
4. $\therefore \triangle OAC \cong \triangle ODC$	**4.** S.A.S.
5. $\therefore \overline{OA} \cong \overline{OD}$	**5.** C.P.C.T.

Since $\overline{OA}$ is the radius and $\overline{OA} \cong \overline{OD}$, then D is on the circle. If D and A are on both the circle and on the tangent, the tangent intersects the circle at two points. This contradicts the definition of a tangent and the original assumption that $\angle OAT \neq 90°$ must be false.

Therefore, $\angle OAT = 90°$, that is, $\overline{OA} \perp \overline{ST}$.

Theorem A tangent to a circle is always perpendicular to the radius at the point of tangency.

Example 2

A circle is given with centre at O and a point P outside the circle. If two tangents from P intersect the circle at A and B, show that $\overline{PA} \cong \overline{PB}$.

GIVEN: Circle with centre at O, a point P outside the circle, and two tangents from P that intersect the circle at A and B.
REQUIRED: To prove that $\overline{PA} \cong \overline{PB}$.
PROOF:

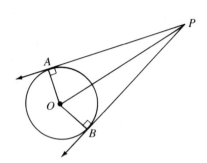

Statement	Reason
1. $\overline{AO} \cong \overline{BO}$	**1.** Radii of same circle
2. $\overline{OP} \cong \overline{OP}$	**2.** Reflexive property
3. $\angle PAO \cong \angle PBO$	**3.** Radii are perpendicular to tangents.
4. $\therefore \triangle PAO \cong \triangle PBO$	**4.** Hypotenuse and one side of right triangle
5. $\therefore \overline{PA} \cong \overline{PB}$	**5.** C.P.C.T.

Theorem Two tangents from a given point to the same circle are equal in length.

Exercises

1. Calculate, correct to one decimal place, the indicated lengths.

a.

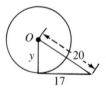

b.

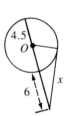

2. A line through M and N is tangent to a circle at R. The radius is 4 cm. M and N are 15 cm and 11 cm respectively from the centre of the circle. Determine the length of $\overline{MN}$.

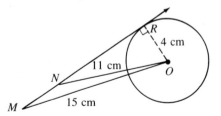

3. Two tangents from a point T outside a circle meet the circle at E and F. Show that $\angle TEF \cong \angle TFE$.

4. Given a circle with centre at O and tangents from P that meet the circle at A and B.

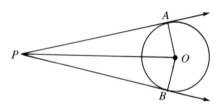

a. Show that $\angle APO \cong \angle BPO$.
b. Show that $\overline{PO}$ bisects $\angle AOB$.

5. Determine the lengths indicated.

a.

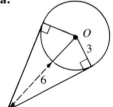

b.

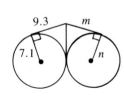

6. Show that the tangents at either end of a diameter of a circle are parallel.

326

7. How many tangents can be drawn to a circle in each situation?
a. from a point on the circle
b. from a point outside the circle
c. from a point inside the circle

8. Two tangents are drawn from a point A to a circle meeting it at B and C. Another tangent at any point P on minor arc BC meets $\overline{AB}$ at D and $\overline{AC}$ at E. Prove that the perimeter of $\triangle ADE$ is twice the measure of $\overline{AB}$.

9. Quadrilateral $PQRS$ circumscribes a circle such that each of the four sides are tangents. Prove that $\overline{PQ} + \overline{RS} = \overline{PS} + \overline{QR}$.

10. Tangents from L meet a circle with radius 8 cm at points M and N. If L is 22 cm from the centre of the circle, calculate the length of $\overline{MN}$.

11. Two tangents are drawn from a point T to meet a circle at X and Y. Prove that the angle between the tangents at T and the central angle $\angle XOY$ are supplementary.

12. If $\overline{AB}$ is a common tangent to two circles of different radii and the centres of the circles are joined by $\overline{OC}$, show that $\angle O \cong \angle C$.

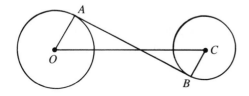

13. Concentric circles are circles which have the same centre. Given two concentric circles where two chords of the outer circle are tangent to the inner circle, prove that the chords are the same length.

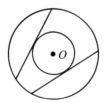

14. For two concentric circles, prove that a chord of the larger circle that is tangent to the smaller circle is bisected at the point of tangency.

15. In two concentric circles, a tangent to the inner circle is a 12 cm chord of the outer circle. If the radius of the inner circle is 5 cm, what is the radius of the outer circle?

16. In a circle, $\overline{SQ}$ and $\overline{PR}$ are perpendicular diameters, each 8 cm in length. From any point V on the minor arc SP, draw $\overline{VT}$ and $\overline{VW}$ perpendicular to the two diameters with T and W on the circle. Determine the length of $\overline{TW}$.

17. Concyclic points are points which lie on the same circle. A, B, and C are concyclic points of a circle with centre O. The tangents from A and B intersect at P and the tangents from B and C intersect at Q such that $\overleftrightarrow{AP} \parallel \overleftrightarrow{CQ}$. Show that $\angle POQ = 90°$.

18. Using the diagram from Exercise 17, extend $\overrightarrow{OP}$ so that it intersects the tangent from C at S and extend $\overrightarrow{OQ}$ so that it intersects the tangent from A at T. Show that $\overline{ST} \parallel \overline{PQ}$.

19. $\triangle ABC$ is inscribed in a circle with centre O. P is a point on the circle. If $\overline{PR} \perp \overline{AB}$, $\overline{PS} \perp \overline{BC}$, and $\overline{PT} \perp \overline{AC}$, show that R, S, and T are collinear.

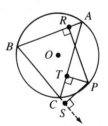

327

12·5 Tangents and Chords

This section examines two specific angular relationships between chords and tangents using some of the properties studied so far.

A theorem states that $\angle a = \frac{1}{2}(\angle b)$.
If $\angle a = 39°$, then we know that $\angle b = 78°$.

Since $\overline{PT}$ is a tangent, $\angle PTO$ is a right angle. Hence $\angle c = 90° - \angle a$. Also, $\triangle OTS$ is an isosceles triangle, so $\angle c \cong \angle d$. Therefore, $\angle d = 90° - \angle a$. The sum of the angles of $\triangle OTS$ is $\angle c + \angle d + \angle b$ or $180°$, so $(90° - \angle a) + (90° - \angle a) + \angle b = 180°$. Solving this we get $\angle b = 2\angle a$ or $\frac{1}{2}(\angle b) = \angle a$.

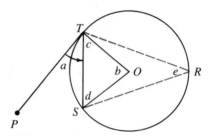

$\overline{PT}$ is a tangent to the circle.

We know also that $\frac{1}{2}(\angle b) = \angle e$. Why? A related theorem states that $\angle a \cong \angle e$. For example, if $\angle a = 39°$, then $\angle e = 39°$.

Exercises

1. Determine the measures of the indicated angles.

a.   **b.**

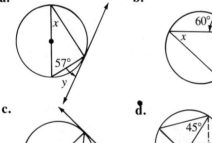

c.   **d.**

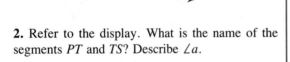

2. Refer to the display. What is the name of the segments PT and TS? Describe $\angle a$.

3. With reference to the chord TS, name $\angle b$ and $\angle e$.

4. State in words the theorem relating each.
a. $\angle a$ and $\angle b$ **b.** $\angle a$ and $\angle e$
c. Write a two-column proof for each theorem.

5. Another theorem states that $\angle m = \frac{1}{2}(\angle n - \angle s)$.
a. If $\angle s = 110°$, then what is the measure of $\angle m$?
b. If $\angle n = 219°$, then what is the measure of $\angle m$?
c. A.T., the "Mathematics Wizard", posed the problem: "If $\angle n = 100°$, what is the measure of $\angle m$?" Explain why there is no answer.

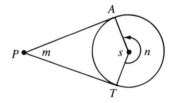

6. Prove the theorem in Exercise 5. (*Hint*: Draw a line from P through centre O to meet the circle at D.)

7. A ball with a diameter of 20 cm is placed in a cone. The ball touches the cone 20 cm from its vertex. How far is the centre of the ball from the vertex?

8. A ball with a diameter of 30 cm rests in a square box with sides of 20 cm and a depth of 10 cm. How far is the bottom of the ball from the bottom of the box?

12·6 Tangents and Secants

Properties relating the tangent and the secant of a circle are developed in this section. Recall that a secant is a line which intersects a circle at two points.

Refer to the diagram. The first property states that the square of the length of the tangent $\overline{PT}$ is equal to the product of the length of the entire secant, $\overline{PA}$, and the section of the external secant, $\overline{PB}$.

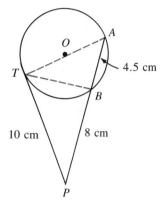

In this case, $\overline{PT}^2 = \overline{PA} \times \overline{PB}$

$$10^2 = 12.5 \times 8$$

This is verified by drawing two triangles, $\triangle TBP$ and $\triangle TPA$, and showing they are similar. Since $\angle PTB \cong \angle PAT$ (why?) and $\angle P \cong \angle P$, then $\angle TBP$ and $\angle ATP$ are equal. Therefore, the two triangles are similar. Then we write the proportion for the ratio of two pairs of corresponding sides.

$$\frac{\overline{PT}}{\overline{PB}} = \frac{\overline{PA}}{\overline{PT}}$$

Hence, $\overline{PT}^2 = \overline{PA} \times \overline{PB}$.

> **Theorem** If a tangent and a secant intersect outside a circle at a point P, then the square of the length of the tangent from P equals the product of the lengths of the secant from P and its external secant.

A corollary to the above tangent-secant theorem states that $\overline{PA} \times \overline{PB} = \overline{PC} \times \overline{PD}$. In this diagram, $7.2 \times 5 = 8 \times 4.5$.

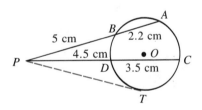

The reasoning follows directly from the tangent-secant theorem. Draw in the tangent $\overline{PT}$. We know that each secant is related to the tangent so that $\overline{PT}^2 = \overline{PA} \times \overline{PB}$ and $\overline{PT}^2 = \overline{PC} \times \overline{PD}$, and hence $\overline{PA} \times \overline{PB} = \overline{PC} \times \overline{PD}$.

> **Corollary** If two secants intersect outside the circle at a point P, then the product of the length of one secant and its external secant is equal to the product of the length of the other secant and its external secant.

Exercises

1. Refer to the diagram to identify each.
a. the tangent **b.** the entire secant
c. the secant outside the circle
d. the square of the length of the tangent
e. the product of the length of the entire secant and the section of the secant outside the circle

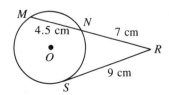

2. Determine the lengths of the indicated line segments correct to one decimal place.

a. **b.**

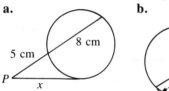

3. Determine the lengths of the indicated line segments correct to two decimal places.

a. **b.**

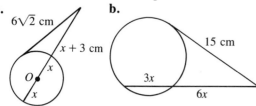

4. Use a dictionary to define the word "corollary". Explain why the two-secants property is a corollary to the tangent-secant theorem.

5. Calculate the lengths of the indicated line segments correct to one decimal place.

a. **b.**

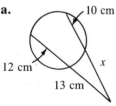
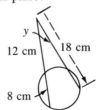

6. A theorem states that $\angle m = \frac{1}{2}(\angle n - \angle s)$.

a. If $\angle s = 42°$ and $\angle n = 86°$, what is the measure of $\angle m$?

b. If $\angle m = 39°$ and $\angle s = 55°$, find the measure of $\angle n$.

c. Prove the theorem. (*Hint*: See Exercise 6 in Section 12·5).

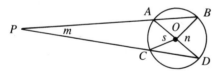

7. The distance between the centres of two circles, having radii of 6 cm and 3 cm, is 18 cm. Calculate the length of the internal tangent $\overline{TS}$.

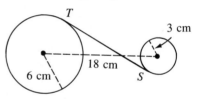

8. A secant from W intersects a circle with centre O and radius 6 at B and C with B the midpoint of $\overline{WC}$.

a. If $\overline{BC}$ subtends an angle of 90° at O, calculate the length of $\overline{WC}$.

b. What is the length of a tangent drawn from W to the circle?

c. Calculate the length of $\overline{WO}$.

9. A spherical watertank with a diameter of 8 m is held by supports as shown. The length of the water pipe from D to the ground B is 18 m. Find the lengths of $\overline{AB}$ and $\overline{CB}$ which are tangent to the tank.

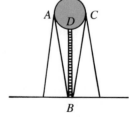

10. Right $\triangle DEF$ is given with an inscribed circle and a circumscribed circle. The diameter of the circumscribed circle can be determined by using the Pythagorean Theorem. Therefore, $\overline{DF^2} = \overline{DE^2} + \overline{EF^2}$.

a. Explain why this is true.

b. Show how the length of the diameter of the inscribed circle can be determined from the side lengths.

12·7 Arc Length and Sector Area

Lily has a circular vegetable garden with a diameter of 10 m. She has decided to divide the garden into 12 equal sections. In each section, she would like to plant a different type of vegetable. Also, she would like to place a fence around the garden to keep away animals.

a. Determine the area each type of vegetable will occupy.

b. What length of fence will enclose each section of the garden?

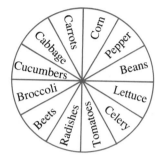

a. The area of a circle is determined by the formula $A = \pi r^2$. Therefore, the area of one section is $\frac{1}{12}$ the area of the entire circle or $\frac{1}{12}\pi r^2$. Also, each sector angle is 30° or $\frac{1}{12}$ of 360°.

Therefore, the area of each section $= \frac{30}{360}(\pi)(5^2)$
$$\doteq 6.5 \text{ m}^2$$

b. The circumference of a circle is given by the formula $C = 2\pi r$, where r is the radius and 2π is the sector angle in radian measure. Recall that $2\pi = 360°$, $\pi = 180°$, $\frac{\pi}{2} = 90°$, and so on. The central angle is 30° or $\frac{\pi}{6}$ rad.

Therefore, the length of fence that will enclose one sector of the garden is $\frac{\pi}{6}(5)$ or approximately 2.6 m.

The area, A, of a sector with a central angle measuring $n°$ is determined by the formula

$$A = \frac{n}{360}(\pi r^2)$$

The length of a circular arc, ℓ, subtending a central angle of $n°$ is determined by the formula

$$\ell = \frac{n}{360}(2\pi r)$$

Example

Calculate the area of the shaded segment subtending an angle of 60° with a radius of 8 cm.

The commonly-used formula $A = \frac{1}{2}bh$ will determine the area of the triangular part. The triangle formed here is an equilateral triangle, therefore, $b = 8$. Using the Pythagorean relationship, we find that $h = 4\sqrt{3}$.

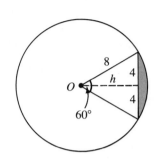

Therefore, the area of the triangle $= \left(\frac{1}{2}\right)(8)(4\sqrt{3})$
$$\doteq 27.7 \text{ cm}^2$$

The sector area $= \frac{60}{360}(\pi)(8^2)$
$$\doteq 33.5 \text{ cm}^2$$

Therefore, the area of the shaded segment is $33.5 - 27.7$ or 5.8 cm^2.

Exercises

1. Calculate the area of each shaded sector.

a.

b.

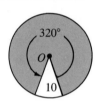

2. Calculate the area of the shaded segment in each circle.

a.

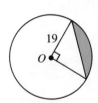

b.

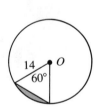

3. Calculate the length of each arc.

a.

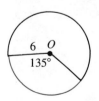

b.

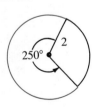

4. How much longer is each arc than the chord subtending it?

a.

b.

5. A sub-lit dance floor is being constructed in the form of a semicircle beside a rectangle. Calculate each measure.
a. the perimeter of the dance floor
b. the area of each of the nine sections of the floor
c. the total length of the nine interior supports

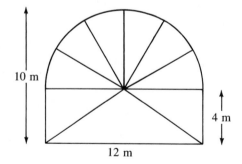

6. The intersection of a plane and a sphere forms a circle. If the radius of the sphere is 26 cm, how far away from the centre of the sphere is the plane that produces a circle with a diameter of 16 cm?

7. Calculate the area of the shaded portion of this circular design with centre O.

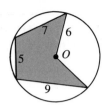

8. Without calculating the circumference of the Earth, how much longer is it around the equator 10 m above the Earth's surface than it is on the surface?

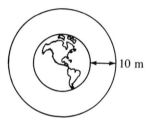

9. A cement storm sewer has an inner diameter of 1.5 m. What is the volume of water in an 8 m length of the sewer when the sector angle subtended by the water line is 90°?

10. The centres of two circular pulleys are 32 cm apart and each pulley has a diameter of 14 cm. What is the length of the belt around them?

11. Two circles with centres O and M lie in parallel planes through a sphere with centre O. The line containing O, M, and L is perpendicular to both planes. If $\angle POL = 60°$ and $\overline{OM} = 17$ m, what is the radius of the sphere?

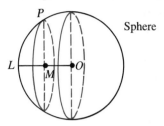

12. Show that in a circle of radius r, the segment cut off by a 60° central angle has an area of $A = \dfrac{r^2(2\pi - 3\sqrt{3})}{12}$.

13. Find the area of a segment of a circle with a radius of 10 cm and an arc measure of 68°. (*Hint*: Use trigonometry.)

14. The area of a ring is 48π cm² and the inner circle has a radius of 8 cm. Find the length of the radius of the outer circle.

15. Find the area of a segment of a circle with a 12 cm radius and an arc measure of 32°.

Historical Note

Emilie du Châtelet (1706-1749)
Marquise du Châtelet was born into nobility in Paris. Being of a wealthy and influential family, she was expected to be clever as well as to make a social appearance, so she decided to concentrate her studies on the works of Euclid and Isaac Newton. One of her most outstanding achievements was the translation of Newton's *Principia Mathematica* from English to French, which she completed shortly before her death.

Du Châtelet also studied functions. The circumference of a circle is a function of its radius. Give three other functions related to the circle or sphere.

333

12·8 Equations of Circles I

A circle is defined by a set of points equidistant from a fixed point known as the **centre** of the circle. The distance from the centre to the points on the circle is known as the **radius**. By applying the skills learned in Analytic Geometry, we can determine the equation of a circle.

Example 1

Determine the equation of a circle with centre at $O(0, 0)$ and radius 7 units.

Let $P(x, y)$ represent a point on the circle.

$$|\overline{OP}| = \sqrt{(x - 0)^2 + (y - 0)^2}$$
$$= \sqrt{x^2 + y^2}$$

Since, $|\overline{OP}| = 7$

Therefore, $\sqrt{x^2 + y^2} = 7$

$$x^2 + y^2 = 49$$

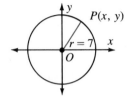

The equation of a circle with centre at $O(0, 0)$ and a radius of 7 units is $x^2 + y^2 = 49$. This is an equation of degree two. Since the centre is at the origin, this circle is said to be in **standard position**. The **unit circle** is a circle in standard position with radius 1 unit and is represented by the equation $x^2 + y^2 = 1$.

> A circle in standard position has a second degree equation of the form $x^2 + y^2 = r^2$, where r is the radius.

Example 2

Determine the x- and y-intercepts and sketch the graph of the circle defined by the equation $x^2 + y^2 = 16$.

x-intercepts

Let $y = 0$.

$\therefore x^2 + y^2 = 16$

$x^2 = 16$

$x = \pm 4$

y-intercepts

Let $x = 0$.

$\therefore x^2 + y^2 = 16$

$y^2 = 16$

$y = \pm 4$

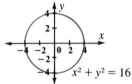

Therefore, the circle goes through the points $(4, 0)$, $(-4, 0)$, $(0, 4)$, and $(0, -4)$. By plotting these points, we can sketch the circle connecting them.

Example 3

Write the equation of a circle in standard position that passes through $P(4, 2)$.

The equation of a circle in standard position is of the form $x^2 + y^2 = r^2$.

Since the point $(4, 2)$ lies on the circle, we can substitute $x = 4$ and $y = 2$ into the equation $x^2 + y^2 = r^2$ to determine r^2.

Therefore, $16 + 4 = r^2$

$$r^2 = 20$$

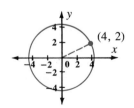

The equation of a circle in standard position that passes through $P(4, 2)$ is $x^2 + y^2 = 20$.

Exercises

1. Write the equation of each circle in standard position.
a. having a radius of 12 units
b. going through the point $(-3, 5)$
c. with x-intercepts at $(4\sqrt{2}, 0)$ and $(-4\sqrt{2}, 0)$

2. Sketch the circles described by each equation using the x- and y-intercepts. State the domain and range.
a. $x^2 + y^2 = 25$ **b.** $x^2 + y^2 = 4$
c. $x^2 + y^2 = 13$ **d.** $x^2 + y^2 = 65$

3. Write an equation for each circle with centre at $(0, 0)$. State the domain and the range.

a.
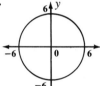

b.
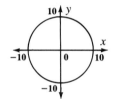

c.
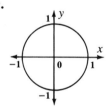

d.
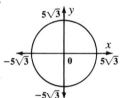

4. Identify three points on each circle.
a. $x^2 + y^2 = 85$ **b.** $x^2 + y^2 = 64$
c. $x^2 + y^2 = 100$ **d.** $x^2 + y^2 = 23$

5. Determine the equation of a circle in standard position whose diameter has one endpoint at $(-1, 5)$.

6. If $P(4, 2)$ and $Q(2, 4)$ are the endpoints of a chord of a circle in standard position, what is an equation of the circle?

7. Determine whether each point is in the interior or the exterior of the circle $x^2 + y^2 = 15$.
a. $(4, 3)$ **b.** $(-2, -3)$ **c.** $(-1, 4)$
d. $(0, \sqrt{15})$ **e.** $(\sqrt{2}, \sqrt{3})$ **f.** $(-\sqrt{3}, 5\sqrt{2})$

8. What is described by each equation?
a. $x^2 + y^2 = 0$ **b.** $y = 2x^2 + 4$

9. Answer these using the equation $x^2 + y^2 = 81$.
a. Solve the equation to give two expressions for y.
b. Solve the equation to give two expressions for x.
c. Each expression in parts **a** and **b** represents a semicircle. Using a calculator, set up a table of values for each equation and graph the points to identify which half of the circle is described.

10. Sketch the graph of each semicircle.
a. $y = \sqrt{9 - x^2}$ **b.** $x = -\sqrt{1 - y^2}$
c. $y = -\sqrt{20 - x^2}$ **d.** $x = \sqrt{25 - y^2}$

11. Write an equation which describes each semicircle.

a.
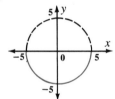

b.
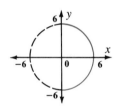

c.
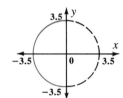

d.
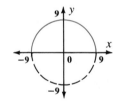

12. A bridge is supported by a 30 m wide arch which is an arc of a circle. Its height is one third the radius of the circle.
a. Draw a labelled diagram on a coordinate grid with centre at $(0, 0)$.
b. Write an equation of the circle.
c. Determine the height of the arch.

13. Draw graphs of each set of points for $x, y \in R$.
a. $\{(x, y) | x^2 + y^2 > 9\}$ **b.** $\{(x, y) | x^2 + y^2 \leq 4\}$
c. $\{(x, y) | x^2 + y^2 \leq 36 \text{ and } y > x\}$

335

12·9 Equations of Circles II

In this section, circles will be translated from the standard position to other positions in which the centre is **not** at the origin. From the equations developed, the coordinates of the centres and the radii can be identified readily.

In the diagram, the circle with centre $(0, 0)$ has been translated 2 units right and 3 units down. This translation is represented by the mapping $(x, y) \rightarrow (x + 2, y - 3)$. The equation of this circle is found by using the distance formula
$|d^2| = (x - x_1)^2 + (y - y_1)^2.$
$|\overline{AP}|^2 = (x - 2)^2 + [y - (-3)]^2$
Since $|\overline{AP}|$ is the radius of the circle, we write
$7^2 = (x - 2)^2 + (y + 3)^2$
$49 = x^2 + y^2 - 4x + 6y + 13$

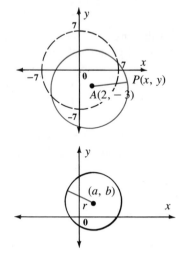

> The equation of a circle with centre at (a, b) and radius r units is $r^2 = (x - a)^2 + (y - b)^2$.

Example

Write an equation of the circle that has a diameter with endpoints $A(3, 2)$ and $B(-1, -2)$.

Understand the Problem
The endpoints of the diameter are given. The centre of the circle is the midpoint of the diameter. Half the diameter is its radius. It is necessary to write the equation of the circle.

Develop a Plan
Find the centre: the coordinates of the centre of the diameter. Then calculate the radius: the length of half the diameter. Use the general equation of the circle and substitute the values of a, b, and r.

Carry Out the Plan
The midpoint of the diameter, $\overline{AB}$, is
$\left(\frac{3 - 1}{2}, \frac{2 - 2}{2}\right)$ or $(1, 0)$.

The length of the diameter is
$|\overline{AB}| = \sqrt{(-1 - 3)^2 + (-2 - 2)^2}$
$\quad\quad = 4\sqrt{2}$
The length of the radius is $2\sqrt{2}$.

The general equation of the circle is $r^2 = (x - a)^2 + (y - b)^2$. Substituting in the values of a, b, and r, we get $(2\sqrt{2})^2 = (x - 1)^2 + (y - 0)^2$
$\quad\quad\quad 8 = (x - 1)^2 + (y - 0)^2$

Look Back
The equation of the circle is $8 = (x - \underline{1})^2 + (y - \underline{0})^2$. Note the underlined numerals. This general equation tells us the radius is $\sqrt{8}$ or $2\sqrt{2}$ units and the centre is at $(1, 0)$.
Another form of the equation is $x^2 + y^2 - 2x - 7 = 0$.

Exercises

1. Give the radius and the coordinates of the centre of the circle whose equation is
$64 = (x - 4)^2 + (y + 5)^2$.

2. Write the equation of each circle.

a.

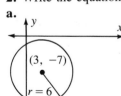

b.

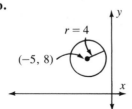

c.

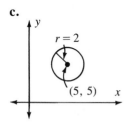

d.

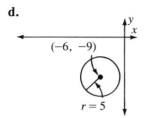

3. Write an equation that describes the image of the unit circle after each translation. Sketch the graph of the image circle.
a. $(x, y) \rightarrow (x + 2, y + 6)$
b. $(x, y) \rightarrow (x - 3, y + 1)$
c. $(x, y) \rightarrow (x - 1, y - 4)$
d. $(x, y) \rightarrow (x, y + 7)$ **e.** $(x, y) \rightarrow (x - 8, y)$

4. Write an equation for each circle with the given centre and radius.
a. $(4, 1), 5$ **b.** $(-2, 3), 3$
c. $(2m, m), m$ **d.** $(4, -c), \sqrt{3}$

5. Write the mapping that translates each circle back to standard position.

a.

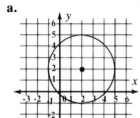

b.

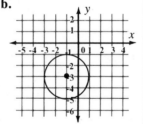

6. Write an equation of each circle and sketch the circle.
a. a circle whose diameter has endpoints at $(-5, -1)$ and $(1, 7)$
b. a circle tangent to the x-axis and with its centre at $(5, -2)$
c. a circle passing through $(1, 2)$ with its centre at $(-3, 4)$
d. a circle tangent to the y-axis at $(0, -2)$ with a radius of 3
e. a circle with x-intercepts at -1 and 14
f. a circle passing through $(0, 2), (2, 6)$, and $(1, -1)$

7. Identify the centre and radius of each circle and sketch the graph. (*Hint*: Complete the squares. The first one is started for you.)

a. $x^2 - 6x + y^2 + 2y = 15$
$x^2 - 6x + \blacksquare + y^2 + 2y + \blacksquare = 15 + \blacksquare$

b. $x^2 + y^2 + 4x - 8y + 4 = 0$
c. $x^2 + y^2 - 6x + 14y + 33 = 0$
d. $x^2 + y^2 + 12y + 4 = 0$
e. $x^2 + y^2 + 10x - 20 = 0$

8. Given the circle defined by the equation $x^2 + y^2 - 2x + 10y - 51 = 0$.
a. Determine the centre and the radius of the circle and sketch the graph of the circle.
b. Locate any four points on the circle and write the equations of two chords formed by these points.
c. Determine equations of the perpendicular bisectors of each chord.
d. Determine their point of intersection. What do you notice about this point?
e. Calculate the distance between the centre and one of the four points in part **b**. What do you notice about this distance?

Braintickler

The numbers are divided into the three groups
$A = \{0, 3, 6, 8, 9, \ldots\}$
$B = \{1, 4, 7, 11, 14, \ldots\}$
$C = \{2, 5, 10, 13, \ldots\}$
In which groups would each be placed?
a. 15   **b.** 16   **c.** 17   **d.** 80

12·10 Analytic Methods

Many of the properties of circles studied earlier in this chapter can be verified using the analytic skills learned in Chapter 6.

Example 1

Verify the tangent-secant theorem given the circle $x^2 + y^2 = 4$ with tangent $y = 2$ from the point $A(2, 2)$ and secant $y = x$ also from point A.

The point of tangency is $T(0, 2)$. Therefore, $|\overline{TA}|$ is 2 units.

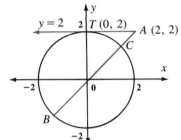

To determine the points of intersection of the secant and circle, substitute $y = x$ into the equation of the circle. Thus $x^2 + y^2 = 4$

$$x^2 + x^2 = 4$$
$$2x^2 = 4$$
$$x^2 = 2$$
$$x = \pm\sqrt{2}$$

The points of intersection are $B(-\sqrt{2}, -\sqrt{2})$ and $C(\sqrt{2}, \sqrt{2})$.

$$|\overline{AC}| = \sqrt{(2 - \sqrt{2})^2 + (2 - \sqrt{2})^2} \qquad\qquad |\overline{AB}| = \sqrt{(2 + \sqrt{2})^2 + (2 + \sqrt{2})^2}$$
$$= \sqrt{4 - 4\sqrt{2} + 2 + 4 - 4\sqrt{2} + 2} \qquad\qquad = \sqrt{4 + 4\sqrt{2} + 2 + 4 + 4\sqrt{2} + 2}$$
$$= \sqrt{12 - 8\sqrt{2}} \qquad\qquad\qquad\qquad = \sqrt{12 + 8\sqrt{2}}$$

According to the tangent-secant theorem, $|\overline{TA}|^2 = |\overline{AC}| \times |\overline{AB}|$.

$$|\overline{TA}|^2 = 2^2 \qquad |\overline{AC}| \times |\overline{AB}| = (\sqrt{12 - 8\sqrt{2}})(\sqrt{12 + 8\sqrt{2}})$$
$$= 4 \qquad\qquad\qquad\qquad = \sqrt{144 - 128}$$
$$= 4$$

Since $|\overline{TA}|^2 = |\overline{AB}| \times |\overline{AC}|$, the tangent-secant theorem holds.

Example 2

Determine an equation of a tangent that intersects the circle $x^2 + y^2 = 16$ at $T(3, \sqrt{7})$.

Let $P(x, y)$ represent any point on the tangent, not on the circle. From the equation, we know that the centre of the circle is $(0, 0)$.

The slope of $\overline{OT}$ is $\frac{\sqrt{7}}{3}$. The slope of $\overline{TP}$ is $\frac{y - \sqrt{7}}{x - 3}$.

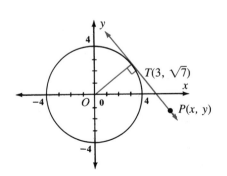

Since the radius is perpendicular to the tangent, their slopes are negative reciprocals.

Therefore, $\dfrac{\sqrt{7}}{3} = -\dfrac{x - 3}{y - \sqrt{7}}$

$$-3x + 9 = \sqrt{7}y - 7$$
$$y = \frac{-3\sqrt{7}}{7}x + \frac{16\sqrt{7}}{7}$$

An equation of the tangent is $3\sqrt{7}x + 7y - 16\sqrt{7} = 0$.

Example 3

Write the equations of the tangents from $T(10, 0)$ to the circle $x^2 + y^2 = 10$.

Let $P(x, y)$ represent the point of tangency.
Since $\overline{OP} \perp \overline{TP}$, $\triangle OTP$ is a right triangle.
Using the Pythagorean Theorem,
$$|\overline{TP}|^2 = |\overline{TO}|^2 - |\overline{OP}|^2$$
$$= (10)^2 - (\sqrt{10})^2$$
$$= 100 - 10$$
$$= 90$$
$$|\overline{TP}| = \sqrt{90} \text{ or } 3\sqrt{10}$$

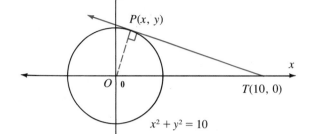

Also, using the distance formula,
$$|\overline{TP}| = \sqrt{(x - 10)^2 + y^2}$$

Equating these two results for $|\overline{TP}|$, we get
$$\sqrt{(x - 10)^2 + y^2} = 3\sqrt{10}$$
or $(x - 10)^2 + y^2 = 90$

This equation describes a circle of points (x, y) all of which are $\sqrt{10}$ units from T. To identify the points on the given circle, we need to find the intersection of the two circles by solving the system of equations.

$$
\begin{array}{lll}
x^2 - 20x + 100 + y^2 = 90 & \quad & \textcircled{1} \\
x^2 \qquad\qquad\quad + y^2 = 10 & \quad & \textcircled{2} \\
\hline
-20x + 100 = 80 & \quad & \textcircled{1} - \textcircled{2} \\
-20x = -20 & & \\
x = 1 \text{ and } y = \pm 3 & &
\end{array}
$$

The circles intersect at $(1, 3)$ and $(1, -3)$. These points of intersection also are the points of tangency. Why?

An equation of the tangent through $P_1(1, 3)$ and $T(10, 0)$ is
$$\frac{y - 3}{x - 1} = \frac{0 - 3}{10 - 1}$$
$$9y - 27 = -3x + 3$$
$$3x + 9y - 30 = 0$$
or $x + 3y - 10 = 0$

An equation of the tangent through $P_2(1, -3)$ and $T(10, 0)$ is
$$\frac{y - (-3)}{x - 1} = \frac{0 - (-3)}{10 - 1}$$
$$9y + 27 = 3x - 3$$
$$3x - 9y - 30 = 0$$
or $x - 3y - 10 = 0$

The equations of the tangents from $(10, 0)$ to the circle $x^2 + y^2 = 10$ are $x + 3y - 10 = 0$ and $x - 3y - 10 = 0$.

Exercises

1. For each point on a circle in standard position, list the coordinates of another point that will form a diameter.
a. (3, 6)   **b.** (−2, −5)   **c.** (−4, 0)   **d.** (a, b)

2. Show that an angle subtended by a diameter of the circle defined by the equation $x^2 + y^2 = 25$ is a right angle. Follow these hints.
a. Given that one endpoint of a diameter of the circle is at $A(-4, -3)$, determine the coordinates of the other endpoint B.
b. Determine coordinates of any other point C that lies on this circle.
c. Calculate the slopes of $\overline{AC}$ and $\overline{BC}$.
d. What do the slopes indicate about $\angle ACB$?

3. Show that the perpendicular bisector of these chords intersect at the centre of the circle.

a. 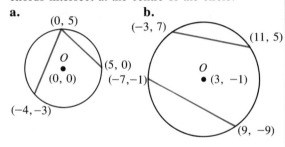 **b.**

4. Determine the centre of a circle that passes through $Q(0, 5)$, $R(9, -1)$, and $S(-4, 2)$.

5. Solving two equations simultaneously will determine the intersection of two graphs. For an equation of a line and an equation of a circle, the result will be either no solution (they do not intersect), one solution (the line is a tangent), or two different solutions (the line is a secant). Solve each pair of equations to determine whether the linear equation describes a tangent, a secant, or a line that does not intersect the circle.
a. $x^2 + y^2 = 16$; $x = y$
b. $x^2 + y^2 = 4$; $x - y = 4$
c. $x^2 + y^2 = 10$; $x + 3y - 10 = 0$
d. $x^2 + y^2 = 20$; $2x + y - 10 = 0$
e. $(x - 3)^2 + (y + 5)^2 = 9$; $x - 3y - 1 = 0$
f. $x^2 - 6x + y^2 - 3 = 0$; $x + 2y - 5 = 0$

6. Determine an equation of a tangent to each circle at the point given.
a. $x^2 + y^2 = 58$ at $(7, 3)$
b. $x^2 + y^2 = 25$ at $(-3, 4)$
c. $x^2 + y^2 = 15$ at $(3, -\sqrt{6})$
d. $x^2 + y^2 = 64$ at $(0, 8)$

7. Show that the line $3x + y + 10 = 0$ is tangent to the circle $x^2 + y^2 = 10$.

8. Calculate the length of a segment of each tangent from the given point to the circle.
a. $2x - 5y - 29 = 0$; from $(7, -3)$ to $x^2 + y^2 = 29$
b. $x + 2y + 5 = 0$; from $(-7, 1)$ to $x^2 + y^2 = 5$

9. Points $A(-5, 0)$, $B(0, -5)$, $C(4, 3)$, $D(3, 4)$, $E(0, 5)$, and $F(-4, 3)$ all lie on a circle described by the equation $x^2 + y^2 = 25$.
a. Draw a diagram of these points on the circle.
b. Extend $\overline{BA}$ and $\overline{DE}$ to meet outside the circle at P.
c. Extend $\overline{AF}$ and $\overline{CD}$ to meet at Q.
d. Extend $\overline{FE}$ and $\overline{BC}$ to meet at R.
e. Determine whether P, Q, and R are collinear.

10. $\triangle MNP$ is inscribed in the circle described by $x^2 + y^2 = 169$ with $M(0, 13)$, $N(-5, -12)$, and $P(12, 5)$.
a. Write the coordinates of some point Q on minor arc $\overline{NP}$.
b. Draw perpendiculars from Q to each of the lines through $\overline{MN}$, $\overline{NP}$, and $\overline{MP}$.
c. Show that the three points at which the perpendiculars meet the lines are collinear.

Using the Library

Write a report on the methods mathematicians have used to determine the value of the irrational number π. Include approximations generated by mathematicians such as Archimedes, Ptolemy, Wallas, and others. Why is π considered a transcendental number? Include references to efforts made by governments to legislate the value of π.

12·11 Transformations of Circles

A circle can be transformed by means of stretches. What happens when we stretch a circle along the y-axis?

We will graph a circle with its centre at the origin and a radius of 5. Its equation is $x^2 + y^2 = 25$. Now apply a vertical stretch with a factor of 2 and sketch the results. First, we will record the coordinates of some points on the circle using the x- and y-intercepts: (5, 0), (0, 5), (−5, 0), (0, −5).

Now apply the stretch mapping: $(x, y) \rightarrow (x, 2y)$. Each x-coordinate remains the same, but the y-coordinate is multiplied by 2.

$(5, 0) \rightarrow (5, 0)$ $(0, 5) \rightarrow (0, 10)$
$(-5, 0) \rightarrow (-5, 0)$ $(0, -5) \rightarrow (0, -10)$

These points are graphed and the curve is sketched. We see the image of the transformation is an ellipse. In this vertical stretch only the y-values have changed.

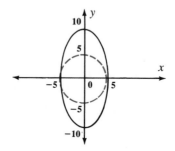

Example 1

Write an equation of the ellipse formed by stretching, with a factor of 3, the circle $x^2 + y^2 = 17$ along the x-axis. Sketch the circle and ellipse.

Understand the Problem
The circle has a radius of $\sqrt{17}$ and its centre is at the origin. The mapping for a stretch with a factor of 3, along the x-axis is $(x, y) \rightarrow (3x, y)$. The equation of the image of the transformation (an ellipse) is to be determined. The circle and ellipse are to be sketched.

Develop a Plan
Write the coordinates of the x- and y-intercepts of the circle. Use the mapping to write the intercepts of the image. Pick a point on the ellipse and write its coordinates in terms of x and y. Substitute these values into the equation of the circle. Simplify and write the general equation.

Carry Out the Plan
The intercepts for the circle are $(\sqrt{17}, 0)$, $(0, \sqrt{17})$, $(-\sqrt{17}, 0)$, and $(0, -\sqrt{17})$. The intercepts for the ellipse are $(3\sqrt{17}, 0)$, $(0, \sqrt{17})$, $(-3\sqrt{17}, 0)$, and $(0, -\sqrt{17})$. These points are plotted on the graph.

Let (u, v) represent any point on the ellipse. Then $u = 3x$ and $v = y$.

Therefore, $x = \dfrac{u}{3}$ and $y = v$.

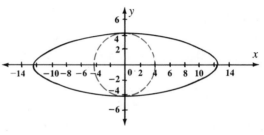

By substituting these values into $x^2 + y^2 = 17$, we obtain the equation of the ellipse.

Therefore, $\left(\dfrac{u}{3}\right)^2 + v^2 = 17$ or $u^2 + 9v^2 = 153$.

341

Look Back

The equation of the ellipse is $x^2 + 9y^2 = 153$. To check, use a point on the circle such as $(1, 4)$. Under the mapping, the image is $(3, 4)$. Substitute this in the equation of the ellipse: $x^2 + 9y^2 = 153$. Therefore $3^2 + 9(4)^2 = 153$. It checks. The image of the circle under a stretch along the x-axis is an ellipse as shown.

Example 2 illustrates a stretch along the x- and y-axes. Notice that the stretch factor is greater than 1 along the x-axis, but less than 1 along the y-axis.

Example 2

Apply the mapping $(x, y) \rightarrow \left(3x, \dfrac{y}{2}\right)$ to the unit circle $x^2 + y^2 = 1$.

a. Determine the x- and y-intercepts and sketch the graph of the ellipse.

b. Write the equation of the resulting ellipse.

a. The intercepts of the circle are $(1, 0)$, $(0, 1)$, $(-1, 0)$, and $(0, -1)$. Using the mapping, we get the intercepts of the ellipse: $(3, 0)$, $\left(0, \dfrac{1}{2}\right)$, $(-3, 0)$, and $\left(0, -\dfrac{1}{2}\right)$. Plot both sets of intercepts and draw a smooth curve through each set.

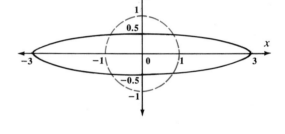

b. If (u, v) represents a point on the ellipse, then $u = 3x$ and $v = \dfrac{y}{2}$. Thus, $x = \dfrac{u}{3}$ and $y = 2v$. Substituting these values into the equation of the circle, we get $\left(\dfrac{u}{3}\right)^2 + (2v)^2 = 1$

$$\dfrac{u^2}{9} + 4v^2 = 1$$

The equation of the ellipse is $\dfrac{x^2}{9} + 4y^2 = 1$ or $x^2 + 36y^2 = 9$.

From the graph, we see that the circle has been stretched vertically by $\dfrac{1}{2}$ (or "shrunk"), and stretched horizontally by a factor of 3.

If a circle described by $x^2 + y^2 = r^2$ is stretched by a factor of k

a. in the y-direction, the resulting ellipse has an equation of $k^2x^2 + y^2 = k^2r^2$.

b. in the x-direction, the resulting ellipse has an equation of $x^2 + k^2y^2 = k^2r^2$.

Exercises

1. Explain what happens to a point $(2, 3)$ under each stretch.

a. horizontally with a factor of 5

b. vertically with a factor of $\dfrac{2}{3}$

c. vertically with a factor of 4 and horizontally with a factor of 8

2. Under what conditions are the absolute values of the y-intercepts of the ellipse less than those of the circle? greater than those of the circle?

3. Describe the stretch factors in each ellipse.

a. $9x^2 + y^2 = 4$ **b.** $x^2 + 25y^2 = 4$

c. $\dfrac{x^2}{9} + 81y^2 = 4$ **d.** $3x^2 + 5y^2 = 4$

4. Apply a horizontal stretch of a factor of 4 to the circle $x^2 + y^2 = 25$ by completing each step.
a. Determine the x- and y-intercepts of the circle and sketch its graph.
b. Write the mapping that describes the given stretch.
c. Apply the mapping to the x- and y-intercepts to determine the intercepts of the ellipse.
d. Sketch the graph of the ellipse.

5. Describe the stretch that transforms the unit circle into each ellipse.

a. 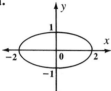 **b.**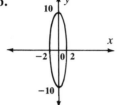

6. Write a mapping to describe each stretch.
a. in the x-direction by a factor of 2
b. in the y-direction by a factor of 6
c. in the y-direction by a factor of $\frac{1}{3}$

7. Sketch the unit circle with the centre at the origin. Then sketch each stretch of the unit circle.
a. by a factor of 5 in the y-direction
b. by a factor of 12 in the y-direction
c. by a factor of 3 in the x-direction
d. by a factor of $\frac{2}{3}$ in the x-direction

8. Graph and determine the equation of each ellipse formed by a vertical stretch of the circle $x^2 + y^2 = 5$ for the given factor.
a. 4   **b.** 16   **c.** 20

9. Identify the factor of the horizontal stretch that transformed the unit circle centred at the origin to each ellipse.

a. 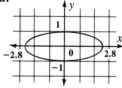 **b.**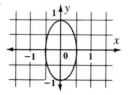

10. Write equations of the image of $x^2 + y^2 = 20$ following a horizontal stretch defined by each factor. Graph each.
a. $\frac{1}{8}$ **b.** $\frac{1}{16}$ **c.** $\frac{3}{2}$ **d.** 4

11. Each of these ellipses has been transformed by a vertical and/or horizontal stretch of the unit circle. Identify the direction and factor of the stretch.

a. 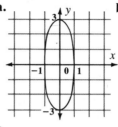 **b.**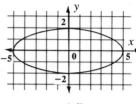

c. 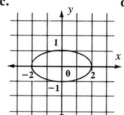 **d.**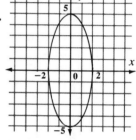

12. Given the equation of a circle and the stretch factors, state in step form how to determine the equation of the resulting ellipse.

13. Graph each ellipse.
a. $\left(\frac{x}{3}\right)^2 + \left(\frac{y}{2}\right)^2 = 4$ **b.** $\left(\frac{x}{5}\right)^2 + \left(\frac{y}{4}\right)^2 = 1$
c. $9x^2 + 4y^2 = 25$ **d.** $x^2 + 16y^2 = 9$

14. A unit circle in standard position is stretched under these conditions. Graph both the unit circle and its image under each. Describe and explain the shape of the image.
a. horizontally and vertically by a factor of 3
b. horizontally by a factor of 0
c. horizontally and vertically by a factor of 0

15. A unit circle in standard position is stretched horizontally by a factor of 2 and vertically by a factor of 3. The image is translated right 3 units and down 2 units. Write equations for the resulting first image and the second image. Draw the graphs.

12·12 Computer Application— Circles

Marvin used this program to identify the centre of a circle given the coordinates of three points on the circle.

```
10 INPUT "ENTER THE THREE POINTS "; X1, Y1, X2, Y2, X3, Y3
20 REM MIDPOINTS OF TWO CHORDS (R1, R2) AND (P1, P2)
30 R1 = (X1 + X2) / 2
40 R2 = (Y1 + Y2) / 2
50 P1 = (X2 + X3) / 2
60 P2 = (Y2 + Y3) / 2
70 REM SLOPES OF THE TWO CHORDS
80 S1 = (Y2 - Y1) / (X2 - X1)
90 S2 = (Y3 - Y2) / (X3 - X2)
100 REM SLOPES PERPENDICULAR TO THE CHORDS
110 M1 = -(1 / S1)
120 M2 = -(1 / S2)
130 REM Y-INTERCEPTS OF PERPENDICULAR BISECTORS OF CHORDS
140 B1 = R2 - M1 * R1
150 B2 = P2 - M2 * P1
160 REM INTERSECTION OF THE BISECTORS
170 X = (B2 - B1) / (M1 - M2)
180 Y = M1 * X + B1
190 REM (X, Y) IS CENTRE OF CIRCLE CONTAINING THE THREE
POINTS
200 PRINT "THE CENTRE IS AT ("; X; ", "; Y; ")."
250 END
```

Exercises

1. Follow each step of the program for the three points $(-3, 4)$, $(5, 0)$, and $(0, -5)$.

2. What centre is calculated for the three points $(-6, 4)$, $(-2, -4)$, and $(2, 6)$?

3. What happens through this program with the input of each set of points?
a. $(3, 1)$, $(6, 1)$, and $(9, 1)$
b. $(2, 8)$, $(2, 11)$, and $(2, -7)$

4. Adapt the program to spot three collinear points and to print "The three points are collinear."

5. Add these lines to the program.
```
210 REM CALCULATE THE RADIUS
220 R = SQR((X1 - X) ^ 2 + (Y1 - Y)
^ 2)
230 PRINT "THE RADIUS IS "; R;
" UNITS.": GOTO 250
```
Run the program using the points in Exercises 1 and 2.

6. Explain what each line or set of lines in the program does.

7. Run the program using the points $(-3, 3)$, $(-3, -5)$, and $(-3, 0)$. Explain why an error message occurs.

8. Write a short report discussing the advantages and disadvantages of computers in supermarkets.

12·13 Chapter Review

1. Identify each part of the circle with centre O, diameter $\overline{TR}$, and tangent $\overleftrightarrow{PT}$.

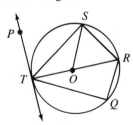

a. a chord **b.** a sector angle subtended by $\overline{TS}$
c. an inscribed angle subtended by minor arc RS
d. an angle one half the measure of $\angle ROS$
e. an angle supplementary to $\angle TQR$
f. three right angles
g. an angle congruent to $\angle PTS$

2. If $\overline{LN}$ is a diameter, $\overline{JK}$ and $\overline{JN}$ are tangents, and $\angle KON = 120°$, determine the measure of each angle.

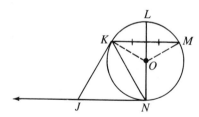

a. $\angle KOL$ **b.** $\angle MOL$ **c.** $\angle JKN$
d. $\angle NKM$ **e.** $\angle NJK$

3. Prove that two triangles formed by two intersecting chords of a circle are similar.

4. The points F, G, H, and K are in counterclockwise order on a circle such that $\angle HGK \cong \angle FHG$. Prove that chords $\overline{GH} \parallel \overline{FK}$.

5. A secant and a tangent from P meet the same circle at A, B, and C respectively. Prove that the angle formed at P by the secant and the tangent is equal to one half the difference between the two central angles subtended by arcs $\overline{AC}$ and $\overline{BC}$.

6. If $\angle MQP = 80°$ and $\angle NPM = 25°$, determine the measures of $\angle NQP$ and $\angle NMP$.

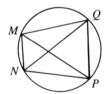

7. Write an equation for each circle?
a. centre at $(0, 0)$ and radius 6 units
b. in standard position through $(5, -1)$
c. diameter from $(-2, -3)$ to $(2, -3)$
d. radius 10 units and centre $(4, -1)$

8. Determine the length of each chord of a circle.
a. 9 cm from the centre; diameter is 24 cm
b. 3.5 m from the centre; radius is 5 m

9. A 25 cm chord is 18 cm from the centre of a circle. What is the radius of the circle?

10. What is the area of a circle that has a 12 cm chord 5 cm from the centre of the circle?

11. Three rolls of newsprint are bound together by a steel band as shown. How long is the steel band if each roll has a 2 m diameter?

12. Determine an equation of the ellipse formed by a stretch of each circle.
a. the unit circle, in the x-direction, by a factor of 2
b. $x^2 + y^2 = 8$, in the y-direction, by a factor of $\frac{1}{2}$.

12·14 Chapter Test

1. Calculate the length of the arc in part **a** and the area of the segment in part **b**.

a.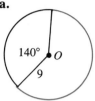

b.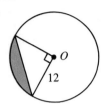

2. Calculate the lengths of the segments indicated by x and y.

a.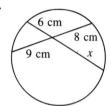

b.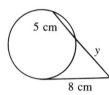

3. Prove that $\overline{PM} \times \overline{PN} = \overline{PR} \times \overline{PS}$.

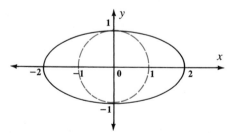

4. Write the equation of the ellipse.

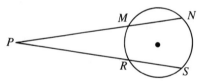

5. The vertices of $\triangle TAB$ lie on a circle. The bisector of $\angle TBA$ meets the circle at P, and the bisector of $\angle TAB$ meets the circle at Q such that $\overline{BQ} \parallel \overline{AP}$. Prove that $\angle QBP = 60°$.

6. Graph each equation on a separate set of axes.
a. $x^2 + y^2 = 36$ **b.** $y = -\sqrt{16 - x^2}$

7. Two circles of different radii intersect at T and S. A line through T intersects one circle at M and the other at P. Another line through T intersects the first circle at R and the other at V. Prove that $\angle RSV \cong \angle MSP$.

8. In preparation for a bonspiel, Matt has been studying the curling rink carefully. He knows that the distance from the hack to the T-line is 38 m, and that the outer circles have radii of 2.4 m, 1.8 m, and 1.2 m. Matt knows that a stone will actually "curl" into the position shown at the back of the 2.4 m circle, but he is calculating straight distances from the front of the hack. If the secant formed by $z + y$ is tangent to the 1.8 m circle, determine the three lengths labelled x, y, and z.

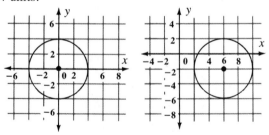

9. Write an equation of each circle with radius 4 units.

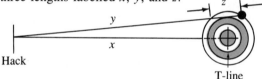

10. A circle with equation $x^2 + y^2 = 17$ is given.
a. Select any point that satisfies the equation.
b. Determine an equation of a tangent at that point.
c. Identify the coordinates of any other point on the tangent.
d. Verify that the triangle with vertices at the point from part **c**, the point of tangency, and the centre of the circle, is right angled.

Cumulative Review   Chapters 10–12

1. Find the slope and y-intercept of $3x + 6y = 12$.

2. Graph the system and state the solution set. Is the system dependent and consistent, independent and consistent, or inconsistent?
$$x - 2y = 9$$
$$-3x + y = 3$$

3. Solve each system of equations.

a. $\quad 2m - n = 9$
$\quad\quad 3m - 7n = 19$

b. $\quad x + y - z = 5$
$\quad\quad 2x - y + 2z = 11$
$\quad\quad 3x + 2y - z = 20$

4. Solve the following system.
$$x^2 + y^2 = 5$$
$$xy = 2$$

5. Use the quadratic formula to solve the equation.
$$2x^2 + 3x + 1 = 0$$

6. The sum of a number and its square is six times the next highest number. Find the number.

7. The perimeter of a rectangular playing field is 270 m and its area is 3500 m². Find the dimensions of the field.

8. Graph the intersection of the regions.
$$\{(x, y)\,|\,y - x < 5 \cap y \geq x^2 - 6\}$$

9. A cyclist traveled 80 km and discovered she could have made the trip in 48 min less had she travelled 5 km/h faster. Find the rate at which she travelled.

10. A rectangular mirror has dimensions 3 dm by 10 dm. If the length and width are increased by the same amount, find the minimum new dimensions which will more than double the mirror surface area.

11. Find the value of the angle correct to the nearest degree.

a. $\sin \theta = 0.1234$
b. $\sec \theta = -0.7710$
c. $\cot \theta = 2.7475$
d. $\cos \theta = -0.5736$

12. Find each value correct to four decimal places.

a. $\tan 25°$
b. $\cos 31°$
c. $\sin 8°$
d. $\cot 460°$
e. $\sin 230°$
f. $\csc 825°$

13. A ladder, leaning against a wall, touches the wall 4.7 m from the ground. If the ladder makes an angle of 62° with the ground, how long is the ladder?

14. The world's steepest railroad gradient by adhesion is a 1 m rise for every 11 m of track. Find the angle this rail line makes with the horizontal.

15. Solve the triangle.

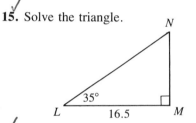

16. A balloonist notes the angle of depression to a farmhouse directly ahead is 36° and the angle of depression to a building directly behind was 70°. If the balloonist is 1000 m high, how far apart are the farmhouse and the building?

17. Find the exact value of each.

a. $\sin 135° \csc 405° - \cos 150° \cot 240°$
b. $\csc(-135°)$

18. Solve. $0° \leq \theta \leq 360°$

a. $\cos \theta + 1 = \dfrac{1}{2}$
b. $\cot^2\theta - 1 = 0$

19. A ball is dropped from a height of 81 m. Each time it lands, it bounces to a height which is $\dfrac{1}{3}$ the distance it last fell. The ball is caught when it bounced to a height of 1 m. Find the total distance travelled by the ball.

20. The radii of two circles whose centres are 25 cm apart are 4 cm and 11 cm. Find the length of their common external tangent segment.

21. A triangular race course was laid out for sailboats as shown in the diagram. Find the total length of the course.

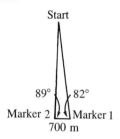

Start

89°　82°

Marker 2　Marker 1
700 m

22. Find the value of each variable.

a.

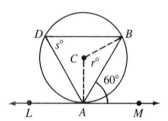

b.

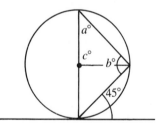

c.

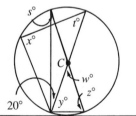

d.

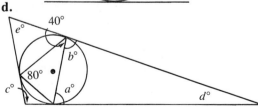

23. A plane travelling at 900 km/h left Hackville, flew north for 45 min, west for 30 min, and landed at Weston.
a. What is the straight line distance from Hackville to Weston?
b. If the plane consumed 1500 L of fuel for every hour of flight, how much fuel was used on the flight from Hackville to Weston?

24. Andrea, Norma, Paul, and Mike reside on each floor of a four-storey apartment building. Their ages are 16, 15, 14, and 11, but not necessarily in that order. Andrea lives immediately above the 15-year old and directly below the 14-year old. Norma has to pass the 11-year old to leave the building from her apartment. Norma is more than one floor away from Mike. Paul is more than one year younger than Norma. Find the ages and the floors on which each person resides.

25. A hockey puck, 8 cm in diameter, is wedged in the corner of a shelf making contact with the two adjacent walls. How far is the edge of the puck from the corner?

26. The Lethbridge Logic Club interviews four prospective members each year and selects only one. The new member selected is the first person who correctly answers and explains the reasoning used to reach the correct answer to the following situation.

A table is set up so that when the four people are seated each can see the person on their right or left but not the person across the table. The four prospective members, unknown to each other, are seated at the table and told when looking right and left to raise their hand if they see at least one woman. Each candidate is told to deduce and announce the sex of the person they cannot see.

One year all four candidates were female and each therefore raised her hand. A few moments passed before the winning candidate announced that she was certain the person opposite her was a woman. Explain how she could arrive at that conclusion logically.

DATA ANALYSIS

Tune Up

1. Calculate the sum.

a. $\dfrac{7 + 20 + 59 + 37 + 42 + 36}{6}$

b. $\dfrac{(3)^2 + (-2)^2 + (5)^2 + (-3)^2 + (0)^2}{5}$

c. $\dfrac{4}{1} + \dfrac{4}{2} + \dfrac{4}{3} + \dfrac{4}{4}$

d. $\dfrac{6}{1} + \dfrac{6}{2} + \dfrac{6}{3} + \dfrac{6}{4} + \dfrac{6}{5} + \dfrac{6}{6}$

Study this table of data and answer the questions that follow.

British Columbia
Traffic Incident Statistics for One Year

Surface Conditions	Property Damage	Injury	Fatalities
Dry	42 627	14 851	288
Wet	18 923	6 449	84
Icy	7 742	1 738	25
Snow	4 957	942	17
Slush	1 248	382	9
Muddy	156	50	1
Other	2 124	311	4
Road Type			
Asphalt	55 535	21 330	386
Gravel	3 562	923	31
Earth	396	109	4
Concrete	290	100	3
Oiled gravel	79	29	4
Brick/Stone	17	7	0
Other	17 898	2 225	0

2. How many Fatalities occurred for each road-surface condition?

a. Snow   **b.** Icy   **c.** Wet   **d.** Dry

3. How many incidents involving Property Damage occurred for each road type?

a. Concrete **b.** Earth **c.** Gravel **d.** Asphalt

4. These statistics appear to imply that the worst road conditions for driving is on dry asphalt. What do you think of this conclusion?

5. According to these statistics, state the best road conditions for driving. What do you think of this conclusion?

6.

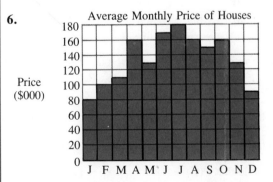

a. Which month has the lowest average price?

b. What is the average price between May and August?

c. Between which months is the largest increase?

13·1 Probability

Assuming a certain number of points is needed to win a game in which each player has an equal chance of winning a single point, how should the stakes be divided between two players if they quit the game before it is finished?

This problem was given to mathematician Blaise Pascal by the French gambler, Antoine Gombaud, Chevalier de Méré. Through a series of letters, Pascal and another French mathematician, Pierre de Fermat, solved the problem thereby developing and laying the foundation for the first theory of **probability**.

The probability of an event, P(*E*), is the measure of the chances that event *E* will occur. The situation which produces an event is called an **experiment**. The set of all possible outcomes of an experiment is called the **sample space**. The **complement** of an event, P($\overline{E}$), is that part of the sample space not in the event.

But what is probability? It is easy to say that the probability of tossing a head when you flip a coin is $\frac{1}{2}$, but what does it mean?

Understand the Problem

Experiment .... A coin is tossed
Sample Space .... A head or a tail ....{H, T}
Event .... A head turns up .... {H}
Complement of the event .. Not a head .. {T}

Develop a Plan

Use the formula to calculate the probability:

$$P(E) = \frac{\text{number of favourable outcomes}}{\text{total number of outcomes}}$$

$$P(H) = \frac{\text{a head}}{\text{a head or a tail}}$$

Carry Out the Plan

There is 1 way for a head to come up.
There are 2 ways for a head or a tail to come up.
So, P(H) $= \frac{1}{2}$.

Look Back

Theoretically, there is a 1 in 2 chance that a coin will land heads up when tossed fairly.

Example 1

A single marble is drawn out of a bag which contains 2 blue, 3 green, and 5 red marbles. Determine the theoretical probability of drawing a green marble.

The total number of ways we can draw a marble is called the sample space. In this case, it is $\{B_1, B_2, G_1, G_2, G_3, R_1, R_2, R_3, R_4, R_5\} = 10$.
The number of favourable outcomes is P(G) $= \{G_1, G_2, G_3\} = 3$.

The probability of obtaining a green marble is $P(G) = \frac{\text{favourable outcomes}}{\text{total outcomes}} = \frac{3}{10}$.

The probability of not obtaining a green marble is $P(\overline{G}) = \frac{\text{ways of not getting a green}}{\text{total outcomes}} = \frac{7}{10}$.

Notice that $P(G) + (\overline{G}) = \frac{3}{10} + \frac{7}{10} = 1$.

If each event of an experiment has an equal chance of happening, then the outcomes are **equally likely** to occur. For example, the chances of rolling a three with a fair die is $\frac{1}{6}$, the same as rolling a five. Hence they are equally-likely events.

The theoretical probability differs from the experimental probability in that the number of favourable outcomes and the total number of outcomes is obtained from the data collected.

Example 2

At West Hill Secondary, 150 Grade 11 students were asked at random if they were enrolled in mathematics. Of these, 92 students said yes. Calculate the probability that the next Grade 11 student asked will be enrolled in mathematics.

The number of favourable replies (yes) was 92. The total number of replies was 150.
We use the experimental probability:

$$P(E_{exp}) = \frac{\text{number of favourable outcomes}}{\text{total number of experimental outcomes}}$$

$$\therefore P(YES) = \frac{92}{150} = 0.61$$

The experimental probability is $\frac{46}{75}$ or 0.61. We say the probability of a yes response is 61 times out of one hundred or 61%.

Exercises

1. In your own words, explain the meaning of the words "random", "sample space", and "event".

2. State whether each event is random.
a. A bus arrives at a bus stop.
b. A winning ticket is drawn in a lottery.
c. A student receives an 'A' lettergrade for Math.
d. Seven turns up on the roll of a pair of dice.

3. State whether each outcome of each pair is equally likely to occur.
a. a tail or a head occurring with one toss of a coin
b. drawing a white or a red marble from a bag containing 4 red and 1 white marble
c. rolling a one or a six with a die

4. State the sample space, the event, and the complement of the event for each experiment.
a. randomly choosing an even digit
b. drawing a heart from a deck of well-shuffled cards
c. drawing a red marble from a bag of 5 red and 8 white marbles

5. Obtain a set of 10 thumbtacks. Drop the set 10 times. Record the number of tacks landing "up" as opposed to "down".
a. Calculate the probability that a thumbtack will land in the "up" position.
b. Explain why one cannot calculate the theoretical probability of a thumbtack landing "up".

6. The letters of the word SHAMATTAWA are placed in a hat and one is drawn at random. Find the probability of each event.
a. P(A)   **b.** P(T)   **c.** P(W)   **d.** P(H or M)
e. Compare the results in parts **a** to **d** with the experimental results obtained by performing the experiment. Draw one letter from a hat containing the letters written on cards 100 times in succession, returning each letter after each draw.

7. A.T., the "Mathematics Wizard", stated, "The probability of a student in your class having blue eyes is $\frac{1}{3}$." Survey your class to see if A.T. is correct. If A.T.'s prediction is incorrect, give the experimental probability.

8. On an assembly line producing computer chips, 14 defective chips were found in 91 000 produced in a month. Estimate the probability that any given computer chip produced during the next month will work satisfactorily.

9. One marble is drawn at random from a bag containing 6 red, 10 white, and 4 green marbles. Find the probability of each event.
a. P(R)   **b.** P(G)   **c.** P(W)   **d.** P(B or W)
e. Compare the results in parts **a** to **d** with the experimental results obtained by performing the experiment. Draw one marble at a time from a bag containing the marbles indicated, returning each marble after each draw.

13·2 Events

The probability that a 3 will turn up on the roll of a fair die is $\frac{1}{6}$. If a 2 turns up on the first roll of the die, this will in no way affect the probability that a 3 will occur on the next roll. Successive events are said to be **independent** when the first event does not affect the second event.

Example 1

Determine the probability that an ace followed by a king will be drawn from a deck if each card is returned to the deck after each draw.

The probability of an ace being drawn is $\frac{4}{52}$ or $\frac{1}{13}$. Since the ace is returned to the deck, the first draw has no affect on the second draw. The probability of a king being drawn is $\frac{1}{13}$ also.

Therefore, the probability of an ace and a king being drawn is $\frac{1}{13} \times \frac{1}{13}$ or $\frac{1}{169}$.

The probability of two or more independent events is $P(A \text{ and } B) = P(A) \times P(B)$.

If the outcome of the first event affects the outcome of the second event, the events are said to be **dependent**.

Example 2

Determine the probability of drawing a diamond from a deck of well-shuffled cards followed by drawing a spade without replacing the diamond to the deck.

The probability of drawing a diamond, P(D), is $\frac{1}{4}$. Since the first card is not returned, there are only 51 cards in the deck. Hence, the probability of now drawing a spade, P(S), is $\frac{13}{51}$. Therefore, the probability of drawing a diamond followed by a spade, P(D and then S), without replacement is:
$P(D \text{ and then } S) = \frac{1}{4} \times \frac{13}{51} = \frac{13}{204}$.

If A and B are dependent events, then $P(A \text{ and then } B) = P(A) \times P(B \text{ after } A \text{ has occurred})$.

If events cannot occur simultaneously, they are said to be **mutually exclusive**.

Example 3

Two dice are rolled. What is the probability that either the sum is 3 or the sum is 8?

Let P(sum 3) represent the probability that the sum of the dice is 3. A sum of 3 occurs 2 times.
∴ P(sum 3) is $\frac{2}{36} = \frac{1}{18}$.
Let P(sum 8) represent the probability that the sum of the dice is 8. A sum of 8 occurs 5 times.
The probability that sum 3 or sum 8 occurs is
P(sum 3 or sum 8) = P(sum 3) + P(sum 8)
$= \frac{1}{18} + \frac{5}{36} = \frac{7}{36}$

		Blue Die			
1	2	3	4	5	6
(1, 1)	*(1, 2)*	(1, 3)	(1, 4)	(1, 5)	(1, 6)
(2, 1)	(2, 2)	(2, 3)	(2, 4)	(2, 5)	**(2, 6)**
(3, 1)	(3, 2)	(3, 3)	(3, 4)	**(3, 5)**	(3, 6)
(4, 1)	(4, 2)	(4, 3)	**(4, 4)**	(4, 5)	(4, 6)
(5, 1)	(5, 2)	**(5, 3)**	(5, 4)	(5, 5)	(5, 6)
(6, 1)	**(6, 2)**	(6, 3)	(6, 4)	(6, 5)	(6, 6)

Red Die (rows 1–6)

Sample-space Diagram

If A and B are mutually-exclusive events, then $P(A \text{ or } B) = P(A) + P(B)$.

If two events are **not** mutually exclusive then one may occur when the other does. We must take into account any duplication caused by both events happening.

Example 4

What is the probability that one of the dice is a 3 or the sum is 8.

$P(3) = \frac{11}{36}$ since the 3 occurs 11 times in the sample space.

$P(\text{sum } 8) = \frac{5}{36}$ since sum 8 occurs 5 times.

If the two were mutually exclusive, then $P(3 \text{ or sum } 8) = P(3) + P(\text{sum } 8)$

$$= \frac{11}{36} + \frac{5}{36}$$

But they are not mutually exclusive and there is a duplication. The throws (3, 5) and (5, 3) have both a 3 and a sum 8.

The probability that 3 and sum 8 are thrown is $P(3 \text{ and sum } 8) = P(3) \times P(\text{sum } 8)$

$$= \frac{11}{36} \times \frac{5}{36}$$

This amount must be subtracted.

Hence, $P(3 \text{ or sum } 8) = P(3) + P(\text{sum } 8) - P(3) \times P(\text{sum } 8)$

$$= \frac{11}{36} + \frac{5}{36} - \frac{11}{36} \times \frac{5}{36}$$

$$= \frac{16}{36} - \frac{55}{1296} = \frac{521}{1296} \text{ or } 0.4 \text{ (rounded)}$$

If A and B are not mutually-exclusive events, then $P(A \text{ or } B) = P(A) + P(B) - P(A \text{ and } B)$.

Exercises

1. In your own words, explain the meaning of the terms ''independent'', ''dependent'', and ''mutually exclusive''. Use examples to support your explanations.

2. State whether each is a dependent, independent, or mutually-exclusive event. For each event, calculate i) the theoretical probability and ii) the experimental probabilities obtained after 3, 5, and 10 repetitions of each.

a. rolling a seven twice with a pair of fair dice
b. drawing an ace and a king in two successive draws, from a well-shuffled deck of cards
c. tossing a head with a fair coin three successive times
d. How do the results change as the number of times each experiment is performed is increased?

3. Find the theoretical probability of each event when throwing a pair of dice.
a. a sum of 9   **b.** at least the sum of 9
c. at most the sum of 9   **d.** a sum other than 9

4. The letters A, B, and C are written separately on three identical slips of paper. The slips are placed in a hat, randomly drawn one at a time, and replaced after each draw. Find the probability for each event.
a. P(A or B)   **b.** P(A and then B)
c. P(vowel)   **d.** P(D)
e. P(A)   **f.** P(A or B or C)
g. Perform parts **a**, **b**, **c**, and **d** experimentally 30 times. Record the results and calculate the experimental probabilities. How do the two sets of results compare?

5. A white die and a green die are tossed. Find each probability.

a. P(G5 and G6)   **b.** P(W2 and G2)

c. P(W5 or G6)   **d.** P(sum 5)

e. Perform parts **a, b, c,** and **d** experimentally 30 times. Record the results and calculate the experimental probabilities. How do the two sets of results compare?

6. Two people are dealt a card from the same well-shuffled deck without replacements. Find the probability that

a. each person is dealt an ace.

b. each person is dealt a face card.

7. A bag contains 3 white and 4 red marbles. What is the probability of drawing (without replacements)

a. a red ball followed by a white ball?

b. a white ball followed by a red ball?

c. a red and a white ball in no particular order?

8. A special deck of cards consists of only the aces and face cards. What is the probability of drawing (without replacements)

a. a king followed by an ace?

b. a queen followed by a queen?

c. an ace followed by a king followed by a queen?

9. A man knows that there are three children in the family next door but does not know their sexes. If a girl answers the door when the man pays a visit, what is the probability that there are exactly two boys in the family?

10. A sample space for two fair coins can be set up by using this table.

2nd Coin

	H	T
H		HT
T		

1st Coin

a. Copy and complete the table.

b. What is the probability of tossing an H and a T? tossing two heads?

c. Explain why tossing a head and a tail is more likely than tossing two heads.

d. Construct a model to show the sample space for 3 coins. Calculate the probability of tossing HTT.

11. The first team to win four games in a World Series final wins the series. Toronto plays Montreal and the probability of a Toronto win for each game is P(T) = 0.7.

a. What is the probability of the series being over in four straight games?

b. Prepare a sample space for five games.

c. What is the probability of Toronto winning only one of the first two games?

12. In **conditional probability**, only part of the sample space is dealt with. Referring to Example 4 in the display, what is the probability that the sum is 8 given that one of the dice is a 3? This is denoted by P(sum 8 | 3).

Understand the Problem

We are given that 3 is on one of the dice. We are asked for the probability of the other being such as the sum is 8.

Develop a Plan

Refer to the sample space in Example 3 of the display to see how many times a three is in a throw and in these cases how many have a sum of 8. Then using basic principles, the probability is:

$$P(\text{sum } 8 | 3) = \frac{\text{favourable outcomes}}{\text{total outcomes}}.$$

Carry Out the Plan

For P(sum 8 | 3) we have a sample space of 11 cases with 3, and we have 1 favourable case with a sum of 8.

Therefore, $P(\text{sum } 8 | 3) = \frac{1}{11}$.

Look Back

The probability of rolling a sum of 8 given that a 3 has been rolled is $\frac{1}{11}$. Solve these problems.

a. What is the probability that a sum of 7 will be rolled given that one of the dice is 5?

b. A box contains 3 red balls and 7 blue balls. Two balls are drawn in succession without replacement. Find the probability of drawing a red ball given a blue ball was drawn first.

c. Explain how the above situations relate to this formula: $P(A|B) = \frac{P(A \text{ and } B)}{P(B)}$

13·3 Approximating Probabilities

An experimental method of determining the probability of an event is to simulate an actual situation using a model. Once we have determined the probability of a successful outcome and, where appropriate, assumed the independence of events, we can then select a model of the random situation. We then assign outcomes of experiments in the model to match possible events in the "real-life" situation. The experiment must be performed with the model many times to obtain a large enough sample. The resulting data may then be analysed and inferences can be made about the general situation.

Example

A child is equally likely to be born male or female. What is the probability that exactly two male children occur in a four-child family?

Understand the Problem

The birth of each child is an independent event with the probability of $\frac{1}{2}$. If B stands for Boy and G for Girl, some examples of 4 consecutive births might be BBGG, BGBG, GBBG, GGBB, and GBGB.

Develop a Plan

Since the chances of a child being born male is $\frac{1}{2}$, an appropriate model can be chosen from:

Plan 1—Coin: female—head; male—tail. Toss 4 coins at once, or
Plan 2—Dice: female—even; male—odd. Roll 4 dice at once, or
Plan 3—Random digits: female—odd; male—even. Pick random digits in groups of 4.

An experiment represents a single four-child family.
A successful event occurs when:
Plan 1—exactly 2 tails turn up when the coins are tossed.
Plan 2—exactly 2 odd numbers appear when four dice are rolled.
Plan 3—exactly 2 even digits appear in each group of four randomly-chosen digits.
Since a random number table is readily available, we choose plan 3.

Carry Out the Plan

The more experiments conducted, the more reliable the approximation will be. The following is the result of 50 experiments using a random number table. Those in bold are successful events.

7043	**5188**	**2349**	**5982**	1451	8575	3563	**5025**	1931	7345
9184	9879	**8378**	4911	8284	8880	5813	0063	3271	9846
1507	**6794**	**2190**	7958	**5021**	7839	1813	**1623**	**6309**	6860
2202	2302	6250	**6495**	9529	4640	6050	**8013**	3967	2746
4395	**7342**	1642	8784	6654	**4853**	5371	**1225**	**5038**	9979

Look Back

The data shows 18 successful events in 50 experiments. Therefore, $\frac{18}{50} = 0.36$. The approximate probability that exactly two male children will occur in a four-child family is 0.36.

Extension

What is the probability that the first two children born will be male?

The data shows 12 successful events of this kind in 50 experiments. The approximate probability that the first two children born will be male is $\frac{12}{50} = 0.24$.

Exercises

1. Using the example in the display, find the approximate probability of each.
a. three female children in a family of four
b. one female child in a family of four
c. all female children in a family of four

2. What model would you choose to simulate these situations?
a. Forty percent of the Canadian labour force is female. A company employs 200 people of which 55 are women. Find the probability that this could happen by chance.
b. A baseball player is hitting 0.200. Approximate the probability of the player getting a hit in the next five times at bat.
c. A woman has 6 dresses to wear to work. She chooses a dress at random each day. What is the probability that she wears the same dress more than twice in a 5 d week.
d. A salesman claims that no more than 2% of the matches he sells are defective. Since the matches are destroyed when tested, devise a sampling plan to test the accuracy of the salesman's claim.

3. The Integrated Commercial Bank has two tellers serving customers. When a customer arrives, they form a line. During any minute, the probability a customer arrives is 0.9. Each customer takes 3 min to serve. Let 0, 1, 2, 3, 4, 5, 6, 7, and 8 mean a customer arrives and 9 means no customer arrives. The 20 random digits selected to represent the arrival or nonarrival of a customer for a 20 min period were 75223250916320843704.
a. Copy and complete the table and answer the questions.

RND Digit	Min	Teller A	Teller B	Customers Queued
7	1	C1		
5	2	C1	C2	
2	3	C1	C2	C3
2	4	C3	C2	C4
3	5	C3	C4	C5
2	6	C3	C4	C5, C6
...	...	...	...	...

b. Find the average length of a queue.
c. Find the number of customer-free-minutes for Teller A, Teller B.
d. Find the average number of minutes each customer spends standing in a queue.
e. If you were the bank manager, would you increase the number of tellers based on this queuing model?

4. During any minute, the probability that a customer arrives at Sidney's fast-food outlet is 0.80. The manager has three cashiers serving customers who have queued for service. Each customer takes 2 min to be served. Answer the questions for a 45 min period.
a. Find the average number of minutes each customer waits for service.
b. Find the average length of a queue.
c. How many minutes of free time does each cashier have?

5. The probability that a well-drilling company will find water is 0.30. Each well drilled, whether successful or not, costs $450. Design and run a simulation to approximate each situation.
a. the average cost of drilling to find the first successful well
b. the average number of wells needed to be drilled to find 10 water-producing wells

6. Visit a local supermarket or fast-food outlet and record the following data. A stopwatch, if available, would be useful. Obtain appropriate permission first.
a. How long does a queue get?
b. How many minutes does each clerk have that is customer free?
c. How long does each customer wait to be served?
d. How long does it take to serve each customer?
e. How many clerks are serving customers?
Determine the appropriate times and probabilities. Create a simulation of the queue at this site.
Explore the affects on the customer-waiting time of increasing the number of clerks using your simulation model.
Discover the average waiting time of a customer when the number of clerks is reduced.

13·4 Collecting Data—Sampling

Collecting data is an important part of today's society. Scientists collect data for their experiments. Politicians collect information about public opinions. Consumer advocates collect data about product quality. Statisticians conduct polls and censuses to gain information about a population. Sampling provides an efficient and accurate way of collecting data.

These definitions are useful when discussing sampling.

Population: The group of objects or people about which information is needed.
Example: All sixteen-year-old students in Canada.

Sample: A subset of the population which is used to obtain information about the whole population.
Example: All sixteen-year-old students in B.C.

Parameter: A numerical feature of the population which is usually not known.
Example: The number of left-handed sixteen-year-old students in Canada.

Statistic: A numerical feature of the sample which is known when the sample is taken. The statistic changes from sample to sample.
Example: The number of left-handed sixteen-year-old students in B.C. determined by the sample.

Strata: One or more groups within the population which have a special feature.
Example: Rural or urban students in the sample.

Precision of a statistic depends on the size of the sample. The larger the sample size, the greater the precision. The Census is a method of collecting data where the sample is the entire population. In ancient times, people were counted for tax purposes or military service. In 1666, Canada's first census was conducted in New France to account for the resources and population needs. Today the Canadian Census is taken every five years.

Example 1

A school census is conducted to determine a school profile based on information about the student population. The following census form was given to each student in the school at the same time and collected after five minutes.

Do NOT put your name on this form.
The individual responses to this census will be kept confidential.

AGE: _____   SEX: ___ M ___ F   DATE OF BIRTH: _____ _____ _____
                                                       Day   Month   Year

PLACE OF BIRTH: _____
                    City or Town   How do you travel to school? Walk _____

                    _____   Bus _____
                    Province or State
                                                                         Car _____
                    _____
                    Country   Bicycle _____

                                                       Other (specify) _____

What distance, in kilometres, do you travel from home to school? _____ km
Favourite Radio Station _____   Favourite TV program _____

How many hours per week do you spend:
Watching TV _____   Listening to music _____   Studying _____
On sports activities _____   Working at a job _____   Other (specify) _____

Another method of collecting data is to take a **simple random sample** of the population. The sample is taken so that each member of the population has an equal chance of being selected.

Example 2

Outline a method, using a simple random sample, to check the quality of canned fish produced at a fish-packing plant. The size of the sample is 10 drawn from 1000 lots of canned fish.

Understand the Problem
From 1000 lots, we must pick 10 of them, ensuring that each lot has an equal chance of being selected.

Develop a Plan
Assign each lot a 3-digit number and use a random number table to find which lots will be selected.

Carry Out the Plan
Label the 1000 lots 000, 001, 002, 003,..., 999, in any order. Select a line in the random number table at the back of this book and read across. For example, a line in the table reads:
82806 82277 88300 29832 22806 92486.

Read groups of three digits. Each group represents a label attached to a lot of canned fish. The simple random sample is the set of lots labelled:
828, 068, 227, 788, 300, 298, 322, 280, 692, 486.

Look Back
Ten numbers from 000 to 999 have been chosen. The lots having these numbers would then be opened and their contents examined.

If we wish to divide a population into groups based on a common feature, then we use a **stratified random sample**.

Example 3

Government inspectors decided to sample the quality of 20 lots of canned fish produced on Monday, Wednesday, and Friday of a particular week. The days of the week are the strata of the sample. Since the lots of canned fish are opened and thus destroyed during the inspection, this type of sampling is referred to as **destructive sampling**.

Stratum	Size of Stratum	Sample Size	No. of Lots Rejected
Fish canned on Monday	600 lots	12	1
Fish canned on Wednesday	300 lots	6	1
Fish canned on Friday	100 lots	2	1
Total	1000 lots	20	3

The sample size for each stratum was determined by taking the ratio of the stratum size to the total population.

For instance, Stratum (Monday) $\frac{600}{1000} = \frac{x}{20}$
$$x = 12$$

A simple random sample was used to select the sample lots in each of the three strata. An approximation of the percent of inferior quality lots in the population is $\frac{3}{20} = 0.15$ or 15%.

The total number of rejected lots is a statistic. The 15% estimation of the inferior quality lots in the total population is a parameter.

Exercises

1. List some advantages of sampling over taking a census.

2. List some of the possible ways the information on the census form from Example 1 in the display could be used.

3. Census questions are often asked to detect changes in society. How could a school census be used to detect changes in student interests?

4. In the past, census-takers knocked on every door and asked census questions of a responsible adult who happened to be present. Today a questionnaire is left with each household with instructions that the form is to be completed on a certain date.
a. Discuss the advantages of this change in census taking.
b. What problems might a census-taker have in ancient times that census-takers today don't have, and vice versa?
c. Why is the Canadian Census not taken every year?

5. Few people realize how dangerous potatoes are. A survey presents this evidence.
a. 99.9% of all people who die of cancer have eaten potatoes.
b. All potato eaters born between 1900 and 1910 have wrinkled skin, have lost most of their teeth, and have failing hearing and/or eyesight, if they have not already died.
c. 99.8% of all people who were at fault in a car accident have eaten potatoes.
d. 99.99% of all people who ate potatoes in 1888 later died.
Discuss the above evidence and point out the errors that result in the false conclusions that potatoes are dangerous.

6. A shipment of 432 sockeye and 433 pink salmon lots were to be inspected. Devise a method, using a random number table, to select a sample size of 20. The method used must allow the sampler to know whether the lot sampled is sockeye or pink salmon.

7. Each number in bold print is either a parameter or a statistic. In each case, state which is correct.
a. Of all the workers interviewed, **92%** expressed job satisfaction.
b. A manufacturer advertised that the average life of the battery the company produced was **35.2 h**. A random sampling procedure inspected 500 batteries and found the average life to be **36.1 h**. The order was purchased.
c. A random telephone survey was conducted across Canada. Of the first 100 phone calls, **61** people answering the phone were between the ages of 18 and 64. This was not surprising because **62.2%** of the Canadian population is between the ages of 18 and 64.

8. List three sources of sample error that can occur in a telephone survey.

9. A truck manufacturer received a shipment of 1000 lots of wheel bearings. Each lot was labelled with a number from TB 749 to TB 1748. A random sample of 150 lots is to be selected for inspection.
a. Describe how this can be done using a random number table.
b. How could the precision of the sample be increased?

10. A squadron has 300 male and 60 female personnel. A personnel relations officer takes a stratified random sample of 30 male and 30 female squadron members.
a. What is the chance that a male member will be selected?
b. What is the chance that a female member will be selected?

11. Each member of the sample in Exercise 10 is asked, ''Do female personnel in this squadron have the same chance of promotion as male personnel with the same qualifications?''
2 of the 30 males answered ''No''.
28 of the 30 females answered ''No''.
The officer reported that ''30 out of 60 personnel (50%) in the squadron stated that females with the same qualifications do not have the same chance of promotion as males.'' Explain the error in this conclusion.

13·5 Percent Frequency Table

The purpose of organizing large amounts of data is to answer certain questions about a population or to find patterns in a population. Organizing data and describing patterns is called **descriptive statistics**. The **percent frequency table** allows us to find patterns in a set of data and to compare the patterns with another related set of data. By expressing frequencies as percents, we can compare sets of data.

Example

The number (D) of defective integrated circuits (chips) found in 20 boxes of 1000 chips each which were listed.

35, 42, 31, 27, 28, 51, 37, 45, 34, 16,
32, 34, 19, 35, 26, 29, 43, 31, 46,   7

a. How many boxes had less than 30 defective chips? 40 defective chips?
b. What percent of the boxes shipped had less than 4% defective chips?

The boxes of chips are divided into various **classes** of equal width for purposes of comparison. An example is the class $10 \leq D < 20$, where 10 is the **lower class boundary**, 20 is the **upper class boundary**, and $\frac{10 + 20}{2} = 15$ is the **class mark**. The class $10 \leq D < 20$ records the instances where there are 10 to 19 inclusive, defective chips per box of 1000. The lower class boundary is included in the class interval and the upper class boundary is not.

Class	Tally	Frequency	Percent Frequency	Cumulative Percent Frequency
$0 \leq D < 10$	I	1	5	5
$10 \leq D < 20$	II	2	10	15
$20 \leq D < 30$	IIII	4	20	35
$30 \leq D < 40$	⊬⊬ III	8	40	75
$40 \leq D < 50$	IIII	4	20	95
$50 \leq D < 60$	I	1	5	100

> Frequency is the number of boxes in each class.

a. The number of boxes with less than 30 defective chips (3%) is 7, the sum of the frequencies of the first three classes.
The number of lots with less than 40 defective chips (4%) is 15.
b. The percent of lots with less than 4% defective chips (less than 40 chips per box) is the cumulative frequency of the fourth class, that is, 75% of the lots had less than 4% defective chips.

To find the size of the intervals to set up a frequency table, first decide on the number of intervals required. Then divide the difference between the **lower limit** (the lower class boundary rounded down) and the **upper limit** (the upper class boundary rounded up) by the number of intervals required.

From the above example, this lower limit is 0 and the upper limit is 60. The interval width is $\frac{60 - 0}{6} = 10$.

A **histogram** gives a graphical representation of the above percent frequency table.

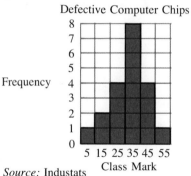

Defective Computer Chips

Frequency

Class Mark

Source: Industats

Notice the axes are properly labelled, the graph has a title, and the source of the data is given.

Exercises

1. Explain the meaning of each term.
a. upper limit
b. lower class boundary
c. class mark
d. upper class boundary
e. histogram
f. lower limit

2. Refer to the display for parts **a** to **f**.
a. From the percent frequency table, explain how the Percent Frequencies and the Cumulative Percent Frequencies are determined.
b. Find the class mark for each class.
c. How many boxes had less than 2% defective chips?
d. What percent of the boxes had less than 5% defective chips?
e. What percent of the boxes had between 1% and 4% defective chips?
f. What is the upper class boundary for the third class?

3. Two sporting goods stores recorded the number of customers each had during a 20 d period of operation.
Store A: 26, 38, 47, 39, 56, 72, 44, 28, 68, 69, 72, 89, 86, 78, 87, 53, 52, 98, 74, 68
Store B: 35, 95, 76, 83, 38, 59, 60, 70, 56, 63, 73, 40, 77, 82, 83, 73, 77, 81, 71, 84
a. Construct a percent frequency table and histogram.
b. Compare the number of customers the two stores had. If the stores were to hire additional staff, how might they be deployed?

4. Sixteen coho salmon were caught each spring. Their masses were recorded in kilograms.

Year 1: 4.08, 3.49, 3.45, 3.32, 3.34, 5.52, 5.21, 2.7, 3.10, 4.10, 4.37, 6.80, 5.5, 4.6, 2.2, 3.41
Year 2: 3.8, 3.45, 3.42, 3.12, 3.6, 3.52, 4.25, 4.39, 3.35, 3.21, 7.26, 3.85, 3.5, 3.47, 2.85, 3.49

a. Construct a percent frequency table with interval size 0.50 kg, and construct a histogram.
b. Compare the masses of the salmon in the two years.
c. It is estimated there are 750 000 salmon in the fishing area. Approximate the number of fish between 2.5 and 3.5 kg.

5. The following data represents the gas consumption in litres per 100 km of 50 cars selected at random from a shipment of one make and model. The manufacturer claimed the fuel consumption to be better than 5.05 L/100 km.

4.9, 5.1, 5.1, 5.0, 4.8, 4.8, 5.3, 4.9, 5.0, 5.1,
5.2, 5.3, 5.1, 5.0, 5.0, 5.2, 5.0, 5.2, 5.1, 5.2,
5.1, 5.1, 5.1, 5.0, 5.2, 5.0, 5.2, 5.0, 4.8, 5.0,
5.1, 5.0, 5.1, 4.9, 5.0, 5.1, 5.2, 5.3, 5.2, 4.8,
4.9, 5.3, 5.0, 5.2, 5.0, 5.0, 5.2, 4.8, 5.0, 5.1

a. Construct a percent frequency table with class length 0.1, starting at 4.75.
b. What percentage of the cars tested exceed the manufacturer's claim for fuel consumption?
c. If the shipment had 2500 cars, approximately how many cars would have fuel consumption in the range $4.75 \leq C < 5.15$ L/100 km?

13·6 Stem and Leaf Plots

A **stem and leaf plot** has the advantage of preserving the original data after the table is constructed.

Example 1

The number of wins during a major league baseball season was recorded for each of the teams in the league. Construct a stem and leaf table using this data to see the distribution of the wins.

83, 71, 74, 57, 66, 91, 77, 81, 62, 60, 84, 99, 97,
62, 101, 83, 85, 90, 84, 95, 83, 98, 77, 77, 75, 89

Stem	Leaf
10	1
9	0, 1, 5, 7, 8, 9
8	1, 3, 3, 3, 4, 4, 5, 9
7	1, 4, 5, 7, 7, 7
6	0, 2, 2, 6
5	7

First digit of 71

Last digit of 101

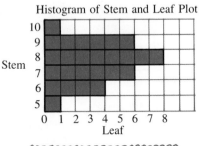

Histogram of Stem and Leaf Plot

Each stem represents a class.

The table shows the outline of a horizontal histogram based on the data. The histogram provides a visual summary and permits a quick interpretation of the data. For instance, the average number of wins is in the range $80 \leq w < 90$.

Example 2

A company wanted to know how effective a sales-training program was for their sales staff. The number of contracts signed the month before and the month after the training program by the same 15 salespeople were recorded. Construct a stem and leaf plot to organize and display these data.

Sales before training: 65, 64, 26, 34, 43, 49, 58, 91, 12, 27, 58, 47, 39, 48, 59
Sales after training: 22, 50, 69, 41, 83, 72, 11, 59, 58, 81, 65, 92, 73, 57, 66

Leaf Before	Stem	Leaf After
1	9	2
	8	1, 3
	7	2, 3
4, 5	6	5, 6, 9
8, 8, 9	5	0, 7, 8, 9
3, 7, 8, 9	4	1
4, 9	3	
6, 7	2	2
2	1	1

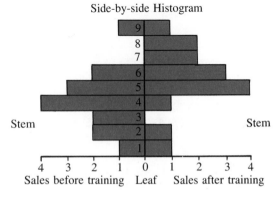

Side-by-side Histogram

Sales before training   Leaf   Sales after training

This table is a **double stem and leaf plot**. It is used to make quick comparisons of the distribution and data of two different sets. The side-by-side histogram based on this data provides an easy-to-read picture of the distribution of the data.

362

Exercises

1. List the advantages of a double stem and leaf plot.

2. In what situations is a stem and leaf plot more useful than a frequency table?

3. Referring to Example 1 in the display, how many teams ended the season with wins in each class.
a. $90 \le w < 100$ **b.** $80 \le w < 90$
c. $50 \le w < 60$

4. Referring to Example 1 in the display, state the class having each frequency.
a. 1   **b.** 4   **c.** 6

5. In Example 1, if there were two more teams in the league, both having total win counts in the 70's, would the average for the league still be in the 80's?

6. Refer to Example 2 in the display.
a. Approximately what is the average number of contracts sold before the training program? after the training program?
b. What can you conclude about the value of the training program for the 15 salespeople who took the course?

7. A soft-drink distributor recorded the monthly sales of Blast-cola (in kilolitres) for 48 months. Construct a stem and leaf plot based on the data.
26.3, 21.5, 22.8, 23.3, 24.6, 25.1, 26.6, 27.2, 28.4, 29.3, 30.3, 31.4, 32.0, 31.5, 30.7, 29.0, 28.6, 27.7, 26.4, 25.1, 24.9, 23.2, 22.2, 21.3, 22.3, 23.4, 24.5, 25.3, 26.1, 27.7, 28.1, 29.2, 30.9, 29.5, 28.6, 27.1, 25.5, 24.6, 23.7, 24.5, 28.7, 27.4, 26.5, 25.6, 25.8, 26.9, 27.8, 26.7
a. Which class has a frequency of 2? 7?
b. Which class has a frequency of 3? 5? 6?
c. What is the approximate average number of kilolitres of Blast-cola sold per month during the 48-month period?

8. The times for the 100 m breaststroke event were recorded for the top 25 boys in the 15 to 17 a age group in Canada. Construct a stem and leaf plot based on the data.
1:10.96, 1:09.32, 1:08.25, 1:10.14, 1:10.18, 1:09.94, 1:07.51, 1:10.46, 1:10.76, 1:10.89, 1:08.52, 1:05.96, 1:10.51, 1:10.06, 1:09.63, 1:06.87, 1:10.88, 1:10.25, 1:09.84, 1:09.56, 1:07.39, 1:09.13, 1:10.76, 1:09.58, 1:09.94
a. Which class has a frequency of 8? 11?
b. Comment on the distribution of times in the table.

9. The batting averages for a baseball team are listed.
0.297, 0.291, 0.310, 0.361, 0.281, 0.301, 0.288, 0.310, 0.280, 0.280, 0.289, 0.300, 0.300, 0.314, 0.311, 0.335, 0.309, 0.340, 0.310, 0.312, 0.320, 0.305, 0.280, 0.295, 0.300, 0.300, 0.295, 0.295, 0.300, 0.284
During mid-season break, a batting training program was conducted. The averages for the next two months are listed.
0.300, 0.305, 0.289, 0.335, 0.320, 0.300, 0.309, 0.297, 0.293, 0.309, 0.312, 0.295, 0.320, 0.303, 0.293, 0.291, 0.296, 0.300, 0.368, 0.297, 0.317, 0.324, 0.302, 0.295, 0.293, 0.277, 0.311, 0.314, 0.299, 0.307
a. Construct a double stem and leaf plot and a double histogram.
b. Make inferences on the effectiveness of the training program. Can all the changes be attributed to the training program? Comment.

10. Construct a stem and leaf plot based on this data showing the mean monthly precipitation (in millimetres) over a 30-month period in a line running through Windsor, London, Toronto, to Ottawa.
65.3, 61.0, 67.6, 65.8, 66.3, 60.7, 63.3, 62.0, 76.2, 49.5, 59.9, 78.2, 81.0, 82.8, 63.5, 57.7, 55.4, 74.9, 70.1, 77.0, 73.2, 74.9, 81.3, 86.6, 78.5, 81.5, 72.6, 83.1, 83.6, 82.3
a. Arrange the data in classes of size 10.
b. What class has the greatest frequency?
c. State the range of values in the class $50 \le p < 60$.
d. An unusually dry year would occur in this region if the mean monthly rainfall was below what value?

13·7 Box and Whisker Plots

Although stem and leaf plots have the advantage of preserving all the data while maintaining a graphic representation for comparative purposes, they do not inform about such questions as: What is the centre of the data?, What are the extremes of the data?, and Is the data spread symmetrically about the centre? A graphic way of communicating these and other observations is called the **box and whisker plot**.

Geological experts in the Mexican government were assigned to collect data about earthquakes over a two-year period. The magnitude on the Richter Scale of 23 earthquakes for each year were recorded at a seismic station. This was the data collected:

Year 1: **3.2**, 4.1, 5.1, 5.2, 5.4, *5.7*, 5.8, 5.9, 6.1, 6.3, 6.3, **6.5**, 6.5, 6.5, 7.0, 7.0, 7.3, *7.5*, 7.6, 7.7, 7.8, 8.3, **8.5**

Year 2: **3.0**, 3.1, 3.5, 3.5, 4.2, *4.4*, 4.5, 4.6, 4.7, 4.8, 5.4, **5.5**, 5.6, 5.6, 5.8, 6.1, 6.2, *6.3*, 6.5, 7.0, 7.1, 7.2, **8.5**

How can the experts display this data so it clearly demonstrates and compares the strength and frequency of an average earthquake as well as the ranges? The median, the upper and lower extremes, and the upper and lower hinges of the data can be used. Then box and whisker plots can be made.

First order the data from least to greatest magnitude.
The **median** or middle value in the data is **6.5** for Year 1 and **5.5** for Year 2. It is ranked 12th from the bottom or top of both data lists. When there is an even number of data, the median is the average of the two middle numbers.
The **upper and lower extremes** are *8.5* and *3.2* respectively for Year 1, and *8.5* and *3.0* respectively for Year 2.
The **upper and lower hinges** are *7.5* and *5.7* which are the medians for the upper and lower halves respectively for Year 1. The upper and lower hinges for Year 2 are *6.3* and *4.4* respectively.
The median hinge plot of this data consists of a box extending from hinge to hinge and whiskers extending from each hinge to the extreme.

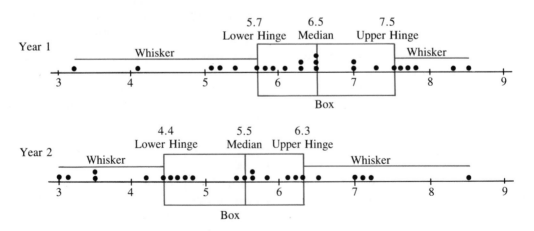

The boxes contain 50% of the data for each year.
The following information and conclusions can be determined easily from the two graphs.

1. The severity of earthquakes decreased in Year 2.

2. The range of magnitudes of earthquakes for Year 1 was 3.2 to 8.5, and 3.0 to 8.5 in Year 2. Therefore, the range of magnitudes was slightly greater in Year 2.

3. A typical earthquake for Year 1 had a magnitude between 5.7 and 7.5. A typical earthquake for Year 2 had a magnitude between 4.4 and 6.3.

Can we conclude from these plots that a trend toward less severe earthquakes is evident? Discuss. Care must be taken when drawing conclusions based on data.

Exercises

1. Find the median, hinges, and extremes in each set of numbers. Construct box and whisker plots.
a. 8, 12, 15, 2, 4, 13, 6, 12, 20, 4, 10
b. 90, 40, 30, 70, 100, 50, 20, 60, 80, 10
c. 0.080, 0.071, 0.066, 0.068, 0.079, 0.081, 0.085, 0.081, 0.072, 0.067, 0.054, 0.072, 0.067, 0.075, 0.081, 0.072, 0.069, 0.081
d. $95 500, $87 000, $85 000, $97 800, $93 000, $92 000, $96 250, $87 000, $95 000

2. The number of goals scored by two hockey players in their eleven best games during a season were recorded.
Player A: 3, 4, 2, 3, 4, 5, 3, 3, 2, 4, 3
Player B: 2, 1, 3, 3, 2, 4, 1, 2, 2, 1, 1
Construct box and whisker plots based on these data. Compare the performance of the two players. Which player showed greater consistency in goal scoring?

3. Diet Cola A and Diet Cola B were tested to determine the number of calories per 100 mL. Random samples of each type of cola produced the following results.
Cola A: 0.44, 0.41, 0.40, 0.42, 0.43, 0.38, 0.40, 0.47, 0.44, 0.43, 0.43, 0.41, 0.39, 0.45, 0.41, 0.38, 0.40, 0.43, 0.46
Cola B: 0.41, 0.36, 0.37, 0.38, 0.37, 0.39, 0.39, 0.39, 0.37, 0.39, 0.40, 0.38, 0.38, 0.39, 0.38, 0.39, 0.36, 0.38, 0.35
a. Construct box and whisker plots for these data.
b. Which cola showed the greatest variability?
c. If the manufacturers of Colas A and B claimed that their colas contained 0.42 and 0.38 calories per 100 mL respectively, are their claims accurate?
d. Which cola typically was closest in calories per 100 mL to its claim?

4. What does a small box indicate about the data?

5. What does the plot tell us about the data if one of the whiskers is very short and the other very long?

6. Can the box extend over all the data?

7. Can a box and whisker plot look like the diagram below? Describe the distribution of the data displayed by this plot.

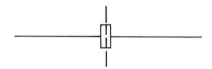

8. How does an extremely high score affect the mean? Does an extreme score alter the position of the box appreciably? Explain.

9. The percentage of the Canadian population under the age of 17 in the provinces and territories in 1961 and 1981 are listed. Construct box and whisker plots for these data and answer the questions.

	Nfld.	P.E.I.	N.S.	N.B.	Que.	Ont.
1961	48	41.5	40.3	43.8	41	36.6
1981	36.5	31.2	29.4	31.2	27.3	27.4

	Man.	Sask.	Alta.	B.C.	Yukon	N.W.T.
1961	37.4	39	39.9	35.6	39.2	44.5
1981	28.8	30.5	29.9	26.5	32.1	41.7

a. What is the median value for 1961? 1981?
b. What is a "typical" percentage of the population between the ages of 0 and 17 a during 1961? 1981?
c. What happened to the population between the ages of 0 and 17 from 1961 to 1981? Suggest reasons for this change.

13·8 90% Box and Whisker Plot

Often surveys and polls are designed so that responses to questions are either positive or negative. The percentage of positive responses in a population is called the **parameter** or **p-value** of that population.

To understand how to find the *p*-value of a population, start by taking 100 samples from a population whose *p*-value is known and record the frequency of the samples. Based on this data, a **90% box and whisker plot** may be drawn to contain 90% of the sample responses.

Example 1

It is known that 30% of the adult residents of a town hold at least one university degree. A poll is conducted asking 20 adults in the town if they have a university degree. A simulation of this poll will be made using a random number table.

Since we know 30% of the population will answer yes to the question, the digits 1, 2, and 3 will simulate a yes response.
Since we know 70% of the population will answer no to the question, the digits 4, 5, 6, 7, 8, 9, and 0 will simulate a no response.
The results of one random sample of size 20, for example, are:
96749 **37823** 71868 **121**49
The number of yeses (numbers 1, 2, and 3) in this particular sample is 7.
A frequency table recording the results from all 100 samples each of size 20 is constructed where the number of times a yes response was given is recorded in the frequency row.

No. of Yeses	0	1	2	3	4	5	6	7	8	9	10	11	12	13	14	15	16	17	18	19	20
Frequency	1	2	2	9	12	16	20	14	10	9	2	1	1	1	0	0	0	0	0	0	0

A histogram shows the distribution of yes responses. Notice that 90% of the positive responses occur between 3 and 9 inclusive. This interval is known as the **confidence interval** since we are 90% confident that 3 to 9 adults (inclusive) out of any 20 will have a university degree.

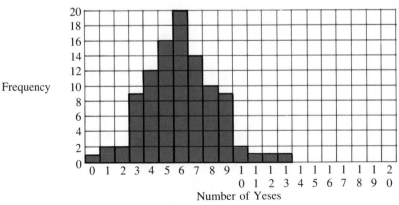

Histogram of Yes Responses in
100 Random Samples Size 20

Frequency

Number of Yeses

A box and whisker plot readily shows that a "typical" number of yes answers in a sample of size 20 would be 3 to 9 inclusive. The box contains 90% of the yes responses. The **common class** is 3-9. The whiskers contain 10% of the yes responses. The **rare class** is 0-2 and 10-13. Also, 30% of a randomly chosen sample of size 20 will give between 3 and 9 yes responses, 90% of the time.

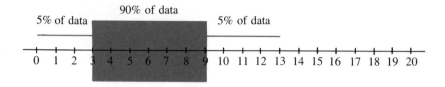

If this simulation is repeated for known *p*-values from 5% to 95%, a useful graph emerges. As the percent of positive responses is increased, the histogram of each distribution would slide to the right and so would the corresponding box and whisker plots. The box and whisker plots for sample sizes of 20 and 100 are illustrated in the tables section in the back of this book. Note that if 70% of a population answers yes to a question, then in a random sample of 20 people, 90% of the time we will get 11 to 17 yes responses. This is outlined by the solid coloured lines in the graph below. Try the procedure outlined in Example 1 for known *p*-values of 40% and 60% to verify this.

Example 2

Use the graphs in the back of the book to answer each question.

a. Find the *p*-value likely to occur when 10 yes responses are obtained in a random sample size 20.

b. Find the *p*-value likely to occur when 69 yes responses are obtained in a random sample size 100.

a. According to the graph of sample size 20, 35% to 65% of the population will respond yes. The *p*-value range is 65-35 or 30%. This is outlined by the solid black lines in the graph to the right.

b. According to the graph of sample size 100, 65% to 75% of the population will respond yes. The *p*-value range is 75-65 or 10%.

Notice that the range of *p*-values or confidence interval decreases as the sample size increases.

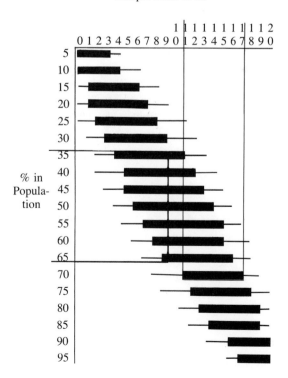

90% Box and Whisker Plots for Sample Sizes of 20

367

Exercises

1. In your own words, explain the meaning of the terms ''confidence interval'', ''parameter'', and ''*p*-value''.

2. State the *p*-value containing each sample value using the graph of sample size 20 in the back of this book.
a. 18   **b.** 8   **c.** 4   **d.** 16

3. State the number of samples that each *p*-value (percent of positive responses) contains using the graphs of sample size (i) 20, (ii) 100.
a. 45%   **b.** 95%   **c.** 15%   **d.** 60%

4. State the *p*-value containing each sample value using the graph of sample size 100 in the back of this book.
a. 73   **b.** 39   **c.** 9   **d.** 80

5. In your own words, explain what ''the range of *p*-values decreases as the sample size increases'' means.

6. A sample, size 100, is randomly removed from a shipment of Christmas tree light bulbs. The sample contained 6 defective bulbs. What percent of the shipment is likely to have defective bulbs?

7. What percentage of private aircraft have defective compasses?
a. 7 out of 20 randomly chosen private aircraft had defective compasses.
b. 26 out of 100 randomly chosen private aircraft had defective compasses.

8. Given the following, what percent of Canadians will vote Liberal in the next federal election?
a. 12 out of 20 voters said they would vote Liberal.
b. 26 out of 100 voters said they would vote Liberal.
c. What reason could be given for the different result in part **b**.

9. The two box and whisker plots show the number of days that the sun shone 75% of the time, for cities A and B, over a 12-month period.

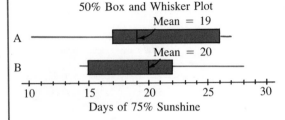

Days of 75% Sunshine

a. Analyse the plots and explain what they tell the reader.
b. If you were planning to experiment with solar heat units, in which city should you locate? Explain.
c. In calculating the mean, how does one extremely low score affect the mean? Is the box in these diagrams affected by extreme scores?

10. What percentage of the population have the Rh-positive factor in their blood?
a. 17 out of 20 randomly chosen individuals had Rh-positive factor in their blood.
b. 92 out of 100 randomly chosen individuals had Rh-positive factor in their blood.

11. A randomly chosen sample of 20 students were asked if they watched television the previous evening. Sixteen said they did.
a. Predict what percent of the student population at that school watched television the previous evening.
b. A national survey said that 74.8% of high school students watch TV every night. Account for the different results.

Using the Library

Recently Environment Canada began reporting weather in terms of percentages. For instance, ''today there is a 40% chance of rain.''
a. Explain what this statement means and how the meteorologists arrive at these values.
b. Is this method more or less accurate than saying, ''there is a chance of rain with showers following''?

13·9 Central Tendencies I

Often it is useful to locate a single value in a set of data that is representative of the whole set. There are several single values around which all the values are clustered. They are called **measures of central tendency**. The four commonly used are **mean**, **median**, **mode**, and **weighted mean**.

Example 1

Nine golfers agreed to play 3 rounds of golf. Player number 9 decided to drop out after the first round. Find the measures of central tendency for each round.

Player	Round 1	Round 2	Round 3
1	72	76	68
2	73	71	74
3	75	72	74
4	75	70	73
5	74	73	75
6	71	74	76
7	76	75	71
8	70	77	71
9	107	***	***

The mean score, $\bar{x}$, for the first round is the arithmetic average of the numbers in the first round.

That is, $\bar{x} = \dfrac{x_1 + x_2 + x_3 + \ldots + x_n}{n}$

$= \dfrac{693}{9}$

$= 77$

The mean score for the golfers in Round 1 is 77.

Ordered Data

Round 1:
70, 71, 72, 73, **74**, 75, 75, 76, 107

Round 2:
70, 71, 72, 73, 74, 75, 76, 77
                    ∧
             73.5

Round 3:
68, 71, 71, 73, 74, 74, 75, 76

To find the median, order the data in each round. The median score is the middle number when the numbers are arranged in numerical order.

The median score for the golfers in Round 1 is **74**.

Since there is an even number of scores in Round 2, the median is the arithmetic mean of the two middle scores. In this case, the median is **73.5**.

The mode is the score which occurs most frequently in each round. In Round 1, the mode is 75. In Round 2 there is no mode. In Round 3 there are two modes, 71 and 74, and the set of scores is said to be **bi-modal**.

Any one of the three values can represent a typical score in each round. It depends on the user's interpretation as to which measure is the most meaningful. Each score may provide a bias to the message. If one wishes to console Player 9, one may describe Round 1 by saying, "The mode was 75." However, if one wishes to indicate how good the golfers are, one could say, "The median was 74."

Both measures of central tendency were used accurately. However, one tends to make the scores seem higher and the other makes them seem lower. This is an example of how measures of central tendency can be interpreted in a variety of ways.

369

Example 2

Calculate the mean green fee for a round of golf and find the mode. The green fees are: for a member $2, an associate member $5, and a nonmember $20.

Green Fee	Frequency	(Green Fee) × (Frequency)
$2	50	100
$5	390	1950
$20	210	4200
Total	650	6250

The mode can be found by inspecting the frequency column. The mode for the green fees is $5, since it occurs 390 times.

The calculation of the arithmetic average of the three green fees, $\frac{2 + 5 + 20}{3} = 9$ or $9, is inappropriate because some fees occur more than others. Therefore, the weighted mean is used.

$$\text{Weighted mean} = \frac{\text{total green fees paid}}{\text{total number of golfers}}$$

$$= \frac{6250}{650}$$

$$\doteq 9.62$$

The mean green fee is $9.62.

Exercises

1. In your own words, explain the meaning of the terms "mean", "median", "mode", and "weighted mean".

2. Predict each measure of central tendency in each. Then calculate them and compare.
a. each round of Example 1 in the display
b. the green fees in Example 2 in the display
c. If 50 more members paid green fees, how would this affect the mode? mean?
d. Which is the better measure of central tendency, the median or mean? Explain.

3. Calculate the weighted mean and the mode for the February daily low temperatures.

Temp. (°C)	−40	−38	−30	−20	−15	−10	0	5	10
Frequency	4	2	5	4	2	3	6	1	1

Explain which measure of central tendency you would use if you were preparing an advertisement to promote
a. the sale of heavy winter wear.
b. an outdoor recreational facility.
c. the sale of skiing equipment.

4. Find the four measures of central tendency of nine linesmen on a football team.

Player	1	2	3	4	5	6	7	8	9
Mass (kg)	70	73	73	75	76	83	83	90	105

a. Which measure of central tendency would you use to psychologically i) overwhelm your opponent with the bulk on the team?, ii) create false confidence in your opponent by down playing the size of the team?
b. Which measure is affected by every value in the set?

5. A hockey team has 4 goaltenders, 12 defensemen, and 21 forwards. This list outlines the cost to outfit each player.
Goaltender—$1612.50
Defenseman
   without plastic shields—$690
   with plastic shields—$725
Forward
   without plastic shields—$650
   with plastic shields—$685
If 2 defensemen and 5 forwards do not wear a plastic shield, find the weighted mean and the mode costs to equip a player on the team.

6. A city freeway had three lanes in each direction. A study to determine driver lane preference involved recording the number of cars in each lane in five-minute intervals for one hour of the evening rush hour. These were the results.

Lane 1: 283, 275, 289, 244, 260, 235, 220, 240, 250, 290, 220, 180

Lane 2: 235, 255, 280, 272, 240, 230, 210, 222, 195, 210, 170, 220

Lane 3: 270, 260, 272, 248, 252, 240, 205, 230, 240, 255, 180, 190

a. Calculate the measures of central tendency for each lane.

b. Rank the lanes in order from most preferred to least preferred during the evening rush hour. Provide your rationale.

7. A manufacturer tested the braking distance of 50 randomly-chosen automobiles. The measurement was the distance, in metres, required to stop when the brakes were applied at 65 km/h. The results are listed.

35.1, 34.7, 35.9, 36.8, 35.9, 36.3, 35.8, 37.4, 36.9, 36.1, 37.4, 36.7, 35.2, 36.2, 36.4, 34.2, 36.5, 36.1, 35.9, 36.8, 33.5, 36.1, 36.3, 36.8, 36.1, 36.1, 35.8, 36.5, 36.7, 35.4, 35.9, 36.9, 37.0, 36.1, 34.9, 35.7, 36.8, 35.2, 36.0, 35.7, 35.8, 36.4, 35.6, 37.2, 35.9, 34.9, 36.0, 36.5, 36.8, 35.8

a. Calculate the measures of central tendency for this data.

b. A car is the same make and model as those tested and its braking distance, when tested, is 39.4 m. List the factors that might contribute to the difference between the manufacturer's statistics and the individual results.

c. Explain which measure you would use if you were an advertising agent for i) the car manufacturer, ii) a competing company.

8. Calculate the central measures of a cross-country runner who recorded the distances, in kilometres, for each day for a week.

10, 7, 12, 20, 15, 12, 10

Which measure best describes the distance the runner travels? Explain.

9. The players on a basketball team had heights in centimetres as follows.

180, 210, 170, 190, 200, 180, 220, 205, 210, 180

a. Calculate the central measures for this data.

b. Which measure best describes the heights of the players? Explain.

c. Which measure would the coach be best advised to announce in order to lull his opponents? Explain.

10. What does it mean when the median and mean are very different? Use this example to explain.

Salaries paid per week to nine employees of a small firm: $600, $600, $625, $675, $680, $690, $700, $3000, $5000

11. What does it mean when the mode and mean are very different? Use this example to explain.

Shoe sizes of ten students: 6, 6, 6, 6, 7, 8, 10, 12, 13, 16

12. What does it mean when the mode and median are very different? Use this example to explain.

Marks of nine students on a Math exam: 30, 40, 45, 75, 80, 85, 90, 95, 95

Using the Library

Statistics Canada is Canada's central statistical agency. It was established in 1918 under the name Dominion Bureau of Statistics and is a scientific research organization. Under the 1971 Statistics Act, it has the responsibility to "collect, compile, analyse, abstract, and publish statistical information relating to the commercial, industrial, financial, social, economic, and general activities and condition of the people of Canada."

a. Using the library, research the responsibilities and major programs of Statistics Canada.

b. Outline some of the different types of research performed by Statistics Canada and how information is collected and analysed.

13·10 Central Tendencies II

Often there is a need to determine the measures of central tendency for large amounts of data. In many cases, exact figures may not be as important as the grouping of the data.

Example

An auto manufacturer stated that the Model X car leaving his factory had an average fuel consumption rate of between 7 and 7.5 L/100 km of driving. An independent agency tested 50 Model X cars. The test included city and highway driving conditions. Did the auto manufacturer give an honest report of the fuel consumption of the Model X car?

Understand the Problem

Did the auto manufacturer accurately describe the fuel consumption rate of the Model X car? On what driving conditions was the auto manufacturer's report based?

Develop a Plan

Group the data into convenient classes. Construct a histogram and find the modal class by inspection. Construct a table. Calculate the measures of central tendency for this data using the data grouped by classes.

Carry Out the Plan

Class	Class Mark (CM)	Frequency (F)	CM × F	Percent Frequency	Cumulative Percent Frequency
$6 \leq c < 6.5$	6.25	1	6.25	2	2
$6.5 \leq c < 7$	6.75	4	27	8	10
$7 \leq c < 7.5$	7.25	18	130.5	36	46
$7.5 \leq c < 8$	7.75	4	31	8	54
$8 \leq c < 8.5$	8.25	1	8.25	2	56
$8.5 \leq c < 9$	8.75	6	52.5	12	68
$9 \leq c < 9.5$	9.25	10	92.5	20	88
$9.5 \leq c < 10$	9.75	5	48.75	10	98
$10 \leq c < 10.5$	10.25	1	10.25	2	100
Total		50	407	100	

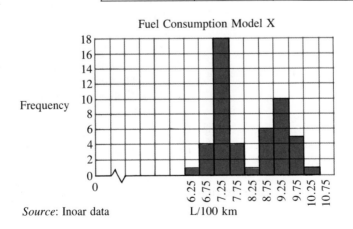

Fuel Consumption Model X

Frequency

L/100 km

Source: Inoar data

The modal class can be seen in the histogram. The range of the modal class is 7 to 7.5 and has a class mark of 7.25. The mean of this data is calculated using the formula:

$$\text{Mean} = \frac{\text{total of (CM} \times \text{F)}}{\text{total frequency}} = \frac{407}{50}$$

$$= 8.14$$

The median lies between the 25th and 26th values in the list which are found in the class $7.5 \leq c < 8$. This class has width $0.5 = 8.0 - 7.5$ and contains 4 values. We say the class frequency is 4.
The 25th value is the 2nd value (n) in the class $7.5 \leq c < 8$.
The 26th value is the 3rd value ($n + 1$) in the same class.
Since we do not know the specific values we **assume even distribution of data** within each class and calculate the median using the formula:

$$\text{Lower class boundary} + \frac{n}{\text{class frequency}} \times \text{class width}.$$

The 25th value is calculated as $7.5 + \frac{2}{4} \times 0.5 = 7.75$.

The 26th value is calculated as $7.5 + \frac{3}{4} \times 0.5 = 7.875$.

The mean of these two values is the median.

Therefore, $\frac{7.75 + 7.875}{2} = 7.8125$.

Look Back
The modal class is 7-7.5. The median class is 7.5-8. The mean class is 8-8.5. The auto manufacturer was honest in citing 7-7.5 L/100 km as this is the modal class. Competitors may disagree and cite the mean or median class since these are less favourable.

Exercises

1. Refer to the example in the display.
a. Explain why the median lies between the 25th and 26th values.
b. Why were the mean and median values greater than the modal class values?

2. State the class width for each.
a. $0 \leq n < 8$ **b.** $12 \leq n < 32$
c. $-10 \leq n < 20$ **d.** $205 \leq n < 221$

3. Find the class mark (CM) for each.
a. $8 \leq n < 20$ **b.** $-5 \leq n < 32$
c. $-30 \leq n < -15$ **d.** $166 \leq n < 232$

4. In your own words, explain the meaning of the terms "modal class", "class mark", and "cumulative percent frequency".

5. Copy and complete the table.
a. Calculate the mean and the median.
b. Find the modal class.
c. Construct a frequency histogram based on this data.

Class	CM	Freq.	CM × F	% Freq.	Cum. % Freq.
$140 \leq c < 150$	145	1			
$150 \leq c < 160$		2			
$160 \leq c < 170$		9			
$170 \leq c < 180$		10			
$180 \leq c < 190$		18			
$190 \leq c < 200$		11			
$200 \leq c < 210$		9			
Total					

6. Given the following information, construct a frequency table, calculate the mean and the median, and find the modal class. Construct a frequency histogram.
The first class is $0.10 \leq p < 0.20$. The number of classes is 9. The data, p, is the chlorine concentration in the air, in parts per million (ppm).
0.85, 0.66, 0.34, 0.87, 0.33, 0.29, 0.65, 0.62, 0.25, 0.82, 0.24, 0.14, 0.55, 0.54, 0.42, 0.41, 0.47, 0.19, 0.95, 0.41, 0.45, 0.57, 0.60, 0.57, 0.70, 0.21, 0.91, 0.51, 0.30, 0.55

13·11 Graphs of Distributions

Graphs give visual summaries of data sets. The data may be of a sample or a population. Histograms, **frequency polygons**, and **ogives** are examples of graphs of distributions which will be examined in this section. From the ogive (**cumulative frequency polygon**), the **percentiles** and **quartiles** of a set of data may be found.

Example 1

The table shows the heights, in centimetres, of 80 players competing for positions on a football team. What does the distribution of their heights look like on a graph? Are their heights evenly distributed? Is there a "typical" height for a player?

Height (cm)	Frequency	Class Mark	% Frequency	Cumulative % Frequency
$173 \leq h < 176$	4	174.5	5	5
$176 \leq h < 179$	8	177.5	10	15
$179 \leq h < 182$	12	180.5	15	30
$182 \leq h < 185$	16	183.5	20	50
$185 \leq h < 188$	16	186.5	20	70
$188 \leq h < 191$	12	189.5	15	85
$191 \leq h < 194$	8	192.5	10	95
$194 \leq h < 197$	4	195.5	5	100
Total	80	***	100	

The data listed in this table can be shown on a frequency histogram.

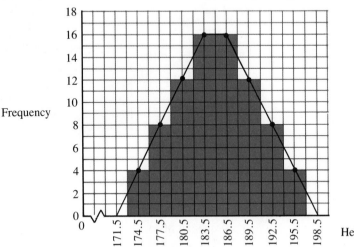

Note the vertical bars, with no spaces between them, are drawn to a height proportional to their frequency. Each bar is centred at its corresponding class mark and extends from the lower to the upper class boundary.

A histogram gives a clear picture of distribution of the data. Joining the midpoints (class mark) of the top of each bar by a series of straight line segments, a line graph called a frequency polygon can be constructed. Two zero points are added at the class mark above and below the extreme intervals.

374

An ogive (cumulative frequency polygon) can be constructed using the values in the cumulative frequency and percent frequency columns in the table.

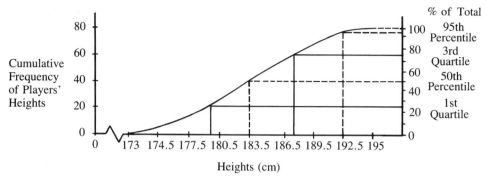

The line extends up and to the right until it levels out at 100%. Why?
The left scale is the number of players less than the stated height while the right scale is a percent scale. The ogive may be used to find the measures called percentiles and quartiles.
The first quartile is the value such that 25% (one quarter) of the distribution is below it.
The second quartile has 50% (one half) of the distribution below it. The second quartile coincides with the median.
The third quartile has 75% (three quarters) of the distribution below it.
The 60th percentile is the value such that 60% of the distribution lies below it.

To find the 95th percentile in the distribution, draw a straight line horizontal from 95 on the right scale until the line intersects the polygon. Draw a vertical line to the horizontal scale and read the value. The 95th percentile is approximately 192.5 cm. 95% of the players are 192.5 cm tall or less.

Exercises

Use the cumulative frequency polygon in the display to answer Exercises 1 and 2.

1. Find the value representing each in the distribution.
a. the mean value   **b.** the third quartile
c. the 30th percentile   **d.** the 90th percentile

2. Which percentile, approximately, does each value have in the distribution.
a. 186.5   **b.** 176.5   **c.** 195
d. 188.5   **e.** 181.5   **f.** 182.5

3. Why does the cumulative frequency polygon always start at 0 and end at 100? Explain.

4. Can an ogive decrease as it goes to the right? Why or why not?

5. Explain in your own words what it means for a student's score to be in the 99th percentile?

6. The table shows the number of three-bedroom homes sold during one month for each price range.

Price Range ($000)	Frequency
20-30	1
30-40	2
40-50	4
50-60	18
60-70	21
70-80	12
80-90	4
90-100	1

Construct a histogram, frequency polygon, and ogive based on these data.
a. Determine from the ogive the 20, 40, 55, 70, 80, and 95th percentile for the price range of three-bedroom homes sold.
b. What percent of the homes sold for more than $56 000. Find the first, second, and third quartile values.

13·12 Mean Deviation

Another aspect of data analysis is the measure of spread or dispersion of data. The simplest measure of spread is called the **range**. Other measures are **deviation** and **mean deviation**.

Example

The sunrise times for a Canadian town on the 50°N latitude were recorded on the first day of each month for a year.

Date	Sunrise (minutes after midnight—y)	Deviation Score $(y - \bar{y})$	$\lvert y - \bar{y} \rvert$
Jan. 1	498	$498 - 372 = 126$	126
Feb. 1	474	$474 - 372 = 102$	102
Mar. 1	423	$423 - 372 = 51$	51
Apr. 1	356	$356 - 372 = -16$	16
May 1	296	$296 - 372 = -76$	76
Jun. 1	257	$257 - 372 = -115$	115
Jul. 1	256	$256 - 372 = -116$	116
Aug. 1	290	$290 - 372 = -82$	82
Sep. 1	333	$333 - 372 = -39$	39
Oct. 1	377	$377 - 372 = 5$	5
Nov. 1	428	$428 - 372 = 56$	56
Dec. 1	476	$476 - 372 = 104$	104
Total	4464	0	888

The deviation score is the difference between an item value and the mean.

The sum of the **deviation scores** is always zero.

The mean sunrise time is calculated as $\bar{y} = \frac{4464}{12}$

$$= 372$$

the total minutes after midnight / the number of months

The mean sunrise time is 372 min after midnight.

The range of this data is the difference between the greatest and least values. Therefore, the range is $498 - 256$ or 242 min.

The mean deviation gives a measure of how much a set of data varies and is calculated by adding the absolute values of all the deviation scores and finding their mean.

$\therefore$ Mean deviation of n items $= \dfrac{\Sigma \lvert y - \bar{y} \rvert}{n}$

The symbol Σ means the "sum of".

$$= \frac{888}{12} = 74$$

The mean deviation of the sunrise time over the year is 74 min.

Exercises

1. In your own words, explain the meaning of the term "mean deviation".

2. Explain why the sum of the deviation scores is zero?

3. From the example in the display, what does it mean to have a large deviation score?

4. Explain the meaning of the range of the sunrise times in the example in the display.

5. The number of games won over a ten-year period were recorded by two teams.
Lions: 5, 10, 7, 9, 8, 10, 9, 11, 12, 13
Tiger-cats: 8, 5, 5, 6, 8, 11, 8, 5, 6, 8
a. Find the mean deviation for each team's win record.
b. Which team showed a more consistent win record?
c. Explain what this data tells a coach about the two teams.

6. Find the mean deviation of this set of exam scores.

Suzanne	35	Sean	50
Erica	19	Gordon	47
Mai	20	Michael	39

7. The maximum daily temperatures, in degrees Celsius, recorded in January at selected Canadian cities were:

Yellowknife	2.8	Toronto	16.7
Vancouver	14.4	Montreal	12.8
Calgary	16.1	Halifax	13.9
Regina	8.9	Charlottetown	11.7
Winnipeg	7.8	St. John's	13.3

a. Find the mean maximum temperature.
b. Find the median maximum temperature.
c. Find the mean deviation of the maximum temperatures.
d. Describe a situation in which a company would be able to use this information in making a decision.

8. An investment company was presented with a proposal to fund a ski lodge which was to be constructed on one of two sites. Data showing the median number of days of snow cover over a ten-year period for both sites was obtained. Which site consistently provided good ski conditions for a longer period of time? Use the mean deviation of this data to determine your answer.
Site A: 99, 72, 98, 99, 93, 86, 87, 88, 85, 83
Site B: 85, 92, 89, 95, 83, 94, 87, 88, 83, 94

9. The number of times ten new cars from each of Company A and Company B were returned for required repairs in the first year were recorded and analysed. What does each analysis tell you about the difference in the service required by the cars in each company?
a. The means for both companies were the same (20). However, the mean deviation for Company A was higher (1.8) than that of Company B (0).
b. The mean for Company A was higher (1.5) than that for Company B (1) but the mean deviation for Company B was higher (1.6) than for Company A (0.5).
c. The means and mean deviations were nearly the same for both companies.

10. The lengths of terms of office for 22 Canadian Governors-General are listed in years.
1, 3, 6, 5, 5, 5, 5, 6, 7, 5, 5, 5, 5, 4, 5, 6, 6, 7, 8, 7, 5, 5
a. Find the mean length of term of office.
b. Find the mean deviation for this data.

Braintickler

A soft drink company hired an investigator to survey the number of people who drink cola and soda water. This is his report.

Number of people interviewed	100
Number who drink cola	78
Number who drink soda water	71
Number who drink both	48
Number who drink neither	0

The investigator was fired for making an error in the report. Can you find the error?

13·13 Variance and Standard Deviation

Another useful measure of dispersion in statistics is called **variance**. The variance is determined by adding the squares of each deviation score and then finding their mean. If we wish to say something more specific about a set of data, we find the **standard deviation**. It is the amount of deviation from the mean. The standard deviation of a set of n samples is equal to the square root of the variance.

Example

A train conductor recorded the number of passengers boarding and leaving the train at the ten stops during a trip.
Passengers boarding: 44, 42, 42, 51, 42, 42, 42, 31, 42, 42
Passengers leaving train: 43, 42, 10, 42, 42, 42, 73, 42, 42, 42

The two sets of data have the same mean, median, and mode, namely 42. The second set of data is more spread out showing greater dispersion than the first.
Calculating the variance (S^2) or measure of the spread of the data on the number of passengers boarding the train is done using the following steps.

1. Calculate the mean. $\bar{y} = \dfrac{y_1 + y_2 + \ldots + y_n}{n}$

$$\bar{y} = \frac{420}{10} = 42$$

2. Subtract the mean from each member in the data set. $(y - \bar{y})$

3. Square each difference. $(y - \bar{y})^2$

4. Find the sum of the squares of the differences. $\Sigma(y - \bar{y})^2$

5. To get variance, divide this sum by 1 less than the number of data values, $(10 - 1) = 9$.

$$S^2 = \frac{\Sigma(y - \bar{y})^2}{n-1} \quad S^2 = \frac{206}{9} \doteq 22.9$$

Data	$\bar{y}$	$(y - \bar{y})^2$	$(y - \bar{y})^2$
44	42	2	4
42	42	0	0
42	42	0	0
51	42	9	81
42	42	0	0
42	42	0	0
42	42	0	0
31	42	−11	121
42	42	0	0
42	42	0	0
		Sum	206

6. For standard deviation we use $S.D. = \sqrt{S^2}$. Hence $S.D. = \sqrt{22.9} \doteq 4.8$. This tells us that in one standard deviation from the mean there are 4.8 people.

It has been determined that using $(n - 1)$ in the variance formula, 1 less than the number of data values, gives a better estimate of small population variance than using just n. Using only n tends to underestimate the population variance. Thus $(n - 1)$ introduces a correction factor in the calculation of variance. An explanation and use of standard deviation will be provided in Section 13·15.

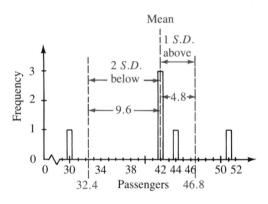

378

Exercises

1. Outline the steps used in calculating a sample variance (S^2).

2. Outline the steps used in calculating the standard deviation (S.D.) when you know the variance (S^2).

3. Consider these three lists of numbers.

I: 1, 1, 1, 5, 9, 9, 9
II: 1, 3, 5, 5, 5, 7, 9
III: 1, 4, 4, 5, 5, 7, 9

a. Calculate the mode, median, mean ($\bar{y}$), and range of each.
b. Prepare a chart with the data, $\bar{y}$, $y - \bar{y}$, and $(y - \bar{y})^2$. Calculate the S^2 and S.D. for each.
c. A histogram can show the spread of the data. Mark a standard deviation on each as illustrated in the first. Compare the three distributions.

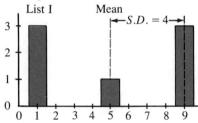

4. Calculate the mean ($\bar{y}$), the variance (S^2), and the standard deviation (S.D.) for each set of data.
a. 98, 117, 156, 210, 271, 253, 337, 293, 194, 169, 96, 83
b. 47, 84, 149, 190, 245, 249, 317, 278, 205, 129, 60, 39
c. −32.8, −30.4, −24.3, −13.7, −1.1, 7.2, 11.4, 9.9, 3.6, −4.1, −18.1, −27.8

5. To determine the speed of sound in dry air, ten tests each at 0°C and 20°C were conducted. The tests produced the following results. The measurements are in metres per second. Calculate $\bar{y}$, S^2, and S.D. for this data. Compare the means, medians, and modes, and the variance and standard deviation.
At 0°C: 331.5, 331.9, 331.7, 331.4, 331.5, 331.5, 331.4, 331.5, 331.4, 331.2
At 20°C: 337.2, 338.4, 340.4, 340.4, 341.5, 344.5, 346.5, 346.5, 348.7, 349.9

6. For the number of passengers leaving the train in the example, calculate the variance and the standard deviation.

7. The graphs show distributions of red chickens taken from different pens in the same flock purported to have 30% red chickens. The size of each sample is given. Discuss what affect the size of the sample has on the distribution of red chickens in the sample.
a. 100 samples of 5   **b.** 100 samples of 10
c. 100 samples of 50

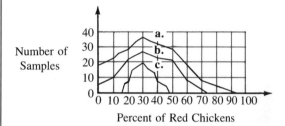

Percent of Red Chickens

Historical Note

Barbara McClintock (1902-   )
Barbara McClintock was born in Hartford, Connecticut. After receiving a doctorate degree in Botany, Barbara began her study of the chromosomes of the maize (Indian corn) plant. McClintock's achievements included perfecting the method of viewing chromosomes under a microscope. Her genetic work was so far ahead of its time that other geneticists around the world were highly skeptical of her findings. In 1983, Barbara McClintock's achievements were officially recognized when she received the Nobel Prize for Physiology and Medicine.

Geneticists interested in the inheritance of a single trait may use the binomial expansion $(p + q)^2 = p^2 + 2pq + q^2$.
If the trait of interest is non-blue eye colour, B, or blue eye colour, b, and BB or Bb combination produce non-blue eyes, while only bb combination produces blue eyes, find the offspring probabilities in the first generation of a $(B + b)^2$ cross.

13·14 Normal Distributions

Frequency histograms are helpful when we wish to make inferences about data. A curve connecting the midpoints of the tops of the bars of a histogram produces a **frequency curve**. A **normal curve** is symmetrical and bell shaped. Frequency curves are described by comparing them with the normal curve. Notice how the curves below compare with the normal curve.

In a frequency curve, the mode is the point where the curve reaches its greatest value. The median occurs at the point which divides the area under the curve into two equal regions to its right and left. The mean can be thought of as the balance point for that shape as noted in the diagrams.

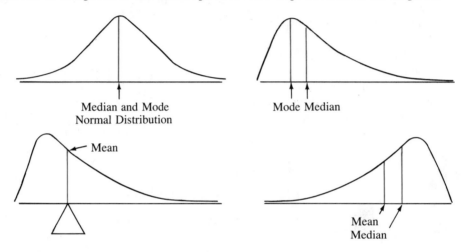

Median and Mode
Normal Distribution

Mode Median

Mean

Mean
Median

When the mean and median occur at the same point, the normal curve is produced and the symmetry of the curve can be seen.

If the mean is located further toward the long tail of the frequency curve than the median, the curve is said to be **skewed**.

Example

The number of goals scored during a season by each of the 34 players on a hockey team were recorded and a histogram of the data was drawn. Was the frequency curve produced normal or skewed?

Class	CM	F	CM × F
$0 \le g < 9$	5	3	15
$10 \le g < 20$	15	5	75
$20 \le g < 30$	25	8	200
$30 \le g < 40$	35	7	245
$40 \le g < 50$	45	5	225
$50 \le g < 60$	55	3	165
$60 \le g < 70$	65	2	130
$70 \le g < 80$	75	1	75
Total		34	1130

The modal class is $20 \le g < 30$.

The mean is $\frac{1130}{34}$ or 33.2.

The median is calculated as follows.
$$30 + \frac{1}{7} \times 10 \doteq 31.43$$
$$30 + \frac{2}{7} \times 10 \doteq 32.86$$
$$\frac{31.43 + 32.86}{2} \doteq 32.15$$

380

Goals Scored During Season

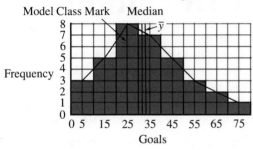

Goals Scored During Season

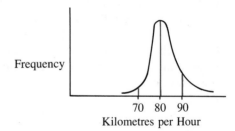

The frequency curve is skewed. Notice that the mean is closer to the long tail of the frequency curve than the median.

Describe what would have to happen to the number of goals scored in the next hockey season to make the frequency curve of that data a normal curve.

Exercises

1. Using these graphs, i) state whether each curve is skewed or normal, and ii) match the mean, median, and mode with the correct letter. Explain each choice.

a.

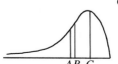

A BC

b.

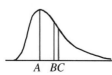

A

c.

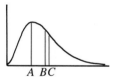

AB C

d.

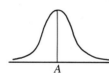

A BC

2. Curve 1 was based on a sample size of 100. Curve 2 was drawn from the results of a sample size of 1000.

Curve 1   Curve 2

a. Discuss how the curve is affected by an increase in sample size.
b. Which curve would produce more confidence in a prediction about the population?
c. Which sample took less time and energy to obtain?

3. A traffic survey revealed the following frequency curve for motorists clocked on a section of highway having an 80 km/h speed limit.

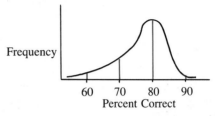

Frequency

70 80 90
Kilometres per Hour

a. Is this distribution skewed?
b. Explain the distribution in terms of the driving habits of those motorists sampled.

4. The results of a math test produced the following distribution curve.

Frequency

60   70   80   90
Percent Correct

a. Was student achievement high on this test?
b. Was this an easy test for those who wrote it?
c. Was the student population writing this test normally distributed with regard to abilities?
d. Describe the student achievement on the test.

13·15 Standard Deviation

Using the mean, median, and mode to describe a set of data can be misleading and incomplete. We need to know how the data is spread out. For instance, it may all be bunched up or it may be spread out evenly. It may be bunched on one side of the mean and spread out on the other side. In the last section we used variance to help us. Since variance is measured in square units it is much better to use a measure that is in "linear units" instead. A modified form of variance that does this is called standard deviation. It is calculated by taking the square root of the variance. The formula for standard deviation $(S.D.)$ is $S.D. = \sqrt{S^2} = \sqrt{\dfrac{\Sigma(y - \bar{y})^2}{n - 1}}$. In standard deviation we make a comparison of the distribution of the data with that of the normal frequency distribution curve. Standard deviation is a measure of the spread about the mean.

Primarily, the larger the standard deviation the more the data is spread out. But you may ask what is a large standard deviation? It depends on several things. If we are talking about the distribution of the mass of fully-grown elephants, then a $S.D. = 50$ kg is not large, but if we are dealing with the mass of a group of office workers, then $S.D. = 50$ kg would be excessively large. Large and small have only relative meaning. We have to look at the situation in question.

The normal frequency curve with standard deviations is so constructed that most scores are in the middle, and as one moves away from the middle in either direction the number of scores at any given value decrease with increasing distance from the mean value. The diagram shows that in a normal distribution 68% of the cases fall within one standard deviation of the mean,
95% of the cases fall within two standard deviations of the mean, and
99.7% of the cases fall within three standard deviations of the mean.

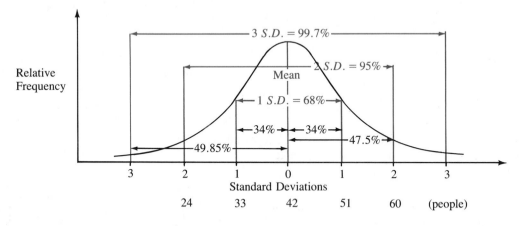

If we are given the number of cases, the mean, and the standard deviation (or variance), we can describe the distribution of any normal frequency curve.

Example 1

In a meeting of 20 people gathered to discuss investments, the mean amount that individuals had to invest, in hundreds of dollars, was 42 with a variance of 81. Assuming the distribution is normal, describe the distribution of the wealth.

Since the variance is 42, then the $S.D. = \sqrt{81}$ or 9.

From the diagram above we know that 34% of the people are within one standard deviation above the mean of 42 or $42 + 9 = 51$ and 34% within one standard deviation below which is $42 - 9 = 33$. Altogether, there are 68% of 20 or approximately 14 people within one standard deviation of the mean. This all translates into the fact that 14 people have from $3300 to $5100 to invest. Similarly, two standard deviations about the mean, the interval of which is $42 \pm 2(9)$ or 24 to 60 contains, 95% of 20, or 19 people. These 19 have from $2400 to $6000 to invest. See the standard deviation chart above.

Example 2

The mean waiting time for patients in the waiting room of a large clinic is 20 min, and the standard deviation is 5 min. The average number of people waiting is 20. Assume the distribution of waiting time is a normal distribution.

a. What percent of the waiting times would be between 10 and 30 min?

b. Studies show that patients who wait more than 30 min get annoyed. What percent of the patients in the waiting room are annoyed?

a. The range for two standard deviations is $20 \pm 2(5)$ or 10 and 30 min. 95% of the waiting time is in this interval.

b. Patients who are annoyed because they wait more than 30 min are in the region beyond the two standard deviations, at the higher end. This region represents 2.5% of the cases. Hence only 2.5% of the people are annoyed. In a group of 20 people, this is less than one person (0.5).

Exercises

1. In a meeting of 20 people gathered to discuss investments, the mean amount individuals had to invest, in hundreds of dollars, was 50 and the variance 64. Describe the distribution of the wealth. Compare this situation with that in Example 1.

a. In which situation is the mean the highest? the variance the highest? there the most money?

b. How many people are within three standard deviations of the mean?

c. Write an explanation of how the mean and variance affect the distribution of the money and the total money present.

d. If you represented an investment firm, at which meeting would you prefer to be? Explain.

2. In a normal frequency distribution curve

a. how many standard deviations wide is the curve?

b. what percent of measurements lie within three standard deviations on either side of the mean?

c. what percent of the measurements lie below one standard deviation above the mean?

d. what percent of the measurements lie above two standard deviations below the mean?

3. Standard deviations can be in rational numbers. Explain approximately what percentage of the population you would be above if you were at a point

a. 0.5 $S.D.$ above the mean.

b. 1.5 $S.D.$ above the mean.

4. The length of the take-off times of 600 commercial aircraft had a normal distribution with a mean of 35 s and a standard deviation of 9 s. Approximately, how many take-off times would be

a. in the interval 26 s to 44 s?

b. expected to exceed 53 s?

5. The mean daily minimum temperature during the month of May in Penticton, B.C., is 5.9°C, and $S.D. = 5.9$°C. If, during the month of May, the temperature drops below freezing, there is a threat that the fruit crop may be wiped out. If the temperatures for May form a normal distribution, what number of days is it likely to be cold enough to endanger the fruit crops?

6. Make up more questions for discussion in class about each of the situations in the exercises above.

13·16 Computer Application—Data Analysis

This computer program can be used to quickly calculate the mean, variance and standard deviation of a large set of numbers.

```
10 DIM X(100)
20 INPUT "HOW MANY NUMBERS DO YOU WISH TO ENTER? (UP TO 100)";
NUM
30 FOR I = 1 TO NUM
40 INPUT "ENTER A NUMBER";X(1)
50 A = A + X(I)
60 B = B + X(I) ^ 2
70 NEXT I
80 M = A / NUM
90 V = B / (NUM − 1) − A ^ 2 / (NUM ^ 2 − NUM)
100 S = SQR(V)
110 PRINT "THE MEAN IS "; M; ", THE VARIANCE IS "; V; ",
AND THE STANDARD DEVIATION IS "; S; "."
120 END
```

Exercises

1. In your own words, explain each line in the computer program.

2. Run this program several times by entering your own numbers.

3. Alter this program to accept up to 500 numbers.

4. Enter the following winning times in seconds for the men's 110 m hurdles from the 1896 to the 1984 Olympic Games and find the mean, variance, and standard deviation.
17.6, 15.4, 16, 16.2, 15, 15.1, 14.8, 15, 14.8, 14.6, 14.2, 13.9, 13.7, 13.5, 13.8, 13.6, 13.3, 13.24, 13.30, 13.39, 13.2

5. Obtain a set of marks from a class exam or test and use the program to find the mean, variance, and standard deviation for that data.

6. Statistics can be used to help prove a point or to help ease a potentially bad situation. Polls are often part of news stories. When the results of a poll are reported, important questions about how the poll was conducted should be answered in the reports to avoid misuse or misunderstanding. Using examples found in newspapers, write a short report on the uses and misuses of data and statistics.

Braintickler

Jot down any three-digit number, then repeat it to make a six-digit number. Now divide this six-digit number by 7, then divide the quotient by 11, and finally divide that quotient by 13. Repeat with other three-digit numbers until you see the pattern. Explain the pattern.

13·17 Chapter Review

1. What is the probability of drawing each, with replacements, from a well-shuffled deck of cards.
a. a heart   **b.** a jack   **c.** a jack and a queen

2. Find the probability of throwing each with a pair of dice.
a. a sum of seven   **b.** at least seven
c. at most seven   **d.** a four with a sum of seven

3. A manufacturer claims that no more than 1.5% of the fireworks the company makes are defective. Since the fireworks are destroyed when tested, devise a sampling plan to test the accuracy of the manufacturer's claim.

4. A production manager kept a daily record of the number of defective parts produced for 14 d before and 14 d after an assembly-line overhaul. Construct a double stem and leaf plot based on these data.
Defective parts after overhaul: 33, 24, 28, 15, 23, 36, 41, 32, 28, 35, 11, 26, 13, 12
Defective parts before overhaul: 24, 30, 41, 41, 52, 29, 51, 34, 44, 42, 55, 26, 45, 47
a. What conclusion can be made about the value of the overhaul?
b. What is the mean, median, and mode of the defective parts produced before the overhaul? after the overhaul?
c. Comment on which measure in part **b** is the best one for use to show that the overhaul was worthwhile.

5. A study to determine consumer preference involved recording the amount of Dentudaze and Molarmarvel toothpaste sold during seven shopping days. The results were as follows.
Dentudaze: 147, 182, 135, 198, 206, 195, 127
Molarmarvel: 197, 135, 201, 182, 197, 188, 146
a. Find the mean, median, and mode for each set of data.
b. Which brand was preferred? Explain which measure you would use and why.

6. A hang glider company wanted to locate in either Ottawa or Toronto. In order to demonstrate their product, the city with the greatest variation in mean monthly wind speeds (in metres per second) would be chosen. Construct a box and whisker plot for each set of data and answer the questions.
Ottawa: 4.6, 4.7, 4.7, 4.7, 4.4, 3.9, 3.4, 3.4, 3.8, 4.1, 4.4, 4.4
Toronto: 6.2, 5.8, 5.5, 5.1, 4.4, 3.8, 3.6, 3.7, 4.0, 4.3, 5.4, 5.6
a. Find the median values for Toronto and Ottawa.
b. Find the extreme values for Toronto and Ottawa.
c. Find the hinges for Toronto and Ottawa.
d. What is the difference between the two medians for the cities? Account for these differences.
e. Which city has the greater variability in mean monthly wind speeds?
f. In which city should the company locate? Explain.

7. Calculate the mean, sample variance, and standard deviation for the set of marks on a Math exam.
54, 65, 75, 69, 59, 39, 63, 92, 70, 46, 59, 68, 27, 73, 77, 65, 65, 80, 60, 52, 51, 78, 88, 94, 45, 64, 72, 82, 73

8. Construct a histogram, frequency polygon, and ogive, based on the number of cars in each price range on a dealer's lot.

Price Range ($000)	Freq.	Cum. % Freq.
$0 \leq p < 5$	0	0
$5 \leq p < 10$	10	10
$10 \leq p < 15$	25	
$15 \leq p < 20$	40	
$20 \leq p < 25$	20	
$25 \leq p < 30$	5	

a. Determine from the ogive the 20, 40, 80, and 95th percentiles.
b. What percent of the cars were priced more than $15 000?
c. Find the first, second, and third quartile values.
d. Is the distribution a "normal frequency distribution"? Explain.

13·18 Chapter Test

1. Calculate the probability of drawing from a bag containing 8 white and 10 red balls
a. a red ball?
b. a red and a white with replacements?
c. a red followed by a white without replacements?

2. Calculate the probability of rolling 2 fair dice to produce
a. at least one 3.   **b.** a sum of 14.
c. a sum of 5.   **d.** a 2 with a sum of 7.

3. A popcorn supplier claims that no more than 0.5% of its kernels fail to pop. Since the kernels cannot be sold as popping corn once popped, devise a sampling plan to test the accuracy of the supplier's claim.

4. Construct a percent frequency table based on the elevation in metres of 16 weather observation stations. (*Hint*: Use a class width of 100.)
325, 53, 335, 102, 229, 410, 91, 343, 280, 198, 369, 126, 198, 202, 242, 496
a. Find the class mark for each class.
b. How many weather stations have an elevation less than 300 m?
c. What percentage of the weather stations have an elevation between 200 and 400 m?
d. What is the upper boundary for the first class?

5. The number of airports with scheduled flights in 18 countries on two continents, A and B, were recorded. Construct a double stem and leaf plot based on these data.
A: 26, 19, 65, 21, 16, 13, 32, 10, 60, 13, 73, 79, 17, 13, 14, 12, 13, 10
B: 37, 21, 60, 32, 25, 26, 29, 23, 70, 36, 72, 35, 39, 72, 36, 41, 53, 52

6. The following measurements are the gains or losses in the closing prices of a stock for 14 consecutive days. Calculate the mean, variance, and standard deviation for the data.
-5, 3, -8, -1, 3, 10, -2, 5, 2, 5, -1, -5, 9, -4

7. The owner of 9 taxis recorded the fuel consumption before and after a tune up had been done on all the cabs. The results in litres per 100 km of city driving were as follows.
Before tune up: 17, 11, 20, 6, 12, 11, 15, 9, 14
After tune up: 13, 6, 10, 18, 9, 9, 15, 7, 12
Construct a 50% box and whisker plot for each set of data and answer the questions.
a. Find the median and hinge value for the "before tune up" data and for the "after tune up" data.
b. Find the difference between the two median values.
c. Comment on the affect of the tune up on gas consumption.

8. The highest elevations (in metres) in each of the ten provinces and two territories are listed.
a. Find the mean, median, and mode.

Alta.	3747	B.C.	4663	Man.	832
N.B.	820	Nfld.	1573	N.S.	532
Ont.	665	P.E.I.	142	Que.	1268
Sask.	386	N.W.T.	2762	Yuk.	6050

b. Suggest a display for these data with a comment that says something about Canadian geography.

9. The two ogives shown below represent the performance of two-year-old chimpanzees and Rhesus monkeys in a behavioural performance test.

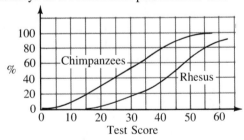

a. Define, in your own words, the 95th percentile.
b. Determine the score of each group for the 60th and 95th percentiles.
c. What percent of the chimpanzees achieved more than 35 on the behavioural test?
d. Find the first, second, and third quartile values.
e. What conclusion can you reach? Explain.

CHAPTER FOURTEEN

SEQUENCES, SERIES, AND ANNUITIES

Tune Up

1. Evaluate if $a = 3$, $b = -0.5$, and $c = 5$.
a. $ab - bc$
b. $a^2 - b^2$
c. $f(a) = 5a^2 - 3a$
d. $f:b \rightarrow 3b - 8b^2$
e. $f(c) = c^3 - 3c + 7$
f. $f:a \rightarrow 2a^3 - a^2 + 4a$

2. Evaluate.
a. $(1.05)^3$
b. $(1.0275)^{10}$
c. $(1.12)^{25}$
d. $(1.0833)^{40}$
e. $(1.15)^{20}$
f. $(1.0725)^8$
g. $(1.03)^5$
h. $(1.05)^2$
i. $(1.09)^{24}$
j. $(1.015)^8$
k. $(1.07)^{24}$
l. $(1.065)^6$

3. Solve for the variables.
a. $a + 2b = 9$
$a + 7b = 19$
b. $a + 13b = 1$
$a + 5b = 25$
c. $x + 7y = 35$
$x + 21y = -70$
d. $x + 19y = 123$
$x + 49y = 666$

4. Factor.
a. $a + ab$
b. $p + pi$
c. $(a + i) + (a + i)i$
d. $(x + r)^2r + (x + r)^2$
e. $\dfrac{a+b}{3} + \dfrac{a+b}{6} + \dfrac{a+b}{8}$

5. Simple interest is calculated by multiplying principal (p), rate (r), and time (t) using the formula $I = prt$. The amount (A) of an investment after interest is paid is $A = p + I$. Copy and complete the tables.

	a.	b.	c.
p	$563.15	$2179.50	
r	9.75%	5.25%	12.30%
t	3 a	18 months	0.3 a
I			$765.21
A			

	d.	e.	f.
p			
r	8.15%		
t	125 d	5.5 a	30 d
I	$23.79	$6589.20	$903.00
A		$125 000	$12 500

6. Give the calculator keying sequence and evaluate.
a. $\dfrac{2.732 + (7.326)^2}{(4.91)^4}$
b. $\dfrac{4678.21[(1.0833)^5 - 1]}{1.083\,33 - 1}$

7. The sum of three consecutive odd numbers is 141. What are the numbers?

14·1 Sequences

Number patterns have fascinated people over the ages. One such pattern involves $\{0, 2, 4, 6, 8, ...\}$ and $\{1, 3, 5, 7, ...\}$. This pattern is used in a game in which one person picks up a number of small objects and another guesses "odd" or "even". If the guess is correct, then that person wins. Another number pattern is that formed by dots in square arrays called square numbers. The set of numbers is called a sequence of perfect squares.

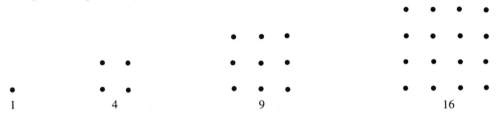

We must use caution when looking at sequences and predicting the subsequent terms. An interesting case is shown here.

1   2   4   8   16   ...

What do you think is the next number in the sequence?
One possibility is 32. However, if this is the sequence of the number of regions formed by connecting points on the circumference of a circle, we get a different sixth term.

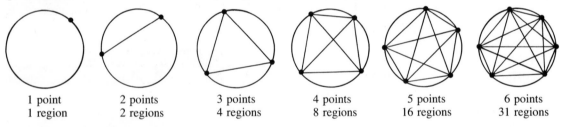

| 1 point | 2 points | 3 points | 4 points | 5 points | 6 points |
| 1 region | 2 regions | 4 regions | 8 regions | 16 regions | 31 regions |

Another interesting set of numbers is the **Fibonacci sequence**: 1, 1, 2, 3, 5, 8, ... The patterns of leaves on a stem and the growth of seeds on a flower sometimes follow this sequence. This pattern may be written as a function in the form of ordered pairs: (1, 1), (2, 1), (3, 2), (4, 3), (5, 5), (6, 8), ..., where the first number in the ordered pair is the number of the term in the sequence and the second number is the term.

In mathematics, we refer to the first term of a sequence as t_1, the second term as t_2, and the **general term**, often called the nth term, as t_n. The subscript identifies the number of the term.

> A **sequence** is any set of numbers appearing in a definite order. Each member of the set is called a **term**. The domain of the sequence is a subset of the natural numbers and the range is the set of terms of the sequence.

As illustrated above, we can define a sequence by listing a number of consecutive terms. Also, we can state a rule, in words or algebraically, that generates the terms; or we can use a mapping notation as we did with functions.

Example 1

Find the first three terms in each sequence.

a. Add 2 to the preceding term and multiply by 3, given that the first term is 5.

b. $t_n = 3n - 5$

c. $f(k) \rightarrow \dfrac{k(3k - 2)}{k + 1}$, $k \in N$

a. Start with the first term 5. To get the second term, add 2 to 5; then multiply by 3 to get 21. The third term is $3(21 + 2) = 69$. The first three terms are 5, 21, and 69.

b. The nth term is $t_n = 3n - 5$. To find the first term, substitute $n = 1$.

$$t_1 = 3 \times 1 - 5 \qquad \text{Similarly,} \quad t_2 = 3 \times 2 - 5 \qquad t_3 = 3 \times 3 - 5$$
$$= -2 \qquad\qquad\qquad\qquad\quad = 1 \qquad\qquad\qquad\quad = 4$$

The three terms in the sequence are -2, 1, and 4.

c. Substitute, in turn, the numbers 1, 2, and 3 for k in each mapping.

$$f(1) = \frac{1(3 \times 1 - 2)}{1 + 1} \qquad f(2) = \frac{2(3 \times 2 - 2)}{2 + 1} \qquad f(3) = \frac{3(3 \times 3 - 2)}{3 + 1}$$
$$= \frac{1}{2} \qquad\qquad\qquad = \frac{8}{3} \qquad\qquad\qquad = \frac{21}{4}$$

The three terms are $\frac{1}{2}, \frac{8}{3},$ and $\frac{21}{4}$.

A sequence may be described by a formula relating a term to its preceding term or terms. This formula is called a **recursive formula**.

Example 2

Find the first five terms defined by the recursive formula $t_n = 2t_{n-1} - 3$, $t_1 = -5$, $n > 1$.

The first term is -5. For the second term, multiply the first term by 2; then subtract 3. Also, n is greater than 1 since the first term is given. Substitute 2, 3, 4, and 5 for n and substitute the value of the immediately preceding term for t.

$$t_n = 2t_{n-1} - 3 \qquad t_n = 2t_{n-1} - 3 \qquad t_n = 2t_{n-1} - 3 \qquad t_n = 2t_{n-1} - 3$$
$$t_2 = 2t_1 - 3 \qquad\quad t_3 = 2t_2 - 3 \qquad\quad t_4 = 2t_3 - 3 \qquad\quad t_5 = 2t_4 - 3$$
$$t_2 = 2(-5) - 3 \qquad t_3 = 2(-13) - 3 \qquad t_4 = 2(-29) - 3 \qquad t_5 = 2(-61) - 3$$
$$t_2 = -13 \qquad\qquad t_3 = -29 \qquad\qquad t_4 = -61 \qquad\qquad t_5 = -125$$

The five terms are -5, -13, -29, -61, and -125.

Can you write a recursive formula for a sequence? The next example shows a way to do this.

Example 3

Given the sequence $-3, 1, 7, 15, \ldots$, find a recursive formula defining the sequence. Look for a pattern relating to the number of the term.

$$t_1 = -3 \quad t_2 = 1 = -3 + 4 \qquad\qquad \text{Each constant added is } 2 \times \text{(the term number).} \qquad t_2 = -3 + 2(2) = 1$$
$$t_3 = 7 = 1 + 6 \qquad\qquad\qquad\qquad\qquad\qquad\qquad\qquad\qquad t_3 = 1 + 2(3) = 7$$
$$t_4 = 15 = 7 + 8 \qquad\qquad\qquad\qquad\qquad\qquad\qquad\qquad\qquad t_4 = 7 + 2(4) = 15$$

The recursive formula is $t_n = t_{n-1} + 2n$.

Exercises

1. Continue the Fibonacci sequence in the display for the next four terms. Define a rule for finding the subsequent terms in the Fibonacci sequence.

2. Play the Odds and Evens game described in the display. First make a prediction of who will win and by what margin. After the game, discuss your prediction.

3. Why do we substitute natural numbers for the variables in the examples in the display?

4. Describe a possible sequence of steps for each.
a. a computer program that computes the sum of a set of numbers
b. buying a used car
c. a trip around the world starting at Vancouver

5. Given the general term, find the first three terms of the sequence.
a. $t_n = 2n - 3$
b. $t_n = n - 5$
c. $t_n = 1^n$
d. $t_n = 2^{n-3}$
e. $t_n = n^2$
f. $t_n = 3(5^n)$
g. $t_n = 3 - 2n$
h. $t_n = 1 - 2(n + 4)$
i. $t_n = \dfrac{n+1}{n-1}$
j. $t_n = (-1)^n$

6. Determine a rule and state the general term.
a. 1, 3, 5, 7, ...
b. $1, \dfrac{1}{2}, \dfrac{1}{3}, \dfrac{1}{4}, \dfrac{1}{5}, \ldots$
c. 3, −3, 3, −3, ...
d. 2, 5, 10, 17, 26, ...
e. 5, 10, 15, 20, ...
f. $a, ar, ar^2, ar^3, \ldots$

7. Find the first five terms of each sequence.
a. $f(n) = 2n - 1$
b. $f(k) = k^2(k - 1)$
c. $f(n) = \dfrac{(n+1)(n-1)}{3}$
d. $f : k \rightarrow \dfrac{3k+2}{2k-1}$
e. $f : n \rightarrow \dfrac{n^3 + 2n^2}{n+1}$
f. $f : k \rightarrow \dfrac{k(k-1)}{3k+1}$
g. $f(n) = (-1)^{n+1}3n$
h. $f : n \rightarrow 2^{n-1}$

8. Find the next two rows in Pascal's triangle.

9. A sequence of squares is made by joining the midpoints of sides as illustrated.

a. Copy and complete the chart.

Number of squares (n)	1	2	3	4	5
Number of regions (t_k)	1	5	9		
Change in number of regions		4	4		

b. Write the defining function for t_k.
c. Write the recursive formula for the sequence.
d. Determine the values of t_{39}, t_{365}, and t_{900}.

10. The first four triangle numbers are 1, 3, 6, and 10.

a. Copy and complete the chart.

Number of term in sequence (n)	1	2	3	4	5 ... 9
The term (t_n)	1	3	6	10	
Change in t_n		2	3	4	
Change in change			1	1	

b. Since there are two differences before a constant occurs, this is a quadratic relation. The relation is $t_n = an^2 + bn + c$. Determine the values of a, b, and c.
c. Determine the values of t_{12}, t_{25}, and t_{50}.
d. Write a recursive formula for the sequence.

11. Find the first five terms of the sequence determined by the recursive function.
a. $t_1 = 3$, $t_n = 2t_{n-1} + 1$, $n > 1$
b. $t_1 = 1$, $t_k = (t_{k-1})^2 + 3k$, $k > 1$
c. $t_1 = 4$, $t_k = t_{k-1} - 5k$, $k > 1$
d. $t_1 = 1$, $t_2 = 1$, $t_{n+2} = t_{n+1} + t_n$

12. Write a recursive formula for each sequence.
a. 4, 1, −2, −5, ...
b. 2, 6, 10, 14, ...
c. 4, 8, 16, 32, ...
d. $1, \dfrac{1}{2}, \dfrac{2}{3}, \dfrac{3}{4}, \ldots$

13. A sequence has a first term of -8 with each succeeding term being three more than twice the preceding term.
a. Find the first five terms.
b. State the general term, t_n.
c. Define the sequence using a recursive formula.

14. A solid, square-based pyramid 7 m high is constructed with cubic blocks measuring 1 m on a side.
a. Write a sequence giving the number of blocks used at each level from the top down.
b. What is the general term for this sequence?
c. Can this sequence be written as a recursive formula? Give your reasons.
d. Repeat parts **a** to **c** for the total number of blocks in each pyramid.

15. Given the general term, i) calculate the first four terms; and ii) determine a recursive formula.
a. $t_n = (2n - 1)^2$ **b.** $t_n = 3^n$
c. $t_n = \dfrac{3n}{n + 1}$ **d.** $t_n = \dfrac{n^2 - 1}{n}$
e. $t_n = \dfrac{n(n - 1)}{2}$ **f.** $t_n = 3^{-n}$

16. An example of a constant sequence is 403, 403, 403, ...
a. State the nth term.
b. Describe the sequence in words.
c. Write a recursive formula.

17. Refer to Exercise 9.
a. Copy and complete this table given that the first square has a side of 4 cm.

Square	1	2	3	4	5	6
Length of side	4					
Perimeter of square	16					

b. Write a function for the
i) length terms.   ii) area terms.
c. Write a recursive function for the
i) length terms.   ii) area terms.

18. A growing small business doubles its sales every day. After the first day, the sales were $4.
a. Write the sequence to represent the sales for seven consecutive days.
b. Write a recursive formula and a general term to describe the sequence.

19. Some sequences are easier to describe by a recursive formula than by a general term.
i) Determine the first six terms in each.
ii) State in words, the rule for the sequence.
a. $t_1 = 4$, $t_2 = 6$, $t_n = 2t_{n-2} - t_{n-1}$, $n > 2$
b. $t_1 = 5$, $t_2 = 10$, $t_3 = 4$, $t_n = 5t_{n-3} - 4t_{n-2} + t_{n-1}$, $n > 3$

20. There is a disadvantage to the recursive formula as compared to the general term. Find the tenth term in each sequence. Which method is easier?
a. $t_n = 2n^2 - 5n + 1$
b. $t_1 = 1$, $t_2 = 3$, $t_n = t_{n-1} + 10 + 6(n - 3)$, $n > 2$

Historical Note

Johann Elert Bode (1747-1826)
This German astronomer studied the relative distances from the Sun to the planets. Bode developed a rough approximation of the mean distances based upon empirical data. The sequence developed from Bode's Law is 0.4, 0.7, 1.0, 1.6, 2.8, 5.2, ... Earth's relative distance is third in the sequence. The scientists of the day thought that there was no planet at the relative distance of 2.8. Armed with this sequence, astronomers began to look for another planet. In 1801, Giuseppi Piazzi discovered Ceres in a cluster of asteroids that filled the 2.8 position. Later, Neptune and Pluto were added to the list of planets to complete a one-to-one match with the first ten terms of Bode's Law. This is an example of how mathematicians sometimes are able to predict a scientific discovery.

1. How can the balance of the sequence be generated? Use this sequence to generate the first ten terms: $t_1 = 0$, $t_2 = 3$, $t_n = 2t_{n-1}$, $n > 2$.
Now add 4 to each term in the sequence and then divide by 10 to create Bode's sequence.

2. Match the ten terms with the nine planets and with Ceres between Mars and Jupiter. If the distance from Earth to the Sun is 1.495×10^8 km, use the sequence to calculate the distances of the other planets from the Sun.

14·2 Arithmetic Sequences

An airplane takes off from a runway and climbs at a steady rate of 500 m/min. The altitudes at one-minute intervals are shown in this sequence.

Time (minutes)   0   1   2   3   ...
Altitude (metres)   0   500   1000   1500

Change in altitudes   500   500   500

The difference between two consecutive terms is 500. The **common difference** is 500. The sequence 0, 500, 1000, 1500, ... is an arithmetic sequence. Each term is found by adding 500 to the preceding term.

> A sequence which increases or decreases by a common difference is an arithmetic sequence.

Arithmetic sequences are often called **linear sequences** since the graphs of the ordered pairs form straight lines. Consider the sequence formed when a deposit of $30 is placed in a savings account, then $25 is deposited each week. The table shows the amount at the end of each week. The graph shows the linear function.

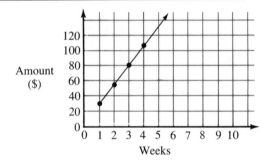

Week	1	2	3	4	...	t_n
Deposit	30	55	80	105	...	$f(n)$

Example 1

How much is in the bank at the end of 10 weeks?

Understand the Problem and **Develop a Plan**
The sequence of amounts in the bank in successive weeks is given by 30, 55, 80, 105, ... The tenth term in the sequence represents the amount in the savings account at the end of the tenth week. To find the tenth term, a sequence showing the amounts in the account at the end of each week is set up and a pattern is found.

Carry Out the Plan
This sequence shows the amounts for four successive weeks.

$t_1 = 30$	Initial term	$t_1 = a$
$t_2 = 30 + 25$	First term + common difference	$t_2 = a + d$
$t_3 = 30 + 25 + 25$	First term + 2 common differences	$t_3 = a + d + d$
$t_4 = 30 + 25 + 25 + 25$	First term + 3 common differences	$t_4 = a + d + d + d$

We can see from the pattern that the tenth term is the first term plus 9 common differences; or $30 + 9(25)$.

Look Back
The amount in the bank at the end of 10 weeks is $255.

> The **general term** or nth term, t_n, of an **arithmetic sequence** with the first term, a, and a common difference, d, is found by the formula $t_n = a + (n - 1)d$.

Example 2

Which term is 55 in the sequence 13, 19, 25, 31, ...?

Understand the Problem and Develop a Plan
Since $19 - 13 = 6$, $25 - 19 = 6$, and $31 - 25 = 6$, this is an arithmetic sequence. We have to determine which term of the sequence 55 is. The general-term formula can be used to solve for n.

Carry Out the Plan
The common difference, d, is 6. The first term is 13. The nth term is 55. Substitute in the formula:

$$t_n = a + (n - 1)d$$
$$55 = 13 + (n - 1)6$$
$$6n - 6 = 55 - 13$$
$$n = 8$$

Look Back
55 is the eighth term in the sequence. Is this reasonable? Extending the sequence by adding 6 to each successive term to check the answer: 13, 19, 25, 31, 37, 43, 49, 55. This shows that 55 is t_8.

Example 3

The tenth term of a sequence is 67 and the fifteenth term is 107. Write the first five terms of the sequence.

Understand the Problem
We know $t_{10} = 67$ and $t_{15} = 107$. We are to find t_1, t_2, t_3, t_4, and t_5.

Develop a Plan
Write each term given using the general-term formula. The tenth term is $67 \rightarrow 67 = a + 9d$. The fifteenth term is $107 \rightarrow 107 = a + 14d$. Since there are two equations in two unknowns, this system of equations can be solved using a method learned in Chapter 10. Then substitute the values of a, d, and n in the general-term formula to calculate t_1, t_2, t_3, t_4, and t_5.

Carry Out the Plan
Use the formula for the general term: $t_n = a + (n - 1)d$.

The 10th term is 67.
The 15th term is 107.

$$
\begin{array}{lll}
67 = a + 9d & \quad ① \\
107 = a + 14d & \quad ② \\
\hline
40 = 5d & \quad ② - ① \\
d = 8 \\
\end{array}
$$

Substitute in ① to solve for a. $\qquad a = -5$

The general term is $t_n = -5 + (n - 1)d$. Now we can find t_1, t_2, t_3, t_4, and t_5.

$t_1 = -5$	$t_2 = -5 + 8$	$t_3 = -5 + 2(8)$	$t_4 = -5 + 3(8)$	$t_5 = -5 + 4(8)$
	$= 3$	$= 11$	$= 19$	$= 27$

Look Back
The first five terms of the sequence are -5, 3, 11, 19, and 27. Is this reasonable? Check to see that there is a common difference. Also check the general-term formula for t_{10} and t_{15}.

Exercises

1. In your own words, describe an arithmetic sequence. List three examples of arithmetic sequences.

2. An interesting sequence is obtained from the pentagons shown.

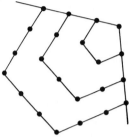

a. Write the sequence showing the number of dots in each pentagon.
b. Write a general term for the number of dots in the *n*th pentagon.

3. A sky diver jumped from a balloon at an altitude of about 3.2 km. She fell almost 0.6 km before pulling the rip cord. The distances, in metres, that she fell in the first several seconds were 4.8, 14.4, 24.0, 33.6, 43.2, ...
a. Find the common difference.
b. What is the value of *a* for the general-term formula?
c. Calculate the distance she fell in the 20th second.

4. Several years ago, students in a school in Ontario formed the world's largest human pyramid. They formed the pyramid by lying on the ground. The number of students in the rows starting at the top were 1, 2, 3, 4, 5, ...
a. How many students were in the 16th row of the pyramid?
b. How many students are in the *n*th row?

5. Draw a graph of the terms of each sequence. Which are arithmetic? For each arithmetic sequence, determine the values of *a* and *d*, and find an expression for t_n.
a. 3.8, 4.7, 5.6, 6.5, 7.4, 8.3
b. 19, 15, 11, 7, 3, −1, −5
c. 2, 4, 8, 16, 32, 64
d. 7, 7, 7, 7, 7, 7, 7, 7, 7

6. Determine which represent an arithmetic sequence.

a. 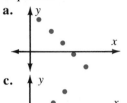   **b.**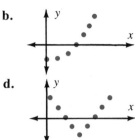

c.   **d.**

7. Indicate the sequences which are arithmetic and find the common difference.
a. 1, 5, 9, 13, 17, ...
b. 0.1, 0.2, 0.3, 0.4, 0.5, ...
c. $\frac{1}{4}, \frac{1}{2}, \frac{3}{4}, 1, \frac{5}{4}, ...$

8. Find the common difference and state the next three terms of the arithmetic sequence.
a. −1, −2, −3, −4, −5, ...
b. 3.6, 4.1, 4.6, 5.1, 5.6, ...
c. $1 + i, 3 + 2i, 5 + 3i, 7 + 4i, ...$
d. $\frac{1}{2}, 1, \frac{3}{2}, 2, \frac{5}{2}, ...$

9. Find the general term of each arithmetic sequence.
a. −13, −19, −25, ...   **b.** 12, 17, 22, ...
c. $x - a, x, x + a, ...$ **d.** $2x^2, 5x^2, 8x^2, ...$
e. $\frac{3}{8}, \frac{1}{8}, -\frac{1}{8}, ...$ **f.** 1.21, 1.34, 1.47, ...

10. Write the first three terms of each arithmetic sequence.
a. $a = -1, d = 4$ **b.** $a = 2, d = -5$
c. $a = 4, d = 3$ **d.** $a = 7, d = -6$

11. An arithmetic sequence is defined by the function $f(n) = 3n - 4$. Find the value of each.
a. $f(1)$ **b.** $f(3)$
c. $f(10)$ **d.** $f(a)$
e. $f(a + 1)$ **f.** $f(a + 1) - f(a)$

12. The general term of a sequence is given by $t_n = 3n + 5$.
a. Draw a graph showing the first four terms.
b. What type of sequence is this? Why?

13. Carol is to receive a \$5 allowance in the first week, \$8 in the second, \$11 in the third, and so on. What allowance would she receive in the 20th week?

14. Johann's job guarantees annual raises such that he earns \$25 000 in the third year and \$33 500 in the fifth year. What was his beginning salary and his annual raise?

15. Find the indicated term for each arithmetic sequence.
a. 4, 7, 11, 16, ..., t_{20}
b. 5, 15, 25, 35, ..., t_{35}
c. $-1, -5, -9, -13, ..., t_{11}$
d. $a(r-1), ar, a(r+1), ..., t_9$

16. Calculate the first term, the common difference, and the general term for each arithmetic sequence.
a. $t_2 = 9, t_7 = 33$ **b.** $t_{11} = -25, t_{20} = -43$
c. $t_5 = -5, t_{10} = -23$ **d.** $t_3 = 13, t_{12} = 40$
e. $t_4 = 6, t_9 = 1$ **f.** $t_6 = -5, t_{13} = -19$

17. A pile of bricks is arranged in rows. There are 45 bricks in the 5th row and 33 bricks in the 11th row.
a. How many bricks are in the first row?
b. Write the general term for the sequence.
c. What is the maximum number of rows of bricks possible?

18. Which of the sequences are arithmetic?
a. $t_n = 2n - 7$ **b.** $t_n = 3 + 5n$
c. $t_n = n(2 + n)$ **d.** $t_n = n^2 + 3n - 2$
e. $t_n = \dfrac{5}{7n}$ **f.** $t_n = \dfrac{n-9}{n+1}$

19. Find the first three terms and the general term of the sequence defined by $t_1 = -7, t_n = t_{n-1} + 5, n > 1$.

20. A sequence is defined by $t_1 = 5, t_k = t_{k-1} - 9, k > 1$. Show that the sequence is arithmetic.

21. The terms $4x - 1, 5x + 2,$ and $7x - 3$ form an arithmetic sequence. Determine the value of x.

22. A sequence is defined by $t_n = 8 - 3n$. Find each.
a. the first three terms **b.** t_{10}
c. n, if $t_n = -55$ **d.** t_{n-1}
e. $t_{n-1} - t_n$ **f.** n, if $t_n = -115$

23. Given that $3x + 1, x^2,$ and $4x - 7$ form an arithmetic sequence, find the value of x.

24. How many terms are in each sequence?
a. $-1, 3, 7, 11, ..., 47$ **b.** 2, 4, 6, 8, ..., 100
c. 2, 9, 16, ..., 149 **d.** 97, 92, 87, ..., -3

25. Find the first positive term for the sequence whose general term is $t_n = 2n - 99$.

26. Equal numbers of passengers get on an outbound train at each station after the first station. There were 35 passengers on board when the train left the first station and 95 passengers when it left the fifth station. Write a sequence to show the number on board as the train left the first five stations. Assume nobody gets off. (*Hint*: Use the four-step problem-solving model and this chart.)

Station	1	2	3	4	5
Number Boarding					
Total on Board	35				95

The terms between two given arithmetic terms are called the **arithmetic means**.

27. Use the process of Exercise 26 for each case.
a. Find six arithmetic means between -12 and 23.
b. Find one arithmetic mean between 930 and 124. What is another name for this number?

28. Find the number of arithmetic means indicated in each case.
a. three between 9 and 27
b. six between 21 and -35
c. two between $x + 2y$ and $4x - y$
d. four between $2m - 3n$ and $2n - 8m$

29. The first 30 numbers in the sequence 4, 44, 444, 4444, 44 444, ..., are added. What digit is in the ten's place?

14·3 Geometric Sequences

Suppose you receive a letter instructing you to send $5 to the first person at the top of a six-name list. You cross out the top name, add your name to the bottom, and send a copy to five friends. Your five friends are to do the same. If all people receiving letters cooperate, 15 625 letters will have been sent when your name reaches the top of the list, and you will receive $78 125! (These "chain letters" are considered a form of gambling in many places and are illegal. Why do you think they are prohibited?)

Number of term (n)	1	2	3	4	5	6	7
Number of letters (t_n)	1	5	25	125	625	3125	15 625

Common ratio   5   5   5   5

The ratio of successive terms or the **common ratio**, r, is constant. In this case the common ratio is 5. A sequence such as 1, 5, 25, 125, 625, ..., is called a **geometric sequence**. A geometric sequence is one in which each term after the first is found by multiplying the previous term by a common ratio.

Example 1

Suppose a ball, dropped from an initial height of 30 m, bounces up 0.9 of its previous height. How high does the ball bounce on the tenth bounce?

Understand the Problem and **Develop a Plan**
The ball bounces to 0.9 of its previous height. We are to find the height of the ball on the tenth bounce. We can look for a pattern by setting up a sequence of the heights of each bounce.

Carry Out the Plan
This table shows the heights of the first four bounces.

Bounce number	1	2	3	4	...
Height of bounce	27.0	24.3	21.9	19.7	...

Now look for a pattern.

$t_1 = 27.0$	Initial term	$t_1 = a$
$t_2 = 27.0 \times 0.9$	First term $\times 0.9$	$t_2 = ar$
$t_3 = 27.0 \times 0.9 \times 0.9$	First term $\times 0.9 \times 0.9$	$t_3 = ar^2$
$t_4 = 27.0 \times 0.9 \times 0.9 \times 0.9$	First term $\times 0.9 \times 0.9 \times 0.9$	$t_4 = ar^3$

Notice that the tenth term in the sequence is the first term times 0.9, nine times.

Calculator Keying Sequence

$t_{10} = 27.0 \times (0.9)^9$ 0.9 $\boxed{y^x}$ 9 $\boxed{=}$ $\boxed{\times}$ 27 $\boxed{=}$ **10.460353**

$\phantom{t_{10}} = 10.5$

Look Back
On the tenth bounce, the ball reaches a height of 10.5 cm.

The general term, or nth term, t_n, of a **geometric sequence** with the first term, a, and a common ratio, r, is found by the formula $t_n = ar^{n-1}$.

Example 2

Find the first four terms of each geometric sequence.

a. $a = 3$, $r = \frac{1}{2}$

b. $t(n) = \frac{1}{3}(-2)^{n-1}$

a. $t_1 = 3\left(\frac{1}{2}\right)^0 = 3$

$t_2 = 3\left(\frac{1}{2}\right)^1 = \frac{3}{2}$

$t_3 = 3\left(\frac{1}{2}\right)^2 = \frac{3}{4}$

$t_4 = 3\left(\frac{1}{2}\right)^3 = \frac{3}{8}$

b. $t(1) = \frac{1}{3}(-2)^0 = \frac{1}{3}$

$t(2) = \frac{1}{3}(-2)^1 = \frac{-2}{3}$

$t(3) = \frac{1}{3}(-2)^2 = \frac{4}{3}$

$t(4) = \frac{1}{3}(-2)^3 = \frac{-8}{3}$

The sequence is 3, $\frac{3}{2}$, $\frac{3}{4}$, $\frac{3}{8}$, ...

The sequence is $\frac{1}{3}$, $\frac{-2}{3}$, $\frac{4}{3}$, $\frac{-8}{3}$, ...

Example 3

Find the geometric sequence in which the fifth term is 48 and the ninth term is 768.

Write the equation for each term and find the ratio of the equations.

Solve for r.

$t_9 = ar^8 \rightarrow 768$ $ar^8 = 768$

$t_5 = ar^4 \rightarrow 48$ $ar^4 = 48$

$\frac{ar^8}{ar^4} = \frac{768}{48}$

$ar^4 = 16$

$r^4 = 16$

$r = 2$ or -2

Solve for a.

$ar^4 = 48$

$16a = 48$

$a = 3$

$(2)^4 = 16$

$(-2)^4 = 16$

The sequence is 3, 6, 12, 24, ..., or 3, -6, 12, -24, ...

Values that increase by a constant amount, x, have a common ratio of $(1 + x)$. If the values decrease by the constant amount, the common ratio is $(1 - x)$.

Example 4

If, due to inflation, the value of money has been decreasing at the rate of 3.4%/a, then what is the 1992 value of money valued at $100 in 1989?

Year	Value in Dollars
1989	100
1990	$100 - 0.034(100) = 100(1 - 0.034)$ $= 96.60$
1991	$100(1 - 0.034) - 0.034[100(1 - 0.034)] = 100(1 - 0.034)^2$ $= 93.32$
1992	$100(1 - 0.034)^2 - 0.034[100(1 - 0.034)^2] = 100(1 - 0.034)^3$ $= 90.14$

The 1992 value is $90.14.

Exercises

1. What is your opinion of chain letters?
a. Explain why it is extremely unlikely one would get back $78 125 as described in the display.
b. Explain what you would do if you received a chain letter.
c. What do you think about the warning that normally is included in each chain letter that, if you break the chain, bad luck will befall you?

2. If no one ever broke the chain, which term in the sequence would contain enough letters for everyone in Canada?

3. State the value of the initial term, a, the ratio, r, and the fifth term for each.
a. 1, 3, 9, 27, ...   **b.** 4, 20, 100, 500, ...
c. 5000, 500, 50, 5, ... **d.** 81, 54, 36, 24, ...

4. Identify the sequences which are geometric. State the common ratio and the next three terms.
a. 4, 12, 36, 108, ...   **b.** 2, 7, 9, 14, 16, ...
c. 5, 9, 13, 17, ...   **d.** a, ar, ar^2, ar^3, ...
e. $\frac{1}{8}$, $\frac{1}{16}$, $\frac{1}{32}$, ...   **f.** 1, $\sqrt{2}$, $\sqrt{3}$, 2, $\sqrt{5}$, ...
g. 5, -1, $\frac{1}{5}$, ...   **h.** -36, 6, -1, $\frac{1}{6}$, ...

5. Find the first four terms of each geometric sequence.
a. $a = 2$, $r = 3$ **b.** $a = -3$, $r = -4$
c. $a = -1$, $r = \frac{1}{5}$ **d.** $a = 4$, $r = -3$

6. Write an equation for the given information.
a. The fifth term of a geometric sequence is 55.
b. The 17th term of a geometric sequence is 1.0078.

7. Write the first five terms of the sequence.
a. $t_n = 5(3)^{n-1}$ **b.** $t_n = 3(2)^{n-1}$
c. $t_n = -7(5)^{n-1}$ **d.** $t_n = \frac{1}{4}(-3)^{n-1}$

8. An office building, worth $780 000 in 1989, sold for $967 200 in 1990. At this rate of increase, how much will the building sell for in 1991? in 1992?

9. The Smiths had three children. Each of these children had three children, and so on. How many great, great grandchildren do the Smiths have if all are living? What is the value of a? r?

10. Write a formula for t_n and use it to find the indicated term.
a. 54, 36, 24, ..., t_6
b. $7\sqrt{2}$, $\frac{7}{3}\sqrt{6}$, $\frac{7}{3}\sqrt{2}$, ..., t_{13}
c. $\frac{1}{6}$, $\frac{1}{5}$, $\frac{6}{25}$, ..., t_7
d. 0.0035, 0.035, 0.35, ..., t_{11}

11. Find the 12th term in the sequence 7, 14, 28, 56, ... Which term is 1792?

12. Find the first four terms of the geometric sequence with the fourth term $\frac{1}{2}$ and the seventh term $\frac{1}{16}$.

13. Find the geometric sequence in which $t_1 = 5$ and $t_7 = 320$.

14. How many terms are in the sequence?
a. 4, 12, 36, ..., 2916
b. 243, 81, 27, ..., $\frac{1}{81}$
c. 5, -10, 20, ..., $-10\,240$
d. 3, $3\sqrt{3}$, 9, ..., 177 147

15. After a new industrial park is built, the population of a town is expected to increase an average of 25%/a for a period of 5 a. If the population is now 12 756, what will it be in 5 a?

16. The number of a bacteria increases by 50%/h. If the current number of bacteria is 500, how many will there be in 7 h?

17. The amount of money in an account increases by 2.5% every six months. If a $5000 deposit is made, then what is the amount after 3 a?

18. If $2x - 7$, $x + 4$, and $6x - 3$ are consecutive terms in a geometric sequence, find x.

19. These sequences start with the same two terms.
1, 5, 25, …
1, 5, 9, …
Show that every term in the geometric sequence is also a term in the arithmetic sequence.

20. A sequence of squares is made by inscribing successive squares in a square with a side length of 4 cm by joining the midpoints of sides.

a. Set up a sequence for the length of the sides of the successively smaller squares.
b. Derive an expression for the length of the eighth square in the sequence.
c. Write the keying sequence you would use to evaluate the expression on a calculator.
d. Set up a sequence for the perimeter of the successively smaller squares.
e. Derive an expression for the length of the tenth square in the sequence. Evaluate the expression.

21. Each side of an equilateral triangle is 40 cm long. Another triangle is inscribed in it by joining the midpoints of the sides of the previous triangle. This process is continued as indicated in the diagram. Find the perimeter of the sixth triangle in the sequence.

22. A car depreciates 30%/a. Find the value of a $15 000 car after 3 a.

23. A swimmer is increasing her distance by 10% each week to reach a goal of 30 km. If she can swim 3 km now, when will she reach her goal?

24. Franca's father offers her two different plans for paying her allowance: either $10.00 each week, or an allowance starting at $0.10, doubling each week for 1 a. Which plan would give Franca the most money over the year? Show the solution.

25. A study indicates that the population of a mining town fell from 10 000 to 6561 in the 4 a after the closing of the mine. If the population decreases geometrically, what were the populations of the town at the end of each month? (*Hint*: Use a method similar to that of finding an arithmetic mean.)

> The terms between two given geometric terms are called the **geometric means**.

26. Use the process of Exercise 25 in each case.
a. Find three geometric means between 4 and 324.
b. Find two geometric means between 48 and 0.75.
c. Find three geometric means between $x^5 + x^4$ and $x + 1$.
d. Find one geometric mean between $x^3 + x^2 - x - 1$ and $x - 1$.

27. Determine the geometric means in each case.
a. two between 81 and 3
b. two between $\frac{3}{2}$ and $\frac{81}{16}$
c. three between 5 and 405
d. three between 1250 and 2

28. A vacuum pump removes one fifth of the air from a sealed tank on each stroke of the piston. How much air remains after five strokes. (*Hint*: Assume the original amount of air is 1 unit.)

29. In a provincial study, it was projected that the number of deaths in highway accidents would decrease by 14.5% each year after seat-belt legislation was passed. The number of deaths in the province the year before the legislation was passed was 614.
a. About how many deaths would there be after 3 a of such legislation?
b. Do you think seat-belt legislation is warranted? Explain your answer.

14·4 Series

In medieval England, a court jester asked to be paid 4 pennies for the first year of his service, 8 pennies for the second, 16 pennies for the third, and so on. In eight years of service, the jester explained that his payment in pennies would be 4, 8, 16, 32, 64, 128, 256, 512. The total payment in pennies is the **series** $4 + 8 + 16 + 32 + 64 + 128 + 256 + 512$.

This is a series of eight terms with the first term 4 and the last term 512. Mathematicians distinguish between sequences and series: a sequence is a set of ordered items and a series is the sum of the terms of a sequence of numbers. We indicate the sum of n terms by S_n. For example, the sum of the eight terms is S_8. The amount the jester would earn in eight years is 1020 pennies.

$$S_8 = 4 + 8 + 16 + 32 + 64 + 128 + 256 + 512$$
$$= 1020$$

A series may be written as $S_n = t_1 + t_2 + t_3 + \ldots + t_n$.
In mathematics, the Greek letter sigma, Σ, is used to write a sum.

$$\sum_{n=1}^{5} 2n$$

This is read "the summation from $n = 1$ to 5 of 2 times n". The n is the **index of summation**.

$$\sum_{n=1}^{5} 2n = 2(1) + 2(2) + 2(3) + 2(4) + 2(5)$$
$$= 2 + 4 + 6 + 8 + 10$$
$$= 30$$

Example 1

Given $\displaystyle\sum_{k=0}^{3} (3^k - k)$, write the corresponding series in expanded form and find the sum.

$$\sum_{k=0}^{3} (3^k - k) = (3^0 - 0) + (3^1 - 1) + (3^2 - 2) + (3^3 - 3)$$
$$= 1 + 2 + 7 + 24$$
$$= 34$$

The sum of the series is 34.

The **general term** of a series is found by the formula $t_n = S_n - S_{n-1}$, where $n > 1$ and $t_1 = S_1$.

Example 2

The sum of n terms of a series is given by $S_n = 2n^2 - n$.
a. What is the general term? **b.** What is t_5?

a. $t_n = S_n - S_{n-1}$
$= (2n^2 - n) - [2(n-1)^2 - (n-1)]$
$= 2n^2 - n - [2(n^2 - 2n + 1) - n + 1]$
$= 2n^2 - n - (2n^2 - 5n + 3)$
$= 4n - 3$

b. $t_n = 4n - 3$
$t_5 = 4(5) - 3$
$= 17$

The general term is $t_n = 4n - 3$.

t_5 is 17.

400

Exercises

1. The jester served the English king for twelve years. Write the expanded form for S_{12} and calculate his total payment.

2. Write the corresponding series.
a. 3, 5, 7, 9, 11, ...
b. 8, 4, 2, 1, $\frac{1}{2}$, $\frac{1}{4}$, $\frac{1}{8}$, ...

3. Identify each as a sequence or a series.
a. 7, 1, −5, −11, −17, ...
b. $3 - 3 + 3 - 3 + 3 - 3$
c. 1, 3, 9, 27, 81, ...
d. $2 + 4 + 8 + 16 + 32$

4. Find the first three sums of each series whose general sum is given.
a. $S_n = 2n + 1$ **b.** $S_n = 3n^2 - 2$
c. $S_n = n^2 + n$ **d.** $S_n = 5 - 4^n$
e. $S_n = n^3 - 3n$ **f.** $S_n = 15 - 3n^4$

5. Find t_7 for the series in which $S_7 = 5$ and $S_6 = -12$.

6. Write the sum of a, ar, ar^2, and ar^3 in sigma notation.

7. Write in expanded form and find the sum.
a. $\sum_{n=3}^{7} (3n - 2)$ **b.** $\sum_{n=2}^{5} 3(4)^{n-2}$
c. $\sum_{p=4}^{7} (p + 2)$ **d.** $\sum_{m=6}^{8} (-m)$

8. The first four partial sums of the sequence 1, 2, 3, 4, ..., 10 are: $S_1 = 1$, $S_2 = 3$, $S_3 = 6$, and $S_4 = 10$. Can you predict the sum of the first ten terms of this sequence? of the first n terms?

9. Evaluate.
a. $\sum_{n=0}^{4} (3n - 1)$ **b.** $\sum_{k=0}^{3} (2k + 3)$
c. $\sum_{m=1}^{5} 3^m$ **d.** $\sum_{n=1}^{p} \cos nx$
e. $\sum_{n=3}^{7} (n^2 + 1)$ **f.** $\sum_{n=5}^{10} (1 - n) + n^2$

10. Determine the sum of the corresponding series. Write the series in sigma notation, if possible.
a. 3, −3, 3, −3, 3, −3
b. 5, 10, 15, 20, 25, 30, 35
c. 1, 4, 16, 64
d. 1, 4, 7, 10, 13, 16, 19
e. 1, $\frac{1}{3}$, $\frac{-1}{3}$, −1, $\frac{-5}{3}$

11. For the sequences 9, 9, 9, 9, 9, 9, ..., write the series and an expression for S_n.
a. Calculate the value of each.
i) S_{12} ii) S_{40} iii) S_{300}
b. State the value of $S_{40} - S_{39}$.

12. A sequence is made by inscribing successive squares in a square with a side length of 8 cm by joining the midpoints of the sides of the previous square.

a. Write a series for the total length of the sides of 6 squares.
b. Calculate S_6 for the series.

13. In a curve-stitching design, this pattern is made. Each side of the largest equilateral triangle is 80 cm. Other triangles are inscribed by joining the midpoints of the sides of the previous triangle. This process is continued until 6 triangles are formed. What is the length of yarn that is needed to make the design?

401

14·5 Arithmetic Series

A series in which the terms form an arithmetic sequence is called an **arithmetic series**. For example, $3 + 8 + 13 + 18 + \ldots$ is an arithmetic series. The general formula for calculating the sum of a series may be found by investigating the sum of a limited number of terms. In the series $1 + 3 + 5 + 7 + 9 + 11$, certain pairs have the same sum.

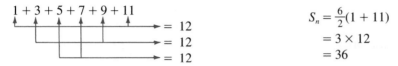

$1 + 3 + 5 + 7 + 9 + 11$

$= 12$
$= 12$
$= 12$

$$S_n = \frac{6}{2}(1 + 11)$$
$$= 3 \times 12$$
$$= 36$$

The sum of the first 100 natural numbers may be found using a related method based on the sum of the corresponding terms. It is reported that Gauss used this method mentally to find the sum of a series of consecutive numbers.

Example 1

Find the sum of the first 100 natural numbers.

$$S_{100} = 1 + 2 + 3 + \ldots + 98 + 99 + 100$$
$$S_{100} = 100 + 99 + 98 + \ldots + 3 + 2 + 1 \quad \text{← Reverse the series.}$$
$$2S_{100} = 101 + 101 + 101 + \ldots + 101 + 101 + 101 \quad \text{← Add.}$$
$$= 100(101)$$
$$S_{100} = \frac{100(101)}{2} \quad \text{There are 100 terms in the series.}$$
$$= 5050$$

The sum of the first 100 natural numbers is 5050.

The formula for the sum of a general arithmetic sequence of n terms, with a first term, a, and a common difference, d, can be developed following the method of Example 1.

Example 2

Find the sum of the general arithmetic series.
$$a + (a + d) + (a + 2d) + \ldots + [a + (n - 1)d]$$

$$S_n = a + (a + d) + \ldots + [a + (n - 2)d] + [a + (n - 1)d]$$
$$S_n = [a + (n - 1)d] + [a + (n - 2)d] + \ldots + (a + d) + a$$
$$2S_n = n[2a + (n - 1)d]$$
$$S_n = \frac{n}{2}[2a + (n - 1)d]$$
$$S_n = \frac{n}{2}[a + a + (n - 1)d] \quad \text{Modify the expression in the bracket to give the first term and the general term.}$$
$$S_n = \frac{n}{2}(a + t_n)$$

The sum of an arithmetic series is $S_n = \frac{n}{2}(a + t_n)$ or $S_n = \frac{n}{2}[2a + (n - 1)d]$.

402

In general, the terms or the sum of an arithmetic series may be found given different information, such as: i) the first three terms and the value of n; ii) two different partial sums and a value of n; or iii) a term and the sum.

Example 3

Find the sum of the first 16 terms of the arithmetic series $1 + 3 + 5 + \ldots$. The first term is 1, the difference is 2, and the number of terms n is 16. Use the formula for the sum of an arithmetic series.

$S_n = \frac{n}{2}[2a + (n - 1)d]$

$S_n = \frac{16}{2}[2 \times 1 + (16 - 1)2]$

$S_n = 256$

The sum of the first 16 terms of the series is 256.

Example 4

The sum of the first two terms of an arithmetic series is 11, and the sum of the first four terms is 42. Find the first six terms of the series, and the sum of the first six terms.

Make replacements in the formula $S_n = \frac{n}{2}[2a + (n - 1)d]$.

$11 = \frac{2}{2}[2a + (2 - 1)d] \rightarrow 11 = 2a + d$ ①

$42 = \frac{4}{2}[2a + (4 - 1)d] \rightarrow 42 = 4a + 6d$ ②

$\quad\quad\quad\quad\quad\quad\quad 22 = 4a + 2d$ ③ $\quad$ Multiply ① $\times$ 2.

$\quad\quad\quad\quad\quad\quad\quad 20 = \quad\quad 4d$ ② $-$ ③

$\quad\quad\quad\quad\quad\quad\quad\quad d = 5$

Substituting $d = 5$ in ①, we have $a = 3$.

The first six terms of the series are $3 + 8 + 13 + 18 + 23 + 28$.

The sum of $S_6 = \frac{6}{2}(6 + 25)$ or 93.

Example 5

In a given series, the 12th term is 28 and the sum of the first 20 terms is 470. Find the series.

Write t_{12} and S_{20} in terms of a, n, and d using the expressions for the general term and the sum of n terms.

$t_n = a + (n - 1)d$ $\quad\quad\quad\quad\quad\quad\quad\quad\quad S_n = \frac{n}{2}[2a + (n - 1)d]$

$t_{12} = a + 11d$ $\quad\quad\quad\quad\quad\quad\quad\quad\quad S_{20} = \frac{20}{2}[2a + 19d]$

$28 = a + 11d$ ② $\quad\quad\quad\quad\quad\quad\quad 470 = 20a + 190d$

$\quad\quad\quad\quad\quad\quad\quad\quad\quad\quad\quad\quad\quad\quad 47 = 2a + 19d$ ①

Solve equations ① and ② simultaneously. The balance of the solution is left as an exercise.

Exercises

All series in these exercises are arithmetic.

1. Find the sum of each series using the method of Example 1 in the display.
a. $11 + 15 + 19 + 23 + 27$
b. $-32 - 22 - 12 - 2 + 8 + 18$
c. $2\sqrt{3} + 4\sqrt{3} + 6\sqrt{3} + 8\sqrt{3}$
d. $x + 2x + 3x + 4x + 5x + 6x + 7x + 8x$
e. $\frac{1}{2} + 1 + \frac{3}{2} + 2 + \frac{5}{2} + 3 + \frac{7}{2} + 4$

2. Find t_{20} and S_{20} for each series.
a. $3 - 3 - 9 - 15 - \ldots$
b. $12 + 19 + 26 + \ldots$
c. $53.8 + 41.1 + 28.4 + \ldots$
d. $2a + 5a + 8a + \ldots$
e. $(5 + i) + (7 + 4i) + (9 + 7i) + \ldots$
f. $\frac{1}{7} + \frac{2}{7} + \frac{3}{7} + \ldots$

3. Find the sum.
a. $2 + 9 + 16 + \ldots + t_{10}$
b. $-10 - 13 - 16 - \ldots + t_{25}$
c. $5 + \frac{14}{3} + \frac{13}{3} + \ldots + t_{11}$
d. $0.001 + 0.011 + 0.021 + \ldots + t_{43}$
e. $-11m - 2m + 7m + \ldots + t_{70}$
f. $7\sqrt{2} + 13\sqrt{2} + 19\sqrt{2} + \ldots + t_{150}$

4. Sanjay's weekly allowance of \$7 is to increase by \$3 each week that he keeps his grades up. He achieves this for a period of 10 weeks.
a. What is his allowance after 10 weeks?
b. What is the total he received for that period?

5. Jocelyn opens an account into which she deposits \$50. Each month she increases the deposit \$15 over the previous month.
a. What is the amount of her 11th deposit?
b. What is the total of her first 11 deposits?

6. A tortoise prepares for a race by increasing the distance walked each day by 3 m. It begins by walking 5 m the first day.
a. What distance is walked on the 18th day?
b. What is the total distance for the 18 d?
c. Will the tortoise be ready for the 100 m race by the 30th day?

7. Find the sum.
a. $3 + 9 + 15 + \ldots + 105$
b. $-5 + 2 + 9 + \ldots + 100$
c. $4 + 15 + 26 + \ldots + 213$
d. $43 + 31 + 19 + \ldots - 521$
e. $21.5 + 14.2 + 6.9 + \ldots - 715.8$
f. $2\sqrt{7} + 5\sqrt{7} + 8\sqrt{7} + \ldots + 83\sqrt{7}$

8. Evaluate.
a. $\sum\limits_{n=1}^{11} (n + 7)$ **b.** $\sum\limits_{k=1}^{40} (5 - k)$

9. Are the series in Exercise 8 arithmetic? Why?

10. Write two arithmetic series in sigma notation.

11. Find t_{17} and S_{17}. The first term and the common difference are given.
a. $a = -7$, $d = 3$ **b.** $a = -23$, $d = 9$
c. $a = 5.9$, $d = -0.8$ **d.** $a = 6\sqrt{7}$, $d = -\sqrt{7}$

12. The recursive function, $t_1 = 5$, $t_n = t_{n-1} - 7$, $n > 1$, defines an arithmetic sequence.
a. Find the first six terms.
b. Calculate S_6.

13. Complete the solution to Example 5 in the display.

14. An arithmetic series has a first term of 37 and the sum of the first 12 terms is 1434.
a. Find the common difference.
b. Calculate S_{21}.

15. Find the sum of the first 100 even natural numbers.

16. Develop a general formula for the sum of the first n even integers.

17. Develop a general formula for the sum of the first n odd integers.

18. The sum of the first 13 terms of an arithmetic series is 507, and the sum of the first 25 terms is 2025. Find the series.

14·6 Geometric Series

How much would you have in an account after ten deposits, if on day one you deposit $1, on day two you deposit $2, day three $4, and so on, each day doubling the previous day's deposit? The sequence of deposits would be: 1, 2, 4, 8, 16, 32, 64, 128, 256, 512.

The sum of this geometric sequence is a series which is also geometric.
$1 + 2 + 4 + 8 + 16 + 32 + 64 + 128 + 256 + 512$

A **geometric series** is the sum of a geometric sequence.

The general formula for finding the sum of a geometric series may be found by investigating the sum of a simple known geometric series.

Example 1

Find the sum of the geometric series $1 + 5 + 25 + 125 + 625$.

$$S_5 = 1 + 5 + 25 + 125 + 625 \qquad ①$$
$$\underline{5S_5 = \quad 5 + 25 + 125 + 625 + 3125 \qquad ②} \qquad \text{Multiply } S_5 \text{ by the}$$
$$S_5 - 5S_5 = 1 - 3125 \qquad\qquad ① - ② \quad \text{common ratio, 5.}$$
$$-4S_5 = -3124$$
$$S_5 = 781$$

Apply the same method to the general geometric series with first term, a, common ratio, r, and n terms.

$$S_n = a + ar + ar^2 + \ldots + ar^{n-1} + ar^n \qquad ①$$
$$\underline{rS_n = \quad ar + ar^2 + \ldots + ar^{n-1} + ar^n + ar^n \qquad ②} \quad \text{Multiply ① by } r.$$
$$S_n - rS_n = a - ar^n \qquad\qquad ① - ②$$
$$S_n(1 - r) = a(1 - r^n) \quad \text{Factor.}$$
$$S_n = \frac{a(1 - r^n)}{1 - r} \quad \text{Divide. } r \neq 1$$

If $r < 1$, then both $(1 - r^n)$ and $1 - r$ will be positive. However, if $r > 1$, then both $(1 - r^n)$ and $1 - r$ will be negative. Since it is often easier to work with positive quantities, we multiply both the numerator and denominator by -1.

$$S_n = \frac{a(1 - r^n)(-1)}{(1 - r)(-1)}$$
$$S_n = \frac{a(r^n - 1)}{r - 1} \quad r > 1$$

The sum of a geometric series is $S_n = \dfrac{a(r^n - 1)}{r - 1}$ when $r > 1$, and $S_n = \dfrac{a(1 - r^n)}{1 - r}$ when $r < 1$.

Example 2

Given the series $27 + 9 + 3 + 1 + \ldots + \frac{1}{243}$.

a. How many terms are in the series?   **b.** Calculate the sum.

a. $a = 27$

$r = \frac{9}{27} = \frac{1}{3}$

$t_n = \frac{1}{243}$

$n = ?$

$t_n = ar^{n-1}$

$\frac{1}{243} = 27\left(\frac{1}{3}\right)^{n-1}$

$\frac{1}{243 \times 27} = \left(\frac{1}{3}\right)^{n-1}$

$\frac{1}{3^5 \times 3^3} = \left(\frac{1}{3}\right)^{n-1}$

$\left(\frac{1}{3}\right)^8 = \left(\frac{1}{3}\right)^{n-1}$ Powers of the same base.

$\therefore n - 1 = 8$ The exponents are equal.

$n = 9$

There are nine terms in the series.

b. $S_n = \dfrac{a(1 - r^n)}{1 - r}$ $r < 1$

$S_9 = \dfrac{27\left[1 - \left(\frac{1}{3}\right)^9\right]}{1 - \frac{1}{3}}$

$\doteq 40.497\ 942\ 4$

$\doteq 40.5$

Calculator Keying Sequence

27 ✕ ((1 − ((3 y^x 9 +/−))))

÷ ((1 − ((1 ÷ 3)))) =

The sum of the series is approximately 40.5.

Example 3

Find the sum of the first 100 terms of the geometric series with the first term 5 and the common ratio is -2.

Since $r < 1$, the formula to use is $S_n = \dfrac{a(1 - r^n)}{1 - r}$

$= \dfrac{5[1 - (-2)^{100}]}{1 - (-2)}$

$= \dfrac{5(1 - 2^{100})}{3}$ The solution is left in this form since it is an extremely large negative number.

Example 4

The amount of a sequence of deposits invested at the rate of 3% each interest period after five deposits is $100 + 100(1.03) + 100(1.03)^2 + 100(1.03)^3 + 100(1.03)^4$. Find the sum.

$a = 100$

$r = 1.03$ $(r > 1)$

$n = 5$

$S_n = \dfrac{a(r^n - 1)}{r - 1}$

$= \dfrac{100(1.03^5 - 1)}{1.03 - 1}$

$= 530.913\ 567$

$= 530.91$

Calculator Keying Sequence

100 ✕ ((1.03 y^x 5

− 1)) ÷ 0.03 =

The deposits amount to $530.91.

Exercises

In these exercises, all series are geometric.

1. Why is the series multiplied by the common ratio in Example 1 of the display?

2. Apply the method of Example 1 to calculate the sum.
a. $1 + 3 + 9 + 27 + 81 + 243$
b. $2.1 - 4.2 + 8.4 - 16.8 + 33.6$
c. $\sqrt{7} + 7 + 7\sqrt{7} + \ldots + t_8$
d. $75 + 15 + 3 + \ldots + t_{10}$

3. Explain the calculator keying sequence in Example 2 of the display. Why is the $\boxed{+\!/\!-}$ key used?

4. Explain the calculator keying sequence of Example 4 of the display. Explain why 0.03 is used. What keys could be used instead?

5. Find S_n.
a. $1 + 2 + 4 + \ldots + t_n$
b. $231.5 + 23.15 + 2.315 + \ldots + t_n$
c. $5\sqrt{3} + 15\sqrt{3} + 45\sqrt{3} + \ldots + t_n$
d. $1 - \dfrac{a}{3} + \dfrac{a^2}{9} - \ldots + t_n$

6. A series of \$550 deposits invested at the rate of 12%/a after 6 a is worth $550 + 550(1.12) + 550(1.12)^2 + 550(1.12)^3 + \ldots + 550(1.12)^5$. Find the amount at the end of 6 a.

7. Given the geometric series $2 + 10 + 50 + \ldots$, find t_9 and S_9.

8. For each series, calculate the given sum.
a. $4 + 8 + 16 + \ldots; S_{19}$
b. $8 + (-8) + 8 + \ldots; S_{50}$
c. $5.72 + 57.2 + 572 + \ldots; S_{13}$
d. $x\sqrt{2} + 2x + 2\sqrt{2}x + \ldots; S_{32}$
e. $\dfrac{1}{2} + \dfrac{1}{4} + \dfrac{1}{8} + \ldots; S_9$

9. Ken walked 5 km on the first day of training. He increased this distance by 10% each day. The series is $5 + 5(1.1) + 5(1.1)^2 + \ldots$.
a. What distance did he walk on day 30?
b. What is the total distance he walked in 30 d?

10. Cyrus has \$10 000 to give to needy causes in Hull. Each receives half of his remaining money and he donates to ten causes. How much money is left after the donations?

11. The balance in Frederika's savings account (in dollars) is represented by the series $100 + 100(1.035) + 100(1.035)^2 + \ldots$ to 12 terms. What is the balance?

12. A ball bounces to 65% of its previous height. It is dropped from a height of 100 m. What is the total distance the ball travels from the time it is dropped until it hits the ground the sixth time? (*Hint*: $\{100 + 2[100(0.65) + 100(0.65)^2 + 100(0.65)^3 + \ldots + 100(0.65)^5]\}$.)

13. A pyramid system is used to contact delegates at a political convention. The person in charge of the contact committee relays the information to four people, each of whom notifies four people, who in turn notify four people each, and so on.
a. Write the corresponding series for the people contacted.
b. Calculate the sum of 20 levels of this system.

14. Find the sum.
a. $3 + 6 + 12 + \ldots + 1536$
b. $5 + 15 + 45 + \ldots + 10\,935$
c. $7 + 3.5 + 1.75 + \ldots + 0.109\,375$
d. $2\sqrt{5} + 10 + 10\sqrt{5} + \ldots + 31\,250$
e. $1 + \dfrac{1}{3} + \dfrac{1}{9} + \ldots + \dfrac{1}{729}$
f. $34.2 + 3.42 + 0.342 + \ldots + 0.000\,034\,2$
g. $0.3 + 0.03 + 0.003 + \ldots + 0.000\,000\,000\,03$

15. Given the series $1 + 0.5 + 0.25 + \ldots$, find S_{100}.

16. The ratio of a geometric series is $\dfrac{1}{3}$ and the sum of the first five terms is 121. Find the series.

Braintickler

What is the average of the first 35 even numbers?

14·7 Compound Interest—Amount

Interest earned on an investment is compounded if, at the end of each interest period, the interest is added to the principal and allowed to accumulate. A savings account allows the option of withdrawing the interest or allowing it to accumulate. Some investments do not permit withdrawals of the interest. For example, a five-year Investment Certificate at 6.75%, compounded annually, can only be cashed after 5 a.

Example 1

A sum of $1000 is invested at 7.25%/a (7.25% per annum), compounded annually. Compute the amount of the investment at the end of each of the first three years. How does this compare to simple interest at the same rate?

End of Year	Principal	Calculation of Interest	Interest	Amount
1	$1000.00	$1000.00 \times 0.0725 \times 1$	$72.50	$1072.50
2	$1072.50	$1072.50 \times 0.0725 \times 1$	$77.76	$1150.26
3	$1150.26	$1150.26 \times 0.0725 \times 1$	$83.39	$1233.65
			$233.65	

The total compounded interest is $233.65.

The total simple interest at 7.25%/a for three years is:
Principal $\times$ interest rate $\times$ time
$1000.00 \times 0.0725 \times 3 = 217.50$

Compound interest pays $16.15 more.

The period for which interest is calculated is the **interest period**. The equation for calculating the amount of a sum of money invested at compound interest can be developed as in Example 2.

Example 2

Develop a formula for finding the amount, A, of a sum of money, P, invested for a number of interest periods, n, at $i\%$ per period.

Time	Principal	Interest	Amount
0	P		P
1	P	Pi	$P + Pi = P(1 + i)$
2	$P(1 + i)$	$P(1 + i)i$	$P(1 + i) + P(1 + i)i = P(1 + i)(1 + i)$
			$= P(1 + i)^2$
.			
.			
.			
n			$P(1 + i)^n$

The growth of this investment may be shown on a time line.

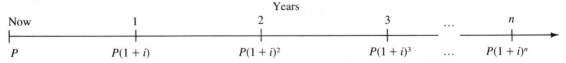

The amounts form a geometric sequence in which the first term is P and the common ratio is $(1 + i)$.

The formula used to find the amount of a compounded investment is
$$A = P(1 + i)^n$$
where P is the amount invested, i is the interest rate per compound (interest) period, and n is the number of interest periods.

Example 3

Sally inherited $3000 which she invested at a local bank in Moose Jaw at 8.5%/a, compounded semi-annually. After 4 a, she withdrew the funds to purchase a used car costing $3800.
a. What is the amount of the investment after 4 a?
b. Does she have enough cash left to purchase a $1200 video-sound system?

a. Understand the Problem and Develop a Plan
Since this is an investment problem using compound interest, the formula $A = P(1 + i)^n$ applies. Since the interest is compounded semiannually, the interest period is for six months and the interest rate per period is the annual rate divided by two. Substitute the given information into the formula and calculate the unknown amount.

Carry Out the Plan

$A = ?$

$P = \$3000$

$i = \dfrac{8.5}{2} = 0.0425$

$n = 4 \times 2 = 8$

$A = P(1 + i)^n$
$= 3000(1 + 0.0425)^8$
$= 4185.330\ 54$
$= 4185.33$

Calculator Keying Sequence
$3000\ \boxed{\times}\ 1.0425\ \boxed{y^x}\ 8\ \boxed{=}$

The investment amounts to $4185.33 after 4 a.

b. After paying for the used car, Sally has $385.33 (i.e. $4185.33 - 3800.00$), which is not sufficient to buy the video-sound system.

Exercises

All interest rates are per annum.

1. In your own words, describe the difference between simple interest and compound interest?

2. Calculate the amount of each investment.
a. $4250 invested at 13.5%, compounded annually for 5 a
b. $275 invested at 3.5%, compounded annually for 3 a
c. $7287 invested at 8.25%, compounded annually for 7 a

3. Extend the table in Example 2 of the display for 3 a and 4 a.

4. Calculate the amount of each investment.
a. $510 invested at 12.3%, compounded semi-annually for 8 a
b. $719 invested at 7.5%, compounded semi-annually for 5 a
c. $10 755 invested at 9.25%, compounded semi-annually for 3 a
d. $35 800 invested at 18.5%, compounded semi-annually for 20 a

5. Find the amount of each investment.

	a.	b.	c.	d.
P	$560	$1250	$15 000	$6980
i	12.50%	6.75%	13.50%	8.25%
n	annual	quarterly	monthly	semiannually
t	5 a	3.5 a	2 a	8 a

6. Which investment earns more interest? Explain your answer.
a. $100 at 9%, simple interest for 1 a
b. $100 at 9%, compounded annually for 1 a
c. $100 at 9%, compounded semiannually for 1 a

7. Calculate the amount of each investment.
a. $500 invested at 7.25%, compounded annually for 3 a
b. $893 invested at 10.75%, compounded semiannually for 30 months
c. $23 650 invested at 8%, compounded quarterly for 18 months

8. To purchase camera equipment, Amir borrowed $2390 from his father at 6% simple interest for 3 a.
a. How much does he owe after 3 a?
b. How much would he owe if the interest had been compounded semiannually?

9. Beth wishes to invest her $1000 savings in a local bank in Dartmouth. Which of these plans would give her the greatest amount after 2 a? Explain your answer using calculations.
a. an interest of 11.50%, compounded annually
b. an interest of 11.25%, compounded semiannually
c. an interest of 11.00%, compounded quarterly
d. an interest of 10.00%, compounded monthly

10. The value of Kaori's property increased by 15%/a for 3 a, after which she sold it. Originally, it had been valued at $55 000. What was the value after 3 a?

11. Norris borrowed $2000 at 10.5%, compounded semiannually. He invested this in gold bullion which increased in value by 28% over one year, after which he sold the bullion. What was his profit?

12. One type of Canada Savings Bond pays compound interest at 10.25%, compounded annually. Calculate the value of a $5000 bond over the nine-year period to maturity.

13. Jennifer has saved $5000 towards her university education which she plans to begin in 4 a. She will need $8500 for the first year. What interest rate, compounded semiannually, will give her the required amount?

14. What is the amount of $100 when invested for 5 a at each rate?
a. 10%, compounded annually
b. 20%, compounded annually
c. Does doubling the interest rate double the amount accumulated? Explain your answer.

15. What is the amount of $100 when invested at 10%, compounded annually, for each time?
a. 5 a
b. 10 a
c. If the length of the investment is twice as long, is the amount accumulated twice as much? Explain your answer.

16. In 1935, grandfather Alex loaned Joe $200 to start a homestead in British Columbia. The agreed interest rate was 1%, compounded annually. Joe was very successful, but he forgot about the loan for 50 a, after which time he computed the amount owing. How much does he owe Alex's heirs?

17. Approximately how long does Valerie have to wait for her $100 investment to double if it is invested at 11.5%, compounded monthly?

18. Aristotle believes that he can triple his money in 5 a. What interest rate is necessary for each compounding method?
a. annually   **b.** semiannually
c. quarterly   **d.** monthly

Braintickler

You have $3.30 in change, made up of an equal number of nickels and quarters. You challenge a classmate as follows, "If you can tell me how many nickels and quarters there are, I'll split my change with you." What should the answer be?

14·8 Using Compound Interest

One of the easiest ways to calculate compound interest is by using a calculator.

Example 1

Two different types of investments are offered by the local trust company in Flin Flon. Jill wishes to know which of the two yields the greater interest on $3000 after 3 a. One pays 10.25%, compounded annually. The other pays 10.00%, compounded quarterly. She uses these keying sequences on a calculator and records the amounts after each $\boxed{=}$.

10.25%, compounded annually

3000 $\boxed{\times}$ 1.1025 $\boxed{=}$ **3307.5**
$\boxed{=}$ **3646.51875**
$\boxed{=}$ **4020.286922**

10.00%, compounded quarterly $\left(i = \frac{0.1000}{4}\right)$

3000 $\boxed{\times}$ 1.025 $\boxed{=}$ **3075.**
$\boxed{=}$ **3151.875**
$\boxed{=}$ **3230.671875**
$\boxed{=}$ **3311.438672** (after 1 a)
...
$\boxed{=}$ **4034.666473** (after 3 a)

The 10.00%, compounded quarterly, paid $14.38 more than the 10.25%, compounded annually.

Example 2

The "Rule of 72" states that an investment with interest, compounded annually, doubles in about $(72 \div i)$ years, where i is the interest rate in percent. Confirm the Rule of 72 by calculating how long it takes for $1000 to double when it is invested at:

a. 10%, compounded annually.

b. 7%, compounded annually.

a. By the Rule of 72, the amount should double in about 7 a $(72 \div 10)$.
Using Jill's keying method:
1000 $\boxed{\times}$ 1.1 $\boxed{=}$ $\boxed{=}$ $\boxed{=}$ $\boxed{=}$ $\boxed{=}$ $\boxed{=}$ $\boxed{=}$
1948.72

b. By the Rule of 72, the amount should double in about 10 a $(72 \div 7)$.
Using Jill's keying method:
1000 $\boxed{\times}$ 1.07 $\boxed{=}$ $\boxed{=}$ $\boxed{=}$ $\boxed{=}$ $\boxed{=}$ $\boxed{=}$ $\boxed{=}$ $\boxed{=}$ $\boxed{=}$ $\boxed{=}$
1967.15

Example 3

Sometimes interest is calculated and compounded on a daily basis. This is often called **continuous compounding**. The value for n is 365. The annual interest rate is divided by 365 to get the value for i to use in the formula $A = P(1 + i)^n$. Calculate the amount needed to repay a short-term loan of $8000, taken out on July 3 and due on September 16, if the annual interest rate is 18% and the interest is compounded daily.

The number of days must be counted:

July 3-July 31	= 29 d
August 1-31	= 31 d
September 1-16	= 16 d
Total	76 d

The number of interest periods is $n = 76$, and the value of i is $0.18 \div 365$.
$A = 8000[1 + (0.18 \div 365)]^{76}$
The calculator keying sequence is:
0.18 $\boxed{\div}$ 365 $\boxed{+}$ 1 $\boxed{=}$ $\boxed{y^x}$
76 $\boxed{=}$ $\boxed{\times}$ 8000 $\boxed{=}$ **8305.44**

The amount needed to repay the loan is $8305.44. Is this reasonable? At 20% simple interest, the interest would be about one fifth of 0.2×8000 or about $320. So, a compounded interest of $305 is reasonable.

Exercises

1. Use the constant function on a calculator to find the amount of each.

	Principal	Rate Compounded	Term
a.	$350	8% annually	3 a
b.	$350	16% annually	3 a
c.	$8000	12.5% annually	5 a
d.	$16 000	12.5% annually	5 a
e.	$9000	9% annually	4 a
f.	$9000	9% annually	8 a

2. Use your answers for Exercise 1 to answer the following.
a. If the annual interest rate doubles, does the interest double?
b. If the amount is doubled, is the interest doubled?
c. If the time doubles, does the interest double?
d. If the number of compounding periods increases, does the interest increase?

3. Use the Rule of 72 to approximate the time it takes each investment to double in value. Indicate whether it will be slightly more or less than the number of years you give.

	Principal	Rate Compounded
a.	$4800	10%
b.	$9000	6%
c.	$9000	12%
d.	$8677	18%

e. If the rate doubles, is the time needed to double the value cut in half?

4. In Example 3, explain why one fifth of 0.2×8000 is used.

5. Calculate the interest on each loan. Interest is compounded daily.

	Principal	Rate	Loan Dated	Repaid
a.	$540	12%	88/03/23	88/06/14
b.	$2100	9.75%	88/06/24	88/10/03
c.	$9150	10.875%	88/01/30	88/03/28*
d.	$450	12.65%	88/02/24	88/05/08
e.	$4559	8.66%	88/10/20	89/02/26*
f.	$500	15.5%	88/10/15	89/02/05

*Requires special attention.

6. On April 8, Chester's Hardware takes out a short-term loan to pay for some merchandise that has just arrived. The loan is for $6200 at 16%, compounded daily. The loan is retired (paid off) on June 2. What is the amount needed to retire the loan?

7. A farmer in Red Deer needs to borrow $3500 to meet harvesting expenses. When the harvest is over and the grain is sold, the loan can be repaid. The interest on the loan is 16.5%, compounded daily. The date of the loan is 1988/09/24 and the due date is 1988/10/15. What is the amount necessary to retire the loan?

8. Describe five situations in which a person might want to take out a short-term loan. In each case, indicate whether you think it would be wise to do so. Remember that the person taking the loan must pay it back, with interest.

9. Some firms which issue credit cards charge daily interest though they list the interest rate as an annual rate. Calculate the true interest rate when an annual rate of 18% is compounded daily.

10. As a summer job, two students open a painting company and take out a short-term loan to get started. A $500 loan is given on June 24. The interest is cited as 18%/a, compounded daily. The loan is to be paid back on July 24. The banker says, "The interest is taken off the $500. You get the balance." How much did the two students get? Is the interest truly 18%? Explain your answer.

Braintickler

A grandfather gives half the money in his pocket to his daughter, a fourth of what is left to his granddaughter, and a third of what is left to his grandson. He then splits the balance with you. If you get $2.00, how much did he have in the beginning?

14·9 Present Value

An investment made today of $1000 at an interest rate of 10.5%/a, compounded annually, will yield a larger sum of money two years from now. Conversely, an investment which will amount to $1000 in two years requires less than $1000 to be invested today.

Now ⟵—————➤ Two Years from Now
$1000 $1000(1 + 0.105)²
  ? $1000

Example 1

The average cost of spending one year in Mexico studying and travelling is $8000. Terry plans to study and travel there in four years. How much should he invest today at 6.75%, compounded semiannually, to have $8000 in four years?

Apply the formula for compound interest $A = P(1 + i)^n$.

$A = \$8000$ $\qquad\qquad\qquad$ $A = P(1 + i)^n$ $\qquad\qquad$ Calculator Keying Sequence

$P = ?$ $\qquad\qquad\qquad\qquad$ $8000 = P(1.033\ 75)^8$ $\qquad$ 8000 $\boxed{\div}$ $\boxed{(}$ 1.03375 $\boxed{y^x}$

$i = \dfrac{0.0675}{2} = 0.033\ 75$ $\qquad\qquad$ $P = \dfrac{8000}{(1.033\ 75)^8}$ $\qquad$ 8 $\boxed{)}$ $\boxed{=}$

$n = 4 \times 2 = 8$ $\qquad\qquad\qquad$ $= 6134.311\ 25$

$\qquad\qquad\qquad\qquad\qquad\quad$ $\doteq 6134.31$

Terry should invest $6134.31 today in order to have $8000 in four years.

> A future sum of money, A, invested at a rate of $i\%$ per interest period, for n interest periods has a **present value**, P, given by: $P = \dfrac{A}{(1 + i)^n}$ or $P = A(1 + i)^{-n}$.

A time diagram may be used to illustrate the relationship between a future amount of money, A, and earlier values if the money is invested at a rate, i, compounded annually, for a period of four years.

Time Line in Years

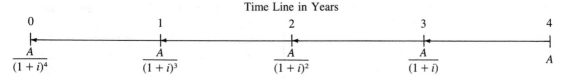

Example 2

What sum of money invested today would amount to $50 000 in 3 a at an interest rate of 8.75%, compounded monthly.

$A = \$50\ 000$ $\qquad\qquad\qquad\qquad\qquad$ $P = A(1 + i)^{-n}$

$i = \dfrac{0.0875}{12}$ $\qquad\qquad\qquad\qquad\qquad$ $= 50\ 000(1.007\ 291\ 666)^{-36}$

$n = 12 \times 3$ $\qquad\qquad\qquad\qquad\qquad\quad$ $\doteq 38\ 493.05$

$P = ?$

A sum of $38 493.05 will grow to $50 000 if invested for 3 a at 8.75%, compounded monthly.

Exercises

All interest rates are per annum.

1. Use a time line diagram to show the value of $1000 in today's dollars from 5 a ago to 5 a from now. The interest rate is 8%, compounded annually.

2. Is the present value of money, dollar for dollar, more or less than the future value?

3. Calculate the present value of each investment.
a. $3175 invested at 6.8%, compounded annually, for a period of 5 a
b. $529 invested at 8.23%, compounded annually, for a period of 9 a
c. $12 848 invested at 10.6%, compounded annually, for a period of 15 a
d. $31 673 invested at 14.8%, compounded annually, for a period of 23 a

4. Calculate the present value of each investment.
a. $965 invested at 12.5%, compounded semiannually, for a period of 3 a
b. $5178 invested at 9.25%, compounded semiannually, for a period of 17 a
c. $159 invested at 3.75%, compounded semiannually, for a period of 2 a
d. $57 890 invested at 16.7%, compounded semiannually, for a period of 2.5 a

5. Shen-yi purchases a boat from his uncle and agrees to pay him $5000 in 2 a. If the interest rate is 9.5%, compounded monthly, how much is the boat worth today?

6. Joanne wishes her daughter to have $20 000 on her eighteenth birthday in 10 a. How much should she invest today at 10.23%, compounded semiannually, to achieve this goal?

7. Twenty years ago, Charles invested $1500. Today he has $10 769. What was the interest rate if it was compounded annually?

8. An investment of $2500 doubles over 5 a. What is the interest rate if the compounding was semiannually? monthly?

9. Jack's inheritance was invested for him on his fifth birthday. It amounted to $11 257 on his twenty-first birthday. If the interest rate was 6.75%, compounded semiannually, then how much was invested?

10. Olga's salary in her first year of working was $27 900. Over a four-year period, this increased to $34 789. What interest rate, compounded annually, would yield this increase in salary?

11. A bond is valued at $1000 in three years. If the current interest rate is 9.85%, compounded annually, what is the present value of the bond? Is $930 a good price for this bond?

12. Suppose the purchasing power of money decreased an average of 3.4%/a for the last 7 a. What was the value, 7 a ago, of money valued at $100 today?

Using the Library

Carl Friedrich Gauss (1777-1855) was an eminent mathematician who contributed extensively to the study of mathematics.
a. Using the library, research his life and contribution to mathematics.
b. Write a short report on his life or on his mathematical endeavours.
c. In 1796, he developed a theory which showed that a regular polygon with a prime number of sides can be constructed using compasses and a straightedge if and only if the prime number is of the form $f(n) = 2^{2n} + 1$, where $n \in W$.
 i) How did Gauss develop this theory?
ii) At the early age of 19, Gauss constructed a regular polygon of 17 sides with a straightedge and compasses. Explain how he was able to do this. Construct a regular polygon of 17 sides using Gauss' method.

Braintickler

If
$$2^{\blacksquare} \bullet 3^{\blacksquare} \bullet 4^{\blacksquare} = 5,$$
$$3^{\blacksquare} \bullet 4^{\blacksquare} \bullet 5^{\blacksquare} = 112,$$
and
$$4^{\blacksquare} \bullet 5^{\blacksquare} \bullet 6^{\blacksquare} = 2267,$$
then
$$\blacksquare^{\blacksquare} \bullet \blacksquare^{\blacksquare} \bullet \blacksquare^{\blacksquare} = \blacksquare\blacksquare.$$

14·10 Effective Interest Rate

Credit card companies usually quote the rate of interest on unpaid balances as a per month charge. Common rates are 1.50%, 1.75%, or 2.00% per month. This is the same as compounding the interest monthly.

To determine the effective rate ($E.R.$) of interest per year, we equate the amount, compounded monthly, for a one-year period to the amount for one year if the interest is compounded annually. For example, if a credit card company advertises a monthly interest rate of 1.50%, we can find the effective rate by equating the amounts as compounded monthly and annually. Suppose that the balance is \$1.

$$P(1 + E.R.)^1 = P(1 + i)^n$$
$$1(1 + E.R.)^1 = 1(1 + 0.015)^{12}$$
$$1 + E.R. = 1.195\ 618\ 17$$
$$E.R. \doteq 0.1956$$

Though the advertised, or nominal, interest rate is 1.50% per month, the effective interest is higher, approximately 19.56%/a.

In general, $(1 + i)^n = 1 + E.R.$ and $E.R. = (1 + i)^n - 1$, where i is the interest per period and n is the number of interest periods.

Exercises

1. When is the effective rate of interest the same as the advertised or nominal rate?

2. Why does the effective rate of interest differ from the nominal rate of interest if the compounding period is less than one year?

3. Show if the following pairs of rates are equivalent.
a. 10% compounded quarterly; 10.38% compounded annually
b. 2% compounded monthly; 24% compounded annually
c. 27% compounded monthly; 30.6% compounded annually
d. 15.5% compounded semiannually; 16.1% compounded annually

4. A credit card company charges 18.3% on the unpaid balance each month. What is the effective annual rate?

5. Which rate offers the greater yield on an investment?
a. 9% compounded annually or 8.75% compounded quarterly
b. 10.25% compounded semiannually or 10.5% compounded annually
c. 15% compounded monthly or 16% compounded annually
d. 6.35% compounded annually or 6.25% compounded semiannually

6. Calculate the equivalent annual rate.
a. 12.3% compounded weekly
b. 29% compounded monthly
c. 3.75% compounded daily
d. 17.9% compounded monthly

7. Because of the continual lowering in value of its currency, a foreign country increased the fare on its national airline by 10% each week. What is the effective annual rate of increase?

8. What interest rate compounded semiannually is equivalent to 11% compounded annually? 10.5% compounded monthly?

14·11 Annuities

An **annuity** is a sequence of payments which may be made regularly, or received regularly, over a specific period of time, e.g., weekly, monthly, semiannually, or annually. For example, a regular income of $10 000 a year from a trust fund is one type of annuity. Other types are mortgage payments, buying on credit, pensions, and retirement savings.

A person whose income is in large isolated sums, could invest such sums in an annuity and receive regular payments for a specified time period. The opposite is also true. By depositing a regular amount into an annuity, a person could accumulate a larger sum of money.

Example 1

What sum of money would be accumulated after 4 a at an interest rate of 7.5%/a, compounded annually, if $5000 is deposited annually, at the end of each year? The deposits start one year from today.

Construct a time diagram showing the time, the payment, and the value of each payment after 4 a.

Time Payment Value Diagram

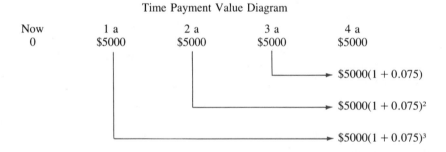

Now	1 a	2 a	3 a	4 a
0	$5000	$5000	$5000	$5000

$5000(1 + 0.075)

$5000(1 + 0.075)^2$

$5000(1 + 0.075)^3$

The sum accumulated is: $5000 + 5000(1 + 0.075) + 5000(1 + 0.075)^2 + 5000(1 + 1.075)^3$. This is a geometric series with a first term of $5000, a common ratio of $(1 + 0.075)$, and four terms. To find the accumulated amount, we can use the equation for the sum of a geometric series when $r > 1$.

$$S_n = \frac{a(r^n - 1)}{r - 1}$$

$$= \frac{5000(1.075^4 - 1)}{1.075 - 1}$$

$$\doteq 22\ 364.6093$$

$$\doteq 22\ 364.61$$

Calculator Keying Sequence

5000 $\boxed{\times}$ $\boxed{(}$ 1.075 $\boxed{y^x}$ 4 $\boxed{-}$ 1 $\boxed{)}$
$\boxed{\div}$ $\boxed{(}$ 1.075 $\boxed{-}$ 1 $\boxed{)}$ $\boxed{=}$

After 4 a, the accumulated amount would be $22 364.61.

416

Sometimes we have a specific goal, such as a house, a car, education, or travel towards which to save. How much should be saved on a regular basis to achieve that goal?

Example 2

Louisa is planning to take a trip around the world in three years time. If she can invest money at 8%/a, compounded semiannually, how much should she deposit semiannually, starting six months from today, to have $10 000 for the trip?

Let R represent the amount of the regular payment. We will use a time payment value diagram to determine the deposits.

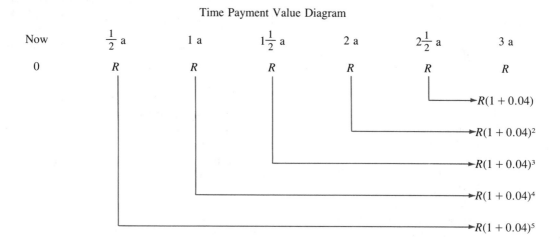

Time Payment Value Diagram

These payments represent a geometric sequence with $a = R$, $r = 1.04$, and $n = 6$.
The sum of the sequence for $r > 1$ is:

$$S_n = \frac{a(r^n - 1)}{r - 1}$$

$$10\ 000 = \frac{R(1.04^6 - 1)}{1.04 - 1}$$

$$R = \frac{10\ 000(1.04 - 1)}{1.04^6 - 1}$$

$$\doteq 1507.619\ 02$$

$$\doteq 1507.62$$

Calculator Keying Sequence

10 000 ⊠ 0.04 ⊡ ⬚ 1.04
⬚ 6 ⊟ 1 ⬚ ⊟

Louisa would have to deposit $1507.62 every six months to accumulate $10 000 in 3 a.

The annuities in Examples 1 and 2 are each ordinary annuities. The periodic payment of an ordinary annuity is made at the end of each time period. The **term** of the annuity is the length of time over which payments are made. The time between payments is the **payment period**. The compounding period for the interest and the payment period must be the same for an annuity.

Exercises

1. Which of the following investments are annuities?
a. $1000 invested for 5 a
b. an investment of $500 each month for 3 a
c. an investment of $2000 now, $500 in 6 months, and $1000 in 1 a

2. Draw a time payment value diagram for each and calculate the amount of the annuity.
a. $750 is deposited each year for 3 a at 9.56%, compounded annually
b. $125 is paid into a fund each month for 6 months at 12.5%, compounded monthly

3. Calculate the amount of the annuity.
a. 12 monthly payments of $275 at 8.7%, compounded monthly
b. 8 annual payments of $5800 at 7.45%, compounded annually

4. Sarah deposits $55 each month into a fund paying 11.23%, compounded monthly. What is the value of her fund after 18 months?

5. On his 15th birthday, Horace deposited $10 in an educational fund paying 9.75%, compounded monthly. Each month until and including his 18th birthday, Horace deposited $10 in this fund. Draw a time payment value diagram and determine the value of his fund after his 18th birthday.

6. Don saves $575 each month for his retirement fund. How much is this worth after 25 a if the fund pays 6%, compounded monthly?

7. Kelly is repaying a loan in 12 monthly payments of $167. The interest rate on the loan is 12.75%, compounded monthly. What is the amount of these payments?

8. Which annuity has the higher value after 5 a?
a. monthly payments of $100 at 12%, compounded monthly
b. annual payments of $1200 at 12%, compounded annually

9. What is the amount of a court award of $500 per month at 10%, compounded monthly, for a period of 15 a?

10. Some car owners regularly save money to pay for a new car. What monthly saving is necessary to cover the cost of a new car in 3 a, with an estimated cost of $17 500? The interest rate is 5.5%, compounded monthly.

11. Meegan agreed to pay Charles $13 750 in 4 a. What semiannual payment is necessary if the current rate of interest is 11.25%, compounded semiannually?

12. Peggy paid $1000 into a university fund for her baby Hugh on the day he was born. Ten years later, she began making annual payments of $1000 into the fund. If the fund pays 6.75%, compounded annually; then what is the balance in the fund after Hugh's 21st birthday?

13. For 5 a, Alex made semiannual payments of $1350 into an account paying 12.5%, compounded semiannually. After that, the account remained dormant for 3 a until he withdrew the balance. Draw a time payment value diagram to find how much he withdrew.

Braintickler

What rate of interest would be necessary to produce the amount indicated in the puzzle?

Invest $10 each month for 444 months. What do you get?

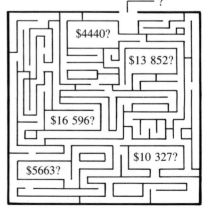

418

14·12 Present Value of an Annuity

The present value of an annuity may be found by adding the present values of each of the periodic payments.

Example 1

Jane wishes to invest in an annuity that will pay her $5000 at an interest rate of 12%, compounded semiannually, for a period of 3 a. What amount must she invest today to receive the payments beginning 6 months from now?

The formula for present value of a sum of money is applied to each payment. The rate of interest for each time period is 6% and there are 6 payments.

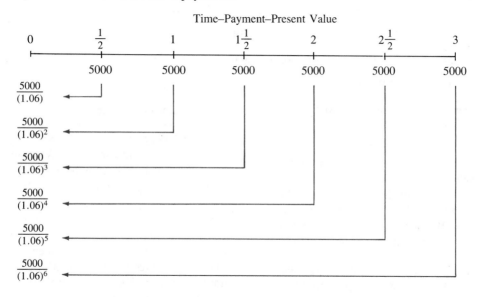

Time–Payment–Present Value

The sum of the terms can be written as: $\dfrac{5000}{(1.06)} + \dfrac{5000}{(1.06)^2} + \dfrac{5000}{(1.06)^3} + \dfrac{5000}{(1.06)^4} + \dfrac{5000}{(1.06)^5} + \dfrac{5000}{(1.06)^6}$

This is a geometric series in which the first term, a, is $\dfrac{5000}{1.06^6}$, $r = 1.06$, and $n = 6$.

Since $r > 1$, $S_n = \dfrac{a(r^n - 1)}{r - 1}$ $\quad \therefore\ S_6 = \dfrac{5000}{1.06^6}\left[\dfrac{1.06^6 - 1}{1.06 - 1}\right]$

$$= \dfrac{5000}{1.06^6}\left[\dfrac{1.06^6 - 1}{0.06}\right]$$

$$\doteq 24\ 586.62$$

Calculator Keying Sequence

5000 $\boxed{\times}$ $\boxed{(}$ 1 $\boxed{-}$
$\boxed{(}$ 1 $\boxed{\div}$ 1.06 $\boxed{)}$
$\boxed{y^x}$ 6 $\boxed{)}$ $\boxed{\div}$ 0.06

Jane must invest $24 586.62 now to receive $5000 every 6 months for the next 3 a.

> The present value of an annuity is $P.V. = \dfrac{a(r^n - 1)}{r - 1}$.

Suppose you receive a large sum of money and wish to invest some of this for a lifetime income. "What annual payment can you expect to receive?", is an important question to consider.

Example 2

Sam won $50 000 in a recent lottery. He decided to invest this in an annuity that would provide a monthly income for the next 4 a while he furthers his education. If the interest rate is 8%, compounded monthly, what monthly income will he receive for 4 a?

Let R represent the amount of the monthly payment. Since the payments are compounded monthly over 4 a, there is a total of 48 payments.

$$a = \frac{R}{1.0067^{48}}$$
$$n = 48$$
$$P.V. = 50\ 000$$

$$P.V. = \frac{a(r^n - 1)}{r - 1},\ r > 1$$

$$50\ 000 = \frac{R}{1.0067^{48}}\left[\frac{1.0067^{48} - 1}{1.0067 - 1}\right]$$

$$= \frac{R}{1.0067^{48}}\left[\frac{1.0067^{48} - 1}{0.0067}\right]$$

$$R \doteq 1221.58$$

$$i = \frac{0.08}{12} = 0.0067$$

Sam will receive a monthly income of approximately $1221.58 for 4 a. Since the actual interest rate was $\frac{2}{3}$%, this is an approximate amount.

Rework the example using $r = 1.006\ 666$. Is the difference significant? Comment.

Exercises

1. Use a time-payment-value diagram to show the present value of each annuity.
a. $500 payable semiannually for a period of 2 a with interest of 11.2%, compounded semiannually
b. $175 payable monthly for a period of 7 months with interest of 8%, compounded monthly

2. Which annuity has the greater present value?
i) 36 monthly payments of $100 at 10.24%, compounded monthly
ii) 3 annual payments of $1200 at 10.75%, compounded annually
iii) 6 semiannual payments of $600 at 10.5%, compounded semiannually

3. Frank repays a car loan in thirty-six monthly payments of $89. If the loan carried an interest rate of 14.8%, compounded monthly, then what is the present value of the loan?

4. An investment of $1000 today yields a monthly income of $100 starting one month from today for a period of 1 a. What is the rate of interest?

5. A scholarship fund is to pay $1500 to the top mathematics student each year. What amount invested today at 12.8%, compounded annually, will provide this scholarship for the next 20 a?

6. Keith has the option of receiving six annual payments of $15 000 or total payment of $68 000 today. At an interest rate of 0.75%, compounded annually, from which option will Keith receive the most money? Show calculations.

7. Barbara wants some flexibility in her income from investments. She has a total of $125 000 to invest in three annuities. From one she wants a monthly income of $1750 for 3 a. From a second she wants a semiannual income of $5000 for 3 a. The third annuity is to provide an annual income for 3 a, using the balance of her funds. The interest rates are 12.4% compounded monthly, 12.8% compounded semiannually, and 13% compounded annually, respectively. Determine her income from the annual annuity.

14·13 Deferred Annuities

A deferred annuity has the first payment delayed. However, once the payments begin, the annuity has all the features of an ordinary annuity. For example, regular monthly payments on an annuity that runs for 10 payments could begin 7 months from today. Six payments would then be "missed" and the first payment is deferred by 6 months.

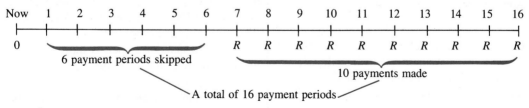

Example

Katrina wants to know the present value of an annuity of $1000 which is deferred for three years and runs for six years. The prevailing rate of interest is 8%, compounded semiannually.

Understand the Problem
Draw a diagram and put on all the information.

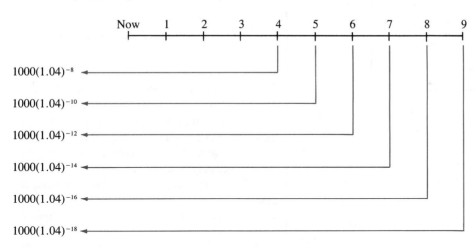

Develop a Plan
Use the Present Value formula after calculating the values for a, r, and n.

Carry Out the Plan
$a = 1000(1.04)^{-18}$, $r = (1.04)^2$, $n = 6$

$$P.V. = \frac{a(r^n - 1)}{r - 1}$$
$$= \frac{1000(1.04)^{-18}[(1.04)^{12} - 1]}{(1.04)^2 - 1}$$
$$\doteq 3635.86$$

Look Back
The present value of the annuity is $3635.86. Can you do a similar problem on your own? This is left to the exercises.

Exercises

1. Would you think the present value of a deferred annuity would be worth more or less than a regular annuity for the same number of payments? Explain.

2. Under what situations would deferred annuities be suitable over regular annuities?

3. If the same amount of money (present value) is invested to buy an annuity, which will yield the highest payments, a 20-payment annuity deferred 10 a or a regular 20-payment annuity? Explain.

4. Interpret this diagram by explaining each amount or groups of numbers.

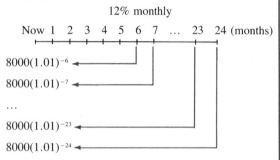

5. Marcus has an annuity of $500 which is deferred for 5 a and runs for 4 a. The interest rate is 12%/a. Marcus wants to take all the money now to invest in his business. What is the present value?

6. Gloria and Hart have a joint 10-payment annuity; the first payment of $900 is to be made eight years hence at an interest rate of 13%/a, compounded semiannually. They want to collapse the annuity and take the funds now to start a business. What amount will they be able to get from the annuity?

7. An annuity of $1500 is payable every July 1 from 1988 to 1999 inclusive. If the rate of interest is 16%, compounded semiannually, what is the value of the annuity on July 1, 1987?

8. Quinten wants to invest a sum of money on June 1, 1988 to provide an annuity with the first payment of $1000 to be on June 1, 2000. There are to be a total of 50 annual payments. How much will Quinten have to invest if money earns 10%, compounded annually?

9. A mother gives each of her 2 twin children an annuity of $1000 with the first of 5 payments on their twenty-fifth birthday. If money earns 10%, compounded annually, what is the value of each annuity on their eighteenth birthday?

10. Interpret this diagram by explaining each amount or groups of numbers.

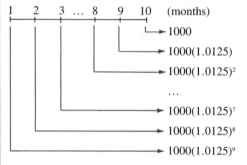

11. A woman, just prior to her fortieth birthday, decides to purchase a $500 monthly annuity to start on her fifty-fifth birthday. The annuity is based on the premise she will receive the annuity for twenty years. She wants to make monthly payments starting immediately and ending when she turns fifty-five. The interest rate is fixed at 10%, compounded monthly.
a. What amount must accumulate by her fifty-fifth birthday?
b. What amount must she deposit monthly during the next fifteen years?

Using the Library

Research the use of actuarial tables by insurance companies and the variables which determine the insurance rates for car insurance. Why do certain age groups pay higher insurance rates than those in other age groups?

14·14 Bonds

Each September and October, the federal government advertises the sale of Canada Savings Bonds for purchase starting on November 1. Newspapers carry ads regularly for other bond issues. For example, in 1986, Maritime Telegraph and Telephone issued $50 million worth of bonds maturing in 20 a.

The **face value** of a bond is the amount stated on the bond and payable to the owner on the due date. The **market value** of a bond is the price at which it sells. The **date of maturity** or due date is the date on which the corporation redeems or buys back the bonds.

A bond is a contract between a lender and a borrower. The purchase of a bond is a form of investment whereby money is loaned to the issuer of the bond. Utility companies, large corporations, and governments are the most common issuers of bonds.

The buyer of a bond is guaranteed
  i) the rate of interest stated, or higher,
 ii) the method by which the interest is paid, simple or compound,
iii) the face value of the bond on the due date (maturity date),
iv) the interest is paid on the face value (or par value) of the bond.

The rate of interest on a bond is called the **bond rate**. A **coupon bond** is one which has dated coupons representing the interest owing on the bond. These coupons are to be "clipped" and redeemed from the issuer.

When purchasing Canada Savings Bonds, you may choose either Regular or Compound Interest Bonds. Regular Interest Bonds pay interest each year, whereas Compound Interest Bonds compound the interest to the date you cash the bond.

Example 1

A $1000 Canada Savings Bond carries 8.75% interest compounded annually. Calculate the value of the bond if it is cashed on November 1, 3 a after the purchase date.

$A = ?$ $A = (1 + i)^n$
$P = \$1000$ $= 1000(1.0875)^3$
$i = 8.75\%$ $\doteq 1286.138\ 67$
$n = 3$ $\doteq 1286.14$

The cash value of the bond after 3 a is $1286.14.

There is a certain amount of risk involved in investing in bonds. The interest rate is thus set high enough to attract buyers. One factor in determining the "attractiveness" of a bond issue is the **yield rate**, the rate of interest you actually receive on the bond. Bonds may sell at prices that are higher or lower than their face value because the market value affects the yield rate.

Example 2

A $100 Bell Canada bond paying 12.65% with a due date of November 15, 2005, sold for $117.125 on July 7, 1988.
a. What is the annual interest?
b. Calculate the yield rate for the first year, to 3 decimal places, if a commission of $5 was charged.

a. Interest = Face Value × Rate of Interest × Time
$$= 100 \times 0.1265 \times 1$$
$$= 12.65$$

The annual interest is $12.65.
b. Cost of the Bond $= \$117.125 + \$5.00$
$$= \$122.125$$
Interest Received = Cost of Bond × Yield Rate
$$12.65 = 122.125 \times Y.R.\%$$

Yield Rate $(Y.R.) = \frac{12.65 \times 100}{122.125}$
$$= 10.358\ 2395$$

The yield rate for the first year is 10.358%.

Note that the yield rate and the bond rate can differ according to the market value of the bond. If a bond sells for its face value, it is said to be **at par**. If the bond sells for more than the face value, it sells at a **premium**. If the bond sells for less than the face value, it sells at a **discount**.

The value of a bond issue in today's terms can be obtained by adding the present value of the face value of the bond and the present value of the interest payments, using the desired yield rate as the rate of interest.

Example 3

Calculate the amount an investor should pay for a $5000, 10.25%, 5 a bond bearing annual coupons if the investor wishes to have a yield of 12%, compounded annually, on this investment.

Annual Interest = Face Value × Rate of Interest × Time
$$= 5000 \times 0.1025 \times 1$$
$$= 512.50$$

Present value of $5000
$$P = A(1 + i)^{-n}$$
$$= 5000(1 + 0.12)^{-5}$$
$$\doteq 2837.12$$

Present value of interest payments
$R = \$512.50$
$i = 0.12$
$n = 5$
$$P.V. = \frac{R[1 - (1 + i)^{-n}]}{i}$$
$$= \frac{512.50[1 - (1.12)^{-5}]}{0.12}$$
$$\doteq 1847.45$$

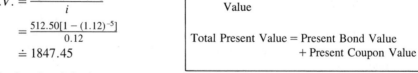

Total Present Value of a Bond

0 1 2 3 4 5 (years)
Bond
Present Value $5000

0 1 2 3 4 5 (years)
Coupon
Present Value   R

Total Present Value = Present Bond Value
                    + Present Coupon Value

The present value of the bond and the interest
$$= \$2837.12 + \$1847.45$$
$$= \$4684.57.$$

An investor would realize a yield rate of 12% if the bond was purchased for $4684.57.

Exercises

1. What is meant by the "issuer" of a bond series?

2. Explain the value of "R" and "i" in Example 3 of the display.

3. In your own words, explain each term.
a. face value   **b.** market value
c. coupon bond   **d.** yield rate
e. date of maturity **f.** bond rate
g. premium   **h.** discount

4. Find the value of the coupon on each bond.
a. a \$5000, $11\frac{5}{8}\%$ bond with monthly coupons

b. a \$1000, $12\frac{1}{2}\%$ bond with semiannual coupons

c. a \$10 000, $9\frac{1}{4}\%$ bond with quarterly coupons

d. a \$2000, 12% bond with annual coupons

5. A \$1000, $12\frac{3}{4}\%$ Province of Prince Edward Island bond dated December 12, 2004, is quoted at \$118.624 per \$100 on August 30, 1986.
a. What is the face value of the bond?
b. What is the market value of the bond on August 30, 1986?
c. What is the due date?
d. Calculate the present value of the bond 10 a before the due date.
e. Calculate the present value of the coupon 10 a before the due date.
f. Calculate the present value of the bond and the coupon 10 a before the due date.

6. If a Province of Manitoba $11\frac{3}{4}\%$ bond with a face value of \$100 sells for \$90.145, then what is the price of a \$1000 bond?

7. Calculate the yield rate for the first year.
a. A $10\frac{1}{2}\%$ \$5000 bond with a purchase cost of \$4625. A commission of $\frac{1}{2}\%$ is charged.

b. A $12\frac{5}{8}\%$ \$1000 bond with a purchase price of \$1125.60. The commission is $\frac{1}{4}\%$.

8. Sue purchased a $12\frac{7}{8}\%$ \$10 000 Province of Newfoundland bond quoted at \$106.682.
a. What was the cost of the bond?
b. What is the annual coupon value?
c. What is the yield rate if a commission of \$25 is charged?

9. A \$1000 bond is purchased for \$957.80. The bond rate is 7%. Calculate the annual yield rate if a $\frac{1}{4}\%$ commission is charged.

10. Which investment will provide the greater yield for the first year?

a. Government of Canada paying $12\frac{3}{4}\%$ and due March 1, 2008, is quoted at \$120.428 per \$100.
b. Bell Canada paying 12.65% due on November 15, 2003, is quoted at \$110.25 per \$100.

11. Nova Scotia Power floated a bond issue paying $12\frac{1}{2}\%$ with a due date of December 20, 2003. The current market value is \$109.83 per \$100. Calculate the yield on a purchase of \$6000 face value of bonds at the market price. The commission is 0.3%.

12. Josefa bought a \$3000 Province of Saskatchewan bond paying $12\frac{1}{2}\%$ semiannually costing \$119.64 per \$100. The bond is due in 15 a.
a. What did she pay for the bond?
b. What price on the bond would provide a 10.65% annual yield?

13. An Ontario Hydro $10\frac{3}{4}\%$ bond due in 3 a is currently selling for \$104.97 per \$100. Interest payments are made semiannually. What should you pay for this bond to receive a 9.85% annual yield rate?

14. Determine the present value of a \$500 Government of Canada $10\frac{3}{4}\%$ bond due in 1.5 a if interest payments are semiannual and the desired yield rate is 9.24%.

15. A \$7000 bond paying 12.375% and due in 5 a has quarterly coupons.
a. What is the value of each coupon?
b. What is the present value of the coupons if the desired yield rate is 11.82%?
c. What is the present value of the par value of the bond?
d. What purchase price would yield the desired yield rate?

14·15 Computer Application— Sum of Geometric Series

It is usually easier and faster to do complicated calculations with a computer. Many of the exercises in this chapter can be done using computer programs. This program will calculate the sum of a geometric series given the first term of the series, the number of terms in the series, and the common ratio.

```
10  REM TO CALCULATE THE SUM OF A GEOMETRIC SERIES
20  INPUT "THE FIRST TERM OF THE SERIES IS "; A
30  INPUT "THE NUMBER OF TERMS IN THE SERIES IS "; N
40  INPUT "THE COMMON RATIO IS "; R
50  S = (A * (R ∧ N − 1)) / (R − 1)
60  PRINT "THE SUM OF THE GEOMETRIC SERIES WITH THE FIRST
TERM "; A; ", THE COMMON RATIO "; R; ", AND "; N;" TERMS IS ";
S; "."
70  END
```

Exercises

1. Run the program inputting these values for A, N, and R. Record your answers.
a. $A = 2$, $N = 4$, $R = 5$
b. $A = 0.5$, $N = 8$, $R = -4$
c. $A = 22$, $N = 13$, $R = -\frac{1}{3}$

2. Explain the purpose of line 50.

3. Modify line 50 to read
`50 S = (A * (1 − R ∧ N)) / (1 − R)`
a. Input the values of A, N, and R from Exercise 1 and record your answers.
b. Compare the answers. What do you notice?
c. Is there a difference as to which equation is used to calculate the sum of a geometric series? Explain.

4. Modify the program to calculate the first term of the geometric series given the sum of the series, the common ratio, and the number of terms in the series.

5. Input these values for S, R, and N in the modified program. Record your answers.
a. $S = 26.984$, $R = 0.36$, $N = 9$
b. $S = -0.4596$, $R = 0.04$, $N = 16$
c. $S = 2789.361$, $R = 36.89$, $N = 12$

6. Write a program to find the sum of an arithmetic series given the first term of the series, the common difference, and the number of terms in the series. Input these values for A, D, and N. Record your answers.
a. $A = 12$, $D = 4$, $N = 56$
b. $A = -72$, $D = -34$, $N = 15$
c. $A = -53$, $D = 45$, $N = 100$
d. $A = 32$, $D = -0.5$, $N = 50$

7. Modify the program in Exercise 6 to find the common difference of an arithmetic series. Input these values for S, A, and N. Record your answers.
a. $S = -59$, $A = -2$, $N = 24$
b. $S = 78$, $A = 6$, $N = 35$
c. $S = -367$, $A = -57$, $N = 49$
d. $S = -7965$, $A = -375$, $N = 275$

8. Write a program which will calculate compound interest. Redo the exercises in Section 14·7 using this program and compare your answers.

9. In recent years, the use of computers by the medical profession to keep records of patients has increased dramatically. Comment on the efficiency of such a system. What are the possibilities and consequences of inputting the wrong information?

14·16 Chapter Review

1. In your own words, define an arithmetic sequence and a geometric sequence.

2. How does a sequence differ from a series?

3. Find the indicated term of each sequence.
a. 1, −2, −5, −8, ..., t_{17}
b. 7, −7, 7, −7, ..., t_{151}

4. The fifth term of an arithmetic sequence is 17 and the twenty-second term is 102.
a. Find the first term and the common difference.
b. Write the first five terms of the sequence.

5. Evaluate.
a. $\sum\limits_{n=1}^{4} n(3n-1)$ **b.** $\sum\limits_{k=0}^{5} (2n-1)$

6. Calculate the sum.
a. $1 + 3 + 5 + \ldots + t_9$
b. $54 + 27 + 13.5 + \ldots + t_{27}$
c. $0.3 + 0.03 + 0.003 + \ldots + t_{35}$

7. On his tenth birthday, Jim's parents deposited $50 in an account for his education. The next month and each succeeding month up to and including his eighteenth birthday, they increased the deposit by $15. What is the total of the deposits?

8. The mass of sand removed from a riverbed in one day was 2.3 t. The amount removed was increased by 10% each day for the next 14 d. What was the total mass of sand removed from the riverbed in those 15 d?

9. In your own words, explain the difference between simple and compound interest.

10. Calculate each amount.
a. $1750 invested at 10.25% simple interest for 2 a
b. $5325 invested at 12.75%, compounded semiannually for 7 a
c. $235 invested at 5.5%, compounded monthly for 18 months

11. Calculate the present value.
a. $5000 due in 6 a at 11.7%, compounded annually
b. $3798 due in 3 a at 8.4%, compounded monthly
c. $23 892 due in 8 a at 13%, compounded semiannually

12. Al has $25 000 to invest. Which plan provides the greatest return on his investment over a 4 a period?
 i) 13% simple interest
 ii) 12.25% compounded quarterly
 iii) 12.75% compounded annually

13. Calculate the effective annual rate.
a. 10.25% compounded every three months
b. 15% compounded semiannually

14. Calculate the amount of each annuity.
a. 48 monthly payments of $120 at 8.5%, compounded monthly
b. 16 annual payments of $2300 at 10.2%, compounded annually

15. Find the present value of each annuity.
a. annual payments of $10 000 at 8.75%, compounded annually, for a period of 7 a
b. semiannual payments of $3800 at 11.8%, compounded semiannually, for a period of 13 a

16. Roger invests $550 each month in an annuity in preparation for his retirement 15 a from today. The fund pays 9.25%, compounded monthly. Calculate the value of the fund in 15 a.

17. A $5000 Province of British Columbia 12% bond dated October 20, 1993, is quoted at $112.063 on August 30, 1986.
a. What is the face value of the bond?
b. What is the market value of the bond on August 30, 1986?
c. What is the bond rate?
d. What is the redemption date of the bond?
e. Calculate the annual coupon value.
f. What is the yield rate?

14·17 Chapter Test

1. Give one example of each.
a. an arithmetic sequence
b. a geometric sequence
c. an arithmetic series
d. a geometric series

2. Given the sequence, find the indicated term.
a. 1, 1, 2, 3, 5, ..., t_{10}
b. 586.1, 117.22, 23.444, ..., t_{17}
c. $3\sqrt{7} + \sqrt{3}$, $5\sqrt{7} - \sqrt{3}$, $7\sqrt{7} - 3\sqrt{3}$, ..., t_{13}
d. $\frac{1}{2}$, $\frac{11}{10}$, $\frac{17}{10}$, ..., t_{27}

3. Find the sum.
a. $7\sqrt{2} + 5\sqrt{2} + 3\sqrt{2} + ... + t_{16}$
b. $3.45 + 0.345 + 0.0345 + ... + t_7$
c. $1.1r + 1.21r + 1.331r + ... + t_9$

4. The fourth term of an arithmetic sequence is -13 and the seventeenth term is -91. Find the sequence.

5. The fifth term of a geometric sequence is 324 and the eighth term is 8748. Find the sequence.

6. A new paint loses only 8.5% of its colour each year, in a climate where 90% of the days are sunny. What percentage of the colour of a new paint job remains after 6 a in this climate?

7. Calculate the amount.
a. $537 invested for a period of 6 months at 9%, compounded monthly
b. $5812 invested for a period of 3.5 a at 12.75%, compounded semiannually
c. $53 610 invested for a period of 15 a at 14.25%, compounded annually

8. Calculate the present value.
a. $4275 due in 3 a at 13.6%, compounded annually
b. $823 due in 1 a at 9%, compounded semiannually
c. $1090 due in 4 a at 12.3%, compounded monthly

9. Faye deposited her summer earnings of $2390 in an account paying $7\frac{7}{8}\%$, compounded monthly. One year later she checked the account. What was the balance at that time?

10. In 3 a, after John has completed 1 a of working after college, he owes $4000 to his brother Jim. What is the present value of the loan at $11\frac{5}{8}\%$ compounded semiannually?

11. Which plan provides the greatest amount after 7 a?
 i) a deposit of $3000 at 10% simple interest
 ii) a deposit of $3000 at $9\frac{5}{8}\%$ compounded semiannually
 iii) seven annual payments of $430 at 9.5% compounded annually

12. Calculate the effective annual rate of interest.
a. 13.5% compounded semiannually
b. 27.5% compounded quarterly

13. Calculate the amount.
a. 12 annual payments of $1250 at 11.8%, compounded annually
b. 60 monthly payments of $75.90 at 12.9%, compounded monthly
c. quarterly payments of $520 at 9.85%, compounded quarterly, for a period of 8 a

14. Calculate the present value.
a. 10 semiannual payments of $712 at 10.25%, compounded semiannually
b. 25 annual payments of $12 679 at 8.75%, compounded annually

15. Sally and Fred, both 20, are planning to purchase a suitable franchise by age 25. Towards this goal, they deposit $600 each month, beginning today, in an annuity paying 11.3%, compounded monthly. How much will they have in the fund after their last payment 5 a from today?

428

BUSINESS APPLICATIONS

Tune Up

1. Identify each sequence as arithmetic or geometric. Then state the next three terms for each sequence.

a. 2, 5, 8, ...
b. 1, 3, 9, ...
c. 3, −3, 3, ...
d. 1, $\frac{1}{2}$, $\frac{1}{4}$, ...
e. a, $a(x+1)$, $a(x+1)^2$, $a(x+1)^3$, ...

2. Find the sum.

a. $1 + 3 + 9 + 27 + 81$
b. $1 + \frac{1}{2} + \frac{1}{4} + \frac{1}{8} + \frac{1}{16}$
c. $1 + r + r^2 + r^3 + r^4 + r^5 + r^6$
d. $a + a(1 + i) + a(1 + i)^2 + ... + a(1 + i)^5$

3. Evaluate to five decimal places.

a. $(1.03)^{10}$
b. $(1.065)^{15}$
c. $(1.125)^{25}$
d. $(1.1875)^{13}$

4. Evaluate to two decimal places.

a. $10 + 10(1.07) + 10(1.07)^2 + 10(1.07)^3$
b. $15 + 15(1.025) + 15(1.025)^2 + ... + 15(1.025)^5$
c. $100(1.065) + 100(1.065)^2 + ... + 100(1.065)^{10}$

5. Copy and complete the table. $I = prt$

Principal	Rate	Time	Interest	Amount
$700	5%	3 a		
$2350		6 months		$2493.50
$9378	12.5%		$3750	

6. Copy and complete the table. $A = P(1 + i)^n$

Principal	Rate per Annum	Compound Period	Time	Amount
$5000	8.25%	semi-annually	3 a	
$25 000	10.5%	monthly	2 a	
	13.75%	annually	5 a	$123 467
	18.5%	semi-annually	10 a	$5682
$1000	12%	annually		$2000

7. Armand loans $1000 to his friend Guy at an interest rate of 7%/a, simple interest. How much should Guy pay Armand on the due date of the loan five years later?

8. Cheryl deposits $1000 in an account paying interest at 7%/a, compounded semiannually. How much will she have in five years in principal plus interest?

9. Explain why Cheryl (in Exercise 8) will receive more money than Armand (in Exercise 7) after the same five-year period.

10. Milos lent $1000 to his younger brother to help him pay for a used car. His brother promised to repay Milos $1097 in one year's time.
a. What is the interest rate on the loan?
b. What would the interest rate be if Milos had asked his brother to repay $1120 in one year's time?

15·1 Mortgages

A house is usually the most expensive purchase an individual will make in his or her lifetime. Because of the high cost, a loan or **mortgage** often is needed in order to buy a home. The lenders of mortgages are banks, trust companies, credit unions, mortgage companies, insurance companies, the seller or vendor of the house in a "vendor-take-back" mortgage, and private individuals.

A mortgage is money borrowed for property which is used as collateral or security against the value of the loan.

The **amortization period** is the maximum length of time that money can be borrowed. A mortgage with an amortization period of 25 a is common.

Options for Repaying the Mortgage

1. The **term** of a mortgage is a period of time during which the interest rate payable on the amount borrowed is determined. The term of the mortgage could be as long as the amortization period, but because of fluctuating interest rates, it is often for a shorter period of time, ranging from six months to five years. The **due date** of the mortgage is at the end of the term.

2. The **interest rate** may be fixed for the term of the mortgage, or it may vary each year, or it may vary with each payment period depending upon the conditions set by the borrower and lender. After the term is up, a new interest rate can be set, or the borrower might pay off the mortgage entirely, or the loan might be renegotiated with a different lender.

3. In a "variable rate mortgage", the interest rate is set for a period of time, after which it may change based on the current market rates.

4. Nonblended payments consist of a payment on the principal plus a separate payment on the interest owed to that date. The interest is compounded usually on a monthly basis. Credit unions often use this method. **Blended payments** consist of a payment on the interest due plus a payment on the principal. In this case, the interest is compounded annually or semiannually.

5. A **fully open mortgage** is one which may be prepaid, either in full or in part, at any time without penalty to the borrower. A **closed mortgage** includes a penalty to the borrower for prepayment, but is usually at a lower interest rate than an open mortgage. In a closed mortgage, the interest rate and the amount of the regular payments may be altered only at the end of the term. If the borrower wishes to repay all or part of a closed mortgage prior to the end of the term, a **penalty**, usually of 3 months interest on the balance owing, is charged to the borrower.

6. Some mortgages have prepayment privileges, such as a "double up" payment (twice the scheduled payment) on the regular due date. Other options are to make payments on a weekly, as opposed to a monthly basis; or to pay a percentage of the outstanding balance on the anniversary date of the mortgage.

Example 1

A trust company offers a 3 a term mortgage amortized over 25 a at an annual interest rate of 10.25%, compounded semiannually.

a. When is the mortgage due?

b. What are the options available to the borrower at that time?

a. Although the amortization period is 25 a, the mortgage is due after 3 a.

b. The borrower has three options at the end of 3 a: i) the balance owing may be repaid in full; ii) the mortgage may be renewed; iii) the mortgage may be refinanced with a new lender and the original lender paid in full.

Example 2

Mr. Salinger wishes to prepay the balance of his mortgage. He negotiates with his local bank in Comox to pay the balance plus a three-month interest penalty. The interest rate on his mortgage is 12.75% and the balance owing is $9700. What amount is he required to pay?

The interest penalty on the balance owed is:

$$9700 \times \frac{3}{12} \times 0.1275 = 309.19$$

The amount payable is $9700.00 plus the interest penalty of $309.19, or $10 009.19.

Exercises

For the exercises, assume that the maximum that one can borrow is 40% of one's yearly income.

1. What is the maximum amount a person with an annual income of $15 790 could borrow to start a business?

2. Two college students have designed a computer game. They estimate that $4700 is needed to complete the programming and testing of the game. Is their total summer income of $10 350 sufficient to obtain a loan of $4700? Explain.

3. The terms of Carol's loan from the credit union require that she pay $50 on the first of each month plus the interest owed from the previous month. If the interest rate for January was 10.25%/a and her loan balance was $1350, what amount must Carol pay on February 1?

4. What factors might determine the type of mortgage suitable for a person?

5. Make a list of the mortgage lenders in your area. Check the newspapers for advertisements. The classified section may list private lenders.

6. Assemble the latest information about the options available for residential home mortgages from a variety of lending institutions. Summarize the options in a table showing prepayment privileges, terms of the mortgages, amortization periods, fixed versus variable interest rates, penalties for early repayment, and any other options.

7. Check the business pages in newspapers for the latest information about mortgage interest rates. Compare the rates and terms for different lenders, and the rates for open and closed mortgages. What is the penalty for prepayment of a closed mortgage?

8. In a "double up" mortgage, an extra payment can be made against the principal without penalty. Frank Lisky has a "double up" mortgage with monthly payments of $563.21. This year, Frank plans to make five "double up" payments. Without considering the interest saved, by how much will these extra payments reduce the principal?

9. The local bank in Rainy River offers these mortgages: a three-year, fully open mortgage at a rate of 13.5%/a, compounded semiannually; or a closed mortgage for six months at 12.75%/a. Discuss reasons that would affect your choice.

15·2 Mortgage and Loan Payments

For most people, the purchase of a car, land, or a house is a major transaction. If we do not have the total purchase price in cash, we might consider applying to a bank, trust company, private individual, or other lending institutions for a loan or mortgage for the balance owed. A common arrangement is to repay the debt with regular, monthly payments over a period of time. The interest rate usually is compounded semiannually. The amount of the monthly payments can be found by referring to a precalculated table, or by performing the calculations ourselves. An expanded version of this table is available at the back of the text.

MONTHLY PAYMENTS TO AMORTIZE A LOAN OF $10 000, COMPOUNDED SEMIANNUALLY									
Years	10%	11%	12%	13%	14%	15%	16%	17%	18%
1	878.22	882.68	887.13	891.58	896.03	900.47	904.90	909.33	913.76
2	460.52	464.95	469.38	473.83	478.28	482.74	487.20	491.68	496.15
3	321.72	326.23	330.76	335.31	339.88	344.46	349.06	353.68	358.32
4	252.66	257.27	261.92	266.60	271.30	276.04	280.80	285.60	290.42
5	211.48	216.21	220.98	225.80	230.66	235.55	240.49	245.46	250.47
6	184.24	189.09	194.00	198.96	203.97	209.02	214.13	219.28	224.47
7	164.97	169.94	174.98	180.08	185.24	190.46	195.73	201.06	206.44
8	150.67	155.77	160.94	166.18	171.49	176.87	182.31	187.81	193.37
9	139.69	144.91	150.21	155.60	161.05	166.58	172.18	177.85	183.58
10	131.03	136.37	141.80	147.32	152.92	158.60	164.36	170.19	176.08

In the table, find the row for the amortization period (1 a to 10 a) and then move to the right to locate the column for the appropriate interest rate (10% to 18%). The value in dollars and cents is the monthly payment per $10 000 of the loan. For example, a $10 000 loan amortized over 10 a with an interest rate of 17%/a requires a monthly payment of $170.19. In other words, monthly payments of $170.19 over 10 a are required to repay the amount, plus interest, on a loan of $10 000.

Example 1

Frederika Piper wishes to finance a new home computer system costing $8900. The local bank in Burnaby approves a loan for the total cost at an interest rate of 13%/a, amortized over a 5 a period.
a. What is the monthly payment?
b. What is the total amount paid over the 5 a period and how much of this is interest?

a. From the table, the monthly payment for a loan of $10 000 amortized over 5 a at 13%/a is $225.80. Since Frederika is borrowing only $8900, her monthly payment is found as follows.
$$\frac{8900}{10\ 000} \times 225.80 = 200.96$$
Frederika's monthly payment is $200.96.

b. The total amount paid over the 5 a is found by multiplying the number of years by the number of months in a year by the amount of the monthly payments.
$$5 \times 12 \times 200.96 = 12\ 057.60$$
The total amount paid over the 5 a period is $12 057.60.

432

To find the interest paid, subtract the principal of the loan from the total amount paid.

12 057.60 − 8900.00 = 3157.60

The interest on the loan is $3157.60.

Payments for periods less than one month are calculated as a fraction of the monthly payment. For example, the weekly payment for Example 1 may be calculated as the monthly payments over a year divided by the number of weeks in a year: ($200.96 × 12) ÷ 52 = $46.38.

Also, we can calculate the amount of a loan or mortgage payment by applying the appropriate formulas. First, it is necessary to compute the payment for the compound period: annual or semiannual. Then, the payment is divided into monthly compounded payments.

P(principal), i(annual interest rate), n(amortization period)

	Compounded Annually	Compounded Semiannually
Payment per Compound Period (R_c)	$R_c = P\left[\dfrac{1-(1+i)^{-n}}{i}\right]^{-1}$	$R_c = P\left[\dfrac{1-(1+0.5i)^{-2n}}{0.5i}\right]^{-1}$
Monthly Payment (R_m)	$R_m = R_c\left[\dfrac{\left(1+\frac{i}{12}\right)^{12}-1}{\frac{i}{12}}\right]^{-1}$	$R_m = R_c\left[\dfrac{\left(1+\frac{i}{12}\right)^{6}-1}{\frac{i}{12}}\right]^{-1}$

Example 2

At her local bank in Regina, Frances Kim arranged a $100 000 mortgage with a 5 a term at an annual interest rate of 10%, compounded semiannually. The amortization period was 25 a.

a. Calculate the semiannual payment.   **b.** Find her monthly payment.

a. If $P = 100\ 000$, $i = 0.10$, and $n = 25$, then the semiannual payment R_c is

$R_c = P\left[\dfrac{1-(1+0.5i)^{-2n}}{0.5i}\right]^{-1}$

$= 100\ 000\left[\dfrac{1-(1.05)^{-50}}{0.05}\right]^{-1}$

$= 5477.67$

Calculator Keying Sequence

1.05 $\boxed{y^x}$ 50 $\boxed{+/-}$ $\boxed{=}$ $\boxed{+/-}$ $\boxed{+}$ 1 $\boxed{=}$
$\boxed{\div}$ 0.05 $\boxed{=}$ $\boxed{1/x}$ $\boxed{\times}$ 100 000 $\boxed{=}$

The semiannual payment is approximately $5477.67.

b. The semiannual payment R_c (due six months from the date of the mortgage) is the future value of an annuity whose compound period is monthly. $\dfrac{i}{12} = \dfrac{0.10}{12}$ or about 0.0083.

$R_m = R_c\left[\dfrac{\left(1+\frac{i}{12}\right)^{6}-1}{\frac{i}{12}}\right]^{-1}$

$= 5477.67\left[\dfrac{(1.0083)^6-1}{0.0083}\right]^{-1}$

$\doteq 894.18$

Calculator Keying Sequence

1.0083 $\boxed{y^x}$ 6 $\boxed{=}$ $\boxed{-}$ 1 $\boxed{=}$ $\boxed{\div}$
0.0083 $\boxed{=}$ $\boxed{1/x}$ $\boxed{\times}$ 5477.67 $\boxed{=}$

The monthly payment is approximately $894.18.

Differences between amounts calculated using the formula and those found in the table are due to differences in rounding.

Exercises

1. In Example 1, part **a**, of the display, why is $8900 divided by $10 000?

2. In your own words, explain how the total amount of interest paid over the period of the loan in Example 1 of the display was found.

3. In Example 2 of the display, why is it necessary to calculate the semiannual payment first?

4. In Example 2 of the display, why do we not divide $5477.67 by 6 to obtain the monthly payment?

5. If the monthly payment on a loan of $1000 is $56.24, then what is the monthly payment of a loan of $5000 with the same interest rate and amortization period?

6. Find the monthly payment on a mortgage of $10 000 amortized over 7 a at each interest rate.
a. 10%   **b.** 13%   **c.** 18%

7. Determine the monthly payment on a mortgage of $60 000 at an interest rate of 15% for each amortization period.
a. 5 a   **b.** 18 a   **c.** 35 a

8. Increase each monthly payment in Exercise 7 by a maximum of 5%. What would be the new amortization period for each? (*Hint*: Use the table at the end of this book.)

9. Find the weekly payment for the given monthly mortgage payment.
a. $567.87   **b.** $1349.61   **c.** $7102.11

10. Calculate the twice-monthly payment for the given monthly payment.
a. $1324.65   **b.** $837.55   **c.** $668.40

11. Phyllis estimates that she can afford a maximum monthly mortgage payment of $750. What is the largest mortgage she could arrange, amortized over 10 a, if the current interest rate is 11%/a, compounded semiannually?

12. Given a loan of $10 000 amortized over 13 a at 12%/a, compounded semiannually, how many years can be cut from the amortization period by increasing the payment by $50 each month?

13. William Seahawk's part-time job gives him a take-home salary of $235 each week. He calculates that he can afford to pay 20% of this towards a car loan. The bank offers him an interest rate of 14%/a, compounded semiannually, and a maximum amortization period of 5 a. What is the most he can borrow for the car? Approximate your answer to the nearest $100.

14. Calculate the annual and the monthly payments on a $70 000 mortgage amortized over 15 a at an interest rate of 14%/a, compounded annually.

15. Compute the semiannual and the monthly payments on a $57 000 mortgage amortized over 20 a at 12.5%/a, compounded semiannually.

16. Does doubling the rate of interest cause the payment to be doubled? Explain your answer. Use examples to support your answer.

17. Does doubling the amortization period cut the interest rate in half? Explain your answer. Use examples to support your answer.

18. A mortgage of $23 500 has an interest rate of 14%/a, compounded semiannually, and is paid monthly. Assume that the rate of interest remains constant.
a. What is the total amount paid on this mortgage over a 25 a amortization period?
b. If the payments are increased by a maximum of $10 each month, then what would be the amortization period?
c. What would be the decrease in total interest paid if the payments were increased as in part **b**?

19. Write a short report discussing the advantages and disadvantages of amortizing a mortgage on a house for 20 a compared to 30 a.

15·3 Amortization of a Mortgage

We can determine the balance owing on a mortgage at any time from an **amortization table**. The table entries provide the portion of each payment assigned to the principal and to the interest.

We can calculate the amount of interest owing by applying the **Interest Factor Formula** to the outstanding balance. The formula is used only when payments are more frequent than the compound period; for example, when payments are monthly and the compound period is semiannual.

The interest rate for one month, when compounded for six months, must be equivalent to the semiannual interest rate. Let j and k represent the interest rate for one and six months, respectively. Then,

$$(1 + j)^6 = 1 + k$$
$$1 + j = (1 + k)^{\frac{1}{6}}$$
$$j = (1 + k)^{\frac{1}{6}} - 1$$

Remember.
$$(x^6)^{\frac{1}{6}} = x$$

	Interest Factor Formulas (i = annual rate of interest)	
	Compounded Semiannually	Compounded Annually
Monthly Payment	$(1 + 0.5i)^{\frac{1}{6}} - 1$	$(1 + i)^{\frac{1}{12}} - 1$

The calculation of interest by any other method is not permissible for blended payments since the principal is being reduced during the compounding period.

Example 1

A loan, compounded semiannually, at an interest rate of 14%/a is payable monthly. The amortization period is 10 a.
a. Calculate the interest factor.
b. Find the interest for one month on a balance of $65 900.
c. Prepare an amortization table for the first three payments if the monthly payment is $1007.74.

a. Use the Interest Factor Formula for semiannual compounding. $i = 14\%$
Interest Factor $= (1 + 0.5i)^{\frac{1}{6}} - 1$ Calculator Keying Sequence
$\qquad = (1.07)^{\frac{1}{6}} - 1$ $1.07 \boxed{y^x} \boxed{(} 1 \boxed{\div} 6 \boxed{)} \boxed{=} \boxed{-} 1$
$\qquad \doteq 0.011\ 340\ 26$
The interest factor is approximately 0.011 340 26.

b. The amount of the $1007.74 payment which is applied against interest is found as follows.
Interest Paid $=$ (Interest Factor) $\times$ (Balance)
$\qquad = 0.011\ 340\ 26 \times 65\ 900$
$\qquad \doteq 747.32$
The interest paid for one month on a balance of $65 900 at 14%/a, compounded semiannually, is approximately $747.32.

c. The amortization table for the first three payments is given below.

		AMORTIZATION TABLE			
Principal: $65 900.00			Rate of Interest: 14%/a		
Compound Period: semiannual			Amortization Period: 10 a		
Payment: $1007.74, monthly			Interest Factor: 0.011 340 26		
Payment Number	Balance Owing ($)	Total Payment ($)	Interest ($)	Amount on Principal ($)	New Balance ($)
0	65 900.00				
1	65 900.00	1007.74	747.32	260.42	65 639.58
2	65 639.58	1007.74	744.37	263.37	65 376.21
3	65 376.21	1007.74	741.38	266.36	65 109.85

Nonblended payments have the interest calculated on the balance and the number of days for which it has been outstanding. The rate of interest is determined monthly depending on the Bank of Canada rate.

Example 2

On March 1, Clovis borrowed $6000 from the Sydney Credit Union for a new car. The amortization period was one year. Monthly payments are $500 on the principal, plus the amount of interest owing on the outstanding balance. Prepare an amortization table for the first three payments. The interest rates for the first three months are: March—11.50%/a; April—12.00%/a, and May—11.75%/a.

Understand the Problem

The amount owing on the principal is reduced by $500 on the first of each month, beginning one month after the loan is obtained. The interest owed for the outstanding balance from the previous month is added to the $500 payment to obtain the total payment due.

Develop a Plan

The amortization table can be rearranged with the headings for Total Payment and Amount on Principal interchanged. Then calculate the interest for the number of days in the previous month using $I = prt$.

Carry Out the Plan

			AMORTIZATION TABLE		
Principal: $6000.00			Rate of Interest: varies		
Compound Period: monthly			Amortization Period: 1 a		
Payment: $500 + interest, monthly					
Date	Balance Owing ($)	Amount on Principal ($)	Interest ($)	Total Payment ($)	New Balance ($)
March 1	6000.00				
April 1	6000.00	500.00	$6000 \times 0.115 \times \frac{31}{365} = 58.60$	558.60	5500.00
May 1	5500.00	500.00	$5500 \times 0.1200 \times \frac{30}{365} = 54.25$	554.25	5000.00
June 1	5000.00	500.00	$5000 \times 0.1175 \times \frac{31}{365} = 49.90$	549.90	4500.00

Look Back

The total interest paid for any period of time also can be obtained from an amortization table. A computer program could be written to update the total with each calculation.

Exercises

1. Calculate the interest factor for each.

a. a $20 000 mortgage at 9.75%/a, compounded annually and payable monthly

b. a $500 000 mortgage at 10.25%/a, compounded annually and payable weekly

c. a $73 500 mortgage at 11%/a, compounded semiannually and payable monthly

d. a $112 500 mortgage at 8.5%/a, compounded semiannually and payable weekly

2. Calculate the interest payment for the given mortgage balance and the interest factor.

Balance	Interest Factor
a. $135 789	0.010 050
b. $210 000	0.001 832

3. Explain the conditions under which a large mortgage can have a smaller monthly payment than a smaller mortgage.

4. In your own words, explain how to calculate the interest payment given the following information.

a. the mortgage balance and the interest factor

b. the mortgage balance and the rate per annum, compounded annually and payable monthly

5. On starting his first job, Hans borrowed $4300 to finance a new car. The loan has an interest rate of 13%/a, compounded semiannually, and is paid monthly over 3 a. Provide an amortization table showing the first three payments on the loan.

6. Modify the Interest Factor Formula for a twice-monthly payment when the interest is compounded annually and semiannually.

7. The Niro family has arranged a mortgage of $66 000 amortized over 19 a, at 12%/a, compounded semiannually, and payable monthly. However, the terms of the mortgage allow them to double their payment each month. Assuming that they double their first five payments, prepare an amortization table to determine the balance owing after five months.

8. The Malkowskis purchased a house for $59 800, with a down payment of $20 000. They arranged to finance the balance owed with a mortgage amortized over 12 a at 11%/a, compounded semiannually. The local bank in Fredericton offered two payment plans: i) monthly payments; or ii) semiannual payments.

a. Draw up an amortization table for both plans for the first year.

b. Which plan might be preferable to the Malkowskis? Explain your answer.

9. Ken inherited a trust fund which guarantees to pay him $10 000 each month for the rest of his life. He decided he could afford to retire to Florida, and to buy a house on a canal, a houseboat, and a Ferrari. After down payments, he would owe $98 000 on the house, $16 000 on the houseboat, and $20 000 on the car. The local bank has offered him a loan at 10.5%/a, compounded semiannually. How should he arrange his loan to maintain a lifestyle costing $7500 each month? Will he have to use his capital from the trust fund if he wants to repay the loan within 10 a?

10. On August 1, a local bank in Smith Falls approved a mortgage of $45 000 to the Flamingo Golf Club for improvements to the club house. The payments were to be $3000, plus interest on the outstanding balance each month. The interest rates for August, September, October, and November were 13.0%/a, 12.5%/a, 12.0%/a, and 11.25%/a, respectively.

a. Prepare an amortization table showing payments for the first four months.

b. What balance is owing after ten months, assuming that all payments have been made on time?

Using the Library

Investigate the effects of high interest rates on the national economy by researching the period 1981-82, when the interest rates rose to 19.5%/a. Indicate the effects on homeowners renewing mortgages, construction companies, business in general, and banks and trust companies.

15·4 Savings as an Investment

Banks and trust companies offer a variety of savings accounts, ranging from daily interest to no-charge chequing. Some accounts have interest rates which are dependent on the balance and involve service charges which decrease the interest earned (especially some daily interest accounts). Others have free chequing privileges on accounts with a minimum balance.

A **daily interest** account is one in which interest is calculated on the minimum daily balance and the interest is credited to the account monthly. A **monthly interest** account is one in which interest is calculated on the minimum monthly balance and the interest is credited to the account twice a year on October 30 and April 30. A **term deposit** or **Guaranteed Investment Certificate** (G.I.C.) is an account in which money is invested for a given term. Money is "locked in" such an account in that, if the investor withdraws the money before the completion of the term, no interest is paid. Term deposits and investment certificates require a deposit of $500 or more; and funds must be on deposit for a minimum of thirty days in a term deposit, and for a minimum of one year in a G.I.C. Interest rates may vary according to the length of the term.

Example

On June 10, Mei-lee has $10 000 to invest for 1 a. The Northern Trust Company in Whitehorse offers a one year G.I.C. paying 9.75%/a, compounded semiannually. A local bank has a 180-270 d term deposit, paying 8.00%/a. The term deposit can be renewed for the balance of the year at an interest rate of 8.75%/a. The bank also offers a daily interest savings account paying a fixed rate of 3.50%/a, compounded monthly. Compare the interest paid by each type of account over the 1 a period.

The amount Mei-lee would have after 1 a if she invests in the G.I.C. is calculated as follows.

$$A = P(1 + i)^n$$
$$= 10\ 000(1.048\ 75)^2$$
$$= 10\ 000(1.099\ 876\ 56)$$
$$= 10\ 998.77$$

P (Principal) = 10 000
i (interest rate per period) = 0.048 75
n (number of interest periods) = 2

Mei-lee would have $10 998.77 at the end of 1 a if she invests in the G.I.C.

If she invests in the term deposit, the amount at the end of the first 180 d period is as follows.

$$I = prt$$
$$= 10\ 000 \times 0.08 \times \frac{180}{365}$$
$$= 394.52$$

For the balance of the year, $365 - 180 = 185$, she would have $10\ 000 + 394.52 = 10\ 394.52$ to invest at 8.75%/a.

$$I = prt$$
$$= 10\ 394.52 \times 0.0875 \times \frac{185}{365}$$
$$= 460.99$$

After 365 d she would have $10 394.52 + $460.99, or $10 855.51, if she invests in the term deposits.

If she invests in the daily interest account, the amount after 1 a can be approximated as follows.

$$A = P(1 + i)^n$$
$$= 10\ 000(1 + 0.002\ 917)^{12}$$
$$= 10\ 355.71$$

$$i = \frac{0.035}{12}$$
$$= 0.002\ 917$$
$$n = 12$$

Mei-lee would have approximately \$10 355.71 at the end of 1 a if she invests in the daily interest account. To find the exact amount, the interest would have to be calculated for each month separately; for example, for the 20 d remaining in June, the 31 d in July, and so on, compounding it each month.

Exercises

1. Calculate the exact interest on the daily interest account in the example in the display.

2. Under what circumstances is a daily interest account preferable? a term deposit? a G.I.C.?

3. Calculate the interest payable on these savings accounts for the month of July.
a. a monthly account with a minimum balance of \$5700 and a rate of 6.5%/a
b. a daily interest account with a balance of \$5700 and a rate of 5%/a

4. Find the amount of the investment on maturity (at the end of the term).
a. a two year G.I.C. for \$5000 at 10%/a, compounded annually
b. a 179 d term deposit for \$5000 at 9.5%/a, renewed for 4 consecutive terms of 179 d at 9.75%/a, 9.25%/a, 8.50%/a, and 9.00%/a
c. Explain which investment you would choose.

5. Chloe plans to open a savings account on August 15 with a deposit of \$150. How much interest would she earn in each case for the month of August?
a. The account is a daily interest account paying 3.5%/a compounded monthly.
b. Interest is paid on the minimum monthly balance at 5%/a.
c. Explain which account she might choose.

6. Mr. Johanssen has \$25 000 to invest for a period not to exceed 6 months. Which of these plans will provide the greatest return?
a. a savings account paying 6.75%/a, compounded monthly
b. a 120-179 d term deposit paying 7.25%/a

7. Anna has received an inheritance of \$100 000. She will use the inheritance to purchase a house with a closing date (the date she must pay for the house) in three months. In the meantime, what is her best option for investing the money?
a. a daily interest account paying 6.25%/a, compounded monthly
b. a 60-89 d term deposit paying 7.00%/a
c. a regular savings account paying 7.50%/a

8. What type of account would be best for a person who is unsure as to when it might be necessary to withdraw the money? Explain your answer.

9. Since 1981, Michael has kept \$10 000 in \$100 bills hidden in a shoe box. Due to inflation, the buying power of \$100 has dropped to about \$70. Suggest ways that Michael could have maintained or increased the buying power of this money.

10. Obtain information from banks and trust companies on various types of savings accounts. Compare the interest rates, service charges, minimum balance requirements, and any other features. List the advantages and disadvantages of each type of account.

11. Use newspapers to find current interest rates payable on term deposits and G.I.C.'s. Use this information to determine the best return on \$1000 for each time period.
a. one month
b. two months
c. one year
d. two years
e. five years
f. ninety days

15·5 The Stock Market

Many companies issue stock, or shares in the company, to raise money from investors. A stock market is used by companies, investors, and stockbrokers to buy, sell, and trade shares. In Canada, the markets are the Toronto (TSE), Montreal (MSE), Alberta (ASE), and Vancouver (VSE) Stock Exchanges.

When purchasing shares in a company, one buys part ownership of the company. There are two types of shares: preferred and common. **Preferred shares** have a fixed rate of return on their **par** or initial value. For example, the Hudson's Bay Company issued 10 000 000 preferred shares with a par value of $25 and an annual return of 7.5%/a. Holders of these shares are paid before holders of common shares, and do not have voting privileges at the annual shareholders' meeting. Preferred shares usually offer good security with moderate **dividends** or return on the investment during a twelve-month period. On the other hand, the price of **common shares** is set by whatever people are willing to pay—this is the **market value** of the common share. The holder of common shares may receive dividends from the company after all other expenses have been met, and ownership typically entitles the shareholder to vote at the annual meeting. An individual may also profit through **capital gains** on the value of the shares one owns—a capital gain (or loss) is an increase (or decrease) in the market value of the share.

$250 000 000

Hudson's Bay Company

Convertible Preferred Shares Series H

Price: $25 per share to yield 7.50% per annum

Individuals must be willing to assume a certain amount of **risk** when purchasing shares. If the company does not make a profit, no dividends may be paid; if the market price of the shares decreases, the shareholder will not be able to sell the shares at the original purchase price; and if the company goes bankrupt, the shares lose all value. High risk is associated usually with new companies producing unproven products or with natural resource, exploration companies such as oil or mining. Typically, high-risk companies must offer high returns or dividends to attract investors. A lower level of risk is associated with long-standing companies producing proven products, or with banks and utilities having a long record of success and a constant or growing demand for their services. Low-risk companies are sometimes referred to as "blue chip" companies and they typically are able to attract investment with lower dividend levels.

An individual can minimize risk by doing research into areas of a company's background, such as its past performance, its history of dividend payments, and by forecasting the future demand for the company's products. Another method of evaluating a company for investment is to determine the ratio of price per share versus earnings (total income) per share (P/E). Companies which have P/E ratios of between 20:1 to 12:1 are usually considered safe investments. Those with ratios as low as 6:1 are excellent investments.

LOWEST PRICE-EARNINGS RATIOS	
(1986 ESTIMATES)	
Canadian Imperial Bank of Commerce	6:1
ATCO	6:2
Royal Bank of Canada	6:5
Bank of Nova Scotia	6:5
National Bank of Canada	6:7
Meridian Technologies	6:7
Bank of Montreal	6:9

Example 1

A rumour of a new product breakthrough causes the price of a company's shares to rise from $3.50 to $61.00 on the stock market. The company had 3 300 000 shares outstanding, but the earnings were only $114 164.

a. Calculate the earnings per share.

Earnings ÷ number of shares = earning per share

114 164 ÷ 3 300 000 = $0.0346

The earnings per share is $0.0346.

b. Calculate the *P/E* ratio.

Price per share ÷ earnings per share = *P/E*

61.00 ÷ 0.0346 = 1763

The *P/E* ratio is 1763.

The dividend is the amount paid to a shareholder per share owned for a twelve-month period. The **dividend yield** is the dividend per share divided by the share price. It is usually expressed as a percent.

Example 2

A fish processing company in St. John's has 125 000 shares outstanding and a total of $118 750 in dividends is paid to the shareholders. The average price per share during the year was $10.25.

a. Find the dividend paid per share.

118 750 ÷ 125 000 = 0.95

The dividend paid is $0.95 per share.

b. Find the yield per share.

$$\text{yield} = \frac{\text{dividend}}{\text{share price}} \times 100$$

$$= \frac{0.95}{10.25} \times 100$$

$$= 9.27$$

The yield is approximately 9.27%.

Exercises

Refer to the examples in the display to answer Exercises 1 through 6.

1. How much capital (money) was raised by the Hudson's Bay Company in the sale of 10 000 000 preferred shares?

2. What is the annual dividend on one preferred share of the Hudson's Bay Company?

3. What are two advantages of preferred over common shares?

4. List three factors which might affect your decision whether to buy shares.

5. Would the shares in the company of Example 1 in the display be considered high or low risk? Explain.

6. Which Canadian bank had the best *P/E* ratio in the 1986 estimates? Does that factor alone make those shares the best in which to invest?

7. Calculate the *P/E* ratio.
a. a share costing $47.50, paying 5%/a
b. a share costing $13.75, paying $1.25/share

8. Sal inherited these shares from her grandmother. Calculate the dividend from each.
a. 1000 preferred shares at 7.50%/a of Paper Unlimited with a par value of $50.00
b. 500 preferred shares at 8.625%/a of SEDCO with a par value of $10.00

9. Calculate the yield of these shares.
a. McDoug shares selling for $9.375/share paying $0.215/share
b. Hacker shares selling for $27.75/share paying $3.84/share

Using the Library

Research and write a short essay on one of these topics: selling short, penny stocks, blue chip stocks, capital gains on common stock versus dividend income from preferred stock, or choosing stock with the best potential.

15·6 The Stock Market Report

After each business day, newspapers report the volume of trading and the prices for shares listed on local stock exchanges. One line from such a report is shown below.

				Last			52 weeks	
Stock	**Div**	**High**	**Low**	**Price**	**Ch'ge**	**Vol**	**High**	**Low**
Algoma	2.00	\$19	$18\frac{3}{4}$	$18\frac{3}{4}$	$-\frac{1}{4}$	850	19	10

The company name is listed first (Algoma) in the stock market report. The dividend declared, if any, is given next. The highest price for Algoma shares traded during the day is given as \$19/share, and the lowest price for the day is given as $18\frac{3}{4}$ or \$18.75/share. The closing (last) price per share at the end of the business day is the same as the lowest price for that day. Today's closing price over the closing price of the last business day (Ch'ge) is shown to have decreased by one quarter of a dollar. The volume (Vol) is the total number of shares traded for the day. The highest and lowest prices at which the company's shares have traded in the last 52 weeks is indicated at the far right.

Shares can be purchased through a stockbroker who charges a commission or fee based on the size of the transaction. In purchasing shares, a buyer may choose to operate a cash account or a margin account. A **cash account** requires full payment for any purchases; while a **margin account** requires only partial payment with the balance borrowed from the stockbroker.

The format of stock market reports vary with the exchange.

Toronto Stock Exchange

				Last			52 weeks	
Stock	**Div**	**High**	**Low**	**Price**	**Chge**	**Vol**	**High**	**Low**
Banister C		\$12¾	12⅝	12⅝	−⅛	1400	13½	7¼
Bk Alberta		\$6¼	6¼	6¼		200	8	6
Bank BC		56	56	56		15032	365	55
Bk BC 228	2.28	\$22⅞	22½	22⅞	+⅞	400	24⅞	21
Bk BC 222	2.22	\$22⅜	22⅛	22¼		1300	25⅛	20⅛
Bank Mtl	2.00	\$34⅛	33⅞	33⅞		21291	39¼	29⅞
Bk Mtl 250	2.50	\$27	26⅞	26⅞		1582	28½	26¼
Bk Mtl 3p	2.12	\$26⅛	26	26⅛	+⅛	1950	27⅜	25⅞
Bk Mtl w		\$5¼	5	5⅛	+⅛	28800	8¼	400
Bank N S	.72	\$18¼	18	18	−⅛	107326	21⅝	15
Bk N S 1p	1.61	\$23¾	23¾	23¾		3700	26⅝	22⅞
Bankeno o		320	310	310	−20	1000	5	100
Barons Oil		405	400	400	−5	8300	420	280
Barincor f	.16	\$8¼	8¼	8¼	+⅜	900	8¾	6⅞
Barincor w		160	150	160	+15	5300	200	85
Bathrst p	1.05	\$13¾	13¾	13¾	+½	400	14	12¼
Baton	.20	\$12¾	12⅝	12¾	+⅛	9900	14⅛	9¾
Battle MA	.10	\$50⅝	48⅞	50½	+1½	25000	59	16¾
Bay Mills	.12	\$12¾	12⅝	12¾	+⅛	9200	12¾	7⅞
Beau CA o		90	87	87	−3	9600	145	20
Beaufield o		130	127	127	−3	8824	185	100
Beaver R o		405	385	395	+10	94500	450	275
Becker B f	.75	\$40	41	43		nt	48⅛	41

Vancouver Stock Exchange

Complete tabulation of Wednesday transactions. Quotations in cents unless marked \$. q—Restricted, Subordinate, or Non-voting shares, i—Development stocks, z—Odd lot. Net change is from previous close of same lot type.

Stock	**Sales**	**High**	**Low**	**Close**	**Net Ch'ge**
Aabco oil	10000	48	45	45	−3
Aby inv a i	4000	11	11	11	
Abc tech	13300	180	171	180	
Aber res i	59520	310	270	290	−20
Abo res	20500	85	81	85	
Absorptve i	1100	296	290	290	−10
Access tc i	29000	90	90	90	
Achates rs i	1500	60	60	60	+5
Acheron	3125	21	21	21	−1
Achilles i	3000	42	42	42	
Acquest i	6000	37	37	37	
Acquisitor i	9900	\$6¾	6⅝	6¾	+¼
Acu sys i	24700	275	265	270	+10
Ad com i	8500	23	22	22	
Ad dome i	1000	25	25	25	
Adams ex i	7000	47	45	45	−2
Adola i	21500	16	16	16	
Adriatic rs i	4500	52	50	50	

Alberta Stock Exchange

Complete tabulation of Wednesday transactions. Quotations in cents unless marked \$. Net change is from previous close of same lot type.

Stock	**Sales**	**High**	**Low**	**Close**	**Net Ch'ge**
Aaron	2000	20	20	20	
Accord	3000	250	230	230	−20
Adv sprt	4000	20	20	20	
Aladin	200	\$5	5	5	
Alta res	3000	215	200	215	+15
Albury	600	80	80	80	+5
Aldrsht	11000	60	52	52	
Alert a	1500	55	51	51	
Alta mira	13000	22	22	22	
Alta pac	6000	35	33	33	
Alterio	2000	55	55	55	
Amaril	3000	30	30	30	+10
Am chr b	10000	36	35	35	−1
Amer env	1500	130	123	123	−17
Amr ore	60800	61	55	58	+6
Amuse int	2000	30	30	30	
Anadm	113000	50	50	50	
Anglo	1000	70	70	70	
Anyox	22300	150	145	145	
Argus	21000	46	45	45	

Exercises

1. Use the Toronto Stock Exchange report to answer the following.

a. How many Bk Alberta shares were traded?

b. What was the high for Bankeno o?

c. What was the low for Banister C?

d. What was the closing price for Barons Oil?

e. What was the change for Bay Mills?

f. What was the 52 week high for Baton?

g. What was the 52 week low for Beau CA o?

2. Use the Toronto Stock Exchange report to answer the following.
a. What stock showed the largest gain? the largest loss?
b. How much would it cost to buy 500 shares of Bk Mtl 3p at the lowest trading price during the day?
c. How much would it cost to buy 800 shares of Battle MA at the highest trading price?

3. Use the Vancouver and Alberta Stock Exchange reports to answer the following.
a. Three quotations are underlined in each report. Explain all the information underlined.
b. The closing price for Abo res one month ago was $0.77. How has the current closing price changed as compared to one month ago?
c. Use a newspaper to compare the current report for the VSE and ASE with those quotations shown. Which companies are still listed? How have the share prices changed?

4. A.T., "the Mathematics Wizard", claimed that you should never invest in the stock market unless you can afford to lose your investment. Comment on this claim.

Use any current stock market report for three consecutive days to answer Exercises 5 to 8.

5. Choose the fourth company listed under the "B's". What is the closing price for the company's shares on the third day?

6. Which companies listed under the "B's" showed the greatest increase in share price from day 2 to day 3? Which showed the greatest decrease?

7. What was the highest share price for the first company listed on day 1?

8. Find the fifth company listed under the "B's".
a. If you bought 350 shares of that company at the lowest price on day 1, how much would the shares cost?
b. If your stockbroker charged 3.5% of the purchase price as commission, what is your total cost?

Use the current listing for three consecutive days from the TSE to answer Exercises 9 to 12.

9. How much did Mr. Ho pay for 1000 shares of Dylex Ltd if he bought them at the closing price on the day 2 quotation?

10. Ms. Waleski bought 50 shares of Midland Doherty at the lowest price on day 2. Mr. Gucci bought 100 shares of Inter-City Gas at the closing price on day 1. Who paid more and how much more?

11. Mrs. Loney bought 875 shares of Domtar at its lowest price on day 3.
a. What is the lowest price at which she could have bought the shares?
b. If her broker charged $0.20/share, what was the total cost?

12. Which of the companies listed in the "B's" had the greatest change in stock price on day 2?

13. Find out what "volume trading" means and how it is done.

14. Use a recent copy of the Financial Times or the Financial Post to find an example of how such factors as a change in interest rates, a new federal budget, or an election can effect share prices.

15. Investigate to find the advantages and disadvantages of having a cash account versus a margin account with a stockbroker.

Using the Library

Research and write a short essay on one of the following topics: the 1929 stock market collapse, the possible effect of a merger between two companies on the value of their shares, or the effect of changes in interest rates on the prices of shares.

15·7 Interpreting the Stock Market Reports

When buying some stock, there are several things you might do to help predict the Market. The first thing to do is to get several daily newspapers or financial papers which list the averages that serve as barometers of the business in addition to the stock market quotations illustrated in the previous section. Each average indicates the average movement on the exchange to which it refers. The Dow-Jones Index is an American index. In Canada each stock exchange produces its own index. The Toronto Stock Exchange (TSE), being one of the largest in Canada, is of most significance. By studying the TSE index, we notice that averages in late December were up (from 183 to 184) compared to the previous year (173.01) and a little under the high of the previous year (188.94).

TORONTO STOCK EXCHANGE INDEX					MONTREAL STOCK EXCHANGE INDEX				
	153	12	29	19		65	13	7	8	85
	Ind.	Golds	B.M.	W.O.		Ind.	Util.	Banks	Papers	Comp.
Dec. 27 ..	HOLIDAY				Dec. 27 ..	HOLIDAY				
Dec. 24 ..	183.50	143.40	77.20	217.26	Dec. 24 ..	188.09	157.34	231.24	81.05	187.03
Dec. 23 ..	183.06	143.46	77.10	217.80	Dec. 23 ..	188.25	156.98	231.57	81.07	187.10
Dec. 22 ..	184.12	143.50	76.96	219.66	Dec. 22 ..	188.94	157.13	233.80	81.02	187.83
Dec. 21 ..	183.76	143.07	76.51	220.25	Dec. 21 ..	188.86	156.97	236.04	80.99	187.96
Mo. Ago .	165.58	152.50	70.23	194.76	Mo. Ago .	169.00	145.07	211.31	68.49	169.15
Yr. Ago ..	173.01	161.42	89.32	197.54	Yr. Ago ..	175.85	151.86	176.21	91.30	171.93
1986 High	188.94	202.66	103.01	242.60	1986 High	188.94	161.39	236.04	95.35	187.96
1986 Low	158.33	132.40	67.86	180.30	1986 Low	162.59	142.11	172.04	64.73	163.80

Financial papers help make the interpretation of stock market reports easier by presenting data in graph form. Consider the graphs of the data shown in the TSE Index.

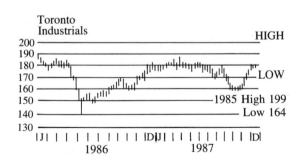

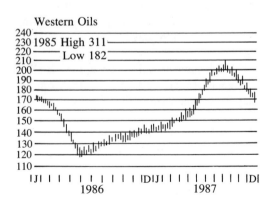

When buying or selling stock, your agent, or stockbroker, will charge a **brokerage fee** (commission) according to some scale or schedule. Two charts representative of the schedules are shown.

Exercises

1. Find the commission that must be paid on each purchase.

a. 200 shares at $9.75/share

b. 350 shares at $22.36/share

c. 50 shares at $190.40/share

2. Mr. Wheatly sold and bought the following stock in one day.

Sold: 200 shares—Algoma St at $18\frac{3}{4}$

150 shares—Bestar at $5\frac{1}{8}$

200 shares—Excel W at $33

Bought: 100 Mitel Corp at $6\frac{1}{2}$

50 Coho A at $210

Calculate the excess or amount he had to pay.

3. Discuss each in small groups and prepare a report on the conclusions reached by your group. Present the reports to the whole class and compare your conclusions with those of other groups.

a. Do you agree graphs are easier to interpret than the figures in a chart? Give examples.

b. Do you think there is a time of the year that is best for selling on the TSE? for buying?

c. What do you think happened to stock prices in January 1986?

d. What trend started in the latter part of 1987 with reference to Western Oil?

4. From newspapers collect as many articles as you can in one week that would indicate trends in stocks.

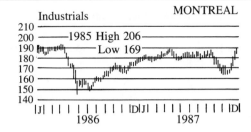

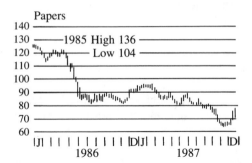

5. Discuss each in small groups and prepare a report on the conclusions reached by your group. Present the reports to the whole class and compare your conclusions with those of other groups.

a. Do the TSE and MSE reflect the same trends in Industrials? Explain.

b. If you bought into paper stock in 1986, what would you do now?

c. What do you think caused a drop in trading volumes of Industrials in the fall of 1987?

d. Describe what happened in the prices of Papers in 1986 and 1987.

e. Generally, which of the stocks shown would be the best to buy into in 1988? to sell (if you held any) for a quick profit in 1988?

15·8 The Financial Report

Companies listed on a stock exchange publish annual, and sometimes quarterly, financial reports for their stockholders. The third quarter financial report for Scotiabank on the following page was published in the local newspapers. The terms used in financial reports vary according to the type of business in which the companies are engaged.

Exercises

Use the third quarter financial report from Scotiabank to answer Exercises 1 to 11.

1. What is meant by "total assets"?

2. What is the value of the cash resources (assets) on July 31, 1986?

3. What is the value of "other" assets on July 31, 1985?

4. What is meant by "total liabilities, capital, and reserves"?

5. What was the average number of common shares for the three months ended July 31, 1986?

6. What was the value of the provision for loan losses for the nine months ended July 31, 1985? July 31, 1986?

7. What was the value of the total non-interest expenses for the nine months ended July 31, 1985? July 31, 1986?

8. What was the net income for the three months ended July 31, 1985?

9. What was the net income per common share for the three months ended July 31, 1986?

10. What was the value of common dividends paid for the nine months ended July 31, 1985?

11. Explain the difference between the net income available to common shareholders and common dividends paid.

12. Use a textbook on finance or financial accounting to investigate the difference between the following.
a. income and expenses
b. assets and liabilities
c. accounts payable and accounts receivable
d. a balance sheet and a statement of income
e. stocks and bonds

13. Do research on two major corporations listed on a Canadian stock exchange. Obtain their annual reports and use current stock market listings from a newspaper. Compare the value of the following for the companies.
a. assets
b. liabilities
c. capital surplus
d. retained earnings
e. net income
f. earnings per common share
g. the current closing price per common share

Historical Note

Ellen L. Fairclough (1905-   )
Born in Hamilton, Ontario, in 1905, Fairclough was a chartered accountant and owner of a Hamilton accounting firm. She was elected to Parliament and became the first woman federal Cabinet minister, as Secretary of State, in 1957. She introduced a bill requiring equal pay for equal work and advocated equal opportunity in the work place for both men and women.

Write to the provincial Ministry of Labour to obtain information on wages and salaries. Do the statistics indicate that progress is being made in such issues as equal pay for equal work?

Scotiabank
THE BANK OF NOVA SCOTIA

Third Quarter Financial Report

Interim Consolidated Statement of Income

(Unaudited)
(in $ thousands)

	For the three months ended July 31		For the nine months ended July 31	
	1986	1985	**1986**	1985
Interest income				
Income from loans, excluding leases	**$ 1 079 881**	$ 1 079 133	**$ 3 334 226**	$ 3 283 758
Income from lease financing	**4 866**	3 873	**14 514**	12 418
Income from securities	**132 806**	107 252	**369 996**	320 374
Income from deposits with banks	**176 609**	239 864	**561 167**	793 674
Total interest income, including dividends	**1 394 162**	1 430 122	**4 279 903**	4 410 224
Interest expense				
Interest on deposits	**956 338**	1 036 831	**3 009 489**	3 272 712
Interest on bank debentures	**15 581**	16 310	**59 639**	52 196
Interest on liabilities other than deposits	**4 538**	949	**8 903**	3 207
Total interest expense	**976 457**	1 054 090	**3 078 031**	3 328 115
Net interest income	**417 705**	376 032	**1 201 872**	1 082 109
Provision for loan losses	**104 000**	79 200	**306 300**	224 200
Net interest income after loan loss provision	**313 705**	296 832	**895 572**	857 909
Other income	**115 227**	91 438	**319 444**	259 876
Net interest and other income	**428 932**	388 270	**1 215 016**	1 117 785
Non-interest expenses				
Salaries	**165 448**	150 848	**478 663**	439 048
Pension contributions and other staff benefits	**15 999**	13 320	**43 886**	39 433
Premises and equipment expenses, including depreciation	**56 410**	51 611	**166 284**	152 238
Other expenses	**57 141**	54 600	**169 192**	158 830
Total non-interest expenses	**294 998**	270 379	**858 025**	789 549
Net income before provision for income taxes	**133 934**	117 891	**356 991**	328 236
Provision for income taxes	**50 500**	41 400	**118 400**	108 900
Net income before minority interests in subsidiaries	**83 434**	76 491	**238 591**	219 336
Minority interests in subsidiaries	**1 119**	380	**2 480**	1 589
Net income for the period	**$ 82 315**	$ 76 111	**$ 236 111**	$ 217 747
Preferred dividends paid	**$ 6 584**	$ 5 944	**$ 20 003**	$ 16 255
Net income available to common shareholders	**$ 75 731**	$ 70 167	**$ 216 108**	$ 201 492
Average number of common shares outstanding	**161 873 088**	146 352 659	**154 124 871**	145 640 050
Net income per common share: Basic	**$ 0.46**	$ 0.47	**$ 1.40**	$ 1.38
Fully diluted	**$ 0.46**	$ 0.45	**$ 1.36**	$ 1.31
Common dividends paid	**$ 27 513**	$ 24 849	**$ 77 846**	$ 74 192
Dividends per common share	**$ 0.17**	$ 0.17	**$ 0.51**	$ 0.51

Consolidated Balance Sheet Highlights

(Unaudited)
(in $ millions)

As at July 31

	1986	1985
Cash resources	**$ 9 372**	$ 11 028
Securities	**5 165**	4 254
Loans	**42 572**	39 074
Other assets	**4 684**	3 710
Total assets	**$ 61 793**	$ 58 066
Demand deposits	**$ 3 245**	$ 3 285
Notice deposits	**11 798**	11 086
Fixed-term deposits	**37 593**	36 714
Total deposits	**52 636**	51 085
Other liabilities	**5 443**	3 762
Subordinated debentures	**750**	686
Capital and reserves		
— preferred	**350**	350
— common	**2 614**	2 183
Total liabilities, capital and reserves	**$ 61 793**	$ 58 066

15·9 Investing in Gold and Silver

Because of its properties, gold is a commodity that has always been in demand. Traditionally, investors have purchased gold in times of high inflation because its value tends to rise as fast, or faster, than the rate of inflation. In the past, silver has been used in the same way, but recent discoveries in metallurgy have provided alternatives to its use and its price has fallen or remained steady. There are several ways of investing in precious metals. An investor might buy bullion in the form of bars or wafers, bullion coins, Precious Metal Certificates, or futures and options contracts.

Current prices for precious metals are listed on the financial pages of newspapers. An article in the April, 1986, issue of Canadian Consumer by Hermine G. Baylen discusses the risks involved in such investments.

Exercises

Use the library or materials provided by a brokerage firm that deals in commodities to answer the following. Obtain information on the types of gold and silver investments, selling and buying prices, service fees and commissions, storage and insurance fees, and the forms of payment.

1. What is meant by bullion, bullion coins, and Precious Metal Certificates?

2. What is the unit for measuring precious metals?

3. What are the standard sizes of gold and silver bars?

4. What are the risks in investing in gold bars, coins, or certificates?

5. What is meant by an "assay" of the metal content in a gold bar?

6. What is meant by the "premium" on a gold coin and by the "bar charge" on bullion?

7. What is meant by the "spread" when buying or selling precious metals?

8. What countries produce gold coins and in what sizes are they produced?

9. Assume that the rate of inflation has been 4%/a. The price of gold in February, 1987, was $540 per troy ounce. Compare this with the current price. At what price should gold now sell to have kept pace with inflation?

10. Al bought 100 troy ounces of gold at $630 and sold it 2 a later at $685. Would he have made a greater profit if he had invested the money at 8%/a, compounded annually? Explain.

11. List the advantages and disadvantages of investing in gold coins, bullion, and in gold futures.

12. What is the difference between a futures contract and an options contract?

13. What are the risks in buying futures contracts? Compare these to the risks in buying options contracts.

14. How does the premium on gold coins compare with the bar charge on gold bars on a per ounce basis? As a broker, which of these would you advise a client to buy? Explain.

15. Ms. Mayo paid $1500 towards an option contract to purchase twenty 200 ounce silver contracts at $8.32/ounce. On the due date of the contract, the market price had fallen to $7.15/ounce. Should Ms. Mayo let the option lapse? Explain.

16. On May 22, Mr. Lee purchased ten 20 ounce gold contracts at $484.93/ounce for delivery in December of that year. He made a $20 000 deposit on the contract. Two weeks before delivery, he sold 5 contracts at $535.24/ounce. On the due date, Mr. Lee took delivery of the gold and promptly sold it through a broker for $588.35/ounce. What was his profit on these transactions?

15·10 Computer Application— Mortgages

One practical use of home computers can be to calculate monthly mortgage payments and compare various options. The first program calculates the interest factor; the second, monthly payments.

Use these programs to solve Exercises 7 and 8 from Section 15·2, and Exercise 1 from Section 15·3. Compare these answers to those you obtained earlier and account for any discrepancies.

```
10   REM INTEREST FACTOR
20   INPUT "THE ANNUAL RATE OF INTEREST (%) IS "; I
30   I = I / 100
40   INPUT "COMPOUNDED ANNUAL (A) OR SEMIANNUAL (S)"; CP$
50   INPUT "PAYMENTS MONTHLY (M) OR WEEKLY (W)"; P$
60   GOSUB 1010
70   PRINT "THE INTEREST FACTOR IS "; FACT
80   END
1010  IF CP$ <> "S" THEN 1060
1020  Z = 1 + 0.5 * I
1030  IF P$ <> "M" THEN 1050
1040  FACT = Z ^ (1 / 6) - 1: RETURN
1050  FACT = Z ^ (1 / 26) - 1: RETURN
1060  Z = 1 + I
1070  IF P$ <> "M" THEN 1090
1080  FACT = Z ^ (1 / 12) - 1: RETURN
1090  FACT = Z ^ (1 / 52) - 1: RETURN
```

```
10   REM MONTHLY PAYMENT
20   INPUT "ANNUAL RATE OF INTEREST (%) IS "; I
30   I = I / 100
40   INPUT "COMPOUNDED ANNUAL (A) OR SEMIANNUAL (S)"; CP$
50   INPUT "AMOUNT OF MORTGAGE IS "; P
60   INPUT "AMORTIZATION PERIOD (YEARS) IS "; N
70   IF CP$ <> "S" THEN 120
80   A = ((1 - (1 + 0.5 * I) ^ (-2 * N)) / ^ (0.5 * I)) ^ -1
90   RC = P * A
100  B = (I / 12) / (((1 + I / 12) ^ 6) - 1)
110  RM = RC * B: GOTO 160
120  A = 1 - (1 / (1 + I)) ^ N
130  RC = P * I / A
140  B = (1 + I / 12) ^ 12 - 1
150  RM = RC * I / 12 / B
160  PRINT "THE MONTHLY PAYMENT IS "; RM
170  END
```

15·11 Chapter Review

1. What is the amortization period of a mortgage?

2. Why can we not use one twelfth of the annual interest rate to calculate the monthly interest on a mortgage rate that is compounded semiannually?

3. What is the advantage in making extra payments on the principal of a mortgage?

4. Use the table at the back of the text to calculate the monthly payments. The interest is compounded semiannually.
a. $50 000 at 18%/a amortized over 8 a
b. $73 400 at 11%/a amortized over 23 a

5. Calculate the amount of the monthly payment on each mortgage.
a. a $35 700 mortgage at 11.50%/a amortized over 25 a, compounded semiannually
b. a $47 890 mortgage at 10.75%/a amortized over 15 a, compounded annually

6. Calculate the interest factor for each mortgage in Exercise 5.

7. Mr. Sehdeu wants to use a one-year amortization table so that he might decide on various options. His mortgage will be for $100 000 amortized over 20 a at 12%/a, compounded semiannually.
a. Prepare an amortization table for 1 a using the chart at the back of the text to calculate the monthly payment.
b. How much interest was paid for the year?

8. Stephanie keeps $100 bills in a metal safe for emergencies. Over 3 a, she has accumulated $3600 at the rate of $100/month. A savings account would have paid 4.5%/a, compounded semiannually; a term deposit would have paid 6.75%/a, compounded monthly; and a G.I.C. would have paid 7.25%/a, compounded annually. Due to inflation, the value of the cash dropped by 4%/a over the three years. Suggest a better strategy for Stephanie to have followed as she accumulated these funds.

9. Mr. Sehdeu considers doubling each payment for the first year (see Exercise 7). Alter the amortization table accordingly.
a. Has the total interest paid changed?
b. How much more would be paid on the mortgage by doubling each payment?
c. How much interest has been saved?

10. Inge purchased a 5 a G.I.C. for $13 500 that paid 12.5%/a, compounded annually. What is the value of the certificate after 5 a?

11. Ms. Blaut purchased 1000 ounces of gold for $850.00/ounce in 1980. As the price began to fall, she sold 500 ounces for $710.00/ounce. When she felt that the price had "bottomed out", she purchased 500 ounces at $270.00/ounce. By February 23, 1987, the price was $403.00/ounce.
a. Did Ms. Blaut reach a breakeven point on her investments by early 1987?
b. Would an investment in a savings account paying 6.50%/a, compounded semiannually, have paid a better return? Explain.

12. Explain the difference between preferred and common shares.

13. How can an investor reduce the risk involved in buying stocks?

14. Corporation B has a P/E ratio of 12.4:1, but its earnings per share have doubled since that was calculated and the price per share has increased by 50%. What is the actual P/E ratio? Would you consider this stock as an investment? Explain.

15. Loman Companies Limited issued 3 000 000 preferred shares with a par value of $25.00/share and paying $1.825/share each year.
a. Calculate the amount raised by the company.
b. Calculate the yield on the shares.
c. What would be the annual income from 10 000 of these shares?

15·12 Chapter Test

1. What are the advantages and disadvantages of making extra payments on a loan or mortgage?

2. Alice has borrowed $3750 to pay expenses during her year at university. The loan is to be amortized over 5 a at an interest rate of 14%/a, compounded semiannually.
a. Calculate her monthly payments.
b. Prepare an amortization table showing the first three payments.

3. Mrs. Fortier plans to purchase a building costing $275 000 with a $75 000 down payment and a mortgage for the balance. She has narrowed her choice of lenders to two. One offers a 5 a term mortgage amortized over 25 a at an annual interest rate of 13.5%, compounded annually. The other offers a mortgage amortized over 20 a at 12.5%/a, compounded semiannually.
a. Calculate and compare the monthly payments on the mortgages.
b. Give reasons for choosing either plan.

4. Mr. Kynd plans to set up a fund to assist graduating students from Sanford High to further their education. The income from the invested funds must be available each June 30. Donations to the fund are to be made every six months. Which investment would provide the best income and suit the needs of the fund? Give reasons for your answer.
a. a 1 a G.I.C. paying 7.75%/a, compounded semiannually, and renewed each year
b. a 120-179 d term deposit paying 7.50%/a
c. a savings account paying 6.75%/a, compounded monthly
d. preferred stock in Bajk Corporation paying 7.25%/a annually
e. gold certificates

5. Ben purchased ten 100 ounce bars of silver at a price of $7.94/ounce. The bar charge was $0.75/ounce. He sold the bars later for $6.97/ounce total. Calculate his loss on this investment.

6. Bank A had a *P/E* ratio of 6.1:1 when the price of the shares begins to fall because of information on the poor quality of its loans. How will this effect the *P/E* ratio?

7. Trilea Corporation offers 500 000 preferred shares with a yield of 10.25%/a for sale. The par value of each share is $100.00.
a. Calculate the amount raised by Trilea assuming that all shares are sold.
b. Calculate the annual dividend on 5000 shares.

8. MNP Corporation reported common share earnings of $4.1 million for the previous year.
a. Calculate the earnings per share on 3.5 million outstanding common shares.
b. The current value of the stock is $15.75/share. Calculate the *P/E* ratio.

9. Itza Corporation had an excellent profit this year, but decided to build its cash reserves and offer a stock split to its shareholders. The offer gave three shares for each original share. Before the split, the share price was $33 and $11 after. After the split, the price rose to $12.25, and then to $13.75. Clair held 1000 of the original shares and sold 1000 new shares at $13.75. Her broker charged a 3% commission.
a. Calculate the proceeds from the sale.
b. Compare the value of Clair's stock holdings before and after the split and sale.

10. Ron's broker charges 3.5% commission. Ron purchases 500 shares of Consolidated Computers at $20.00/share and sold 5000 shares of Equis Mining at $1.30/share.
a. What is the balance of his account with the broker?
b. Ron had purchased Equis Mining for $0.05/share 1 a ago. What is his capital gain?
c. Due to inflation, the buying power of $100 has decreased to $97.75 over the year. What is the buying power of his capital gain in terms of the previous year?

451

Cumulative Review   Chapters 13–15

1. Find the probability of throwing each with a pair of dice.

a. a sum of 11

b. at most a sum of 7

c. at least a sum of 7

2. A television manufacturer received a shipment of 5000 colour picture tubes. The tubes were numbered from EA1073 to EA6072. A random sample of 350 tubes is to be selected for inspection. Describe how this sample can be chosen using a random number table.

3. On August 21, a major computer manufacturer offered a free software package valued at $800 to all purchasers of their Zeida 2000 computer. The mass advertising campaign began on August 31. One chain's daily sales totals before and after the campaign were as follows.

Before	8	10	4	11	17	12	15	5	3
After	21	13	12	19	25	30	11	8	12

Construct a box and whisker plot for each set of data and answer the following.

a. Find the median value for the before data.

b. Find the median value for the after data.

c. Find the hinge values for the before data.

d. Find the hinge values for the after data.

e. Find the difference between the two median values.

f. Comment on the effect of the advertising on the sales totals.

4. Calculate the mean, variance, and standard deviation for this set of marks on a computer studies exam.

76, 82, 91, 45, 54, 76, 82, 60, 79, 58

5. The mean flying time for amateur pilots is 130 min with a standard deviation of 15 min. The distribution of flying time is a normal distribution.

a. What percent of the flying time is between 115 min and 145 min?

b. What percent of the amateur pilots fly longer than 160 min?

6. Calculate the indicated term.

a. 1, 5, 25, ..., t_{12}

b. $-7, -3, 1, ..., t_{23}$

c. 3, 1, -1, ..., t_{11}

d. 8, 1, $\frac{1}{8}$, ..., t_9

e. 2, 0.4, 0.08, ..., t_8

7. Evaluate the indicated sum.

a. $2 + (-6) + 18 + ... + t_{10}$

b. $-0.5 + 0.5 + 1.5 + ... + t_{100}$

c. $1 + \frac{1}{2} + \frac{1}{3} + \frac{1}{4} + \frac{1}{5}$

d. $100 + 100(1.12) + 100(1.12)^2 + ... + t_7$

8. Toma's mother deposited $500 in an account on the day he was born. Assume a constant rate of interest of 6%/a, compounded semiannually. What is the balance of the account on Toma's 18th birthday if the interest was allowed to accumulate and no other deposits or withdrawals were made?

9. Calculate the amount.

a. $2130 invested at 12.40%/a, compounded annually for 5 a

b. $175 invested at 7.75%/a, simple interest for 3 a

c. $7689 invested at 15.30%/a, compounded monthly for 1 a

d. 20 monthly payments of $340 at 8.50%/a, compounded monthly, on the day the last payment is made

e. 12 semiannual payments of $525 at 13.25%/a, compounded semiannually, on the day the last payment is made

10. Calculate the present value.

a. $5235 due in 4 a at 9.75%, compounded semiannually

b. $500 due in 6 months at 5.50%/a, compounded monthly

c. $1500 due in 6 a at 11.00%/a, compounded annually

d. 15 annual payments of $5000 at 11.25%/a, compounded annually

Cumulative Review   Chapters 13–15

11. Olga Romano agrees to make 24 monthly payments of $466.48 to pay fully for a $10 000 car.
a. What is the total amount of interest charged?
b. Describe how the effective interest rate can be determined.

12. Answer the following given a mortgage of $35 780 at 15%/a, compounded semiannually, and amortized over 10 a.
a. Determine the monthly payment.
b. Calculate the interest factor.
c. Draw up an amortization table showing the first four payments.

13. Calculate the cost of 100 shares of Bell Canada quoted at $41.38/share if the broker charges a commission of 5%.

14. Kam Lee purchased 5000 shares of Hilco 7.5% preferred shares with a par value of $25. The income from these shares is paid semiannually.
a. Calculate his semiannual income.
b. Calculate the first year's yield if he paid $23.50/share.

15. Name three items on a financial report that can give an investor insight into the financial strength of a company.

16. In 1987, the value of gold increased from $540 to $620 per troy ounce over a 6-month period.
a. What was the capital gain on an ounce wafer over that 6 months?
b. Would a savings account paying 4.5%/a have been a better investment? Explain.

17. Fred Ince invested the larger portion of his summer earnings in Douk shares selling for $2.375/share paying $0.625/share semiannually. The broker charged a 3.5% commission on the purchase transaction. His other option was to invest in a one-year G.I.C. paying 8.5%/a. Did he make the right decision? Explain your answer using calculations.

18. A game show uses seven chips, three of which are labelled X, and the remaining four are labelled as the numbers 7, 8, 3, and 1. The chips are placed in a drum. A contestant blindly draws one chip at a time and guesses the location of the number in the price of a car. The X's are strikes and three strikes eliminates the contestant. What is the probability of a contestant choosing an X for each of the first three draws?

19. Ace Supermarket recorded the number of customers at the checkouts at 16:00 on 30 consecutive business days.

15, 21, 34, 18, 12, 26, 31, 23,
21, 18, 11, 20, 19, 16, 15, 31,
28, 27, 25, 10, 37, 41, 28, 43,
21, 29, 35, 48, 16, 32

a. Construct a percent frequency table.
b. On how many days did the supermarket have between 30 and 40 customers at 16:00?
c. What percent of the days recorded did the supermarket have less than 30 customers?
d. Construct a histogram based on this data.

20. Jim was offered a summer job paying $1.00 on the first day and an increase of $0.50/d on each subsequent working day.
a. How much would he earn on the 40th day?
b. What would be the total earnings from this job over 50 d?
c. Another employer offered a salary beginning with $2.00 for the first day and 110% of the previous day's salary on each succeeding day. Show calculations comparing these two offers.

21. On the issue date of October 20, 1978, Jay White Feather purchased a twenty-year $1000 Arcom Corporation 10.25% bond.
a. Determine the present value of the semiannual interest payments on October 20, 1988, if money is compounded semiannually at 8.25% at that time.
b. Calculate the present value of the face amount of the bond on that date.

Powers, Roots, 1-100

n	$\sqrt{n}$	n	$\sqrt{n}$
1.0	1.0000	5.5	2.3452
1.1	.0488	5.6	.3664
1.2	.0954	5.7	.3875
1.3	.1402	5.8	.4083
1.4	.1832	5.9	.4290
1.5	1.2247	6.0	2.4495
1.6	.2849	6.1	.4698
1.7	.3038	6.2	.4900
1.8	.3416	6.3	.5100
1.9	.3784	6.4	.5298
2.0	1.4142	6.5	2.5495
2.1	.4491	6.6	.5690
2.2	.4832	6.7	.5884
2.3	.5166	6.8	.6077
2.4	.5492	6.9	.6268
2.5	1.5811	7.0	2.6458
2.6	.6125	7.1	.6646
2.7	.6432	7.2	.6833
2.8	.6733	7.3	.7019
2.9	.7029	7.4	.7203
3.0	1.7321	7.5	2.7386
3.1	.7607	7.6	.7568
3.2	.7889	7.7	.7749
3.3	.8166	7.8	.7928
3.4	.8439	7.9	.8107
3.5	1.8708	8.0	2.8284
3.6	.8974	8.1	.8460
3.7	.9235	8.2	.8636
3.8	.9494	8.3	.8810
3.9	1.9748	8.4	.8983
4.0	2.0000	8.5	2.9155
4.1	.0248	8.6	.9326
4.2	.0494	8.7	.9496
4.3	.0736	8.8	.9665
4.4	.0976	8.9	2.9833
4.5	2.1213	9.0	3.0000
4.6	.1448	9.1	.0166
4.7	.1679	9.2	.0332
4.8	.1909	9.3	.0496
4.9	.2136	9.4	.0659
5.0	2.2361	9.5	3.0822
5.1	.2583	9.6	.0984
5.2	.2804	9.7	.1145
5.3	.3022	9.8	.1305
5.4	2.3238	9.9	3.1464

n	n^2	n^3	$\sqrt{n}$	$\sqrt[3]{n}$	n	n^2	n^3	$\sqrt{n}$	$\sqrt[3]{n}$
1	1	1	1.000	1.000	51	2 601	132 651	7.141	3.708
2	4	8	1.414	1.260	52	2 704	140 608	7.211	3.733
3	9	27	1.732	1.442	53	2 809	148 877	7.280	3.756
4	16	64	2.000	1.587	54	2 916	157 464	7.348	3.780
5	25	125	2.236	1.710	55	3 025	166 375	7.416	3.803
6	36	216	2.449	1.817	56	3 136	175 616	7.483	3.826
7	49	343	2.646	1.913	57	3 249	185 193	7.550	3.849
8	64	512	2.828	2.000	58	3 364	195 112	7.616	3.871
9	81	729	3.000	2.080	59	3 481	205 379	7.681	3.893
10	100	1 000	3.162	2.154	60	3 600	216 000	7.746	3.915
11	121	1 331	3.317	2.224	61	3 721	226 981	7.810	3.936
12	144	1 728	3.464	2.289	62	3 844	238 328	7.874	3.958
13	169	2 197	3.606	2.351	63	3 969	250 047	7.937	3.979
14	196	2 744	3.742	2.410	64	4 096	262 144	8.000	4.000
15	225	3 375	3.873	2.466	65	4 225	274 625	8.062	4.021
16	256	4 096	4.000	2.520	66	4 356	287 496	8.124	4.041
17	289	4 913	4.123	2.571	67	4 489	300 763	8.185	4.062
18	324	5 832	4.243	2.621	68	4 624	314 432	8.246	4.082
19	361	6 859	4.359	2.668	69	4 761	328 509	8.307	4.102
20	400	8 000	4.472	2.714	70	4 900	343 000	8.367	4.121
21	441	9 261	4.583	2.759	71	5 041	357 911	8.426	4.141
22	484	10 648	4.690	2.802	72	5 184	373 248	8.485	4.160
23	529	12 167	4.796	2.844	73	5 329	389 017	8.544	4.719
24	576	13 824	4.899	2.884	74	5 476	405 224	8.602	4.198
25	625	15 625	5.000	2.924	75	5 625	421 875	8.660	4.217
26	676	17 576	5.099	2.962	76	5 776	438 976	8.718	4.236
27	729	19 683	5.196	3.000	77	5 929	456 533	8.775	4.254
28	784	21 952	5.292	3.037	78	6 084	474 552	8.832	4.273
29	841	24 389	5.385	3.072	79	6 241	493 039	8.888	4.291
30	900	27 000	5.477	3.107	80	6 400	512 000	8.944	4.309
31	961	29 791	5.568	3.141	81	6 561	531 441	9.000	4.327
32	1 024	32 768	5.657	3.175	82	6 724	551 368	9.055	4.344
33	1 089	35 937	5.745	3.208	83	6 889	571 787	9.110	4.362
34	1 156	39 304	5.831	3.240	84	7 056	592 704	9.165	4.380
35	1 225	42 875	5.916	3.271	85	7 225	614 125	9.220	4.397
36	1 296	46 656	6.000	3.302	86	7 396	636 056	9.274	4.414
37	1 369	50 653	6.083	3.332	87	7 569	658 503	9.327	4.431
38	1 444	54 872	6.164	3.362	88	7 744	681 472	9.381	4.448
39	1 521	59 319	6.245	3.391	89	7 921	704 969	9.434	4.465
40	1 600	64 000	6.325	3.420	90	8 100	729 000	9.487	4.481
41	1 681	68 921	6.403	3.448	91	8 281	753 571	9.539	4.498
42	1 764	74 088	6.481	3.476	92	8 464	778 688	9.592	1.514
43	1 849	79 507	6.557	3.503	93	8 649	804 357	9.644	4.531
44	1 936	85 184	6.633	3.530	94	8 836	830 584	9.695	4.547
45	2 025	91 125	6.708	3.557	95	9 025	857 375	9.747	4.563
46	2 116	97 336	6.782	3.583	96	9 216	884 736	9.798	4.579
47	2 209	103 823	6.856	3.609	97	9 409	912 673	9.849	4.595
48	2 304	110 592	6.928	3.634	98	9 604	941 192	9.899	4.610
49	2 401	117 649	7.000	3.659	99	9 801	970 299	9.950	4.626
50	2 500	125 000	7.071	3.684	100	10 000	1 000 000	10.000	4.642

Table of Trigonometric Functions

ANGLE deg	sin	cos	tan	csc	sec	cot	ANGLE deg	sin	cos	tan	csc	sec	cot
0	0.0000	1.0000	0.0000	undefined	1.0000	undefined	45	0.7071	0.7071	1.0000	1.4142	1.4142	1.0000
1	0.0175	0.9998	0.0175	57.299	1.0002	57.2900	46	0.7193	0.6947	1.0355	1.3901	1.4396	0.9657
2	0.0349	0.9994	0.0349	28.654	1.0006	28.6363	47	0.7314	0.6820	1.0724	1.3673	1.4663	0.9325
3	0.0523	0.9986	0.0524	19.107	1.0014	19.0811	48	0.7431	0.6691	1.1106	1.3456	1.4945	0.9004
4	0.0698	0.9976	0.0699	14.336	1.0024	14.3007	49	0.7547	0.6561	1.1504	1.3250	1.5243	0.8693
5	0.0872	0.9962	0.0875	11.474	1.0038	11.4301	50	0.7660	0.6428	1.1918	1.3054	1.5557	0.8391
6	0.1045	0.9945	0.1051	9.5668	1.0055	9.5144	51	0.7771	0.6293	1.2349	1.2868	1.5890	0.8098
7	0.1219	0.9925	0.1228	8.2055	1.0075	8.1443	52	0.7880	0.6157	1.2799	1.2690	1.6243	0.7813
8	0.1392	0.9903	0.1405	7.1853	1.0098	7.1154	53	0.7986	0.6018	1.3270	1.2521	1.6616	0.7536
9	0.1564	0.9877	0.1584	6.3925	1.0125	6.3138	54	0.8090	0.5878	1.3764	1.2361	1.7013	0.7265
10	0.1736	0.9848	0.1763	5.7588	1.0154	5.6713	55	0.8192	0.5736	1.4281	1.2208	1.7435	0.7002
11	0.1908	0.9816	0.1944	5.2408	1.0187	5.1446	56	0.8290	0.5592	1.4826	1.2062	1.7883	0.6745
12	0.2079	0.9781	0.2126	4.8097	1.0223	4.7046	57	0.8387	0.5446	1.5399	1.1924	1.8361	0.6494
13	0.2250	0.9744	0.2309	4.4454	1.0263	4.3315	58	0.8480	0.5299	1.6003	1.1792	1.8871	0.6249
14	0.2419	0.9703	0.2493	4.1336	1.0306	4.0108	59	0.8572	0.5150	1.6643	1.1666	1.9416	0.6009
15	0.2588	0.9659	0.2679	3.8637	1.0353	3.7321	60	0.8660	0.5000	1.7321	1.1547	2.0000	0.5774
16	0.2756	0.9613	0.2867	3.6280	1.0403	3.4874	61	0.8746	0.4848	1.8040	1.1434	2.0627	0.5543
17	0.2924	0.9563	0.3057	3.4208	1.0457	3.2709	62	0.8829	0.4695	1.8807	1.1326	2.1301	0.5317
18	0.3090	0.9511	0.3249	3.2361	1.0515	3.0777	63	0.8910	0.4540	1.9626	1.1223	2.2027	0.5095
19	0.3256	0.9455	0.3443	3.0716	1.0576	2.9042	64	0.8988	0.4384	2.0503	1.1126	2.2812	0.4877
20	0.3420	0.9397	0.3640	2.9238	1.0642	2.7475	65	0.9063	0.4226	2.1445	1.1034	2.3662	0.4663
21	0.3584	0.9336	0.3839	2.7904	1.0711	2.6051	66	0.9135	0.4067	2.2460	1.0946	2.4586	0.4452
22	0.3746	0.9272	0.4040	2.6695	1.0785	2.4751	67	0.9205	0.3907	2.3559	1.0864	2.5593	0.4245
23	0.3907	0.9205	0.4245	2.5593	1.0864	2.3559	68	0.9272	0.3746	2.4751	1.0785	2.6695	0.4040
24	0.4067	0.9135	0.4452	2.4586	1.0946	2.2460	69	0.9336	0.3584	2.6051	1.0712	2.7904	0.3839
25	0.4226	0.9063	0.4663	2.3662	1.1034	2.1445	70	0.9397	0.3420	2.7475	1.0642	2.9238	0.3640
26	0.4384	0.8988	0.4877	2.2812	1.1126	2.0503	71	0.9455	0.3256	2.9042	1.0576	3.0716	0.3443
27	0.4540	0.8910	0.5095	2.2027	1.1223	1.9626	72	0.9511	0.3090	3.0777	1.0515	3.2361	0.3249
28	0.4695	0.8829	0.5317	2.1301	1.1326	1.8807	73	0.9563	0.2924	3.2709	1.0457	3.4203	0.3057
29	0.4848	0.8746	0.5543	2.0627	1.1434	1.8040	74	0.9613	0.2756	3.4874	1.0403	3.6280	0.2867
30	0.5000	0.8660	0.5774	2.0000	1.1547	1.7321	75	0.9659	0.2588	3.7321	1.0353	3.8637	0.2679
31	0.5150	0.8572	0.6009	1.9416	1.1667	1.6643	76	0.9703	0.2419	4.0108	1.0306	4.1336	0.2493
32	0.5299	0.8480	0.6249	1.8871	1.1792	1.6003	77	0.9744	0.2250	4.3315	1.0263	4.4454	0.2309
33	0.5446	0.8387	0.6494	1.8361	1.1924	1.5399	78	0.9781	0.2079	4.7046	1.0223	4.8097	0.2126
34	0.5592	0.8290	0.6745	1.7883	1.2062	1.4826	79	0.9816	0.1908	5.1446	1.0187	5.2408	0.1944
35	0.5736	0.8192	0.7002	1.7435	1.2208	1.4281	80	0.9848	0.1736	5.6713	1.0154	5.7588	0.1763
36	0.5878	0.8090	0.7265	1.7013	1.2361	1.3764	81	0.9877	0.1564	6.3138	1.0125	6.3925	0.1584
37	0.6018	0.7986	0.7536	1.6616	1.2521	1.3270	82	0.9903	0.1392	7.1154	1.0098	7.1853	0.1405
38	0.6157	0.7880	0.7813	1.6243	1.2690	1.2799	83	0.9925	0.1219	8.1443	1.0075	8.2055	0.1228
39	0.6293	0.7771	0.8098	1.5890	1.2868	1.2349	84	0.9945	0.1045	9.5144	1.0055	9.5668	0.1051
40	0.6428	0.7660	0.8391	1.5557	1.3054	1.1918	85	0.9962	0.0872	11.4301	1.0038	11.474	0.0875
41	0.6561	0.7547	0.8693	1.5243	1.3250	1.1504	86	0.9976	0.0698	14.3007	1.0024	14.336	0.0699
42	0.6691	0.7431	0.9004	1.4945	1.3456	1.1106	87	0.9986	0.0523	19.0811	1.0014	19.107	0.0524
43	0.6820	0.7314	0.9325	1.4663	1.3673	1.0724	88	0.9994	0.0349	28.6363	1.0006	28.654	0.0349
44	0.6947	0.7193	0.9657	1.4396	1.3902	1.0355	89	0.9998	0.0175	57.2900	1.0002	57.299	0.0175
45	0.7071	0.7071	1.0000	1.4142	1.4142	1.0000	90	1.0000	0.0000	undefined	1.0000	undefined	0.0000

Random Numbers

1	67983	60852	09916	43596	20363	53315	37287	07662	26401	28650
2	19010	91956	31795	41845	25190	06991	66521	93755	02166	79003
3	41830	13963	52289	51633	77785	31712	93500	19449	77822	36645
4	50115	21246	09195	09502	53413	26357	63992	52872	42570	80586
5	22712	09067	51909	75809	16824	41933	97621	68761	85401	03782
6	82806	82277	88300	29832	22806	92486	36042	34590	55743	85297
7	68885	23670	25151	14619	33069	05296	14748	43282	62802	30626
8	41971	29316	23695	60065	62854	01237	72575	98475	61743	66763
9	86818	10485	28018	57382	70220	77420	94651	05024	24716	63746
10	61411	17729	56740	10634	56007	05873	36764	41765	97918	49916
11	20240	11618	52392	19715	20334	01124	39338	73458	63616	72057
12	47935	98490	99047	20071	81921	13627	99672	26523	53766	01219
13	28555	86201	62668	98919	54425	52470	21863	38900	96199	02418
14	59767	56647	35868	12109	29037	72768	45163	69121	72091	48070
15	99784	67224	77465	88593	61371	05036	41838	02224	34532	14840
16	69823	11868	50659	64782	20491	11303	41774	80579	09599	00703
17	89585	58666	00566	73433	67326	86922	42271	45800	59208	94299
18	93707	06735	84194	51810	19421	68021	05152	06217	57168	95760
19	04063	28256	83450	70758	00038	24278	55795	30155	78395	65622
20	89294	03751	09422	22965	09888	95835	80131	65972	16145	59876
21	60301	16519	51348	36322	70572	48637	05309	08369	79567	67699
22	74006	15355	95718	91467	30481	31576	84764	67417	19343	01920
23	86117	80403	42385	64085	70178	07265	87005	48570	25755	81223
24	87860	70624	75971	40430	43435	34945	70220	32445	18369	01990
25	10484	39599	04817	06980	22037	43080	52425	77667	67793	92230
26	45635	80376	17981	83957	91343	18249	85861	90149	59239	10040
27	89884	99155	65450	31432	60782	51442	31091	91187	81633	54164
28	08854	49077	20318	73772	85867	61524	78601	92812	34536	97897
29	43755	12282	84744	58693	25640	66247	58618	40854	85560	00699
30	36381	94203	18050	28540	97769	63915	65191	04638	76462	13106
31	05478	49611	27465	72222	56456	82646	09667	43683	33611	15020
32	30900	37036	68577	43276	57609	88486	16952	46799	49171	19846
33	87097	50134	42000	51378	60900	70086	51319	51408	85037	15608
34	84951	45154	20051	46979	79305	46375	16686	96475	54604	14795
35	52243	19460	67237	95379	78426	75457	05919	05828	13052	51831
36	48397	03688	27314	19086	58143	56293	78283	87702	17610	97741
37	36108	73699	01494	88477	18706	86938	40590	38087	22757	04249
38	73798	17752	23699	42632	77518	34777	66590	12061	35079	14551
39	26577	40103	74102	06328	43037	77254	78000	61577	41810	85898
40	81004	57367	28642	02357	23267	76973	29206	69086	42603	49297

Monthly Payments to Amortize a Loan of $10 000, Compounded Semiannually

Years	10%	11%	12%	13%	14%	15%	16%	17%	18%
1	878.22	882.68	887.13	891.58	896.03	900.47	904.90	909.33	913.76
2	460.52	464.95	469.38	473.83	478.28	482.74	487.20	491.68	496.15
3	321.72	326.23	330.76	335.31	339.88	344.46	349.06	353.68	358.32
4	252.66	257.27	261.92	266.60	271.30	276.04	280.80	285.60	290.42
5	211.48	216.21	220.98	225.80	230.66	235.55	240.49	245.46	250.47
6	184.24	189.09	194.00	198.96	203.97	209.02	214.13	219.28	224.47
7	164.97	169.94	174.98	180.08	185.24	190.46	195.73	201.06	206.44
8	150.67	155.77	160.94	166.18	171.49	176.87	182.31	187.81	193.37
9	139.69	144.91	150.21	155.60	161.05	166.58	172.18	177.85	183.58
10	131.03	136.37	141.80	147.32	152.92	158.60	164.36	170.19	176.08
11	124.06	129.51	135.07	140.72	146.46	152.29	158.19	164.18	170.23
12	118.34	123.92	129.60	135.37	141.25	147.21	153.26	159.39	165.60
13	113.60	119.28	125.08	130.99	136.99	143.09	149.28	155.55	161.89
14	109.61	115.41	121.32	127.35	133.48	139.70	146.02	152.42	158.89
15	106.23	112.13	118.16	124.30	130.55	136.90	143.34	149.86	156.46
16	103.33	109.35	115.48	121.74	128.10	134.56	141.12	147.75	154.46
17	100.84	106.96	113.20	119.56	126.03	132.61	139.27	146.01	152.83
18	98.69	104.90	111.24	117.71	124.28	130.96	137.72	144.56	151.47
19	96.81	103.12	109.56	116.12	122.79	129.56	136.42	143.35	150.35
20	95.17	101.56	108.10	114.75	121.52	128.38	135.32	142.34	149.42
21	93.72	100.21	106.83	113.58	120.43	127.37	134.40	141.49	148.65
22	92.45	99.02	105.73	112.56	119.49	126.51	133.62	140.78	148.00
23	91.33	97.98	104.77	111.67	118.68	125.78	132.95	140.18	147.47
24	90.33	97.06	103.93	110.91	117.99	125.15	132.39	139.68	147.01
25	89.45	96.25	103.19	110.24	117.39	124.61	131.91	139.25	146.64
26	88.66	95.54	102.54	109.66	116.87	124.15	131.50	138.89	146.32
27	87.96	94.90	101.97	109.15	116.42	123.76	131.15	138.59	146.06
28	87.33	94.34	101.47	108.71	116.03	123.41	130.85	138.33	145.84
29	86.77	93.84	101.03	108.32	115.69	123.12	130.60	138.11	145.65
30	86.27	93.39	100.64	107.98	115.39	122.87	130.38	137.93	145.49
31	85.82	93.00	100.29	107.68	115.14	122.65	130.20	137.77	145.36
32	85.41	92.64	99.99	107.42	114.92	122.46	130.04	137.64	145.25
33	85.05	92.33	99.72	107.19	114.72	122.30	129.90	137.53	145.16
34	84.72	92.05	99.48	106.99	114.55	122.16	129.79	137.43	145.08
35	84.42	91.80	99.27	106.81	114.41	122.04	129.69	137.35	145.01

90% Box and Whisker Plots for Sample Sizes of 20

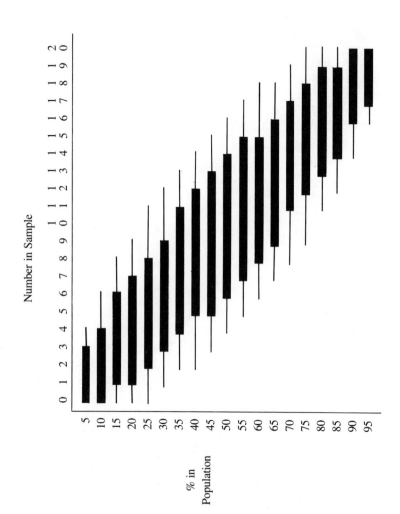

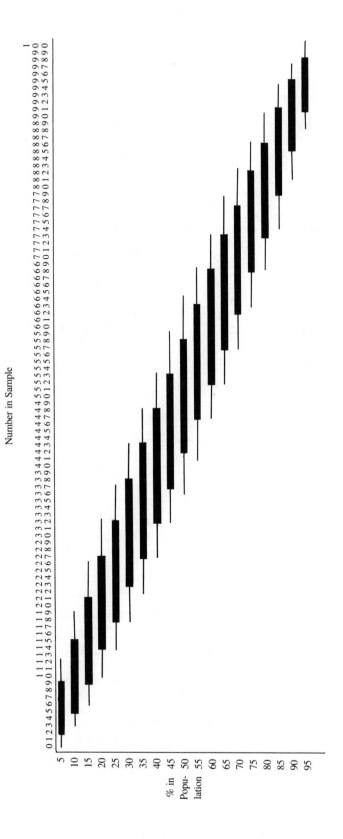

90% Box and Whisker Plots for Sample Sizes of 100

Number in Sample

Glossary

Abscissa The horizontal or *x*-coordinate of an ordered pair plotted on a coordinate grid.

Amortization period The time over which a loan is repaid in regular, equal payments.

Amount The future value of a sum of money.

Amplitude One half the distance between the maximum and minimum values of a trigonometric function.

Annuity A specified payment made (or payable) at stated intervals for a fixed period of time.

Arithmetic sequence A sequence of terms in which each successive term is determined by the addition of a constant to the preceding term.

Arithmetic series The terms of an arithmetic sequence combined by addition.

Asymptote A line which a curve approaches indefinitely without meeting it.

Box and whisker plot A graphic representation of confidence intervals and extreme values of a population.

Central angle An angle formed by two radii at the centre of a circle.

Circumscribed circle One that passes through each vertex of a polygon.

Closed half planes The union of a half plane and its boundary.

Collinear points Points that lie on the same straight line.

Combined variation A combination of both a joint and an inverse variation.

Common difference The difference between successive terms of an arithmetic sequence.

Common ratio The ratio between successive terms of a geometric sequence.

Common tangent A line that is tangent to more than one circle.

Compound interest Interest paid on the principal and the accrued interest.

Compound period The length of time between interest payments.

Convex polygonal regions The intersection of a finite number of closed half planes.

Coplanar points Points which lie on the same plane.

Coterminal angles Angles with the same initial and terminal arms when placed on the coordinate axes in standard position.

Degree of a term A measure of the number of variable factors forming a term.

Degree of an equation The degree of the highest term in the equation.

Direct variation When two quantities, *x* and *y*, are related so that $\frac{x}{y} = k$, a constant, then *y* varies directly as *x*.

Discriminant The algebraic expression $b^2 - 4ac$, where *a*, *b*, and *c* are the coefficients of the quadratic equation $ax^2 + bx + c = 0$, where *a*, *b*, $c \in R$ and $a \neq 0$.

Due date The date by which a bond or preferred share is redeemed by the issuer.

Ellipse A curve formed by applying a horizontal and/or vertical stretch to a circle.

Exponential equation An equation which contains a quantity whose exponent is a variable.

Exterior angle The angle formed outside a polygon between the extended side and the side adjacent to the extended side of the polygon.

Face value The redemption value of a bond or preferred share on the due date.

Family of lines A set of lines that have a common property.

Function A relation in which every member of the domain corresponds to exactly one member of the range.

Geometric sequence A sequence of terms in which each successive term is determined by multiplying the preceding term by a constant.

Geometric series The terms of a geometric sequence combined by addition.

Half line That part of a straight line on either side of a point on the line.

Half plane boundary A line which divides a plane into two half planes.

Identity An equation which is true for all values of the variable(s).

Inconsistent equations Simultaneous equations having no common root.

Intersection The set of elements belonging to two or more sets.

Inverse variation When two quantities, x and y, are related so that $xy = k$, a constant, then y varies inversely as x.

Irrational number A number which cannot be expressed as a quotient of two integers.

Joint variation The relationship which occurs when the value of a variable changes directly as the product of two or more variables.

Linear equation An equation that describes a set of collinear points.

Linear function Any straight line where the slope is a linear function.

Linear programming A procedure which uses inequalities to maximize or minimize a given variable.

Major arc The longer arc between two fixed points on a circle.

Median of a triangle A line segment from one vertex to the midpoint of the opposite side.

Minor arc The shorter arc between two fixed points on a circle.

Ordinate The verticle or y-coordinate of an ordered pair plotted on a coordinate system.

Parabola The graph of a quadratic function is called a parabola.

Parameter A numerical feature of a population which is usually not known.

Partial variation A variation resulting from a combination of a direct variation and a constant.

Period The length of one complete cycle in a trigonometric function.

Phase shift The horizontal translation of a periodic function.

Point of tangency The point on a curve at which a tangent intersects it.

Population The group of objects or people about which information is needed.

Postulate A statement which is accepted as true without proof.

Proportion An equation that states that two ratios are equal.

Quadrantal angle An angle with its terminal arm coterminal with one of the axes of the coordinate system when placed in standard position.

Quadratic equation An equation which can be written in the form $ax^2 + bx + c = 0$, where a, b, $c \in R$ and $a \neq 0$.

Quadratic function Any function which can be written in the form $y = ax^2 + bx + c$, where a, b, $c \in R$ and $a \neq 0$.

Quadratic formula $x = \dfrac{-b \pm \sqrt{b^2 - 4ac}}{2a}$

Radian A unit of measure of an angle. One radian is the measure of an angle subtended at the centre of a circle by an arc the same length as the radius.

Radical The root of a quantity denoted by an expression written under the radical sign, $\sqrt{}$.

461

Radicand The quantity under a radical sign.

Rate A comparison of numbers which have different or unlike units of measure.

Ratio A comparison of numbers which have the same units of measure.

Rational number A number which can be expressed as a quotient of two integers.

Rationalizing a denominator The process of removing the radical sign in the denominator without changing the value of the expression.

Recursive formula A formula which determines successive terms of a sequence from one or more of the preceding terms.

Reference angle The angle between the terminal arm of an angle and the nearest x-axis.

Regular payment Equal valued payments made at equal time intervals.

Relation Any set of ordered pairs.

Resultant vector A single vector that is the sum of two or more vectors.

Scalar A quantity which has magnitude only.

Secant A straight line intersecting a circle at two points.

Sector angle An angle at the centre of a circle between two radii.

Sequence A set of elements to which there is an order.

Series The indicated addition of a sequence of terms.

Simple random sample A sample chosen in such a way as to allow each member of the population an equal chance of selection.

Skew lines Nonintersecting, nonparallel lines in three-dimensional space.

Slope The ratio of the vertical and horizontal distances between two points in the plane.

Standard deviation The positive square root of the variance of a set of measurements.

Standard position Centred at the origin of the coordinate grid.

Stem and leaf plot A frequency distribution table that shows all the data collected.

Strata Group of a population having special features or which in some way share a common feature.

Stratified random sample A sample chosen from a population divided into strata.

System of linear equations Any set of linear equations having the same variables.

Tangent to a circle A straight line intersecting a circle at only one point.

Theorem A general statement which must be proven before it is accepted as true.

Transversal A line or line segment which intersects two or more lines at unique points.

Unit circle A circle with centre at $(0, 0)$ and a radius of 1 unit.

Variance The mean of the square of the deviations of the measurements about their mean.

Vertex The vertex of the graph of a parabola is the turning point of the graph.

Vector A quantity that has both magnitude and direction.

x-intercept The abscissa of the point at which a line crosses the horizontal axis.

y-intercept The ordinate of the point at which a line crosses the vertical axis.

Answers

Chapter 1

Page 1 **1. a.** 2 **b.** 13 **c.** 7 **d.** 2 **2. a.** x^2 **b.** 3
c. y^2 **d.** a^3 **4. a.** 252 **b.** 3213 **c.** xyz **d.** $60x^3y^3$
5. b. $\left(\frac{16}{5}, -\frac{6}{5}\right)$ **7.** 13 **8.** 101 **9. a.** 4 **b.** -6 **c.** 3
d. 0 **e.** 7 **f.** -4 **10.** 0 m **11. a.** $3x + 18$
b. $2x^2 - 2x$ **c.** $2a^2 + 2ab$ **d.** $3xy + 6y^2$

Page 2 **1. a.** coefficient; numerical **b.** 1
c. trinomial **d.** constant **2. a.** monomial **b.** trinomial
c. binomial **d.** monomial **e.** trinomial **f.** binomial
3. a. yes **b.** no **c.** yes **d.** yes **4. a.** -7 **b.** -27
c. 38 **d.** 4 **5. a.** 60 cm^2 **b.** 136 cm^2 **c.** $\frac{1}{2}$ and b

Page 3 **1. a.** $5a + 2b + 4$ **b.** $6m + n$
2. a. $7a - 4b$ **b.** $-p - 9q$ **c.** $-6u + 8v$
d. $-x^2 + 10x - 13$ **3. a.** $18ab + a^2b - 11ab^2$
b. $8pq + 7pq^2 + 4pq^3$ **c.** $3x^2yz + 16xy^2z + 7xyz^2$
4. $5x + 2y$ **5.** $-9x + 15y$ cm

Pages 4-5 **1. a.** $8q^2 + 24q + 18$
b. $ac + ad + ae + bc + bd + be$
2. a. $2x^2 + 6xy - xy - 3y^2 = 2x^2 + 5xy - 3y^2$
b. $4 - 4(2x - y) + (2x - y)^2$
$= 4 - 8x + 4y + 4x^2 - 4xy + y^2$
3. a. $10a^2b - 6ab$ **b.** $-28x^2 - 8x^2y$ **c.** $24p^3 - 20pq$
d. $12x^2 + 20x - 8$ **e.** $6m^3n - 3m^2n^2 - 27mn^3$
f. $-36ab - 3b^2 + 24bc$ **4. a.** $x^2 - 2x - 3$
b. $5x^2 - 7x - 6$ **c.** $36p^2 - 1$ **d.** $20 - 19a + 3a^2$
e. $36k^2 + 63k + 20$ **f.** $10s^2 - 7st - 12t^2$
g. $25y^2 + 20yz + 4z^2$ **h.** $25 - 30ab + 9a^2b^2$
5. $\pi(a^2 + 16b^2 + c^2 + 8ab - 2ac - 8bc)$
6. a. $4x^2 - 26x + 40$ **b.** $-18 - 51p + 9p^2$
7. a. $20a^2 + 24a - 3$ **b.** $-x^2 - 6x + 1$
c. $33m^2 + 40mn + 6n^2$ **d.** $14x^2 + 53x - 47$
e. $16 - 26x + 3x^2$ **f.** $2a^2 + 45ab + 13b^2$
g. $5p^2 - 12pq + 4q^2$ **8.** $3p^2 - \frac{3}{2}pq$
9. a. $4x^2 + 14x - 1$ **b.** $7x^2 - 34x - 4$
10. $38a^2 + 18ab - 2b^2$
11. a. $9 + 6a + 12b + a^2 + 4ab + 4b^2$
b. $x^2 - 2xy + y^2 - 8x + 8y + 16$
c. $p^4 + 2p^2q - 6p^2r + q^2 - 6qr + 9r^2$
d. $x^2 + 4x + 4 - 10xy - 20y + 25y^2$
e. $9m^2 + 24mn + 16n^2 - 6mp - 8np + p^2$
f. $4u^2 + 4uv + v^2 - 4uw + 2vw + w^2$
g. $a^4 + 2a^2b^2 + b^4 - 1$ **h.** $x^6 - 4x^2 + 4xy - y^2$
i. $y^4 + 12y^3 + 36y^2 - 16$ **j.** $m^2 - 9n^2 + 6np - p^2$
k. $16a^2 - b^2 - 25c^2 - 10bc$
12. $11x^2 - 15xy + 5xz + 7yz + 7y^2 - 14z^2$
13. a. $4p^2 - 5pq + 27q^2$ **b.** $4a^2 - 16ac - 8bc$
c. $17m^2 + 17n^2$ **d.** $10a^4 - 30a^2 + 21$

e. $2x^2 + xy + 14y^2$ **f.** $-3u^2 - 8uv + 17v^2$
g. $3p^4 + 28p^2 - 55$ **h.** $2a^4 + 8b^2c^2 + 6a^2bc$

Page 6 **1. a.** 2 **b.** $5x$ **c.** 15 **d.** a **e.** 8 **f.** c
g. 9 km **h.** h **i.** r **j.** xy **2. a.** $2(k^2 + 4k - 2)$
b. $10s(s - 4t - 6t^2)$ **c.** $2a(4a + 5b - 3bc^2)$
d. $5xy(3x - 4z + 8z^2)$ **e.** $3ps(6ps + 9s + 2)$
f. $12(1 - 4mn - 3n^2)$ **g.** $3c(18 + 3d - 10cd^2 - d^3)$
3. 5 cm and $3a - 9b + c^2$ cm **4. a.** $4m(3n + 5)$
b. $5s(1 + t^2)$ **c.** $2\pi(r^2 + 4R^2)$ **d.** $-6p(3p + q^2)$
e. $3uv(3x + 5y - 2z)$ **f.** $rs(4r^2s - 5r - rs + 8)$
5. a. $(4m + 5n)(p + q)$ **b.** $(r - 6)(x - 2)$
c. $(b - c)(3x + 1)$ **d.** $(r + 1)(2p - 5)$
e. $(m - 4)(2x - 3y + z)$ **f.** $(2a + b)(4a + 3b - c)$
6. $16x^2 - 80x + 100 - 4\pi x^2 + 20\pi x - 25\pi$

Page 7 **2. a.** $-\frac{3}{7}$ **b.** 0 **c.** 2 **d.** $\frac{3}{2}$ **e.** $\frac{17}{4}$ **f.** $\frac{19}{5}$
3. a. 6 **b.** 2 **c.** $-\frac{15}{2}$ **d.** $-\frac{3}{2}$ **e.** $\frac{3}{41}$ **f.** $\frac{29}{6}$ **4.** 9 kg,
24 kg **5.** 0.7 km by 3.6 km **6.** 98°; 57°; 25°
7. a. 44 **b.** 1 **c.** $\frac{11}{3}$ **d.** $\frac{19}{2}$ **e.** $0.\dot{7}$ **f.** 9.65 **g.** 6
h. $\frac{125}{9}$ **i.** 70 **j.** -4

Page 8 **1. a.** $x = y + 18$ **b.** $m = 2n - 1500$
c. $x = 2(m + r)$ **2.** $2k - 5$ **3.** $10n + 25(15 - n)$
4. Compstore 9 000; Compworld 29 000 **5.** 39, 47
6. $265.00; $155.00 **7.** 120 km **8.** Y 420 000;
A 210 000; M 140 000 **9.** width 6 cm; length 21 cm

Pages 9-11 **3.** 12; 18; 25 **4.** 240 **5.** 8
6. 3 m by 7 m **7.** $2200 at 10%; $2800 at 12%
8. 15 cm **9.** 6 km **10.** 140 km **11.** 36; 38; 40
12. 6 km **13.** 12; 36 **14. a.** 27; 24 **b.** 34
15. $24 000 **16.** adult 180; student 460 **17.** 295
18. 17

Pages 12-13 **2. a.** infinitely many **b.** 5 **c.** no
9. yes **10.** $\frac{5}{3}$ **11.** no **12.** 21

Pages 14-15 **1. a.** 12 **b.** $\frac{44}{5}$ **c.** -7 **d.** $-\frac{3}{11}$
e. $\frac{9}{5}$ **f.** $\frac{28}{19}$ **2. a.** 21 **b.** $\frac{7}{3}$ **c.** 35 **d.** 14 **e.** 7 **f.** 10
3. 3 **4.** $-\frac{28}{5}$ **5.** $\frac{81}{4}$ **6.** $\frac{40}{3}$ **7.** $\frac{3}{2}$ **8.** $-\frac{30}{7}$ **9.** 0 **10.** 0
11. -3 **12. a.** $3s$ **b.** s **14.** $\frac{25}{26}$; $\frac{1}{2}$ **19.** $z + 2w$ **20.** 0
21. 0 or -1 **22.** 0 or -2 **25.** -2 **26.** listing number
of trucks first (22, 2), (19, 4), (16, 6), (13, 8),
(10, 10), (7, 12), (4, 14), (1, 16)

Pages 16-17 **2.** yes **3.** 180 ha; 20 ha; 100 ha
4. \$95.15 **5.** 33, 19 **7. a.** $a = 1$, $b = 8$ **8.** no **9.** 1,
2, 3 **10.** 200 **11.** 38 **12.** 56 units² **13.** 21 min

14. no **15.** $\frac{5}{8}$ m/min

Pages 18-19 **2. a.** 34 m **b.** 77.7 cm **3. a.** 44 m
b. 60 m **c.** 104 m² **4.** \$12 991.97 **5.** \$245.12
6. refinish **7.** 7 **10.** \$2100.00 **11.** 170 cm²

Pages 20-21 **1.** circle **2. a.** 32.86 m; 85.93 m²
b. 637.74 m; 32 365.47 m² **3.** \$7755.80 **4.** 314 m²
5. $\frac{72}{100}$ of a day **6.** 706.86 cm² **7.** 863.94 cm²;
471.24 cm² **8.** $(2800 - 49\pi)$ m² **9.** The larger has
four times the area. **10.** 1 cm; 2.046 cm
11. $24 + \frac{14\pi}{3}$; 87.96 cm² **12.** 35° **13.** 48π cm²

14. 10 **15.** $s = \frac{2A}{r}$ **BRAINTICKLER** 204

Pages 22-23 **3. a.** 166 cm² **b.** 338.16 cm²
c. 504 cm² **4. a.** 363.23 cm² **b.** 289.2 cm²
c. $52 + 6\pi$ cm² **d.** 967.6 cm² **5.** \$334.11
6. 252 cm² **7.** 56.25% **8.** 162 cm² **9.** \$1.38
10. b. 324π cm² **c.** \$105.56 **11.** 265.46 m²

Pages 24-25 **1.** $V = \frac{b^2}{3}\sqrt{s^2 - \frac{b^2}{2}}$

2. $V = \frac{b^2}{3}\sqrt{s^2 - \frac{b^2}{2}} - \left(\frac{1}{3}\left(\frac{s_1 b}{s}\right)^2 \sqrt{s_1^2 - \frac{1}{2}\left(\frac{s_1 b}{s}\right)^2}\right)$

3. b. 1 548 944.6 cm³ **c.** 18 769 cm² **4.** 185.6 cm³
5. 360 cm³

6. $V = \frac{\pi}{3}\left(\sqrt{S^2 - R^2} - \sqrt{s^2 - \left(\frac{Rs}{S}\right)^2}\right) \times (R^2 + Rr + r^2)$

7. 55% **8.** $\frac{6x^2}{\pi}$ **9.** 4 times **10.** the larger cantaloupe
11. The volume increases fourfold.

Pages 26-27 **2. a.** $\frac{17}{24}$ **b.** $1\frac{1}{1000}$ **c.** $\frac{a}{b}$ **4. c.** no
5. 72% **b.** 70.6% **6.** 140 km **BRAINTICKLER**
neither one

Page 28 **2.** line 60 **3.** line 100 **6.** 33 quarters,
56 nickels, and 42 nickels **7.** change 50 INPUT
"GUESS THE NUMBER OF NICKELS "; X •
60 LET TX = 0.25 ∗ (X − 9) + 0.1 ∗
(2∗X − 28) + 0.05 ∗ X • 100 PRINT "THERE ARE
"; X; " NICKELS, "; 2 ∗ X − 28; " DIMES, AND
"; X − 9; " QUARTERS" **8.** change
30 REM IN \$8.00 • 60 LET TX = 0.25 ∗ X + 0.1 ∗
(3 ∗ X − 4) + 0.05 ∗ (7 ∗ X − 12) • 100 PRINT
"THERE ARE "; X; " QUARTERS, "; 3 ∗ X − 9;
" DIMES, AND "; 7 ∗ X − 12; " NICKELS" •
THERE ARE 10 QUARTERS, 26 DIMES, AND 58
NICKELS

Page 29 **1. a.** -11 **b.** 12 **c.** 8 **d.** 79
2. a. $13x - 8y$ **b.** $2a + 12b - 8c$ **c.** $11x^2 + 18x - 13$
d. $-3m^2 + 4mn + 16n^2$ **3. a.** $-2x + 20y$ **b.** $6x - 12y$
c. $-3x + 14y$ **4.** $15a - 5b + 20c$
5. a. $-3x + 17y - 11z$ **b.** $6m + 19n + 14p$
6. a. $-15a^3b^3$ **b.** $16x^3y^3z^2$ **c.** $x^2 + 6x - 27$
d. $x^2 - 11x + 30$ **e.** $8x^2 + 42x + 27$ **f.** $36x^2 - 1$
g. $4x^2 + 20x + 25$ **h.** $12 - 5x - 2x^2$ **7. a.** $13a - 19b$
b. $8 + 6x^2$ **c.** $24ab$ **8.** $10x - 6$ cm **9. a.** $-\frac{7}{2}$ **b.** $\frac{19}{13}$
c. $-\frac{22}{3}$ **d.** $-\frac{20}{7}$ **10.** $2\pi r(r + h)$ **11.** 28, 30, 32

12. 14 quarters, 30 dimes **13.** 17 **14. a.** $\frac{4}{3}\pi r^3$
b. $\frac{1}{3}b^2h$ **c.** $\frac{1}{3}\pi r^2h$ **d.** πr^2h **15.** \$4200
16. a. cylinder **b.** 75π units³ **17.** Jenette has \$34
and Bradley has \$65.

Page 30 **1. a.** 12 **b.** 10 **c.** 41 **d.** -19 **e.** 7
f. 30 **2. a.** $4x + 12y + 11z$ **b.** $15a - 6b - 4c$
3. a. $-6p - 13q + 3r$ **b.** $5x^2 + 9xy - 6y^2$
4. a. $3a + 13b - c$ **b.** $-18x + 12y + 3z$
c. $9x^2 - 10x - 20$ **d.** $3m^2 + 7mn - 2n^2$
6. $10p^2 - 11pq + 3q^2$ cm² **7. a.** $15x - 9y$
b. $5a - 23b$ **c.** $2p + 14q$ **d.** $8x^2 + 4x + 14$
e. $-15x - 31$ **f.** $14x^2 - 22x + 12$ **8.** $10\frac{2}{3}$ km
9. \$800 **10. a.** $-\frac{10}{7}$ **b.** 1 **c.** $\frac{7}{4}$ **d.** -1 **e.** 0
11. 32, 56 **12.** 244.4 m³ **13. a.** 96 cm²; 64 cm³
b. $\pi(9h + 10.2)$ cm²; 5.1πh cm³ **14. a.** 20 450 cm³
b. \$19.95

Chapter 2

Page 31 **1. a.** $2y - x$ **b.** $-2a - 5b$ **c.** $2p + 8m$
d. $x^2(a - 4) + y(2 + b)$ **e.** $3a(x^2 + 1)$ **2. a.** $3a^2$
b. $-6xy$ **c.** $-10rs$ **d.** $-2abx$ **e.** $12a^2x^2$ **f.** a^2b^2
3. a. $4x + 4y$ **b.** $-10x + 5y$ **c.** $-3ax + 2ay$
d. $15ax + 9ay$ **e.** $-12x^2 + 4xy - 20xz$
f. $3ax + 2ay - 7az$ **4. a.** 12 **b.** -8 **c.** 12 **d.** -34
e. 0 **f.** -42 **5.** 280 m² **6.** 47 cm **7. a.** $2(x + 2y)$
b. $3(x - 3y + 8)$ **c.** $a(2x + 5y)$ **d.** $2ab$ **e.** $5ax(1 - 4y)$
f. $ab(x + y - 3z)$ **8. a.** $3x + 1$ **b.** 56

Page 32 **1. a.** $x^2 - 4x - 21$ **b.** $x^2 - 2x - 8$
c. $x^2 - 3x - 28$ **d.** $x^2 - 8x - 9$ **2. a.** $6x^2 - 24x + 24$
b. $15x^2 + 7x - 2$ **c.** $2x^2 - 24x + 54$
d. $abx^2 + x(4b - 7a) - 28$ **3. a.** $9x^2 - 16$ **b.** $4x^2 - 49$
c. $16x^2 - 4$ **d.** $a^2x^2 - b^2$ **4. a.** $9x^2 + 12x + 4$
b. $16x^2 + 8x + 1$ **c.** $4x^2 - 20x + 25$
d. $49x^2 - 70x + 25$ **e.** $a^2x^2 + 2abx + b^2$
f. $a^2x^2 - 2abx + b^2$ **5.** $x^3 + y^3$ **6. a.** a^2x^2
b. $a^2x^2 + 2abx + b^2$ **c.** $(ax - b)^2$ **7. a.** $a^3 + 27$
b. $m^3 - 64$ **c.** $125 + y^3$ **d.** $8x^3 - 27$ **e.** $27b^3 + 125$
f. $125a^3 - 8b^3$ **g.** $x^3 + y^3$ **h.** $x^3 - y^3$

Page 33   **1. a.** 6, -5 **b.** 2, 8 **c.** -3, -5
2. a. $(x-7)(x+2)$ **b.** $(x-2)^2$ **c.** $(x+3)(x+4)$
d. $(x-1)(x-6)$ **e.** $(x-5)(x+3)$ **f.** $(x+8)(x-4)$
3. a. ± 11, ± 4, ± 1 **b.** ± 8, ± 16 **c.** ± 23, ± 10,
± 5, ± 2 **d.** ± 8, 0 **4. a.** $(x-3y)(x+y)$
b. $(p+3q)(p+9q)$ **c.** $(m-12n)(m+n)$
d. $(r-5s)(r-4s)$ **5. a.** $(x+8)(x-1)$
b. $(t+6)(t-3)$ **c.** $(x-2)(x-12)$ **d.** $(x+6)(x+8)$
6. a. $(x^2+3)(x^2+2)$ **b.** $(x^2-5)(x^2+4)$
c. $(s^2-3)(s^2+9)$ **d.** $(p^2-3)(p^2-10)$
e. $(x^2+3y)(x^2+6y)$ **f.** $(m^2-5n)(m^2+n)$
7. a. $2(x+6)(x-1)$ **b.** $3(x-4)(x-2)$
c. $2(x+8)(x-5)$ **d.** $5(x+4)(x-1)$
8. a. $[(x+a)+3][(x+a)+1]$

Pages 34-35   **1. a.** 8, -5 **b.** -9, -4 **c.** 3, 6
d. -7, 4 **3. a.** ± 9, ± 3 **b.** ± 13, ± 7, ± 8
c. ± 23, ± 10, ± 5, ± 2 **d.** ± 19, ± 11, ± 9 **4.** $4x$;
$5x$; $(x-2)$; $(5x+4)$ **6. a.** $(3x-5)(x-1)$
b. $(6x+1)(x-2)$ **c.** $(4x+3)^2$ **d.** $(4x+15)(2x+1)$
7. a. $(2x-1)(x+4)$ **b.** $(3x+2)(x-3)$
c. $(2x+3)(x-5)$ **d.** $(3x-1)(x+4)$
e. $(3k-2)(k-2)$ **f.** $(2s-5)(s+1)$ **g.** $(2t-3)(t-4)$
h. $(3m-5)(m+1)$ **8.** $18x$; $2x$; $2x$; $2x$; $2x$; $6x$
a. $2(2x+5)(x-3)$ **b.** $2(4x-1)(x-2)$
c. $4(3x+2)(x-1)$ **d.** $3(5x+4)(x+1)$ **9.** yes
10. a. $(2x-1)(2x+3)$ **b.** $(3x-2)(2x+1)$
c. $(4p+1)(3p-5)$ **d.** $(5y+1)^2$ **e.** $(3h-4)(h+2)$
f. $(6z-5)(z-3)$ **g.** $2(4x^2-7x+2)$
h. $(2u-1)(3u+4)$ **11.** Length is $2x+5$ or $4x+10$;
height is $2x-2$ or $x-1$. **12. a.** $(2x-y)(x+3y)$
b. $(4x-y)(x-3y)$ **c.** $(2x+5z)(x+3z)$
d. $(2r-3q)(r-q)$ **e.** $(5t+4u)(t+2u)$
f. $(6x-y)(3x+2y)$ **13. a.** $x(x+5)$ **b.** $(x+5)(x-3)$
c. $(2x-5)(2x+1)$ **d.** $(3x+17)(x+1)$
e. $(5x-9)(x+1)$ **14. a.** $(x+8)(x-6)$ **b.** $2x(4x-3)$
c. $(5x+2)(x-3)$ **d.** $(6-x)(5+3x)$
e. $(4x+1)(2x+7)$ **f.** $3x(x+y)$ **g.** $(x-4)(x-12)$
h. $(2x-3)(5x-4)$ **i.** $(2x+9)(x-4)$
j. $3(x+5)(x-3)$ **k.** $5a(x-3)(x-2)$
l. $[3(a+2b)+4][2(a+2b)-5]$
m. $[4(x-y)+5][(x-y)+1]$

Page 36   **2. a.** 144 **b.** $4x^2$ **c.** $2x$ **d.** y^2 **e.** 9; 3
f. $(x^2+y^2)(x+y)(x-y)$ **3. a.** $(x+5)(x-5)$
b. $(x+6)(x-6)$ **c.** $(2x+1)(2x-1)$
d. $(4x^2+9)(2x+3)(2x-3)$ **e.** $(6x+5)(6x-5)$
f. $(8x+3)(8x-3)$ **4. a.** $(x+y-1)(x-y+7)$
b. $(6a+b)(4a+5b)$ **c.** $(8x+3y-17)(8x-3y-23)$
5. a. $(2a+b+c)(2a+b-c)$
b. $(x-y+2z)(x-y-2z)$ **c.** $(2x+4)(2x-2)$
d. $(x-1)(x-9)$ **e.** $(6x+23)(6x+13)$
f. $(6x+3y+z)(6x+3y-z)$
6. a. $(x+y-z)(x-y+z)$
b. $(a+3b+4c)(a-3b-4c)$
c. $(p+q-5r)(p-q+5r)$
d. $(3x+2u+v)(3x-2u-v)$ **7. a.** $2(x+3)(x-3)$

b. $5(2x+1)(2x-1)$ **c.** $\left(\dfrac{1}{6}m+\dfrac{1}{2}n\right)\left(\dfrac{1}{6}m-\dfrac{1}{2}n\right)$

d. $\left(\dfrac{1}{5}p+\dfrac{1}{9}qr\right)\left(\dfrac{1}{5}p-\dfrac{1}{9}qr\right)$ **e.** $(x+2)(x-2)(x^2+4)$
f. $(x^2+y^2)(x+y)(x-y)$

Page 37   **1. a**, **c**, **d**, **e** **2. a.** $4x$ **b.** $4x^2$ **c.** $28x$
d. $48b^2$ **3. a.** $(x+3)^2$ **b.** $(a-2)^2$ **c.** $(a-1)^2$
d. $(3x-8)^2$ **e.** $(3y+2)^2$ **f.** $3(2a-5)^2$ **g.** $(2+5x)^2$
h. $(2a-9c)^2$ **i.** $(3x-5yz)^2$ **j.** $2xy(x+2y)^2$
5. $2a^2-4b^2$ **6. a.** 4; 2304 **b.** 2704 **c.** $10\ 816$
d. 9604 **7. a.** 4; 8096 **b.** 6384 **c.** 9975 **d.** 1564
8. a. $(4x^2+y^4)(2x+y^2)(2x-y^2)$ **b.** $(x+5y)(x-5y)$
c. $(2p+3q)(2p-3q)$ **d.** $(6m+7n)(6m-7n)$
e. $(4x^2+25y^2)(2x+5y)(2x-5y)$
f. $(p+2qr)(p-2qr)$ **g.** $(x^2+2x+3)(x-3)(x+1)$
h. $(x+1)(x+4)(x^2-5x-4)$

Pages 38-39   **1. a.** $(x+2)^2-4$ **b.** $(x-2)^2-4$

c. $4\left(x+\dfrac{1}{2}\right)^2-1$ **d.** $4\left(x-\dfrac{1}{2}\right)^2-1$ **2. a.** $(x+4)^2-1$

b. $(x-1)^2-16$ **c.** $(x-2)^2-9$ **d.** $\left(x-\dfrac{5}{2}\right)^2-\dfrac{1}{4}$

e. $\left(x-\dfrac{7}{2}\right)^2-\dfrac{81}{4}$ **f.** $\left(x+\dfrac{3}{2}\right)^2-\dfrac{1}{4}$

5. a. $2\left(x+\dfrac{7}{4}\right)^2-\dfrac{81}{8}$ **b.** $3\left(x-\dfrac{3}{2}\right)^2-\dfrac{51}{4}$

c. $-3\left(x-\dfrac{8}{6}\right)^2+\dfrac{1}{3}$ **d.** $\left(x-\dfrac{3}{2}\right)^2-\dfrac{9}{4}$

e. $\left(x+\dfrac{5}{2}\right)^2-\dfrac{25}{4}$ **f.** $\dfrac{1}{3}\left(x-\dfrac{3}{2}\right)^2-\dfrac{3}{4}$

g. $\dfrac{1}{2}(x+1)^2-\dfrac{1}{2}$ **h.** $9\left(x+\dfrac{1}{2}\right)^2-\dfrac{9}{4}$

6. a. $(x+2)^2-1$ **b.** $\left(x-\dfrac{7}{2}\right)^2-\dfrac{9}{4}$ **c.** $(x+3)^2-2$

d. $3\left(x-\dfrac{2}{3}\right)^2-\dfrac{4}{3}$ **e.** $5\left(x+\dfrac{25}{2}\right)^2-\dfrac{3125}{4}$

f. $2\left(x+\dfrac{3}{4}\right)^2-\dfrac{25}{8}$ **g.** $6\left(x-\dfrac{1}{12}\right)^2-\dfrac{49}{24}$

h. $8\left(x-\dfrac{1}{8}\right)^2-\dfrac{9}{8}$ **7.** digits **8. a.** $(6x-1)(x-1)$
b. $(x+5y)(x-5y)$ **c.** $x(3-x)(4+7x)$
d. $3(x+2)^2$ **e.** $14x^2(x-2y)(x+2y)$

f. $2\left(a+\dfrac{3}{4}\right)^2-\dfrac{21}{8}$ **g.** $3(2y^4+5)(2y^4-5)$

h. $2(a+2)(a+10)$ **i.** $(2x+1)(x-2)$ **j.** $(y+3)^2$
k. $3(x-2y^2)(x^2+2xy^2+4y^4)$ **l.** $[(x-y)+2]^2$
m. $4(a-3b)(3a-b)$ **9. a.** $10x^2$; $(x^2+5)^2-4x^2$;
$[(x^2+5)+2x][(x^2+5)-2x]$ **b.** $-6x^2$;
$(x^2-3)^2-25x^2$; $[(x^2-3)+5x][(x^2-3)-5x]$
c. $-4x^2$; $(x^2+2)^2-4x^2$; $[(x^2+2)+2x][(x^2+2)-2x]$
d. x^2+9; $16x^2$; $[(x^2+9)+4x][(x^2+9)-4x]$
10. a. $(x^2+1+x)(x^2+1-x)$
b. $(m^2+3-2m)(m^2+3+2m)$
c. $(k^2+3+3k)(k^2+3-3k)$
d. $(p^2+4-2p)(p^2+4+2p)$
e. $(s^2+2+2s)(s^2+2-2s)$
f. $(2a^2+5+3a)(2a^2+5-3a)$

11. a. $4\left(x^2 + \frac{3}{4}\right)^2 - \frac{109}{4}$ **b.** $(x^2 + 3)^2 - 34$
c. $x^2(x - 1)(x + 1)$ **d.** $x^4(x - 1)(x + 1)$
e. $(a^2 + 3)(a^2 - 3)$ **f.** $t^3(t + 1)(t^2 - t + 1)$
12. b; b, b, $4a$; b; b; b, $2a$, $4a$

Page 40   2. a. x, $3y$, $3xy$, x^2, $9y^2$;
$(x - 3y)(x^2 + 3xy + 9y^2)$ **b.** 2, r, $2r$, 4, r^2;
$(2 + r)(4 - 2r + r^2)$ **c.** $5m$, $2n$, $10mn$, $25m^2$, $4n^2$;
$(5m + 2n)(25m^2 - 10mn + 4n^2)$ **d.** 1, $3p$, $3p$, 1, $9p^2$;
$(1 - 3p)(1 + 3p + 9p^2)$ **e.** x, $10y$, $10xy$, x^2, $100y^2$;
$(x + 10y)(x^2 - 10xy + 100y^2)$ **f.** $4u$, $5v$, $20uv$, $16u^2$,
$25v^2$; $(4u - 5v)(16u^2 + 20uv + 25v^2)$
3. a. $(x + y)(x - y)(x^4 + x^2y^2 + y^4)$
b. $(4a^2 + b^3)(16a^4 - 4a^2b^3 + b^6)$
c. $(1 + x^2)(1 + x)(1 - x)(1 + x^4 + x^8)$
d. $(3a^3 - 5x^6)(9a^6 + 15a^3x^6 + 25x^{12})$
e. $(6x^2 - y^8)(36x^4 + 6x^2y^8 + y^{16})$
4. a. $x^3 + 3xy^2 + 3x^2y + y^3$ **b.** $8a^3 - 12a^2b + 6ab^2 - b^3$
c. $-26a^3 + 36a^2b + 18ab^2 + 28b^3$
5. a. $(ab^2 + 1)(a^2b^4 - ab^2 + 1)$
b. $(p^2q^3 - r)(p^4q^6 + rp^2q^3 + r^2)$
c. $2(2mn - 3)(4m^2n^2 + 6mn + 9)$
d. $(5 + xy^3)(25 - 5xy^3 + y^6)$
6. a. $(3c - 2d)(9c^2 + 6cd + 4d^2)$
b. $(5 - s)(25 + 5s + s^2)$ **c.** $\left(\frac{m}{7} - \frac{n}{4}\right)\left(\frac{m^2}{49} + \frac{mn}{28} + \frac{n^2}{16}\right)$
d. $\left(\frac{1}{9} - \frac{5p}{6}\right)\left(\frac{1}{81} + \frac{5p}{54} + \frac{25p^2}{36}\right)$
e. $\left(\frac{r}{10} - \frac{s}{4}\right)\left(\frac{r^2}{100} + \frac{rs}{40} + \frac{s^2}{16}\right)$ **f.** $\left(\frac{1}{4} - \frac{3z}{2}\right)\left(\frac{1}{16} + \frac{3z}{8} + \frac{9z^2}{4}\right)$
7. yes

Pages 41-43   1. a. $(2a + 7b)(3c - d)$
b. $(4x + y)(5z + 3)$ **c.** $(2p - q)(m - 6n)$
d. $(5s + 12r)(r - 3t)$ **e.** $(8v - 3u)(v - 2w)$
f. $(c + 6a)(c + 4b)$ **g.** $(2x + 3y)(x - 5)$
h. $(3p + 2s)(3p + 4r)$ **i.** $(5x - 2y)(2x - 5z)$
2. a. $5(m + 2n)(m - 2n)$ **b.** $3a(2a + 3b^2)(2a - 3b^2)$
c. $2(6x + 1)(x - 2)$ **d.** $y(y - 4)^2$
e. $2(x^2 + 4)(x + 2)(x - 2)$ **f.** $pq(2p + 1)(2p - 3)$
g. $m^2(2m - 1)(m + 5)$ **h.** $(x + y)(x - y)(x - 3y)$
3. a. $(m + 5 + n)(m + 5 - n)$
b. $(b + 3a + 3)(b + 3a - 3)$
c. $(x - 2y + 2z)(x - 2y - 2z)$
d. $(c + 4d - 2a)(c + 4d + 2a)$
e. $(5p + 2q + 1)(5p + 2q - 1) - 10pq$
f. $(4r - s + 4t)(4r - s - 4t)$
g. $(3v + 2u + w^2)(3v + 2u - w^2)$
h. $(3 + a + b)(3 - a - b)$ **i.** $(5 + 2m - n)(5 - 2m + n)$
4. $(2p + 2q + r)(2p + 2q - r) + 2pq$
a. $4p(4p + q) + (2p - r)(2p + r)$ **b.** no
d. $4p(p + 4q) + (2q + r)(2q - r)$
5. a. $-4a(3a + b)(2a - b)$ **b.** $(q + 3)(q - 3)(p + 4)^2$
c. $(x^4 + 9)(x^2 + 3)(x^2 - 3)$ **d.** $5(3km + 4)(km - 5)$
6. a. $3x(x + 3)(x^2 - 3x + 9)$ **b.** $p(q - p)(q^2 + pq + p^2)$
c. $3[1 + 2(a + b)][1 - 2(a + b) + 4(a + b)^2]$

d. $x[(x - 2y) - 1][(x - 2y)^2 + (x - 2y) + 1]$
e. $(ab + 5a)(a^2b^2 + 5a^2b + 25a^2)$
f. $2p^2(r + q^2)(r - q^2)(r^2 + q^4)$
g. $(3x + 3 + y)(3x + 3 - y)$
h. $(a^3 - a^2b - c)(a^3 - a^2b + c)$ **i.** $(a - b)(a + b)^2$
j. $r^2(2 - s)(4 + 5s)$ **k.** $(x + 2y)(x - 2y)(x^2 + 2y^2)$
l. $4(k^2 + 3t^2)(k + t)(k - t)$
m. $a(2a^2 - b^2)(a - b)(a + b)$ **7. a.** $(3a + b)(c - 4d)$
b. $(x + 1)^2$ **c.** $(x + 1)(x - 8)$ **d.** $3x(x^4y - 2x + 4yz)$
e. $(2xy + 1)(xy - 4)$ **f.** $8(x - 3y)(x^2 + 3xy + 9y^2)$
g. $(2m + 3n^2)(2m - 3n^2)(4m^2 + 9n^4)$
h. $[5(a + b + c) + 1][(a + b + c) + 2]$
8. $(x - 1)(x + 2)(x - 2)$
9. a. $y^2(2x - 1)(2x + 1) - 4(x - 1)(x + 1)$
b. $(x + 1)(x^2 - x + 1)(y + 1)(y - 1)$
c. $(a + 4b)(a - 4b)(a + 2b)$
d. $(2x - 1)(4x^2 + 2x + 1)(y^2 + 2)$
e. $(3y + 2x - 4)(3y - 2x + 4)$
f. $2(m + 5)(m - 5)(n + 3)$
g. $5(p + q)(p + 1)(p^2 - p + 1)$
h. $(5 + 4a + 6b)(5 - 4a - 6b)$
i. $3s(r + 1)(r - 1)(t + 1)(t - 1)$
j. $(y - 1)(y^2 + y + 1)(x + 4)(x - 4)$
10. a. $(3a - 4)(a + 2)$ **b.** $(7y + 4)(y - 1)$
c. $2(6m^2 - 2n + 3mn^2 - 4m^8 - 9)$
d. $(x^2 + y^4)(x^4 - x^2y^4 + y^8)$ **e.** $[(a + b)^2 + 1]^2$
11. a. $(3x - 5y)(2x - 3y)$ **b.** $(2a - 5b)(a + 6b)$
c. $(p - 3q^2)(4p + q^2)$ **d.** $(3m + 8n)(m + 2n)$
e. $(5r - 6s)(r - 3s)$ **f.** $(2u - v)(9u + 4v)$
g. $(3a + 2bc)(a + 3bc)$ **h.** $(x^2 - 2y)(x^2 - 5y)$
i. $(s^3 + 3t^2)(4s^3 - 9t^2)$ **j.** $(2cd^2 + 5)(cd^2 - 3)$
k. $(6p + r^4)(p + 4r^4)$ **12. b.** yes **13. a.** $3(2x - 5) = 9$
b. $2x - 5 = 3$ **c.** 1 **14.** -3 **16.** 16
17. $V = \frac{1}{3}\pi h(x^2 + xy + y^2)$; if $x = y$, $V = \frac{1}{3}\pi h(3x^2)$ or
$\frac{1}{3}\pi h(3y^2)$; $V = \pi x^2 h$ or $\pi y^2 h$ **18.** no

Pages 44-45   1. a. $x(x + 8) - 3$
b. $x(5x - 4) - 10$ **c.** $x[2x(2x + 3) - 12] + 5$
d. $x\{x[2(4x^2 - 1) + 1] + 3\} - 6$ **e.** $x[-3x(2x - 5) + 2]$
f. $x[x(2x - 9) + 14] - 22$ **2.** yes **3. a.** $x(4x - 5) + 3$;
29, 12, 3, 2, 9, 24 **b.** $x[x(x - 2) + 8] - 12$; -44,
-23, -12, -5, 4, 21 **c.** $x[x^2(2x + 3) - 5] + 3$; 21, 7,
3, 3, 49, 231 **d.** $x[x(3x - 4) - 1] + 10$; -28, 4, 10,
8, 16, 52 **4. a.** 54 **b.** 0 **c.** 51 **d.** 6 **e.** 4 **f.** 27
5. $x(x + 4) - 5$ **a.** -8, -9, -8, -5, 0, 7, 16, 27, 40
b. $x = 1$ **6.** -3, -1.766, -0.248, 1.578, 3.736
7. -2, -1.58, -1.17, -0.75, -0.34, 0.07
8. b. $V = \pi L(R^2 - r^2) \rightarrow \pi L(R + r)(R - r)$
c. $57\,000\pi$ **d.** $1{:}1.04$ or $25{:}26$ **9.** -16, -10.36,
-4, -1.24, 2.25, -0.86, -0.49, -0.12, 0.24 **10.** 6
a. yes **11.** 0.88π cm^2 **12. a.** $(x + 1)(x - 4)$
b. $(3x + 5)(2x - 7)$ **c.** $2(x + 1)(x + 11)$ **d.** $(x - 3)^2$
e. $8(x - 1)(x^2 - x + 1)$ **f.** $16(x^2 - 2y^2)(x^6 + 2y^2)$
g. $(3x - 4)(x + 2)$ **h.** $c[3(ab + 2d + 3e) + b]$
i. $(x + 5y)(x - 4y)$

Pages 46-47   1. $3x^2$; $-18x$, 0   4. a. $x - 20$
b. $x + 4$ c. $x + 5$ d. $x^2 - 3x - 9$ e. $2x^2 + 5x - 4$
f. $8x^2 - x - 2$ 5. a. $6x + 5$; 1 b. $x^2 + 5x + 3$; 25
c. $3x^2 - 2x + 2$; -11 d. $4x^2 + 3x + 1$; 6
e. $6x^3 + 15x^2 - 11x - 6$; -34 6. a. $x^3 + 2x^2 - 6x - 3$
b. $x^2 + 2x + 4$ c. $3x^2 - 2x - 4$ d. $3x^3 - 11x^2 + 5x - 1$
e. $4x^2 + x + 6$ 7. yes 9. $x + 1$ **HISTORICAL
NOTE** 1. one billionth of a second 2. Common
Business Oriented Language 3. 138 889.89/s

Page 48   1. a. 0 b. 0, 5 c. -3, -2 d. $\frac{5}{2}$, -1
e. 5, -3 f. 0, 4 g. 0, 1, 2 h. $-\frac{7}{2}$, $\frac{3}{5}$ 2. a. 5, -1
b. -1, -2 c. 6, -6 d. 0, $\frac{5}{2}$ e. -6, 3 f. 3, 9
3. a. $y = -2$, $x = \frac{5}{4}$ b. $x = \frac{3}{4}$, $y = -2x$ c. $y = \frac{1}{2}$,
$x = 6$ 4. a. $y = 0$, 7, -1 b. $x = -1$ c. $m = -13$, 4
d. $x = \pm 1$ e. $p = 0$, -6, 2 f. $x = -\frac{7}{2}$, $\frac{2}{3}$
5. a. $x = -3$, $\frac{1}{2}$ b. $x = 1$, -1, $\frac{1}{2}$ c. $x = -1$, $\frac{4}{5}$
6. a. $x = \frac{9}{5}$, -4 b. $x = -\frac{1}{3}$, -1 c. $x = \frac{4}{3}$, $-\frac{1}{2}$
d. $x = 0$, -5 e. $y = 1$, 8 f. $p = -1$, $-\frac{3}{4}$ 7. 13 cm

Pages 49-50   2. yes 4. $x - 6$ 5. a, b, e, and f
6. a. ± 1, ± 3, ± 9 b. ± 1, ± 2, ± 3, ± 6 7. yes
8. a. $(x - 2)(x + 4)(x + 5)$ b. $(x - 1)(x^3 - x^2 + 8x + 7)$
c. $(x - 3)(x^2 + 3x + 12)$ d. $(m + 2)(m - 4)(m + 1)$
e. $(y - 3)(y + 3)^2$ f. $x(x^2 - 3x - 2)$ 10. a. 24 b. 12
c. 20 d. -18 e. -5 f. -54 g. 3 h. 24
11. a. $(y - 2)(y - 3)(y + 1)$ b. $(x - 3)(x - 2)(x + 4)$
c. $(x - 1)(2x + 3)(x + 7)$ d. $(x + 1)(x^3 + 5x^2 - 5x + 4)$
e. $(x + 1)(x - 2)(2x - 1)(x + 4)$ 13. no 15. x^3, $-abc$
16. $x^2 + x + 3$

Page 51   2. a. 2 b. -31 c. 17 d. 1313 4. -22
6. $x^3 + 3x^2 + 3x + 5$ 7. $k = \pm 2$ 8. $23 + 41 + 5$
9. b. $-\frac{49}{27}$, $\frac{47}{8}$, $-\frac{29}{64}$

Pages 52-53   1. a. a, $b \neq 0$ b. $x \neq 2$, $-\frac{3}{4}$
c. $x \neq \frac{1}{2}$ d. $x \neq -\frac{5}{2}$, 3 e. $x \neq \pm 2$ f. $x \neq 0$, 1
3. a. $a - 3$ b. $\frac{1}{2}x - \frac{7}{2}$ c. $2(3x + 1)$
d. $h = 4(2m + 8)$ 5. a. $5x$; $y \neq 0$ b. $\frac{3}{7} + \frac{1}{x}$; $x \neq 0$
c. $\frac{4a}{-3b^2}$; a, $b \neq 0$ d. $\frac{pr^2}{4}$; p, $q \neq 0$ e. $\frac{x - 2y}{3xy}$; x, $y \neq 0$
f. $\frac{3}{c - 4}$; $c \neq \pm 4$ 5. a. $\frac{-1}{m + 5}$; $m \neq 6$, -5
b. $\frac{(r + 1)}{r}$; $r \neq 0$, 8 c. $\frac{a + 4}{a + 2}$; $a \neq 9$, -2 d. $\frac{k - 3}{k + 5}$;

$k \neq 3$, -5 6. $4x + 1$ 7. a. $\frac{x + 3}{x - 2}$; $x \neq \frac{1}{4}$, 2
b. $\frac{5k - 1}{2k + 3}$; $k \neq -\frac{3}{2}$ c. $\frac{2n - 5}{6n + 1}$; $n \neq \pm \frac{1}{6}$
d. $\frac{5p + 1}{3p - 2}$; $p \neq 4$, $\frac{2}{3}$ e. $\frac{2y - 3}{y + 5}$; $y \neq -\frac{1}{2}$, -5
f. $\frac{2u}{4u - 5}$; $u \neq \frac{5}{4}$ g. $\frac{-(2a + 3)}{2a - 3}$; $a \neq 5$, $\frac{3}{2}$
h. $\frac{8r + 3}{r + 3}$; $r \neq \frac{1}{2}$, -3 8. $(6t - 15)$ km/h 9. a. no
b. $\frac{2(x - 1)}{3x - 4}$; $x \neq \frac{4}{3}$, $-\frac{7}{2}$ 10. a. $\frac{2x + 1}{4x^2 + 2x + 1}$; $x \neq \frac{1}{2}$
b. $a + 3$ c. $\frac{25p^2 - 5p + 1}{2p - 1}$; $p \neq -\frac{1}{5}$, $\frac{1}{5}$
d. $\frac{a^2 + 2ab + 4b^2}{a - 2b}$; $a \neq 2b$ e. $\frac{-(2t + 3s)}{9s^2 + 6st + 9t^2}$; $s \neq \frac{2}{3}t$
f. $\frac{k^2 + 6km + 36m^2}{2k + m}$; $k \neq 6m$, $-\frac{1}{2}m$
11. $25x^2 + 10x + 4$ cm² 12. $2n + 10$

Pages 54-55   2. a. $a \neq -1$ b. $a \neq -1$
c. $k \neq 0$, 3, -3, $-\frac{1}{4}$ d. $m \neq \pm 2$, $\frac{10}{3}$ 3. a. $\frac{1}{3}$ b. $\frac{1}{4}$
c. $\frac{10}{x}$; $x \neq 0$ d. $\frac{14}{3y}$; $y \neq 0$ 4. a. $\frac{2}{5xy}$; x, $y \neq 0$
b. $-\frac{b}{4}$; a, $b \neq 0$ c. $\frac{2n^2}{m^4}$; m, $n \neq 0$ d. $\frac{3}{28}$; a, $b \neq 0$
5. $\left(\frac{1}{100(x - 3)}\right)$ 7. $\frac{1}{x(x - 4)}$; $x \neq -\frac{1}{3}$, 4, 0
8. $\pi\left(4m - \frac{5}{2}\right)^2$ cm² 9. a. $\frac{b - 3}{2b + 4}$; $b \neq \pm 2$, $\frac{1}{5}$
b. $\frac{4m^2 + 2m + 1}{2}$; $m \neq 3$, $\frac{1}{2}$, $-\frac{5}{6}$
c. $\frac{-4a(a - b)}{3a^2 - 2a + b^2}$; $d \neq \pm 2c$ d. $\frac{4k + 2}{3k}$; $k \neq 0$, -3
e. $\frac{p - 6q}{2(p^2 - pq + q^2)}$; $p \neq q$, $\pm \frac{3}{4}q$
f. $\frac{3(y + 4z)(x + 3)}{10}$; $x \neq 3$, $y \neq -4z$
g. $\frac{(3a - b - 4c)(a^2 + 2ab + 4b^2)}{4(a + 2b)(a^2 - 2ab + 4b^2)}$; $a \neq -2b$ 10. $84.00
11. $(x^6 - x^3y^3 + y^6)$ 12. a. $\frac{m - 1}{m}$; $m \neq 0$, ± 1
b. $\frac{4x^2 - 10x + 25}{3}$; $x \neq -2$, $\pm \frac{5}{2}$
c. $\frac{c + d}{5(c - 3d)}$; $a \neq -\frac{5}{3}$, $d \neq 2c$, $c \neq d$, $c \neq \pm 3d$ d. -1;
$m \neq -3$, $\frac{5}{2}$, $n \neq 2$ e. $\frac{25(2p - q)(p + 1)}{(q + 2p)(5p - 1)}$; $p \neq 3$, $\frac{1}{5}$, -1,
$q \neq -2p$ 13. $\frac{2x - 5}{6y(2x + 5)}$; $x \neq \pm \frac{5}{2}$, $\frac{9}{2}$, $y \neq 0$

Pages 56-57   1. a. 6 b. 225 c. $198xy$ d. $12x^2y^2$
e. $6(x - 4)$ f. abc 2. a. $\frac{28abc}{4ab}$ b. $\frac{16a^2bc}{20ab}$
c. $\frac{8a^2b + 12abc}{4ab}$ d. $\frac{4a^2b + 4ab^2 + 4abc + 36ab}{4ab}$

3. $a, b \neq 0$; yes **4. a.** $\dfrac{11}{3ac}$ **b.** $\dfrac{13}{x+2}$ **c.** $\dfrac{2}{x}$ **d.** $\dfrac{2t-3}{t-3}$

e. $\dfrac{11m}{m+5}$ **f.** $\dfrac{2(s+3)}{s-3}$ **5. a.** $\dfrac{1}{xy}$ **b.** $\dfrac{4}{5x}$ **c.** $\dfrac{7y-6}{y-1}$

d. $-\dfrac{2b+5}{b+4}$ **e.** $\dfrac{2}{a}$ **f.** $\dfrac{3x^2-5x+4}{x^2}$ **6. a.** $\dfrac{13}{4x}$ **b.** $\dfrac{32-a}{10}$

c. $\dfrac{c-3}{abc}$ **d.** $\dfrac{5}{2}$ **e.** $\dfrac{7+3y}{y}$ **f.** $\dfrac{9a-10b}{5a^2b^2}$ **g.** $\dfrac{11y+25}{2(y+3)^2}$

7. $\dfrac{1}{2}$ **8.** $\dfrac{17}{2(x+2)}$ **9.** $\dfrac{x-9}{2(x+3)}$ **10.** $\dfrac{3x+5}{x-3}$

11. $x = 15$ cm **12. a.** $\dfrac{-3x^2-22x-4}{(5x+1)(3x-2)}$ **b.** $\dfrac{12m-13}{5(m+1)}$

c. $\dfrac{3x^2-14x-3}{(x-6)(x-3)(x+3)}$ **d.** $\dfrac{-8m^2-14m-1}{(m+3)(2m-1)}$

e. $\dfrac{g(10p^2+27)}{15p}$

Pages 58-59

1. a. $x \neq \dfrac{4}{5}, y \neq -\dfrac{3}{2}$

b. $a \neq -\dfrac{1}{4}, 3, p \neq \pm\dfrac{5}{2}$ **c.** $x \neq 4y, -2y, m \neq 5n,$

$-\dfrac{1}{2}n,$ **2.** no **3. a.** $\dfrac{4x^2-2x-8}{3(x-4)}; x \neq 4$

b. $\dfrac{a^2+8a-17}{(a+3)(a-5)}; a \neq -3, 5$ **c.** $\dfrac{6k-5}{3k-1}; k \neq \pm\dfrac{1}{3}$

d. $\dfrac{2m^2+14m+3}{(2m+1)(2m+8)}; m \neq -\dfrac{1}{2}$

e. $\dfrac{3p^2+7p+9}{10(p+1)}; p \neq \pm1, p \neq \dfrac{3}{2}$

f. $\dfrac{2x^2+x+18}{(x-3)(x^2+3x+9)}; x \neq 3$ **4. a.** $\dfrac{26x-5}{3x(x-1)}; x \neq 0, 1$

b. $\dfrac{2(5x+7)}{(x+1)(x+2)}; x \neq -1, -2$

5. a. $\dfrac{(3x^2+6x+3)}{(2x+1)(2x-1)}; x \neq \pm\dfrac{1}{2}$

b. $\dfrac{6s^2+25s+16}{5(2s-1)}; s \neq \dfrac{1}{2}, 5, t \neq 2$

c. $\dfrac{(2+x)(x-y-2)-(x+y)}{(2+x)}; x-y \neq 2, x \neq \pm2$

d. $\dfrac{5a^3-3a^2-48a+14}{2(a+1)(a-2)}; a \neq -1, 2$

e. $\dfrac{-p^3-p^2+72p-48}{2p(p-4)^2}; p \neq -3, 4, 0$

6. a. $\dfrac{11x-26}{3x(x-1)}; x \neq 0, 1$ **b.** $\dfrac{7(x-1)}{x^2}; x \neq 0$

7. $\dfrac{(x^2+3x+9)(x-1)-5x}{(x-3)(x^2+3x+9)}; x \neq 3$

8. $\dfrac{3a^3+8a^2b-3ab^2+8a-2b}{(4a-b)(a+3b)}; a \neq -3b, \dfrac{b}{4}$

10. a. $\dfrac{12n+52}{(n+1)(n+3)}; n \neq -1, -3$

b. $\dfrac{24x-13}{(2x+1)(x-2)}; x \neq 2, -\dfrac{1}{2}$

Pages 60-61

2. a. 24 **b.** $60ab^2$ **c.** $4c^2-6c$
d. $3x^2-2x-5$ **e.** $8k^2+24k$ **f.** y^2-9 **g.** $30xy^2$

h. $30m^2n^2$ **3. a.** $\dfrac{17}{5}$ **b.** $-\dfrac{17}{5}$ **c.** $-\dfrac{59}{6}$ **d.** -10 **e.** $\dfrac{28}{13}$

f. $-\dfrac{33}{26}$ **4. a.** $\dfrac{5}{4}; x \neq 0$ **b.** $-4; c \neq -1$

c. $-\dfrac{26}{11}; x \neq -6, \dfrac{2}{3}$ **d.** $\dfrac{25}{4}; a \neq 0$ **e.** $-\dfrac{6}{7}; y \neq 0, 2$

f. $-\dfrac{2}{3}; m \neq 0$ **5. a.** $\dfrac{6}{17}$ **b.** $-\dfrac{1}{2}$ **c.** $\dfrac{29}{11}$ **d.** $\dfrac{17}{4}$ **e.** $\dfrac{4}{5}$

f. $-\dfrac{3}{17}$ **g.** $\dfrac{3}{4}$ **h.** $\dfrac{8}{5}$ **6.** 36 km **7. a.** $\dfrac{17}{3}; x \neq \pm3, 0, \dfrac{7}{2}$

b. $-\dfrac{13}{4}; p \neq -3, 0$ **c.** $-2; k \neq -3, 0, 2$ **d.** $\dfrac{3}{5};$

$n \neq \pm1$ **e.** $-\dfrac{3}{7}; a \neq -1, -\dfrac{2}{5}, -\dfrac{1}{4}, 0, \dfrac{1}{2}$

8. a. $\dfrac{10}{3}$ ohms **b.** $p = 12, q = 6$ **9.** 72 cm²

10. 8, 18, 40 **11.** $\dfrac{-(x+14x-16)}{2(x-1)}$

Page 62
1. line 40 **3.** when $y>0$ **4.** to print the number **5.** 1.6190001 **a.** 1.618 033 99 **c.** the Golden Ratio **7.** 20 REM THE EQUATION $X - 1 / X - 1 = 0$ • 40 LET $Y = X - 1 / X - 1$

Page 63
1. a. $10a^2-51a+27$
b. $12p^2-51p-45$ **c.** $4s^2+4s+1$ **d.** $8k^2-48k+72$
e. $4x^3-5x^2y-10xy^2-3y^3$ **f.** $a^2+6ab+9b^2-16c^2$
2. a. $7x^2+x+13$ **b.** $38-11t$ **c.** $40m^2+22m+60$
d. $39s+12$ **3. a.** $(2a-3b)(a+5d)$
b. $(2y-3z)(4x-y)$ **c.** $(2m^2+5)(3n-5)$
d. $(3a-b)(4a+1)$ **4. a.** $(x+5+y)(x+5-y)$
b. $(3+2a-b)(3-2a+b)$
c. $(3n+2m+2p)(3n+2m-2p)$
d. $(x-3+y+z)(x-3-y-z)$
5. a. $(x-3y)(x^2+3xy+9y^2)$
b. $(5a+1)(25a^2-5a+1)$
c. $(2p-3q)(4p^2+6pq^2+9q^4)$
d. $2(5m+2n)(25m^2+10mn+4n^2)$
e. $(x+2-y)[(x+2)^2+y(x+2)+y^2]$
f. $(4+a-3b)[16-4(a-3b)+(a-3b)^2]$
6. $(2x-1)$ units
7. a. $(2+j)(4-2j+j^2)(k+2)(k-2)$
b. $(x+1)(x^2-x+1)(2y-5)$
c. $(y+2)(y-2)(2x+1)(2x-1)$
d. $(y+2)(y-2)(x+1)(x+2)$
8. a. $(p^2+3q^2+2pq)(p^2+3q^2-2pq)$
b. $(2c^2-d^2+4cd)(2c^2-d^2-4cd)-d^4$
c. $(5x^2-4y^2)^2+31x^2y^2$
d. $(3a^2-b^2c^4+2abc^2)(3a^2-b^2c^4-2abc^2)$ **9.** d and f
10. a. $x+1$ **b.** $x+2$ **c.** $x-3$ **11.** $k = 16$
12. a. $x \neq 0$ **b.** $x \neq -\dfrac{5}{2}, 3$ **13. a.** $\dfrac{4m}{3n^2}$ **b.** $-\dfrac{3y}{4x^5}$

c. $\dfrac{2}{3t}$ **d.** $\dfrac{m+1}{m-5}$ **e.** $\dfrac{4a-b}{2a+b}$ **f.** $\dfrac{8c+3d}{c^2+2cd+4d^2}$ **g.** $\dfrac{2p+3q}{2p-5q}$

h. $\dfrac{2}{3x+1+y}$ **14.** -20 **15. a.** $\dfrac{x+2}{3x}$ **b.** $\dfrac{2x}{3x+5}$

c. $\dfrac{2c+d}{(4a^2+6ab+9b^2)}$ **d.** $\dfrac{(m-3n)(5n)}{p(n-3m)(m-n)}$ **16. a.** $\dfrac{17(a+1)}{24}$

b. $\dfrac{3(5x-7)}{4x(x-3)}$ **c.** $\dfrac{-5x^2-8x+8}{(3x+1)(x-4)}$ **d.** $\dfrac{34x-3}{5x(2x+1)}$

Page 64   **1. a.** $3m^2 - 14mn + 8n^2$
b. $6x^2 + 27xy - 15y^2$ **c.** $4a^3 - 7a^2b - 23ab^2 - 10b^3$
d. $p^2 + q^2 + 25r^2 - 2pq + 10pr - 10qr$
2. a. $(2a + 3b)(2c + d)$ **b.** $(5b^2 + 1)(25b^4 - 5b^2 + 1)$
c. $2x(x + 3y)(x - 3y)$ **d.** $(x - 2y + z)(x - 2y - z)$
e. $2(k + 2)(k^2 - 2k + 4)$ **f.** $(3y + 2)(x + 4)(x - 1)$
g. $(2x - 3 + y)(2x - 3 - y)$
h. $4s(3s - 1)(9s^2 + 3s + 1)$ **i.** $b^2(2a - 1)(2a + 9)$
j. $(1 - 50m^2)(3q - 2p)$
4. a. $(4x^2 + 1 + x)(4x^2 + 1 - x)$
b. $(2a^2 - 3b^2 + 4ab)(2a^2 - 3b^2 - 4ab)$
c. $(m^2 + n^4 + 5mn^2)(m^2 + n^4 - 5mn^2)$
d. $(2r^2 + 2t^2 - 3rt)(2r^2 + 2t^2 + 3rt)$
5. $(x - 1)(x + 2)(x - 4)$ **6.** $x = 0, \dfrac{5}{2}, -6$
7. a. $k = 6.5$ **b.** $k = 40$ **c.** $k = -13$
8. $2a^3 - 4a^2b + 2ab^2 + 36b^3$ **9. a.** $x \neq 0$ **b.** $x \neq \pm 2$
10. a. $\dfrac{-3(a + 3)}{10}$ **b.** $\dfrac{3k^2 - 7k + 10}{k(k - 2)}$
c. $\dfrac{-x - 3}{(2x - 1)(x + 6)(x - 4)}$ **d.** $\dfrac{p^2 - 6p - 21}{(2p + 5)(p + 3)}$
e. $\dfrac{15y^3 - 76y^2 - 11y - 6}{2y(9y^2 + 1)}$ **11.** $\dfrac{4b^2 + 40b + 75}{3(2b + 9)}$
12. $2x^2 + 11x + 44$ remainder 128
13. $\dfrac{3m^2 + 13mn - 10n^2}{10}$ **14.** $(3x - 1)(x + 4)$
15. a. $\dfrac{7a}{-2b^2}$ **b.** $-\dfrac{1}{3}$ **c.** $\dfrac{2p - 3}{6p - 1}$ **d.** $\dfrac{3x - 1}{x + 8}$ **e.** $\dfrac{4a - b}{3a + b}$
f. $\dfrac{9m^2 + 3mn + n^2}{m - 5}$ **g.** $\dfrac{x + 2 + 3y}{2}$ **h.** $x + 2$
16. $d = \dfrac{4p^2 - 10pq + 25q^2}{p - q}; p \neq -\dfrac{5q}{2}, q$

Chapter 3

Page 65   **1. a.** $\dfrac{58}{103}$ **b.** $\dfrac{5x^2}{y^2}, y \neq 0$ **c.** $\dfrac{x}{x + 2}$,
$x \neq \pm 2$ **d.** $11 + x, x \neq 11$ **e.** $3t$ **f.** $1, z \neq -6, -1$
g. $\dfrac{17s}{31t}, t \neq 0$ **h.** $x^3 + 1, x \neq 0$ **i.** $ab - 2t, ab \neq -2t$
j. $\dfrac{1}{3}$ **k.** $\dfrac{1}{x - y}, x \neq \pm y$ **l.** $\dfrac{r}{2}, r \neq 0$ **2. a.** 1 **b.** $\dfrac{16}{x}, \dfrac{16}{3}$
c. $\dfrac{(x - 2)^2}{4t}, \dfrac{1}{8}$ **3.** factoring **4. b.** $\dfrac{8}{3\pi} = \dfrac{y}{x}$ **c.** $\dfrac{2}{5} = \dfrac{y}{x}$
d. $\dfrac{7}{6} = \dfrac{y}{x}$ **e.** $\dfrac{24}{9t + 4s} = \dfrac{y}{x}$ **5. a.** $x = -10$ **b.** $x = -3$
c. $x = -1$ **d.** no solution **6.** $\dfrac{x - 8}{x}; \dfrac{6}{14} = \dfrac{3}{7}$ **7. g.** a,
b, e, f **h.** c, d; c **9.** no

Pages 66-69   **1. a.** 1:3 **b.** 3:4 **c.** 9:16 **d.** 1:2
e. 2:1:4 **f.** 34:17:26 **2. a.** $3y$:1:$9yz$ **b.** 5:13:16:21
c. 1:$(x + 1)$ **d.** $3y$:4 **e.** x:$(x + 4)$
f. $(x + 2)$:$(2x + 3)$:$(x + 5)$ **g.** $(2a + 1)$:$(2a + 3)$:a
4. a. 125:1 **b.** 65:3 **c.** 3:80 **d.** 10:3 **5.** 2:5
6. a. 3:8 **b.** It is a ratio, 375:1000. **c.** 24 **7.** 40

8. 173 333.33:476 666.67 **9. a.** 35 wins, 45 losses
b. 7 wins, 9 losses **c.** wins + losses = games played
10. a. 1:4 **b.** 100:1 **11. a.** 1:27 **b.** 1000:1:1000
12. 95 857.99 **13.** 8:11:2 **14.** 15, 30, 55
15. 62.1 m/s, 20.7 m/s **16.** 224 847 km/s **17.** 16 m,
6 m, 4 m **18. a.** 1.625 **b.** 1.618 03... **19.** 12 girls
20. a. 5:14 **b.** 360 cm² **c.** 30:7 **d.** c **21.** perimeter
of the top **22.** 4:1 **23.** 10 L **24.** $7806.12
27. a. 5.625 cm **b.** 5.3̇ cm **c.** 33.33 mm

Pages 70-71   **2. a.** 432 **b.** 15; 59.5 **c.** 18; $3\dfrac{1}{2}$
d. 15; $7x$; 2.5 **e.** 17; 1; 255 **f.** 5; bc **3. a.** $1229.41
b. $1005.88 **c.** 732.06 **4.** $x = \dfrac{1}{2}$ **5. a.** 16.875 **b.** 9
c. $3\sqrt{8}$ **d.** 16 **6. a.** 25 **b.** 9 **c.** $\sqrt{xy}$ **7.** $\dfrac{11}{6}$
8. 87.5 kPa **9. a.** $\dfrac{a}{b} = \dfrac{c}{d}$ then $\dfrac{a}{c} = \dfrac{b}{d}$ **b.** $\dfrac{a}{b} = \dfrac{c}{d}$
then $\dfrac{b}{a} = \dfrac{d}{c}$ **c.** $\dfrac{a}{b} = \dfrac{c}{d}$ then $\dfrac{a + b}{b} = \dfrac{c + d}{d}$ **d.** $\dfrac{a}{b} = \dfrac{c}{d}$
then $\dfrac{a + kb}{b} = \dfrac{c + kd}{d}$ **11. a.** yes **b.** no **c.** no **d.** yes
e. no **12.** $\dfrac{2}{3}$ **13.** 15 hockey, 35 football

Pages 72-73   **2. a.** 9600 **b.** 48 000 **c.** 1920
d. 3200 **e.** 640 **f.** 533 **4. a.** 4230 **5.** 100 kN
6. 26.25 L³ **7.** 24 000 mL of salad oil, 11 840 mL of
mild vinegar **8.** no **9.** 89 **10. a.** $\overline{DE}$ = 7.5 cm;
$\overline{DF}$ = 13.5 cm **b.** $\overline{XY}$ = 4.8 m; $\overline{PR}$ = 2.9 m
11. a. 32.625 kg/s **12.** 700 cm³ **13. a.** no **c.** 80

Pages 74-76   **1.** 2 **3.** no, joint variation
4. a. $a \propto b$ and $a = kb$ **b.** $x \propto y^2$ and $x = ky^2$ **c.** $M \propto DV$
and $M = kDV$ **6.** The graph is a straight line and
passes through (0, 0). **7. a.** 40 **b.** 108 **c.** 3 **d.** −88
8. F is doubled; F is halved. **9.** 7.8 kW; 78 kW;
130 kW **10.** 21 093.75 cm³/s **11.** 106.82 m
12. b. direct variation **c.** 130.7 m **13. b.** direct
c. Time increases by $\sqrt{2}$; time decreases by $\dfrac{1}{\sqrt{2}}$.
14. b. joint **c.** It will increase fourfold. **d.** 400 J

Pages 77-79   **2.** no **3. a.** $x \propto \dfrac{1}{y}$ and $x = \dfrac{k}{y}$
b. $x \propto \dfrac{y}{z^2}$ and $x = \dfrac{ky}{z^2}$ **c.** $x \propto \dfrac{1}{yz}$ and $x = \dfrac{k}{yz}$ **d.** $a \propto \dfrac{y^2}{xz}$ and
$a = \dfrac{ky^2}{xz}$ **4. a.** 43.75 **b.** 104.2 **c.** 17.5 **d.** 437.5
5. $\dfrac{1}{63}$ **6. a.** 500 **b.** 6 **c.** $\dfrac{10}{7}$ **d.** $55x$ **7.** y increases
by $\sqrt{2}$ **8.** yes **9.** 3.16 h **10.** $296 **11. b.** 9.375 L
12. 180 rev/s **13.** 3 m **14.** no **15. a.** $F = \dfrac{km_1m_2}{d^2}$
b. $1.\dot{3} \times 10^{-10}$ **16.** 469
Pages 80-81   **2. a.** $200.00 **b.** $262.50
c. $325.00 **d.** $450.00 **3. a.** $C = 2.25 + 0.9n$

469

b. $34.38 **4. b.** $C = 43 + 7.38(n - 6)$, $n \geq 6$
c. $61.45 **5. a.** $I = 110\ 000 + 10g + 12r + 16b$
b. $210 180 **6. a.** $C = 10\ 000 + 0.045b$ **b.** $32 500
7. a. $-38°C$ **b.** $10.3°C$ **c.** 6 600 m
9. a. $C_A = 600 + 25d$, $C_B = 300 + 50d$, $C_C = 100d$
b. Plan A **c.** Plan C

Pages 82-85 **2.** direct variation
3. 3.5×10^{13} cd **4.** 6 h, 40 min **6. a.** partial
c. $C = 300 + 6.5n$, $n \leq 75$ **7. a.** t is directly
proportional to P and inversely proportional to k. **b.** x
is directly proportional to the product of p and y. **c.** T
is directly proportional to x^2 and inversely proportional
to y. **8.** 759 **9. b.** direct variation **c.** 158 400 m
10. 5960 kW **11. a.** combined **b.** C is reduced by
$\frac{1}{3}$. **12. a.** $P = k\frac{v}{r^2}$ **b.** combined **c.** P will be
quadrupled. **13.** $22 857 **15. a.** joint variation
16. yes **17.** 70°, 90°, 20° **18.** 18, 24 **19.** $x = \frac{17}{2}$

20. a. $\frac{a+b}{b} = \frac{c+d}{d}$ and $\frac{a-b}{b} = \frac{c-d}{d}$, therefore
$\dfrac{\frac{a+b}{b}}{\frac{a-b}{b}} = \dfrac{\frac{c+d}{d}}{\frac{c-d}{d}}$ therefore $\frac{a+b}{a-b} = \frac{c+d}{c-d}$ **b.** proven the
same way **21. a.** 4:3 **b.** 7:3 **c.** 7:−1 **d.** 5:4
22. a. $m \propto \frac{1}{n}$ **b.** yes **c.** no **d.** increase by $-\frac{1}{4}$
23. 2.5 t **24.** $\frac{7}{1536}$ units **25.** $66\frac{2}{3}$ s **26.** 761.7 N

BRAINTICKLER $\frac{\pi(r+n)}{2}$

Page 86 **1.** calculation of the unknowns in the
proportion **2.** to determine that the proportion is
defined **4. a.** $\frac{12}{11}, \frac{15}{11}$ **b.** $\frac{5}{9}, \frac{5}{3}$ **c.** 0, 0 **d.** undefined
e. $\frac{200}{51}, \frac{202}{51}$ **5. a.** to solve proportions in which the
terms of each ratio are in fractional form
b. $x = \frac{36}{35}$, $y = \frac{12}{35}$ **6.** 10 REM A PROGRAM TO
FIND A QUADRUPLE RATIO • 20 REM OF THE
FORM X:Y:Z:Q = A:B:C:D • 30 REM WHERE X,
Q, B, C, D ARE GIVEN • 40 INPUT "ENTER
CONSTANTS X, Q, B, C, D"; X, Q, B, C, D •
50 IF D = 0 THEN 120 • 60 IF Q = 0 THEN 120 •
70 LET Z = Q / D * C • 80 LET Y = Q / D * B •
90 LET A = D / Q * X • 100 PRINT "THE RATIO
IS "; X; ":"; Y; ":"; Z; ":"; Q; " = "; A; ":"; B;
":"; C; ":"; D • 110 GOTO 140 • 120 PRINT
"RATIO IS UNDEFINED. ENTER NEW DATA" •
130 GOTO 40 • 140 END

Page 87 **1. a.** 1:2 **b.** 1:3 **c.** 18:5 **d.** 1:4
e. $3xy:51$ **f.** 9:20:43 **g.** $(x - 3):3$
h. $(x - 1):2z(x^2 - 1):3$ **2. b.** a right triangle **c.** $\frac{20}{3}, \frac{25}{3}$

4. 1:16 **5. a.** $400 savings bonds; $333 guaranteed
interest certificates; $267 simple stocks **b.** $444,
$370, $296 **6. a.** $56\frac{1}{4}$ **b.** $2\sqrt{2}$ **c.** $\frac{221}{270}$ **d.** $100\sqrt{2}$
e. $\frac{156}{51}$ **f.** $\frac{a}{b}$ **8.** 6:3 **9.** 600 L **10. b.** joint variation
11. 9.1×10^{-5} m **12.** no **13. a.** $C = 45 + 8.55t$
b. partial variation **c.** $1011.15 **14. a.** 3:4 **b.** 7:12
c. 9:16 **d.** $-1:\frac{3}{4}$ **e.** 4:3 **f.** 1:−1

Page 88 **1. a.** 23:96 **b.** $1:x^2 + 1$ **c.** $mn:qr$
d. $3:x$ **e.** $x^2 + 3x + 9:4$ **f.** $3:8y:16yz$ **2. a.** $x = \frac{80}{29}$,
$y = \frac{96}{29}$ **b.** $x = \frac{12}{13}$, $y = 39$ **3. a.** $\frac{2}{3}r^2:1$ **b.** Volume
would increase eightfold. **5. a.** $-\frac{73}{13}$ **b.** 9 **c.** 16
d. $-\frac{1}{3}$ **e.** $27\sqrt{3}$ **6.** Division by zero is undefined,
so a ratio with respect to zero has no meaning.
7. a. $53\frac{1}{3}$ min on physics, 1 h $46\frac{2}{3}$ min on math and
5 h 20 min on chemistry **b.** 6:2:1 **8.** 285.6 g of nuts,
499.8 g of raisins, 214.2 g of dried fruits **9.** 1667
deer **10.** 625.2 g nuts, 1094.1 g raisins, 468.9 g
dried fruits, 312.6 g granola **11. a.** $k = 170$ **c.** direct
variation **12. a.** partial variation **b.** $C = 4500 + 125n$
c. 84 pages **13. a.** 7:1, 15:1, 31:1 **b.** $2^n - 1:1$

Cumulative Review Chapters 1-3

Pages 89-90 **1. a.** $11x - 5$ **b.** $7x + 21$
c. $11a^2 + 12ab - 8b^2$ **d.** $-3m^2 - 4mn + 14n^2$
2. a. $x \neq 0$; $-\frac{4}{x}$ **b.** $x \neq 4$; $\frac{4}{x-4}$ **c.** $x \neq \pm2$; $\frac{x+1}{2(x+2)}$
d. $x \neq 3$, $-\frac{5}{2}$; $\frac{2x+5}{x-3}$ **3. a.** $\frac{3}{x-5}$ **b.** $\frac{x-2}{2x(2x-3)}$
c. $\frac{13a+18}{2a(a+6)}$ **d.** $\frac{7}{(m+1)(m-3)}$ **4. a.** $a = -\frac{9}{4}$
b. $p = \frac{81}{8}$ **c.** $p = \frac{1}{25}$ **d.** $x \geq -6$ **e.** $x > 5$ **f.** $m = -\frac{11}{4}$
g. 17 **5.** 4 cm by 18 cm **6.** $4a^2 + 10a - 12$
7. a. $8a^2 - 22ab + 15b^2$ **b.** $4m^2 + 30mn - 16n^2$
c. $6x^3 + 15x^2 - 8x - 20$ **d.** $3p^3 + 2p^2 - 9p - 2$
8. a. $(3y + 2)(2x - 5)$ **b.** $3(2x + 1)(2x - 1)$
c. $(2a + 1)(6a - 5)$ **d.** $(p + 3)(p - 2)(p + 2)$
e. $(3 + m + 2n)(3 - m - 2n)$ **f.** $(2x - 3)(4x^2 + 6x + 9)$
9. a. $(x^2 + 2x - 2)(x^2 - 2x - 2)$
b. $(p^2 + 3pq + q^2)(p^2 - 3pq + q^2)$ **10. a.** $k = -12$
b. $k = 4$ **11. a.** $\frac{a^2 + ab + b^2}{c}$ **b.** $\frac{4(x + y)}{x + 2y + z}$
12. a. $\frac{2x^2 - 2x + 16}{(x + 2)(x - 5)}$ **b.** $\frac{24x^2 - 20x + 8}{(3x^2 + 5x - 2)(3x^2 - 5x + 2)}$
c. $\frac{-a^2 + 9a + 6}{(a - 2)(a + 3)}$ **d.** $\frac{2m^2 + 9mn + 4n^2 + m - 3n}{(m - 3n)(2m + n)}$

13. $6x^3 + 11x^2 - 13x + 2$ cm² **14. a.** 2:7 **b.** 3:15:7
c. 3:2 **d.** 2:(x − 1) **15.** 25 cm **16.** 19.2 cm
17. 24 dimes, 84 quarters **18.** 84°, 96° **19. a.** 8
b. $4\sqrt{6}$ **20. a.** $n = \frac{100}{9}$ **b.** $n = \frac{200}{3}$ **c.** $n = 6\sqrt{10}$
d. $n = \frac{9}{7}$ **21.** 3.7 h **22.** one ninth as intense
23. $692.50 **24.** 315 × 15 = 4725 **25.** The ratios are
not as specified in the will. **27.** division by zero in
step 3 **28.** $\frac{r}{R} = \frac{1}{\sqrt{2}}$ **29.** 0 **30.** $\frac{3}{52}$ **31.** 3 tables seating
6 and 6 tables seating 10

Chapter 4

Page 91 **1. a.** {1, 2, 3, 4, 5, 6, 7, 8, 9, 10}
b. {0, 1, 2, 3, 4, 5, 6, 7, 8, 9}
c. {−5, −4, −3, −2, −1, 0, 1, 2, 3, 4} **2.** rational
and irrational **3. a.** −14 **b.** 6 **c.** $\frac{17}{13}$ **d.** $\frac{10}{7}$ **e.** −3
f. $\frac{4}{11}$ **g.** 5 **4. a.** $35x^2y + 40xy^2$ **b.** $x^4y^2 - 3x^3y^3$
c. $6x^2 - 15xy + 9xz$ **d.** $x^2 + 2xy - 15y^2$
e. $4x^2 - 28xy + 49y^2$ **f.** $25x^2 - 81y^2$
5. a. $(x + 5)(x + 1)$ **b.** $(x + 10)(x − 8)$
c. $(x − 3)(6 − 7x)$ **d.** $(x − 5)(x + 3)$
e. $(3x + 2)(3x − 2)$ **f.** $(x + 0.2)(x − 0.1)$
g. $(3x + 1)(2x + 3)$ **h.** $5(2x − 1)(x − 3)$ **6. a.** 4, 5
b. $-\frac{7}{3}$, 1 **c.** 4, −4 **d.** $-\frac{4}{5}$, 2 **e.** $-\frac{3}{8}$, 4
f. $-\frac{3}{2}, -\frac{3}{14}$ **g.** $\frac{5}{4}, -\frac{5}{4}$ **h.** −2, 2 **7. a.** $3x − 4y$
b. $12xy^3 + 9y − 1$ **8. a.** $-\frac{699}{25}$ **b.** −33 **c.** 68
d. $\frac{127.125}{32}$ **9.** $200 674.90 **10. a.** 4 **b.** 3 **c.** 0
11. $40\sqrt{9.8}$ m/s

Pages 92-93 **1. a.** irrational **b.** rational
c. rational **d.** rational **e.** rational **f.** irrational
g. rational **h.** rational **i.** irrational **j.** irrational
3. a. 763; 3 **b.** 5; 1 **c.** 56; 2 **d.** 2122; 4 **4. a.** 0.375
b. $0.\overline{7}$ **c.** −3.5 **d.** $0.\overline{923\ 076}$ **e.** $0.\overline{142\ 857}$ **f.** 0.625
5. a. $\frac{71}{100}$ **b.** $\frac{3}{10}$ **c.** $\frac{5}{8}$ **d.** $\frac{7}{9}$ **e.** $\frac{41}{333}$ **f.** $\frac{1504}{3333}$ **g.** $\frac{2}{3}$
h. $\frac{47}{99}$ **i.** $\frac{2957}{9999}$ **6.** $\frac{4}{9}$ t **7.** $\frac{1}{4}$ of the circumference
8. $\frac{17}{90}$ **9.** $3.\overline{142\ 857}$ **10.** $0.\overline{142\ 857}$, $0.\overline{285\ 714}$,
$0.\overline{428\ 571}$ **a.** $0.\overline{571\ 428}$, $0.\overline{714\ 285}$, $0.\overline{857\ 142}$
11. a. $\frac{29}{90}$ **b.** $\frac{23}{30}$ **c.** $\frac{14}{15}$ **d.** $\frac{277}{99}$ **e.** $\frac{44}{75}$ **f.** $\frac{31}{165}$ **g.** $\frac{21}{55}$
h. $\frac{262}{1665}$ **i.** $\frac{217}{9900}$ **12. a.** $\frac{1}{6}$

Pages 94-95 **1. a.** reflexive **b.** transitive
2. a. no **4. a.** $b = 0$; $b<0$ **b.** $c = b + c$; $c<b + c$

c. = bc; $< bc$ **d.** $ac = bc$; $< bc$ **5. a.** no
b. multiplication property for $c<0$ **6. a.** identity
multiplication **b.** additive inverse **c.** closure
d. reflexive **e.** commutative addition **f.** distributive
g. distributive **h.** transitive **i.** trichotomy
j. transitive **k.** transitive **l.** multiplication for $c<0$
7. a. $x + 5>2x − 5$ **b.** $−3<m$ **c.** $q + p$ **d.** $y<w$
e. $< −3n$ **f.** $p>q$ **8. a.** $x<8$ **b.** $m>−12$ **c.** $y>−3$
d. $p<17$ **e.** $x<−4$ **f.** $x<−7$ **g.** $x>−26$
h. $x>−18$ **i.** $x>0$ **j.** $x>0$ **k.** $y≥3$ **l.** $d≤25$
10. a. 2800 **b.** 1245.4 **c.** 0 **HISTORICAL NOTE**
2. a. 9 **b.** 24

Pages 96-97 **1. a.** x^8 **b.** m^5 **c.** q^{19} **d.** p^{13} **e.** y^{48}
f. s^{33} **g.** c^5d^5 **h.** $32x^5$ **i.** a^6b^{16} **j.** $p^{25}q^{35}$
2. 268.1 cm³, 193 g **3.** 3.141 59 **4.** $1973.82
5. a. $-243x^{15}$ **b.** $16p^{12}q^8$ **c.** $p^{8x}q^{4y}$ **d.** $k^{10n^2 + 5n}m^{10n^2}$
e. $\frac{3}{2}x^4$ **f.** $\frac{-a^2}{56}$ **g.** $1600m^{18}n^{27}$ **h.** $-a^{37}b^{18}c^{41}$ **i.** $a^3b^9c^{15}$
j. $d^{4m}f^{4m}g^{4m}$ **k.** $-75m^{10}n^{15}$ **6. a.** $3^{(2^4)}$ **b.** 6561,
43 046 721 **7. a.** 318.596 **b.** 1296 **c.** 3125
d. 16 384 **e.** 169.835 63 **f.** 1.410 598 8
g. 1.050 844 9 **8.** 1.073 74 × 10⁹ **9. a.** $2^{4x − 4}$
b. $7^{−x + 2}$ **c.** $2^{−9x − 25}x^{2x + 3}$ **d.** $3^{−5x + 22}$ **e.** $2.5^{4x + 10}$
10. a. 1 **b.** 27 **c.** $\frac{3}{7}$ **11. a.** 67.265 557
b. 134.531 11 **c.** 47.085 89 **12.** for 2: 1.866 066,
1.414 213 6, 1.071 773 5; for 3: 1.933 182,
1.245 730 9, 1.056 467 3 **a.** 1 **b.** They all do.
13. a. 23 **b.** 109 **c.** 1024 **d.** 15 625 **e.** 11 025
f. $-\frac{216}{125}$ **14.** $0.\overline{304\ 347\ 826\ 086\ 956\ 521\ 739\ 1}$

Pages 98-99 **3.** 343 **4. a.** $\frac{1}{8}$ **b.** 1 **c.** −1
d. $-\frac{1}{27}$ **e.** $\frac{1}{64}$ **f.** $\frac{1}{49}$ **g.** undefined **h.** 8 **i.** $\frac{25}{9}$
j. −100 **k.** 16 **l.** 1 **5. a.** $\frac{1}{xy}$ **b.** x^5 **c.** $\frac{5}{m^5}$ **d.** $\frac{x^3}{3}$
e. $\frac{2y^3}{5x^2}$ **f.** $\frac{ac^3d}{b^5}$ **7.** no **8. a.** $24x^2$ **b.** $8x^3$ **c.** $2\sqrt{3}x$
9. a. x^9 **b.** $\frac{1}{m^7}$ **c.** p^2 **d.** $\frac{1}{x}$ **e.** c^2 **f.** d^{50} **10. a.** 1, 2
11. a. $\frac{1}{2x}$ **b.** $\frac{1}{25y^2}$ **c.** 1 **d.** $\frac{r^{21}}{216}$ **e.** $\frac{n^{12}}{m^8}$ **f.** 1
12. a. $\frac{1}{a^6b^9}$ **b.** $35x^2y^2$ **c.** x^2y^{10} **d.** $-\frac{4}{3}m^4n$
13. a. $16x^4y^2$ **b.** $4\sqrt{3}x^2y$ **14. a.** $-\frac{1}{3}$ **b.** $\frac{9}{2}$ **c.** $\frac{9}{64}$
d. $9\frac{1}{4}$ **e.** $-\frac{29}{54}$ **f.** 72 **15. a.** 1 **16.** $253 539.50
17. a. 2 **b.** −2 **18. a.** 0.708 92 **b.** 0.307 95
c. 0.362 45 **d.** 0.082 40 **19.** $7411.62 **20. a.** $\frac{n^7}{16m^4}$
b. $\frac{n^3r^2}{m^5}$ **c.** $\frac{z^8}{49x^8y^7}$ **d.** $\frac{486a^8c^{10}}{b^2}$ **e.** $\frac{r^{22}}{25p^2q^8}$ **f.** $\frac{18b^7}{a^2}$
g. $\frac{1}{81x^5y^9z^4}$

Pages 100-101 2. a. $5\sqrt{7}, \sqrt{175}$ b. $4\sqrt{6}, \sqrt{96}$
c. $6\sqrt{3}, \sqrt{108}$ d. $7\sqrt{5}, \sqrt{245}$ e. $9\sqrt{7}, \sqrt{567}$
f. $8\sqrt{5}, \sqrt{320}$ 3. a. $\sqrt{28}$ b. $\sqrt{75}$ c. $\sqrt{605}$
d. $\sqrt{468}$ e. $\sqrt{450}$ f. $\sqrt{700}$ g. $\sqrt{405}$ h. $\sqrt{192}$
i. $\sqrt{735}$ 4. a. $4\sqrt{3}$ b. 8 c. 6 d. 12 e. 15 f. $6\sqrt{3}$
5. a. 0.5 b. 0.4 c. 15.0 d. 7.4 e. 5.8 f. 0.03
g. 0.05 h. 9.6 i. 6.6 6. a. $5\sqrt{3}$ b. $7\sqrt{2}$ c. $4\sqrt{2}$
d. $6\sqrt{2}$ e. $4\sqrt{3}$ f. $15\sqrt{2}$ g. $6\sqrt{5}$ h. $8\sqrt{3}$
7. a. $x\sqrt{y}$ b. $a\sqrt{ab}$ c. $x\sqrt[3]{y^2}$ d. $mn\sqrt[3]{m^2n}$
e. $p^2q\sqrt{pq}$ f. $c^2\sqrt[3]{cd^2}$ g. $f^4g^2\sqrt[3]{g^2}$ h. $w^5x^7\sqrt{wx}$
8. all true 11. a. $4x^2y^4\sqrt{x}$ b. $3mn\sqrt{3m}$
c. $3p^2q^2\sqrt[3]{3p}$ d. $2c\sqrt{cd}$ e. $7ab\sqrt{b}$ f. $2r^3t^4$
g. $mn^2\sqrt[3]{p^2}$ h. $a^5b^3c^7\sqrt{b}$ 12. 44.4 s 13. 114 km
14. 7.07 m 15. 79.24 cm² 16. 14.14 s 17. 15 cm²

Pages 102-103 1. a. $7\sqrt{3}$ b. $5\sqrt{7}$ c. $18\sqrt{2}$
d. $20\sqrt{3}$ e. $11\sqrt{5}$ f. $7\sqrt{2}$ 2. yes 3. a. $2\sqrt{2}$
b. $100\sqrt{7}$ c. $20\sqrt{3}$ d. $\sqrt{3}$ 4. a. $5\sqrt{3}$ b. $3\sqrt{3}$
c. $2\sqrt{2}$ d. $13\sqrt{3}$ e. $6\sqrt{5}$ f. $9\sqrt{2}$ 5. a. $12\sqrt{3}$
b. $11\sqrt{2}$ c. $20\sqrt{2}$ d. $17\sqrt{3}$ e. $82\sqrt{2}$ f. $50\sqrt{3}$
g. $\sqrt{2}$ h. $19\sqrt{7}$ 6. $100\sqrt{2}$, 141.42 8. a. $4x\sqrt{y}$
b. $2a^2b\sqrt{b}$ c. $7xy\sqrt{x}$ d. $16pq\sqrt{pq}$ 9. a. $43\sqrt{3}$
b. $9\sqrt{2}$ c. $54\sqrt{2}$ d. $47\sqrt{5}$ e. $49\sqrt{2}$ f. $11\sqrt{6}$
g. $24\sqrt{5}+6\sqrt{6}$ h. $24\sqrt{6}-10\sqrt{7}$
10. $10\sqrt{2}-75\sqrt{3}$ 11. a. $2\sqrt{2}$ b. $7\sqrt{2}$ c. $2\sqrt{3}$
d. $\frac{5}{2}\sqrt{2}+2\sqrt{3}$ e. $5\sqrt{7}$ f. $\frac{5}{2}\sqrt{6}-9\sqrt{3}$
12. a. $\sqrt{7}>\sqrt{5}$ b. $13>3\sqrt{16}$ c. $5\sqrt{2}>4\sqrt{3}$
d. $7\sqrt{6}>6\sqrt{7}$ e. $3\sqrt{2}>2\sqrt{3}$ f. $10\sqrt{12}>20\sqrt{2}$
13. 1 h, 59 min 14. b. $2\sqrt{3}+3\sqrt{5}$
c. $12\sqrt{3}+18\sqrt{5}$ 15. $200\sqrt{3}$

Page 104 1. a. 3 b. 7 c. 5 d. 11 e. 12 f. 15
g. 133 h. 17 2. a. $a-b$ b. $\sqrt{a}-\sqrt{b}$ c. $a-b$
d. $(\sqrt{a}+\sqrt{b})(\sqrt{a}-\sqrt{b})=a-b$ 3. a. $3a$ b. $18a$
c. $a+b$ d. $2a-b$ e. $12a-4b$ f. $18x-36$
g. $7+4\sqrt{3+b}+b$ h. $4+4\sqrt{3a+b}+3a+b$
4. rectangular prism 5. a. $10\sqrt{21}$ b. $72\sqrt{6}$
c. 140 d. $30\sqrt{2}$ e. $7\sqrt{2}-5\sqrt{7}$ f. $20+\sqrt{15}$
g. $3\sqrt{5}-5\sqrt{3}$ h. $17+\sqrt{102}$ 6. $(\sqrt{15}-\sqrt{5})$ m
7. $20+2\sqrt{5}$ cm² 8. a. 6 b. 7 c. 243 d. 372
e. 837

Page 105 1. yes 3. a. 3 b. 0.6 c. $\sqrt{6}$
d. 0.857 e. $\sqrt{7}$ f. 3 4. a^2b-c^2d 5. a. $\frac{7+\sqrt{7}}{21}$
b. $\frac{2\sqrt{2}-2\sqrt{5}}{5}$ c. $\frac{9\sqrt{5}-15\sqrt{3}}{40}$ d. $\frac{65\sqrt{2}-2\sqrt{13}}{26}$
e. $\frac{\sqrt{10}-2}{3}$ f. $3+\sqrt{6}$ g. $\frac{12+2\sqrt{3}}{11}$ h. $\frac{175+30\sqrt{7}}{139}$
6. a. 3 b. 7 c. 5 d. 11 e. 3 f. 3
7. $\frac{240\sqrt{5}+160}{41}$ m

Pages 106-108 1. yes 2. b. 5 3. a. 25 b. no
solution c. 9 d. 49 e. no solution f. 225
5. a. $x+3$ b. $x^2-10x+25$ c. a^2+2a+1
d. x^2+6x+9 e. $x-6\sqrt{x+6}+15$

f. $51-14\sqrt{2-x}-x$ 6. a. 22 b. no solution c. 41
d. 4 e. -7 f. no solution 7. no 9. a. $\frac{4}{3}$ b. 6
c. $-\frac{4}{3}$ d. 4 10. a. no solution b. 4 c. 6 11. 108
12. $\sqrt{82}$ cm 13. a. $r=\sqrt{\frac{A}{\pi}}$ b. 6.9 cm
14. a. $t=\sqrt{2gs}$ b. 98 s 15. a. $d=\sqrt[3]{54t^2}$
b. 2.4 km 16. a. $\frac{25}{9}$ b. 16 c. $\frac{9}{4}$ d. 9 e. $\frac{1}{9}$
f. no solution 17. a. 5 b. no solution c. 4 d. 2, 6
e. 2, 38 f. 7 18. $x=3, \sqrt{x}=\sqrt{3}$,
$\sqrt{2x+7}=\sqrt{13}, \sqrt{3x-4}=\sqrt{5}$

Page 109 1. a. $s=\frac{v^2}{g}$ b. 637 755.1 m
2. a. $d=\sqrt[3]{54t^2}$ b. 0.97 km 3. a. $\ell=\frac{T^2g}{4\pi^2}$
b. 0.99 m 4. 14.9 m 5. a. $h=\frac{d^2}{13}$ b. 11.1 km
6. 1960 units

Pages 110-111 1. a. $\sqrt{5}$ b. $\sqrt[4]{15}$ c. $\sqrt[6]{259}$
d. $\sqrt[3]{12}$ e. $\sqrt[5]{100}$ f. $\sqrt{1000}$ 2. a. $(\sqrt{x})^3$
b. $(\sqrt[3]{-y})^4$ c. $(\sqrt[5]{56})^3$ d. $(\sqrt[6]{m})^5$ e. $(\sqrt{p})^5$
f. $(\sqrt[3]{-111})^7$ 3. a. $3^{\frac{4}{2}}$ b. $9^{\frac{2}{3}}$ c. $-9^{\frac{2}{3}}$ d. $y^{\frac{3}{5}}$ e. $(xy)^{\frac{1}{4}}$
f. $(xy^2)^{\frac{2}{3}}$ 5. a. 2 b. 2 c. -3 d. 5 e. 2 f. 2
6. a. 4 b. 32 c. 243 d. $\frac{1}{32}$ e. 8 f. 3 g. 4 h. $\frac{1}{4}$
i. 125 j. 8 7. 31.25 kg 8. 768 000 9. 1 d
10. a. $\frac{a^4}{b^2}$ b. $-243p^{10}$ c. $\frac{y^2}{x^3}$ d. $k^{\frac{1}{4}}$ 11. a. $\frac{2}{3}$ b. $\frac{4}{9}$
c. $\frac{243}{100\,000}$ d. $-\frac{8}{27}$ 13. 20:00 14. 108 h
BRAINTICKLER 50 km

Pages 112-113 1. after the fourth payment
2. \$13 492.33 3. 41% of the light 4. 2 700; 19 683
5. 1.041 cm³ 7. 5.7×10^9 8. \$9011.20 9. b. no
10. $\sqrt{3}(1-\sqrt{5})$ 11. \$12 278.27 12. 147 months or
12.25 a 13. 20 508 708 14. \$14 693.28
BRAINTICKLER 70

Pages 114-115 1. a. 5 b. 7 c. $\frac{3}{4}$ d. 9 e. 0
f. -4 g. 5 h. 1 i. 1 j. 1 2. 3, 3, 3, 3 3. a. 3
b. 4 c. 4 d. 3 e. 2 f. -1 g. 0 h. -3 i. 3 j. -2
k. -6 l. -3 4. 54 h 5. 4.5 d 6. c. 1 7. the fourth
8. a. $\frac{7}{2}$ b. 1 c. $\frac{4}{5}$ d. $\frac{1}{2}$ e. 7 f. 0 g. 3 h. 3 i. 7
j. -2 k. -3 l. $-\frac{1}{4}$ 9. all real numbers 10. a. -2
b. 2 c. $\frac{1}{2}$ d. $-\frac{1}{2}$ e. $\frac{1}{3}$ f. 0 g. 0 h. $-\frac{1}{4}$ i. $-\frac{1}{5}$
j. $-\frac{1}{3}$ 11. 183 months or 15.25 a 12. 598 d
13. 7.375 a

Page 116 **1.** 4 **2.** to set up a loop that will evaluate 5.2^x for $x = 1$ to 20 **3.** 10 REM TO EVALUATE THE VALUE OF X GIVEN A AND B • 20 REM IN THE EXPRESSION A ∧ X = B • 30 INPUT "ENTER THE VALUES OF A AND B "; A, B • 40 FOR X = − 10 TO 10 • 50 LET ANS = A ∧ X • 60 PRINT "DOES "; ANS; " ="; B; "?" • 70 INPUT A$ • 80 IF A$ = "YES" GOTO 100 • 90 NEXT X • 100 PRINT "X ="; X • 110 END **a.** 5 **b.** 5 **c.** 0 **d.** −1 **e.** −2 **f.** 6 **g.** −1 **h.** 6 **4.** increment of index would be in tenths **5.** 50 FOR X = 0 TO 10 STEP 0.1 • Everything else the same as in Exercise 3. **a.** 1.5 **b.** 2.2 **c.** 0.2 **d.** 3.4 **e.** 3.5 **f.** 1.5 **g.** 2.5 **h.** 0.2 **7.** 10 REM A PROGRAM TO EVALUATE HOW LONG IT TAKES • 20 REM FOR A BACTERIA CULTURE TO INCREASE 100 TIMES • 30 GET NO • 40 FOR X = 10.1 TO 101 ∗ NO STEP 0.1 • 50 LET N = NO ∗ 2 ∧ (X / 10) • 60 IF N = 100 ∗ NO GOTO 80 • 70 NEXT X • 80 PRINT "X ="; X; " HOURS" • 90 END

Page 117 **1. a.** $\overline{Q}$ **b.** Q **c.** Q **d.** Q **2. a.** $0.\overline{285\ 714}$; 6 **b.** $0.8\overline{6}$; 1 **c.** -0.625; terminating decimal **3. a.** $\frac{5623}{1000}$ **b.** $\frac{71}{99}$ **c.** $\frac{29}{9}$ **d.** $\frac{8}{15}$ **5. a.** 2^{4x+4} **b.** 3 **6.** 12 **7. a.** x^{13} **b.** $\frac{1}{y^3}$ **c.** m^{21} **d.** p^5q^5 **e.** $\frac{r^8}{t^8}$ **f.** 1 **g.** $-\frac{6}{x}$ **h.** $\frac{y}{3x^2}$ **i.** $125a^9b^6$ **j.** $\frac{3cd^5}{5}$ **k.** $2a^2b$ **l.** $\frac{1}{a^4b^3}$ **8. a.** 3 **b.** 1 **c.** 3 **d.** 4 **e.** 4 **f.** $\frac{1}{2}$ **g.** $\frac{1}{125}$ **h.** $\frac{1}{8}$ **i.** 8 **9. a.** 1.242 297 **b.** 0.836 39 **c.** 0.921 51 **d.** 1.912 93 **e.** 1.515 72 **f.** 3.823 62 **10. a.** 80 **b.** 327 **c.** $2\sqrt{3}$ **d.** $\frac{16}{25}$ **e.** no solution **11.** 10 240 **12.** $3757.84 **13. a.** $3\sqrt{2}$ **b.** $20\sqrt{2}$ **c.** $70\sqrt{3}$ **d.** xy^2 **e.** $nm\sqrt{m^2}$ **f.** $3xy^2\sqrt[3]{x}$ **14. a.** $10\sqrt[4]{3}$ **b.** $12 - 4\sqrt{7}$ **c.** $2\sqrt{3} + 3\sqrt{2} + 2\sqrt{6}$ **d.** $24\sqrt{2}$ **e.** $2\sqrt{5}$ **f.** $2\sqrt{13} - 2\sqrt{7}$ **g.** $12\sqrt[3]{x} - \sqrt{x}$ **h.** $5x^2y^2\sqrt{xy}$ **15. a.** $\sqrt{21} - 6$ **b.** $105 + 56\sqrt{5}$ **c.** $3 + 8\sqrt{6}$ **d.** $364 + 210\sqrt{3}$ **16. a.** 6 **b.** −30 **17. a.** $\frac{\sqrt{3}}{7}$ **b.** $\frac{7\sqrt{2} + 4\sqrt{7}}{21}$ **c.** $\frac{8\sqrt{42} - 10\sqrt{6}}{29}$ **d.** $\frac{117 + 25\sqrt{21}}{47}$

Page 118 **1. a.** $\overline{Q}$ **b.** Q **c.** Q **d.** $\overline{Q}$ **2. a.** $0.\overline{714\ 285}$; 6 **b.** $0.\overline{315\ 789\ 473\ 684\ 210\ 526}$; 18 **c.** $0.\overline{008\ 264\ 462\ 809\ 917\ 355\ 371\ 9}$; 22 **3.** $\frac{77}{90}$ km **4. a.** m^{11} **b.** $\frac{1}{a^2}$ **c.** m^{15} **d.** $27h^3$ **e.** $\frac{625}{p^4}$ **f.** 1 **g.** $1183k^{23}$ **h.** $\frac{6g^6}{f^5k^2}$ **i.** $216r^{12}s^{21}$ **j.** $\frac{x^6}{27w^{12}}$ **k.** $3m^3n^2$ **l.** $\frac{1}{32p^3}$ **5.** 8 **6. a.** 1.131 408 2 **b.** 0.130 093 7 **c.** 0.875 391 **d.** 2.930 156 **7. a.** 5 **b.** 3 **c.** −4

8. a. 5 **b.** 1 **c.** 2 **d.** 9 **e.** 4 **f.** $\frac{1}{5}$ **g.** $\frac{1}{216}$ **h.** $\frac{1}{27}$ **i.** 27 **9. a.** 8 **b.** 327 **c.** $3\sqrt{2}$ **d.** $\frac{49}{9}$ **e.** −5 **10.** about 36% **11. a.** $4\sqrt{3}$ **b.** $21\sqrt{2}$ **c.** $2ab\sqrt[3]{a^2}$ **12.** no **13. a.** $\sqrt{3} - 3\sqrt{7}$ **b.** 0 **c.** $4\sqrt{2} - 2\sqrt{6} + 2\sqrt{11}$ **d.** $21\sqrt{3} + 12\sqrt{7}$ **e.** $30\sqrt{5} - 27\sqrt{3}$ **f.** $5\sqrt{6} - 2\sqrt{2}$ **g.** $\sqrt[4]{x} - \sqrt{y}$ **h.** $6a^3b^3\sqrt{b}$ **14. a.** $\sqrt{30} - 35$ **b.** $54 - 21\sqrt{6}$ **c.** $46 + 27\sqrt{3}$ **d.** $668 - 96\sqrt{30}$ **15. a.** 1 **b.** 145 **16. a.** $\frac{2\sqrt{42}}{21}$ **b.** $\frac{9\sqrt{5} - 5\sqrt{6}}{75}$ **c.** $\frac{-3\sqrt{15} - 7\sqrt{3}}{2}$ **d.** $\frac{144 + 34\sqrt{10}}{37}$

Chapter 5

Page 119 **2. a.** 2 **b.** 3 **c.** 3 **4. a.** 133° **b.** 105° **c.** 43° **d.** 81° **e.** 11° **f.** $180° - a°$ **g.** $180° - 5x°$ **h.** $155° - x°$ **5. a.** 53° **b.** 89° **c.** 5° **d.** 4° **e.** 37° **f.** $90° - k°$ **g.** $2(45 - a)°$ **h.** $3(5 + x)°$ **7.** all three sides equal—equilateral; two sides equal—isosceles; no sides equal—scalene **8.** all angles less than 90°—acute-angled triangle; one angle equal to 90°—right-angled triangle; one angle greater than 90°—obtuse-angled triangle **9. a.** 37 **b.** −8 **c.** 3 **12. a.** a triangle with all angles less than 90° **b.** a triangle with one right angle **c.** a triangle with one angle greater than 90° **d.** a triangle with two sides of equal length **e.** a triangle with no right angle **f.** They have three sides and the angles all add up to 180°. **13.** 30°, 110°, 40°

Pages 120-122 **5. a.** If it's a salmon, then it's a fish. **b.** If you're a Grade 11 student, then you're a brilliant mathematician. **c.** If it's a triangle, then its angles add up to 180°. **d.** If you live in Dartmouth, then you live in Nova Scotia. **e.** If you drive in Ontario, then you must wear a seat belt. **f.** If two planes are parallel, then they never meet. **g.** If you are the sun, then you never set on the British Empire. **h.** If you live in Saskatchewan, then you know how to drive in Waskesiu. **i.** If you were at the 1988 Winter Olympics, then you were in Calgary. **j.** If you drive in North Bay, then you drive in the snow. **6. a.** HYP: A school has good mathematics students. CONCL: The school will win the mathematics competition. **b.** HYP: An angle is a right angle. CONCL: Its measure is 90°. **c.** HYP: A figure is a square. CONCL: All its sides are congruent. **d.** HYP: You live in British Columbia. CONCL: You have seen the Rocky Mountains. **e.** HYP: You pass the final examination in the Grade 11 mathematics course. CONCL: You will study mathematics in Grade 12. **f.** HYP: You lived through the Depression. CONCL: You know the value of a dollar.

7. a. GIVEN: △ABC is isosceles; REQUIRED: To prove $\angle B = \angle C$. **b.** GIVEN: ℓ_1 and ℓ_2 are parallel; REQUIRED: To prove ℓ_1 does not intersect ℓ_2. **c.** GIVEN: $ABCD$ is a rectangle; REQUIRED: To prove $\overline{AC} = \overline{BD}$. **d.** GIVEN: There are six rows of five desks each in the classroom; REQUIRED: To prove there are a total of 30 desks in the classroom.

8. $20\frac{2}{5}$ cm

Pages 123-125 **1. a.** $\angle c$ and $\angle e$; $\angle d$ and $\angle f$ **b.** $\angle a$ and $\angle c$; $\angle h$ and $\angle f$; $\angle e$ and $\angle g$; $\angle b$ and $\angle d$ **c.** $\angle a$ and $\angle e$; $\angle h$ and $\angle d$; $\angle b$ and $\angle f$; $\angle c$ and $\angle g$ **d.** $\angle a = 126°$; $\angle b = 54°$; $\angle c = 126°$; $\angle d = 54°$; $\angle e = 126°$; $\angle f = 54°$; $\angle g = 126°$; $\angle h = 54°$ **2.** yes **3. a.** $\angle a = 111°$; $\angle b = 69°$; $\angle c = 111°$; $\angle d = 111°$ **b.** $\angle a = 59°$; $\angle b = 61°$; $\angle c = 121°$ **4. a.** $\angle QRS = 50°$ **b.** $\angle QRS = 156.25°$ **5. a.** $\angle a = 107°$; $\angle b = 73°$; $\angle c = 26°$; $\angle d = 154°$; $\angle e = 73°$ **b.** $\angle a = 43°$; $\angle b = 66°$; $\angle c = 71°$; $\angle d = 109°$ **6.** $\angle 2$ and $\angle 3$ form a line; $\angle 1 + \angle 2 = \angle 3 + \angle 2$ (transitive property); $\angle 2$ was subtracted; $\angle 2 + \angle 3 = 180°$, $\angle 3 + \angle 4 = 180°$, $\angle 2 + \angle 3 = \angle 3 + \angle 4$, $\angle 2 = \angle 4$ **7. f.** alternate interior and corresponding angles **g.** 180° **h.** $\angle 1 + \angle 2 = 180°$ (form a line), $\angle 1 = \angle 3$ (alternate interior angles), $\angle 3 + \angle 2 = 180°$ (substitution property) **8. a.** Join AC, $\angle BAC = \angle DCA$, $\angle DAC = \angle BCA$, $\therefore \angle BAC + \angle DAC = \angle DCA + \angle BCA$, $\therefore \angle A \cong \angle C$ **b.** parallelogram **c.** The opposite interior angles of a parallelogram are equal.

Pages 126-127 **1.** $\ell_1 \parallel \ell_2$, $\ell_2 \parallel \ell_4$, $\ell_1 \parallel \ell_4$, $\ell_3 \parallel \ell_5$ **2. a.** If it flies, then it's an airplane. **b.** If you're a prospector, then you discover gold. **c.** If one competed in Alberta, then one competed in the 1988 Winter Olympics. **d.** If you swim for a swim team, then you're a swimmer. **e.** If krings krong, then blings blong. **f.** If it has feathers, then it's a bird. **6. a.** yes **b.** no **c.** yes **d.** yes **7. a.** $\angle 2 = \angle 6$, $\angle 1 = \angle 5$, alternate angles **b.** $\angle 7 = \angle 3$, $\angle 8 = \angle 4$, alternate angles **8.** $\angle 4 \cong \angle 6$, $\angle 3 \cong \angle 5$, $\angle 5 \cong \angle 2$ **9. a.** $\angle 3$ **b.** congruent **c.** corresponding angles **d.** parallel by congruence of corresponding angles **10. a.** If a transversal cuts two lines and the consecutive interior angles are supplementary, then the two lines are parallel. **b.** GIVEN: Two lines cut by a transversal and that consecutive interior angles are supplementary. **c.** REQUIRED: To prove the two lines are parallel. **d.** 180° **e.** corresponding or alternate **f.** Referring to diagram in Exercise 9: $\angle 2 + \angle 3 = 180°$ (given), $\angle 1 + \angle 2 = 180°$ (form a line), $\angle 1 = \angle 3$ (transitive property), corresponding angles are equal so the lines are parallel. **11.** Each pair of planes intersects in a line parallel to the third plane. **12.** Interior alternate angles are congruent. Corresponding angles are congruent. Consecutive interior angles are supplementary.

Pages 128-129 **1.** $\angle CPA \cong \angle PLN$ by construction **2. f.** Draw a perpendicular to the given line. Draw a second perpendicular to the first perpendicular through the given point. **3.** $\angle CPA$; corresponding angles congruent **5.** The perpendicular bisector of the noncongruent side bisects the vertex opposite this side. **6. a.** $\overline{XZ}$ is too long for the other two sides. **b.** $\overline{CD}$ does not reach $\overline{JD}$. **7. a.** alternate angles congruent by construction **b.** $\angle RST$ and $\angle XTV$ are corresponding angles. **8. a.** X is the midpoint of $\overline{PR}$ **b.** $\overline{AX} \parallel \overline{QR}$, $\angle PAX$ and $\angle PQR$ are corresponding angles. **c.** $\angle PXA \cong PRQ$ **d.** $\overline{AX} = \frac{1}{2}\overline{QR}$ **e.** The midpoint line of a triangle is one half the length of the third side of the triangle.

Pages 130-132 **1. a.** 57° **b.** 72.5° **c.** 104° **2. a.** $\angle a = 43°$, $\angle b = 43°$, $\angle c = 90°$ **b.** $\angle w = 115°$, $\angle x = 65°$, $\angle y = 80°$, $\angle z = 35°$ **c.** $\angle r = 39°$, $\angle s = 51°$, $\angle t = 39°$ **d.** $\angle w = 100°$, $\angle x = 60°$, $\angle z = 60°$ **3. a.** 77° **b.** 18° **c.** 42.1° **d.** $180° - r° - t°$ **e.** $180° - a° - b°$ **f.** yes **4. a.** $x = 70°$, $2x - 100 = 40°$ **b.** $x - 5 = 30°$, $x - 15 = 20°$, $4x - 10 = 130°$ **c.** $4x = 80°$, $2x - 10 = 30°$, $5x + 10 = 110°$ **d.** $x + 8 = 40°$, $5x - 20 = 140°$, $2x + 11 = 75°$, $y = 65°$ **6.** exterior angles equal opposite interior angles; $x + 15$, $5x - 20$; substitution; 25; solving for x; 105; substitution; $\angle ACD = 105°$ **8. b.** since $\overline{AD} \perp \overline{BC}$, $\angle ADB \cong \angle ACD = 90°$, so $\angle BAD + \angle B = 90° = \angle CAD + \angle C$, but $\angle B \cong \angle C$ $\therefore$ $\angle BAD \cong \angle CAD$ **9.** $\angle B \cong \angle B$ (reflexive), since $\overline{AC} \perp \overline{BD}$ and $\overline{DE} \perp \overline{AB}$, $\angle DEB \cong \angle ACB = 90°$, so $\angle A + \angle B = 90° = \angle D + \angle B$, $\therefore$ $\angle A \cong \angle D$ **10. a.** 360° **b.** 540° **c.** 1080° **d.** 1440°

Page 133 **1. a.** $\overline{CB} \cong \overline{RS}$, $\overline{BA} \cong \overline{ST}$, $\overline{AC} \cong \overline{TR}$, $\angle B \cong \angle S$, $\angle A \cong \angle T$, $\angle C \cong \angle R$, $\triangle ABC \cong \triangle TSR$ **b.** $\overline{MP} \cong \overline{XY}$, $\overline{MQ} \cong \overline{XW}$, $\overline{PQ} \cong \overline{YW}$, $\angle M \cong \angle X$, $\angle P \cong \angle Y$, $\angle Q \cong \angle W$, $\triangle MPQ \cong \triangle XYW$ **2.** $\overline{RS} \cong \overline{VW}$, $\overline{RT} \cong \overline{VX}$, $\overline{ST} \cong \overline{WX}$, $\angle R \cong \angle V$, $\angle S \cong \angle W$, $\angle T \cong \angle X$ **3. a.** $\overline{EF} \cong \overline{RM}$, $\overline{EG} \cong \overline{RN}$, $\overline{FG} \cong \overline{MN}$, $\angle E \cong \angle R$, $\angle F \cong \angle M$, $\angle G \cong \angle N$ **b.** $\overline{QR} \cong \overline{CB}$, $\overline{QS} \cong \overline{CA}$, $\overline{RS} \cong \overline{BA}$, $\angle Q \cong \angle C$, $\angle R \cong \angle B$, $\angle S \cong \angle A$ **c.** $\overline{XY} \cong \overline{XZ}$, $\overline{XZ} \cong \overline{XY}$, $\overline{YZ} \cong \overline{ZY}$, $\angle X \cong \angle X$, $\angle Y \cong \angle Z$, $\angle Z \cong \angle Y$ **4. a.** 34.5 **b.** 65° **5.** no **6.** They are congruent.

Pages 134-137 **3.** $\overline{KR}$ between $\angle K$ and $\angle R$, $\overline{KP}$ between $\angle K$ and $\angle P$, $\overline{RP}$ between $\angle R$ and $\angle P$ **5. a.** $\overline{AB} \cong \overline{MN}$, $\overline{BC} \cong \overline{NP}$ **b.** $\overline{KI} \cong \overline{SP}$, $\overline{KJ} \cong \overline{SR}$ **6. a.** $\angle A \cong \angle L$, $\angle C \cong \angle M$ **b.** $\angle V \cong \angle X$, $\angle VTW \cong \angle XRY$ **7.** no **8. a.** S.A.S **b.** S.S.S. **c.** S.A.S. or A.S.A **d.** A.S.A. **e.** S.S.S. or S.A.S. **f.** S.A.S. **9. a.** $\overline{SR} \cong \overline{MP}$, $\angle S \cong \angle M$, $\overline{ST} \cong \overline{MN}$, $\therefore$ $\triangle RST \cong \triangle PMN$ (S.A.S.) **b.** $\overline{ED} \cong \overline{HG}$, $\overline{FD} \cong \overline{IG}$, $\overline{EF} \cong \overline{HI}$, $\therefore$ $\triangle EDF \cong \triangle HGI$ (S.S.S.) **c.** $\angle R \cong \angle K$, $\overline{TR} \cong \overline{CK}$, $\angle T \cong \angle C$, $\therefore$ $\triangle RVT \cong \triangle KPC$ (A.S.A.) **10.** $\overline{AB} \cong \overline{AC}$ (given), $\angle B \cong \angle C$ (given), $\overline{BM} \cong \overline{CM}$ ($\overline{AM}$ bisects $\overline{BC}$), $\therefore \triangle ABM \cong \triangle ACM$ (S.A.S.) **11. a.** Given; $\overline{QR} \cong \overline{SR}$;

Given; $\triangle QKR \cong \triangle SKR$; S.A.S.; $\overline{KQ} \cong \overline{KS}$
b. $\angle Q \cong \angle S$, $\angle QKR \cong \angle SKR$, $\overline{KQ} \cong \overline{KS}$
12. a. $\angle BAC \cong \angle DCA$; Definition of a parallelogram; $\angle DAC \cong \angle BCA$; Alternate angles; $\overline{AC} \cong \overline{AC}$; $\angle ADC \cong \angle CBA$; A.S.A. **b.** yes; C.P.C.T.
c. Opposite sides of a parallelogram are congruent.
13. a. $\angle M \cong \angle P$ (given), $\overline{KM} \cong \overline{KP}$ (given), $\angle K \cong \angle K$ (reflexive property), $\therefore \triangle KMN \cong \triangle KPL$ (A.S.A.)
b. $\overline{KL} \cong \overline{KN}$ (C.P.C.T.)

Page 138   **2.** $\angle BAD \cong \angle CAD$ (construction), $\overline{AB} \cong \overline{AC}$ (given), $\overline{AD} \cong \overline{AD}$ (reflexive property), $\triangle ABD \cong \triangle ACD$ (S.A.S.), $\therefore \angle B \cong \angle C$ (C.P.C.T.); for the second proof notice $\overline{DB} \cong \overline{DC}$ and use (S.S.S.)
3. a. $53°$ **b.** A.S.A. **c.** True because A.S.A. is true.
4. a. $x = 48°$; third angle is $66°$. **b.** Two congruent angles are $42°$; third angle is $96°$. **5.** Draw $\angle ABC$, bisect $\angle A$. $\angle BAD \cong \angle CAD$ (construction), $\angle B \cong \angle C$ (given), $\overline{AD} \cong \overline{AD}$ (reflexive property), $\triangle ABD \cong \triangle ACD$ (S.A.A. congruence corollary), $\therefore \overline{AB} \cong \overline{AC}$ (C.P.C.T.) **6.** $\overline{QT} \parallel \overline{RX}$ (given), $\angle 1 \cong \angle 2$ (given), $\angle 1 \cong \angle x$ (corresponding angles), $\angle 2 \cong \angle R$ (alternate angles), so $\angle X \cong \angle R$ (transitive property), so $\overline{QX} \cong \overline{QR}$, $\therefore \triangle QRX$ is isosceles.

Pages 139-141   **1. a.** adjacent **b.** opposite
c. adjacent **d.** opposite **e.** adjacent **f.** opposite
5. a. true. **b.** square **c.** true. **d.** equiangular **e.** true
f. true **g.** parallelogram **h.** square, rectangle **i.** true
j. trapezoid **7. a.** square, rectangle **b.** square, rectangle, rhombus, parallelogram **c.** square, rhombus
d. square, rectangle **e.** parallelogram, rhombus, square, rectangle **f.** all parallelograms **g.** all but trapezoid, quadrilateral **h.** square, rhombus **8.** no
11. If a figure is a parallelogram, then opposite sides are congruent. GIVEN: parallelogram $ABCD$; REQUIRED: To prove $\overline{AB} \cong \overline{DC}$ and $\overline{AD} \cong \overline{BC}$; PROOF: Join $\overline{AC}$, $\overline{AB} \parallel \overline{DC}$, so $\angle BAC \cong \angle DCA$, $\overline{AD} \parallel \overline{BC}$, so $\angle DAC \cong \angle BCA$, $\overline{AC} \cong \overline{AC}$ (reflexive property), $\angle ADC \cong \angle CBA$ (A.S.A.), $\therefore \overline{AB} \cong \overline{DC}$ and $\overline{AD} \cong \overline{BC}$ (C.P.C.T.) **12.** If a figure is a parallelogram, then consecutive angles are supplementary. GIVEN: Parallelogram $ABCD$; REQUIRED: To prove that each pair of consecutive angles is supplementary; PROOF: $\overline{AB} \parallel \overline{DC}$, so $\angle A + \angle D = 180°$, $\angle B + \angle C = 180°$, $\overline{AD} \parallel \overline{BC}$, $\therefore \angle A + \angle B = 180°$, $\angle D + \angle C = 180°$, and each pair of consecutive angles is supplementary. **13.** If a figure is a parallelogram, then the diagonals bisect each other. GIVEN: Parallelogram $ABCD$; REQUIRED: To prove that the diagonals bisect each other; PROOF: Join $\overline{AC}$ and $\overline{BD}$, Let the point of intersection be E, $\overline{AB} \cong \overline{DC}$ (from Exercise 11), $\overline{AB} \parallel \overline{DC}$ (definition of a parallelogram), $\angle ABE \cong \angle CDE$ (alternate angles), $\angle BAE \cong \angle DCE$ (alternate angles), $\triangle ABE \cong \triangle CDE$ (A.S.A.), $\overline{AE} \cong \overline{CE}$ (C.P.C.T.), so $\overline{BD}$ bisects $\overline{AC}$, $\overline{BE} \cong \overline{DE}$ (C.P.C.T.), $\therefore \overline{AC}$ bisects $\overline{BD}$. **14.** If a

figure is a rectangle, then its diagonals are congruent. GIVEN: Rectangle $ABCD$; REQUIRED: To prove $\overline{AC} \cong \overline{BD}$; PROOF: Join $\overline{AC}$ and $\overline{BD}$. In $\triangle ABD$ and $\triangle BAC$ $\overline{AB} \cong \overline{AB}$ (reflexive property), $\overline{BC} \cong \overline{AD}$ (definition of a parallelogram), $\angle A \cong \angle B = 90°$ (definition of a rectangle), so $\triangle ABD \cong \triangle BAC$ (S.A.S.), $\therefore \overline{AC} \cong \overline{BD}$ (C.P.C.T.) **15.** If a figure is a rhombus, then the diagonals are perpendicular to each other. GIVEN: $ABCD$ is a rhombus; REQUIRED: To prove $\overline{AC} \perp \overline{BD}$; PROOF: Join $\overline{AC}$ and $\overline{BD}$, Let the point of intersection be E, In $\triangle ABE$ and $\triangle CBE$ $\overline{AB} \cong \overline{CB}$ (definition of a rhombus), $\overline{BE} \cong \overline{BE}$ (reflexive property), $\overline{AE} \cong \overline{CE}$ (diagonals of a parallelogram bisect each other), so $\triangle ABE \cong \triangle CBE$ (S.S.S.), and $\angle AEB \cong \angle BEC$ (C.P.C.T.), but $\angle AEB$ and $\angle BEC$ are supplementary, so $\angle AEB = 90° = \angle BEC$, $\therefore$ the diagonals are perpendicular. **16.** If the figure is a rhombus, then the diagonals bisect the vertices of the rhombus. GIVEN: $ABCD$ is a rhombus; REQUIRED: To prove the diagonals bisect the vertices; PROOF: Follow the proof of Exercise 15 to $\triangle ABE \cong \triangle CBE$ (S.S.S.), and $\angle ABE \cong \angle CBE$ (C.P.C.T.), Similarly the other diagonal can be shown to give the same result, hence the diagonals bisect the vertices. **17.** No, a rectangle is a parallelogram. **18.** Exercises 11, 12, and 13 apply also to rectangles, squares, rhombuses; Exercises 14, 15, and 16 apply also to squares.
19. Exercise 11: If opposite sides of a figure are congruent, then the figure is a parallelogram; Exercise 12: If consecutive angles of a figure are supplementary, then the figure is a parallelogram; Exercise 13: If the diagonals of a figure bisect each other, then the figure is a parallelogram; Exercise 14: If the diagonals of a figure are congruent, then the figure is a rectangle; Exercise 15: If the diagonals of a figure are perpendicular to each other, then the figure is a rhombus; Exercise 16: If the diagonals of a figure bisect the vertices of the figure, then the figure is a rhombus. *All converses are true. **20. a.** 62 units
b. $\angle T = 110°$, $\angle V = 70°$ **21. a.** $116°$, $32°$, $58°$
b. 10 units, 7 units **c.** 10 units **22. a.** both are 46 units, **b.** 26 units. **HISTORICAL NOTE** $x = 2$, $p = 3$

Pages 142-143   **1.** $\angle ADF \cong \angle ABF$ (parallel by corresponding angles) **2.** $\angle FXY \cong \angle FIH$ (parallel by corresponding angles) **3. a.** Bases are $\overline{KL}$ and $\overline{ST}$, median is $\overline{RU}$. **b.** Bases are $\overline{AB}$ and $\overline{DC}$, median is $\overline{WY}$. **4. a.** 12 units **b.** 12.6 units **c.** 28 units
d. 39.2 units **5. a.** 19 units **b.** 33 units **c.** 14 units
d. 19 units **e.** 46 units **6.** PROOF: Going from B to A and then from A to C is the same as going from B to C, so $\overline{BA} + \overline{AC} = \overline{BC}$, but $\overline{BA} = 2\overline{DA}$, and $\overline{AC} = 2\overline{AF}$, so $2(\overline{DA} + \overline{AF}) = \overline{BC}$, but $\overline{DA} + \overline{AF} = \overline{DF}$, $\therefore 2\overline{DF} = \overline{BC}$. **7.** yes **8. a.** 5, 5, 4 **b.** 20, 7, 3
c. 34, 17, 9 **9. a.** 168 units^2 **b.** 204 units^2 **c.** 246 units^2

10. $\overline{XY} = \dfrac{\overline{BC}}{2}$, $\overline{YZ} = \dfrac{\overline{AB}}{2}$, $\overline{XZ} = \dfrac{\overline{AC}}{2}$, perimeter of

$\triangle XYZ = \overline{XY} + \overline{YZ} + \overline{XZ} = \dfrac{\overline{BC}}{2} + \dfrac{\overline{AB}}{2} + \dfrac{\overline{AC}}{2}$ = perimeter of

$\triangle ABC \div 2$. **11.** GIVEN: Isosceles trapezoid $ABCD$; Join $\overline{AC}$ and $\overline{BD}$, Let point of intersection be X, $\overline{AX} \cong \overline{BX}$ (symmetry), $\overline{DX} \cong \overline{CX}$ (symmetry), $\overline{AX} + \overline{CX} = \overline{BX} + \overline{DX}$ (addition), $\therefore \overline{AC} \cong \overline{DB}$ (substitution) **12.** 5, 3

Pages 144-145 **1. a.** Ducks have webbed feet. Ducks do not have webbed feet. (Assume the second one.) **b.** In $\triangle XYZ$, $\angle X \ncong \angle Y$. In $\triangle XYZ$, $\angle X \cong \angle Y$. (Assume the second one.) **c.** In $\triangle HIG$, $\angle G$ is a right angle. In $\triangle HIG$, $\angle G$ is not a right angle. (Assume the second one.) **d.** $a \neq b$. $a = b$. (Assume the second one.) **e.** ℓ_3 is parallel to ℓ_4. ℓ_3 is not parallel to ℓ_4. (Assume the second one.) **f.** $\triangle RST$ is equilateral. $\triangle RST$ is not equilateral. (Assume the second one.) **g.** Quadrilateral $ABCD$ is a square. Quadrilateral $ABCD$ is not a square. (Assume the second one.) **h.** In $\triangle ABC$, $\angle 3$ is not an exterior angle. In $\triangle ABC$, $\angle 3$ is an exterior angle. (Assume the second one.) **2.** Assume ℓ_1 is not parallel to ℓ_2. If $\angle 1$ and $\angle 2$ are alternate angles $\angle 1 \ncong \angle 2$. But $\angle 1 \cong \angle 2$ so the assumption is false. Thus ℓ_1 is parallel to ℓ_2. **3.** Assume you didn't do homework. Then you can't do well on a test. But you did do well on a test. So you did do your homework. **4.** GIVEN: $\triangle PQR$ where $\angle Q = 55°$, $\angle R = 75°$; REQUIRED: To prove $\angle P \neq 40°$; PLAN: Assume $\angle P = 40°$ and find a contradiction; PROOF: 1. Only two possibilities; 2. To prove opposite; 3. Sum of angles in a triangle; 4. 176°; Addition; 5. $\angle P \neq 40°$; Indirect reasoning. **5.** PROOF: Assume $\angle B = 90° = \angle C$, $\angle A + \angle B + \angle C = 180°$, $\angle A + 90° + 90° = 180°$, so $\angle A = 0°$, so $\triangle ABC$ is not a triangle thus assumption is wrong, $\therefore$ $\angle B$ and $\angle C$ cannot both be right angles. **6.** PROOF: Assume two sides parallel, say $\overline{AB}$ and $\overline{AC}$, thus $\angle B + \angle C = 180°$ (consecutive interior angles), but $\angle A + \angle B + \angle C = 180°$, so $\angle A = 0°$, $\triangle ABC$ is not a triangle, thus assumption is wrong, $\therefore$ $\overline{AB}$ is not parallel to $\overline{AC}$. **7.** GIVEN: $\triangle ABC$ where D is not the midpoint of $\overline{BC}$ and $\overline{AD}$ bisects $\angle A$; REQUIRED: To prove $\overline{AB} \ncong \overline{AC}$; PLAN: Assume $\overline{AB} \cong \overline{AC}$ and reach a contradiction; PROOF: 1. Only two possibilities; 2. To reach a contradiction; 3. Assumption; 4. Given; 5. Definition of bisection; 6. Reflexive property; 7. $\triangle ABD \cong \triangle ACD$; S.A.S.; 8. $\overline{BD} \cong \overline{CD}$; C.P.C.T.; $\therefore$ D is midpoint by definition which is a contradiction, thus $\overline{AB} \cong \overline{AD}$. **8.** 1. Two possibilities; 2. To prove opposite; 3. Given; 4. Definition of an even number; 5. Definition of a prime number; 6. $2n$ is not prime; Indirect reasoning. **BRAINTICKLER** Joan borrowed Doreen's skirt and Ellen's sweater; Doreen borrowed Ellen's skirt and Simone's sweater.

Page 146 **1.** Triangles are not congruent. **2.** To calculate the lengths of the sides and compare them. **3. a.** congruent **b.** congruent **c.** not congruent **4.** Change: 50 M = SQR((Y2 − Y1) ∧ 2 + (X2 − X1) ∧ 2) • 51 N = SQR((B2 − B1) ∧ 2 + (A2 − A1) ∧ 2) • 52 J = SQR((Y3 − Y1) ∧ 2 + (X3 − X1) ∧ 2) • 53 K = SQR((B3 − B1) ∧ 2 + (A3 − A1) ∧ 2) • 54 L = SQR((Y3 − Y2) ∧ 2 + (X3 − X2) ∧ 2) • 55 P = SQR((B3 − B2) ∧ 2 + (A3 − A2) ∧ 2) • 56 IF M<> N THEN 90 • 57 If J<> K THEN 90 • 58 IF L<>P THEN 90 • 80 PRINT M, J, L, N, K, P, ''THE TRIANGLES ARE CONGRUENT.'' • 85 GOTO 99 • 90 PRINT M, J, L, N, K, P, ''THE TRIANGLES ARE NOT CONGRUENT.'' • 99 END **7.** Change: 31 M = (Y2 − Y1) / (X2 − X1) • 32 N = (Y3 − Y1) / (X3 − X1) • 33 P = (Y3 − Y2) / (X3 − X2) • 34 J = (B2 − B1) / (A2 − A1) • 35 K = (B3 − B1) / (A3 − A1) • 36 L = (B3 − B2) / (A3 − A2) • 40-70 Same, just change the letter names of M to L • 80 PRINT M, N, P, J, K, L, ''THE TRIANGLES ARE CONGRUENT.'' • 85 GOTO 99 • 90 PRINT M, J, L, N, K, P, ''THE TRIANGLES ARE NOT CONGRUENT.'' • 99 END

Page 147 **1. a.** 70° **b.** 40°, 140° **2. a.** 62°, 71°, 47° **b.** 24°, 38°, 118° **4. a.** $\angle G \cong \angle X$ **b.** $\overline{AB} \cong \overline{KC}$ **5.** PROOF: $\overline{AB} \parallel \overline{MN}$ (given), $\angle A \cong \angle N$ (alternate angles), $\overline{AX} \cong \overline{NX}$ (given), $\angle AXB \cong \angle NXM$ (vertically opposite), $\therefore$ $\triangle ABX \cong \triangle NMX$ (A.S.A.). **6.** PROOF: In isosceles $\triangle ABC$ bisect angle A and meet $\overline{BC}$ at X, $\overline{AB} \cong \overline{AC}$ (given), $\angle B \cong \angle C$ (given), $\angle BAX \cong \angle CAX$ (definition of bisector), $\triangle BXA \cong \triangle CAX$ (A.S.A.), $\therefore$ $\overline{BX} \cong \overline{CX}$ (C.P.C.T.). **7.** PROOF: $\overline{XP} \cong \overline{XR}$ and $\overline{XQ} \cong \overline{XS}$ (definition of bisection), $\angle PXQ \cong \angle RXS$ (vertically opposite angles), $\triangle PXQ \cong \triangle RXS$ (S.A.S.), $\overline{PQ} \cong \overline{RS}$ (C.P.C.T.), $\angle PQX \cong \angle RSX$ (C.P.C.T.), $\overline{PQ} \parallel \overline{SR}$ (alternate angles), $\therefore$ $PQRS$ is a parallelogram. **9. a.** quadrilateral **b.** true **c.** rhombus **d.** square **e.** true **10.** PROOF: In $\triangle JKN$ and $\triangle JRM$, $\overline{JM} \cong \overline{JN}$ (given), $\angle JMR \cong \angle JNK$ (sides opposite congruent angles), $\overline{KM} \cong \overline{NR}$ (assumption), $\triangle JKN \cong \triangle JRM$ (S.A.S.), so $\angle KJN \cong \angle RJM$ (C.P.C.T.), so $\angle KJM \cong \angle RJN$ (subtraction of same angle from both), but this is a contradiction, $\therefore$ assumption is false and $\overline{KM} \cong \overline{RN}$. **11.** 50

Page 148 **1. a.** 2 and 3; 3 and 4 **b.** 1 and 2 **c.** 1 and 3 **d.** 1 and 4 **e.** 1 and 5 **2. a.** 1 and 2 (alternate interior), 1 and 3 (consecutive interior), 1 and 4 (corresponding) **4. a.** 72° **b.** 95° **c.** 57° **d.** 106° **5. a.** rectangle and square **b.** rectangle and square **c.** square and rhombus **d.** square and rhombus **e.** trapezoid **f.** all except trapezoid **g.** rhombus and square **6.** PROOF: $\overline{AC} \cong \overline{AD}$, $\overline{BC} \cong \overline{ED}$, $\angle ACD \cong \angle ADC$ (angles opposite congruent sides), $\angle ACB \cong \angle ADE$ (supplements of congruent angles), $\triangle ABC \cong \triangle AED$ (S.A.S.), $\therefore$ $\angle BAC \cong \angle EAD$

476

(C.P.C.T.) **7.** PROOF: In $\triangle ADB$ and $\triangle ACE$, $\angle B \cong \angle E$ (given), $\overline{AB} \cong \overline{AE}$ (opposite congruent angles), $\overline{BC} \cong \overline{ED}$ (given), $\overline{BD} \cong \overline{EC}$ (adding $\overline{CD}$ to both), $\therefore \triangle ADB \cong \triangle ACE$ (S.A.S.) **8.** PROOF: $\overline{NL} \cong \overline{PL}$, and $\overline{KL} \cong \overline{ML}$ (both given), $\angle KLN \cong \angle MLP$ (vertically opposite), so $\triangle KLN \cong \triangle MLP$ (S.A.S.), $\angle KNL \cong \angle LPM$ (C.P.C.T.), $\therefore \overline{KN} \parallel \overline{PM}$ by alternate angles. **9.** PROOF: Assume n^2 is even, n is of the form $2n + 1$, so $n^2 = (2n + 1) = 4n^2 + 4n + 1$ which is odd thus contradicting the original assumption. **10.** 6 vertices $\times$ 4 lines = 24 triangles.

Chapter 6

Page 149   **1.** $1875:$3125$ **2. a.** 24 **b.** $\frac{33}{2}$

3. a. IV **b.** II **c.** III **d.** I **4. a.** on the negative x-axis **b.** on the positive y-axis **5. a.** $(x, 0)$ **b.** $(0, y)$ **c.** $(2, y)$ **d.** $(x, -5)$ **e.** $(x, \pm y)$ **f.** $(x, y) \rightarrow (-x, -y)$ **6.** x: 0, 2; y: 5, yes **7.** (1, 250), (2, 300), (3, 450), (4, 650)

Pages 150-151   **2. a.** 10, -6 **b.** -6, -1 **c.** $-3x$, $5y$ **d.** $x_2 - x_1$, $y_2 - y_1$ **3.** yes **4. a.** $\frac{1}{2}$ **b.** $\frac{-5}{7}$ **c.** $\frac{7}{3}$ **d.** $\frac{3}{4}$ **e.** 0 **f.** undefined **6. a.** $\frac{2b}{-7a}$ **b.** p **c.** a **d.** $\frac{6 - 2s}{3 - r}$ **e.** 0 **f.** $\frac{1 + m}{2 + m}$ **g.** undefined **7.** They are on a vertical line. **8.** 4.37 m **9.** 16 m **10.** 0.4 m **11. a.** $\frac{-48}{5}$ **b.** 5 **c.** 1 **d.** 5 **12.** 0, $\frac{5}{8}$, undefined, $\frac{-2}{3}, \frac{3}{2}$ **13.** They are equal.

Page 152   **5.** yes **HISTORICAL NOTE a.** $Ax^2 + Bx + C$ **b.** $2x^2 - 7x^3 - 42x$ **c.** $3a^2 - 12a^3b^2$ **d.** $-8m - 24m^2x$

Page 153   **2.** yes **3. a.** yes **b.** no **c.** yes **d.** no **5.** no **7.** no **9.** 20

Pages 154-155   **3. a.** $6x + y + 34 = 0$ **b.** $3y + 5x - 12 = 0$ **c.** $y - 4x + 31 = 0$ **d.** $7y - 3x + 22 = 0$ **e.** $4y + x + 2 = 0$ **4. a.** $2y + x - 11 = 0$ **b.** $3y - 2x - 4 = 0$ **c.** $3y - x + 5 = 0$ **d.** $y + x - 7 = 0$ **5. b.** $3y + 4x - 21 = 0$ **c.** yes **d.** collinear **6.** neither **8. a.** $y = 4$ **b.** $y = 1$ **c.** $y = 3$ **d.** $y = 0$ **9. a.** $x = 2$ **b.** $x = -5$ **c.** $x = 0$ **d.** $x = -1$ **10. a.** $y = 1$ **b.** $2y + 5x - 6 = 0$ **c.** $4y - x + 4 = 0$ **d.** $x = 4$ **e.** $y - 3x - 18 = 0$ **f.** $x = 5$ **11. a.** $12k - L + 45 = 0$ **b.** 45 cm **12. a.** $y + 3x - 24 = 0$; $5y - 4x + 13 = 0$; $13y - 18x - 27 = 0$ **b.** $y = 3$; $x = 9$; $y = -10$; $x = -4$ **13.** $\overline{JL}$ is $2y - x - 3 = 0$; $\overline{KM}$ is $y + 2x - 4 = 0$

Pages 156-158   **2. a.** 5; (2, 3) **b.** -2; (1, -6) **c.** 0.5; (-4, -12) **d.** 6; (-3, 1) **e.** $\frac{1}{2}$; (1, -4) **f.** $\frac{-5}{3}$; (-6, -2) **3. a.** $y - 5 = -4x$ **b.** $y - 4 = -1(x + 3)$ **c.** $y + 5 = \frac{5}{3}(x + 2)$ **d.** $y - 6 = -(x + 1)$ **e.** $y - 3 = \frac{3}{4}x$ **f.** $y = \frac{-7}{9}x$ **6.** $y - 6 = \frac{-7}{8}(x + 9)$ **7. a.** $y - 8 = \frac{25}{16}(x - 6.74)$ **c.** 15.70 **8. a.** -1, 4 **b.** $\frac{-7}{3}, \frac{5}{2}$ **c.** 2, 2 **d.** 2, $\frac{-5}{3}$ **e.** $\frac{-2}{5}, \frac{4}{5}$ **f.** $\frac{5}{2}$, 4 **9. a.** $y = -2x + 4$ **b.** $y = \frac{6}{7}x + 7$ **c.** $y = \frac{-3}{4}x - \frac{4}{5}$ **d.** $y = 8x - 5$ **e.** $y = -x - \frac{1}{3}$ **10. a.** $y = 3x + 7$ **b.** $y = \frac{1}{2}x - \frac{9}{4}$ **c.** $y = 4x + 13$ **d.** $y = \frac{5}{3}x + \frac{4}{3}$ **e.** $y = \frac{2}{3}x - \frac{2}{3}$ **f.** $y = \frac{5}{3}x - 6$ **11. a.** $y - 0 = 5\left(x - \frac{2}{5}\right)$ **b.** $y - 0 = \frac{-3}{2}\left(x - \frac{4}{3}\right)$ **c.** $y - \frac{5}{3} = \frac{-1}{3}(x - 1)$ **d.** $y + 5 = \frac{-1}{2}(x - 2)$ **13. a.** $a = 55w + 200$ **b.** 55, 200 **d.** 1025 **e.** 28 weeks

Pages 159-161   **1. a.** $3x - 5y - 16 = 0$ **b.** $2x - y + 1 = 0$ **c.** $2x - y + 5 = 0$ **d.** $3x - 10y + 4 = 0$ **3. a.** $x + y - 1 = 0$ **b.** $5x - 2y + 3 = 0$ **c.** $5x - 7y - 1 = 0$ **d.** $3x - 2y + 8 = 0$ **e.** $3x + y + 1 = 0$ **f.** $3x + 7y - 5 = 0$ **4. a.** $x - 3y - 2 = 0$ **b.** $x + 6y - 2 = 0$ **c.** $5x + 14y + 105 = 0$ **d.** $x - y + 8 = 0$ **5. a.** $2x + y - 3 = 0$ **b.** $2x - 3y + 5 = 0$ **c.** $4x - 3y + 6 = 0$ **d.** $x = 0$ **8. a.** $x - y + 3 = 0$ **b.** $x + y + 3 = 0$ **9. a.** $x - 5y = 0$ **b.** $7x + 5y + 1 = 0$ **c.** $x - 2y + 6 = 0$ **d.** $x - 7y - 7 = 0$ **e.** $3x + y - 3 = 0$ **10. b.** $0.6x - y + 3.1 = 0$ **d.** 0.60 **11.** $6x - 5y + 147 = 0$ **12.** $y + 1 = \frac{-10}{4 - a}(x - 4)$ **a.** $a = 4$ **b.** slope is positive when $a > 4$, slope is negative when $a < 4$ **13. a.** $16p - c + 120 = 0$ **c.** 120 **d.** 16 **e.** $1720, 6120 **14. a.** point-slope; $\frac{-2}{5}$, -2, -5 **b.** standard; $\frac{-7}{4}$, 7, 4 **c.** slope y-intercept; $\frac{2}{7}$, -2, 7 **d.** standard; $\frac{p}{m}, \frac{p}{n}, \frac{m}{n}$ **e.** point-slope; $\frac{fg - e}{f}$, $fg - e$, $-f$ **f.** slope y-intercept; $\frac{q}{p}$, $-q$, p **g.** standard; $\frac{-3a - 4b - c}{3}, \frac{3a + 4b + c}{4}, \frac{3}{4}$ **h.** standard; $\frac{-(e + f)}{a + b}, \frac{-(e + f)}{c + d}, \frac{-(a + b)}{c + d}$ **15. a.** $y = 4$, $y = 8x - 12$, $y = -2x - 2$ **b.** $y = 1$, $x = 1$, $y = -1$,

477

$x = -1$ **c.** $y = \frac{1}{2}x + 2$, $x = 2$, $y = \frac{1}{2}x - 2$, $x = -2$

d. $y = 2$, $y = -2x + 6$, $y = \frac{1}{2}x - \frac{3}{2}$, $y = -2x - 4$

16. a. -7 **b.** $p\epsilon R$ **c.** $p = 3$ **d.** $\frac{-8}{33}$

17. a. $\frac{57}{8}$ **b.** $\frac{-59}{5}$ **c.** $\frac{-37}{5}$ **d.** $\frac{186}{5}$ **e.** $\frac{99}{20}$ **f.** $\frac{-39}{4}$

18. a. $c = 0.06h + 27.09$ **b.** \$27.09 **c.** \$0.06

BRAINTICKLER exponents: 0, 1, 2; operation signs: +; 74

Page 162 **1.** 0, $y = 4$; $\frac{4}{3}$, $y = \frac{4}{3}x + \frac{16}{3}$; -2,

$y = -2x + 2$ **2. a.** $y = m(x - 4) - 2$
b. $y = m(x + 1) + 5$ **c.** $y = m(x + 3) - 7$
d. $y = mx - 8$ **e.** $y = m(x - 2)$ **f.** $y = m(x - 6) - 9$
3. a. $(3, -2)$ **b.** $(-1, 6)$ **c.** $(-4, 0)$ **d.** $(0, -3)$
4. a. $y = -3(x - 2) + 4$ **b.** $y = -3(x + 1) + 5$
c. $y = -3(x + 3) - 1$ **d.** $y = -3x - 3$ **5.** yes
7. a. $y = \frac{-1}{2}(x - x_1) + y_1$ **b.** $y = mx - 6$ **8. a.** $x = c$
b. $y = m(x - 1) - 2$

Page 163 **2. a.** $2x - y + 17 = 0$
b. $x + 6y + 4 = 0$ **c.** $16x + 12y + 109 = 0$
d. $3x - 4y + 22 = 0$ **3.** 110 **4. a.** perpendicular
b. parallel **5. a.** parallel **b.** no relation **c.** no relation
d. parallel **6.** parallel: a and f, b and c, e and h;
perpendicular: a and d, f and d

Pages 164-166 **1.** $\left(\frac{-11}{2}, 4\right)$ **3.** 13 **4. a.** 5
b. $5\sqrt{2}$ **c.** 7 **d.** $4\sqrt{5}$ **e.** 6.5 **f.** 11.4 **5. a.** yes
b. yes **c.** no **d.** no **e.** yes **f.** yes **6. a.** $(4, 1)$
b. $(-1, 1)$ **c.** $\left(\frac{3}{2}, \frac{3}{2}\right)$ **d.** $\left(-5, \frac{3}{2}\right)$ **e.** $\left(\frac{1}{2}, 0\right)$
f. $(-0.95, 1.75)$ **7.** Each side is $\sqrt{29}$ units in length.
8. $(0, 6)$ or $(0, 2)$ **9.** 31.14, $\left(\frac{-3}{2}, \frac{9}{2}\right)$ **10. a.** no
b. no **c.** no **d.** no **e.** yes **f.** yes **11.** $5x - 12y = 0$,
$2x + 5y = 0$, 13, 9.3; $5x + 3y - 50 = 0$, $7x - 5y = 0$,
5.8, 33.8; $10x - 9y - 50 = 0$, $x = 14$, 13.5, 10
12. a. $(-2, 4)$, $\left(\frac{7}{2}, \frac{5}{2}\right)$, $\left(0, \frac{-5}{2}\right)$, $\left(\frac{-11}{2}, -1\right)$
b. parallelogram **c.** One pair of opposite sides has
length 6.1 and slope -0.27; the other pair has length
5.7 and slope 1.43 **13. a.** $(2, 3)$ **14. a.** 206 units
b. $(22.5, 187.5)$ **c.** $y = \frac{201}{45}(x - 200)$ **d.** 182; 348.4
15. a. yes **b.** no **c.** yes **d.** no **16.** no
17. a. $(4, -5)$ **b.** $(-3, 1)$ **c.** $(a, -b)$
d. $(m + 2, 3 - n)$ **18. a.** $(-3, -2)$
b. $(-2, 4)$ **c.** $(-p, q)$ **d.** $(-k - 2, k - 3)$
19. a. 3, $\left(\frac{7}{2}, a\right)$ **b.** $(p - q)$, $\left(\frac{p + q}{2}, -1\right)$
c. $\sqrt{(m - 1)^2 + (n - 1)^2}$, $\left(\frac{m + 1}{2}, \frac{n + 1}{2}\right)$

d. $\sqrt{13}$, $\left(a - 1, b + \frac{3}{2}\right)$ **e.** $\sqrt{p^2 + 4q^2}$, $\left(\frac{5p}{2}, 5q\right)$
f. $\sqrt{(3 - 2t)^2 + 4}$, $\left(\frac{3 + 2t}{2}, t\right)$ **20. a.** $(4, 1)$
b. perpendicular **c.** 12 **21.** 11.17 m

USING THE LIBRARY **b.** $\left(-\frac{5}{6}, -\frac{1}{2}\right)$, (a, b)
c. $x + 3y + 1 = 0$

Pages 167-168 **1. a.** 2:5 **b.** 3:2 **c.** 1:1 **d.** 3:2
2. 1:2 **3. a.** $\sqrt{26}:1$ **b.** 32:37 **4.** $\left(\frac{-7}{5}, \frac{7}{5}\right)$
5. a. $(1, 3)$ **b.** same **c.** 1:1 **6. a.** $\left(\frac{-2}{7}, \frac{-1}{7}\right)$
b. $\left(\frac{-13}{7}, \frac{-17}{7}\right)$ **c.** $\left(\frac{-9}{4}, -3\right)$ **d.** $\left(\frac{-63}{11}, \frac{-13}{11}\right)$
e. $\left(0, \frac{3}{11}\right)$ **f.** $\left(\frac{-5q + 6p}{q + p}, \frac{-7q + 9p}{q + p}\right)$ **g.** $\left(\frac{a + 6}{2a + 1}, \frac{2a + 9}{2a + 1}\right)$
h. $\left(\frac{-5 + 6s - 6a}{1 + s - a}, \frac{-7 + 9s - 9a}{1 + s - a}\right)$ **7.** $(13, 8)$
8. a. $(12, 7)$ **b.** $\left(\frac{1}{3}, 5\right)$ **c.** $(3, -5)$ **9. a.** 1:1

Pages 169-171 **2.** $\overline{PQ} = 5$, $\overline{QR} = 5$, $\overline{PR} = 5\sqrt{2}$
3. a. slopes of $\overline{PQ} = \overline{SR} = 2$ **b.** Slopes of the pairs of
parallel sides are 0 and $\frac{-5}{2}$. **4. a.** All sides have the
same length. **b.** All sides have the same length and
the adjacent sides are perpendicular. **5. a.** $\overline{QT} \cong \overline{TR}$
b. $\overline{AT} \perp \overline{CB}$ **6.** $m_{DE} = m_{BC}$ and calculate lengths
of the line segments. **7.** Find lengths of $\overline{ST}$ and $\overline{QR}$
and compare. **8. a.** Product of slopes is -1.
b. and **c.** Calculate lengths of the line segments.
d. Find all lengths equal.

Pages 172-174 **1. a.** $(-7, 4)$, $(4, 4)$, $(4, -3)$
b. $(-3, 12)$, $(10, 12)$, $(-3, -7)$ **2. a.** 5.5 units²
b. 22.5 units² **c.** 20 units² **3. a.** 16 units²
b. 253 units² **4.** 12, 10, and 10 units² **5.** 21 units²
6. 10.5 units² **9.** 63 units²

Page 175 **1. a.** $\frac{3\sqrt{10}}{2}$ **b.** $\frac{7\sqrt{13}}{13}$ **2. a.** $\frac{79\sqrt{113}}{113}$
b. $\frac{86\sqrt{89}}{89}$ **3. a.** $p = 2$ **b.** $q = 8$ **4.** Distance is zero.
The point is on the line.

Pages 176-178 **2. a.** scalar **b.** vector **c.** scalar
d. scalar **e.** scalar **f.** vector **g.** vector **h.** vector
4. $\vec{a}$ and $\vec{b}$ **8. a.** 5 **b.** 5 **c.** 12 **d.** 9.2 **e.** 20.5
f. 6 **9. a.** $(4, 8)$ **b.** $(-2, 10)$ **c.** $(-6, 4)$ **d.** $(1, 9)$
e. $(1, 4)$ **f.** $(-2, 7)$ **10.** $\vec{b} = \vec{c}$, $\vec{g} = \vec{h}$, $\vec{f} = \vec{e}$ **11.** -2
12. $\frac{1}{2}$ **13.** $\overrightarrow{DH} = \overrightarrow{HA}$, $\overrightarrow{AE} = \overrightarrow{EB}$, $\overrightarrow{BF} = \overrightarrow{FC}$,
$\overrightarrow{DG} = \overrightarrow{GC}$ **BRAINTICKLER** 250 m; two different
events are being observed.

Pages 179-181 **3. a.** $[-2, 3]$ **b.** $[4, 3]$
c. $[0, -2]$ **d.** $[-3, 0]$ **4.** 20 km/h [S53°E] **6.** yes

7. b. $[-4, 9]$ **d.** $[-2, -5]$ **g.** yes **8.** $[1, -2]$
9. a. six times, same direction **b.** three times, opposite direction **c.** one half times, same direction
10. a. $\vec{e}$ **b.** $\vec{b}$ **c.** $\vec{e}$ **d.** $\vec{g}$ **e.** $\vec{d}$ **f.** $\vec{g}$ **11. a.** $\vec{j}$ **b.** $\vec{j}$
c. $-\vec{z}$ **d.** $\vec{m} - \vec{j}$ **e.** $\vec{z} + \vec{j}$ **f.** $\vec{z} + \vec{m}$ **g.** $\vec{z} + \vec{j} + \vec{m}$
h. $\vec{m} - \vec{j} - \vec{z}$

Pages 182-183 **1.** 123 km/h **2.** $[8, -2]$
3. 652 N; N57.5°E **5.** 75 km/h **6. a.** 15.3 km/h
b. 7.7 km/h **c.** 18.6 km/h **d.** 33.3 km/h
e. 27.8 km/h **7.** 26 km/h **8.** 22.4 N **9.** 79 km/h
10. 80.2 km/h **11.** 12.8 km/h
BRAINTICKLER 3 m

Pages 184-185 **1.** Answers may vary.
2. Answers may vary. **12.** Answers may vary.

Page 186 **3.** once **4. a.** 4.5 **b.** 8 **c.** 7 **d.** 15.5
e. 0 **5.** collinear points **6.** Change: 10 REM
CALCULATE THE AREA OF A REGULAR
4-SIDED POLYGON • 30 INPUT "ENTER THE
COORDINATES OF THE VERTICES ";
X1, Y1, X2, Y2, X3, Y3, X4, Y4 •
40 LET A = SQR((Y2 − Y1) ∧ 2 + (X2 − X1) ∧ 2) •
50 LET B = SQR((Y3 − Y2) ∧ 2 + (X3 − X2) ∧ 2) •
60 LET C = SQR((Y3 − Y1) ∧ 2 + (X3 − X1) ∧ 2) •
70 LET D = SQR((Y4 − Y1) ∧ 2 + (X4 − X1) ∧ 2) •
80 LET E = SQR((Y3 − Y4) ∧ 2 + (X3 − X4) ∧ 2) •
90 LET S = (A + B + C) / 2 • 100 LET
T = (C + D + E) / 2 • 110 LET A1 = SQR(S ∗
(S − A) ∗ (S − B) ∗ (S − C)) • 120 LET
A2 = SQR(T ∗ (T − C) ∗ (T − D) ∗ (T − E)) •
130 LET AR = A1 + A2 • 140 PRINT "THE AREA
OF THE REGULAR 4-SIDED POLYGON IS ";
AR; "SQUARE UNITS." • 150 END **7.** Change:
10 REM CALCULATE THE PERIMETER OF A
REGULAR POLYGON • 20 INPUT "ENTER THE
NUMBER OF SIDES AND COORDINATES OF
TWO ADJACENT VERTICES "; N, X1, Y1, X2,
Y2 • 30 LET A = SQR((Y2 − Y1) ∧ 2 + (X2 − X1) ∧
2) • 40 LET P = N ∗ A • 50 PRINT "PERIMETER
OF THE POLYGON IS "; N ∗ A; " UNITS" • 60
END

Page 187 **1. a.** -1 **b.** 0 **c.** undefined **d.** $\frac{6}{7}$

5. a. 6.4 **b.** 19.7 **6. a.** $(6, 3)$ **b.** $\left(\frac{5}{2}, 2\right)$ **c.** $(0, 0)$

d. $\left(\frac{5}{2}, \frac{-7}{2}\right)$ **7. a.** $y + 4 = \frac{-3}{2}(x - 1)$ **b.** $y = \frac{1}{4}(x - 3)$

c. $y = \frac{1}{3}(x - 2)$ **d.** $y - 8 = \frac{4}{5}(x - 1)$

e. $y + 4 = \frac{3}{5}(x - 4)$ **8.** a and f; b and c; d and e

9. $y + 2 = \frac{-5}{16}(x + 3)$ **10.** $\left(3, \frac{3}{5}\right)$ **11. a.** 31 units²

b. 33 units² **c.** 0 units² **d.** They are collinear. **12.** $\frac{21}{5}$

14. a. $[5, -5]$ **b.** $[-8, -14]$ **c.** $[-17, -8]$
d. $[3, -4]$ **e.** $[3, -10]$ **f.** $[11, 28]$ **15. b.** 35.8 N,
9° below the horizontal

Page 188 **2.** no **3. a.** $y + 1 = \frac{3}{5}(x - 2)$

b. $y = \frac{-5}{2}(x + 2)$ **c.** $y = -5x + 7$

d. $y + 5 = \frac{2}{3}(x - 4)$ **e.** $y - 4 = 3(x + 2)$

f. $y + 5 = \frac{-1}{3}(x - 5)$ **5.** $y = \frac{5}{2}(x + 3)$

6. 17 **7. a.** $(-3, 0)$ **b.** $\left(\frac{3}{2}, 2\right)$ **8.** no

9. a. $y - 1 = \frac{5}{4}(x + 1)$ **b.** $\left(\frac{4}{3}, \frac{11}{3}\right)$ **10.** Both are
$\sqrt{29}$ units in length. **11.** $\sqrt{17}$ **13.** 25 units²
14. b. $\sqrt{58}$ **c.** $[4, -1]$ **d.** $[24, 25]$
e. $\vec{m} - \vec{n} = [7, 6]$, $\vec{n} - \vec{m} = [-7, -6]$ **15. c.** 318 N

Cumulative Review Chapters 4-6

Pages 189-190 **1. a.** Q **b.** Q **c.** Q **d.** $\overline{Q}$ **e.** $\overline{Q}$
f. $\overline{Q}$ **2.** $0.\overline{45}$ **3.** $4\frac{53}{99}$ **4. a.** $\frac{2}{m^7}$ **b.** $-3qr$ **c.** $6x^9$

d. $8p^3q^6$ **e.** $-2m^3$ **f.** $\frac{1}{3ab^3}$ **g.** $\frac{a^2}{16b^8}$ **h.** $\frac{n^9}{m^3}$ **5. a.** 16

b. 3 **c.** $\frac{1}{16}$ **d.** $\frac{1}{125}$ **6. a.** 3^{7x} **b.** 7^{3x+2} **7. a.** 20

b. $-\frac{1}{5}$ **c.** 36 **d.** $\frac{1}{16}$ **8. a.** $2a^2b\sqrt{3b}$ **b.** $3k^2m^3\sqrt[3]{2k}$
9. a. $\sqrt{5}$ **b.** $4\sqrt{3}$ **10. a.** $6\sqrt{3} - 12$

b. $x - 4\sqrt{xy} + 4y$ **11. a.** $\sqrt{6}$ **b.** $\frac{19 - 16\sqrt{6}}{25}$

12. a. $x = 12.5$ **b.** $x = \frac{3}{2}$ **13. a.** Both are 100°.

b. $3x - 5 = 28°$, $7x - 21 = 56°$, $4x + 40 = 84°$
21. a. $\sqrt{5}$ **b.** $-\frac{4}{7}$ **c.** $\left(-\frac{1}{2}, -\frac{1}{2}\right)$ **d.** $\sqrt{65}$

e. $-\frac{5}{9}$ **f.** $\left(-4, \frac{3}{2}\right)$ **22.** parallel: a and e;
perpendicular: a and f, b and d, e and f
23. $y + 2 = -\frac{3}{5}(x - 4)$ **24.** $y + 1 = \frac{6}{5}(x + 4)$

25. $y - 1 = -\frac{1}{4}(x + 3)$ **26.** $y = -4x - 2$

27. a. $y - 2 = \frac{2}{9}(x + 5)$ **b.** $y = \frac{7}{2}(x + 1)$

c. $\left(-\frac{85}{59}, -\frac{91}{59}\right)$ **28.** $y - 1 = -\frac{1}{4}(x + 3)$ **29.** $\frac{10\sqrt{34}}{17}$

30. $2\sqrt{30}$ **31.** $\frac{43}{127}$ **32.** 4 **33.** 6 **34.** 16
35. a. $[-2, 9]$; $\sqrt{85}$ **b.** $[-3, 6]$; $3\sqrt{5}$
c. $[-19, -22]$; $13\sqrt{5}$ **d.** $[-21, -27]$; $3\sqrt{130}$
36. 1050 **37.** 39 m **38.** 42°N, 107°W

Chapter 7

Page 191   1. a. 0 **b.** −2 **c.** undefined **d.** $\frac{d-b}{c-a}$

2. m is the slope and b is the y-intercept. **3. a.** II
b. I **c.** III **d.** IV **e.** on the negative x-axis **f.** on the
positive y-axis **4. a.** ±7 **b.** no solution **5. a.** 1
b. 2 **c.** 1 **d.** 2 **6.** Part b is the reflection of part a in
the y-axis. **c.** yes **7.** Part b is the reflection of part a

in the line $y=x$. **c.** no **8. b.** $y=4x-6$ **c.** $\frac{3}{2}$, −6

9. a. $y=-x+8$ **b.** $y=4x-2$ **11. a.** min, (0, 0)
b. max, (0, 2)

Pages 192-193   2. a. $D=\{-5,-1,2,4\}$,
$R=\{-4,0,3,5\}$ **b.** $D=\{0,4,9,16\}$,
$R=\{0,2,3,4\}$ **c.** $D=\{5,6,7,8\}$, $R=\{-3\}$
d. $D=\{-5,-3,0,3,5\}$, $R=\{5,3,0\}$
e. $D=\{-2,-1,0,1,2\}$, $R=\{-8,-1,0,1,8\}$
f. $D=\{2\}$, $R=\{-7,-4,0,3,7\}$ **3. a.** yes
b. $y=\sqrt{x}$ **c.** $y=-3$ **d.** $y=|x|$ **e.** $y=x^3$ **f.** $x=2$
5. a. one-to-one **b.** one-to-one **c.** many-to-one
d. many-to-one **e.** one-to-one **f.** one-to-many
6. a. $D=\{-7,-3,-2\}$, $R=\{7,3,2\}$
b. $D=\{4,9,36\}$, $R=\{4,-2,5,-1,8,-4\}$
c. $D=\{-5,5,-2,2,0\}$, $R=\{25,4,0\}$
d. $D=\{7,0,-8\}$, $R=\{60,5,-40\}$ **7. a.** one-to-one
b. one-to-many **c.** many-to-one **d.** one-to-one
8. a. (10, $106.50) **b.** (24, $256.60)

c. (44, $468.60) **9. a.** 24 **b.** −41 **c.** −1 **d.** $\frac{2}{5}$

e. −51 **f.** −1 **10. a.** $x \to 2x+9$ **b.** $x \to |x|-3$

c. $x \to 2|x|+4$ **11. a.** 3 **b.** ±4 **c.** 11 **d.** $\pm\frac{3}{2}$

e. $-\frac{3}{2}$ **f.** 29 **12.** (1, $15.25), (2, $30.50),

(5, $76.25), (8, $122.00), $(n, \$15.25n)$
13. a. $x \to 2x+1$ **b.** $x \to -4x+3$ **c.** $x \to -6x+7$
14. (6, $6.50), (9, $14.00), (15, $29.00),
$(n, \$4.00+\$2.50(n-5))$ **15. a.** (−2, −10), (0, −2),
(2, 6) **b.** (−10, 0), (0, −10), (10, 0) **c.** (−4, 9),
(0, 1), (4, 9)

Pages 194-195   1. no **2.** yes
5. a. $D=\{2,3,4,5,6\}$, $R=\{2,3,4,5,6\}$
b. $D=\{0,1,2,3,4\}$, $R=\{0,1,4,9,16\}$
c. $D=\{10,7,4,3,1\}$, $R=\{-10,-7,-4,-3,-1\}$
d. $D=\{-5,-10,-15,-20,-25\}$, $R=\{8,6,4,2,0\}$
e. $D=\{-1,0,1,2,3\}$, $R=\{3\}$ **f.** $D=\{7\}$,
$R=\{5,4,3,2,1\}$ **6. a.** $D=\{x\,|\,x\epsilon R,\,|x|\leq 1\}$,
$R=\{y\,|\,y\epsilon R,\,|y|\leq 2\}$ **b.** $D=\{x\,|\,x\epsilon R,\,x\geq -4\}$,
$R=\{y\,|\,y\epsilon R\}$ **c.** $D=\{x\,|\,x\epsilon R\}$, $R=\{y\,|\,y=2;\,x\geq 2,$
$y=-2;\,x<2\}$ **d.** $D=\{x\,|\,x\epsilon R\}$, $R=\{y\,|\,y\epsilon R\}$
e. There is a "jump" discontinuity at $x=2$.
8. a. $D=\{x\,|\,x\epsilon R,\,x\neq 9\}$, $R=\{y\,|\,y\epsilon R,\,y\neq 0\}$
b. $D=\{x\,|\,x\epsilon R,\,x\neq -2,-1\}$,
$R=\left\{y\,|\,y\epsilon R,\,y\geq 6 \text{ or } y\leq\frac{1}{6}\right\}$

c. $D=\{x\,|\,x\epsilon R,\,x\neq 5,-7\}$, $R=\{y\,|\,y\epsilon R,\,y\neq 0\}$
9. a. $D=\{x\,|\,x\epsilon R\}$, $R=\{y\,|\,y\epsilon R\}$ **b.** $D=\{x\,|\,x\epsilon R\}$,
$R=\{y\,|\,y\epsilon R\}$ **c.** $D=\{x\,|\,x\epsilon R\}$, $R=\{y\,|\,y\epsilon R,\,y\geq 0\}$
d. $D=\{x\,|\,x\epsilon R\}$, $R=\{y\,|\,y\epsilon R,\,y\leq 0\}$
e. $D=\{x\,|\,x\epsilon R\}$, $R=\{y\,|\,y\epsilon R,\,y\geq 0\}$
f. $D=\{x\,|\,x\epsilon R\}$, $R=\{y\,|\,y\epsilon R,\,y>0\}$
11. b. $D=\{d\,|\,d\epsilon R,\,d\geq 0\}$, $R=\{t\,|\,t\epsilon R,\,t\geq 0\}$
12. b. $D=\{T\,|\,T\epsilon R,\,20\leq T\leq 100\}$,
$R=\{t\,|\,t\epsilon R,\,0\leq t\leq 5\}$

Pages 196-197   3. a. no **b.** no **c.** no **d.** yes

5. a. $y<5-x$ **b.** $y>-\frac{2}{3}x$ **c.** $y>x-4$ **d.** $y<\frac{1}{2}x$

e. $y<-1+|x|$ **f.** $y<\frac{3}{2}x-6$ **7. a.** $2w+t\geq 10$

8. a. $1.5c+5t\leq 30$ **c.** no **9. a.** $y\geq -\frac{6}{5}x+6$

b. $y<-\frac{4}{3}x-4$ **10. a.** $3g+14f\leq 420$

11. a. $20k-15h>3000$ **b.** yes **12.** $x\geq 0,\,y\geq 0,$

$x<8,\,y<\frac{5}{8}x+5$

Pages 198-199   2. For both $D=\{x\,|\,x\epsilon R\}$,

$R=\{y\,|\,y\epsilon R\}$ **3.** $\left(-\frac{5}{2},\,-\frac{5}{2}\right)$ **4. a.** Inverse =

$\{(0,4),(-1,4),(1,4),(-2,4),(2,4)\}$; For the
Relation—$D=\{4\}$, $R=\{-2,-1,0,1,2\}$; For the
Inverse—$D=\{-2,-1,0,1,2\}$, $R=\{4\}$

b. Inverse = $\left\{\left(\frac{1}{\sqrt{2}},\,\sqrt{2}\right),\left(\frac{1}{\sqrt{3}},\,\sqrt{3}\right),\left(\frac{1}{\sqrt{5}},\,\sqrt{5}\right),\right.$

$\left.\left(\frac{1}{\sqrt{6}},\,\sqrt{6}\right)\right\}$; For the Relation—

$D=\{\sqrt{2},\sqrt{3},\sqrt{5},\sqrt{6}\}$, $R=\left\{\frac{1}{\sqrt{2}},\frac{1}{\sqrt{3}},\frac{1}{\sqrt{5}},\frac{1}{\sqrt{6}}\right\}$;

For the Inverse—$D=\left\{\frac{1}{\sqrt{2}},\frac{1}{\sqrt{3}},\frac{1}{\sqrt{5}},\frac{1}{\sqrt{6}}\right\}$,

$R=\{\sqrt{2},\sqrt{3},\sqrt{5},\sqrt{6}\}$ **c.** Inverse = $\{(V,a),(W,b),$
$(X,c)\,(Y,d),(Z,e)\}$; For the Relation—
$D=\{a,b,c,d,e\}$, $R=\{V,W,X,Y,Z\}$; For the
Inverse—$D=\{V,W,X,Y,Z\}$, $R=\{a,b,c,d,e\}$
5. part a **6. c.** $(0,-2)\to(-2,0)$, $(4,0)\to(0,4)$
e. (−4, −4) **7.** yes **8. a.** $D=\{x\,|\,x\epsilon R,\,x\geq 0\}$,
$R=\{y\,|\,y\epsilon R,\,y\geq 0\}$ **b.** $D=\{x\,|\,x\epsilon R,\,x\geq 0\}$,

$R=\{y\,|\,y\epsilon R,\,y\geq 0\}$ **9. a.** $y=\frac{1}{4}(x+7)$ **b.** $y=2x$

c. $xy=1$ **d.** $|y|x=-1$ **e.** $|y|=5-x$ **f.** $y=x^3$
10. a. For the Relation—$D=\{x\,|\,x\epsilon R\}$,
$R=\{y\,|\,y\epsilon R,\,y>0\}$; For the Inverse—
$D=\{x\,|\,x\epsilon R,\,x>0\}$, $R=\{y\,|\,y\epsilon R\}$ **b.** For
the Relation—$D=\{x\,|\,x\epsilon R\}$, $R=\{y\,|\,y\epsilon R\}$; For the
Inverse—same as the relation **c.** For the Relation—
$D=\{x\,|\,x\epsilon R\}$, $R=\{y\,|\,y\epsilon R,\,y\leq 0\}$; For the Inverse—
$D=\{x\,|\,x\epsilon R,\,x\leq 0\}$, $R=\{y\,|\,y\epsilon R\}$ **d.** For the
Relation—$D=\{x\,|\,x\epsilon R,\,x\neq 0\}$, $R=\{y\,|\,y\epsilon R,\,y\neq 0\}$;
For the Inverse—$D=\{x\,|\,x\epsilon R,\,x\neq 0\}$,
$R=\{y\,|\,y\epsilon R,\,y\neq 0\}$ **11.** no **12.** $D=\{x\,|\,x\epsilon R,\,x\neq 0\}$,

$R = \{y | y \epsilon R, y \neq 0\}$ **b.** yes **13.** $D = \{x | x \epsilon R, x \neq 0\}$, $R = \{y | y \epsilon R, y \neq 0\}$ **b.** The graph is its own inverse. **14.** Joe

Pages 200-202   **1.** yes **2.** Parts b, c, and d are functions. **4.** Parts a, b, c, e, and f are functions. **5. a.** two **b.** yes **c.** no **6.** no **7.** yes **8. a.** It is a function. **9.** yes **10.** no, a vertical line **11. a.** $R = \{20, 20.1, 20.2, 20.4\}$ **b.** It is a function. **12. a.** $V = \dfrac{10}{D + 10}$ **c.** yes

Page 203   **1. a.** 3 **b.** 0 **c.** $3\frac{1}{2}$ **2. a.** 17 **b.** $3x^2 + 2$ **c.** $3x^4 + 2$ **3. a.** 16 **b.** 0.25 **c.** 0.25 **4. a.** $\frac{2}{3}$ **b.** 3 **c.** $-\frac{3}{5}$ **d.** $\frac{1}{2}$ **e.** $D = \{x | x \epsilon R, x \neq -2\}$, $R = \{y | y \epsilon R\}$ **5.** no **6. a.** 14 **b.** 14 **c.** 828 **d.** 2 **7. a.** $D = \{n | n \epsilon R, n \neq \pm 1\}$, $R = \{h(n) | h(n) \epsilon R\}$ **b.** 0 **c.** 1, -1 **8.** no **9.** $2x + h + 3$ **10. a.** 16 **b.** 0 **c.** 4 **d.** $y^2 + 4y + 4$ **e.** $y^4 + 4y^2 + 4$ **f.** $y^2 + 8y + 16$ **g.** y^2 **h.** $4\sqrt{3} + 7$ **i.** $9x^2 + 6x + 1$ **11. a.** 1 **b.** 8 **c.** $\frac{1}{4}$ **d.** 32 **e.** -64 **f.** 8 **g.** $\frac{1}{4}$ **h.** 16 **i.** 16

Pages 204-205   **1. a.** For the Relation— $D = \{x | x \epsilon R\}$, $R = \{y | y \epsilon R, y \geq -3\}$; For the Inverse— $D = \{x | x \epsilon R, x \geq -3\}$, $R = \{y | y \epsilon R\}$ **c.** yes **d.** yes **2.** $f^{-1}(x) = \pm \sqrt{x}$ **a.** For the Relation—$D = \{x | x \epsilon R\}$, $R = \{y | y \epsilon R, y \geq 0\}$; For the Inverse— $D = \{x | x \epsilon R, x \geq 0\}$, $R = \{y | y \epsilon R\}$ **c.** no **3. a.** 0 **b.** -4 **c.** 6 **d.** 2 **e.** x **f.** x **h.** The result will be the identity function $y = x$. **4.** yes **5. a.** $x = 0$, inverse a function **b.** inverse a function **c.** no **d.** no **e.** $|t| \leq 3$, inverse a function **f.** $u \geq 0$, inverse a function **6. a.** yes **b.** $n = 1000(1.08)^4$ **c.** yes **7. a.** yes **b.** $m = 100(0, 99)^t$ **8. a.** yes **b.** $t = -3|d - 0.5| + 1.5$ **c.** no **9. b.** yes **c.** $N = k_u R - k_c R^2$ **d.** yes **10.** no **BRAINTICKLER** $250(4 - \pi)$ cm³

Pages 206-207   1. The first is 8 units higher. **2.** $f(x) - 9$ **4. a.** For $f(x) = |x| + 2$—$D = \{x | x \epsilon R\}$, $R = \{y | y \epsilon R, y \geq 2\}$; For $f(x) = |x| - 2$—$D = \{x | x \epsilon R\}$, $R = \{y | y \epsilon R, y \geq -2\}$ **5. a.** $D = \{x | x \epsilon R\}$, $R = \{y | y \epsilon R, y > 0\}$ **b.** no **c.** It will be raised 3 units. **d.** The range will be different. **e.** yes **6.** yes **8. b.** $D = \{x | x \epsilon R\}$, $R = \{y | y \epsilon R, y > 0\}$ **c.** yes **9.** yes **10. a.** The price will go down and more oil will be sold. **c.** yes **d.** $D = \{p | p \epsilon R, p \neq 5\}$, $R = \{f(p) | f(p) \epsilon R, f(p) \neq 0\}$ **11. c.** $x \neq 0$ **12.** $x = \dfrac{1}{3}$, $x = -1$, $x \neq 0$

Pages 208-209   **1.** The first is moved down two units and the second is moved right two units.

2. $f(x) = 2^{(x-8)}$ **4. c.** Part a is moved 2 units left and part b is moved 3 units right. **d.** Moved p units left if $p < 0$ and p units right if $p > 0$. **5. c.** $|x - 4|$ is $|x|$ 4 units to the right; $|x + 3|$ is $|x|$ 3 units to the left. **e.** They are the same graph vertically separated 7 units. **f.** no **6.** $N = 2^{t-5}$, $t \geq 5$ **7.** $f(t) = 80(t - 5)$, $t \geq 5$ **8. a.** The second is three units to the left. **b.** The inverse of the second is three units lower. **9. a.** $D = \{x | x \epsilon R, x \neq 0\}$, $R = \{y | y \epsilon R, y \neq 0\}$ **b.** The graph of part a shifted 3 units left. **c.** $D = \{x | x \epsilon R, x \neq -3\}$, $R = \{y | y \epsilon R, y \neq 0\}$ **e.** Graph of part a shifted 2 units right, $D = \{x | x \epsilon R, x \neq 2\}$, $R = \{y | y \epsilon R, y \neq 0\}$ **f.** The graph will be shifted a units right if $a > 0$ and a units left if $a < 0$. **10. a.** The first graph shifted one unit right.

Pages 210-211   **1.** $y = \dfrac{1}{8}|x|$ **2.** stretch by a factor of three **4. a.** $y = 7\sqrt{x}$ **b.** $y = \dfrac{1}{2}x$ **c.** $y = \dfrac{1}{2}|x|$ **d.** $y = 4(3^x)$ **5. a.** compression by a factor of 4 **b.** stretch by a factor of 5 **c.** compression by a factor of 12 **d.** reflection in x-axis and stretch by a factor of 9 **e.** reflection in x-axis **f.** compression by a factor of 5 **g.** stretch by a factor of 7 **h.** reflection in x-axis and stretch by a factor of $\dfrac{4}{3}$ **6. a.** compression by a factor of 9 **b.** reflection in x-axis **c.** stretch by a factor of 6 **d.** reflection in x-axis and compression by a factor of 2

Pages 212-213   **1. a.** vertical translation of 1 **b.** vertical translation of -2 **c.** stretch by a factor of $\dfrac{3}{4}$ **d.** compression by a factor of 4 **e.** reflection in x-axis and a vertical translation of 3 **f.** vertical translation of -3 and stretch by a factor of 5 **g.** vertical translation of 7 and reflection in x-axis **h.** compression by a factor of 2 and vertical translation of 4 **3. a.** reflection in x-axis **b.** reflection in $y = x$ **c.** translation of 7 left and 2 down **d.** translation of 3 right and 5 up **e.** translation 3 right and stretch by a factor of 2 **f.** translation 1 unit right and compression by a factor of 4 **g.** translation 3 units right and 1 unit up and compression by a factor of 3 **h.** reflection in y-axis of a reflection in $y = x$ and a stretch by a factor of 4 **i.** reflection in $y = x$, translation 10 units right and compression by a factor of 6 **j.** translation 9 units right, 7 units up and compression by a factor of 3 **5. a.** $D = \{t | t \epsilon R\}$, $R = \{f(t) | f(t) \epsilon R, f(t) \geq 1\}$ **c.** $1000 **d.** no **6.** a is a horizontal translation, b is a vertical translation, and k is a stretch or compression. **7. b.** 1000 m **c.** when $t = 10$ **d.** 10 min **e.** no **8. a.** $S(r) = 4\pi r^2$ **a.** yes **b.** no **HISTORICAL NOTE** 3.017 071 8 It would be if enough terms of the series were used.

1. $y = 0.005x^2$, yes **2.** Change line 50 LET Y = X + 2 **3.** to prevent the graph from exceeding screen capacity **4.** because the inverse will need to be restricted to the column space of 280 **5.** Change line 50 LET Y = X ∧ 2 − 2 ∗ X + 3 **6.** Change: 45 INPUT "ENTER VALUES FOR A, B, AND C "; A, B, C • 50 LET Y = A ∗ X ∧ 2 + B ∗ X + C

Page 215 **1. a.** $D = \{1, 4, 7, 10, 13\}$, $R = \{0, 5, 10, 15, 20\}$ **b.** $D = \{x|x\epsilon R\}$, $R = \{y|y\epsilon R\}$ **c.** $D = \{x|x\epsilon R, |x|<3, x \neq -1\}$, $R = \{y|y\epsilon R\}$ **d.** $D = \{x|x\epsilon R\}$, $R = \{y|y\epsilon R, y<|x|+3\}$ **3.** For the Relation—$D = \{x|x\epsilon R\}$, $R = \{y|y\epsilon R, y\geq 9\}$; For the Inverse—$D = \{x|x\epsilon R, x\geq 9\}$, $R = \{y|y\epsilon R\}$; They are interchanged. **4. a.** $y = \sqrt[3]{x}$, $D = \{x|x\epsilon R\}$, $R = \{y|y\epsilon R\}$ **b.** $x = (3\pi)^{2y}$, $D = \{x|x\epsilon R, x>0\}$, $R = \{y|y\epsilon R\}$ **c.** $xy = \frac{5}{8}$, $D = \{x|x\epsilon R, x \neq 0\}$, $R = \{y|y\epsilon R, y \neq 0\}$ **5.** Interchange x and y.

7. a. $I = \frac{64}{D^2}$ **c.** yes **8. a.** 54.1 **b.** 0.1 **c.** $y^4 - y^3 + 0.1$ **d.** 0.0375 **e.** $81w^4 - 27w^3 + 0.1$ **f.** 0.001 234 5 **9. a.** translation of 2 units down **b.** translation of 1 unit left and a reflection in the x-axis **c.** compression by a factor of 3 **d.** translation of 5 units down, compression by a factor of 2, reflection in the x-axis **e.** translation of 21 units down, compression by a factor of 5, reflection in the x-axis **f.** translation of 3 units left and 5 units up, compression by a factor of 7 and reflection in the x-axis **10. a.** $x = y^3 - 3y^2 + 9y$, no **b.** $x = 3$, no **c.** $9x + 4y = -11$, yes **d.** $x = \sqrt{1 - 3y^2}$, no **12.** no **13.** $C(d) = \pi d$, yes **14. a.** $150 + 5n$ **b.** yes **c.** yes **d.** $n\geq 120$ **16.** $k = 1$, $b = 0$, $a = 0$

Page 216 **1. a.** $D = \{x|x\epsilon R\}$, $R = \{y|y\epsilon R\}$ **b.** $D = \{-1, 0, 1, 2, 3\}$, $R = \{2, 5, 10, 1, 0\}$ **c.** $D = \{x|x\epsilon R\}$, $R = \{y|y\epsilon R, y\geq 0\}$ **d.** $D = \{x|x\epsilon R, x \neq \pi\}$, $R = \{y|y\epsilon R, y \neq 3\}$ **2. a.** $D = \{x|x\epsilon R, |x|\leq 3\}$, $R = \{y|y\epsilon R, 0\leq y\leq 4\}$ **b.** $D = \{x|x\epsilon R, |x|\leq 3\}$, $R = \{y|y\epsilon R, |y|\leq 4\}$ **c.** $D = \{x|x\epsilon R\}$, $R = \{y|y\epsilon R, y\geq 0\}$ **d.** $D = \{x|x\epsilon R, x\leq \pi\}$, $R = \{y|y\epsilon R\}$ **4.** $xy = k$ **5. a.** $y = -2(x - 4)$ **b.** $\sqrt[5]{\frac{x}{4}} = y$ **c.** $x = 10^{2y}$ **d.** $x = \sqrt{y^2 + 3y - 1}$ **6. a.** 4 **b.** −1 **c.** $3a + 2$ **d.** undefined **e.** $\frac{(a + 2)(a - 1)}{3}$ **f.** −6 **7. a.** $V = \left(\frac{1}{2}\right)\frac{M}{25\ 000}$ **b.** \$4307.62 **c.** yes **8.** $x = \frac{1 \pm \sqrt{21}}{2}$ **10. a.** $7x + 6y\geq 420$ **c.** no **12.** $3x - 1$ **13.** translation of 1 up, reflection in the x-axis, stretch by a factor of 3 **14.** $y = mx + b$ **a.** $y = 4x - 3$ **b.** $y = -x + 10$ **c.** $y = \frac{2}{3}x + \frac{1}{2}$

Chapter 8

Page 217 **1. a.** 2 **b.** 1 **c.** 1 **d.** 3 **3. a.** yes **b.** no **c.** yes **d.** yes **e.** no **f.** yes **4. a.** $2x + 6$ **b.** $x^2 + 3x - 10$ **c.** $3xy^2 - 27x$ **d.** $-80x^2 - 120xy - 45y^2$ **e.** $a^3 + b^3$ **f.** $20 - 4a - 5ab + a^2b$ **5. a.** $2x(1 - 2x)$ **b.** $(5x - 1)^2$ **c.** $x^2(3 - 4x^2)$ **d.** $(2a - 4b)(4a^2 + 8ab + 16b^2)$ **6. a.** yes **b.** yes **c.** yes **d.** yes **e.** yes **f.** yes

7. a. $-\frac{1}{2}$ **b.** 2, −2 **c.** 0, −3 **d.** $-\frac{b}{a}$

8. $\frac{48x^4 - 364x^3 + 38x^2 + 68x - 14}{3x^4 - 28x^3 + 38x^2 + 80x - 21}$ **9. a.** yes **b.** no

c. no **d.** yes **10.** $x = -\frac{52}{37}$, $x \neq \pm 2$, −3 **11.** no

Page 218 **1. a.** yes **b.** no **c.** yes **d.** no **e.** yes **f.** no **2. a.** $2x^2 - 10x + 24$; 2, −10, 12 **b.** $-3x^2 - 12x - 12$; −3, −12, −12 **c.** $x^2 - 2x - 9$; 1, −2, −9 **d.** $-9x^2 - 30x + 25$; −9, −30, 25 **e.** $5x^2 - 32x + 131$; 5, −32, 131 **f.** $-12x^2 + 42x + 4$; −12, 42, 4 **3.** no **4.** $r^2(4 - \pi)$

Pages 219-220 **2.** yes **3. a.** $(0, -2)$, $(-2, 2)$, $x = 0$, parabola **b.** $(1, 4)$, $(-1, 2)$, $x = 1$, parabola **4. a.** $x\epsilon R$, $y>0$, $(0, 0)$, $x = 0$, upward, $\{0\}$ **b.** $x\epsilon R$, $y\leq 0$, $(0, 0)$, $x = 0$, downward, $\{0\}$ **c.** $x\epsilon R$, $y\geq -9$, $(0, -9)$, $x = 0$, upward, $(3, -3)$ **d.** $x\epsilon R$, $y\leq 9$, $(0, 9)$, $x = 0$, downward, $(3, -3)$ **e.** $x\epsilon R$, $y\geq -16$, $(0, -16)$, $x = 0$, upward, $(4, -4)$ **f.** $x\epsilon R$, $y\leq 16$, $(0, 16)$, $x = 0$, downward, $(4, -4)$ **g.** $x\epsilon R$, $y\leq -\frac{3}{2}$, $\left(\frac{-3}{2}, \frac{-3}{2}\right)$, $x = -\frac{3}{2}$, upward, $\left(\frac{-3 + \sqrt{3}}{2}, \frac{-3 - \sqrt{3}}{2}\right)$ **5. a.** reflection in $y = 0$ **6. a.** min **b.** max **c.** max **d.** max **7. a.** −9 **b.** 1 **c.** 5 **d.** 61 **8. a.** $(-1, 0)$, $(5, 18)$ **b.** $(0, 0)$, $(-1, -3)$ **9. a.** $0\leq t\leq 50$; $0\leq h\leq 3062.5$ **b.** 3062.5 m **c.** 0 **d.** no **10. b.** 10, 64 **c.** 37; \$291.60 **12. b.** $0\leq t\leq 10$; $0\leq v(t)\leq 490$ **c.** quadrupled

Pages 221-222 **6. a.** $y = 3x^2$ **b.** $y = 5x^2$ **c.** $y = -3x^2$ **d.** $y = -\frac{1}{2}x^2$

Page 223 **5.** $y = x^2 + 6$; $y = x^2 - 4$ **6. b.** 17.1 s **c.** 20 s

Page 224 **1.** yes **4.** $y = (x + 4)^2$; $y = (x - 3)^2$ **7. a.** upward, $(0, 2)$, $x = 0$, y-intercept = 2, $x\epsilon R$, $y\geq 2$ **b.** upward, $(4, 0)$, $x = 4$, x-intercept = 4, y-intercept = 16, $x\epsilon R$, $y\geq 0$ **c.** downward, $(-2, 0)$, $x = -2$, x-intercept = −2, y-intercept = −4, $x\epsilon R$, $y\leq 0$ **d.** upward, $(0, -5)$, $x = 0$, x-intercept = $\pm \sqrt{5}$, y-intercept = −5, $x\epsilon R$, $y\geq -5$ **e.** upward, $(4, 0)$, $x = 4$, x-intercept = 4, y-intercept = 32, $x\epsilon R$, $y\geq 0$ **f.** downward, $(4, 0)$, $x = 4$, x-intercept = 4, y-intercept = −8, $x\epsilon R$, $y\leq 0$ **8. a.** 625 m/s; 225 m/s **b.** 25 s

Pages 225-226   **3. a.** $\frac{1}{4}(x-2)^2 - 3$

b. $y = 4(x+1)^2 + 2$ **4. a.** upward, (3, 2), $x = 3$,
y-intercept = 11, $x \epsilon R$, $y \geq 2$ **b.** upward, (4, −8),
$x = 4$, x-intercept = $8 \pm 4\sqrt{2}$, y-intercept = 8,
$x \epsilon R$, $y \geq -8$ **c.** downward, (−2, −3), $x = -2$,
y-intercept = −5.8, $x \epsilon R$, $y \leq -3$ **d.** upward,
(0, −5), $x = 0$, x-intercept = $\pm \sqrt{5}$, y-intercept = −5,
$x \epsilon R$, $y \geq -5$ **e.** upward, (4, −2), $x = 4$,
x-intercept = $4 \pm \sqrt{\frac{2}{3}}$, y-intercept = 46,

$x \epsilon R$, $y \geq -2$ **f.** downward, (4, −5), $x = 4$,
y-intercept = −85, $x \epsilon R$, $y \leq -5$
6. $y = -(x-5)^2 + 2$ **7.** $y = 2(x-1)^2 - 2$

9. a. $y = x^2 + 4$ **b.** $y = \frac{1}{2}(x-4)^2 - 2$ **c.** $y = 2x^2 - 3$

13. a. $y = -(x-3)^2$ **b.** $y = (x+5)^2 + 2$
c. $y = (x-2)^2 + 6$ **d.** $y = -(x+1)^2 - 1$
e. $y = (x-4)^2 + 10$ **f.** $y = (x+3)^2$ **g.** $y = -x^2 + 2$
14. $y = (x-700)^2 + 160$ **15.** $x - 1 = 0$
BRAINTICKLER a. J, A, S, O, N, D
b. 522, 652, 982
Pages 227-228   **1. a.** 9 **b.** 4 **c.** 36

d. 20.25 **e.** 6.25 **f.** $\frac{1}{4}$ **2. a.** $[x - (-3)]^2 + 1$

b. $\left[x - \left(-\frac{3}{2}\right)\right]^2 + \left(-\frac{13}{4}\right)$ **3. a.** $y = (x-4)^2 - 12$;
$x \epsilon R$; $y \geq -12$; (4, −12); $x = 4$; upward; −12 at $x = 4$
b. $y = (x+5)^2 - 28$; $x \epsilon R$; $y \geq -28$; (−5, −25);
$x = -5$; upward; −28 at $x = -5$ **c.** $y = (x+3)^2 - 9$;
$x \epsilon R$; $y \geq -9$; (−3, −9); $x = -3$; upward; −9 at

$x = -3$ **d.** $y = \left(x + \frac{7}{2}\right)^2 - \frac{69}{4}$; $x \epsilon R$; $y \geq -\frac{69}{4}$;

$\left(-\frac{7}{2}, -\frac{69}{4}\right)$; $x = -\frac{7}{2}$; upward; $-\frac{69}{4}$ at $x = -\frac{7}{2}$

e. $y = \left(x - \frac{3}{2}\right)^2 + \frac{39}{4}$; $x \epsilon R$; $y \geq \frac{39}{4}$; $\left(\frac{3}{2}, \frac{39}{4}\right)$; $x = \frac{3}{2}$;

upward; $\frac{39}{4}$ at $x = \frac{3}{2}$ **f.** $y = \left(x - \frac{1}{2}\right)^2 + \frac{35}{4}$; $x \epsilon R$;

$y \geq \frac{35}{4}$; $\left(\frac{1}{2}, \frac{35}{4}\right)$; $x = \frac{1}{2}$; upward; $\frac{35}{4}$ at $x = \frac{1}{2}$

4. a. $3(x-2)^2 - 7$ **b.** $-2\left[x - \left(-\frac{5}{4}\right)\right]^2 + \frac{17}{8}$

5. a. $y = 3(x+1)^2 + 5$ **b.** $y = 2\left(x + \frac{1}{4}\right)^2 + \frac{31}{8}$

c. $y = 5\left(x - \frac{3}{10}\right)^2 + \frac{31}{20}$ **d.** $y = -2\left(x - \frac{3}{4}\right)^2 + \frac{17}{8}$

e. $y = -4\left(x + \frac{5}{8}\right)^2 + \frac{103}{16}$ **f.** $y = \frac{1}{2}(x-3)^2 - \frac{21}{2}$

6. a. $y = \left(x - \frac{7}{2}\right)^2 - \frac{29}{4}$ **b.** $y = 4\left(x + \frac{1}{8}\right)^2 - \frac{33}{16}$

c. $y = -3\left(x - \frac{1}{3}\right)^2 + \frac{28}{12}$ **d.** $y = 5\left(x + \frac{12}{10}\right)^2 - \frac{164}{20}$

e. $y = (x+1)^2 - 1$ **f.** $y = 2\left(x - \frac{1}{8}\right)^2 + \frac{97}{32}$

7. a. $y = \frac{1}{5}(x+15)^2 - 44$ **b.** $y = \frac{2}{3}(x-4.5)^2 - 13.5$

c. $y = -\frac{3}{4}(x-6)^2 + 29$ **d.** $y = \frac{2}{3}\left(x - \frac{3}{4}\right)^2 + \frac{6}{48}$
8. $y = -20(x-16)^2 + 5120$; $5120 on 16 apartments
Pages 229-230   **1.** $a = -6$, $b = 8$, $c = -5$;
max = −2.3 at $x = 0.6$ **2. a.** 8 at $x = -1$ **b.** 29 at
$x = -1.5$ **c.** 8.08 at $x = 0.83$ **d.** 10.125 at $x = 0.75$
e. 15.0625 at $x = -0.875$ **f.** −6.95 at $x = 0.1$
g. 21.25 at $x = 3.5$ **h.** 0 at $x = -0.3$ **i.** −2.0625 at
$x = -0.875$ **j.** 6.3 at $x = 1.3$ **3. a.** −7 at $x = -1$;

$1 \pm \frac{1}{3}\sqrt{21}$ **b.** 18 at $x = 3$; $-3 \pm 3\sqrt{2}$ **c.** 1.125 at

$x = 1.25$; 2, $\frac{1}{2}$ **d.** −6 at $x = 1$; 0 or 2 **e.** −0.75 at

$x = 0.5$ **f.** −4 at $x = 0$ **g.** −1 at $x = 5$; 6, 4 **h.** 0 at

$x = 7$; 7 **i.** −10.125 at $x = 0.375$; $\frac{3}{2}, \frac{-3}{4}$ **j.** 0 at

$x = 1.6$; $\frac{5}{3}$ **4.** $5625.00 at $7.50 per ticket **5.** 3 m
by 1 m; 3 m² **7.** 14 suits; $19 601.00 **8. a.** 100 m
by 100 m; 10 000 m² **b.** $66\frac{2}{3}$ m by 50 m each;

$3333\frac{1}{3}$ m² each **c.** 25 m by 50 m each; 1250 m² each

d. one $66\frac{2}{3}$ m by 40 m; $2666\frac{2}{3}$ m²; two $33\frac{1}{3}$ m by

40 m; $1333\frac{1}{3}$ m² **9.** $x + 5 = 0$ **10.** $x - 2 = 0$
BRAINTICKLER no

Pages 231-233   **1. a.** min = 0 at $x = 3$
b. min = −5 at $x = 0$ **c.** max = 2 at $x = -1$

d. min = −7 at $x = 3$ **e.** max = $2\frac{1}{3}$ at $x = \frac{2}{3}$

4. 11, 11 **5.** $\frac{7}{2}$, $-\frac{7}{2}$ **6.** 100 m by 200 m

8. 125 m by 125 m **9.** 3 plots of 12.5 m by $8\frac{1}{3}$ m

10. 19¢; $3.61 **11.** $280; $11 760 per week
12. 5 cm by 5 cm **13.** −2, 1 **14.** 4 fields of

80 m by 50 m **15.** 22 **16.** 4 **17.** $\frac{3}{2}$ **18. a.** $a < 0$

b. max/min = $\frac{4ac - b^2}{4a}$; $x = -\frac{b}{2a}$ **19.** $x = 4, 5$

Page 234   **1. b.** $y = x^2$, $x \epsilon R$, $y \geq 0$; $y = -x^2$, $x \epsilon R$,
$y \leq 0$ **c.** $y = x^2$ upward; $y = -x^2$ downward **d.** $x = 0$,
(0, 0) for both **2. a.** $f(x)$ and a **b.** $f(x)$ and a
3. a. $y = \pm\sqrt{x - 5}$ **b.** $y = \pm\sqrt{x + 4}$
c. $y = \sqrt{x + 8} + 4$ **d.** $y = \sqrt{x - 2} - 6$

e. $y = \pm\sqrt{\frac{1}{3}x + 2} + 4$ **f.** $y = \pm\sqrt{-\frac{1}{2}x + 4} - 3$

4. a. no **b.** no **5. a.** yes **b.** no **c.** yes **d.** no
Page 235   **2. a.** (0, 0), no **b.** (3, 3), no
c. (0, 2), no **d.** (−4, 5), no **e.** (−2, −6), no

f. (5, 1), no **g.** $\left(\frac{3}{2}, \frac{7}{4}\right)$, yes **h.** (0, 9), yes

BRAINTICKLER 8

Page 236   **2.** lines 50 or 80   **4. a.** 1.75
b. −2.875   **c.** −1   **d.** 25.25   **5. a.** −7.3   **b.** 6.0625
c. −16.125   **d.** −8.25   **e.** 22   **f.** 0   **6. a.** no   **b.** Insert
these lines: 45 IF A = 0 THEN 95 • 94 GOTO 100 •
95 PRINT "THERE IS NO MAXIMUM OR
MINIMUM VALUE."   **7.** Insert these lines: 55 LET
VER = −B / (2 ∗ A) • 85 (same as 55) • 60 PRINT
"Y = "; A; "X ∧ 2 + "; B; "X + "; C; " HAS A
MINIMUM VALUE OF "; MIN; " AND THE
VERTEX "; VER; MIN; "." • 90 (same as 60 except
put maximum for minimum)

Page 237   **1. a.** $5x^2 - 6x + 3$; 5, −6, 3
b. $-2x^2 + 16x - 32$; −2, 16, −32   **c.** $3x^2 + 12x + 7$;
3, 12, 7   **d.** $x^2 + 1$; 1, 0, 1   **2. a.** upward, $x = 0$,
(0, −3)   **b.** downward, $x = 3$, (3, 0)   **6. a.** upward,
(0, −1), $x = 0$ **b.** upward, (−5, 0), $x = -5$
c. downward, (8, −3), $x = 8$ **d.** downward, (1, 6),
$x = 1$ **7. a.** $y = x^2 + 4$ **b.** $y = -(x - 3)^2 + (-2)$
c. $y = [x - (-6)]^2$ **d.** $y = (x - 5)^2 + 2$
8. a. $x \epsilon R$, $y \leq 0$ **b.** $x \epsilon R$, $y \geq 2$ **c.** $x \epsilon R$, $y \leq 2$
d. $x \epsilon R$, $y \geq -8$ **9. a.** $y = (x - 5)^2 - 22$
b. $y = -2\left(x - \frac{3}{2}\right)^2 + \frac{19}{2}$ **c.** $y = 4\left(x + \frac{3}{8}\right)^2 - \frac{9}{16}$
d. $y = \frac{1}{2}(x - 1)^2 + \frac{5}{2}$ **10. a.** −27   **b.** 5   **c.** $-\frac{3}{4}$
d. $7 - 12\sqrt{2}$ **11. a.** min = −14 at $x = 4$
b. min = −5 at $x = -6$ **c.** min = −5.125 at $x = 0.25$
d. max = 2 at $x = 3$ **12.** 15, 15   **13.** 125   **15.** $\frac{4ac - b^2}{4a}$
at $x = -\frac{b}{2a}$ **16.** yes

Page 238   **1. a.** yes   **b.** no   **c.** yes   **d.** no
2. a. $y = 4x^2 - 8x + 1$ **b.** $y = -2x^2 + 20x - 50$
c. $y = 3x^2 - 7x + 20$ **d.** $y = 2x^2 - 19x + 9$
e. $y = 8x^2 - 14x - 15$ **4. a.** (0, −8)   **b.** (0, 0)
c. (1, 0)   **d.** (−3, −4)   **e.** (1.25, −3.125)
5. a. $y = (x - 3)^2 + 1$ **b.** $y = -[x - (-2)]^2 + 5$
6. a. $y = (x + 6)^2$ **b.** $y = -x^2$ **c.** $y = x^2 - 3$
d. $y = (x + 2)^2 + 4$ **e.** $y = -x^2 - 5$
7. a. $y = -\left(x - \frac{3}{2}\right)^2 + \frac{29}{4}$ **b.** $y = 2\left(x + \frac{5}{2}\right)^2 - \frac{31}{2}$
8. a. 7.5   **b.** 8.25   **9.** −1.6̇   **10.** 8, −8   **11.** \$60;
\$1800   **13.** no   **14. a.** 2.875 at $x = 0.75$
b. −7.3 at $x = 0.6$

Chapter 9

Page 239   **2. a.** 7   **b.** −15   **c.** $-6\sqrt{3}$
d. $10\sqrt{14}$ **e.** $9\sqrt{3}$ **f.** $4\sqrt{2}$ **g.** $72\sqrt{2} - 5\sqrt{6}$
h. $24\sqrt{10} + 12\sqrt{15} - 20\sqrt{3}$ **3. a.** $\sqrt{3}$ **b.** $-\sqrt{6}$
c. $1 + \sqrt{5}$ **d.** $2 - \sqrt{37}$ **e.** $-\sqrt{162} + 5$
f. $8\sqrt{216} + 3$ **4. a.** $2x - 3x^2$ **b.** $x^2 - 2x - 15$
c. $4x^2 - 5x^3 + 4 - 5x$ **d.** $-21xy + 3x^2 + 30y^2$
e. $9x^2 - 36x\sqrt{6} + 216$ **f.** −12   **5. a.** −3   **b.** −6

c. −4   **d.** −35   **e.** 157   **f.** 13 815   **6. a.** $\frac{1 + \sqrt{3}}{2}$
b. $\frac{10 + \sqrt{2}}{49}$ **c.** $\frac{12\sqrt{3} - \sqrt{15}}{48}$ **d.** $\frac{10y - y\sqrt{x} - 3x}{x - 4y^2}$
e. $\frac{x^3 + x^2\sqrt{y} + 4x\sqrt{23y} + 4x^2\sqrt{23}}{x^2 - y}$
f. $\frac{-24y + 12y\sqrt{5y} - 48\sqrt{7x} + 24\sqrt{35xy}}{4 - 5y}$ **7. a.** $2(x - 2y)$
b. $4(3x^2 + xy - 2y)$ **c.** $7x(4y - 1) + 4y$ **d.** $5x(2 - 7x)$
e. $(x + 2)(3x - 1)(5x + 3)$ **f.** $4(x - 7)^2$
g. $(4x + 9y)(4x - 9y)$
h. $(4a + 9b)(16a^2 - 36ab + 81b^2)$ **8. a.** 0 or $\frac{7}{2}$ **b.** 5
or −4   **c.** $\frac{1}{3}$ or $-\frac{5}{2}$ **d.** −3 or $\frac{1}{4}$ **e.** 4 or $-\frac{7}{3}$ **f.** 0
or $-\frac{3}{4}$ or $\frac{2}{5}$

Pages 240-242   **1. a.** ±4   **b.** 0 or 7   **c.** 0 or −2
d. 5 or −4   **e.** $\frac{1}{2}$ or −4   **f.** 0   **g.** ±2   **h.** 2   **i.** −5
2. a. 2, 8   **b.** $-\frac{1}{2}, \frac{7}{3}$ **c.** ±6   **d.** 0, $\frac{12}{5}$ **e.** $-\frac{5}{2}$, 3
f. 0, $-\frac{33}{6}$ **g.** $\frac{1}{4}, \frac{5}{4}$ **h.** $-\frac{4}{3}$, 3   **i.** $-\frac{2}{5}, -\frac{4}{3}$
j. ±5   **k.** $-\frac{7}{2}$ **l.** ±2   **3. a.** −3, 18   **b.** −3, 18
4. −5, −10 or 11, 6   **5. a.** −3, 5   **b.** $\frac{1}{2}$, 4
c. $\frac{1}{4}$, −2   **d.** $\frac{5}{3}$ **6. a.** no roots   **b.** 2 roots   **c.** 2 roots
7. a. $x = \frac{1}{6}$, −3; $x \epsilon R$, $y \geq -\frac{361}{24}$ **b.** $x = -4, \frac{5}{2}$; $x \epsilon R$;
$y \geq -\frac{507}{8}$ **c.** $x = \frac{7}{8}$, −2; $x \epsilon R$; $y \geq -\frac{529}{32}$ **d.** $x = 6$,
$-\frac{2}{3}$; $x \epsilon R$; $y \geq -\frac{200}{3}$ **e.** $x = \frac{2}{5}$, 2; $x \epsilon R$; $y \geq -\frac{16}{.5}$
8. −10, −3, −31; 5, 12, 14   **9.** 9 s   **10. a.** 7.6
b. 1.5   **11.** The radius of the large circle is 6 units
and the radius of the small circle is 3 units.   **12.** $\frac{6 - \pi}{6}$

Pages 243-245   **2. a.** $(x + 3)^2$ **b.** $(x - 4)^2$
c. $\left(x - \frac{1}{2}\right)^2$ **d.** $\left(x + \frac{5}{2}\right)^2$ **e.** $\left(x - \frac{1}{3}\right)^2$ **f.** $\left(x + \frac{3}{8}\right)^2$
3. a. $x = 5.4$, −0.4   **b.** $x = 1.8$, −2.8   **c.** 1.3, 0.3
d. 3.3   **e.** 0.5, 6.5   **f.** 1.5, 1.25   **4. a.** 6.54, 0.46
b. 7.41, −0.41   **c.** 0.6, −0.5   **d.** 0.43, −0.77
e. 16.18, −6.18   **f.** 4.22, −0.55   **5. a.** 16   **b.** 36
c. 20.25   **d.** 12.25   **e.** 0.16   **f.** 0.694   **6. a.** $p = 3$
b. $p = -\frac{1}{3}$ **c.** $x = \frac{4}{5}$ **d.** $p = 9$ **e.** $p = -5$
f. $p = 4$ **7. a.** $2(x + 3)^2 - 9$ **b.** $2\left(x + \frac{7}{4}\right)^2 - \frac{25}{8}$
8. a. $-5 \pm 3\sqrt{2}$ **b.** $3 \pm \sqrt{6}$ **c.** $4 \pm 2\sqrt{6}$
d. $-\frac{9}{2} \pm \frac{\sqrt{73}}{2}$ **e.** −2, −3   **f.** $-3.5 \pm \frac{\sqrt{37}}{2}$

g. $3 \pm 2\sqrt{3}$ **h.** $-1 \pm \sqrt{11}$ **i.** $\dfrac{5}{2} \pm \dfrac{\sqrt{21}}{2}$

j. $-\dfrac{3}{2} \pm \dfrac{\sqrt{41}}{2}$ **k.** $-\dfrac{11}{2} \pm \dfrac{\sqrt{41}}{2}$ **l.** $-\dfrac{7}{2} \pm \dfrac{\sqrt{33}}{2}$

m. $1, -3$ **n.** $-1, -4$ **9.** 30 min **10.** 1 or -6
11. 2.4 m by 1.8 m **12.** 75 km/h and 55 km/h
13. 10 m, 8 m **14.** no **15.** 520 km/h

16. a. $-4 \pm \dfrac{\sqrt{66}}{2}$ **b.** $2 \pm \dfrac{\sqrt{21}}{3}$ **c.** $-1 \pm \dfrac{2\sqrt{10}}{5}$

d. $1 \pm \dfrac{3\sqrt{2}}{2}$ **e.** $\dfrac{3}{4} \pm \dfrac{\sqrt{41}}{4}$ **f.** $-\dfrac{5}{6} \pm \dfrac{\sqrt{37}}{6}$

g. $\dfrac{1}{10} \pm \dfrac{\sqrt{41}}{10}$ **h.** $0.5, -1.5$ **i.** $-2 \pm \dfrac{\sqrt{22}}{2}$

j. $2 \pm \dfrac{\sqrt{33}}{3}$ **k.** $2 \pm \sqrt{5}$ **l.** $-4 \pm \dfrac{\sqrt{74}}{2}$

m. $\dfrac{1}{4} \pm \dfrac{\sqrt{33}}{4}$ **n.** $-3, 15$ **18. a.** $-1 \pm \sqrt{7}$

b. $3 \pm \sqrt{21}$ **c.** $-6 \pm \sqrt{30}$ **d.** $2 \pm \sqrt{10}$

e. $-4 \pm 2\sqrt{3}$ **f.** $\dfrac{5}{6} \pm \dfrac{\sqrt{85}}{6}$ **19.** 8.2 s

20. division by zero

Pages 246-248 **2. a.** $2x^2 + 3x + 8 = 0$; 2, 3, 8
b. $-7x^2 + 2x - 4 = 0$; $-7, 2, -4$
c. $-6x^2 - x + 5 = 0$; $-6, -1, 5$ **d.** $5x^2 - 6 = 0$;
$5, 0, -6$ **e.** $x^2 + 4 = 0$; 1, 0, 4 **f.** $3x^2 - 6x + 2 = 0$;
$3, -6, 2$ **3. a.** $6x^2 - 11x + 8 = 0$; 6, -11, 8
b. $4x^2 + x + 3$; 4, 1, 3 **c.** $7x^2 - 26x + 18 = 0$;
7, -26, 18 **d.** $5x^2 + 9x + 3 = 0$; 5, 9, 3

4. a. $4 \pm \dfrac{4\sqrt{2}}{2}$ **b.** $-3 \pm \sqrt{7}$ **c.** $-\dfrac{5}{2} \pm \dfrac{\sqrt{33}}{2}$

d. $\dfrac{1}{2} \pm \dfrac{\sqrt{13}}{2}$ **e.** $1, -2.5$ **f.** $\dfrac{5}{6} \pm \dfrac{\sqrt{19}}{6}$ **g.** $\dfrac{5}{4} \pm \dfrac{\sqrt{41}}{4}$

h. 1, 0.2 **5. a.** not real **b.** $\dfrac{9}{2} \pm \dfrac{\sqrt{77}}{2}$ **c.** not real

d. $\dfrac{1}{8} \pm \dfrac{\sqrt{33}}{8}$ **e.** not real **f.** not real **g.** -1.7

h. $\dfrac{9}{4} \pm \dfrac{\sqrt{105}}{4}$ **6. a.** 0, -1, -4 **7.** 2 cm by 11 cm

8. a. 0.3, -3.3 **b.** 7.4, 1.6 **c.** 0.8, -0.6
d. not real **9. a.** $-1.67, 0.67$ **b.** $-0.44, -1.36$
c. 0.45, -4.45 **d.** 1.21, 0.41 **e.** $-0.13, 2.47$

f. $-3.50, 1.00$ **10. a.** $\dfrac{-7}{10} \pm \dfrac{\sqrt{129}}{10}$ **b.** $5 \pm \sqrt{19}$

c. $-\dfrac{5}{4} \pm \dfrac{\sqrt{113}}{4}$ **d.** $2.00, -1.67$

e. $-\dfrac{1}{5} \pm \dfrac{\sqrt{6}}{5}, x \neq -1$ **f.** $-\dfrac{5}{2} \pm \dfrac{\sqrt{33}}{2}, p \neq -2, -4$

g. $\dfrac{15}{24} \pm \dfrac{\sqrt{417}}{24}, t \neq -\dfrac{1}{4}$ **h.** $\dfrac{1}{2}, -5; x \neq \pm 2$

11. a. $-2, 1.67$ **b.** 1.5, -6 **12. a.** ii **b.** i
13. a. $-1, -2, 2$ **b.** 1, 1.22 **c.** $-3, 4.24, -0.24$

d. 6.22, -3.22 **e.** $-\sqrt{2}, \dfrac{3}{2}\sqrt{2}$ **f.** 1.78, -0.56

g. 1.19, -2.52 **h.** 1, 0.71 **14. a.** $0.\dot{3}, -1.5$
b. x not in R

Pages 249-250 **1. a.** $d = 0$; $x = -2$ **b.** $d = 4$;
$x = -1, -3$ **c.** $d = -32$; x not in R **4. a.** $d = 13$,
2 roots **b.** $d = 16$, 2 roots **c.** $d = -4$, no roots
d. $d = 44$, 2 roots **e.** $d = 40$, 2 roots **f.** $d = 0$, 1 root

5. a. $m < \dfrac{9}{16}$, 2 roots; $= \dfrac{9}{16}$, 1 root; $> \dfrac{9}{16}$, no roots

b. $m < 2\sqrt{26}$, no roots; $= 2\sqrt{26}$, 1 root; $> 2\sqrt{26}$,
2 roots **c.** $m < \dfrac{4}{3}$, 2 roots; $= \dfrac{4}{3}$, 1 root; $> \dfrac{4}{3}$, no

roots **d.** $m < 0$, no roots; $= 0$, 1 root; > 0, 2 roots
e. $m < 18$, 2 roots; $= 18$, 1 root; > 18, no roots

6. $k = \dfrac{5}{4}$ **7.** $d > 0$, real, distinct, both; $d = 0$, real,

equal, both; $d < 0$, not real, distinct, both
8. $-24 \pm 16\sqrt{2}$ **9.** 25; they are least common
multiples. **10. a.** i **b.** iii **c.** ii **11. a.** yes **b.** yes
c. no **d.** no **12. a.** 2 roots **b.** 2 roots **c.** 2 roots
BRAINTICKLER 132

Pages 251-252 **1.** first row: 1, 3, -2, $\dfrac{-3 + \sqrt{17}}{2}$

and $\dfrac{-3 - \sqrt{13}}{2}$, -3, -2; second row: 1, -3, -4, 4

and -1, 3, -4; third row: 2, 0, 7, no roots; fourth

row: 2, -5, 3, $\dfrac{3}{2}$ and 1, $\dfrac{5}{2}, \dfrac{3}{2}$ **2. a.** $\dfrac{1}{5}$ **b.** $-\dfrac{4}{5}$

3. $\dfrac{7}{12}; -\dfrac{5}{24}$ **4. a.** $-8, -20$ **b.** $\dfrac{5}{4}, \dfrac{1}{4}$ **c.** $-\dfrac{1}{3}, -\dfrac{10}{3}$

d. $0, -\dfrac{4}{9}$ **e.** $\dfrac{6}{5}, 0$ **f.** $\dfrac{17}{12}, \dfrac{1}{2}$ **g.** 6, -4 **h.** $\dfrac{1}{6}, -\dfrac{2}{3}$

5. a. $x^2 + x - 6$ **b.** $x^2 - 5x + 4$ **c.** $x^2 - 6x$
d. $2x^2 + 9x - 5$ **e.** $20x^2 + 7x - 6$ **f.** $x^2 - 4x + 1$

7. $k = 48$ **8. a.** $1\dfrac{1}{3}$ **b.** $1\dfrac{1}{9}$ **c.** $\dfrac{4}{9}$ **d.** $-3\dfrac{1}{3}$ **e.** $\dfrac{8}{9}$

f. $\dfrac{16}{9}$ **9. a.** -1 **b.** $\dfrac{4}{3}$ **c.** $\dfrac{3}{2}$ **10. a.** $k = \dfrac{1}{3}$ **b.** $k = 14$

c. $k = -1, -2$ **12.** $\dfrac{5}{2}$ or $\dfrac{1}{6}$ **13.** $k = 0$ **14. a.** $\dfrac{61}{16}$

b. $9.\dot{4}$ **c.** $\dfrac{q^2 - 2pr}{p^2}$ **15.** $\dfrac{7}{3}$, 1; $3x^2 - 7x + 3 = 0$

16. 5, 6, 25, 76

Pages 253-256 **1. a.** $5i$ **b.** $11i$ **c.** $9i\sqrt{3}$ **d.** $20i$
e. $-39i\sqrt{2}$ **f.** $-7i\sqrt{5}$ **g.** -3 **h.** 24 **i.** 90 **j.** -256
k. $-i$ **l.** -4 **m.** i **n.** -625 **o.** -27 **2. a.** $3 - 2i$
b. $-5 - 5i$ **c.** $-2 - 5i$ **d.** $8i - 1$ **e.** $9 + 6i$ **f.** $5 + i$
g. 0 **h.** $2a - 2bi$ **3. a.** $4i + 12$ **b.** $-35 + 25i$
c. $3 - i$ **d.** $4 + 47i$ **e.** 13 **f.** $9 + 40i$ **g.** $a^2 + b^2$
h. $a^2 + 2abi - b^2$ **5. a.** $1 \pm i\sqrt{5}$ **b.** $-4 \pm i\sqrt{3}$

c. $2 \pm i\sqrt{5}$ **d.** $3 \pm \dfrac{1}{5}i\sqrt{10}$ **e.** $-3, -1$

f. $-7 \pm \dfrac{1}{2}i\sqrt{5}$ **g.** $\dfrac{2}{3} \pm \dfrac{1}{3}i\sqrt{14}$ **h.** 1, 2.5

i. $\dfrac{-17 \pm i\sqrt{251}}{-30}$ **j.** $\dfrac{11 \pm i\sqrt{15}}{34}$ **k.** $\dfrac{13 \pm i\sqrt{139}}{22}$

l. $\dfrac{-5 \pm i\sqrt{371}}{-18}$ **6. a.** $-\dfrac{9}{4} \pm \dfrac{1}{4}i\sqrt{7}$ **b.** $-\dfrac{1}{13} \pm \dfrac{1}{13}\sqrt{14}$

c. $\pm\dfrac{4\sqrt{7}}{7}$ **d.** $-1\pm\sqrt{5}$ **7.** yes **9. a.** 10 **b.** 20

c. 97 **d.** p^2+q^2 **10. a.** a^2+b^2 **b.** r^2+s^2 **c.** real
11. a. $(1+i)$ **b.** $(2-3i)$ **c.** $(15-2i)$ **d.** $(-5-4i)$
e. $(-7i+3)$ **f.** $(-8i-7)$ **g.** 5 **h.** $12i$ **12. a.** 2 **b.** 13
c. 229 **d.** 41 **e.** 58 **f.** 113 **g.** 5 **h.** 144 **13. a.** $\dfrac{i-1}{2}$

b. $\dfrac{5-2i}{3}$ **c.** $\dfrac{46+37i}{85}$ **d.** $\dfrac{11+68i}{73}$ **e.** $\dfrac{21+i}{26}$

f. $\dfrac{-453-103i}{116}$ **g.** $\dfrac{-125-733i}{4225}$ **h.** $\dfrac{33-19i}{25}$

16. a. $5+2i$ **c.** $90°$ **17. a.** $\sqrt{34}$ **b.** $\sqrt{29}$ **c.** 5
d. 13 **e.** 7 **f.** $\sqrt{145}$ **g.** 13 **h.** $\sqrt{17}$ **i.** 34

Pages 257-259 **2.** 6.5 cm by 14 cm **3.** 7, 15;
-7.5, 14 **4.** 125 m, 5 s, 10 s **5.** (90, 50) km/h;
(50, 30) km/h **6.** 24, 26 or -24, -26 **7.** 17, 19, 21
8. 9 cm by 12 cm **9.** 12 cm **10.** 12, 16 **11.** 8, 15,
17 **12.** 37 cm by 39 cm **13.** height 3 cm, width 6 cm
14. a. 1.1 m **b.** no, discriminant<0 **15.** James
20 km/h, Wayne 60 km/h **16.** 320 km/h **17.** 3 m

18. $\dfrac{1}{4}$ s and 7.9 s **19.** \$135 **20.** \$63 **21.** 12 rows

with 16 students **22.** 16 min **23.** $\dfrac{4a^2(b^2-2ac)}{b^4-b^3+4a^2c^2}$

24. $(84+15\pi)$ cm **25.** ±4, $\pm i\sqrt{5}$ **26. a.** ±2
b. ±3, $\pm\sqrt{3}$ **c.** 25, 81 **d.** 1, 64
27. a. $x^2-10x+29=0$ **b.** $2x^2+4x+3=0$

Page 260 **6.** Add these lines: 92 IF X1 <> X2
THEN 100 • 95 PRINT ''THERE ARE TWO EQUAL
ROOTS. THEY ARE ''; X1; '' AND ''; X2 • 97
GOTO 130 **9.** Omit line 95 and insert 100 PRINT
''THE FACTORED FORM OF THE EQUATION IS

(X − ''; X1; '')(X − ''; X2; '').'' **10. a.** $\dfrac{5}{6}$, $-\dfrac{3}{2}$

b. 2, $-\dfrac{3}{4}$ **c.** $-\dfrac{1}{2}$, $-\dfrac{4}{3}$ **d.** $\dfrac{8}{3}$, $\dfrac{1}{3}$ **e.** $\dfrac{5}{12}$, -3

f. 2, $-\dfrac{5}{8}$ **11.** Change and add these lines: 100

PRINT ''THE ROOTS ARE ''; X1; '' + 0i AND ''';
X2; '' + 0i'' • 120 LET D = −D • 122 LET
P1 = SQR(D) / (2 ∗ A) • 123 LET P = INT(P1 ∗
100 + 0.5) / 100 • 125 PRINT ''THE COMPLEX
ROOTS ARE ''; −B / (2 ∗ A); '' + ''; P; ''i AND ''
−B / (2 ∗ A); '' − ''; P; ''i.''

Page 261 **1. a.** $\dfrac{5}{3}$ **b.** ±5 **2. a.** $\dfrac{3}{2}$, -4

b. 1, -1.6 **4. a.** $3\pm\sqrt{11}$ **b.** $-2\pm\dfrac{1}{2}\sqrt{26}$

c. $\dfrac{1}{4}\pm\dfrac{i}{4}\sqrt{31}$ **d.** $\dfrac{-9\pm\sqrt{87}}{2}$ **5.** $r=5$ cm

6. a. 44; 2 roots **b.** -23; no roots **c.** 44; 2 roots

d. 49; 2 roots **8. a.** $\dfrac{5}{2}\pm\dfrac{1}{2}\sqrt{13}$ **b.** $-\dfrac{1}{6}\pm\dfrac{1}{6}\sqrt{97}$

c. $\dfrac{7}{4}\pm\dfrac{1}{4}\sqrt{41}$ **d.** $-6\pm\sqrt{31}$ **9. a.** 6.3, -0.3

b. -0.1, -2.1 **c.** 4.3, -0.8 **d.** 0.9, -2.2 **10. a.** 2,

---

$\dfrac{1}{3}$ **b.** -10, -3 **c.** $\dfrac{1}{4}$, $-\dfrac{5}{4}$ **d.** $-\dfrac{7}{2}$, $-\dfrac{1}{2}$ **11.** -22,

-21; 21, 22 **12. a.** $15x^2-x-2=0$

b. $x^2-2x-4=0$ **13.** $k=\dfrac{5}{2}$ **14.** 13 cm

15. a. 0.7 s **b.** 3.7 s **c.** 16.5 m **16.** 7 m by 13 m

17. a. $22+6i$ **b.** $7+22i$ **18. a.** $\dfrac{5}{4}\pm\dfrac{i}{4}\sqrt{7}$

b. $\dfrac{3}{2}\pm\dfrac{1}{2}\sqrt{5}$ **19.** $x^2-4x+13=0$

Page 262 **1. a.** $\pm\dfrac{3}{4}$ **b.** $-\dfrac{5}{2}$ **c.** $\dfrac{2}{3}$, $-\dfrac{1}{6}$

2. a. 3, -1 **b.** -2, $-\dfrac{23}{8}$ **3. a.** $4\pm\sqrt{21}$

b. $-3\pm\dfrac{1}{2}\sqrt{30}$ **4. a.** 69, 2 roots **b.** 164, 2 roots

c. 0, 1 root **d.** -80, no roots **5. a.** $\dfrac{15}{2}\pm\dfrac{1}{2}\sqrt{185}$

b. $-\dfrac{1}{3}\pm\dfrac{1}{3}\sqrt{7}$ **c.** $-\dfrac{9}{4}\pm\dfrac{1}{4}\sqrt{57}$ **d.** $\dfrac{1}{10}\pm\dfrac{1}{10}\sqrt{61}$

6. -9, -8, -7; 7, 8, 9 **7. a.** 0.9, -5.9 **b.** 2, $\dfrac{1}{4}$

c. -1.2, -2.8 **d.** -0.8, 3.7 **8. a.** $\dfrac{4}{7}$, $\dfrac{10}{7}$ **b.** -15,

-12 **c.** $\dfrac{-5}{3}$, $-\dfrac{14}{3}$ **d.** -3, $\dfrac{1}{2}$ **9.** 9 cm by 9 cm

10. a. $8x^2-14x+5=0$ **b.** $5x^2-3x-2=0$

11. $k=5$ **12.** 22 **13.** $k=-\dfrac{1}{2}$ **14. a.** 2.6 s **b.** 1.7 s

c. $0\le t\le2.6$, $0\le h(t)\le60$ **16. a.** $\dfrac{1}{5}\pm\dfrac{i}{5}\sqrt{29}$

b. $\dfrac{5}{4}\pm\dfrac{1}{4}\sqrt{17}$ **17.** $x^2-8x+25$ **18.** $\dfrac{8}{9}$

Cumulative Review Chapters 7-9

Pages 263-264 **1. a.** $D=\{R\}$, $R=\{R\}$
b. $D=\{R\}$, $R=\{y|y\ge-2\}$ **c.** $D=\{x|-5\le x\le5\}$,
$R=\{y|-5\le y\le5\}$ **4. b.** $y<-4x+3$

d. $y=-\dfrac{1}{4}x+\dfrac{3}{4}$ **6. a.** 6 **b.** 2 **c.** t^2-3t+2

d. a^2+5a+6 **7.** $g^{-1}(x)=\dfrac{1}{3}x+\dfrac{2}{3}$, $\dfrac{1}{g(x)}=\dfrac{1}{3x-2}$

12. $y=7x-2$ (linear, first degree); $y=x^2-3x+5$
(quadratic, second degree); $4x+9t-3=0$ (linear,
first degree); $x^2+y^2=6$ (second degree) **13. a.** opens
downward, (0, 0), $x=0$ **b.** opens downward, (1, 0),

$x=1$ **15. a.** $(-4, -13)$ **b.** $\left(\dfrac{7}{2}, -\dfrac{45}{4}\right)$ **16. a.** -30

b. -0.3 **19. a.** $x=5$, 2 **b.** 4, $-\dfrac{2}{3}$ **20. a.** 5, -1

b. $\dfrac{1+\sqrt{33}}{4}$, $\dfrac{1-\sqrt{33}}{4}$ **21. a.** 1, $-\dfrac{1}{2}$ **b.** 1.24, -3.24

23. $\dfrac{25}{24}$ **24.** sum is $-\dfrac{b}{a}$; product is $\dfrac{c}{a}$ **25. a.** \$0.534

c. 37.45 L **26.** 9 **27. b.** \$63.50 **c.** \$365.90

28. a. 156.25 m **b.** 3.125 s **29.** 32, −9 **30.** −9, −8, −7 or 9, 8, 7 **31.** 1.2 m **32.** 39.1 m²
33. square = 35.25 m; rectangle = 26.5 m by 53 m
34. 9 cm

Chapter 10

Page 265 **1. a.** −3 **b.** ±6 **2. a.** $y > -9$
b. $x \geq -\frac{34}{5}$ **d.** no **3. a.** 5 **b.** −2 **4. a.** $x = \pm 4$;
$y = \pm 4$ **b.** circle **5. a.** ±8 **b.** 2, −1 **c.** −13, 12
d. −1, $-\frac{2}{3}$ **6.** $y = \pm 6$; $x = \pm 2\sqrt{6}$ **7. a.** $x \neq 0$
b. $\frac{4x - 4 - 3x^2 - 2x}{4x} = 5$ **c.** yes **d.** $3 \pm \frac{\sqrt{69}}{3}$ **e.** no
8. no **9. a.** $a = -3$, $b = 0$, $c = 48$ **b.** ±4
10. a. $\frac{4}{5}$, −3 **b.** $-\frac{13}{3}$, $\frac{11}{3}$

Pages 266-267 **1.** yes **2. a.** yes **b.** no **c.** no
d. yes **3. a.** (4, 2) **b.** (2, 2) **c.** (8, −3) **d.** (2, 3)
e. (4, −2) **f.** (2, −3) **g.** no solution **h.** (−3, −5)
4. a. 52.8 units² **b.** 25 units² **6.** $y = 2$; $2x + y = 8$;
$2x - 3y = 0$ **7.** yes; 2 km east and 1 km north
9. a. $x + y = 10$; $x - y = 4$; (7, 3) **b.** $x - y = 5$;
$x + y = 1$; (3, −2) **c.** $4p + 3n = 11$; $p = n + 1$; pens
$2 each, notebooks $1 each **d.** $0.10d + 0.05n = 0.60$;
$d + n = 9$; 6 nickels and 3 dimes **e.** $2h + f = 13$;
$h + f = 8$; 5 hamburgers and 3 fries **10.** 200, $1000

Pages 268-269 **2. a.** $x = 6y + 7$ **b.** $x = \frac{y}{2} + 5$
c. $x = -\frac{5}{3}y + \frac{17}{3}$ **d.** $x = \frac{7}{5}y + \frac{19}{5}$ **3. a.** $y = 4x - 2$
b. $y = \frac{1}{3} - \frac{x}{3}$ **c.** $y = \frac{2}{3}x - \frac{8}{3}$ **d.** $y = \frac{4}{3}x - \frac{8}{3}$
7. a. (15, 3) **b.** (5, 15) **c.** (−8, −2) **d.** (9, 7)
e. (1, −1) **f.** (−13, −12) **g.** (−1, 2) **h.** $\left(\frac{6}{5}, \frac{8}{5}\right)$
8. a. $\left(-\frac{9}{2}, \frac{1}{4}\right)$ **b.** (1, −1) **c.** (1, 6) **d.** (3, 2)
e. (1, −6) **f.** $\left(-\frac{1}{2}, \frac{1}{2}\right)$ **g.** (200, 500) **h.** (0, −3)
9. 17 kg, 11 kg **10.** 23, 48 **11.** $3500 at 7% and
$1500 at 12% **12.** 350 adults and 850 students
13. a. (5, 4) **b.** (15, 4) **14.** 4 bricklayers and 8
labourers **15.** 18 $2 bills and 24 $10 bills **16.** 89 kg,
161 kg **17.** $\frac{3}{7}$, $\frac{2}{5}$

Pages 270-271 **1.** equation ① by ②, equation
② by ③; yes **3. a.** (10, −6) **b.** (7, 1) **c.** $\left(2, \frac{4}{3}\right)$
d. (2, −1) **e.** $\left(-\frac{1}{3}, 3\right)$ **f.** (0.6, 6) **4. a.** (5, 1)
b. (4, −2) **c.** (2, 3) **d.** $\left(-\frac{13}{11}, \frac{42}{11}\right)$ **e.** (1, 2)

f. $\left(\frac{299}{128}, \frac{79}{64}\right)$ **5.** no solution **6. a.** (1, 6) **b.** (7, 2)
7. a. (2, 7) **b.** (3, 2) **c.** (10, 8) **d.** (6, −4)
8. a. (−2, −3) **b.** (−1, −1) **c.** (2, 1) **d.** (2, 4)
e. (1, 1) **f.** (10, 6) **9. a.** $x + y = 63$; $x - y = 19$;
$x = 41$; $y = 22$ **b.** $x + y = 20$; $20x + 50y = 430$;
$x = 19$; $y = 1$ **c.** $5.36; $0.28 **10.** (5, 1)
11. a. $\frac{p + q}{3}$, $\frac{8 - 2p}{3}$ **b.** $\frac{bv}{a^2 + b^2}$, $\frac{av}{a^2 + b^2}$
12. a. (−24, 60) **b.** (14, 15) **c.** (6, 24) **d.** (−5, −2)

Pages 272-273 **3. a.** (3, 11) **b.** $\left(\frac{1}{2}, -\frac{13}{2}\right)$
c. (−4, −10) **d.** (−13, −69) **4. a.** (2, 3) **b.** (4, −1)
c. (−2, −1) **d.** (−2, 4) **e.** (4, −4) **f.** (−4, 8)
5. a. $\left(\frac{4}{7}, \frac{6}{7}\right)$ **b.** $\left(-\frac{3}{7}, \frac{9}{7}\right)$ **c.** infinite number of
solutions **d.** $\left(-\frac{5}{2}, 2\right)$ **e.** no solution **f.** $\left(\frac{6}{7}, \frac{-23}{7}\right)$
7. 42; 30 **8.** After three days and 400 km, the costs
are the same. **9.** 40 paperbacks and 20 hardbounds
10. 9 L of 15% solution and 15 L of 7% solution
11. a. $\left(\frac{121}{19}, \frac{27}{19}\right)$ **b.** $\left(\frac{44}{10}, \frac{-46}{10}\right)$ **c.** (1.079, −1.9775)
d. (−1.39, −2.82) **e.** (7.5, 0.5) **f.** (46.5, 122.5)
13. 17 **14. a.** $\left(\frac{m + n}{2}, \frac{m - n}{2}\right)$ **b.** $\left(\frac{2a + b}{3}, \frac{b - a}{3}\right)$
c. $\left(\frac{16}{3a}, \frac{-2}{3b}\right)$ **d.** $\left(\frac{a^2 + ab + b^2}{a + b}, \frac{-ab}{a + b}\right)$ **15.** 18
Page 274 **2. a.** (4, 6, 0) **b.** (−1, 2, 5)
c. (2, −5, 0) **d.** $\left(\frac{61}{17}, \frac{31}{17}, \frac{89}{17}\right)$ **4. a.** (2, −1, 3)
b. $\left(\frac{-13}{10}, \frac{39}{10}, \frac{-26}{10}\right)$ **c.** (−3, 5, 7) **d.** (2, 3, 4)
e. (−4, −7, 2) **f.** (−2, 1, 3) **5.** 3 of A; 5 of B;
10 of C
Page 275 **1.** independent and consistent
2. a. dependent and consistent **b.** independent and
consistent **c.** inconsistent **3. a.** independent and
consistent **b.** inconsistent **c.** dependent and consistent
d. inconsistent **4. a.** independent and consistent;
$\left(\frac{20}{17}, \frac{-4}{17}\right)$ **b.** independent and consistent; $\left(\frac{23}{14}, \frac{-8}{14}\right)$
c. independent and consistent; $\left(\frac{7}{5}, \frac{4}{5}\right)$ **d.** dependent
and consistent; infinite number of solutions **6.** no
Pages 276-277 **2. a.** (3, 9), (−1, 1) **b.** (−5, 0)
c. (5, 3), (−3, −1) **d.** no solution **3. a.** (−3, 4),
(4, 3) **b.** (5, 3), (−5, 3) **c.** (0, −2), $\left(\frac{8}{3}, \frac{2}{3}\right)$
d. (2.8, −0.26), (1.88, −1.485) **4. a.** (−1, 1), (3, 9)
b. no solution **c.** (1.075, 9.3), (−2.325, −4.3)
d. (−2, −5), (1.6, 5.9) **5.** (4, −1), (−1, 4)
6. a. (0, −8), **b.** (0, 6), (6, 0) **c.** (3.123, 5.123),
(−5.123, −3.123) **d.** (3, 0) **e.** (0, 8)
f. (1.44, 7.44), (−2.78, 3.225)

Pages 278-279   **1. a.** $(6, 0), (-6, 0)$ **b.** $(5, 5)$, $(-5, -5)$ **2. a.** $(4, 3), \left(-\frac{3}{5}, -20\right)$ **b.** $(3, 4)$, $(-3, 4)$ **c.** $(3, \sqrt{14}), (3, -\sqrt{14}), (-3, \sqrt{14})$, $(-3, -\sqrt{14})$ **d.** $(2, 2), (-2, -2)$ **e.** $\left(-\sqrt{\frac{13}{7}}, \frac{2}{\sqrt{7}}\right), \left(-\sqrt{\frac{13}{7}}, \frac{-2}{\sqrt{17}}\right), \left(\sqrt{\frac{13}{7}}, \frac{2}{\sqrt{7}}\right)$, $\left(\sqrt{\frac{13}{7}}, \frac{-2}{\sqrt{7}}\right)$ **f.** $(0, -4), (\pm\sqrt{7}, 3)$ **4.** 480 **5.** 22 m and 44 m **6.** $\frac{12}{17}$ **7.** 8 d **8.** \$8000 at 8%

9. a. $\left(\frac{1}{2}, \frac{1}{4}\right), (-7, 49)$ **b.** $\left(\frac{1}{2}, 2\frac{3}{4}\right)$ **11.** no **12.** 3, 5

Pages 280-281   **1. a.** solid **b.** dotted **c.** dotted **d.** solid **e.** dotted **f.** solid **3.** yes **10.** $(-3, 5)$, $(1, -3)$ **11.** yes

Pages 282-283   **2. b.** $(0, 15), \left(\frac{10}{7}, \frac{90}{7}\right), (0, 0)$, $(4, 0)$ **c.** $\left(\frac{10}{7}, \frac{90}{7}\right)$ **3. a.** $(0, 0), \left(0, 4\frac{5}{7}\right), (4, 3)$, $\left(5\frac{1}{2}, 0\right)$ **b.** \$29 **c.** \$47.75 **4. a.** $x \geq 0$, $y \geq 0$, $x + y \geq 14$, $x + 2y \geq 20$ **b.** $(0, 14), (8, 6), (20, 0)$ **5.** 3 artists and 4 students **6. b.** 625 kg of peanuts and 125 kg of cashews **7.** \$4.50 each

Page 284   **1. a.** To see if a solution exists. **b.** Calculates x if y is eliminated. **c.** Calculates y if x is eliminated. **d.** Prints the four possible roots. **3.** x is found by eliminating y. **4. a.** no solution **b.** $(2\sqrt{2}, 2), (-2\sqrt{2}, 2), (2\sqrt{2}, -2), (-2\sqrt{2}, -2)$ **5. a.** no solution **6.** Division by zero would cause an error in the program. **7. a.** $(1, 0), (-1, 0)$ **b.** $\left(\frac{2\sqrt{5}}{5}, \frac{4\sqrt{5}}{5}\right), \left(\frac{2\sqrt{5}}{5}, -\frac{4\sqrt{5}}{5}\right), \left(-\frac{2\sqrt{5}}{5}, \frac{4\sqrt{5}}{5}\right)$, $\left(-\frac{2\sqrt{5}}{5}, -\frac{4\sqrt{5}}{5}\right)$

Page 285   **1. a.** $y = 3x - 6;\ 3,\ -6$ **b.** $0,\ -8$ **c.** $y = \frac{-x}{2} + 4;\ \frac{-1}{2},\ 4$ **d.** $y = \frac{-7}{5}x + 7;\ \frac{-7}{5},\ 7$

2. a. $(7, 3)$ **b.** $(5, -4)$ **4. a.** -1 **b.** $\frac{-4}{5}$ **5.** 2 at \$11 and 5 at \$9 **6. a.** $(2, 0)$ **b.** infinite number of solutions **c.** $(2, 0)$ **d.** $\left(\frac{5}{6}, \frac{15}{24}\right)$ **7.** 9000

8. a. $(11, 3)$ **b.** $\left(-66\frac{1}{3}, -30\right)$ **c.** $(6, 16)$ **d.** $(-3, 4)$

9. a. $\left(-\frac{1}{3}, \frac{8}{3}, \frac{-5}{3}\right)$; independent and consistent **b.** $(5, 3, -1)$; independent and consistent **11. a.** $(2\sqrt{2}, \sqrt{2}), (\sqrt{2}, 2\sqrt{2}), (-2\sqrt{2}, -\sqrt{2})$, $(-\sqrt{2}, -2\sqrt{2})$ **b.** $(-5, 21), (4, 12)$ **12. a.** $(-4, -9), (3, -2)$ **b.** no solution **13.** 30 m; 12.5 m **14.** 60¢

Page 286   **3.** $2, \frac{5}{2}, \frac{-5}{4}$ **4.** independent and consistent **5.** $(5, -12)$ **6. a.** $(4, 3)$ **b.** $(3, 5)$ **c.** $(10, 6)$ **d.** $(2, 3)$ **e.** $\left(\frac{44}{17}, \frac{9}{17}\right)$ **f.** $\left(\frac{217}{9}, \frac{53}{3}\right)$ **7.** $(9, 2, -4)$ **8.** ten \$25 sandals and eight \$30 sandals **9.** $\left(\frac{c + 2d}{2}, \frac{c - 2d}{2}\right)$ **10.** $(-3, 4), (3, -4)$ **11.** 120 mm, 22 mm **12.** 450 km/h **13.** $(0.646\,038, 3.095\,573\,6), (-0.64, -3.09)$, $(3.095\,573\,6, 0.646\,038), (-3.09, -0.64)$ **14.** 120 standard and 40 deluxe

Chapter 11

Page 287   **1. a.** 13.2 mm **b.** 9.2 cm

2. a. $a^2 + 2a$ **b.** a^2 **c.** $3a^2 + 7a + 4$ **d.** $\frac{5a + 7}{2a + 9}$ **3. a.** $5y(y - 1)$ **b.** $x(3y - 2)$ **c.** $(a + 2)(x - 2)$ **d.** $(x - 8)(x + 1)$ **e.** $(3x - 4)(5x + 2)$ **f.** $(3y + 4)(3y - 4)$ **g.** $(3a + 2)(2a - 3)$ **h.** $3(1 + x)(5 - 3x)$ **i.** $(x^2 + y^2)(5a - b)$ **j.** $(a^2 + 3)(x - 2)(x + 2)$ **4. a.** 3 **b.** 55 **c.** 60; $x \neq 0$ **d.** $\frac{238}{15}$; $x \neq 2$ **5. a.** 3, 1 **b.** $\frac{-3}{2}$, 1 **c.** $-4a$, a **d.** 3, -1 **6. a.** 25 **b.** 10.6 **c.** 11.1 **d.** 3.6 **e.** 5.64 **7.** $\frac{\overline{AL}}{\overline{GX}} = \frac{\overline{AK}}{\overline{GR}} = \frac{\overline{KL}}{\overline{RX}}$ **8. a.** m **b.** s **c.** $\overline{PR}$ **d.** $\overline{WK}$ **9. a.** $(2, -1)$ **b.** $(3, 5), (-1, -3)$

Page 288   **1. a.** $m = 24$, $l = 21$ **b.** $r = 12$, $l = 56$ **c.** $p = 4.1$, $r = 3.2$ **2.** 1340 m **3.** 4.66 m **4.** $\frac{24}{19} = \frac{\overline{CB}}{22}$, $\overline{CB} = 27.79$ cm **5.** 7 m

BRAINTICKLER The digits are in alphabetical order.

Pages 289-291   **1. a.** tan ratio increases from 0 to 1 **b.** tan ratio increases from 1 to infinity **2. a.** 0.4245 **b.** 1.1918 **c.** 3.2709 **d.** 57.2900 **3. a.** 16° **b.** 41° **c.** 69° **d.** 28° **e.** 55° **f.** 80° **4. a.** 6 **b.** 1.1918 **c.** 0.3527 **d.** 0.1763 **e.** 1.4004 **f.** 2.7475 **g.** 0.0198 **h.** 2.0503 **5.** Can't have two 90° angles in a triangle. **6.** 31.7 cm **7. a.** $\tan K = 1.3333$, $\tan L = 0.7500$ **b.** $\tan K = 1.8750$, $\tan L = 0.5333$ **8.** 1.9 m **9. a.** 55.9 **b.** 37.2 **10. a.** 43° **b.** 35° **11. a.** 5.4 **b.** 28.0 **c.** 9.0 **d.** 35° **e.** 58° **12.** 35° **13.** 11 **14.** 70°

Pages 292-294   **1. a.** 0.8387 **b.** 0.9511 **c.** 0.2250 **d.** 0.6157 **e.** 3.7321 **f.** 1.0000 **3.** 45° **4. a.** $\sin A = \frac{a}{c}$, $\sin B = \frac{b}{c}$, $\cos A = \frac{b}{c}$, $\cos B = \frac{a}{c}$, $\tan A = \frac{a}{b}$, $\tan B = \frac{b}{a}$ **b.** Same as the ratios in part a.

5. a. 34° **b.** 21° **c.** 41° **d.** no solution **e.** 52° **f.** 71° **g.** 49° **h.** 74° **6.** 7:20 or 16:40 **7. a.** 7.2 **b.** 19.8 **8. a.** 44° **b.** 40° **9.** 3° **10. a.** 3.4 **b.** 17.2 **c.** 47° **d.** 36° **11. a.** 35.6 **b.** 25.3 **12.** the rotation about the midpoint on the 5 cm edge **13.** 175 m

Page 295 **1. a.** yes **b.** Small discrepancies could occur from rounding. **2. a.** $\angle B = 49°$, $a = 20.3$, $c = 31$ **b.** $\angle M = 36°$, $k = 14$, $m = 10$ **c.** $r = 14$, $\angle R = 47°$, $\angle Q = 43°$ **d.** $y = 16.2$, $\angle Z = 29°$, $\angle X = 61°$ **3. a.** $\angle C = 55°$, $c = 9.9$, $b = 12.0$ **b.** $\angle C = 43°$, $c = 11.6$, $a = 12.4$ **c.** $a = 16.0$, $\angle A = 40°$, $\angle C = 50°$ **d.** $a = 138$, $\angle A = 75°$, $b = 143$ **e.** $a = 9.6$, $c = 77$, $\angle A = 51°$ **f.** $b = 74.6$, $\angle C = 29°$, $\angle A = 61°$ **4.** $\angle A = 88°$, $c = 20.5$, $b = 42.7$, $a = 46.7$ **5. a.** One is 4.6 m; the other is 3.8 m. **b.** 4.3 m **BRAINTICKLER** 24 cm²

Pages 296-297 **1.** yes **2.** 239 m **3. a.** 29° **b.** They are equal. **4.** 167 m **5.** 6.5 m **6.** 18° **7.** 1.7 m, 2.7 m **8.** 293 m **9.** 21 m **10.** 2252 m **11. a.** 3 m **b.** 68° **12.** 25.0 cm, 67.6 cm, 215.4 cm² **13. a.** 57° **b.** 27.5 cm **14.** 111 m, 448 m

Pages 298-299 **2. a.** 0.6018 **b.** 0.1908 **c.** 1.0355 **d.** 0.9336 **e.** 0.9205 **f.** 0 **i) a.** 1.6616 **b.** 5.2408 **c.** 0.9657 **d.** 1.0711 **e.** 1.0864

f. undefined **3. a.** $\sin 37° = \dfrac{63.5}{m}$ **b.** $\cos 25° = \dfrac{8.3}{m}$ **4. a.** 105.5 **b.** 9.2 **5. a.** 67° **b.** 48° **i)** same values **6. a.** $\sin \theta = \dfrac{-3}{5}$, $\cos \theta = \dfrac{-4}{5}$, $\tan \theta = \dfrac{3}{4}$

b. $\sin \theta = \dfrac{-3}{5}$, $\cos \theta = \dfrac{4}{5}$, $\tan \theta = \dfrac{-3}{4}$

7. a. $\csc \theta = \dfrac{17}{15}$, $\sec \theta = \dfrac{17}{8}$, $\cot \theta = \dfrac{8}{15}$

b. $\csc \theta = \dfrac{\sqrt{58}}{7}$, $\sec \theta = \dfrac{-\sqrt{58}}{3}$, $\cot \theta = \dfrac{-3}{7}$

8. a. $\sin \theta = \dfrac{-12}{13}$, $\cos \theta = \dfrac{5}{13}$, $\tan \theta = \dfrac{-12}{5}$,

$\csc \theta = \dfrac{-13}{12}$, $\sec \theta = \dfrac{13}{5}$, $\cot \theta = \dfrac{-5}{12}$

b. $\sin \theta = \dfrac{4}{\sqrt{17}}$, $\cos \theta = \dfrac{1}{\sqrt{17}}$, $\tan \theta = 4$, $\csc \theta = \dfrac{\sqrt{17}}{4}$,

$\sec \theta = \sqrt{17}$, $\cot \theta = \dfrac{1}{4}$ **9. a.** $\sin \theta = \dfrac{12}{13}$, $\cos \theta = \dfrac{5}{13}$,

$\tan \theta = \dfrac{12}{5}$, $\csc \theta = \dfrac{13}{12}$, $\sec \theta = \dfrac{13}{5}$, $\cot \theta = \dfrac{5}{12}$

b. $\sin \theta = \dfrac{-3}{5}$, $\cos \theta = \dfrac{-4}{5}$, $\tan \theta = \dfrac{3}{4}$, $\csc \theta = \dfrac{-5}{3}$,

$\sec \theta = \dfrac{-5}{4}$, $\cot \theta = \dfrac{4}{3}$ **c.** $\sin \theta = \dfrac{15}{17}$, $\cos \theta = \dfrac{-8}{17}$,

$\tan \theta = \dfrac{-15}{8}$, $\csc \theta = \dfrac{17}{15}$, $\sec \theta = \dfrac{-17}{8}$, $\cot \theta = \dfrac{-8}{15}$

d. $\sin \theta = \dfrac{-4}{5}$, $\cos \theta = \dfrac{3}{5}$, $\tan \theta = \dfrac{-4}{3}$, $\csc \theta = \dfrac{-5}{4}$,

$\sec \theta = \dfrac{5}{3}$, $\cot \theta = \dfrac{-3}{4}$ **10. b.** 37° **c.** (4, 3)

d. $\cos \theta = \dfrac{4}{5}$, $\tan \theta = \dfrac{3}{4}$, $\csc \theta = \dfrac{5}{3}$, $\sec \theta = \dfrac{5}{4}$,

$\cot \theta = \dfrac{4}{3}$ **11.** 1

Pages 300-301 **1.** $\boxed{\text{INV}}$ finds the angle given the ratio; $\boxed{1/x}$ determines the reciprocal ratios. **2. a.** 0° **b.** 90° **c.** 180° **d.** 270° **3. a.** II **b.** IV **c.** II **4. a.** I; 73° **b.** III; 11° **c.** IV; 33° **d.** III; 65° **e.** III; 37° **f.** I; 45° **5. a.** angle given sine ratio **b.** cosecant **c.** angle given cotangent ratio **d.** angle given negative secant ratio **6. a.** -1.3673 **b.** 3.0777 **c.** 0.7986 **d.** 1.2868 **e.** 3.8637 **f.** -0.6157 **g.** -1.1504 **h.** 1.0263 **i.** -0.4663 **7. a.** 47°, 313° **b.** 138°, 318° **c.** 63°, 297° **d.** 199°, 341° **e.** 55°, 235° **f.** 205°, 335° **g.** 123°, 303° **h.** no solution **i.** 60°, 300° **j.** 150°, 330° **8. a.** 22° **b.** 162° **c.** 243° **9. a.** 123°, 303° **b.** 5.0 km **10. a.** 131° **b.** 90° **c.** 52° **d.** 180° **e.** 293° **f.** 212° **11. a.** 329° **b.** 248° **c.** 214° **d.** 90° **e.** 71° **f.** 360° **12.** sin, tan, and sec increase; cos, cot, and csc decrease **13.** 2.5 **14. a.** (3, −5); 301° **b.** (−4, −1); 194° **c.** (−2, 5); 112° **d.** (1, 7); 82°

Pages 302-303 **2.** $\sec = \dfrac{\text{hyp}}{\text{adj}}$, $\csc = \dfrac{\text{hyp}}{\text{opp}}$, $\cot = \dfrac{\text{adj}}{\text{opp}}$ **3.** The ratios are proportional. **4. a.** $x = 8$, $y = 4$

b. $a = b = \dfrac{5\sqrt{2}}{2}$ **5. a.** $\dfrac{-\sqrt{3}}{2}$ **b.** $\dfrac{-\sqrt{3}}{2}$ **c.** $\dfrac{1}{\sqrt{3}}$ **d.** $\dfrac{-1}{\sqrt{2}}$

e. -2 **f.** -1 **g.** -2 **h.** $-\sqrt{2}$ **6. a.** T **b.** F, $\cos(-\theta) = \cos \theta$ **c.** T **d.** F, $\sec(-\theta) = \sec \theta$ **e.** T **f.** T **7. a.** 120°, 240° **b.** 60°, 120° **c.** 45°, 225° **d.** 150°, 210° **e.** no solution **f.** 150°, 330°

8. $\sin \theta = \dfrac{y}{r}$, $\cos \theta = \dfrac{x}{r}$, $\dfrac{\sin \theta}{\cos \theta} = \dfrac{y}{r} \div \dfrac{x}{r} = \dfrac{y}{x} = \tan \theta$

9. a. $\dfrac{-1}{2}$ **b.** 2 **c.** $\sqrt{2} + 2\sqrt{3}$ **d.** 2

10. $48\pi - 36\sqrt{3}$ cm² **11. a.** 0 **b.** −1

Page 304 **2. a.** 30°, 150°, −210°, −330° **b.** 60°, 120°, −240°, −300° **c.** 45°, 315°, −45°, −315° **d.** 60°, 120°, −240°, −300° **e.** 180°, −180° **f.** 135°, 315°, −45°, −225° **3. a.** 90°, 270° **b.** 60°, 300° **c.** 76°, 256°, 304°, 124° **4. a.** 45°, 315° **b.** 270° **c.** 72°, 252°, 288°, 108° **d.** no solution **5. a.** 210°, 330°, −30°, −150°, −90°, 270° **b.** 83°, 277°, −83°, −277° **c.** 124°, 304°, −56°, −236°, 76°, 256°, −104°, −284° **6.** 12°, 168°

Pages 305-306 **1.** no, $\angle C = 46°$ **2.** Draw $\triangle ABC$ with $\angle B$ greater than 90°. Draw $\overline{CD} \perp$ to $\overline{AB}$ produced. $\dfrac{\overline{CD}}{b} = \sin A$, so $\overline{CD} = b \sin A$, $\dfrac{\overline{CD}}{a} = \sin(180 - B) = \sin B$, so $\overline{CD} = a \sin B$, so $a \sin B = b \sin A$, so $\dfrac{a}{\sin A} = \dfrac{b}{\sin B}$ **3.** from C, $h = b \sin A$; from B, $h = a \sin C$ **4. a.** $b = 30$ **b.** $k = 63$ **c.** $\angle P = 95°$ **d.** $\angle T = 72°$ **5.** 13 km **6. a.** 15 **b.** 86 **c.** 40° **7.** Two angles and a side opposite one of the angles. Two sides and an angle opposite one of the sides. **9. a.** $\angle R = 41°$, $\angle T = 66°$, $t = 49$ **b.** $\angle H = 28°$, $g = 15.4$, $f = 26.6$ **c.** $\angle P = 44°$, $\angle D = 73°$, $d = 11.2$ **10.** 29 km from Rock Port, 20 km from Pirate's Cove **11.** 320 m or 169 m **12.** 9.8 m **HISTORICAL NOTE** $\cos n\theta = 2 \cos(n-1)\theta \cos \theta - \cos(n-2)\theta$

Page 307 **2.** 6 or 18 **3. a.** 2 **b.** 0 **c.** 1 **d.** 1 **e.** 2 **4. a.** $\angle B = 66°$, $\angle C = 66°$, $c = 16$; or $\angle B = 114°$, $\angle C = 18°$, $c = 5.4$ **b.** no solution **c.** $\angle B = 90°$, $\angle C = 60°$, $c = 10.4$ **d.** $\angle F = 47°$, $\angle D = 9°$, $d = 1.5$ **e.** $\angle F = 47°$, $\angle D = 97°$, $d = 13.5$; or $\angle F = 133°$, $\angle D = 11°$, $d = 2.7$ **6. a.** $\angle A = 80°$, $\angle C = 43°$, $c = 3.7$; or $\angle A = 100°$, $\angle C = 23°$, $c = 2.1$ **b.** $\angle K = 39°$, $\angle Y = 109°$, $y = 114$; or $\angle K = 141°$, $\angle Y = 7°$, $y = 14.7$ **c.** $\angle M = 48°$, $\angle R = 103°$, $r = 30.5$; or $\angle M = 132°$, $\angle R = 19°$, $r = 10.2$ **7.** 3.9 m **8.** Yes, there are two possible directions for her shot.

Pages 308-310 **1. a.** Cosine is negative so the angle lies in the fourth quadrant. **b.** The calculations are easier. **2.** common factor; still in a quadrant where x is positive; reflection in the y-axis to a quadrant with negative cosine **3. a.** $a = 17$ **b.** $x = 46°$ **4.** 126° **5. a.** 45° **b.** 48 **c.** 61° **6.** identical proofs with the letters changed from that of the display **7. a.** $\angle C = 90°$, $\angle B = 67°$, $\angle A = 23°$ **b.** $\angle K = 9°$, $\angle R = 7°$, $\angle S = 164°$ **c.** $u = 11.6$, $\angle V = 41°$, $\angle W = 65°$ **d.** $t = 16.7$, $\angle R = \angle P = 62.5°$ **8.** 6.2 m **9.** 95 km **10.** 9.3° **11.** 6° **12.** 1 **13.** 3 m **14.** Assuming the two lines are equal, 5.6 m.

Pages 311-312 **1. a.** 7.5 **b.** 9.9 cm² **3. a.** $\frac{1}{2}ab \sin C$ **b.** $\sqrt{s(s-a)(s-b)(s-c)}$ **c.** $\frac{(b^2 \sin A \sin C)}{2 \sin B}$ **4. a.** 16.2 m² **b.** 19.4 cm² **c.** 9.0 units² **d.** 32 units² **e.** 3.5 units² **f.** 1177 cm² **6.** 184 cm² **7. a.** 1113 units³ **b.** 107 units³ **8. a.** 110 cm² **b.** 1086 cm² **9. a.** two triangles: 59 cm², 8.4 cm² **b.** no triangle **c.** two triangles: 492 m², 51 m² **10. a.** $\frac{32}{3}$ units³; $24 + 8\sqrt{3}$ units² **b.** 191 units³; 249.76 units² **11.** 1.7 km²

Page 313 **1.** 16.3 m, 16.2 m **2.** 16° **3.** 68 km **4.** 439 m **5.** 1884 m; 158 728 m² **6. a.** 9.1 km **b.** N25°E

Page 314 **1.** 9.9 cm **2.** Lines 20 and 30 get the values; line 70 is where the calculation is performed. **3. a.** 15 cm **b.** 6.8 cm **c.** 9.8 cm **d.** 127 cm **4.** $(1.011\ 562\ 6)A_1$ **5.** 10 REM APPLICATION OF HERON'S FORMULA • 20 INPUT "LENGTHS OF THE THREE SIDES ARE "; A, B, C • 30 LET S = (A + B + C) / 2 • 40 LET AREA = SQR(S ∗ (S − A) ∗ (S − B) ∗ (S − C)) • 50 PRINT "AREA OF THE TRIANGLE IS "; AREA; " SQUARE CM"

• 60 END **a.** 6 cm² **b.** 3.5 cm² **c.** 6.9 cm² **d.** error **e.** yes **f.** square root of a negative number

Page 315 **1. a.** 21.6 **b.** 11.7 **2.** 4.7 m **4.** $\sin \theta = \frac{2}{3}$, $\tan \theta = \frac{-2}{\sqrt{5}}$, $\csc \theta = \frac{3}{2}$, $\sec \theta = \frac{-3}{\sqrt{5}}$, $\cot \theta = \frac{-\sqrt{5}}{2}$ **5. a.** -0.1228 **b.** 1.0306 **c.** -1.0006 **d.** -0.8693 **6. a.** 69.4°, 290.6° **b.** 37°, 143° **c.** 112°, 292° **d.** 127°, 233° **e.** 13°, 167° **f.** 143°, 323° **7. a.** 240°, 300° **b.** 108.5°, 288.5°, 71.5°, 251.5° **c.** 60°, 300°, 109.5°, 250.5° **d.** 90° **8. a.** $\frac{\sin^2\theta}{\cos^2\theta}$ **b.** $\frac{1}{\sin\theta}$ **c.** $\sin \theta$ **d.** $\frac{\sin\theta}{\cos\theta}$ **9.** 175.5 m **10. a.** 330°, 210°, 90° **b.** 0°, 180°, 360° **c.** 330°, 210°, 90° **d.** 30°, 150°, 330°, 210° **11. a.** $\angle A = 19°$, $a = 10$, $b = 30.4$, Area = 153 units² **b.** $\angle J = 47°$, $\angle R = 104°$, $\angle C = 29°$, Area = 2.9 units² **c.** $\angle W = 45.5°$, $\angle U = 96.5°$, $u = 31$, Area = 208 units²; or $\angle W = 134.5°$, $\angle U = 7.5°$, $u = 4$, Area = 27.3 units² **12.** 2001 km **13.** 14° **14.** Use $\boxed{1/x}$ key with sin of 38°.

Page 316 **1. a.** 1102 m **b.** The hill has a uniform rise. **2. a.** $a = 15.2$, $c = 12.4$, $\angle C = 55°$ **b.** $b = 15$, $\angle B = 51°$, $\angle C = 39°$ **3. a.** 5.6 m **b.** 60 m from the tall tree. **4.** $\sin \theta = \frac{-7}{\sqrt{65}}$, $\cos \theta = \frac{4}{\sqrt{65}}$, $\csc \theta = \frac{-\sqrt{65}}{7}$, $\sec \theta = \frac{\sqrt{65}}{4}$, $\cot \theta = \frac{-4}{7}$ **5. a.** 2 **b.** 4 **c.** 1 **d.** 3 **e.** 4 **f.** 3 **6. a.** 533°, $-187°$ **b.** 355°, $-5°$ **c.** 89°, $-631°$ **d.** 558°, $-162°$ **e.** 273°, $-447°$ **f.** 188°, $-172°$ **7. a.** 210°, 330° **b.** 30°, 210° **c.** 0°, 360° **d.** 135°, 225° **e.** 0°, 360° **f.** no solution **8. a.** 45°, 315° **b.** 60°, 120°, 240°, 300° **c.** 0°, 180°, 360° **d.** 0°, 360° **e.** 0°, 360°, 270° **f.** 0°, 360°, 120°, 240° **9. a.** $b = 4.3$, $a = 7$, $\angle C = 64°$, Area = 13.5 units² **b.** $e = 15.1$, $\angle C = 51°$, $\angle E = 65°$, Area = 88.4 units² **c.** $\angle R = 90°$, $\angle Q = 53°$, $\angle P = 37°$, Area = 602 units² **10.** Doran is 17 m closer. **11.** 101.5 m **12.** 27.2 m

Chapter 12

Page 317 **1.** Given; Reflexive property; $\triangle DCA$; $\overline{DC}$ **2. a.** 180° **b.** 360° **3.** $\sqrt{113}$, $\left(\frac{1}{2}, 2\right)$ **4.** 150 m **5.** $x = y = -10$ **6.** $d = \frac{10}{\pi}$ **7. a.** 3.141 59 **8. a.** $(-4, -7)$ **b.** $(4, 7)$ **c.** $(-4, 7)$ **d.** $(-4, 7)$ **9.** yes **10.** $y - 5 = -\frac{4}{5}(x - 4)$

Pages 318-319 **4.** $\angle PRT$, $\angle PYT$, $\angle PXT$ **5. a.** $\angle DFE$ **b.** $\angle DEF$ or $\angle DGF$ **6. a.** $x = 50°$, $y = 80°$ **b.** $x = 35°$, $y = 90°$, $z = 10°$

Pages 320-322   **1. a.** $\angle A = 22.5°$ **b.** $\angle A = 25°$
2. a. $x = 56°$, $y = 28°$, $z = 28°$ **b.** $x = 90°$, $y = 90°$,
$z = 90°$ **3. a.** $x = 42°$, $y = 21°$ **b.** $x = 170°$, $y = 85°$
c. $a = 120°$ **d.** $c = 110°$, $f = 55°$ **5. a.** $x = 190°$,
$y = 35°$ **b.** $p = 29°$, $q = 29°$, $r = 33°$, $t = 61°$
7. a. $x + y = 180°$ **b.** $x + y = 180°$ **9. a.** $a = 85°$,
$b = 95°$ **b.** $x = 60°$, $y = 90°$, $z = 120°$

Pages 323-324   **3. a.** $\sqrt{13}$ **b.** $4\sqrt{5}$ **c.** $2\sqrt{5}$
d. 6 **4.** 1.84 m **6. a.** 13 cm **b.** 877.5 cm²
9. a. $x = \frac{20}{3}$ **b.** $a = 4$

Pages 325-327   **1. a.** $y = \sqrt{111}$ **b.** $x = 3\sqrt{10}$
2. $\overline{MN} = 4.2$ cm **5. a.** $y = 3\sqrt{3}$ **b.** $m = 9.3$, $n = 7.1$
7. a. 1 **b.** 2 **c.** 0 **10.** 14.9 cm **15.** $\sqrt{61}$ cm
16. 8 cm

Page 328   **1. a.** $x = 33°$, $y = 33°$ **b.** $x = 42°$,
$y = 60°$ **c.** $x = 40°$, $y = 50°$ **d.** $x = 10°$, $y = 90°$,
$z = 55°$ **5. a.** 70° **b.** 39° **7.** $10\sqrt{5}$ cm **8.** 6.2 cm

Pages 329-330   **1. a.** $\overline{RS}$ **b.** $\overline{RM}$ **c.** $\overline{RN}$ **d.** 81
e. 80.5 **2. a.** $x = \sqrt{65}$ cm **b.** $y = 5\frac{1}{3}$ cm

3. a. $x = 3$ **b.** $x = 2.04$ **5. a.** $x = 13.7$ **b.** $y = 13\frac{1}{3}$
6. a. 22° **b.** 133° **7.** $6\sqrt{3} + 5$ **8. a.** $12\sqrt{2}$ **b.** 12
c. $9\sqrt{10}$ **9.** 21.6 m

Pages 331-333   **1. a.** 23.625π units²
b. 88.8π units² **2. a.** 102.9 units² **b.** 17.8 units²
3. a. 4.5π units **b.** 2.7π units **4. a.** 5.8 units
b. 0.12 units **5. a.** $6\pi + 20$ units **b.** 6 sections are
3π m², 2 sections are 12 m², and 1 section is 24 m².
c. $42 + 4\sqrt{13}$ **6.** 24.7 cm **7.** 48.535 units²
8. 20π m **9.** 1.28 m³ **10.** $(14\pi + 64)$ cm **11.** 34 m
13. 59.3 cm² **14.** $4\sqrt{7}$ cm **15.** 12.8π cm²

Pages 334-335   **1. a.** $x^2 + y^2 = 144$
b. $x^2 + y^2 = 34$ **c.** $x^2 + y^2 = 32$ **2. a.** $|x| = |y| \le 5$
b. $|x| = |y| \le 2$ **c.** $|x| = |y| \le \sqrt{13}$
d. $|x| = |y| \le \sqrt{65}$ **3. a.** $x^2 + y^2 = 36$; $|x| = |y| \le 6$
b. $x^2 + y^2 = 100$; $|x| = |y| \le 10$ **c.** $x^2 + y^2 = 1$;
$|x| = |y| \le 1$ **d.** $x^2 + y^2 = 75$; $|x| = |y| \le 5\sqrt{3}$
5. $x^2 + y^2 = 26$ **6.** $x^2 + y^2 = 20$ **7. a.** exterior
b. interior **c.** exterior **d.** on the circle **e.** interior
f. exterior **8. a.** point **b.** parabola
9. a. $y = \pm\sqrt{81 - x^2}$ **b.** $x = \pm\sqrt{81 - y^2}$
11. a. $y = -\sqrt{25 - x^2}$ **b.** $x = \sqrt{36 - y^2}$
c. $x = -\sqrt{12.25 - y^2}$ **d.** $y = \sqrt{81 - x^2}$
12. b. $x^2 + y^2 = 405$ **c.** $3\sqrt{5}$ m

Pages 336-337   **1.** 8; $(4, -5)$
2. a. $(x - 3)^2 + (y + 7)^2 = 36$
b. $(x + 5)^2 + (y - 8)^2 = 16$ **c.** $(x - 5)^2 + (y - 5)^2 = 4$
d. $(x + 6)^2 + (y + 9)^2 = 25$ **3. a.** $(x - 2)^2 + (y - 6)^2 = 1$
b. $(x + 3)^2 + (y - 1)^2 = 1$ **c.** $(x + 1)^2 + (y + 4)^2 = 1$
d. $x^2 + (y - 7)^2 = 1$ **e.** $(x + 8)^2 + y^2 = 1$
4. a. $(x - 4)^2 + (y - 1)^2 = 25$

b. $(x + 2)^2 + (y - 3)^2 = 9$ **c.** $(x - 2m)^2 + (y - m)^2 = m^2$
d. $(x - 4)^2 + (y - c)^2 = 3$ **5. a.** $(x + 2, y + 2) \rightarrow (x, y)$
b. $(x - 1, y - 3) \rightarrow (x, y)$
6. a. $(x + 2)^2 + (y + 3)^2 = 25$
b. $(x - 5)^2 + (y + 2)^2 = 4$ **c.** $(x + 3)^2 + (y - 4)^2 = 20$
d. $(x \pm 3)^2 + (y + 2)^2 = 9$
e. $(x - 6.5)^2 + (y + 13)^2 = 225$ or
$(x - 6.5)^2 + (y - 13)^2 = 225$ **f.** $(x - 5)^2 + (y - 2)^2 = 25$
7. a. $(x - 3)^2 + (y + 1)^2 = 25$; centre $(3, -1)$; radius 5
b. $(x + 2)^2 + (y - 4)^2 = 20$; centre $(-2, 4)$; radius
$2\sqrt{5}$ **c.** $(x - 3)^2 + (y + 7)^2 = 25$; centre $(3, -7)$;
radius 5 **d.** $x^2 + (y + 6)^2 = 32$; centre $(0, -6)$; radius
$4\sqrt{2}$ **e.** $(x + 5)^2 + y^2 = 45$; centre $(-5, 0)$; radius
$3\sqrt{5}$ **8. a.** centre $(1, -5)$; radius $\sqrt{77}$ **d.** centre
e. radius **BRAINTICKLER a.** C **b.** C **c.** B **d.** A
Group A has only curved shapes, Group B has only
straight lines, and Group C has both.

Pages 338-340   **1. a.** $(-3, -6)$ **b.** $(2, 5)$
c. $(4, 0)$ **d.** $(-a, -b)$ **4.** $(x - 2)^2 + (y + 2)^2 = 49$
5. a. secant **b.** no intersection **c.** tangent **d.** tangent
e. no intersection **f.** secant **6. a.** $y - 3 = -\frac{7}{3}(x - 7)$
b. $y - 4 = \frac{3}{4}(x + 3)$ **c.** $y + \sqrt{6} = \frac{3}{\sqrt{6}}(x - 3)$
d. $y = 8$ **8. a.** 13 **b.** $3\sqrt{5}$ **9. e.** yes

Pages 341-343   **1. a.** $(10, 3)$ **b.** $(2, 2)$
c. $(16, 12)$ **3. a.** horizontal factor $\frac{1}{3}$ **b.** vertical
factor $\frac{1}{5}$ **c.** horizontal factor 3, vertical factor $\frac{1}{9}$
d. horizontal factor $\frac{1}{\sqrt{3}}$, vertical factor $\frac{1}{\sqrt{5}}$
4. a. ± 5, ± 5 **b.** $(x, y) \rightarrow (4x, y)$ **c.** ± 20, ± 5
5. a. $(x, y) \rightarrow (2x, y)$ **b.** $(x, y) \rightarrow (x, 10y)$
6. a. $(x, y) \rightarrow (2x, y)$ **b.** $(x, y) \rightarrow (x, 6y)$
c. $(x, y)\left(x, \frac{1}{3}y\right)$ **8. a.** $x^2 + 16y^2 = 80$
b. $x^2 + 256y^2 = 1280$ **c.** $x^2 + 400y^2 = 2000$ **9. a.** 2.8
b. $\frac{1}{2}$ **10. a.** $\frac{1}{64}x^2 + y^2 = \frac{5}{16}$ **b.** $\frac{1}{256}x^2 + y^2 = \frac{5}{64}$
c. $\frac{9}{4}x^2 + y^2 = \frac{80}{9}$ **d.** $16x^2 + y^2 = 80$
11. a. 3 vertically **b.** 2.5 horizontally **c.** 2 horizontally
d. 2.5 vertically **15.** first image $9x^2 + 4y^2 = 36$;
second image $9x^2 + 4y^2 - 54x + 16y + 61 = 0$

Page 344   **1.** 10 X1 = -3, Y1 = 4, X2 = 5,
Y2 = 0, X3 = 0, Y3 = $-5 \bullet$ 30 R1 = 1 $\bullet$ 40 R2 = 2 $\bullet$
50 P1 = 2.5 $\bullet$ 60 P2 = $-2.5 \bullet$ 80 S1 = $-0.5 \bullet$ 90
S2 = 1 $\bullet$ 110 M1 = 2 $\bullet$ 120 M2 = $-1 \bullet$ 140 B1 = 0 $\bullet$
150 B2 = 0 $\bullet$ 180 X = 0 $\bullet$ 190 Y = 0 $\bullet$ 210 THE
CENTRE IS AT (0, 0) **2.** 10 X1 = -6, Y1 = 4,
X2 = -2, Y2 = -4, X3 = 2, Y3 = 6 $\bullet$ 30 R1 = $-4 \bullet$
40 R2 = 0 $\bullet$ 50 P1 = 0 $\bullet$ 60 P2 = 1 $\bullet$ 80 S1 = $-2 \bullet$ 90
S2 = 2.5 $\bullet$ 110 M1 = 0.5 $\bullet$ 120 M2 = $-0.4 \bullet$ 140
B1 = 2 $\bullet$ 150 B2 = 1 $\bullet$ 180 X = $-1.11111111 \bullet$ 190

Y = 1.44444444 • 210 THE CENTRE IS AT
(−1.1111, 1.4444) **3. a.** Error message in line 110.
b. Error message in line 80. **4.** Add: 95 IF S1 = S2
THEN 245 • 245 PRINT ''THE THREE POINTS
ARE COLLINEAR'' **5. a.** $r = 5$ **b.** $r = 5.52$
7. vertical line

Page 345   **1. a.** $\overline{TS}$ **b.** $\angle TOS$ **c.** $\angle RTS$ **d.** $\angle RTS$
e. $\angle TSR$ **f.** $\angle TQR$, $\angle PTO$, $\angle TSR$ **g.** $\angle TRS$ **2. a.** 60°
b. 60° **c.** 60° **d.** 60° **e.** 60° **6.** 55° each
7. a. $x^2 + y^2 = 36$ **b.** $x^2 + y^2 = 26$
c. $x^2 + (y + 3)^2 = 4$ **d.** $(x − 4)^2 + (y + 1)^2 = 100$
8. a. $6\sqrt{7}$ cm **b.** 7.1 cm **9.** 22 cm **10.** 61π cm²
11. $\left(6 + \dfrac{3}{2}\pi\right)$ m **12. a.** $4x^2 + y^2 = 4$ **b.** $x^2 + \dfrac{1}{4}y^2 = 2$

Page 346   **1. a.** 14.7 units **b.** 41.1 units²
2. a. $x = 12$ cm **b.** $y = 5.88$ cm **4.** $4x^2 + y^2 = 4$
8. $x = 35.6$; $y = 36.2$; $z = 3.2$ **9. a.** $x^2 + y^2 = 16$
b. $(x − 6)^2 + (y + 2)^2 = 16$

Cumulative Review Chapters 10-12

Pages 347-348   **1.** $−\dfrac{1}{2}$, 2 **2.** (−3, −6);
independent **3. a.** (4, −1) **b.** (3, 9, 7) **4.** (2, 1),
(−2, −1), (1, 2), (−1, −2) **5.** −1, $−\dfrac{1}{2}$ **6.** 6
7. 100 m by 35 m **9.** 20 km/h **10.** less than 5 dm by
12 dm **11. a.** 7° **b.** 140° **c.** 20° **d.** 125°
12. a. 0.4663 **b.** 0.8572 **c.** 0.1392 **d.** −0.1763
e. −0.7660 **f.** 1.0353 **13.** 5.3 m **14.** 5.2°
15. $\angle N = 55°$, LN = 20.14, MN = 11.55
16. 1740.35 m **17. a.** 1.5 **b.** $−\sqrt{2}$ **18. a.** 120° or
−120° **b.** 45° or 225° **19.** 160 m **20.** 24 cm
21. 9605.2 m **22. a.** $\angle s = 60°$, $\angle r = 120°$
b. $\angle a = 45°$, $\angle c = 90°$, $\angle b = 90°$ **c.** $\angle x = 90°$,
$\angle y = 70°$, $\angle z = 70°$, $\angle w = 40°$, $\angle t = 50°$ **d.** $\angle e = 60°$,
$\angle c = 100°$, $\angle a = 80°$, $\angle b = 80°$, $\angle d = 20°$
23. a. 811.25 km **b.** 1875 L **24.** Paul: 16, 4th;
Norma: 14, 3rd; Andrea: 11, 2nd; Mike; 15, 1st
25. 1.66 cm

Chapter 13

Page 349   **1. a.** 33.5 **b.** 9.4 **c.** $8\dfrac{1}{3}$ **d.** 14.7
2. a. 17 **b.** 25 **c.** 84 **d.** 288 **3. a.** 290 **b.** 396
c. 3562 **d.** 55 535 **6. a.** January **b.** $170 000
c. May and April

Pages 350-351   **2. a.** no **b.** yes **c.** no **d.** yes
3. a. yes **b.** no **c.** yes **6. a.** $\dfrac{2}{5}$ **b.** $\dfrac{1}{5}$ **c.** $\dfrac{1}{10}$ **d.** $\dfrac{1}{5}$
8. $\dfrac{45\ 493}{45\ 500}$ **9. a.** $\dfrac{3}{10}$ **b.** $\dfrac{1}{5}$ **c.** $\dfrac{1}{2}$ **d.** $\dfrac{1}{2}$

Pages 352-354   **2. a.** independent; $\dfrac{1}{6}$
b. dependent; $\dfrac{4}{663}$ **c.** independent; $\dfrac{1}{8}$ **3. a.** $\dfrac{1}{9}$ **b.** $\dfrac{5}{18}$
c. $\dfrac{5}{6}$ **d.** $\dfrac{8}{9}$ **4. a.** $\dfrac{2}{3}$ **b.** $\dfrac{1}{9}$ **c.** $\dfrac{1}{3}$ **d.** 0 **e.** $\dfrac{1}{3}$ **f.** 1
5. a. 0 **b.** $\dfrac{1}{36}$ **c.** $\dfrac{1}{6}$ **d.** $\dfrac{1}{9}$ **6. a.** $\dfrac{3}{663}$ **b.** $\dfrac{33}{663}$ **7. a.** $\dfrac{2}{7}$
b. $\dfrac{2}{7}$ **c.** $\dfrac{2}{7}$ **8. a.** $\dfrac{1}{15}$ **b.** $\dfrac{1}{20}$ **c.** $\dfrac{2}{105}$ **9.** $\dfrac{1}{4}$
10. b. $\dfrac{1}{2}$; $\dfrac{1}{4}$ **11. a.** 0.2401 **c.** 0.21; 0.000 510 3
d. $\dfrac{1}{8}$ **12. a.** $\dfrac{1}{11}$ **b.** $\dfrac{1}{3}$

Pages 355-356   **1. a.** 0.3 **b.** 0.08 **c.** 0.06
3. b. 2.55 **c.** 0; 1 **d.** 2.4

Pages 357-359   **7. a.** parameter **b.** 35.2—
parameter, 36.1—statistic **c.** 61—statistic, 62.2—
parameter **10. a.** 0.5 **b.** 0.1

Pages 360-361   **2. b.** 5, 15, 25, 35, 45, 55 **c.** 3
d. 19 **e.** 15 **f.** 30 **4. c.** 375 000 **5. b.** 54% **c.** 1800

Pages 362-363   **3. a.** 6 **b.** 8 **c.** 1
4. a. $50 \le w < 60$, $100, \le w < 110$ **b.** $60 \le w < 70$
c. $70 \le w < 80$, $90 \le w < 100$ **5.** yes **6. a.** 48; 59
b. of some value **7. a.** $21 \le c < 22$; $26 \le c < 27$
b. $22 \le c < 23$ and $30 \le c < 31$; $24 \le c < 25$ and
$28 \le c < 29$; $25 \le c < 26$ and $27 \le c < 28$ **c.** 26.6
8. a. $1{:}09 \le t < 1{:}10$; $1{:}10 \le t < 1{:}11$
10. a. $60 \le p < 70$; $70 \le p < 80$ **b.** $55.5 \le p \le 55.9$
c. below 60 mm

Pages 364-365   **1. a.** 10; 4 and 13; 2 and 20
b. 55; 30 and 80; 10 and 100 **c.** 0.072; 0.0675 and
0.0805; 0.054 and 0.085 **d.** 93 000; 87 000 and
95 875; 85 000 and 97 800 **2.** Player A **3. b.** Cola A
c. yes **d.** Cola B **4.** The middle 50% of the data is
grouped together (small range). **5.** The data is
skewed. The distribution of the data is not symmetric
about the box. **6.** no **7.** Yes, data is clumped about
the median. **8.** It raises the value of the mean; yes.
9. a. 40.1; 30.2 **b.** 38.2-42.65; 28.1-31.65
c. declined

Pages 366-368   **2. a.** 75-95% **b.** 25-60%
c. 10-35% **d.** 65-90% **3. a.** 5-13; 37-53 **b.** 17-20;
91-100 **c.** 1-6; 9-21 **d.** 8-15; 52-68 **4. a.** 65-80
b. 35-45 **c.** 5-15 **d.** 75-85 **6.** 5-10% **7. a.** 20-55%
b. 20-30% **8. a.** 40-75% **b.** 20-30% **9. b.** City A
10. a. 70-95% **b.** 85-95% **11. a.** 65-90%

Pages 369-371   **2. a.** Mean: 77, 73.5, 72.75;
Median: 74, 73.5, 73.5; Mode: 75, 0, 71 and 74;
Weighted Average: 77, 73.5, 72.75 **b.** Mean: $9.00;
Median: $5.00; Mode: $5.00; Weighted Average:
$9.62 **3.** −18.25°C; 0°C **4.** Mean: 80.9 kg; Median:
76 kg; Mode: 73 kg and 83 kg; Weighted Average:

80.9 kg **a. i)** mode of 83 kg, **ii)** mode of 73 kg
b. mean and weighted average **5.** $791.62; $685.00
6. a. Means: 1) 249, 2) 228, 3) 237; Medians: 1) 247,
2) 226, 3) 244; Modes: 1) 220, 2) 210, 3) 240
7. a. Mean: 36.05; Median: 36.1; Mode: 35.9 and
36.8 **8.** Mean: 12.29; Median: 12; Mode: 10 and 12
9. a. Mean: 195; Median: 190; Mode: 180

Pages 372-373 **2. a.** 8 **b.** 20 **c.** 30 **d.** 16
3. a. 14 **b.** 13.5 **c.** -22.5 **d.** 199 **5. a.** 183.5;
184.7 **b.** $180 \leq c < 190$ **6.** 0.523; 0.525;
$0.50 \leq p < 0.60$

Pages 374-375 **1. a.** 183.5 **b.** 187.5 **c.** 180.5
d. 191.5 **2. a.** 75th **b.** 10th **c.** 100th **d.** 80th
e. 35th **f.** 40th **6. a.** 52.6, 60, 64, 70, 75, 84
b. 70%; $54 000, $62 666, $70 700

Pages 376-377 **5. a.** 1.8, 1.6 **b.** Tiger-cats
6. 10.3 **7. a.** 11.84 **b.** 13.05 **c.** 3.04 **8.** Site A:
mean = 89 d, mean deviation = 6.6 d; Site B:
mean = 89 d, mean deviation = 4 d; Site B is more
consistent **10. a.** mean = 5.27 **b.** mean deviation = 0

Pages 378-379 **3. a.** I: 1 and 9, 5, 5, 8; II: 5, 5,
5, 8; III: 4 and 5, 5, 5, 8 **b.** 16, 64, 6.67, 2.58, 6.3,
2.5 **4. a.** 189.75, 7167, 84.7 **b.** 166, 9134.5, 95.6
c. -10.02, 271.4, 16.5 **5.** At 0°C: 331.5, 331.5,
331.5, 0.04, 0.19; At 20°C: 343.4, 343, 340.4 and
346.5, 19.5, 4.4 **6.** 220.67, 14.85 **HISTORICAL
NOTE** BB + 2Bb + bb; 3 non-blue eyes, 1 blue eyes

Pages 380-381 **1. a.** skewed, A Mode, B mean
C median **b.** normal, A mean, median, and mode
c. skewed, A median, B mean, C mode **d.** skewed,
A mode, B mean, C median **2. a.** compressed **b.** B
c. A **4. a.** yes **b.** Drivers tend to exceed the speed
limit. **5. a.** depends on the maximum **b.** depends
c. no

Pages 382-383 **1. b.** 20 **2. a.** 3 **b.** 49.85%
c. 34% **d.** 47.5% **3. a.** 17% **b.** 23.75% **4. a.** 408
b. 15 **5.** 4.8 d

Page 384 **4.** 14.458, 1.367, 1.169 **3.** Change:
10 DIM × (500) • 20 ... (UP TO 500) ...
BRAINTICKLER Repeating the three digit number is
the same as multiplying by 1001, which is the product
of 7, 11, and 13.

Page 385 **1. a.** $\frac{1}{4}$ **b.** $\frac{1}{13}$ **c.** $\frac{1}{169}$ **2. a.** $\frac{1}{6}$ **b.** $\frac{5}{12}$
c. $\frac{7}{12}$ **d.** $\frac{1}{6}$ **4. a.** reduced the number of defective
parts produced **b.** 40.07, 41.5, 41; 22.7, 27, 28
c. mean **5. a.** 170, 182, none; 178, 188, 197
b. Molarmarvel **6. a.** 4.4, 4.75 **b.** 3.6-6.2, 3.4-4.7
c. 3.8 and 5.6, 3.8 and 4.7 **d.** 0.35 **e.** Toronto
f. Toronto **7.** 65.7, 239.6, 15.5 **8. a.** $11 500,
$15 250, $21 000, $30 000 **b.** 65% **c.** $12 500,
$16 750, $19 750

Page 386 **1. a.** $\frac{5}{9}$ **b.** $\frac{20}{81}$ **c.** $\frac{40}{153}$ **2. a.** $\frac{1}{12}$ **b.** 0
c. $\frac{1}{9}$ **d.** $\frac{1}{6}$ **4. a.** 50, 150, 250, 350, 450 **b.** 10
c. 50% **d.** 100 **6.** 0.79, 29.26, 5.41 **7. a.** 12,
10-16; 10, 8-14 **b.** 2 **c.** reduced gas consumption
8. a. 2036.6, 1327, no mode

Chapter 14

Page 387 **1. a.** 1 **b.** 8.75 **c.** 36 **d.** -3.5
e. 117 **f.** 57 **2. a.** 1.1576 **b.** 1.3117 **c.** 17
d. 24.5442 **e.** 16.3665 **f.** 1.7506 **g.** 1.1593
h. 1.1025 **i.** 7.9111 **j.** 1.1265 **k.** 5.0724 **l.** 1.4591
3. a. $a = 5$, $b = 2$ **b.** $a = 40$, $b = -3$ **c.** $x = 87.5$,
$y = -7.5$ **d.** $x = -220.9$, $y = 18.1$ **4. a.** $a(1 + b)$
b. $p(1 + i)$ **c.** $(a + i)(1 + i)$ **d.** $(x + r)^2(r + 1)$
e. $\frac{15(a + b)}{24}$ **5. a.** $l = 164.72, $A = 727.87
b. $l = 171.64, $A = 2351.14 **c.** $P = $20 737.40$,
$A = $21 502.61$ **d.** $P = 852.35, $A = 876.14
e. $118 410.80, $r = 1\%$ **f.** $P = $11 597.00$,
$r = 94.74\%$ **6. a.** 0.0970 **b.** 27 616.41
7. 45, 47, 49

Pages 388-391 **1.** 13, 21, 34, 55;
$t_n = t_{n-2} + t_{n-1}$, $n \geq 2$ **5. a.** -1, 1, 3 **b.** -4, -3, -2
c. 1, 1, 1 **d.** $\frac{1}{4}$, $\frac{1}{2}$, 1 **e.** 1, 4, 9 **f.** 15, 75, 375
g. 1, -1, -3 **h.** -9, -11, -13 **i.** 0, $\frac{1}{3}$, $\frac{1}{2}$ **j.** -1,
1, -1 **6. a.** $t_n = 2n - 1$ **b.** $t_n = \frac{1}{n}$ **c.** $t_n = 3(-1)^{n+1}$
d. $t_n = t_{n-1} + (2n - 1)$ **e.** $t_n = 5n$ **f.** $t_n = ar^{n-1}$
7. a. 1, 3, 5, 7, 9 **b.** 0, 4, 18, 48, 100 **c.** 0, 1, $\frac{8}{3}$,
5, 8 **d.** 5, $\frac{8}{3}$, $\frac{11}{5}$, 2, $\frac{17}{9}$ **e.** $\frac{3}{2}$, $\frac{16}{3}$, $\frac{45}{4}$, $\frac{96}{5}$, $\frac{175}{6}$ **f.** 0,
$\frac{2}{7}$, $\frac{3}{5}$, $\frac{12}{13}$, $\frac{5}{4}$ **g.** 3, -6, 9, -12, 15 **h.** 1, 2, 4, 8,
16 **8.** 1, 5, 10, 10, 5, 1; 1, 6, 15, 20, 15, 6, 1
9. a. number of regions: 13, 17; change in number of
regions: 4, 4 **b.** $t_k = 4k - 3$ **c.** $t_k = t_{k-1} + 4$; $t_1 = 1$;
$k > 1$ **d.** 153; 1457; 3597 **10. a.** the term: 15 ... 45;
change in t_n: 5 ... 9; change in change: 1 ... 1
b. $a = \frac{1}{2}$, $b = \frac{1}{2}$, $c = 0$ **c.** 78; 325; 1275
d. $t_k = t_{k-1} + k$, $t_1 = 1$, $k > 1$ **11. a.** 3, 7, 15, 31, 63
b. 1, 7, 58, 3376, 11 397 391 **c.** 4, -6, -21, -41,
-66 **d.** 1, 1, 2, 3, 5 **12. a.** $t_1 = 4$; $t_k = t_{k-1} - 3$;
$k > 1$ **b.** $t_1 = 1$; $t_2 = \frac{1}{2}$; $t_k = t_k + \frac{1}{(k - 1)k}$; $k \geq 2$
13. a. -8, -13, -23, -43, -83
b. $t_n = -5(2^{n-1} - 3) - 18$ **c.** $t_1 = -8$; $t_k = 2t_{k-1} + 3$;
$k > 1$ **14. a.** 1, 4, 9, 16, 25, 36, 49 **b.** $t_n = n^2$
c. $t_1 = 1$; $t_n = t_{n-1} + 2n + 1$; $n > 1$ **d. i)** 1, 5, 14, 30,

55, 91, 140 **ii)** $t_n = \frac{[n(n+1)(2n+1)]}{6}$ **iii)** $t_1 = 1$,

$t_n = t_{n-1} + n^2$; $n > 1$ **15. a.** 1, 9, 25, 49; $t_1 = 1$;

$t_k = t_{k-1} + 8(k-1)$ **b.** 3, 9, 27, 81; $t_1 = 3$; $t_k = 3t_{k-1}$;

$k > 1$ **c.** $\frac{3}{2}$, 2, $\frac{9}{4}$, $\frac{12}{5}$; $t_1 = \frac{3}{2}$; $t_n = t_{n-1}$; $\frac{3}{n(n+1)}$; $n > 1$

d. 0, $\frac{3}{2}$, $\frac{8}{3}$, $\frac{15}{4}$; $t_1 = 0$; $t_n = t_{n-1} + \frac{n(n-1)+1}{n(n-1)}$; $n > 1$

e. 0, 1, 3, 6; $t_1 = 0$; $t_n = t_{n-1} + (n-1)$; $n > 1$

f. $\frac{1}{3}$, $\frac{1}{9}$, $\frac{1}{27}$, $\frac{1}{81}$; $t_1 = \frac{1}{3}$; $t_n = \frac{1}{3}t_{n-1}$; $n > 1$

16. a. 403 **c.** $t_n = t_{n-1}$, $n > 1$ **17. a.** length of side:

$2\sqrt{2}$, 2, $\sqrt{2}$, 1, $\frac{\sqrt{2}}{2}$; perimeter of square:

$8\sqrt{2}$, 8, $4\sqrt{2}$, 4, $2\sqrt{2}$ **b. i)** $f(n) = \frac{4}{(\sqrt{2})^{n-1}}$

ii) $f(n) = \frac{16}{2^{n-1}}$ **c. i)** $t_1 = 4$; $t_n = t_{n-1} \div \sqrt{2}$; $n > 1$

ii) $t_1 = 16$; $t_n = t_{n-1} \div 2$; $n > 1$ **18. a.** 4, 8, 16, 32,

64, 128, 256 **b.** $t_1 = 4$; $t_n = 2t_{n-1}$; $n > 1$; $t_n = 2^{n+1}$

19. a. 4, 6, 2, 10, −6, 26 **b.** 5, 10, 4, −11, 23, 87

20. a. 151 **b.** 251 **HISTORICAL NOTE 1.** 0, 3, 6,

12, 24, 48, 96, 192, 384, 768; 0.4, 0.7, 1, 1.6, 2, 8,

5.2, 10.0, 19.6, 38.8, 77.2

Pages 392-395 **2. a.** 5, 10, 15

b. $t_n = 5 + 5(n-1)$ **3. a.** 9.6 **b.** 4.8 **c.** 9.6

4. a. 16 **b.** n **5. a.** $a = 3.8$, $d = 0.9$,

$t_n = 3.8 + 0.9(n-1)$ **b.** $a = 19$, $d = -4$,

$t_n = 19 + -4(n-1)$ **c.** not arithmetic **d.** $a = 7$,

$d = 0$, $t_n = 7 + 0(n-1)$ **6. a.** yes **b.** no **c.** yes

d. no **7. a.** yes, 4 **b.** yes, 0.1 **c.** yes, $\frac{1}{4}$ **8. a.** −1;

−6, −7, −8 **b.** 0.5; 6.1, 6.6, 7.1 **c.** $2 + i$; $9 + 5i$,

$11 + 6i$, $13 + 7i$ **d.** $\frac{1}{2}$; 3, $\frac{7}{2}$, 4

9. a. $-13 - 6(n-1)$ **b.** $12 + 5(n-1)$

c. $x - a + a(n-1)$ **d.** $2x^2 + 3x^2(n-1)$

e. $\frac{3}{8} - \frac{1}{4}(n-1)$ **f.** $1.21 + 0.13(n-1)$ **10. a.** −1,

3, 7 **b.** 2, −3, −8 **c.** 4, 7, 10 **d.** 7, 1, −5

11. a. −1 **b.** 5 **c.** 26 **d.** $3a - 4$ **e.** $3a - 1$ **f.** 3

12. b. arithmetic **13.** $62 **14.** $16 500; $4200

15. a. 61 **b.** 345 **c.** −41 **d.** $a(r+7)$ **16. a.** 4.2,

4.8; $t_n = 4.2 + 4.8(n-1)$ **b.** −5, −2;

$t_n = -5 + -2(n-1)$ **c.** 9.4, −3.6;

$t_n = 9.4 - 3.6(n-1)$ **d.** 7, 3; $t_n = 7 + 3(n-1)$ **e.** 9,

−1; $t_n = 9 - 1(n-1)$ **f.** 5, −2; $t_n = 5 - 2(n-1)$

17. a. 53 **b.** $53 - 2(n-1)$ **c.** 27 **18. a.** yes **b.** yes

c. no **d.** no **e.** no **f.** no **19.** −7, −2, 3;

$t_n = -7 + 5(n-1)$ **21.** $x = 8$ **22. a.** 5, 2, −1

b. −22 **c.** 21 **d.** $11 - 3n$ **e.** 3 **f.** 41 **23.** $x = 2$ or

1.5 **24. a.** 13 **b.** 50 **c.** 22 **d.** 21 **25.** t_{50}

26. number boarding: 0, 15, 15, 15, 15; total on

board: 50, 65, 80 **27. a.** −7, −2, 3, 8, 13, 18

b. 527, average **28. a.** 13.5, 18, 22.5 **b.** 13, 5, −3,

−11, −19, −27 **c.** $2x + y$, $3x$ **d.** $-2n$, $-n - 2m$,

$-4m$, $n - 6m$ **29.** 8

Pages 396-399 **2.** 12th **3. a.** 1, 3, 81 **b.** 4, 5,

2500 **c.** 5000, $\frac{1}{10}$, 0.5 **d.** 81, $\frac{2}{3}$, 16

4. a. yes; 3; 384; 1152, 3456 **b.** no **c.** no **d.** yes; r;

ar^4, ar^5, ar^6 **e.** yes; $\frac{1}{2}$; $\frac{1}{64}$, $\frac{1}{128}$, $\frac{1}{256}$ **f.** no **g.** yes;

$-\frac{1}{5}$, $-\frac{1}{25}$, $\frac{1}{125}$, $-\frac{1}{625}$ **h.** yes; $-\frac{1}{6}$, $-\frac{1}{36}$, $\frac{1}{216}$,

$-\frac{1}{1296}$ **5. a.** 2, 6, 18, 54 **b.** −3, 12, −48, 192

c. −1, $-\frac{1}{5}$, $-\frac{1}{25}$, $-\frac{1}{125}$ **d.** 4, −12, 36, −108

6. a. $ar^4 = 55$ **b.** $ar^{16} = 1.0078$ **7. a.** 5, 15, 45, 135,

405 **b.** 3, 6, 12, 24, 48 **c.** −7, −35, −175, −875,

−4375 **d.** $\frac{1}{4}$, $-\frac{3}{4}$, $\frac{9}{4}$, $-\frac{27}{4}$, $\frac{81}{4}$ **8.** $1 199 328.00;

$1 487 167.00 **9.** 81; 1; 3 **10. a.** $54\left(\frac{2}{3}\right)^{n-1}$; $7\frac{1}{9}$

b. $7\sqrt{2}\left(\frac{\sqrt{3}}{3}\right)^{n-1}$; $\frac{7\sqrt{2}}{729}$ **c.** $\frac{1}{6}\left(\frac{6}{5}\right)^{n-1}$; $\frac{7776}{15\,625}$ **d.** 0.0035

$\times (10)^{n-1}$; 35 000 000 **11.** 14 336; 9th **12.** 4, 2, 1,

$\frac{1}{2}$ **13.** 5, 10, 20, 40, 80, 160, 320 ... **14. a.** 7

b. 10 **c.** 12 **d.** 21 **15.** 38 928 **16.** 8543

17. $5798.47 **18.** 5 or $\frac{1}{11}$ **20. a.** 4, $2\sqrt{2}$, 2, $\sqrt{2}$ ...

b. $4\left(\frac{1}{\sqrt{2}}\right)^7$ **c.** 16, $8\sqrt{2}$, 8, $4\sqrt{2}$, 4, $2\sqrt{2}$, 2

d. $4\left(\frac{1}{\sqrt{2}}\right)^9 = \frac{\sqrt{2}}{8}$ **21.** 3.75 cm **22.** $5145.00 **23.** in

25 weeks **24.** the second allowance **25.** 10 000,

9913, 9826, 9740, 9655, 9571, ..., 6561; use

$r = 0.991$ **26. a.** 12, 36, 108 **b.** 12, 3 **c.** $x^4 + x^3$,

$x^3 + x^2$, $x^2 + x$ **d.** $x^2 - 1$ **27. a.** 27, 9 **b.** $\frac{9}{4}$, $\frac{27}{8}$

c. 15, 45, 135 **d.** 250, 50, 10 **28.** $\frac{1024}{3125}$ **29. a.** 328

Pages 400-401 **1.** $4 + 8 + 16 + ... = 16\,380$

2. a. $3 + 5 + 7 + 9 + 11 + ...$

b. $8 + 4 + 2 + 1 + \frac{1}{2} + \frac{1}{4} + \frac{1}{8} + ...$ **3. a.** sequence

b. series **c.** sequence **d.** series **4. a.** 3, 5, 7 **b.** 1,

10, 25 **c.** 2, 6, 12 **d.** 1, −11, −59 **e.** −2, 2, 18

f. 12, −33, −228 **5.** $t_7 = 17$ **6.** $\sum\limits_{n=1}^{4} ar^{n-1}$

7. a. $7 + 10 + 13 + 16 + 19 = 65$

b. $3 + 12 + 48 + 192 = 255$ **c.** $6 + 7 + 8 + 9 = 30$

d. $-6 - 7 - 8 = -21$ **8.** 55; $\frac{n(n+1)}{2}$ **9. a.** 25 **b.** 24

c. 363 **d.** $\dfrac{\sin\left(p + \frac{1}{2}\right)x - \sin\left(\frac{x}{2}\right)}{2\sin\left(\frac{x}{2}\right)}$ **e.** 140 **f.** 316

10. a. 0; $\sum\limits_{n=1}^{6} 3(-1)^{n+1}$ **b.** 140; $\sum\limits_{n=1}^{7} 5n$ **c.** 85; $\sum\limits_{n=0}^{3} 4^n$

d. 70; $\sum_{n=1}^{7} (3n - 2)$ **e.** $\sum_{n=0}^{4} \left(1 - \frac{2n}{3}\right)$

11. $9 + 9 + 9 + 9 + \ldots$; $S_n = 9n$ **a. i)** 108 **ii)** 360 **iii)** 2700 **b.** 9 **12. a.** $8 + 4\sqrt{2} + 4 + 2\sqrt{2} + \sqrt{2}$ **b.** $7(2 + \sqrt{2})$ **13.** 472.5 cm **BRAINTICKLER** 8

Pages 402-404   **1. a.** 95 **b.** -42 **c.** $20\sqrt{3}$ **d.** $36x$ **e.** 18 **2. a.** $t_{20} = -111$, $S_{20} = -1080$ **b.** $t_{20} = 145$; $S_{20} = 1570$ **c.** $t_{20} = -187.5$; $S_{20} = -1337$ **d.** $t_{20} = 59a$; $S_{20} = 610a$ **e.** $t_{20} = 43 + 58i$; $S_{20} = 480 + 590i$ **f.** $t_{20} = \frac{20}{7}$, $S_{20} = 30$ **3. a.** 335 **b.** -1150 **c.** $\frac{110}{3}$ **d.** 9.073 **e.** 20 965 **f.** 68 100$\sqrt{2}$ **4. a.** \$37.00 **b.** \$242.00 **5. a.** \$200.00 **b.** \$1375.00 **6. a.** 56 m **b.** 549 m **c.** no **7. a.** 972 **b.** 760 **c.** 2170 **d.** -11 472 **e.** -35 409.3 **f.** 1190$\sqrt{7}$ **8. a.** 143 **b.** -620 **9.** yes **11. a.** $t_{17} = -41$; $S_{17} = 289$ **b.** $t_{17} = 121$; $S_{17} = 833$ **c.** $t_{17} = -6.9$; $S_{17} = -8.5$ **d.** $t_{17} = -10\sqrt{7}$; $S_{17} = -34\sqrt{7}$ **12. a.** 5, -2, -9, -16, -23, -30 **b.** -75 **13.** $-5 - 2 + 1 + 4 + 7 + \ldots$ **14. a.** 15 **b.** 3927 **15.** 10 100 **16.** $n(n + 1)$ **17.** n^2 **18.** $-1011 - 884.5 - 785 - 631.5 - 505 - \ldots$

Pages 405-407   **2. a.** 364 **b.** 23.1 **c.** $\frac{2400\sqrt{7}}{\sqrt{7} - 1}$ **d.** 93.75 **5. a.** $2^n - 1$ **b.** $\dfrac{231.5\left(1 - \frac{1}{10^n}\right)}{\frac{9}{10}}$ **c.** $\frac{5\sqrt{3}}{2}(3^n - 1)$ **d.** $\dfrac{3\left[1 - \left(-\frac{a}{3}\right)^n\right]}{3 - a}$ **6.** \$4463.35 **7.** $t_9 = 781$ 250; $S_9 = 976$ 562 **8. a.** 2 097 148 **b.** 0 **c.** 6.36×10^{12} **d.** 223 750.48x **e.** 0.998 **9. a.** 79.32 m **b.** 822.47 m **10.** \$10.00 **11.** \$1460.20 **12.** 428.33 m **13. a.** $1 + 4 + 16 + \ldots$ **b.** 3.665×10^{11} **14. a.** 3069 **b.** 16 400 **c.** 13.89 **d.** 56 528.16 **e.** 1.5 **f.** 38 **g.** $\frac{1}{3}$ **15.** 2 **16.** $81 + 27 + 9 + 3 + 1 + \frac{1}{3} + \frac{1}{9} + \frac{1}{27}$

BRAINTICKLER 36

Pages 408-410   **2. a.** \$8005.13 **b.** \$304.90 **c.** \$12 692.41 **4. a.** \$1325.23 **b.** \$1038.99 **c.** \$14 106.63 **d.** \$1 232 369.20 **5. a.** \$1009.14 **b.** \$1580.00 **c.** \$19 619.87 **d.** \$13 327.10 **6.** c **7. a.** \$616.82 **b.** \$1160.22 **c.** \$25 854.25 **8. a.** \$2820.20 **b.** \$2853.79 **9.** b **10.** \$83 648.13 **11.** \$344.49 **12.** \$12 033.10 **13.** 13.7%/a **14. a.** \$161.05 **b.** \$248.83 **c.** no **15. a.** \$161.05 **b.** \$259.37 **c.** no **16.** \$328.93 **17.** 6 a and 1 month **18. a.** 24.6%/a **b.** 23.2%/a **c.** 22.6%/a **d.** 22.2%/a

BRAINTICKLER 11 quarters and 11 nickels

Pages 411-412   **1. a.** \$440.90 **b.** \$546.31 **c.** \$14 416.26 **d.** \$28 832.52 **e.** \$12 704.23 **f.** \$17 933.06 **2. a.** no **b.** yes **c.** no **d.** yes **3. a.** about 7 a **b.** about 12 a **c.** about 6 a **d.** about 4 a **e.** no **5. a.** \$15.12 **b.** \$58.00 **c.** \$162.24 **d.** \$11.85 **e.** \$142.79 **f.** \$24.80 **6.** \$6354.05 **7.** \$3534.97 **9.** 19.72%/a **10.** \$492.42, no **BRAINTICKLER** \$16.00

Pages 413-414   **1.** \$680.58, \$735.03, \$793.83, \$857.34, \$925.93, \$1000.00, \$1080.00, \$1166.40, \$1259.71, \$1360.49, \$1469.33 **2.** less **3. a.** \$2285.00 **b.** \$259.61 **c.** \$2834.27 **d.** \$1324.42 **4. a.** \$670.74 **b.** \$1113.16 **c.** \$147.61 **d.** \$38 766.71 **5.** \$4137.56 **6.** \$7374.56 **7.** 10.36% **8.** 14.36%; 13.92% **9.** \$3891.58 **10.** 5.67% **11.** \$754.40 **12.** \$79.13 **BRAINTICKLER** $5^7 - 6^6 + 7^5 = 48$ 276

Page 415   **3. a.** yes **b.** no **c.** yes **d.** yes **4.** 19.92% **5. a.** 8.75% compounded quarterly **b.** 10.25% semiannually **c.** 15% monthly **d.** roughly the same **6. a.** 13.07% **b.** 33.18% **c.** 3.82% **d.** 19.4% **7.** 141.04% **8.** 10.72%; 10.73%

Pages 416-418   **1. a.** no **b.** yes **c.** no **2. a.** \$2471.95 **b.** \$769.81 **3. a.** \$3434.82 **b.** \$60 479.79 **4.** \$1072.82 **5.** \$429.62 **6.** \$398 471.53 **7.** \$2125.36 **8.** a **9.** \$207 235.19 **10.** \$448.22 **11.** \$1408.06 **12.** \$21 569.51 **13.** \$25 903.09 **BRAINTICKLER** \$16 596

Pages 419-420   **1. a.** \$1748.54 **b.** \$1192.98 **2.** The first is greatest. **3.** \$2574.68 **4.** 35%/a **5.** \$10 665.09 **6.** \$68 000 has a higher present value. **7.** \$7895.22 annually

Pages 421-422   **5.** \$861.74 **6.** \$2515.69 **7.** \$7592.84 **8.** \$3475.08 **9.** \$2139.80 **11. a.** \$52 312.31 **b.** \$124.87

Pages 423-425   **4. a.** \$48.44 **b.** \$62.50 **c.** \$231.25 **d.** \$240.00 **5. a.** \$1000 **b.** \$1186.24 **c.** Dec. 12, 2004 **d.** \$301.19 **e.** \$698.81 **f.** \$1000.00 **6.** \$901.45 **7. a.** 11.3% **b.** 11.19% **8. a.** \$10 668.20 **b.** \$1287.50 **c.** 12.04% **9.** 7.3% **10.** Bell Canada **11.** 11.35% **12. a.** \$3589.20 **b.** \$6299.13 **13.** \$102.89 **14.** \$585.63 **15. a.** \$216.56 **b.** \$3272.37 **c.** \$4004.06 **d.** \$7276.43

Page 426   **1. a.** 312 **b.** -6553.5 **c.** 16.5 **3. a.** 312; -6553.5; 16.5; -61.25 **4.** Change: 10 REM TO CALCULATE THE FIRST TERM OF A GEOMETRIC SERIES • 20 INPUT "THE SUM OF THE SERIES IS "; S • 50 A = (S $*$ (R $-$ 1)) / (R $\wedge$ N $-$ 1) • 60 PRINT "THE FIRST TERM OF A GEOMETRIC SERIES WITH SUM "; S;

", COMMON RATIO "; R; " AND "; N; " TERMS IS "; A • 70 END **5. a.** 17.272 **b.** −0.441 **c.** 1.576 × 10⁻¹⁴ **6.** 10 REM TO CALCULATE THE SUM OF AN ARITHMETIC SERIES • 20 INPUT "THE FIRST TERM OF THE SERIES IS "; A • 30 INPUT "THE NUMBER OF TERMS IN THE SERIES IS "; N • 40 INPUT "THE COMMON DIFFERENCE IS "; D • 50 S = (N / 2) * (2 * A + (N − 1) * D) • 60 PRINT "THE SUM OF THE ARITHMETIC SERIES WITH THE FIRST TERM "; A; ", THE COMMON DIFFERENCE "; D; "AND "; N; " TERMS IS "; S • 70 END **a.** 6832 **b.** −4650 **c.** 217 450 **d.** 987.5 **7.** Change: 10 REM TO CALCULATE THE COMMON DIFFERENCE OF AN ARITHMETIC SERIES • 40 INPUT "THE SUM OF THE SERIES IS "; S • 50 D = ((2 * S) / N − 2 * A) / (N − 1) • 60 PRINT "THE COMMON DIFFERENCE OF THE ARITHMETIC SERIES WITH FIRST TERM "; A; ", THE SUM "; S; " AND "; N; " TERMS IS "; D • 70 END **a.** −0.0399 **b.** −0.221 **c.** 2.063 **d.** 2.526 **8.** 10 REM TO CALCULATE COMPOUND INTEREST • 20 INPUT "THE PRINCIPAL IS "; P • 30 INPUT "THE INTEREST RATE IS "; I; "%" • 40 INPUT "THE NUMBER OF PERIODS IS "; N • 50 A = P * (1 + I) ∧ N • 60 PRINT "THE AMOUNT OF "; P; " DOLLARS AFTER "; N; " PERIODS AT "; I; "% IS "; A • 70 END

Page 427 **3. a.** −47 **b.** 7 **4. a.** −3, 5 **b.** −3, 2, 7, 12, 17 **5. a.** 80 **b.** 24 **6. a.** 81 **b.** $\frac{27}{2^{25}}$ **c.** $\frac{1}{3}$
7. $74 690 **8.** 73 t **10. a.** $2108.75 **b.** $12 649.51 **c.** $255.16 **11. a.** $2574.25 **b.** $2954.57 **c.** $8722.86 **12.** ii **13. a.** 10.65% **b.** 15.56% **14. a.** $6831.78 **b.** $84 118.74 **15. a.** $50 754.51 **b.** $49 897.81 **16.** $212 882.12 **17. a.** $5000 **b.** $5603.15 **c.** 12% **d.** October 20, 1993 **e.** $600 **f.** 10.71%

Page 428 **2. a.** 55 **b.** 3.84 × 10⁻⁹
c. 27√7 − 23√3 **d.** $\frac{161}{10}$ **3. a.** −128√2
b. 3.833 332 95 **c.** 14.94r **4.** 5, −1, −7, −13, −19, … **5.** 4, 12, 36, 108, 324 **6.** 58.68%
7. a. $561.62 **b.** $8957.83 **c.** $395 447.60
8. a. $2916.09 **b.** $753.65 **c.** $668.10 **9.** $2585.16
10. $2849.96 **11.** ii **12. a.** 13.96% **b.** 30.47%
13. a. $29 801.97 **b.** $6350.45 **c.** $24 877.70
14. a. $5464.65 **b.** $127 105.92 **15.** $49 146.50

Chapter 15

Page 429 **1. a.** arithmetic; 11, 14, 17
b. geometric; 27, 81, 243 **c.** geometric; −3, 3, −3

d. geometric; $\frac{1}{8}$, $\frac{1}{16}$, $\frac{1}{32}$ **e.** geometric; $a(x + 1)^4$,
$a(x + 1)^5$, $a(x + 1)^6$ **2. a.** 121 **b.** 1.9375 **c.** $\frac{r^7 - 1}{r - 1}$
d. $\frac{a[(1 + i)^6 - 1]}{i}$ **3. a.** 1.343 92 **b.** 2 571 84
c. 19.002 60 **d.** 9.337 64 **4. a.** 44.40 **b.** 95.82
c. 1437.16 **5.** Rate column: 12.21%; Time column: 3.20 a; Interest column: $105.00, $143.50; Amount column: $805.00, $13 128.00 **6.** Principal column: $64 832.66, $968.44; Time column: 6.12 a; Amount column: $6372.36, $30 813.79 **7.** $1350.00
8. $1410.60 **10. a.** 9.7% **b.** 12%

Pages 430-431 **1.** $6316.00 **2.** no **3.** $61.53
8. $2816.05

Pages 432-434 **5.** $281.20 **6. a.** $164.97
b. $180.08 **c.** $206.44 **7. a.** $1413.30 **b.** $785.76
c. $732.24 **8. a.** 4 a **b.** 14.5 a **c.** 20.5 a
9. a. $131.05 **b.** $311.45 **c.** $1638.95
10. a. $611.38 **b.** $386.56 **c.** $308.49
11. $55 024.22 **12.** 6 a **13.** $2000.00
14. $11 396.63; $890.31 **15.** $3908.30; $634.63
16. no **17.** no **18. a.** $82 759.95 **b.** 16 a
c. $24 961.23

Pages 435-437 **1. a.** 0.007 783 **b.** 0.001 884 2
c. 0.008 963 39 **d.** 0.001 606 4 **2. a.** $1364.68
b. $384.72 **5.** With 3 payments of $144.18 each, the principal is reduced by $98.81, $99.85, and $100.91 respectively. **6.** $(1 + i)^{\frac{1}{24}} - 1$; $(1 + 0.5i)^{\frac{1}{12}} - 1$
7. $61 910.36 **8.** the semiannual plan **9.** to be amortized for at least 9 a; no **10. a.** $3496.85; $3431.51; $3397.48; $3322.88 **b.** $15 000

Pages 438-439 **1.** $355.67 **3. a.** $31.47
b. $24.21 **4. a.** $6050.00 **b.** $6234.35 **5. a.** $0.23
b. $0.00 **6.** b **7.** c

Pages 440-441 **1.** $250 000 000 **2.** $1.875
5. high **6.** C.I.B.C. **7. a.** 19.96 **b.** 11
8. a. $3750.00 **b.** $431.25 **9. a.** 2.3% **b.** 13.84%

Pages 442-443 **1. a.** 200 **b.** 320 **c.** $12\frac{5}{8}$
d. 400 **e.** $+\frac{1}{8}$ **f.** $14\frac{1}{8}$ **g.** 20 **2. a.** Barincor w; Bankeno o **b.** $13 000.00 **c.** $40 500.00
3. b. up $0.08

Pages 444-445 **1. a.** $33.25 **b.** $49.72
c. $52.60 **2.** $141.20

Pages 446-447 **2.** $9372 millions **3.** $3710 millions **5.** 161 873 088 **6.** $224 200 thousands; $306 300 thousands **7.** $789 549 thousands; $858 025 thousands **8.** $76 111 thousands **9.** $0.46
10. $74 192 thousands

Page 448 **2.** troy ounces **4.** 1000 ounces and 400 ounces **10.** yes **16.** $15 373

Page 450   **4. a.** $966.85 **b.** $719.17
5. a. $355.75 **b.** $520.90 **6. a.** 0.009 361 4
b. 0.008 545 0 **7. b.** $11 640.60 **9. a.** yes
b. $13 691.43 **c.** $719.43 **10.** $24 327.44 **11. a.** no
b. yes **14.** 9.3 **15. a.** $75 000 000 **b.** 7.3%
c. $18 250

Page 451   **2. a.** $86.50 **3. a.** $2207.26;
$2226.76 **5.** $1720.00 **6.** It will go down.
7. a. $50 000 000 **b.** $51 250 **8. a.** $1.17 **b.** 13.46
9. a. $13 337.50 **b.** $33 000; $27 500 **10. a.** He
owes $577.50. **b.** $6031.75 **c.** $5886.99

Cumulative Review Chapters 13-15

Pages 452-453   **1. a.** $\frac{1}{18}$ **b.** $\frac{7}{12}$ **c.** $\frac{7}{12}$ **3. a.** 10
b. 13 **c.** 4.5 and 13.5 **d.** 11.5 and 23 **e.** 3 **4.** 70.3,
222.9, 14.9 **5. a.** 68% **b.** 2.5% **6. a.** 5^{11} **b.** 81
c. -17 **d.** 8^{-7} **e.** $2(0.2)^7$ **7. a.** $-29\ 524$ **b.** 4900
c. 2.283 **d.** 1008.90 **8.** $1449.14 **9. a.** $3821.30
b. $215.69 **c.** $8951.52 **d.** $7277.63 **e.** $9186.73
10. a. $3577.18 **b.** $486.47 **c.** $801.96
d. $35 463.30 **11. a.** $1195.52 **12. a.** $567.47
b. 0.012 126 379 **13.** $4344.90 **14. a.** $4687.50
b. 7.98% **16. a.** $80 **b.** no **18.** $\frac{1}{210}$ **19. b.** 6
c. 70% **20. a.** $20.50 **b.** $662.50 **21. a.** $717.27
b. $445.55

Index